D0142962

Henry VI (1422–61) was one of the most spectacularly inadequate kings of England, and his reign dissolved into the conflict known as the Wars of the Roses; yet he held on to his throne for thirty-nine years and, for almost thirty of them, without much difficulty. What was the nature of Henry's inadequacy, and why did it have such ambivalent and complicated results?

This book offers a re-evaluation of politics and government during Henry VI's reign by looking more clearly at the scheme of values, expectations and practices which shaped the relations of king and nobility during the period. Since the 1970s most histories of fifteenth-century England have focused on the individual interests and private connections of politicians as a means of making sense of politics. By contrast, this work argues that we can understand what happened in Henry VI's reign only if we look at common interests and public connections as well, and that the best way to examine these is by looking at contemporary political ideas and their expression in the language of politics and the institutions of government. For Henry's subjects, it is the problem of establishing royal authority which emerges as paramount, and the supposedly factious and 'overmighty' nobility are recast as doomed but devoted servants of the state.

HENRY VI
AND THE POLITICS OF KINGSHIP

HENRY VI
AND THE POLITICS OF
KINGSHIP

JOHN WATTS

University of Wales, Aberystwyth

CAMBRIDGE
UNIVERSITY PRESS

Published by the Press Syndicate of the University of Cambridge
The Pitt Building, Trumpington Street, Cambridge CB2 1RP
40 West 20th Street, New York, NY 10011–4211, USA
10 Stamford Road, Oakleigh, Melbourne 3166, Australia

First published 1996

Printed in Great Britain at the University Press, Cambridge

A catalogue record for this book is available from the British Library

Library of Congress cataloguing in publication data
Watts, John.
Henry VI and the politics of kingship / John Lovett Watts.
p.   cm.
Includes bibliographical references and index.
ISBN 0 521 42039 3 (hc)
1. Great Britain – Politics and government – 1399–1485.   2. Great
Britain – History – Henry VI, 1422–1461.   3. Great Britain – Kings and
rulers – Biography.   4. Henry VI, King of England, 1421–1471.
5. Monarchy – Great Britain – History.   I. Title.
DA257.W38   1996
320.942′09′024–dc20   95–38634 CIP

ISBN 0 521 42039 3 hardback

For
Mandy, Liz and Grattan,
and
in memory of Katie

CONTENTS

PREFACE

I ALWAYS USED TO snigger at the self-deprecating prefaces which fifteenth-century authors attached to their poems and other writings. I did not realise until I was well under way with this book that the strongest impulse I would feel at this time would be to offer an apology – an apology that my work is not more exhaustively researched, better organised, more carefully thought-out, more clearly expressed and so on. There have been many times when I have thought seriously about abandoning altogether the scheme of publishing this revised version of my PhD thesis: now that government-inspired changes to the system of research funding have made such reticence impossible, I sincerely hope that this book is not one more thing to be alleged against them. It has been quite a long time in the making, and in that time the debates of historians of the fifteenth century – if not always their written words – have moved on a certain amount. Even so, I think that there is still room for a re-evaluation of our assumptions about the operation of fifteenth-century government and, indeed, for an attempt to apply the insights gained in the process to the muddled reign of Henry VI. I should stress, perhaps, that what follows *is* an attempt, an experiment. I think that, on the whole, I am asking the right questions, but it is difficult to be supremely confident about many of the answers. This is primarily a work of interpretation and discussion rather than a definitive summation of research: it does not begin to approach the range and depth of new information about the reign which Ralph Griffiths provided for us in his monograph of fifteen years ago; and one or two of its conclusions may already have been challenged in two doctoral theses which emerged while I was working on the book, and which I deliberately did not read, in order to leave their authors to publish their findings for themselves.[1] In the end, if my

---

[1] These are Kate Selway, 'The Religious Life and Religious Patronage of Henry VI and his Circle', Oxford, 1994, and Helen Castor, 'The Duchy of Lancaster in the Lancastrian Polity, 1399-1461', Cambridge, 1993.

treatment interests people and moves them to think more generally about how we should approach the politics of fifteenth-century England, it will have achieved a large part of its purpose.

Over the course of the last nine years, I have notched up a huge number of academic debts, which it is a pleasure to acknowledge, if not to repay. I owe a great deal of my understanding of later medieval England to those who taught and studied with me at Cambridge: to Christine Carpenter, who supervised me as an undergraduate and then again as a research student; to Ted Powell and Rosemary Horrox, whose lectures I attended and who talked with me about many issues of fifteenth-century history, both then and since; and finally to numerous contemporaries of mine – above all, perhaps, Shelley Lockwood, Benjamin Thompson, Helen Castor, Mike Braddick and Julian Turner, the last of whom gave me a striking sense of how intellectually inspiring research into the political history of later medieval England could be. During my time in Cambridge and subsequently, I have also received advice, help and (often) correction from many other scholars. Among these, I am especially grateful to the following: Gerald Harriss, with whom I have discussed quite a few of my ideas, and who, besides helping me with a number of documentary questions, has kindly read and commented upon several papers and articles which I have written – his criticisms have been extremely pertinent and I have learned from them; Barrie Dobson and Rees Davies, who examined my PhD and made a large number of valuable observations both at the time and since; Margaret Condon, who has discussed the king's council with me on several occasions; Michael K. Jones, who has told me a lot about the war in France and given freely of his views on the aims and activities of the Beaufort brothers; Steve Gunn, who got me to think twice about many of my assumptions about the later fifteenth century; Christopher Brooke, who drew my attention to a number of errors I had made, and forced me to think hard about my views on the foundation of Eton and King's; Mark Ormrod, who talked with me about counsel in the reign of Edward III; Cliff Davies, whose kindness and whose advice on a whole range of topics have been vastly helpful. Several of these people have also read drafts of sections and chapters of the present book – indeed, the last-named found the time to plough through the first five chapters and to reassure me at one of my lowest of low moments: I am exceedingly grateful to him and to others who have looked over my work for me; I could not have finished it without their help and encouragement.

I should also like to record my thanks to a number of institutions. I am grateful to the Master and Fellows of Gonville and Caius College, Cambridge, for giving me every assistance, including a handsome amount of financial support, during the preparation of my thesis; and also to the Warden and Fellows of Merton College, Oxford, for electing me to a Junior Research Fellowship, and providing such a stimulating and yet amiable environment for continuing my work. I am most honoured to have been appointed to a junior lectureship in the Department of History and Welsh History here at Aberystwyth. My colleagues have been a great source of friendship and intellectual support, and it has been a particular pleasure to work in such close proximity to Rees Davies, whose unfailing kindness and excellent advice have been an enormous help in bringing this work to its conclusion. Like most students of history, I have relied heavily on the good will and assistance of members of staff in libraries and record offices: it has invariably been forthcoming, but, in particular, I should like to thank the officers in the Round Room at Chancery Lane, for innumerable bits of information and advice. Finally, I should like to thank the staff of Cambridge University Press, and, in particular, Bill Davies, who has listened patiently to three years' worth of excuses and apologies and gently edged me onwards to the finish.

Last of all: how can I thank Christine Carpenter enough? Having been my teacher and friend for over a decade, she has encouraged, cajoled, provoked and inspired me through every academic project I have tackled. I often feel that I owe almost everything to her support, both intellectual and personal: certainly, whatever credit this book deserves is due, above all, to her. For its weaknesses and errors, of course, no one but myself can be held responsible.

ABBREVIATIONS

'Active Policy'	'The Active Policy of a Prince' in M. Bateson (ed.), *George Ashby's Poems*, EETS, extra ser., no. 76, (London, 1899), pp. 12–41.
Aquinas	A. P. D'Entreves (ed.), *Aquinas: Selected Political Writings* (Oxford, 1959).
Basin, *Histoire*	C. Samaran (ed.), *Thomas Basin. Histoire de Charles VII*, 2 vols. (Paris, 1933–44).
'Benet's Chron.'	G. L. and M. A. Harriss (eds.), 'John Benet's Chronicle for the Years 1400–62', *Camden Miscellany XXIV*, 4th ser., IX (London, 1972), pp. 151–233.
BL	British Library.
Brut	F. W. D. Brie (ed.), *The Brut, or The Chronicles of England*, 2 vols., EETS, orig. ser., nos. 131, 136 (London, 1906–8): all references are to vol. II.
CAD	*A Descriptive Catalogue of Ancient Deeds . . .*, 6 vols., HMSO (London, 1890–1915).
CChR	*Calendar of the Charter Rolls.*
CClR	*Calendar of the Close Rolls.*
CFR	*Calendar of the Fine Rolls.*
Chrons. of London	C. L. Kingsford (ed.), *Chronicles of London* (Oxford, 1905).
CIPM	*Calendarium Inquisitionum Post Mortem.*
CMH	*Cambridge Medieval History.*
Collections	J. Gairdner (ed.), *The Historical Collections of a Citizen of London*, Camden Soc., new ser., XVII (London, 1876).
CPL	*Calendar of . . . Papal Letters.*
CPR	*Calendar of the Patent Rolls.*

Crowland	H. T. Riley (ed.), *Ingulph. Chronicle of the Abbey of Crowland* (London, 1854).
CSP Milan	*Calendar of State Papers and Manuscripts . . . of Milan.*
CSP Venice	*Calendar of State Papers and Manuscripts . . . of Venice.*
De Laudibus	S. B. Chrimes (ed.), *Sir John Fortescue: De Laudibus Legum Anglie* (Cambridge, 1942).
De Natura	*De Natura Legis Naturae*, transl. in T. Fortescue, Lord Clermont (ed.), *Sir John Fortescue, Knight, his Life, Works and Family History*, 2 vols. (London, 1869), I, pp. 187–333.
d'Escouchy, *Chronique*	G. L. E. du F. de Beaucourt (ed.), *Chronique de Mathieu d'Escouchy*, 3 vols. (Paris, 1863–4): all references are to vol. I.
de Waurin, *Croniques*	W. and E. L. C. P. Hardy (eds.), *Recueil des Croniques et Aunchiennes Istories de la Grant Bretaigne . . . par Jehan de Waurin*, 5 vols., Rolls ser., (London, 1864–91).
DKR	*Report of the Deputy Keeper of the Public Records.*
EETS	Early English Text Society.
EHD	*English Historical Documents.*
EHL	C. L. Kingsford (ed.), *English Historical Literature in the Fifteenth Century* (Oxford, 1913).
English Chron.	J. S. Davies (ed.), *An English Chronicle . . .*, Camden Soc., old ser., LXIV (London, 1856).
Feudal Aids	*Inquisitions and Assessments relating to Feudal Aids*, 6 vols., HMSO (London, 1899–1920).
Foedera	T. Rymer (ed.), *Foedera, Conventiones, Literae . . .*, 3rd edn, 10 vols. (The Hague, 1745).
GEC	G. E. Cokayne, *The Complete Peerage*, ed. H. V. Gibbs, *et al.*, 13 vols. (London, 1910–40).
Giles, *Chronicon*	J. A. Giles (ed.), *Incerti Scriptoris Chronicon Angliae . . .*, (London, 1848): all references are to pt IV.
Governance	C. Plummer (ed.), *The Governance of England . . . by Sir John Fortescue, Knight* (Oxford, 1885).

Great Chron.	A. H. Thomas and I. D. Thornley (eds.), *The Great Chronicle of London* (London, 1938).
HBC	E. B. Fryde, *et al.* (eds.), *Handbook of British Chronology*, 3rd edn (London, 1986).
HMC	*Historical Manuscripts Commission.*
Leland, *De Rebus*	J. Leland, *De Rebus Britannicis Collectanea*, ed. T. Hearne, 6 vols. (London, 1770): all references are to vol. I, pt II.
Letters and Papers	J. Stevenson (ed.), *Letters and Papers Illustrative of the Wars of the English in France during the Reign of Henry VI*, 2 vols. in 3, Rolls ser. (London, 1861–4).
Letters of Margaret	C. Monro (ed.), *Letters of Queen Margaret of Anjou . . .*, Camden Soc., old ser., no. LXXXVI (London, 1863).
Livre du Corps de Policie	D. Bornstein (ed.), *The Middle English Translation of Christine de Pisan's Livre du Corps de Policie* (Heidelberg, 1977).
Loci e Libro	J. E. T. Rogers (ed.), *Thomas Gascoigne. Loci e Libro Veritatum* (Oxford, 1881).
PL	J. Gairdner (ed.), *The Paston Letters*, Library edn, 6 vols. (London, 1904).
Plumpton	T. Stapleton (ed.), *Plumpton Correspondence*, Camden Soc., old ser., IV (London, 1839).
PPC	N. H. Nicolas (ed.), *Proceedings and Ordinances of the Privy Council of England*, 7 vols., Record Com. (London, 1834–7).
Regement	F. J. Furnivall (ed.), *Hoccleve's Works, iii. The Regement of Princes*, EETS, extra ser., no. 72, (London, 1897).
Registrum Whethamstede	Riley, H. T. (ed.), *Registrum Abbatiae Johannis Whethamstede*, 2 vols., Rolls ser. (London, 1872–3).
RP	*Rotuli Parliamentorum*, 6 vols., Record Com. (n.p., n.d.).
Secreta	R. R. Steele, (ed.), *Three Prose Versions of the Secreta Secretorum*, EETS, extra ser., no. 74, (London, 1898).
'Somnium'	'Somnium Vigilantis', printed by J. P. Gilson as 'A Defence of the Proscription of the Yorkists in 1459', *English Historical Review*, 26 (1911), pp. 512–25.

Stonor	C. L. Kingsford (ed.), *The Stonor Letters and Papers*, 2 vols., Camden Soc., 3rd ser., XXIX–XXX (London, 1919).
Three Chrons.	J. Gairdner (ed.), *Three Fifteenth-Century Chronicles*, Camden Soc., new ser., XXVIII (London, 1880).
'Three Consideracions'	'The III Consideracions Right Necesserye to the Good Governaunce of a Prince', in Genet (ed.), *Political Tracts*, pp. 180–219.
Town Chrons.	R. Flenley (ed.), *Six Town Chronicles of England* (Oxford, 1911).
'Tractatus'	'Tractatus de Regimine Principum ad Regem Henricum Sextum', in Genet (ed.), *Political Tracts*, pp. 53–168.
VCH	*Victoria History of the Counties of England.*

1

INTRODUCTION: IDEAS AND POLITICS IN FIFTEENTH-CENTURY HISTORY

W HAT WAS THE character of public life in fifteenth-century England? That is the biggest question which this book seeks to answer – or to answer, at least, in some measure. Old-fashioned as it sounds, it is actually quite a new question, for the simple reason that until recently fifteenth-century England was thought to possess very little which could be described in such terms. Instead, it has been traditional to argue that in this period the attentions of public figures were focused mainly on their private concerns, their personal interests and those of their lords and servants; and that the framework of public institutions and ideas they had inherited – the 'constitution', as it came to be known – was at best neglected by them, and at worst unpicked. Even before 1500, political commentators and historians were bemoaning the corruption of public life by the private interests of leading politicians. To many of these contemporaries, it appeared that the public good, or 'common weal', faced destruction at the hands of men who put the claims of self, family or party before those of king and community; who abandoned the old political virtues and sought their own material satisfaction instead.[1] Centuries later, the first academic historians took a similar tack. When, in 1878, William Stubbs came to write the third volume of his *Constitutional History*, it seemed to him that the history of England in the fifteenth century contained 'little else than the details of foreign wars and domestic struggles'.[2] The 'parliamentary institutions' which he took to be the natural forum for public affairs had been reduced to 'insignificance among the ruder expedients of arms, the more stormy and spontaneous forces of personal, political and religious passion'. It was not, he thought, going to be easy 'to trace the continuity of national life through this age of obscurity and disturbance'.

Nowadays, the one-time 'cinderella century' is one of the most widely

---

[1] See below, pp. 40–2.
[2] For this quotation and the succeeding ones, see Stubbs 1875–8: III, pp. 2, 4.

researched periods of the middle ages, but the broad lines of its political and constitutional history have changed less than one might have expected.[3] Perhaps because the focus of historical interest has shifted away from the areas to which the Victorians gave priority, their thinking still exerts a significant influence over our views of the nature of government in later medieval England.[4] In many accounts, for example, it remains implicit that the proper venues for the promotion of public interests were the formal structures of the embryonic state: parliament, the law, the king's council; and the king himself only if he was guided by these.[5] Public life and public responsibility continue to be the property of public institutions; yet the whole world of 'the public' is, as before, peripheral to the political story of the fifteenth century. On the whole, modern political histories, like earlier ones, have centred on a different kind of politics, a politics which was not primarily concerned with matters of public policy, but which turned instead on more 'private' affairs: essentially, the struggles of kings, nobles and gentlemen to advance their personal interests and those of their allies.[6] Appropriately enough, this 'private' politics was conducted in 'private' places: the households of the king and other lords; the by-ways and meeting-places of shires and towns.[7] And the key to political success lay in 'private' means and methods: above all, the skilful distribution of 'patronage' – grants of favour, money, lands or offices – to the eager members of this 'hard, mercenary and shamelessly acquisitive society'.[8]

As far as the history of the centre is concerned, 'State' and 'Society' are thus as disjoined in modern writing as they are in any nineteenth-century work: all that has happened is that our interest has shifted from the former to the latter.[9] In many ways, therefore, Stubbs' belief that 'there is no

---

[3]   S. B. Chrimes' appealing phrase (Chrimes, Ross and Griffiths (eds.) 1972: p. vii). For comment on the explosion of research in fifteenth-century history, see Guth 1977 and Carpenter 1983a.

[4]   Campbell 1988: pp. 7, 12–14; Powell 1994: p. 2; Carpenter 1992: pp. 3, 6–7.

[5]   E.g. Brown 1989: esp. pp. 1–3; Griffiths 1981: pp. 28, 284, 562, 592–4; and note the comments of Carpenter 1992: pp. 282–3.

[6]   See e.g. McFarlane 1972: p. 87. It is interesting to note that in DeLloyd Guth's survey of recent historiography (1977), 'Constitutional History' is lumped in with 'Administrative History' to make a single category covering legal and administrative institutions, while 'Political History' is another category, covering kings, households, nobles and rebels (p. 12).

[7]   Starkey 1981: esp. pp. 225, 263; Guth 1977: p. 16.

[8]   Ross (ed.) 1979: pp. 9–10, quoting McFarlane. See also Griffiths 1991b: p. 11; Hicks 1991a: pp. xii, pp. 41–2; Richmond 1983: p. 59; Carpenter 1992: pp. 4, 6; and Powell 1994 for the tendency of political history to focus on the distribution of patronage in this period.

[9]   For this disjuncture, see Kaminsky and Van Horn Melton 1992: pp. xvii–xviii. See Powell 1994: pp. 11–12 for a similar point about the opposition in modern work on fifteenth-century England between the worlds of 'bureaucracy' (government) and

unity of public interest, no singleness of political aim, no heroism of self-sacrifice' among the politicians of the later middle ages has resurfaced in today's accounts.[10] There is no real disagreement with his diagnosis that 'when the pride of wealth and pomp took the place of political aspirations, personal indulgence, domestic tyranny, obsequious servility followed': it is merely doubted that what Stubbs called 'political aspirations' had been of much significance earlier on. Meanwhile, the observation that Richard II's reign saw 'the baronage ... divided against itself, one part maintaining the popular liberties but retarding their progress by bitter personal antipathies, the other maintaining royal autocracy, and although less guilty as aggressors, still more guilty by way of revenge' might almost be a résumé of modern interpretations of what was going on in the 1450s: one would only need to add the suggestion that the maintenance of either 'popular liberties' or 'royal autocracy' was unlikely to be anything but a cover for the advancement of more private interests.[11]

The idea that, at some level, we are still approaching the world of fifteenth-century politics and government from a Victorian perspective may seem almost unbelievable. The assaults of medievalists on what McFarlane called 'the Stubbsian framework' began within years of Stubbs' death, and an aversion to the assumptions of 'Constitutional History' has been a central characteristic of most twentieth-century writing on the English past.[12] However, as several writers have recently suggested, this aversion could actually be the source of some of the unexpected continuities in fifteenth-century history.[13] Scepticism about Victorian views of the constitution and of its productive role in the politics of periods other than the later middle ages has led political historians to reject the whole notion of an integrated, national and self-conscious political body which the constitutional approach assumes. The result, as K. B. McFarlane famously noted in 1938, was that the collapse of the 'Stubbsian framework' was followed not by the erection of 'a new order', a new model for the understanding of contemporary political and governmental arrangements, but instead by a state of 'anarchy'.[14] In many respects, this state persists today. We may look more sympathetically and searchingly at the social networks and practices which earlier historians regarded as corrupt and disruptive, but we are only just beginning to explore their public qualities, to reconsider their place in relation to the

'patronage', and Harriss 1993 for an important discussion of the relationship between government and society in later medieval England.

[10] For this quotation, and others in this paragraph, see Stubbs 1875–8: II, pp. 625–6; III, pp. 269, 542. For examples of modern writing which tend to echo the judgements quoted here, see e.g. Lander 1969: ch. 7; 1980: pp. 217–21; Griffiths 1981: pp. 592–7.

[11] E.g. Jones 1989a.   [12] McFarlane 1973: pp. 279–80.

[13] Carpenter 1992: pp. 5–6; Powell 1994: pp. 8–10.   [14] McFarlane 1973: p. 280.

world of government and of ideas about government; and to revise our sense of this world in the light of what we have found.[15] McFarlane himself, of course, did go on to develop a coherent and comprehensive new interpretation of political society in later medieval England, but, despite its manifest influence on succeeding generations, it has not redeveloped our understanding of national politics in the period. In part, this is because McFarlane's ideas prompted a significant redirection of scholarly effort towards the affairs of the localities, but it is also a result of the Namierite thread that runs through his writing.[16] Albeit with a certain ambivalence, McFarlane lent encouragement to the idea that medieval politics were mainly concerned with the competition for status and influence, and he emphasised that the key to understanding these politics was to explore the lives of leading politicians and the webs of interest which connected them.[17] In the end, therefore, a paradoxical result of his work has been to confirm the limited and broadly negative views of fifteenth-century political culture which Stubbs and others had left behind. Until very recently, the constitutional history of the period has barely advanced.[18] Its political history has focused mainly on the exploration of private networks and connections. The outcome of these trends is a rather aimless and unenlightening politics, free of development, devoid of public pressures, and often detached from the formal institutions and publicly acknowledged principles which surrounded it.

Is this dispiriting picture of the fifteenth-century polity justified? Certainly, the notion of an entirely unprincipled and unconstitutional society demands suspicion: as one scholar has recently remarked, 'all societies have a constitution, even if ... it consists largely of the unspoken assumptions of the politically aware about what may or may not be done'.[19] Even if fifteenth-century England *was* nothing more than an aggregate of private connections, and there is every reason to doubt this, some public phenomena – principles, institutions, places for debate – must surely have grown up to co-ordinate them. The whole, in effect, must have been more than the sum of its parts, and that is

---

[15] See Carpenter 1992: pp. 3–4, 282–3; also Horrox 1992: pp. 391–2, 398–9, for some interesting comment along similar lines.

[16] Many of the points made in this paragraph are explored at more length in Powell 1994.

[17] See e.g. McFarlane 1972: p. 87; 1973: pp. 119–21, 296–7; 1981e: pp. 19–21.

[18] Together with one or two others, those named in n. 22, below, have, since the 1980s, been producing work which develops our understanding of the later medieval constitution. See, in particular, Powell 1989; Carpenter 1983b and 1992; Harriss (ed.) 1985; and also, in a slightly different way, Horrox 1989. Before this, Harriss 1975 stands almost alone in English scholarship as a revision of older constitutional history: it breaks off before the fifteenth century, however. My debt to these works, and in most cases to their authors, will be obvious from everything written here.

[19] Carpenter 1992: p. 5.

full of significance for the way in which historians ought to approach the discussion of each. Not only can we not understand the political history of the realm unless we explore its ruling framework of ideas and institutions, we cannot understand the political activity of any part of it – least of all that of the co-ordinating part: the community of kings and great lords which occupied centre stage – without doing the same thing. McFarlane once remarked that constitutional history is 'not something distinct from political history; it *is* political history', but this well-known observation clearly cuts both ways.[20] Whilst he apparently intended to suggest that political structures and ideas were shaped by men and their needs, his comment invites the response that the needs of men (or, at least, the ways in which those needs were expressed) were also shaped by the surrounding political ideas and structures.[21]

In the last few years, a number of historians have called for a 'new constitutional history' of fifteenth-century England as a means of produc- ing a more satisfying account of politics by reintegrating the study of political events and relationships with the study of government and of ideas about government.[22] They have argued that the reason why nine- teenth-century historians, and several earlier commentators for that matter, found a lot of fifteenth-century politics to be distasteful, or amoral, or unconstitutional was that these politics did not correspond to what they understood to be the political morality, or constitution, of the time. It was the failure of fifteenth-century kings and noblemen to conform to the anachronistic demands of 'a contractual monarchy beholden to a parliament of estates representing "the kingdom"' which accounts for a large part of Victorian hostility to fifteenth-century practice.[23] The appropriate response for us, it is suggested, is not to follow the assumption that 'constitutional' behaviour is inherently lawful, consultative and parliamentary, as these properties were understood in the nineteenth century, but to explore an alternative possibility: namely, that fifteenth-century politics were indeed governed by a 'constitution', but that this was something rather different, in content and perhaps in structure, from the frameworks which earlier historians envisaged.[24] From a historiographical point of view, there is clearly a lot to recommend

---

[20] McFarlane 1973: p. 280.
[21] The extent to which shared ideas in public discourse actually shaped people's *private* perceptions of their needs is a difficult question, which I do not propose to tackle (but see, for example, Pocock 1973: esp. pp. 30–1).
[22] Powell 1989: pp. 6–9; 1994: pp. 10–13; and Carpenter 1992: pp. 5–13. See also Horrox 1992: pp. 391–3.
[23] Quotation from McKenna 1979: p. 482.
[24] *Ibid.*, pp. 485–7 discusses the problems historians have had with the term 'constitu- tion(al)'.

the return to a more structural, or 'constitutional' approach. It could restore an explanatory framework to a political history which is increasingly detailed, but also – one might argue – increasingly difficult to understand at a global level. It would enable us to identify the defining characteristics of politics in our period and to make comparisons with those of other periods; to negotiate, in fact, a new place for the fifteenth century in the national history which, for one reason or another, we continue to wish to understand. It would permit us to explore the connections between central and local government more effectively than at present: we have gone much further in revising our understanding of the latter than we have our understanding of the former, and the two no longer fit together very well. And besides all this, we may emerge with an enriched understanding of fifteenth-century politics themselves. If they were, at some level, shaped by commonly held principles and commonly accepted practices, then they and the politicians who made them may have been quite different from how they have conventionally been presented. Above all, perhaps, it will be possible to re-evaluate the relationship between politics and public interests, once it is recognised that these interests may have been expressed and mediated in different ways: ways which earlier commentators overlooked. How, then, should we proceed?

The obvious starting-point for any attempt to reinterpret the fifteenth-century constitution must be the political and constitutional ideas of contemporaries, because it is only by placing political society in its proper ideological context that we may understand it fully.[25] We know that fifteenth-century men and women possessed a wide range of ideas concerning the workings of their polity, and it can be relatively easily shown that these ideas were a significant feature of their political discourse: indeed, an attempt to show this for a portion of political society in Henry VI's reign is made below.[26] But how can we be sure that a discourse of this kind actually affected political behaviour? After all, the idealistic statements of fifteenth-century politicians have generally been seen as camouflage for more mundane, and often self-interested, designs. Fortunately, the nature of the relationship between ideas, language and action has been explored at some length by the so-called 'Cambridge School' of historians of political thought, and their work is full of

---

[25] See e.g. Skinner 1978: I, p. xii; Carpenter 1992: pp. 3–4, 7–9, and note the comments of Marc Bloch, cited by Guenée 1971: p. 339: 'the full significance of monarchical institutions, of political institutions in general, cannot ... be understood unless their dependence on the undercurrents of ideas – and sentiments as well – beneath them is clearly established'.

[26] Below, pp. 56–74.

significance for the project before us here.[27] In particular, the question of whether or not the principled language of politicians provides any key to their behaviour has been tackled by Quentin Skinner, with specific reference, interestingly enough, to the debate over Namier's reading of eighteenth-century politics which so influenced McFarlane and many of his successors. The essence of the 'Namierite' critique, Skinner argues, was that politicians' professions of principle are no more than '*ex post facto* rationalisations', providing no guide to the 'underlying realities' of politics and therefore of little consequence to political historians. Skinner's response is that the genuineness of individual professions of principle is not the important question: what matters in the analysis of political language is what principles were chosen and with what effect. It does not matter whether individuals are moved by materialistic concerns or by ideas, or – more plausibly – by some amalgam of the two: the point is that each political society is governed by a matrix of ideas to which all its politicians must make reference.[28] People engaging in any behaviour which is not plainly endorsed by prevailing morality, or which for other reasons requires public justification, are forced to justify themselves in terms of principle. The range of available principles therefore determines the range of available actions, so that a political 'agent's professed principles invariably need to be treated as causal conditions of his actions'. As a result, 'the explanation of political action essentially depends on the study of political ideology': in effect, we need to look at the ideas circulating in the fifteenth-century polity because these *were* the 'underlying realities' of its politics.

One substantial attempt to sidestep Victorian assumptions and recover the true 'political ideology' of fifteenth-century England has, of course, already been made. In 1936, S. B. Chrimes, rejecting the 'Lancastrian Constitution' described by Stubbs and others as a Whiggish anachronism, wrote an analytical survey of what he called 'the spirit of the constitution' in the fifteenth century.[29] This he took to be 'opinions, ideas and assumptions as to the nature and distribution of governmental rights', a definition which, in the event, restricted Chrimes to the limited range of material which consciously assigned rights and duties to recognised parts of the political landscape, rather than the much broader array of sources which took the structures of government as given and commented on their performance.[30] To some extent, Chrimes reproduced the old

---

[27] See Pocock 1972 and, in particular for the points made in this paragraph, Skinner 1974 and 1988: esp. pp. 108–11.

[28] Cf. Hicks 1991b, which concentrates more on the idealism of individuals than the action of ideas on society as a whole (and the results of that action for the individual).

[29] Chrimes 1936: p. xx.

[30] Quotation from *ibid.*, p. xx. This may be compared with another statement of his aims on

assumption that the constitution was an entity in itself, distinct from politics and best described by specialists, above all, lawyers.[31] This did little to heal the growing rift between 'constitutional' and 'political' history, and it is interesting to note that McFarlane condemned the work as 'unnecessarily narrow and legalistic'.[32] Chrimes' portrait of the 'constitution' was a one-sided one: it emphasised legal opinion concerning the most formal and global dealings of king and realm – parliaments, coronations, the succession, the king and the law – at the expense of other views and other relationships. Like earlier works of constitutional history, moreover, it dealt only with arrangements at the 'centre', but the focus of scholarly interest would soon be shifting towards the localities. Far from encouraging a more integrated history, therefore, it cleared the way for the modern tendency to regard the 'constitution' as a body of public law and precedent dealing with a limited range of specific and mostly rather large-scale matters; a body which can safely be excluded from discussions of a politics dominated by personal, factional and local transactions.[33]

What is needed now is not so much a study of public law, but an investigation of the patterns and principles governing public life; and, in fact, a reinterpretation of what 'public life' involved. Law, parliament and the formal offices of government were only a part of the fifteenth-century constitutional framework, not the whole of it.[34] What we must do in particular, if we are to restore a sense of structure to the political history of our period and to understand its real meaning, is to look more closely at the ideological and institutional context of those areas of the polity which we have identified as being most important. Since McFarlane, if not before, these have been the affairs of the king and the nobility, 'the natural supports of monarchy'.[35]

Over the last thirty or forty years, it has become clear that, notwithstanding his traditional presentation in constitutional histories as a limited monarch, the later medieval king was very much the leader of political

p. xvi: to get at 'the half-expressed concepts and ideas behind the machinery of government ... assumptions that called for no statement' – an enterprise which more closely resembles what is being attempted here. Cf. Oakley 1973, which argues that medieval literature on politics was generally far more concerned with the performance of those in authority than with the distribution of powers on which their authority rested, and that historians ought to take account of these priorities in their analyses.

[31] In Kern 1939: p. xiii, Chrimes argued that constitutional history was 'a branch of legal history' and his account drew heavily on legal sources: notably the Year Books and the works of Fortescue. Whether or not the constitution should be regarded as the province of lawyers had been a matter of vigorous debate in the nineteenth century (Burrow 1981: pp. 133–4).

[32] McFarlane 1938 (quotation from p. 708).   [33] See below, p. 13.

[34] See Harriss 1993; Carpenter 1983b for an important discussion of the position of law in this respect; and Watts 1991: pp. 279–80 for some comments on the relative constitutional importance of 'counsel' and 'the council'.

[35] McFarlane 1972: p. 59.

society. In practice, if not also in theory, he enjoyed considerable freedom in the management of his leading subjects, and it was his character and abilities, above all, which determined the fortunes of the polity during his reign.[36] This has been widely acknowledged, but the way in which contemporaries apprehended this reality – what they thought about it and what it meant for their views on politics and their beliefs about the political system – has barely been explored. At the same time, it has been generally recognised that the rule of large parts of the realm belonged in effect to the nobility. Even as lesser landowners filled the local offices of the royal administration and, together with urban and mercantile elites, took over the formal representation of the *communitas* in parliament, the dukes, earls and greater barons retained much of their ancient social and political dominance. In this still-hierarchical and deferential society, they continued to act as the principal mediators between king and people, between 'centre' and 'locality'. So it is that the relationship between the king and the nobility has emerged as the backbone of the fifteenth-century polity.[37] There may have been other webs attaching king and people to one another – structures of public finance, of royal justice, of common defence, of economic association, and these have often been investigated – but it is the relationships, the structures, of royal and noble lordship which have dominated political histories, and in many ways, this seems justifiable.[38] The trouble is that these relationships have mostly been treated as if they were both private and, for the most part, ungoverned by public or constitutional principles. Once again, we need to consider the possibility that these relationships performed a recognised public function and to examine more closely what politically active contemporaries expected from the relationship between the king and the nobility, how they envisaged it working and what part they believed it to play in the normal apparatus of government. This book is an attempt to examine these issues and to make use of the results: in effect, to look at the interaction of a particular king and his leading subjects in the light of contemporary ideas about both kingship itself and the dealings of king and nobility.

In many ways, the reign of Henry VI is an ideal choice for an exercise of this kind. On the one hand, there is a lot of source material: the peculiar sequence of minority, 'inanity' and crisis meant that contemporaries

---

[36] See below, p. 14.

[37] See below, pp. 74–80, and, for the points made here, e.g. Carpenter 1992: pp. 287–8, 347–54; Coss 1989; Given-Wilson 1987a: pp. 11–14, ch. 2.

[38] Harriss 1993 usefully discusses the links between of a number of these webs of association.

discussed and recorded their views on political and constitutional issues extensively. On the other hand, since Chrimes, there has been no sustained attempt to use these materials to provide a structural treatment of what might be called the politics of kingship in the period.[39] Thanks to a number of important studies, the fiscal, military and diplomatic contexts of Henry VI's government are now well understood,[40] but the structures of authority which underpinned that government remain obscure. It is almost universally agreed that Henry himself was an inadequate ruler, and that his personal inadequacies go a long way to explaining the disasters which befell the polity in the 1450s, but there is much less certainty over what these inadequacies were and how they took effect, or precisely why and how much they mattered, or how they inter-related with other factors such as public finance or the situation in France; and indeed there *cannot* be much certainty on these matters until there is a better understanding of the constitutional context in which Henry and his subjects were operating. Why was Henry VI able to go on ruling so unsuccessfully for so long; and why did he consistently attract more support than 'oppositional' figures such as Gloucester and York? Why were the first twenty-eight years of the reign so much more peaceful than the last eleven? What were the leading subjects of the period – Gloucester, York, Bedford, Beaufort, Somerset, Suffolk and Queen Margaret – aiming to achieve? Were they, or any of them, or the nobility as a class, responsible for the descent into civil war at the end of the reign? Were the politics of the 1430s, 1440s and 1450s about anything more than faction and patronage? Were there real divisions over policy in France? How was England actually governed while Henry VI was king? It is not that these questions have not been addressed: it is that they cannot be answered fully and fairly without a detailed investigation of the norms of royal and noble power. We need to tackle them alongside an exploration of what kingship was and how it worked; what was actually expected of both the crown and the man who wore it; how the will of the king's government was composed and conveyed; and how authority was distributed, and interests satisfied, in the late medieval realm. The really interesting questions arising from Henry VI's reign concern the polity, as well as its actors. To answer them, we need to place the personalities and individual interests in the context of a wider politics, and politics itself in the context

---

[39] Note the comments in the preface to Griffiths 1981: p. vii. McFarlane's famous essay on the Wars of the Roses (1981f) is full of important insights in this area and, I feel bound to say that, in my view, it anticipates in sketch form many of the conclusions offered in this book.

[40] See especially Harriss 1986 and 1988; Griffiths 1981: chs. 6, 15–18; Wolffe 1971: chs. 4–5 and 1981: chs. 9–11; Keen 1989.

of government and of ideas about government from which it has become detached.

These aims are reflected in the organisation of the book. In chapter 2, an attempt is made to set out the constitutional norms which governed the relations of king and nobility in mid-fifteenth-century England. The treatment falls into three main sections. In the first, some of the most fundamental and commonplace theories of later medieval monarchy are discussed. The principal sources for this discussion are not the ornate products of schoolmen and philosophers but, as in a number of other recent studies,[41] the popularised versions of their ideas which circulated in works of the influential 'mirrors for princes' genre and similar media. The aim, therefore, is to get at what D. W. Hanson neatly called 'operative political thought': perceptions concerning the distribution and operation of authority which are likely to have arisen from exposure to the more accessible sources of ideology.[42] The second section deals with the changes in the tone and content of this kind of theoretical writing which were brought about by the disruption of normal political relations in the mid-century civil wars. This has seemed important not only because the last eleven years of Henry VI's reign were conducted in the shadow (if not the fact) of civil war, but also because some of the commentators of this period of dissonance, notably Sir John Fortescue, have been so influential in shaping historians' perceptions of later medieval politics. The third section aims at discovering to what extent prevailing theories were actually taken up by the nobility themselves. It begins with a brief examination of their literary tastes, and proceeds to a longer exploration of the language and concepts which they employed, first as participants in the public affairs of the realm, and then as rulers of the shires, before closing with an attempt to show how these two identities were reconciled with the aid of the king.

Chapter 3 pursues the implications of this ideological framework in a survey of the forms of royal government, first at the centre, and then, in a second section, in the localities. Here the aim is not to provide detailed documentation of the various recognised institutions of rule – the writing offices, the law-courts and so on – but to examine the interplay between the inherited structures of government and the demands of political society. This has certain implications for two of the most obviously political bodies which have featured in works on medieval government:

---

[41] E.g. Harriss 1985a, and, in much greater length, Kekewich 1987. When I carried out the bulk of the research on which this book is based, I was unaware of Dr Kekewich's fine thesis, which sets out to do something very similar to what I have attempted in ch. 2, below.

[42] Hanson 1970: p. 12.

the royal court and the king's council. Because it is with the relationship between the crown and the nobility that this book is principally concerned, parliament receives no discussion in this chapter.

The remainder of the book is devoted to a study of the polity of Henry VI. Chapter 4 aims to bridge the gap between the general context of late medieval royal government and the specific circumstances of Henry's reign: first, by examining the question of the king's character and its potential constitutional significance; second, by exploring the particular conventions of Henry's minority, many of which appear to have influenced politics as the king moved imperceptibly into adulthood. Chapters 5, 6 and 7, finally, offer accounts of the changing structures of government and politics during the rest of the reign: from 1435 to 1445, 1445 to 1450 and 1450 to 1461, respectively. These accounts are not intended to be exhaustive. Far from providing detailed treatments of events, they set out to document the major political trends and developments of Henry VI's reign, binding together the various themes explored in earlier chapters with what actually happened. The hope is that, from a more detailed examination of the nature of the monarchy in this difficult time, the broad lines of a new and more persuasive account of the politics of the reign will emerge.

2

THE CONCEPTUAL FRAMEWORK

THE 'CONSTITUTION' HAS not entirely disappeared from accounts of later medieval politics. Rather, conceived as a body of
public law and formal precedent and dimly acknowledged as the outer
boundary of public life, it hovers about the edges of a political stage
dominated by personal, factional and materialistic transactions. When
crises occur – whether natural ones, such as the deaths of kings, or
unnatural ones, such as periods of dissonance among the ruling classes –
it is wheeled on and dusted down, and its principles are invoked to
explain what is happening.[1] Otherwise, it is left to one side. To some
extent, of course, this is a justifiable approach. The main business of
political systems is to attend to the present need: it is only when consensus
among the participants breaks down that strict forms and precedents
become important. Even so, this consensus itself usually rests on a series
of less formal arrangements which have their own patterns and principles;
patterns and principles which are probably all the more influential
because they are shared and often unstated. As is suggested above, these
arrangements and the concepts which underlay them may also deserve to
be seen as 'constitutional', in that they delineated the immediate framework of late medieval politics: within their bounds lay all the possibilities
recognised by politicians. A constitution of this kind is principally
important to us not as a body of ideas to which voluntary recourse could
be had, but as the shared dialectic – in a sense, the common language – of
a political society.[2] The intention behind this approach is not to suggest
that the fifteenth-century nobility (or anyone else, for that matter) were
disinterested ideologues, but rather to insist that they perceived their
interests and planned their behaviour within a particular frame of

---

[1] See e.g. Griffiths 1981: pp. 12 (Henry VI's succession), 275–8 (his coming of age), 676–
84 (the parliamentary crisis of 1450 and the lack of any criticism of the king).
[2] See Pocock 1972.

reference. It is to the exploration of this frame of reference, or 'working constitution', which the present chapter is devoted.

A 'working constitution' is at least implicit in current historical writing on the period. Nobody would suggest that later medieval kings ruled through personal force alone. The influence of powerful conventions, such as hierarchy, obedience and sacral authority, and of institutions of consent and co-operation, such as parliament and the royal council, receives universal recognition. It is understood that these conventions and institutions provided sources of communal power upon which the king could draw in the exercise of his functions. At the same time, however, it has almost become axiomatic that for the maintenance of his polity, the king, in his own person, needed to be ingenious, vigorous and imposing: in a period still readily seen as 'ungovernable', 'strong' kingship, on the whole, was 'good' kingship; 'weak' kingship brought disaster.[3] This sort of assumption raises a number of problems. First of all, it is difficult to reconcile with the communitarian values which are acknowledged to be explicit in the constitution, however this is conceived. As a result, the political system appears hypocritical, even schizophrenic, its published principles and formal practices evoking co-operation and consent, while its real dynamics rested on manipulation and threat. For the most part, as we have seen, historians have resolved this kind of paradox by turning away from the more public elements of the system and focusing on the putative 'realities' of politics instead. But this is not an approach we can really afford to take: the public principles and practices of the system need to be addressed and were, in fact, quite as real as the private aims of its participants.[4] A second problem with the notion that a king needed exceptional qualities merely to retain his throne is that it flies in the face of almost everything we have learned from K. B. McFarlane. Far from evoking a 'community of interests' between the king and the nobility, it conjures up a world of wilfully destructive overmighty subjects and constitutionally undermighty kings.[5] This may not matter in itself – McFarlane might have been wrong, though his judgements in this area seem particularly persuasive – but it does make work on national politics harder to reconcile with work on local politics where more clearly McFarlanite perspectives prevail. And beyond all this, the 'strong' king / 'weak' king dichotomy lacks precision. How much force was actually required of the good, 'strong', king, and what was its nature? Why did his

---

[3]   Something of this approach is to be found in e.g. Ross 1974: pp. 323, 331–41; Lander 1969: ch. 7; Ormrod 1985; Pollard 1988: pp. 46–53, 65. See Carpenter 1992: pp. 5–6, for a recent critique.

[4]   Above, p. 7.   [5]   Cf. McFarlane 1973: pp. 2–3, 120–1, 283.

alter ego, the 'weak' king, cause disaster, and how was his weakness manifested?

A central argument of this book is that we might emerge with a clearer and more accurate sense of fifteenth-century kingship, and of the politics which immediately surrounded it, if we based our analysis upon a more thorough study of contemporary comment on the nature of the polity. Evidence has survived in a profusion of materials, ranging from the complex ideas of jurists and theologians, through handbooks and courtly literature dealing with political themes, to royal propaganda, poems, proverbs and the stuff of correspondence and conversation. The account in the first part of this chapter rests on one kind of source in particular: works in the 'mirrors for princes' tradition.[6] These were treatises aimed at kings and noblemen, and their commonest aim was to popularise received opinion on the mores and practices of personal lordship.[7] As a means of gaining insights into political behaviour, they have been surprisingly little used. Their derivative and moralistic nature has generally ruled them out of serious consideration by political, constitutional and intellectual historians alike.[8] In a sense, however, it is precisely because their contents were commonplace that the mirrors are such a useful source in the attempt to find contemporary 'assumptions which called for no statement'.[9] Their preference for developing individual morality rather than describing the operation of institutions has been presented as a sign of their primitiveness, but it may suggest that later medieval politics were governed by a different order of priorities from those which constitutional historians have traditionally focused on.[10] Finally, in a culture in which the application of reason to authorised truths was expected to deliver enlightenment, handbooks like these might reasonably be expected to have influenced the views of the men and women who read them. We can easily show that kings and noblemen commissioned, borrowed and bought this kind of literature, and we might suggest that it helped to shape their understanding of the polity. Later in the chapter, this proposition will be tested in various ways: by comparing the implications of the mirrors with the

---

[6] This is to use the term 'mirrors for princes' in its loosest sense, simply to mean works of advice, instruction or edification concerning the operations of kingship and lordship (see Genet (ed.), *Political Tracts*, pp. ix–xvi, for a discussion which sets out how the genre ought to be defined). I have also looked at poems, verse histories and similar texts which could – like the mirrors – have been seen by contemporaries as sources of political instruction.

[7] Dunbabin 1988: p. 478.

[8] Note the comments of e.g. Lander 1969: p. 189; Ferguson 1965: pp. 8–9, 11, 24, 31–3; and Brown 1981: p. 130. Carpenter 1983b: pp. 209–13 and Harriss 1985a are pioneering examples of the use of this kind of literature as a source for political norms and expectations.

[9] Quotation from Chrimes 1936: see above, p. 7, n. 30.

[10] Cf. Ferguson 1965: esp. pp. 31–3, and see below, p. 20.

model of authority implicit in contemporary chivalric literature; and, second, by analysing the political discourse of the king and nobility in both local and national contexts. First of all, however, we need to gain a sense of the basic workings of the political system as it appeared to the authors of these texts.

THE NORMS OF KINGSHIP IN THE LATER MIDDLE AGES

At the centre of the polity depicted by the mirrors was a king wielding sovereign power.[11] This is rather to be expected, perhaps, but it bears emphasising because of the legacy of nineteenth-century ideas of 'constitutional monarchy' and, specifically, the lingering belief that, even in the later middle ages, English royal authority operated under significant restraints.[12] Although 'Lancastrian constitutionalism' is now a dead letter, the idea of a legally restrained king continues to dominate discussion of the formal framework of government in the period. If the king was not ruled by representative institutions, it is said, he was at least bound by laws. At a certain level, this proposition is undeniable, but it does invite qualifications, and it may be helpful to preface the discussion of the ideas in the mirrors with a few remarks about the nature of later medieval government as the present author understands it.[13] There is no doubt that by the fifteenth century the king was generally subject to the law, that law itself was made with the assent of the lords and commons in parliament and that the king was bound to obtain the consent of the commons in parliament to taxation. However, there is also no doubt that the authority by which laws were made, unmade and upheld, and by which taxation was sought, though not granted, was royal authority, albeit afforced by the counsel of subjects.[14] No temporal jurisdiction exceeded

---

[11] This is more often assumed than declared, but see e.g. *Livre du Corps de Policie*, p. 40 (the edition of Christine's work referred to in this chapter was translated into English between *c.* 1450 and *c.* 1475 and printed in 1521: *ibid.*, pp. 18–19); Byles, (ed.), *Book of Fayttes of Armes*, p. 11; and, perhaps more surprisingly, Whittaker (ed.), *Mirror of Justices*, p. 8.

[12] See McKenna 1979 for a critique, and Chrimes 1936: pp. 60–2, 344–5, 339 n. 68; Hanson 1970: p. 24; Lander 1989; Brown 1989: p. 14 for treatments which emphasise the formally 'limited' nature of the English monarchy. The question of how (to borrow Fortescue's formulation) 'regal' and 'political' elements were balanced in the later medieval polity remains an interesting and important one. I am in the process of preparing a fuller discussion of matters which are dealt with only cursorily here.

[13] Because my principal concern is with the everyday workings of the polity, I have resolved not to give much consideration to matters such as the succession, coronation and death of the king: a substantial literature on topics such as these already exists. See Chrimes 1936: ch. 1, for an introduction.

[14] In their power to grant taxation, the commons in parliament did enjoy a certain independence of royal authority, since they came with full powers to adjudicate the plea of necessity on the basis of their representativeness: Harriss 1975: pp. 46–8; Edwards

that of the king counselled, but the 'king counselled' was still the king, and this is a point of more than semantic significance.[15] The personal will of the king was the one essential prescription for public acts of judgement and so, by analogy, for all legitimate acts of government.[16] This meant that there was an important sense in which the king was, like parliament today, unrestrained. Under normal circumstances, he could not be resisted within his realm, since it was only by his authority, which depended on his personal will, that acts were done while he was king.[17] This is not to say that kings felt free to do as they pleased – a range of pressures existed to encourage them to conform to law and counsel – but that, in the last resort, they enjoyed a monopoly of legitimate power. This is worth stating because it makes the idea of a 'royal prerogative', implicit in the idea of constitutional restraints, wholly inappropriate to the analysis of the mid-fifteenth-century polity: the king did not have a limited area of absolute liberty; there was one jurisdiction, it was his, and it ranged with equal fullness over all the causes in his realm.[18]

The corollary – in some respects, the obverse – of this sovereign power was a sovereign representativeness. Partly through his crown, but also in fact through his own person, since king and crown could not easily be separated, the king was the representative and embodiment of the realm.[19] This representativeness was one of the leading sources of the

1970 (although their obligation to grant supply in cases of 'evident and urgent necessity' is a point particularly emphasised by Harriss: see pp. 23–6, 35, 38–9, 45–8 etc.). For statements of the view that royal will was the fundamental source of authority in the realm (and that this will was ultimately personal and, in many respects, free), see Chrimes 1936: pp. 5, 6, 8–9, 342–5; Willard and Morris (eds.) 1940: pp. 4–7; Post 1964b: pp. 367–8; Tierney 1963: p. 309; McKenna 1979: p. 484.

[15] Kantorowicz 1957: pp. 364–72. Note that in the thirteenth century, 'Bracton' had apparently advanced a more constitutionalist solution to the problems of counsel (Tierney 1963: pp. 314–17). Even so, the complexity of his arguments, which have generated a great deal of debate among historians, draws attention to the difficulty of denying the king the right ultimately to ignore the advice of his counsellors. The crucial matter of the proper relationship between king and counsel in the later middle ages is discussed at length below.

[16] See n. 14, above, also Powell 1989: pp. 30–8, 51ff, 88 (for the king and justice / judgement) and Brown 1964a: pp. 154–5 (for the king's authorising role in the administration).

[17] The point is partly illustrated by the fact that the 'depositions' of 1327 and 1399 were accompanied (and that of Richard II certainly preceded) by abdications, reflecting the fact that the public power continued to be at the king's disposal: Wilkinson 1948–58: II, chs. 4 and 9 (Clarke 1936: pp. 183–5, argues, on the strength of the Pipewell Chronicle, that a parliamentary deposition preceded Edward's abdication). There is thus an important and practical sense in which Edward II and Richard II deposed themselves. See also Powell 1989: p. 34; Peters 1970: pp. 232ff.

[18] See Tierney 1963: pp. 308–9; Oakley 1968: pp. 344–6. Perhaps surprisingly, Chrimes 1936: pp. 42–3 seems to share this view, at least for the period before Henry VII, but notes that (in the second half of the century in particular) royal power was increasingly defined by law, with the result that what was left began to be seen as distinctive.

[19] For more on the crown, see below, p. 22. For the difficulty of separating king from

king's power, and arguably its major justification. The realm itself owed its definition to the king's rule, and the series of ideas which endowed the realm, or the 'community of the realm', with rights and powers generally bestowed the same blessings on the ruler.[20] Even so, the idea that the king represented his people was something of a two-edged sword. On the one hand, it gave him an untouchable legitimacy above that of any, or any group, of his subjects. In this respect, it was the essence of the personal sovereignty discussed above. Any limitation of the king's power would be a limitation of the realm's power: hence the crime of 'accroach-ment', which followed hot on the heels of this conceptual development.[21] On the other hand, the idea of representation emphasised that the king was given his unlimited powers for one reason only: in order to act for the realm. As the English translator of the *Book of Fayttes of Armes* put it, 'Prynces soverayne ... for none other thyng were establysshed but for to doo right to everyche of their subgettis that shold be oppressid for ony extorcion and for to deffende and kepe them.'[22] Not only did this assumption impose upon the king a general responsibility to take account of the interests of the subjects, it also, as we shall see, inspired the growth of concepts, practices and mechanisms which permitted his direct and real representation of the people through the giving and taking of counsel.

This theme of royal representativeness rested on secure academic foundations. Thirteenth-century ideas concerning the purpose of earthly government, dominated by those of St Thomas Aquinas, made clear that it had been provided for the good of the people. Thomist writing reconciled an organic model of the state, based on Aristotle's *Politics*, with the theocratic world-view of late medieval churchmen. States existed because man, a 'political' animal, lived in communities which required

---

crown, except by the drastic expedient of deposition, see Kantorowicz 1957: pp. 364–8; Maitland 1911; Chrimes 1936: pp. 34–7 and note that the late medieval king possessed full authority even before his coronation (*ibid.*, pp. 17, 19–20, 35; McKenna 1979: pp. 491–505). The representativeness of the king in person is discussed below, p. 27, and elsewhere.

[20] The notion of 'iura regni', for example, was as easily taken to mean 'the rights of the kingship' as well as 'the rights of the realm': indeed, in increasing the confusion between the two, it strengthened the king's claims to public and national authority. See Richardson 1941: pp. 131–5 and, more generally, Post 1964a; 1964b: pp. 367–8; Tierney 1963: p. 309. The concept of 'iura regni' had been used against kings as well, of course: Holt 1960–1: pp. 62–4.

[21] Bellamy 1970: pp. 64–5, 95–8. The concept is plain in the moves against Gaveston: see McKisack 1959: p. 12.

[22] Byles (ed.), *Book of Fayttes of Armes*, p. 11. Similar versions of the Thomist dictum 'Rex datur propter regnum' featured in most later medieval mirrors: see e.g. 'Three Con-sideracions', pp. 189, 198; 'Tractatus', p. 118; *Livre du Corps de Policie*, pp. 51, 56, 66; *Governance*, p. 127; 'Active Policy', lines 219–24; *Regement*, st. 309 (implicitly); Moisant (ed.), *De Speculo Regis*, 'Recensio A', p. 83.

guidance in the common interest if he and all his fellows were to achieve their *summum bonum*. Kings and other just authorities were defined by the fact that they ruled 'the people of a city or a province for their common good', which, in turn, lay 'in the preservation of its unity; or, more simply, in peace'. As a result, a king, who was himself a unity, was the ideal form of authority for the realisation of this common good; while a tyrant, defined as 'one man who seeks personal profit from his position instead of the good of the community subject to him', was the most damaging.[23] Meanwhile, if the quality of rule was measurable in these terms – 'government', according to St Thomas, being 'more useful to the extent that it attains peaceful unity' – this was no prescription for political resistance or restraint.[24] Only God, who gave the king his powers, could bind him to the performance of his duties.[25] The king was indeed 'quasi deus noster in terris': his universal authority was shrouded in the mystery of divine appointment and it was inappropriate for subjects to question his judgements.[26]

Clearly enough, all this tends towards a rather different portrait of English kingship – even of the conceptual basis of English kingship – from the one traditionally offered. As I have noted, constitutional and intellectual historians have typically presented a more limited authority, a shared sovereignty, a 'double majesty', as the central mechanism by which England was theoretically governed.[27] Certainly, among the ideological materials of the middle ages, there were some which seemed to justify popular resistance to the king or the imposition of political controls upon him. Concepts of peerage and election, circulating in the early fourteenth century and, for rather different reasons, in the later fifteenth, posited a monarchy which rested squarely on the authority of the people (or of

---

[23] See generally *Aquinas*, pt I, 'On Princely Government'. Many of the points featured here appeared in fifteenth-century mirrors and similar works. To cite one particularly germane example, the 'Tractatus' observed that 'optima est gubernacio in qua per unum regem perfeccior unitas reservatur' (p. 165).

[24] *Aquinas*, p. 6. In Thomist theory, private persons had no power to constrain others or to interpret the common welfare, only to advise (pp. 56, 71) or to withdraw their own obedience under certain conditions (pp. 69, 81, 89–90) and popular toleration of unjust rule was generally recommended (e.g. pp. 15–18).

[25] That rulers faced spiritual judgement was well known: see e.g. *Regiment*, sts. 409, 410, 414. It may have been the unavailability of legitimate temporal sanctions which encouraged so many advice-writers to emphasise the king's answerability to God: see e.g. 'Three Consideracions', p. 189; 'Active Policy', sts. 84–6; *Livre du Corps de Policie*, pp. 50–1; Moisant (ed.), *De Speculo Regis*, 'Recensio A', pp. 103, 109, 122, 'Recensio B', pp. 127, 129–30, 149 (actually two separate works); Kail (ed.), *Twenty-Six Poems*, pp. 1–4 ('Love God and Drede'); *Regiment*, st. 367.

[26] The quotation is from Bishop Russell's speech intended for Edward V's parliament of 1483, printed by Chrimes 1936: pp. 168–78, p. 173.

[27] See e.g. Wilks 1963: ch. II.iii (not dealing with England alone); Chrimes 1936: pp. 60–2, 344–5 and (for useful definitions of 'limited' and 'constitutional' monarchy) p. 339 n. 68; Hanson 1970: pp. 24–5 (for 'double majesty').

some of them: typically the nobility, on the basis of their once feudal representativeness).[28] Common tags, such as 'vox populi, vox Dei', betrayed a sense that the people were free to act, or at least to speak up, if the king failed to represent their interests as they perceived them;[29] and the fact that these very words were taken as the theme for Archbishop Reynolds' sermon announcing the deposition of Edward II reveals the use to which such ideas might be put.[30] However, it is doubtful that this line of thinking had ever enjoyed hegemony, and it had certainly lost ground by the fifteenth century: indeed, it is largely absent from the sources under discussion in this section. References to popular power appear to be purely cautionary, a reminder to the prince of what could happen if he ignored the duties inherent in his office.[31] References to political controls – organised councils, representative assemblies, even human laws – tend to be scarce and rather incidental.[32] In the past, this tendency has sometimes been advanced as a sign of the political naïvety of the mirrors, but it could be that there is a more complex explanation for it.[33] Jean Dunbabin has noted that, in later medieval England, as in later medieval France, the dominant literature of political theory was mostly Egidian in its assumptions: that is to say that, following Giles of Rome, it emphasised the importance of a unified structure of authority and, in consequence,

---

[28] See e.g. Kingsford (ed.), *Song of Lewes*, pp. 49–51; Whittaker (ed.), *Mirror of Justices*, p. 6; Wilkinson 1948–58: III, p. 355 (*Modus Tenendi Parliamentum*, extract); Harcourt 1907: pp. 149–50 (*Tract on the Office of Steward*). See McKenna 1979: pp. 491ff, for election in the fifteenth century; and Holt 1981: pp. 25–8, for the nobility.

[29] See *Regement*, line 2886; *Crowland*, I, pp. 410–11, for fifteenth-century usages; and, for the rather less controversial notion that 'The puple is godes and not youres, / Thow they be soget to youre degre', Kail (ed.), *Twenty-Six Poems*, p. 1, lines 19–20 (turned to seditious use in the *Song of Lewes*, line 709).

[30] McKisack 1959: p. 89.

[31] The authors of mirrors for princes selected and deployed their material to suit their audiences. Christine de Pisan, for example, who had made a rather oblique reference to *vox populi, vox Dei* in the section of her *Livre du Corps de Policie* which was addressed to the king (p. 58), stuck to recommending obedience and service when she addressed the *populus* itself (pp. 116–17, 165, 169, 179, 184).

[32] The king is routinely told to uphold the law in all these texts (e.g. *Regement*, sts. 397–8; *Secreta*, p. 135), though he is also expected to promote justice and mercy, and these are not quite the same thing: see below, pp. 24, 58–9. It is striking that where tyranny is mentioned, it is usually the Thomist meaning – or something like it – which appears, rather than the idea of a king who rules free from the restraint of law. In the *Regement*, for example, tyranny was cruelty, or unmerciful power (st. 484, lines 3410–11); elsewhere, it was variously defined as excessive regard to the interests of foreigners ('Three Consideracions', pp. 198–9), pillaging the possessions of the subjects (*ibid.* and *Regement*, st. 575; implicit in *Secreta*, pp. 130–2), and as in Aquinas, giving priority to one's own interests ('Three Consideracions', pp. 198–9; *Aquinas*, p. 81). Even Fortescue, champion of English law, recognised that a 'dominium tantum regale' was not necessarily tyrannous: e.g. *Governance*, pp. 110, 112, 113. For councils, see below, at various points. Broadly speaking, the king was urged to take counsel, not to have a council. Fortescue, of course, had rather a different view on this matter: see below, pp. 48ff.

[33] Ferguson 1965: ch. 1, esp. p. 33.

rated royal liberty over notions of mixed government.[34] This did not mean that the interests of subjects were sacrificed to royal fancies: the advancement of the common weal remained the fundamental purpose of government, as we shall see.[35] The point is rather that the disruptive and divisive potential of ceding usable authority to subjects was understood and, as a consequence, alternative means of promoting their interests were developed. For the most part, then, the conventional view that royal authority should be representative was not taken to lengths which could vitiate royal sovereignty. If the evidence of the mirrors for princes is anything to go by, it appears that the main endeavour of English political society was not to restrain, or to divide, its executive, but to direct it.[36] Let us take a closer look at how this was to be achieved.

In later medieval England, the king was sometimes described as an officer, and his office was commonly thought to comprise two main functions: the defence of the realm and the provision of justice.[37] It was on these two areas of activity, publicised to political society by such well-known symbols as the royal seal and the royal sceptres and sword, that the advice-books focused a great part of their attention.[38] Just as the king's sovereignty was balanced by his representative responsibilities, so these functions were both powers and duties. This meant that in theory, at least, they were to be exercised in response to demand: defence was only justified by external attack,[39] whilst kings who went out actively to sit

---

[34] Dunbabin 1988: pp. 483–8, 492, and see Martin 1951: pp. 38–9. Note that Giles' *De Regimine Principum*, which is clearly in favour of untrammelled monarchy, was the main textual basis for the 'Tractatus' and the 'Three Consideracions', two of the sources for the discussion in this chapter: Kekewich 1987: pp. 53–72.

[35] Note also Dunbabin 1988: p. 515.

[36] These points are developed in what follows.

[37] E.g. *Governance*, p. 127: 'though his estate be the highest estate temporall in the erthe, yet it is an office, in wich he mynestrith to his reaume defence and justice'. See also *De Laudibus*, p. 3; Chrimes 1936: pp. 14, 15 n. 1; and above at n. 22.

[38] The royal seal bore the king armed in battle on one face and seated in judgement on the other (Warren 1987: p. 19). Clanchy 1983b: p. 156 comments on its importance as the agency for a mass image of kingship. A contemporary interpretation of the seal appears in 'The Libelle of Englysche Polycye': 'On the one syde hathe . . . a prince rydynge wyth his swerde idraue, / In the othere syde sittynge, sothe it is in sawe, / Betokenynge goode reule and ponesshynge'. A marginal note reads 'By septer and swerde', reflecting the known relationship between these two roles – judgement and defence – with the king's regalia (Wright (ed.), *Political Poems*, II, p. 182, lines 16–19). The king had two sceptres. One, topped by a cross, symbolised power and justice. The other, topped by a dove, symbolised mercy and equity (Passingham 1937: p. 125). The emphasis of advice-literature on the military and judicial functions of the king was noted by Born 1928: p. 504.

[39] See below, p. 37, for some discussion of the principle of the 'just war'. Note that the king's defensive powers had significant consequences for his domestic authority. Russell 1975: p. 302, makes the pertinent point that the king's power to declare war on behalf of his realm helped establish his jurisdiction over that realm and hence the 'monopoly of

in judgement where there was no serious disorder awakened memories of King John.[40] The king was to interpret his office with regard to the needs of his subjects.

These needs were wide-ranging and the king's role in meeting them went beyond the provision of defence and justice alone. By doing his job well, the 'just king' brought a host of benefits: not only 'surty of the land' and 'good kepinge' of its people, but peace, health, joy and even 'temperour of the ayre' and 'plentiousnes of the erthe'.[41] It was through the king's rule that the community of the realm achieved its definition and, in particular, the satisfaction of its interests. This grander conception of the royal estate was expressed in two important *topoi* which emphasised the close connections between king, realm and common interest. One of these was the idea of the crown, which played a significant role in public, and especially fiscal, debate during the fourteenth and fifteenth centuries.[42] It was an idea capable of broad application. If it usually called to mind either the royal 'fisc' or the royal power, to one early fifteenth-century writer, it symbolised the unity of 'lordis, comouns and clergye' in obedience to the king's just rule.[43] For a polity founded on unity, however, the crown raised certain problems: it did not make sense to vest the powers, duties and purposes of monarchy in an object potentially detachable from the royal person.[44] Advice-writers, who were, after all, seeking to shape the quality of rule at the most personal and intimate level of the prince's conscience, made more use of a second *topos* which fulfilled a similar conceptual function: the body politic.[45]

In this idea, which was so influential from John of Salisbury onwards, king and realm were parts of one body; in fact, a person, *persona publica*.[46] If the king was usually identified as the head of this body, he

licit violence', which permitted its internal direction. This is an important demonstration of the interdependence of these two royal functions/rights.

[40] See Holt 1963: pp. 12–16; Powell 1989: pp. 88–9.

[41] Fortescue (ed.), *Fortescue: Works*, I, p. 477.

[42] See Harriss 1975: ch. VI; Kantorowicz 1957: ch. VII, pt 2, especially pp. 358–72, 381–2.

[43] Quotation from Kail (ed.), *Twenty-Six Poems*, p. 50, st. 2. Note especially the last two lines of this stanza: 'The leste lyge-man, with body and rent, / He is a parcel of the crowne'.

[44] See above, at n. 19.

[45] The 'ship of state' was, of course, another concept emphasising the interdependence of king and community. It too was widely used in vernacular and publicist literature: see e.g. Haines 1976, for an example from 1421–2 and Robbins (ed.), *Historical Poems*, no. 78, for another from 1458.

[46] Born 1928: p. 503. The development of the concept is traced by Kantorowicz 1957, especially chs. III–V. See also Nederman (ed.), *Policraticus*, bk V and, for the sustained use of the *topos* in later medieval works, *Livre du Corps de Policie*, *passim*, and *De Laudibus*, ch. XIII. Note that it was also possible for the human body to be represented in civic terms: the intellect as king, the head as palace, the senses as messengers (*Secreta*, p. 208).

was still obliged to rule in harmony with the other members.[47] To no limb could he say 'I have no nede of the', for each had its essential part to play in the life of the whole, just as 'every estate ys ordeigned to support other'.[48] One central consequence of organic models of this kind was that the forces which directed the head – the king's virtues – were of central importance in medieval theories of royal government. In a world where the ruler 'se geret personam civitatis', the private disposition of the king determined the public disposition of the realm.[49] This meant that the royal personality was the natural and proper target for those interested in promoting good rule.[50] The writers of mirrors for princes, who set out to define and induce the sort of kingship which would advance the common interest, therefore devoted themselves to prolonged injunctions to be virtuous, wooing their readers with promises of earthly felicity and eternal bliss in a manner reminiscent of their classical forebears.[51] Moral behaviour, princes would find, was rational behaviour: it suited their own interests as well as those of their subjects, and it fitted the divine plan for the government of the world.[52]

Broadly speaking, four cardinal virtues were urged upon the king: Prudence, Justice, Temperance and Fortitude.[53] These took priority over the 'theological' virtues of Faith, Hope and Charity because they were recognised to be the keys to fulfilment in, and through, society. Social

---

[47] This can be pleasingly illustrated from Edward II's reign, in which the disarray of the body politic was so evident and destructive. The *Vita Edwardi Secundi* makes predictable use of organic imagery, calling the baronage 'membrum regis principale' and commenting that 'the limbs fail when the head is removed': Denholm-Young (ed.), pp. 28, 62. The bishop of Winchester preached to the 1327 parliament from the text 'My head is sick' (McKisack 1959: p. 89).

[48] Quotation from Russell's first draft for his speech to Richard III's parliament, printed by Chrimes 1936: pp. 179–84, p. 180 (and see p. 175). See also *Livre du Corps de Policie*, pp. 165–6.

[49] Quotation from Skinner 1986: p. 24. This idea of the personification of the state in the ruler, culled from Cicero's *De Officiis*, was an influential one all over Europe: *ibid.*, pp. 24–5.

[50] The 'Three Consideracions' urged self-knowledge and self-rule upon the prince for exactly this reason, employing the Aristotelian concepts of 'Michrocosme' and 'Machrocosme': 'Three Consideracions', pp. 182–3. See also Wright (ed.), *Political Poems*, p. 226, lines 22–3: 'Cast in thy conciens clerkly to knowe, / Publique and privathe is alle one', and Robbins (ed.), *Historical Poems*, p. 205, line 61: 'O rex, si rex es, rege te'. Note that the whole issue could also be presented in terms of health, the *Secreta* devoting a long section to physiognomy and the good order and diseases of the body (pp. 216–48) and, tellingly, describing the quality of Justice as 'the helth of Subiectis' (p. 208). See also Murray 1978: p. 120.

[51] For example, *Livre du Corps de Policie*, p. 116, claims to be a treatise 'whiche spekithe to prynces for the exhortacion to morall levyng'. See Skinner 1981: pp. 25–6, 36 for classical ideas concerning *virtus* and the way in which it attracted the goddess Fortuna.

[52] Skinner 1981: p. 36 and *Aquinas*, p. 58. For contemporary examples, see e.g. *Secreta*, p. 121; *Regement*, prologue and st. 406. Note especially *Secreta*, p. 146 – 'Many pepill shall ye well governe, whyle that reyson governyth yow.'

[53] For example, *Regement*, lines 4754–5; *Secreta*, p. 146.

well-being was the major earthly goal of men, and it was thus a particular priority for their leaders. It comes as no surprise, therefore, to learn that each of the cardinal virtues was thought to serve the common welfare in some way.[54] Prudence, the 'be-gynnynge of al governaunce' and also of 'al vertues', was the particular virtue of princes.[55] To some extent, it comprehended the other virtues, because it was axiomatic that what was wise must also be both good and useful.[56] In political treatises, it was typically presented in terms of its capacity to guide its bearer towards his proper end, the furtherance of the common interest of the people.[57] Justice, meanwhile, had similar associations. Its main aims were social and collective: peace and harmony, the stuff of the common weal.[58] To rule his realm justly, the king had to 'love especially and principally the comyn profite of the peeple'.[59] If he was to rise to the godlike attributes of his office, his administration of justice had to take account not only of what was right, but also of his subjects' needs.[60] He had, in fact, to modify justice with 'reson',[61] a quality which called to mind the higher and more complex interest of the common good and which shaded into mercy, 'a vertue that moch causeth the sauftie of the werkys of oure lorde God'.[62] Mercy, in turn, was usually associated with Temperance, the virtue which

---

54 Vanderjagt 1981: pp. 35–6, 46–8; Skinner 1986: p. 25; Murray 1978: pp. 132–5. See also Osberg 1986: p. 229 and note the contemporary description of the cardinal virtues as those by which 'every man governeth hymself in this world' (p. 224). Hexter 1967: p. 396 provides a beautifully succinct treatment of later medieval views on the relationship of virtue and society.

55 Murray 1978: pp. 118, 122, 135, and note 'Tractatus', p. 118: 'Hoc enim sonat nomen regis quod a regendo sumpsit exordium, unde alios regere et in debitum finem dirigere fit per virtutem prudencie.'

56 Murray 1978: p. 133; Skinner 1986: p. 26. Quotations from *Secreta*, pp. 134–5.

57 Pocock 1975: p. 24; *Aquinas*, p. 82. For an example of this in a mirror, see 'Tractatus', pp. 118–19.

58 *Aquinas*, p. 83; *Regement*, st. 359; *Secreta*, pp. 207–8. Note also the view of Jean Gerson (d. 1429), quoted by Doe 1990: p. 85: 'opus iustitiae est pax', because 'iustitia et pax ocsulatae sunt'. The latter was a text used by Archbishop Stafford in his sermon at the opening of the 1445 parliament: *RP*, V, p. 66.

59 'Three Consideracions', p. 197. See also Nichols (ed.), *Boke of Noblesse*, p. 21. Although Christine de Pisan, for example, begins her section on justice by reiterating the Roman Law definition ('iustice is a mesure that yeldeth to every man his right') she goes on to argue that the king will best keep justice by taking the advice of wise and true counsellors who know and love the common weal: *Livre du Corps de Policie*, pp. 84–5. The two versions of justice could be easily elided. Note this extract from Moisant (ed.), *De Speculo Regis*, 'Recensio A', p. 83: 'For justice ... gives to each what is his, and neglects private utility in order to serve the common equity.'

60 *Secreta*, p. 207; Robbins (ed.), *Historical Poems*, p. 229, lines 53–4. In many ways, 'Love', the justice of the common weal, was being rated above 'law': for the analysis of this distinction, see Clanchy 1983a: *passim*, but especially pp. 48, 52–5. For more on 'love', see below, p. 71.

61 'Three Consideracions', p. 197. See below, p. 71 for more on 'reason'.

62 'Three Consideracions', pp. 199–200. Without mercy, justice could be considered 'felonye' (*ibid.*, p. 200).

helped the king to master his bestial passions and redirect his attention towards what was rational and moral and, hence, once again, in the common interest.[63] Fortitude, finally, amounted to openness, constancy and high-mindedness.[64] The reliability of the king's word was the basis of the subjects' faith in authority and, hence, of the cohesion of the realm.[65]

The reason why virtue was so important, then, was that it bound the king *internally* to exercise his powers according to the common interest. There was no need for external restraints which raised difficult questions about the location of authority: to achieve the common welfare, the simple and overlapping unities of king and realm could suffice. Just as the Bractonian king was released from the bonds of law partly because he was internally bound to justice,[66] so the four cardinal virtues justified the king's sovereignty by making him inherently responsive to the common interest of the people. There were some difficulties in practice, of course. On the one hand, the pursuit of virtue could be difficult when the recommended forms of behaviour sometimes contradicted each other. This created a further role for the ruler's Prudence in attempting to reconcile them: finding a 'golden mean' of 'fraunchise' between the extremes of parsimony and 'foole largesse',[67] for example; or identifying 'equity' between the extremes of implacable justice and softness.[68] On the other hand, the identification of the common interest was not a simple business. It could not be left to the ruler's virtue alone: he also needed information.[69] He obtained it by listening to the counsels of his subjects.

Men were usually urged to take counsel on two distinct, though inter-related, grounds. On the one hand, the more counsel there was, the better the quality of judgement.[70] On the other, there was a residual

---

[63] The importance of eradicating vengeance and anger from the prosecution of justice, and indeed from rule in general, features in e.g. *Secreta*, pp. 181; *Regement*, sts. 444, 484. For associations between Temperance and self-control, humility and mercy, see *Secreta*, pp. 181, 191; 'Tractatus', pp. 58–9; 'Three Consideracions', pp. 181–2, 200 ('mercy' replaces Temperance altogether in the four virtues prescribed by this text).

[64] *Secreta*, pp. 170–3; 'Three Consideracions', p. 202.

[65] See *Secreta*, p. 143, for a positively Hobbesian view of a society without faith in its ruler; also *Regement*, sts. 315ff.

[66] Nederman 1984.

[67] *Secreta*, p. 130; 'Three Consideracions', p. 186; *Livre du Corps de Policie*, p. 71.

[68] Hoccleve, for example, very properly condemns those who allow evil to continue unchecked and protests about the free availability of pardons (*Regement*, sts. 443, 456), but elsewhere extols mercy above all other virtues, calling them worthless without it (*ibid.*, sts. 474–6). See also the inconclusive discussion in the 'Tractatus' (p. 51) and the observation of the 'Three Consideracions' author that 'mercy with oute justise is no verrey mercy, but rathir it may be seid folye and symplesse'(p. 200). For 'equity' in this sense, see Kantorowicz 1957: pp. 94–6.

[69] Hence the (presumably figurative) suggestion that the king should go in disguise among his common people to learn their views directly: e.g. *Secreta*, pp. 137–8; *Regement*, st. 366.

[70] Encapsulated in the biblical tag 'ubi multa consilia, ibi salus', quoted by Fortescue

belief in the principle that what affected all should be advised by all.[71] These ideas were widely held throughout society, but it is easy to see what particular relevance they had for the king who ruled it. As principal author of his subjects' fortunes, he had to be especially receptive to their counsel and the interests it represented. With this in mind, advice-writers typically urged modesty, humility, 'debonairtee' upon the king,[72] and followed this up with firm injunctions to take counsel in everything he did.[73] In this respect, Hoccleve's section on counsel in the *Regement of Princes* is archetypal, and we may use his account of the process of responding to counsel as a basis for the formulation of a definitive model.[74]

While he recognised that the king probably had his own ideas on a given topic, Hoccleve advised him to keep them quiet and to listen carefully to his counsellors, who should be as representative as possible: the good, rather than the bad (because they would bear in mind the common interest); the old, rather than the young (because they had experienced more and were likely to be rational, rather than passionate); the poor, as well as the great.[75] The king may have his own prior opinion, then, but he must be prepared to alter it if better ideas are put before him by his counsellors.[76] The image used by Hoccleve to remind the king of the value of counsel is one favoured by 'Bracton' in talking about the law – a bridle: it will keep the king from falling if he uses it properly, but it is

---

(*Governance*, p. 144), and by Bishop Beaufort, in his address to the 1425 parliament (*RP*, IV, p. 261). See also *De Natura*, p. 214; 'Three Consideracions', p. 194; *Regement*, lines 4862–5.

[71] This derives from the civil law dictum, 'Quod omnes tangit, ab omnibus approbetur' (see Harriss 1975: p. 46), rendered in the fifteenth century by the 'Tractatus' author, for example, as 'communia regni negocia sunt communi consilio terminanda' (p. 139).

[72] See e.g. 'Three Consideracions', pp. 181–2; Moisant (ed.), *De Speculo Regis*, 'Recensio B', p. 152; *Livre du Corps de Policie*, p. 77.

[73] For example, Nichols (ed.), *Boke of Noblesse*, p. 57; *Secreta*, p. 209; *RP*, IV, p. 3; and note Gerson's comment – 'How much sense has one single man? Wherefore the wise man says: do everything by counsel and you will never repent' (cited by Quillet 1988: p. 548. Green 1980: p. 162, suggests that 'Werk al by conseil, and thou shalt nat rewe' was one of the most popular proverbs of the fifteenth century. 'De Consulatu Stiliconis', a pseudo-mirror owned by Richard of York, proposed that the lesson of the key virtue, Prudence, was 'evir tave counceil / Withoute advise that no thyng passe' (Flugel, 'Claudian-Ubersetzung', lines 112–13).

[74] *Regement*, sts. 695–717. The section is headed 'De consilio habendo in omnibus factis'.

[75] *Ibid.*, lines 4866–72, 4880–90, 4943–9. The king was particularly reminded that advice which went against his wishes may be the best advice (lines 4894–5). See *Livre du Corps de Policie*, pp. 86–8, for various reasons why the advice of the old was likely to be superior.

[76] This is implicit in all the injunctions to take counsel, but note, especially, *Regement*, lines 4866–9, 4872. The *Secreta* took a similar line, emphasising that the king ought to appear to have a policy in mind, though he should act on the basis of the counsel he received (p. 209: see also 'Active Policy', lines 359–60, 366–7, st. 52). This would help to preserve the sense that the will behind every royal action was indeed the king's, as it had to be (see below, pp. 27–8).

otherwise redundant.[77] Part and parcel of using counsel, of course, was making decisions, or judgements, and the duty (or right) of doing this belonged to the king. Having heard and prudently considered all the advice of his counsellors, he should speak his 'wylle' and make arrangements for its swift execution.[78] An ideal-typical royal judgement was therefore made by the will of the king and the advice of his counsel.

In this everyday process, the part played by the king's will was a complex but crucial one. While the dictates of virtuous rule demanded that he be prepared to sublimate his will to the good advice of his counsellors, they also required that the king preserve its integrity and independence.[79] Counsel, opinion, could itself be a form of will, and an important part of the king's task of making decisions which served the common interest of his community was the reduction of the inevitable variety of his subjects' wills to one: 'common policy' could only be 'common' if it was single as well as representative.[80] So it was that the will which provided for the common interest had also to be single – hence personal – and capable of preserving a truly universal representativeness by being free of the control of any counsellor or group of counsellors. Common policy would be unlikely to emerge automatically from counsel: the king had to choose; he had to will a particular solution. But it had to be the king and no one else who made this act of will: even if he resolved to echo the advice of a particular counsellor, or group of counsellors, it had to be clear that the resolution was his, not theirs, because it was he, not they, who bore the responsibility of speaking for the whole body.[81] Counsellors would tend to speak for themselves, for their followers and sometimes for their communities; they represented sectional interests, not the common interest. The realm needed a single voice louder than the voices of those who spoke for its constituent parts: it needed a single and exceeding will to express its common good. This was the very essence of the king's function and its successful discharge ultimately depended on the inviolability of his will. Ideally, therefore, the royal will was flexible; a

---

[77] *Regement*, lines 4929–35. The image also appears in a similar context in *De Natura*, pp. 216, 218. For law as a bridle in 'Bracton', see Tierney 1963: pp. 299, 310–11.

[78] *Regement*, lines 4873–5. Hoccleve leaves prudent consideration to be understood. In his poem 'The Active Policy of a Prince', George Ashby advises the king to 'Heere every man is counseil and advise / Paciently, and chese therof the best' ('Active Policy', lines 359–60). The author of 'De Quadriparta Regis Specie' (printed by Genet (ed.), *Political Tracts*, pp. 31–9) recommends the same, singling out the virtue of Prudence as being the quality enabling the king to carry this out: p. 35.

[79] *Secreta*, p. 209, is particularly emphatic on this point.

[80] See especially *Aquinas*, pp. 2–4.

[81] One of George Ashby's 'Dicta ... Philosophorum' aimed to express something of this idea: 'By advis and goode counseile to governe / Is goode, but not to be in governance / Of his counseil, but of theim for to lerne'; Bateson (ed.), *Ashby's Poems*, 'Dicta', lines 603–5.

motive force to transform the best counsel into the quasi-judgement of a royal action.[82] As such, it had two aspects: on the one hand, it was the king's personal, private will; on the other, it was the 'official', public will of king and realm. The king's public will characteristically incorporated counsel, unless he was so prudent that consultation was unnecessary, but it had also to retain its purely personal basis: if the king did not will 'privately' what he willed 'publicly', the unity of the body politic was undermined.[83] This was to be a serious problem under Henry VI, as we shall see.

Good and representative government was first of all a matter of right royal will, therefore.[84] This was why the mirrors for princes aimed to inspire virtue in their readers rather than simply urging them to take counsel. Virtue acted at the most intimate level of authority, within the private *persona* of the prince: it would ensure that the king took counsel wisely, that he received it well and that he turned it into authoritative and universally satisfying policy.[85] It would guarantee that his private person served its public functions; indeed, that *persona privata* and *persona publica* would be one and the same; that through the king's absorption and good management of his subjects' counsel, the common interest and identity of the realm would be expressed. Royal virtue was the best – in a sense, the only – constitutional safeguard, since the royal will had to be free of temporal interference if the whole system was to work. Even so, we should not lose sight of the fact that the system we are describing was, in

---

[82] Aquinas' comments on legislation seem particularly appropriate here: 'But will, if it is to have the authority of law, must be regulated by reason when it commands. It is in this sense that we should understand the saying that the will of the prince has the power of law. In any other sense the will of the prince becomes an evil rather than law' (*Aquinas*, p. 56). The 'reason' regulating the king's will when he acts is to be drawn from his own prudence and from the counsel he receives: under those circumstances, his actions foster the common weal, as law does, and have the fullest possible authority. The approach to legislation in 'Bracton' is very similar: it is not 'anything rashly put forward of his own will, but what had been rightly decided with the counsel of his magnates, deliberation and consultation having been had thereon, the king giving it *auctoritas*' (cited by Gillespie 1979: p. 50). For further comment on 'reason' as a coded term for the common interest, see below, p. 71.

[83] No king, of course, was likely to be prudent enough to do without counsel: note Christine de Pisan's telling exemplar of the king who acknowledged that he was wise enough to receive good counsel, but not to give it: *Livre du Corps de Policie*, pp. 90–1. Note too the observation of St Thomas Aquinas that Prudence, the key virtue of the prince, was 'perfected' by counsel (quoted by Quillet 1988: p. 545). The making of the experience of the generality into an important adjunct to the limited Prudence of a ruler is outlined in Pocock 1975: pp. 18–28.

[84] See also Gillespie 1979: esp. p. 49.

[85] According to William of St Thierry, writing in the 1130s, virtue constituted the 'rationality' of the mind, struggling with the baser instincts of desire and anger to direct the individual towards what was moral and natural and in its interests (ultimately, of course, what was in the common interest, since people achieved fulfilment through society): Morris 1972: p. 78; *Aquinas*, pp. 81–2. See also *De Natura*, p. 209.

essence, a representative one. If the king's will was the backbone of royal policy, the fairly clear implication of the advice-literature is that much of the flesh was to be supplied by common counsel. Kingship, then, was essentially a means for the authorisation of public opinion; the king himself, a gilded conduit, receiving a flood of catholic, but unsorted, advice from elements within the *communitas* and channelling it back as representative, and now authoritative, policy.

It is not difficult to see how powerful a king of this kind could be. If he was the means by which the *communitas* achieved its interests, he could expect to act with the full co-operation and authority of all right-thinking people. This becomes clear when we examine the 'drede' which the king was supposed to inspire. For the 'Tractatus' author, it was the first condition of virtuous rule, that the subjects should love and fear the prince. These feelings were not to be induced by royal terrorism, however, but by political morality: to create a state of 'drede', the king should be first 'beneficus et liberalis', second 'magnanimis et fortis' and third 'iustus et equalis'.[86] Fear of the ruler, then, was generated by the proper and responsible rendering of his duties.[87] In a sense, therefore, love conquered all: as Hoccleve put it, 'he that is loved, men drede hym offende'.[88] A king who set out to rule in the common interest disposed of a loving and united *communitas* whose combined power would be sufficient to overwhelm criminals, rebels and foreigners. The royal dignity and majesty were primarily sustained not by the king's private resources, but by the communal power of his satisfied subjects. Both the powers and the interests of the king were tied to those of the *communitas*. Rule was less a force imposed by the king upon the realm than a reaction which his proper functioning elicited from it.

Gathering all this together, it should be clear that the mirrors for princes were offering something rather more than 'traditional generalisations of a moral nature'.[89] They depicted a sophisticated polity in which the king was the vehicle of a communal enterprise for the realisation of communal interests. If he governed himself properly, his subjects governed themselves through him: as Thomas Walsingham wrote of

---

[86] 'Tractatus', p. 72.

[87] See also 'Three Consideracions', p. 188; *Livre du Corps de Policie*, p. 89; Robbins (ed.), *Historical Poems*, p. 229, lines 53–60; Erdmann (ed.), *Lydgate's Siege of Thebes*, line 1205.

[88] *Regiment*, line 4803. See also *Secreta*, p. 183, for very similar observations. These views bring to mind Machiavelli's famous comment, 'it is far better to be feared than loved if you cannot be both': Bull (ed.), *The Prince*, p. 96. To fifteenth-century English advisers, rule in the common interest produced a unity among the subjects which was the practical basis of the king's power. Machiavelli had abandoned this view. It was one which Ashby, Fortescue and other writers of the crisis period also appear to reject: see pp. 39–51, below.

[89] Quotation from Brown 1981: p. 130.

Edward III, 'because he had been distinguished by complete integrity of character, under him to live was to reign, as it seemed to his subjects'.[90] In such a polity, the idea that the king and the common interest could ever be in opposition simply does not work at a theoretical level: the king was no separate entity, but a limb of the body politic. If this idea was accepted by contemporaries, it must have been full of significance for their political operations. How, then, did the theory square with the realities?

This, of course, is a matter to be considered throughout this book, but it is worth noting here that the theorists knew what they were dealing with. They knew that individual kings came in all shapes and sizes, and that few indeed would fit the ideal model of a king who innately knew the common weal and ordained for it. This did not lead them, as it has led generations of constitutionalist politicians and historians, to despair of personal authority as a means of rule. Rather, it took them, as it took their contemporaries, down the avenues of persuasion, counsel and assistance. Knowing that they were dealing with a natural as well as political body, they anticipated forcefulness in the royal personality, and countered it with exhortations to humility, mercy and receptiveness. They provided for counsel to supplement deficiencies in royal Prudence. They played on the intrinsic wilfulness of human beings to make personal will – albeit modified by virtue as much as possible – the basis of their polity. The framework they devised was thus both flexible and geared to the realities of royal power and communal life. It permitted a wise and vigorous king – Henry V, for example – to fulfil, in large measure, his private wishes in his public acts.[91] Yet it also enabled less remarkable men to govern sufficiently well for some sort of public peace to be preserved. A willingness to work with the straightforward regimes of counsel and to attend to the obligations of defence and justice was all that was fundamentally necessary, and there was every reason to hope that kings would see this for themselves.

Certainly, the system was not infinitely elastic. On the one hand, a king like Edward II, or Richard II, who was habitually wrong-headed and resistant to counsel, frustrated the delicate and highly personalised processes of representation and destroyed the consensus which they kept in being. A 'bad' king could not be made to amend himself against his will, because his will remained the central means of fulfilling the common interest of the people: it retained its sovereignty whatever the quality of its

---

[90] Barnie 1974: p. 141 (and note also the very similar view of Walter Burley, quoted by Ormrod 1990: p. 200).

[91] Recent work on this reign has plausibly suggested that Henry himself was the major inspiration for much of his policy: see e.g. Harriss (ed.), 1985.

possessor. As a result, this kind of delinquency could not be countered except by breaking the rules; and breaking the rules meant confusion, disorder, division. On the other hand, perhaps, the system was flawed in its presupposition that 'overmighty' kings were the evil most likely to be encountered.[92] What happened when a king had too little force of personality to make a convincing show of independent will?

An answer is to be found in Fortescue's opening remarks in *De Laudibus*: 'the beginning of all service is to know the will of the lord whom you serve'.[93] This may have been a throw-away comment, but its importance for kingship cannot be doubted. Service to the common weal had to be focused upon the crown and was concentrated and directed by the will of the king. Even though this will was to be wholly responsive to the common interest, it had to exist apart from and above the mass of individuals who made up the *communitas*. Only this way could the common interest be preferred before that of any group or individual. Fifteenth-century advice-writers recognised that their polity required direction, but were careful to restrict the freedom of royal will to the purposes for which it was required. 'Rule' was given no intrinsic substance except at the most intimate level of public decision making. Here, however, it was absolutely essential. Only a single independent will, rooted deep in the king's own person, could guarantee a single common interest and the unity of the realm with which it was so closely associated.

. . .

Alongside the ideas of kingship and community culled from the mirrors for princes, the nobility were exposed to another major scheme of values relevant to politics; a scheme which combined 'martial, aristocratic and Christian elements' and which may seem to have offered guidance contrary to the ideas and attitudes discussed in the preceding section – Chivalry.[94] With its emphasis on individual prowess and honour, martial virtue, enterprise and dynamism, Chivalry has the hallmarks of a model for political relations which encourages the exercise of individual rather than communal force, and in which the hierarchy is maintained not by the mutual interdependence of king and people, but by the rule of might overlaid with the thinnest of civil veneers. As the particular ethos of knights, it could, moreover, be put forward as a corpus of ideas far more

---

[92] Peters 1970: p. x: 'most political theory was primarily concerned with the use and misuse of excessive power ... rather than with the deficiency of power'. A similar trend is noticeable in chivalric theories, which presupposed aggressive instincts on the part of men and concentrated on directing them to useful ends: see below.

[93] *De Laudibus*, p. 5.

[94] Keen 1984: p. 16. For a general survey of the influence of Chivalry in later medieval England, see Ferguson 1960: ch. I.

relevant to aristocratic society than the moralising of the predominantly clerical advice-writers. These considerations raise some interesting questions. First of all, did the representation of the common interest really dominate noble thinking about domestic government to the extent suggested above? Second, had landowners really accepted the subordination of their own authority to that of the crown? So far, it has been implicit that they had, but did Chivalry offer them, as knights, a code for independent action perhaps?[95]

It should perhaps be noted at once that part of the apparent contradiction between the values of Chivalry and those of the mirrors for princes lies in the different functions of chivalric theory. It was devoted to prescribing the uses of force – violence in a sense – in both war and government. While the exercise of force was a matter fundamental to all temporal power, and the duties of the king could be presented wholly in terms of defence (whether 'inward' against rebels and criminals, or 'outward' against foreigners),[96] it was possible for works on governance to focus on other themes, notably, of course, how this power was to be directed. Even so, to say that Chivalry dealt in the management of violence is not to say that it encouraged men to revel in it. Its egotistical overtones must not be overlooked, but it is important to note that many of its attributes bolstered the realm-centred view of kingship outlined above. If Chivalry was indeed 'the secular code of honour of a martially oriented aristocracy', then it may have encouraged lords to think about authority in a similar way to the advice-writers.[97] Chivalric thinking set out to channel the violence intrinsic to society into licit forms, acceptable, even valuable, to the common interest.[98]

The very existence of a 'code of honour' has been alleged to be an

[95] See above, p. 20 (and below, p. 35).

[96] See e.g. the appointments of Gloucester and of York as protector: *RP*, IV, p. 326; *RP*, V, pp. 242, 284. Even so, the king's duties were known to be more than simply defensive: note, for example, Bishop Langley's comment from 1423 that the minority council had been appointed 'si bien dehors pur la defense d'icell [the realm], come dedeins touchante la conservation de la Pees, et la bone et due execution de les Leies de la Terre' (*RP*, IV, p. 197); and the loveday award of 1458 – 'non tantum in defensione interius, sed ad providendum pro sanis directione et regimine eorundem [i.e his lands] interius' (*Registrum Whethamstede*, I, p. 298).

[97] Quotation from Keen 1984: p. 249. Note that some of the material discussed in the preceding section was intended for, and used by, a wider audience than kings alone. The 'Three Consideracions', for example, was based on a French text intended to advise all temporal lords: 'Three Consideracions', p. 177.

[98] See Vale 1981: pp. 5–8. There is, perhaps, a parallel here between the ideals and practices of Chivalry and those of 'bastard feudalism'. Both have been seen as causes of violent behaviour, whereas both can be seen as mechanisms for the containment, perhaps even avoidance, of violence. See, for example, the extract from Plummer's introduction to the *Governance*, printed by McFarlane 1981c: p. 23: 'that pseudo-Chivalry, which, under a garb of external splendour and a factitious code of honour, failed to conceal its ingrained lust and cruelty ... that bastard feudalism'.

incitement to self-assertion and violence, partly on the grounds that it gives the individual an independent licence for his actions.[99] The 'honourable' man, it is argued, must be forever having to defend his claims, and 'the ultimate vindication of honour lies in physical violence'. Leaving aside the question of how often it was necessary or appropriate to invoke this ultimate sanction, particularly given other social restrictions on the use of violence,[100] a lot must depend on what are the attributes of honour in a given society. Over the hundred years from 1485, Mervyn James has claimed, the meaning of honour changed. By the early seventeenth century, a 'civil society' had emerged in which the state claimed a monopoly both of honour, which was now linked with humanistic wisdom and established Protestant religion, and of violence. What James identified was not the decline of a code of honour, but a change in its attributes: the exercise of governance, long a subsidiary component of honour, supplanted the pursuit of an individual and martial 'prouesse' as the dominant theme.[101] It seems possible to suggest that this transition to a non-violent code of honour was already well underway before the sixteenth century. It was surely essential to the exercise of lordship that self-assertion and the use of violence should have 'honourable' forms, but equally, given the emphasis on the common weal in later medieval theories of domestic government, it would be surprising if at least some of the concepts associated with late Tudor civil society were not present in fifteenth-century Chivalry.[102]

'Prouesse' was the essential knightly virtue, and a host of chivalric handbooks were written to teach knights what it was and how to acquire it.[103] Covering a multitude of properties synonymous with knighthood, it called to mind the 'noble dedis' of 'noble men in armes', their 'coragious hertis', 'strenght and power', their 'worship and manhode' shown in 'service' against 'the untrewe reproches of oure auncien adversaries'.[104] But 'prouesse' was not the only quality expected of the knight: he was also

---

[99] These are the views of Julian Pitt-Rivers, cited by Barnie 1974: p. 75 and by Vale 1981: p. 9. See also Kaeuper 1988: p. 392, for a pessimistic view and James 1978: p. 1: 'the root of the matter ['pervasive violence'] lies in the mentality defined by the concept of honour'. The opposite is argued by Huizinga in one of his earliest pieces on Chivalry: 1960: p. 205. Lewis 1968: p. 187 also presents honour as a restraining force in aristocratic politics.

[100] See e.g. Maddern 1992: chs. 3 and 7. [101] James 1978: pp. 2–6.

[102] Dr James argues that 'in the company of his equals, the [late medieval] man of honour was expected to assert his "pre-eminence"' (1978: p. 5), but this would seem to be contradicted by the concept of brotherhood in arms, in particular, if not by the recognised duty of service to the state in general: see Keen 1962 and below. See below, pp. 64–6, for the self-assertion of the lord.

[103] These were a parallel development to the 'mirrors for princes'. Originating in the thirteenth century, they were usually written in the vernacular, so that laymen could understand them: Keen 1984: pp. 6, 16.

[104] Nichols (ed.), *Boke of Noblesse*, pp. 1, 4, 78.

urged to be prudent, an exhortation which reflected his participation in, and duty to, a wider society.[105] It is, moreover, striking how ascetic and religious were the lineaments of the knightly office set down by some of the best-known handbooks.[106] If this was partly intended to induce knights to keep themselves in good shape in order to fulfil their functions adequately,[107] it also emphasised the gravity of what these functions involved.[108] As we shall see, the search for 'prouesse' was closely circumscribed. It is clear that it was only when active defence was called for that knights were expected to provide it: in peacetime, jousting, hunting and the duties of the local landowner were the limit of licit activity.[109]

The handbooks placed great emphasis on the social utility of knighthood. Ramon Lull's *Libre del Ordre de Cavayleria*, for example, declared its purpose to be the restraint and defence of the people.[110] This was underlined in the translation of the work which Gilbert Hay wrote in 1456: 'the office of knighthood should have stark place in governance ... for the office is founded aye on good and profitable works that are speedful to the common profit'.[111] Whilst it is important not to overlook the encouragement given to personal achievement in Chivalry, it is equally important not to miss the paramountcy of the common interest.[112] This is particularly noticeable in fifteenth-century chivalric texts, where knightly activities are time and again related to the needs of the realm.[113] In the *Morte Darthur*, for example, there is little doubt that the Round Table is a metaphor for the body politic, and it is significant that the internecine rivalry which leads to the breaking of the one leads

---

[105] See Murray 1978: pp. 125–7 for the concept of the 'prudens miles', also *Secreta*, p. 121: 'Chyvary is not only kepete, savyd, and mayntenyd by dedys of armes, but by wysdome and helpe of lawes, and of witte, and wysdome of undyrstondynge.'

[106] Keen 1984: pp. 6–17; *Livre du Corps de Policie*, pp. 123–5; Vale 1981: p. 27.

[107] E.g. Keen 1984: p. 9.

[108] It was the equivalent of that Temperance which kept the king's mind on his rational, which is to say 'communal', responsibilities: above, pp. 24–5.

[109] Keen 1984: pp. 9–10, 12. See Vale 1982: pp. 58–9 for the significance of tournaments in the training of knights.

[110] Keen 1984: p. 9. Lull ordered knights to defend the Christian faith, their temporal lords and the weak, and, most interestingly, to judge the people and supervise their labours under the king (*ibid.*, pp. 9–10). This text was printed in English by Caxton in 1483–5: James 1978: p. 3.

[111] Cited by Ferguson 1960: p. 118. Georges Duby has shown that the origins of the term 'miles' lay in public service of a non-military kind, notably in assisting the lord in the exercise of his judicial functions (1973: pp. 332–3).

[112] See Ferguson 1960: p. 107; Vale 1981: pp. 15, 23–4; *Livre du Corps de Policie*, pp. 106, 116–17, 123–4. Communal values could even be applied to the battlefield. Sir John Fastolf rated the 'manly' warrior who fought as part of a group and chose his moment with care above the 'hardy' warrior, who fought as an individual and without discretion: Nichols (ed.), *Boke of Noblesse*, pp. 64–5. See also *Livre du Corps de Policie*, p. 128.

[113] Keen 1984: pp. 235–6; Ferguson 1960: ch. IV.

also to the breaking of the other.[114] The tragedy is not only personal and 'chivalric', but also corporate and political.[115] It is interesting, in this connection, that erotic motivations were not prominent in the English chivalric tradition.[116] Courtly love, which provided a source of authority for chivalric action quite divorced from the needs of the *communitas*, appears to be purely destructive in the *Morte Darthur*.[117] Knights were encouraged to aspire to essentially the same array of political virtues as kings, and for the same reasons.[118]

If the handbooks offered the knight a degree of moral autonomy, arising from his acquisition of virtues which would lead him to exercise violence justly, they did so in the interests of the common weal. Could this have affected the relationship between the knight and his royal lord, who possessed essentially the same licence?[119] Was the knight free to interpret the common weal himself, and act on its behalf, regardless of the claims of the king? Chivalric writers were emphatic about the faithful service which the knight owed his lord and they seem to have assumed that the demands of this service would coincide with the promptings of the knight's own virtue.[120] Any conflict of loyalties would be, in the legal language of the time, an 'inconvenience': as the *Morte Darthur* demon-

---

[114] Pochoda 1971: pp. 25–6, 82, 84. Note Edward III's use of the Round Table as a conceptual basis for the community of lords and knights which later became the garter: Barnie 1974: pp. 66–7; Vale 1982: pp. 67–8.

[115] See especially Sir Lancelot's departing speech, in which the knight's assertion of his individual prowess appears as a register of the disintegration of that 'Most noblest Christian realm, whom I have loved aboven all other realms!': Brewer (ed.), *Morte Darthur*, p. 126. The political nature of later Arthurian romances is discussed in Peters 1970: p. 195.

[116] Ferguson 1960: pp. 49–50, 121.

[117] Most obviously, of course, in the dalliance between Lancelot and Guinevere: 'Through this same man and me hath all this war be wrought, and the death of the most noblest knights of the world; for through our love that we have loved together is my most noble lord slain': Brewer (ed.), *Morte Darthur*, p. 151. Note also the episode of the 'Fair Maid of Astolat' (*ibid.*, part VII, ch. 2) and see Pochoda 1971: pp. 124–5.

[118] See e.g. *Livre du Corps de Policie*, pp. 116–17, 141–3 and *passim*.

[119] Traditional expositions of the purpose of both knighthood and nobility identify two original functions: to fight and to judge men (Keen 1984: p. 152). These were, of course, the same as the functions of the king: see above, p. 21, and note *Regement*, lines 2873–4 ('That kyng that knyghtly is of governaunce, / That is to seyn, doth iustly his office'), and *Livre du Corps de Policie*, p. 117 ('to kepe and maynteyn iustice aftir their degre as wel as the prynce').

[120] See Keen 1984: pp. 7, 9, 14; *Livre du Corps de Policie*, pp. 123–4, 141; Crotch (ed.), *Caxton's Prologues*, p. 81; Vale 1981: p. 26. Keen 1962: pp. 6, 8 shows how allegiance to (royal) temporal lordship was always excluded from agreements between knights. Even so, the *Ordene de Chevalerie*, for example, also ordered the knight not to be a party to false judgement, something which, on the face of it, could only lead down the slippery slope to disobedience of temporal authority (Keen 1984: p. 8). Note that the fact that a lot of chivalric literature dealt with the activities of knights errant, who were outside the framework of temporal lordship, meant that the issue was often sidestepped: Kennedy 1988: p. 70.

strated, resistance to royal authority could scarcely be in the common interest.[121] Even so, tensions remained. Royal misrule, which contravened the common interest, surely demanded some response from the true and virtuous knight.[122] This was not an issue which the didactic literature generally addressed directly, but it is an important one, especially given the close associations between knighthood, lordship and nobility.[123] Were lords entitled to question the quality of royal government? The virtuous knight's interest in the defence of the common weal could be a chivalric analogue for the 'representative' claims of lords, and these, in turn, could be thought to constitute an alternative authority to that of the king.[124] It seems reasonable to suggest that the potential conflict could have been resolved in chivalric thinking as it was to be in the sphere of government: not so much by reducing knighthood and nobility to a simple matter of royal appointment,[125] as by reconciling separate jurisdictions; inducing knights, like lords, to accept that the common interest they defended was primarily a local or sectional one, subordinate to the common interest of the realm, which was in turn protected by a royal lordship in which they may participate.[126] However, this rather complex solution cannot be directly deduced from the conflicting implications of chivalric literature and we must acknowledge it to be a grey area, to be illuminated, perhaps, by an informed study of what happened in practice.[127]

Even so, it is clear that it was only in service to the king and common weal that martial activity was explicitly justified in the predominant

---

[121] 'Inconvenience' denoted a failure in the coherence of existing law: Doe 1990: p. 162.

[122] For example, Mathew 1948: pp. 359–60 suggests that knightly justice is expected to 'supplement' that of the ruler.

[123] Even in the fifteenth century, the nobility could be identified as 'tho that oughte defende yow and youre roiaume that halden theire londis of you by that service onlie [i.e. military service], and gyven to that entent by youre noble auncestries': Nichols (ed.), *Boke of Noblesse*, pp. 78–9. Note that the tract 'Somnium Vigilantis' did deal with this topic, and insisted that good knights would only wish to follow their own wills insofar as these accorded with the will of the ruler ('Somnium', p. 521). This text, which is not part of the handbook tradition, was written under somewhat specialised circumstances, however: see below, p. 43.

[124] See above, p. 20, and also Kaeuper 1988: p. 2 for the view that knightly justice and royal justice were in tension.

[125] Some theorists took this line, however. Bartolus, for example, neatly sidestepped the influential debate over whether virtue or lineage was the basis of nobility by arguing that, in civil terms, it derived from neither: instead, the nobility was whoever the prince chose to raise to its ranks (although all princes should be encouraged to dignify those who were, in a moral sense, 'naturally noble'): Keen 1984: p. 149. See below, p. 46 n. 171, for the application of this idea to lordship.

[126] Participation in royal lordship is implicit in the *topos* of the Round Table (see e.g. Pochoda 1971: p. 84: 'by the noble felyshyp of the Rounde Table was kynge Arthur upborne, and by their nobeles, the kynge and all the realme was ever in quyet and reste').

[127] See below, pp. 65ff.

chivalric theories.[128] The sort of service envisaged, moreover, and the virtues associated with it, had, by the fifteenth century at least, a well-developed domestic aspect – governance – in addition to the more familiar military activities. There was plenty in the chivalric code of honour to encourage the nobility to see their role as the 'tuicione and defens' of the realm and to identify a 'trouthe and dutie' to the king and 'the sayde commone wele'.[129] At the same time, the tendency of chivalric literature to restrain individualism and condemn unauthorised aggression was carried over into writing about the matter of war between nations, the king's second major duty of 'defence outward'.[130] 'Just war' theory licensed only defensive war, although, in practice, the lack of binding international arbitration made the king the adjudicator of his own cause.[131] Even so, wars which were pursued for conquest or magnificence alone earned the censure of even the most bellicose of writers.[132] The just war had to suit the interests of the national *communitas*, and this led theorists to stress the king's obligation to consult widely before taking up arms.[133] Certainly, as F. H. Russell has pointed out, 'warfare has been as difficult to justify satisfactorily in theory as it has been endemic in practice' and there is no doubt that the strictures of authoritative texts did nothing to prevent hundreds of wars waged by the crown and nobility on the basis of an apparently light regard for the interests of their subjects.[134] Nonetheless, some of the enthusiasm which war elicited from among the martial elite may have been stimulated, as well as justified, by the opportunity it provided for these men to participate in the active protec-

[128] See e.g. Vale 1981: pp. 26–7, and, for a claim that this principle was established much earlier, at least in the Angevin domains, Gillingham 1988.

[129] Quoted from the letter of the Yorkist lords at Ludlow, 1459, *English Chron.*, pp. 82–3. The fact that even at the height of their rebellion, these three knights continued to identify the common weal, which they were undertaking to defend, with the king (see below, p. 60) shows the bankruptcy of the idea that the nobility had an independent representativeness.

[130] E.g. Nichols (ed.), *Boke of Noblesse*, pp. 58–9, 64–5; *Livre du Corps de Policie*, pp. 128, 134.

[131] Rather as in the case of the crusades, the church hoped that by licensing some forms of military activity, it could contain other, less desirable, ones: see Keen 1984: pp. 44–9; Russell 1975: pp. 45, 48, 305–6. The 'Three Consideracions' only dealt with defensive war, as if no other form of war were conceivable: pp. 187, 207.

[132] Even the *Boke of Noblesse* insisted that there was 'no grettir tiranny, extorcion, ne cruelte' than wars which arose from 'magnificence, pride and wilfulnesse' (pp. 7–8).

[133] War is presented as a last resort, to be pursued only in the common interest, in *Regement*, st. 560, and Byles (ed.), *Book of Faytts of Armes*, pp. 11ff; although in a sense, this is already implicit in the conditions for a just war, particularly the fact that it was only the monarch (guardian of the common interest) who could justly declare war. The king was enjoined to take counsel on the question of his right to go to war by 'Three Consideracions', p. 207; Nichols (ed.), *Boke of Noblesse*, p. 7; Byles (ed.), *Book of Faytts of Armes*, p. 13. There is thus, in all this, a sense that common counsel was protecting the common interest, just as in the related matter of taxation: see Harriss 1975: ch. III.

[134] Russell 1975: p. 292.

tion and defence of the *communitas* and in the demonstration of its unity, a unity which could all too easily vanish from view in the domestic sphere.[135] On the whole, it seems, military and chivalric thinking was as communitarian as the mirrors for princes.

...

J. S. Roskell once remarked that 'the basic English constitutional and political problem of what we call later medieval and early modern times was how to control a monarchy which, though at no time despotic, was never less than a monarchy'.[136] In some respects, the materials discussed above confirm this picture. They are certainly a powerful reminder of what monarchical thinking involves and where it leads. In the world of the mirrors, it is not parliaments, or laws, or councils, or for that matter, some imagined *communitas* of nobility and gentry, which offer representative government to the realm, but a lordship: the lordship of the virtuous king, whose free authority is justified in public terms by his readiness to hear the counsel of lesser lords and by the inescapable need for a superior source of will, which could reduce subordinate wills to one and so preserve the unity on which everyone depends. In this lordship, as in the other lordships of the bastard feudal age, public and private are tightly interlinked: the private person is also a public person; there is no necessary antithesis between personal power and public service, even when this service includes the all-important task of representation.[137] To a large extent, the power which the king wields does not depend on a force emanating from himself: rather, it is conferred upon him for, and in, the fulfilment of particular social and political functions. The community, of which the king forms both whole and part, is a single organism, held in being by a balance of forces which have no separable origins. Within this organism, political power is 'constitutionally' distributed: it accrues to various items in the public landscape in accordance with a series of ideas and expectations which have now been surveyed. If this conceptual framework did indeed dominate the political understanding and activity of the ruling classes, then it is clear that effective royal government in later

---

[135] See the comments of Vale 1981: p. 27. A significant element in the demonstration of unity was the king's personal involvement, demanded in e.g. *Regement*, st. 560, though cf. Byles (ed.), *Book of Faytts of Armes*, p. 19, where, significantly, it is argued that the king should not go in person, in the interests of the domestic common weal: his death or capture would be 'generally to alle his subgettis, londe and contrees, perdicion and infenyte inconvenyent'. Note that a major reason for resuming the French war offered by the *Boke of Noblesse* was that it would reunite 'worshipfulle men, whiche oughte to be stedfast and holde togider' and so restore the fallen 'res publica': pp. 2–4.

[136] Roskell 1963–4: p. 474.

[137] For the mixture of public and private elements in magnate lordship, see Carpenter 1992: pp. 282–3.

medieval England did not depend on the exercise of 'strong' kingship, or success in foreign war, or any other external force beyond the normal modicum of will on the part of the man who bore its crown. Typically, it seems, the king's powers and purposes came from the polity which he ruled and represented: 'welle woste thou', declared the author of the *Secreta*, 'that thy Subiectis bene thy tresure, by whych thy roialme is confermyd'.[138] If this kind of thinking has not always been sufficiently recognised, it is in part because the disintegration of Henry's rule in the 1450s gave rise to a different structure of values and a different kind of kingship. Let us now turn to these.

THE IDEOLOGICAL IMPACT OF THE CIVIL WARS

In the autumn of 1450, Richard duke of York rose up and called for justice on behalf of the community of the realm. 'Desiryng suerte and prosperite of your most roiall person and welfare of this your noble reame', he advised the king in the interests of 'the conversacion (*sic*) of good tranquillite and pesable rewle among alle trew sogetts' to proceed against the alleged traitors who surrounded him.[139] York's intervention came towards the end of a year in which the divergence of royal government from the common weal had been dramatically demonstrated: Normandy was lost; the crown was bankrupt; the king's counsellors were accused of corruption and the men of the south-east had risen up and pillaged London. This dire state of affairs seemed to justify the duke's assertion of a duty to act for both king and *communitas*. Following Henry VI's manifest failure to fulfil the central obligation of his office, it seemed to one of his greatest subjects that, as the king's 'true liegeman and servant' – as a true knight, in a sense – he himself might legitimately claim to interpret the common weal and take action in its name.

As a result of York's rising and the prolonged disorder which followed it, a rather different conception of kingship began to acquire currency in England. The model of authority discussed above, with its emphasis on virtuous rule and its assumption that the position of each king at the head of the realm was organic and uncontested, appeared inadequate to meet the challenges of the 1450s, 1460s and 1480s. In response, the priorities of advice-writers seem to have altered. The earlier emphasis on the king's obligation to defend the common interest was abandoned in favour of a more emphatic statement of the monopoly of authority to which he was entitled, and a readiness to propose reforms which might enable him to affirm and maintain that monopoly. On one level, this is familiar enough,

---

[138] *Secreta*, p. 213.   [139] Griffiths 1991e: pp. 302–3.

of course, but the issue is worth exploring because, while the political and institutional developments which accompanied this shift of values have been much discussed, less attention has been given to the changes in the ideological material which informed and fed off them.[140] Perpetual strife, it seems, bred a loss of confidence among kings and their apologists and this, in turn, provided the basis for the defensive and authoritarian attitudes associated with what used to be known as 'new monarchy'.[141] The scale of this ideological transformation has been rather underplayed by historians: mainly because there has been a tendency to treat the views of writers of this period – in particular those of Fortescue – as if they were both normative and typical of the century as a whole.[142] The inter-related assumptions that politics were dominated by self-advancement, that loyalties were conditional upon material reward, and that the king had thus to be strong and rich to retain control, have dominated accounts of later medieval England. If this sort of thinking can be shown to have arisen from a prolonged and unexpected crisis in the fortunes of the monarchy – and, indeed, from a misdiagnosis of its causes – then its value as a means of understanding the polity of Henry VI, which was formed in less abnormal times, may be questioned.

To begin at the beginning, it seems clear that when critics of the regime which collapsed in 1450 identified greed and ambition, or 'covetise', as the contemporary basis of political behaviour and allegiance, they were drawing a contrast with what they believed to be the norm. Love of money had driven out virtue, and the consequences for the common weal were predictably destructive: justice and good rule were wholly overcome.[143] Apart from its obvious effect on royal resources,[144] the spread of 'covetise' among the king's advisers was believed to frustrate political relations in two ways. First of all, by poisoning the wells of counsel it drew

---

[140] Though see Kekewich 1987 for an account which reaches similar conclusions to those presented here.

[141] See Goodman 1988 for a recent revision and restoration of the concept.

[142] McFarlane, who called the *Governance* an 'overrated and misleading pamphlet' (1981c: p. 23), made a series of attacks on Fortescue's reading of later medieval politics. In 1981f and 1973: ch. 3 he argued against the concept of overmighty subjects and, especially, against their role as causers of the disorders of the mid-century. For a modern reappearance of the overmighty nobility as a systemic problem, see Pollard 1988: pp. 46–53, 65. Fortescue's historiographical influence has recently been discussed by Carpenter 1992: p. 6.

[143] See, for example, the poem against Bishop Booth of Coventry and Lichfield (Wright (ed.), *Political Poems*, II, pp. 225–9). Lydgate's 'Serpent of Division', written soon after Henry V's death, set out to show how 'covetise' gave rise to pride and ambition and these in turn led to division and thence to destruction: see Scattergood 1971: pp. 138–9 and also Erdmann (ed.), *Lydgate's Siege of Thebes*, p. 46 (where 'covetise' replaces brotherhood, leading to internecine war).

[144] E.g. 'So pore a kyng was never seene, / Nor richere lordes alle bydene': Wright (ed.), *Political Poems*, II, p. 230, lines 13–14.

the king away from his most important function: the representation of the wider *communitas*. Whether this was because of the corruption of the great men who typically advised the king,[145] or (as was more commonly suggested in the early 1450s) because the nobility were edged out of government by cliques of lesser men who were unburdened by territorial responsibility and inevitably seduced into flattery and greed by the rewards at their disposal,[146] the results were the same: the government became detached from its constituency.[147] This meant that the king was not receiving the true service he was owed by those who assisted him in the task of rule: in fact, as the interests of his counsellors replaced the interests of the people as the main focus of his concern, he was being led into a form of tyranny, with disastrous consequences for everyone.[148]

These consequences were aggravated by the second major effect of 'covetise', which was emphasised by George Ashby, in his 'Active Policy of a Prince': just as it drew ministers and counsellors away from their responsibilities to subjects, so it broke down their loyalty to the king.[149] He could not rely on their support: their interest was not in him, but in his goods, because the covetous man had 'no regarde to trouthe ne worship, / So [long as] he may come to goode and Lordeship'.[150] 'Covetise' thus led to untruth, falseness, negligence and, in fact, 'subtel treson': it was a betrayal of both king and community.[151] The idea that the highest bidder would obtain the allegiance of the covetous counsellor was developed by

[145] This was a strand in York's case against Somerset, for example: see e.g. *PL*, I, p. 104.

[146] Note, for example, York's condemnation of 'the singularite of the thriftelewe, coveitous and colde kowardise I-broughte up of noughte' who surrounded the king (BL, Add. MS 48031[A], fol. 126r: 'singularite' appears to mean 'self-interest' here) and the observations of Cade's rebels in art. 3 of their first manifesto: Harvey 1991: p. 187. The same theme emerged in the complaints of Gloucester in 1440 (*Letters and Papers*, II, ii, pp. 440–51) and, especially clearly, in those of Warwick and Clarence in 1469: Halliwell (ed.), *Warkworth's Chronicle*, p. 47. 'Gregory's Chronicle', conversely, spoke admiringly of 'the substaunce of men of worschyppe that wylle not glose nor cory favyl for no parcyallyte' (*Collections*, p. 213: see also Denholm-Young (ed.), *Vita Edwardi Secundi*, p. 99).

[147] See below, pp. 233–4, 250–2.

[148] George Ashby identified covetous counsel, probably (*pace* his editor) that of Henry VI in the 1440s and 1450s, as the cause of the wars: 'Active Policy', sts. 16–17, 24–5. The point was reached where these men would rather die than lose their new-found wealth, 'And so loste there maister, theimselfe and goode, / Oonly covetise shedynge their blode' (lines 181–2).

[149] They took on the position of the false counsellor, who flatters the king rather than advises him, and – because of the failure of the representative function – damages his master by misleading him. Warnings against this stereotype appear in *Secreta*, pp. 210–11; Genet (ed.), *Political Tracts*, pp. 38, 194–5 ('he may nevyr soo knowe his owne estate ne the trouth of his chargeable matiers, in soo moche as he yevyth credence and heerith more ... the liere than the sooth seyer'); *Regement*, lines 4915–21.

[150] 'Active Policy', lines 202–3. These ideas were not new: see Moisant (ed.), *De Speculo Regis*, 'Recensio B', pp. 141–2, for an earlier example.

[151] 'Active Policy', line 200. See also st. 27 and lines 187–9.

Fortescue, but he extended Ashby's point to imply that all men were, if not covetous, at least ambitious and that their loyalties were thus primarily to themselves.[152] When a man was as rich as the king, he would inevitably wish to be king, and indeed he would soon be able to be, partly because the people would support him on the grounds that if he were richer, he would be less dependent on them for financial support.[153] As far as Fortescue was concerned, 'the peple will go with hym that best mey susteyne and rewarde ham', and it is significant that the people's sustenance and reward were seen in purely fiscal terms, without regard for the quality of justice, law or representation.[154] Only money mattered in the world of 'covetise'.

These views represent three stages in a conceptual shift. In the first, 'covetise' is condemned principally because of its destructive effects on the common weal. For Ashby, however, it is the danger to the prince himself which is most important: the fact that the covetous neglect their obligations to the realm is placed below their lack of genuine loyalty to the king. Fortescue, finally, abandons the possibility of a more disinterested loyalty altogether and proposes a new structure of government which could take account of men's intrinsic greed. This trend is a register of the breakdown of trust and confidence in familiar political relationships. Instead of the loyal service which true knights would naturally offer their loving sovereign, materialism and ambition were all around. The implication of the works of Ashby, Fortescue and some of the poets of 1450 is that Henry VI had more or less performed his royal duties, but that the viciousness of his contemporaries had prevented successful rule.[155] In response, the traditional framework of kingship, in which virtuous loyalties could be assumed if the right morality prevailed in the ruler, was cast aside in favour of a more dynamic model in which rule was to be a forceful action of the king, and no longer a natural reaction of the realm. Instead of merely providing a resort of judgement, the king would have to go on to the offensive.

'The Active Policy of a Prince' is shot through with a fear of treason which colours much of the advice which Ashby has to offer. The prince is warned against the danger from traditionally rebellious areas like Kent, from evil barons, from pretenders, from those apparently reconciled,

---

[152] E.g. 'for manis corage is so noble, that naturally he aspirith to high thinges, and to be exaltid, and therfore enforsith hym selff to be alway gretter and gretter': *Governance*, p. 128. Notice the use of the word 'noble' to mean aggressive and ambitious rather than protective and dutiful. Ambition had negative connotations at this time: note, for example, Lydgate's criticisms of 'vayne ambicion' as a product of 'covetise' (Scattergood 1971: p. 139).

[153] *Governance*, pp. 128–9: see the discussion of this section, below, p. 46 n. 173.

[154] *Governance*, p. 129.

[155] This is made plainest of all in the tract 'Somnium Vigilantis', discussed below, p. 43.

from disloyal servants, from the poor commons, from livery and maintenance, from his own kin and offspring and from rich lords.[156] To
combat these many perils, he has to adopt some unattractive devices and
these, in turn, distance him from the servants he can no longer afford to
trust.[157] Far away from the traditionally magnanimous king who forgets
wrongs, trusts the true and consults the wise and great, Ashby's prince is
very much the new monarch: defensive, watchful, independent. While the
poem does include more conventional advice on tempering justice with
mercy (and vice versa), on taking counsel and on the value of pursuing
moderation, its main thrust is undoubtedly towards keeping power rather
than knowing what to do with it.[158] Significantly, the familiar emphasis
on the king's obligation to the common weal is altogether transformed.
When Ashby raises the issue, it is not with the king's fundamental *raison
d'être* in mind, but in connection with the well-worn concern for security:
for Ashby, to be attentive to the 'universal / and the comyn wele' means
keeping an eye on even the smallest affairs of the nation, because out of
little troubles, bigger ones may grow.[159] Vigilance replaces public service
as the king's most fundamental concern.

Earlier in the century, it had apparently been assumed that loyalty and
obedience would accrue naturally to the king as a consequence of his
defence of the common weal. However, these properties were also the
fundamental means by which the rule of the king, on which the defence of
the common weal depended, was normally effected. In the tract known as
'Somnium Vigilantis', which was written in 1459 to support the attainder
of the Yorkists,[160] the normal priority of the issue of defending the
common weal over the issue of maintaining loyalty and obedience was
reversed, and the important question of who was qualified to adjudicate
the king's discharge of his duties was addressed. The author was not
afraid to tackle the central claim of the duke of York and his supporters
head-on. To the excuse that 'they entende the commen welthe of alle the

---

[156] 'Active Policy', lines 389–90, 408–10, 419–21, 427–8, 504–5 and sts. 59, 68, 73, 79,
90, 92.

[157] E.g. *ibid.*, st. 89 (investigating tales about his courtiers and keeping the results of his
researches secret from them). Note the comment on Henry VII reported by John
Flamank in the early 1500s: 'Master Porter said yt was grett pitty that the kinge dyd not
tryst hys true knyghtes better, and to geve them credens in suche thynges as they should
shew for hys surtie, for grett hurt may come by that mene' – Pollard (ed.), *The Reign of
Henry VII*, I, p. 245.

[158] 'Active Policy', lines 331–2, 359–60, st. 36, line 253, st. 46.

[159] *Ibid.*, st. 111. Similarly, while Ashby advises the prince to remedy the complaints of the
common people and protect the poor from extortion in st. 95, he doubtless has in mind
the readiness of the destitute to rebel (e.g. st. 73 and see *Governance*, pp. 138–9, for the
same idea).

[160] See Kekewich 1982: pp. 28–30 for a discussion of the likely timing, purpose and
authorship of this document.

royame, for the which it is resonable and worshipfull to expose himselfe to grete jeoperde of goodis and lyfe' (especially considering 'the grete perplexite wherin the royame stode at that tyme, and nobody employnge himselfe to the reformacion tharof'),[161] he composed this devastating reply which is so significant as to merit quoting in full:

> I remember that amonge many thinges by the whiche the commone welthe of a royame stondyth, the most principall is this: a due subjeccion with fayithfull and voluntarie honoure and thair appertenaunce to be yolden to the soverain in the sayd royame and that none incompatible astat be usurped by ony personne; also that thay that have undre the kynge a governaunce of his peple, that thay ben dylygent to the kepynge of the kynges lawes and that no wronge be done in ony wise, but that alle controversies and debates civile or criminalle, realle or personale, ben decided by the kynges lawes withoute mayntenance or wylfull interrupcion of the cours of justice, and in cas that ony thinge falle of the whiche the determinacion is not expressed in the common lawe, thann the prince moste be asked and inquired and by his excedyng auctorite and prudens of his conseyle an expikan shalbe made tharopon, and so that no thinge be done by singular wylle and senceall affeccion.[162]

Apart from illustrating the extent to which the crown had successfully annexed 'law' to itself, what this passage shows is that if the single authority of the crown was not recognised, it could do nothing for the common good. Indeed, there *was* no common good without a common authority. Obedience, therefore, not the common weal, was the fundamental basis of the state: only because obedience was usually forthcoming and incidental to the king's discharge of his duties could advice literature normally afford to focus on the protection of the common weal. The over-riding need to preserve the king's security in the public interest had been the justification for identifying treason and *lèse-majesté* as specific crimes and it is no surprise to find the writers of this period extending the scope of royal rights in this area on populistic grounds.[163] Harsh treatment of those who threatened the distribution of authority was mercy to those who benefited from that distribution.[164]

Once the crown invoked the ruthless logic of its office, that allegiance to

---

[161] 'Somnium', p. 515.

[162] *Ibid.*, p. 518. In a paper given at the University of Kent on 23 November 1991, Dr A. Gross proposed that 'expikan' was a coinage derived from the concept of *epieikeia* – an equitable judgement based on what is taken to be the intention of the legislator – and not 'explication', as Gilson originally suggested.

[163] 'Active Policy', lines 793–5: 'if thoffence touche the subvercion / Of the Realme, puttyng it in disturbance, / Procede sharply to deue execucion'; 'Somnium', pp. 516–17.

[164] Note 'Somnium', p. 517: in the case of those who sought the 'fynall destruccion of this gracyous kynge and . . . the irreparable subversyoun of all his tru lovers . . . it were none other but cruelnes to have mercy apon thamm'.

the common weal could not be put before allegiance to the king, York had no choice but to submit or to abandon his common weal platform and challenge Henry VI's right to the crown. This was essential to his own protection, but it was also a step dictated by the ideology of monarchy. Only if he were king himself could the duke reconcile crown and common weal, because only from the throne could justice be restored and the commonwealth protected.[165] The king's 'excedyng auctorite' – and, as we have seen, it was only authority, not force – had to be recognised and obeyed if the *common* good, as distinct from the 'singular wylle' of rebels or courtiers was to be upheld. No one who preached the contrary could be called 'withoute lesynge [lying], protectoure or procuroure of the commen welthe'.[166]

The 'Somnium' author described the desperate measures forced upon the Yorkist lords in their wrong-headed campaign, concluding an account of how their secret pacts resulted in the deaths of so many of the king's people with the ironic comment 'thes ben notable poyntes of preservynge of the common welth'.[167] Opposition could mean nothing but destruction. Why should the claim of York and the others to speak for the common good be accepted? The community already possessed an executor of its will: it was the king and no other.[168] To some extent, this line of argument demonstrated the subordinate place of seigneurial authority. Inasmuch as the nobility might lay claim to the tutelage, rule or governance of the provinces for the common benefit of the people who lived in them, they had to have it for and from the king, who was the guardian of the common benefit of the nation. Although, as we have begun to see, it was a grey area of political and chivalric thought whether lords had their authority independently as a function of their landed power and knightly right, or whether they received it from the king as a delegation of his rule, there seems to have been little doubt that this authority was subject to royal overlordship.[169] The king could invoke a higher – because national – common interest to set against the lordships of the chivalrous aristocracy and the primarily local interests they represented. In a crisis, this common interest could be held to repose in obedience to the king: so it was that the 'Somnium' author commented that true knights wished to accomplish the will of the sovereign alone, or their own will only insofar as it accorded with his.[170] Here was the conceptual basis of the royal monopoly of service and honour which

---

[165] See Watts 1990 and below, pp. 328–9 and elsewhere, for further discussion.
[166] 'Somnium', p. 518. [167] *Ibid.*, p. 519.
[168] *Ibid.*, pp. 519–20. The argument is neatly summed up by the rhetorical question, 'who made hem juges?' (p. 520). Note *Aquinas*, p. 71.
[169] See above, pp. 20, 35, and below, pp. 65, 91ff. [170] 'Somnium', p. 521.

Mervyn James found in the later sixteenth century: the idea simply awaited forceful expression, and this it had begun to receive. In its first incarnation, amid the divisions of the later fifteenth century, it took the form of a resumption of lordship.[171]

It is in the treatise of Sir John Fortescue on the *Governance of England* that ideas of resumption achieved their fullest expression. The purpose of this well-known work was to explain how, within the framework of the *dominium politicum et regale* by which England was supposedly governed, the king's fiscal resources could be increased and maintained. Such a policy was, it seemed to Fortescue, the key to restoring royal authority from its nadir in the 1450s. While a number of historians have questioned the relevance of the chief justice's well-known view of the constitution, hardly anyone has attacked another guiding principle of the *Governance*: its author's assumption that fiscal supremacy was the basis of royal power.[172] As the famous, but flawed, treatment of overmighty subjects demonstrates, it seemed to Fortescue that the crown's conceptual and political resources were negligible because, to him, hard-headed self-interest and ambition were the realities of politics, not allegiance to the king.[173] The very fact that a lord had greater disposable income than the king gave him a spur, as well as a means, to rebel. In Fortescue's vision, the king had to be able to pay his way, and one of the leading aims of the *Governance* was to show him how to do so.

Much of this excessively pessimistic reading of political loyalties must be traced to Fortescue's experiences under Henry VI and his observation from abroad of the turbulent years of Edward IV's first reign. This is also true of many of his fiscal and conciliar prescriptions, as is suggested by their inclusion in a memorandum addressed to Warwick at the time of the

---

[171] For James' ideas, see above, p. 33. The view that lordship derived from the king applied above all, argued the 'Somnium' author, to York, Warwick and Salisbury, whose 'furste exordye and begenynge cam of the kyngis large munyficence' ('Somnium', p. 521). For the ways in which kings resumed their lordship in the second half of the fifteenth century, see e.g. Condon 1979 and Hicks 1991d. Note that the corollary of resumed lordship was a more personal discharge of his functions by the king. This was captured by Ashby, 'Active Policy', lines 285–7: 'Do youre selfe and all shall be obeying, / Truste to no man is execucion, / So wele as to youre oune inspeccion'.

[172] See e.g. McFarlane 1981c: p. 23; 1981f: pp. 216–17; 1938: pp. 708, 710. Cf. Carpenter 1992: pp. 6, 7, who *does* make this matter the focus of her criticism and Chrimes 1936: ch. IV and Burns 1985: p. 785 and n. 29, who find Fortescue's vision of the constitution a just one.

[173] Overmighty subjects are dealt with in *Governance*, ch. IX. One obvious flaw in Fortescue's argument is the case of John of Gaunt, very rich and very loyal, which he cites on p. 130 (also used by McFarlane as an example of a harmless 'overmighty subject', interestingly: 1973: p. 178). Note that Ashby's views on wealthy lords were similar: 'Active Policy', st. 92. See above, p. 7, for a discussion of 'the realities of politics'.

Readeption.[174] Even so, Fortescue's solution to the problem of Henry's misrule was not political and specific, but constitutional and wide-ranging. The refoundation of the crown which he proposed went far beyond a restoration of the squandered royal patrimony. Rather, it was a complete revision of the mechanisms by which the king fulfilled the obligations of his office. If Fortescue set out from a series of assumptions similar to those of earlier advice-writers, he arrived at conclusions which were significantly different. Communal well-being remained the funda-mental point of royal government,[175] but it was to be achieved more by communal action through a reformed council than by the virtuous rule of the prince.[176] The invocation of the common interest which had justified the new authoritarianism of the crown was, in Fortescue's writings, turned back upon the king himself. As his power advanced, at the expense of the 'overmighty' nobility, for example, so it was increasingly colonised by the will of the *communitas* expressed through formal counsel.

This can be demonstrated from various stages in the argument of the *Governance*. The problems arising from the king's poverty are not borne by him alone, but by the whole realm.[177] Because the king's office existed so that the needs of the realm could be met, and the realm needed his patrimony to be preserved so that he would not be poor, it was no limitation on the king's power, argued Fortescue, to prevent him from making grants out of it.[178] The king gained from this restriction because his office gained and so did the realm. The issue which most of all preoccupied earlier advice-writers – the reconciliation of public responsi-bilities with the inclinations of a man whose private will is the basis of all public action – is simply ignored: the king wishes to do what his office requires; he bears no personal power whatsoever and, in fact, in a major

---

[174] For the advice to Warwick, see *Governance*, p. 350, and the comments of Wolffe 1971: p. 120. Fortescue's fiscal and conciliar prescriptions seem closely attuned to what are usually regarded as the inadequacies of Henry VI's rule: e.g. the recommendation in favour of resuming land and paying cash out of its issues, rather than simply granting the land or assigning its issues (*Governance*, pp. 120–1, 124–5, 126, 131–4 etc.); the view that conciliar control of grants would stop both undue pressure of suitors on the king and public 'grochynge' about those about his person (*ibid.*, p. 144); the determina-tion to restrict the king's access to other sources of counsel (*ibid.*, p. 350).

[175] *Governance*, p. 127; above, p. 29.

[176] Fortescue several times argued that the existence of political elements in a constitution rescued the people from dependence on the presence of virtue in their ruler: e.g. *Governance*, ch. I; *De Natura*, p. 216.

[177] *Governance*, pp. 119–20.

[178] *Ibid.*, pp. 120–1, 127. The point is that a power to do anything against the purposes of his office would be what Fortescue called a 'nown poiar': a purely negative thing. The 'Somnium' made a similar point about restrictions on the king's exercise of his mercy in cases of subversion: 'though his justice have hir place at this tyme, his mercy and grace is never the les, for here is no matere to exercyse mercy tharopon' (p. 517). See below, p. 353, for the different opinion of Henry's advisers in 1459.

change from earlier norms, the exercise of such power, or will, is unnecessary to his office. There is no risk of disjuncture between the interests of Fortescue's king and those of his realm, because the king is a purely public being: this is what enables Fortescue to turn 'Rex datur propter regnum et non regnum propter regem', normally a reminder to the king of his duty to society, into a statement explaining why his subjects are bound to support him.[179] Fortescue's suspension of the independent private will of the king made it clear that he was not really writing about a monarchy at all. His kingly office was a public fisc.[180]

The administration of this fisc was to be largely in the hands of a representative council and its agents.[181] As their expert and functional nature demanded, the councillors enjoyed a considerable degree of independence. Their tenure of office was governed by their own corporate advice and their deliberations were to be guided by a formulary which they themselves would make.[182] Without the council, the king would do little: it was to assess all petitions and advise on all grants and appointments.[183] Its loyalty to the crown was guaranteed by arrangements depriving the councillors of all other means of lordship and support.[184] The same rubrics applied to the king's officers, for, while the council worked to maintain the royal estate at the centre, the officers were

---

[179] From St Thomas' well-known text, Fortescue deduced that 'the reaume is bounde to susteyne hym in every thyng necessarie to his estate': *Governance*, p. 127.

[180] This idea was not wholly new, of course. Notions of a royal fisc began to develop in the thirteenth century: Harriss 1975: ch. VI. Traces of it appear in earlier fifteenth-century advice-literature. The *Secreta*, for example, declared that if a king found he could not manage his money, then he should ordain some true men 'that may duly als hit longeth to a kynge, his goodis to despende and ordeyn' (*Secreta*, p. 131). Even so, Fortescue's statements on the topic are certainly more definite and far-reaching than any earlier ones.

[181] It was to be a fixed group of twenty-four men – twelve temporal, twelve spiritual – 'off the wysest and best disposed men that can be ffounde in all the parties off this lande', supplemented by eight peers, the king's 'consiliarii nati': *Governance*, pp. 146–7.

[182] Fortescue avoids the question of how the non-noble councillors should be chosen by using the passive ('that ther were chosen': p. 146 – cf. the establishment of the minority council in 1422, p. 114, below). They could only be removed if a majority of the rest advised it (*ibid.*). Noble councillors and the chief councillor were to be chosen by the king (*ibid.*). See pp. 148–9 for the formulary and other arrangements. It is possible that, in making these proposals, Fortescue had the position and powers of the judges in mind. These were a group of almost self-selecting men, who followed routines set down largely by themselves and their predecessors. They worked in the royal interest, but were mostly free of the king's interference or direction: see Ives 1983: chs. I.4, II.7, III.10–11.

[183] *Governance*, pp. 143–4, 150, 153–4. Note that the procedure laid down for the council to follow in deciding whether or not a suitor deserved a grant closely resembles that which was sometimes prescribed for kings to follow (e.g. Genet (ed.), *Political Tracts*, p. 186).

[184] The twenty-four non-noble councillors were to swear to be no other man's but the king's and would thus, it was assumed, have no other source of income but their wages as councillors: *Governance*, p. 146. The position of the eight peers was rather different. They were only to be in office for a year each and were not to be paid: *ibid.*, p. 147.

to do so in the provinces, 'ffor thai mowe best rule the contreis wher as ther offices ben'.[185] It was made quite clear that this way of doing things would allow the king to divert local loyalties away from local lords, since men would know that they owed their position directly to conciliar favour and not to the intercession of the local magnate.[186] Central, if impersonal, control of the patronage *nexus* would be complete.

Fortescue's philosophy was thus reasonably coherent. The power of the crown, relative to that of the lords, was increased through a more vigorous exploitation of the rights implicit in its position. This was acceptable because only by the crown could the common good be guaranteed. It was made more acceptable by the creation of an expert council, which guaranteed the king's capacity to govern by actually taking over the reins to a very large extent. The 'political' element in the constitution was supplied not personally, through the king's prudent assessment of counsel and just dispensation of equity, but institutionally, through a body combining the strengths of 'law' with those of representation. With the king's power effectively in the hands of a corporate representation of his public body, there could be no practical difference between the royal interest and the common interest. This was brought home in the local political control exercised by the crown, where, in a society framed by personal ambition, it controlled all the avenues to advancement. Meanwhile, king and nobility, head and limbs of the old body politic, were essentially removed from power: the former had little choice but to endorse the views of his council and parliament; the latter were to become wealthy nonentities, enjoying their lands in peaceful obscurity, but ever-threatened by the accidents of heredity and the king's 'feudal' prerogatives.[187] Fortescue's new England was to be 'a collage in whiche shul syng and pray for evermore al the men of Ingland spirituel and temporel'.[188] As J. R. Lander has recently observed, this was a striking development. No longer was the realm to be an organic, yet hierarchical phenomenon: it has become a community of men equalised in the king's lawful governance and joined by articulate choice.[189]

---

[185] *Ibid.*, p. 151. For the terms of office-holding, see pp. 150, 153.

[186] *Ibid.*, pp. 152, 157.

[187] *Ibid.*, p. 134. These threats were real: see McFarlane 1973: pp. 143, 172–6 for the high rates of failure in the male line and Thorne (ed.), *Prerogativa Regis*, introduction, for the exploitation of feudal rights by the early Tudors. No very secure future awaited the nobility in the England of the *Governance*.

[188] *Governance*, pp. 154–6.

[189] See Lander 1989: pp. 12–13 (also Harriss 1993: p. 57: neither offers quite the interpretation given here). That the king would be transferring personal power to this 'newe ffundacion' of his crown, is made quite clear by Fortescue's observation that this would be no more against his prerogative than the foundation of an abbey (*Governance*, pp. 154–5).

In the event, of course, Fortescue backed away from the enormity of what he was suggesting. Presenting the work to Edward IV, he licensed him to depart from the model in a way which would have significantly undermined it.[190] It is quite clear that what Fortescue prescribed was incompatible with an active king ruling by traditional methods. This raises some interesting questions about the logic of English legal and bureaucratic development which had so profoundly influenced the thought of the old chief justice: what place, for example, did it leave for the free judgement of the sovereign lord? But Fortescue's ideas were also modelled by the pathological politics which surrounded him. Faced with a dramatic functional failure in the private will of the king, on the one hand, and in the conventionally loyal and co-operative nobility, on the other, Fortescue's solution was to devise ways of doing without them. As such, his theories, together with those of Ashby and others, are inseparable from the crisis in the midst of which they were formulated. What is new in them – the emphasis on obedience, the reduction of loyalty to a simple mercenary phenomenon, the suspicion of delegated power, even the 'college' imagery – in all cases relates to the unusual circumstance of competition for the throne.

For this was the real problem of the second half of the fifteenth century. Natural loyalties became unreliable because, for much of the period after 1460 (and, in certain ways, for a decade before this date), there were viable alternatives to the rule of the present king. At the highest level, unity was replaced by diversity. Since the political system of later medieval England was undeniably a monarchy, the withdrawal of the king's uniqueness was bound to produce strange developments in political practice and theory. It was, after all, on the preservation of an all-powerful and all-responsive royal unity that the corporate loyalty which made government possible had depended. The removal of this one element meant the foundering of the entire system and the consequent, but unusual, necessity of rebuilding it from scratch, a task which, at least to begin with, required a different scheme of values. With no unity at the centre to act as a natural focus, loyalty had to be won: hence the mercenary and authoritarian basis of the polity the theorists described. More straightforward forms of royal *quid* for subjects' *quo* briefly replaced the subtler and more sophisticated balance of interests in normal politics. The common weal ceased to be an expression of the effective justice which arose from the personal play of virtuous king and trusting nobility and became a matter of fiscalism, bureaucracy and centralised security. While earlier fifteenth-century writers provided for the maintenance of a

---

[190] *Ibid.*, p. 157.

broadly self-contained and self-sustaining organism, Fortescue, Ashby and the 'Somnium' author looked into a void where collective interests had collapsed, together with the collective authority which had satisfied them. Their central preoccupation was the creation of adequate authority, through a combination of terror and the exploitation of simple patronage, not the fulfilment of representative and judicial functions which normally dominated the prescribed activities of king and nobility. There is every reason to suppose that the priorities of Henry VI's advisers, at least until the last decade of his reign, were vastly more conventional.

THE POLITICAL IDEAS OF THE NOBILITY

So far, a single, if sprawling, ideology of kingship has been identified, and presented as a dominant feature of contemporary political comment; an ideology which emphasised the common good as the proper end of government, but which recognised the pre-eminent role played by the king in the achievement of this end and which, indeed, gave priority to the subject's duty of obedience whenever the royal right to assess the common good was brought into question. The materials which have been used to explore this ideology are the self-proclaimed authorities of the age: mirrors for princes, handbooks and exemplary poems of various kinds, written with the express intention of bringing human behaviour into line with the *corpus* of revealed truth represented by Scripture and the works of the schoolmen. Up to now, then, we have been concerned with the 'producers' of political thought, not the 'consumers'. If, as seems likely, the language and ideas of politics were not wholly dictated by academics, lawyers and clerks, then it will be necessary to look at the activities of practitioners before reaching any conclusions about the operation of this prevailing ideology and the nature of its relationship with political events.

It is, of course, difficult to determine to what extent producers and consumers of political thought were divorced from each other. The middle ages are often regarded as a time in which the 'right reason' of trained minds held sway over the 'sense-perception' of the laity.[191] If this was indeed the case, then the authorised truths purveyed by advice-literature might be expected to have influenced behaviour in a direct way. But the period was not without its sceptics. Surveying the debates at the Diet of Frankfurt in 1442, Niccolo Piccolomini protested that 'only a fool thinks kings and princes are influenced by tomes and treatises'.[192] Fifty

---

[191] See e.g. Murray 1978: pp. 6–14 and Pocock 1975: pp. 4–5. Part of the conceptual basis for this state of affairs appears in *Aquinas*, pp. 57–8.

[192] Cited by Black 1970: p. 114.

years later, meanwhile, a number of Londoners declared that 'the Popys curse wolde not kylle a flye' when they heard news of clerical sanctions against the wearers of long, pointed shoes.[193] Clearly enough, then, lay mentalities were not determined by authoritative opinion alone.[194] On the other hand, it is important to remember that scholars were not wholly sealed off from society.[195] If they followed academic tradition and the derived authority it represented, their evangelical and didactic responsibilities drew them back into the world. They sought *exempla* which would genuinely convince. Increasingly, they wrote in comprehensible forms and languages.[196] More and more, in the fifteenth century, they lived and worked as lawyers or clerks in the service of the government.[197] On the whole, writers of advice-literature consciously tried to link immanent truth, revealed by faith and scholarship, to the daily concerns of their readers. Even so, the fact remains that we cannot make assertions about what those concerns were, or how accurately men like Hoccleve and Fortescue understood and represented them, on the basis of their writings alone. If advice-literature was indeed a synthesis of reason and the world, we need to know as much about the latter as about the former. How is this to be done?

One possible approach is to look at patterns of book ownership and literary patronage among the aristocracy to see what is revealed about their intellectual tastes. A brief investigation appears below, but the exercise is not without its problems. Very little information about secular libraries in England has survived, especially in comparison with those of France and Burgundy.[198] Fifteenth-century inventories of books are very rare and, because of the nature of domestic record keeping, other references to books are scattered and frequently unspecific.[199] In any case, ownership alone proves little. Books were richly produced status symbols and Barclay's satirised picture of the wealthy book collector – 'Styll am I besy bokes assemblynge ... But what they mene do I nat understonde' – probably had some foundation in reality.[200] Even if we assume, with McFarlane and others, that book owners mostly did read

---

[193] *Collections*, p. 238.
[194] This has been a commonplace of modern historical writing on this period. See e.g. Reynolds 1984: pp. 4–5; Holt 1985: preface.
[195] See Skinner 1969: sections i–iii; Powicke 1936: p. 17.
[196] Genet (ed.), *Political Tracts*, p. xiv; Keen 1984: p. 6; see Green 1980: pp. 142, 149ff for the growth in the practice of translation. Orme 1984: p. 154 comments that even works in Latin were still intended to be read by the aristocracy, who would have been easily able to engage the services of an interpreter.
[197] Lawton 1987: p. 788, and *passim*. A bureaucratic training did not, of course, necessarily bestow an understanding of aristocratic politics upon such men.
[198] Green 1980: p. 91.
[199] *Ibid.*, p. 92, although an example appears in *PL*, VI, pp. 65–7.
[200] Quoted by Green 1980: pp. 91–2.

and understand the books they possessed,[201] we are still not necessarily in any position to judge how their reading influenced their daily lives or political views. Moreover, it is difficult to gauge whether the medieval book market was shaped by the interests of consumers or those of authors: if the latter, sales and purchases may tell us little about the attitudes of the laity.[202]

The same difficulty arises with literary patronage: except in a few cases, we do not have much evidence of attempts on the part of patrons to influence the content of the works they sponsored. Did the rich buy treatises and sponsor their authors simply as a matter of social convention, or were they genuinely interested in what they bought? In a sense, of course, this may not be the important question. We have already accepted that the private psyche is not the main concern of the political historian.[203] What later medieval political literature unquestionably did provide for political society was a public treasury of familiar terms and concepts: a clear and coherent conceptual framework for politics and a language in which to express it.[204] If book ownership and patterns of literary patronage cannot tell us what people were actually thinking, they may at least indicate to what extent people were exposed to this rich source of political terminology.

Another way of exploring the impact of the ideas contained in advice-literature is to investigate the language used by the aristocracy in politics, both national and local, and to analyse the concepts it appears to reflect. These, too, are problematic exercises. Inevitably, it is only rarely that political ideas are presented clearly and pristinely in the day-to-day language of politicians. More commonly, principles and concepts are invoked for particular purposes, or fleetingly implied in the unselfconscious pursuit of conventional ends. Although this makes any sort of assessment rather impressionistic, however, it does have the considerable virtue of focusing attention on ideas in their practical application. Evidently, we need to know the intellectual structures which underpinned the ideology we are examining, but the actual manifestations of this ideology are an important key to establishing its influence in politics. The fact that, for example, the correspondence of the Pastons and other families, which are among our richest sources for contemporary political language, deal with the somewhat specialised politics of the local scene (and that from a gentry perspective) need not be a disadvantage.[205] Not only were local politics plainly part of the 'public' sphere of crown and

---

[201] See e.g. McFarlane 1973: ch. 6. Green argues a similar line in 1980: ch. 3.
[202] The question is considered by Doyle 1983.   [203] Above, p. 7.
[204] See Lawton 1987: pp. 771–3, 775, 791–4 and Pocock 1972: ch. I.
[205] McFarlane 1981f: pp. 231–2.

nobility with which we are mostly concerned, but it is also possible to show relationships between the conceptual framework in which they were conducted and that of the realm as a whole. Enough, moreover, survives among the records of 'high' politics to show the nobility employing ideas closely related to those in the authorities. In the end, then, it may indeed be possible to demonstrate not only how much, but also in what ways, the content of political literature was expressed in politics.

. . .

Alongside the taste for romances and devotional works which sometimes seems to typify the literary consumption of the late medieval aristocracy, there was a significant interest in didactic writing.[206] Handbooks of various kinds – moral, political and chivalric treatises, books of etiquette, collections of maxims or domestic wisdoms – were, together with exemplary and often fantastic histories, an immensely popular genre, purveying to an apparently enthusiastic public attitudes and information deemed useful by the educated.[207] The view of St Paul, which Caxton rendered as 'alle that is wryten is wryten unto our doctryne and for our lernyng', seems amply borne out in the utilitarian leanings of the book-buying public.[208] The duke of Gloucester, for example, said of his new copies of the first five books of Plato's *Republic*, 'they shall be to us as companions or counsellors for ruling our life'.[209] Edward III, meanwhile, had six books purveyed for him purely because they 'related to the solemnity of feasts'[210] and Henry VI's tutor, the earl of Warwick, was ordered to use examples culled from history books to teach the young king to 'love, worship and drede God'.[211] Examples like these suggest that the hopes of the writers – that their works would influence attitudes and practices – were justified.[212] They also reflect the enormous importance which medieval men and women attached to the getting of counsel. A certain receptiveness to the morality inherent in this didactic literature was thus assumed by both authors and their readers and patrons. It remains to be seen which texts were actually being read.

The view that the mirror for princes was the dominant form in the

---

[206] Above, p. 15.

[207] Ferguson 1960: pp. 33–50; Bennett 1946–7: pp. 167–78; Green 1980: pp. 135–7; Scattergood 1983; Keen 1984: pp. 6, 10–11, 15–16; Vale 1981: pp. 14–20 (I do not propose to deal with the ownership of chivalric, as distinct from historical or political, texts).

[208] Crotch (ed.), *Caxton's Prologues*, p. 10; Ferguson 1960: p. 34; Green 1980: p. 134.

[209] Green 1980: p. 142.   [210] *Ibid.*, p. 134.   [211] *PPC*, III, p. 299.

[212] Evidence for the existence of these hopes on the part of authors is to be found in almost all written work of the period, but see, for example, Green 1980: pp. 137–8; Bennett 1946–7: pp. 170–1; *Secreta*, pp. 121–3; Nichols (ed.), *Boke of Noblesse*, p. 1; Caxton's prologue to the *Polychronicon*, in Ferguson 1960: p. 38.

determination of political ideology seems to be justified by the wide dissemination of some key texts. Hoccleve based his *Regement of Princes*, written in 1411–12 for Henry V as prince of Wales, on three well-known continental mirrors: *De Ludo Scaccorum*, by James of Cessolis; *De Regimine Principum*, by Giles of Rome; and the pseudo-Aristotelian *Secreta Secretorum*.[213] Copies of all three works were common among the English aristocracy. Latin, French or even English versions of Giles of Rome were owned, among others, by Sir Simon Burley, tutor to Richard II, Thomas of Woodstock, Edward IV and Richard III (probably), Margaret of Anjou, Thomas Lord Berkeley,[214] Humphrey, duke of Gloucester (in both Latin and French versions),[215] Sir Thomas Charleton, second speaker of the 1453–4 parliament,[216] and John Paston.[217] Paston also owned a printed copy of the *De Ludo Scaccorum*, which suggests that this was a popular work,[218] but even more popular was the *Secreta*, of which eight independent prose translations have survived.[219] Three were carried out for Henry VI, the earl of Ormond and Sir Miles Stapleton respectively, and a copy was owned by Edward IV as earl of March.[220] Of Hoccleve's *Regement* itself, forty-five manuscripts have survived, nearly as many as copies of Gower's *Confessio Amantis* (Book VII of which appears to be based on the *Secreta*) or of *Piers the Plowman*.[221] Another work full of political advice was the *Dicts and Sayings of Philosophers*, actually translated for Edward IV by Earl Rivers, who thought 'ful necessary to my said lord the understanding therof'.[222] A translation of the same work – *Dicta et Opiniones Diversorum Philosophorum* – was made for Sir John Fastolf by his step-son, Stephen Scrope.[223] Another version, again in English, was written by George Ashby, the signet clerk and author of 'The Active Policy of a Prince'.[224] This too was a collection, as the name suggests, of pieces of moral advice, many of them with obvious political relevance.

---

[213] *Regement*, frontispiece, sts. 292–4, 302. Hoccleve commented, perhaps out of *politesse*, that his patron was certain to have read all three books already, but that it was maybe convenient to have the useful advice of all three gathered together in one volume (st. 305). Giles' work was itself actually based on the *Secreta* (Green 1980: p. 140).

[214] Green 1980: pp. 75, 140–1. [215] Vickers 1907: pp. 427, 435.

[216] McFarlane 1973: p. 237. [217] *PL*, VI, pp. 66–7 (no. 987).

[218] *Ibid.*, p. 66. See Kekewich 1987: pp. 163–78, for a full discussion of this work.

[219] Green 1980: p. 141. Orme suggests that the *Secreta* was a text used in the education of noble children, which may have made it particularly influential (1984: p. 97).

[220] Green 1980: p. 141. Edward III also had a copy of the *Secreta* (Vale 1982: p. 50) and so did John Blacman (Kekewich 1987: p. 36) and Guy Beauchamp, earl of Warwick (d. 1315): Todd, *Illustrations of Gower and Chaucer*, p. 161.

[221] Orme 1984: pp. 141, 143; Bennett 1946–7: p. 168.

[222] Green 1980: p. 76. Thomas of Woodstock had possessed a book known as 'Dictes Poetarum', which may well have been the same, or a like, collection: Dillon and St John Hope, 'Inventory of Thomas, Duke of Gloucester . . .', p. 301.

[223] Moore 1912: p. 195. [224] Printed by Bateson (ed.), *Ashby's Poems*.

Meanwhile, historical texts of an exemplary kind were also widely liked. John Lydgate described how his patron, the duke of Gloucester, had asked him to include specific and practical morals in each of the stories he related in his *Fall of Princes*.[225] This was, in fact, a hugely popular work, of which thirty-seven manuscripts survive, including one from the library of John Tiptoft, earl of Worcester and another from the Percy family.[226] The earl of Suffolk possessed a copy of Lydgate's *Siege of Thebes*,[227] whilst the duke of York was given a translation of Claudian's *De Consulatu Stiliconis*, which described the exemplary career of the virtuous Stilico and which may have had a particular influence on its important reader.[228]

This brief survey suggests that advice-literature did indeed appeal to the literary tastes of the nobility, that its assumptions regarding the enthusiasm of readers for advice were justified and that it may indeed, therefore, have been the chief literary influence on the formation of political views. Since many of the texts mentioned here form the basis of the analysis in the first section, it seems plausible to argue that the main themes of the mirrors – the emphasis on the common weal, the central role played by counsel in all political relationships, the common identity of moral and political virtues – were familiar to the nobility and other substantial people. Whether or not the same themes were apparent in their political discourse is a matter we must now consider.

. . .

In the parliament of 1467–8, the chancellor, Bishop Stillington, told the lords and commons that justice was 'grounde well and rote of all prosperite, peas and pollityke rule of every Reame, wheruppon all the Lawes of the world been grounde and sette'.[229] This is an emphatically functionalist description: justice was to be admired because it produced peace and prosperity, twin strands of the common weal. By 'justice', in this instance, Stillington had two meanings in mind: both the simple one we have already discussed and a more artful meaning, namely that 'every persone [should] doo his office that he is put yn accordyng to his astate or degre'. Justice, then, was the proper working of the social order: an order which, the bishop explained, was topped by the king, or 'State Riall', whose particular aim it was to set peace throughout the land, largely through the administration of law and justice by advice of the lords spiritual and temporal, and to provide for outward peace in the interests

[225] Green 1980: pp. 147–8.
[226] *Ibid.*, p. 155; Edward 1977: 424–39, p. 429. Worcester was, of course, a highly literate man (see Mitchell 1938).
[227] Moore 1912: p. 203.   [228] Watts 1990.   [229] *RP*, V, p. 622.

of defending the realm. The king thus appears as an estate, or part, of the realm, with a task to perform in the common interest. The reference to the advice of the lords, meanwhile, draws attention to the essential role which counsel played in the manufacture of policy in the common interest. In this speech alone, therefore, many of the key elements of the monarchical ideology described above are to be found: the common weal arises out of a socially responsive justice which is administered by a pre-eminent king, in association with the counsel of his greatest subjects.[230] While it may be argued that a parliamentary sermon is more likely to reflect clerical or 'official' theory than the independent ideas of the lay nobility, there is plenty of evidence to suggest that views of this kind were widely shared.[231]

To begin with the association of king and common weal, it is clear that this was an absolute commonplace of high political discourse in the period. As Bishop Beckington pointed out in 1442, the good of the king 'verraly is, and moost be, the wele of us alle youre trew subgetts', and references to the good of the people were a recurring element in the clauses justifying acts of royal government.[232] While these most commonly followed positive statements of the honour or profit likely to accrue to the king, they could also be used negatively, as further grounds for condemning those who had damaged him and therefore his subjects.[233] Meanwhile, it seems to have been understood that, just as the advice-books prescribed, the central means of maintaining the connection between king and common weal was virtue. On one well-known occasion, for example, Bishop Stafford told parliament of the six moral virtues which served as steps to a royal throne which itself meant the 'bonum regimen per quod bonum publicum cujuslibet regni crescere ... valeat'.[234]

---

[230] Cf. William Lyndwood's address to the 1431 parliament, which identified three forces (called 'virtutes', tellingly) which enabled the kingdom to stand firm: Unity; Peace; Justice/Equity (*ibid.*, IV, p. 367).

[231] All but two of the chancellors of the fifteenth century were clerics. Even so, given the purpose of the chancellor's address (to outline the causes of summons: Davies and Denton (eds.) 1981: pp. 38, 80, 122), it seems reasonable to assume that the concepts it included were at least meaningful, if not relevant, to a predominantly lay audience: note the comments of Crowder 1986: p. 56.

[232] *Letters of Margaret*, p. 81. This is such a commonplace as to be barely worth noting, but see, for example, *RP*, IV, pp. 201 (the weal of the king or of his realm), 295 (the desires of the king and the *res publica*), 423 (the welfare of the king's person and the good government of his lands), 432 (serve the king and content his subjects), 495 (the profit of the king and the *res publica*), *RP*, V, pp. 73 (service to the king and this his land). See Doe 1990: p. 48 for other examples and discussion.

[233] It is in this context that we find the commons accusing Suffolk of treasons against not only the king's person, but also the 'Corones of youre Reames of Englond and Fraunce', the king's other 'enheritaunce's overseas, 'the estate and dignite of the same, and the universall wele and prosperite of all your true subgettes': *RP*, V, p. 177.

[234] *Ibid.*, V, pp. 35–6. Note, also, the 1459 articles attributed to the earl of Warwick: 'the commone wele and the good politik lawz hereaforne notably and vertuously used'; 'our

If such colourful theorising was unusual among the lords in general, there is plenty to show that they thought along similar lines. The lords of Henry VI's minority council, for example, were determined that the king should receive a training in the virtues.[235] In 1434, they advanced his lack of Prudence – presented as 'feling, knouleche and wisdome ... forsight and discrecion to departe and chese' – as a reason for resisting Gloucester's premature attempt to revive normal royal rule.[236] In theory, as we have seen, Prudence played the greatest role in linking king and *communitas*, but Justice, Temperance and Fortitude also had roles to play, and this seems to have been widely apprehended. The commons, in a petition to the 1449–50 parliament, recited 'howe that the honour, welthe and prosperite of every Prynce reynyng uppon his people stondith moost principally upon conservation of his peas, kepyng of Justice and due execution of his lawes, withouten which no Roialme may long endure in quyete nor prosperite'.[237] This could almost be a quotation from a mirror: it stresses the correlation between the royal duty of justice and the preservation of the common weal. In fact, the dependence of the king's 'welthe' on his maintenance of justice could be surprisingly direct. In the following parliament, it was alleged that lack of justice had so impoverished the commons that they would be unable to relieve the king's debts; a demonstration, in effect, of how the failure of the king to perform his communal duties tended to relieve the commons of their communal responsibilities.[238]

Temperance and Mercy were no less significant. They appeared as Clemency in the attainder bill of the 1459 parliament, for example. In this highly idealised account of recent events, the king was praised for being the 'moost Cristen Prynce whos clemens is to be noted whiles the world endureth'.[239] The bill was endorsed with a proviso that the king should not be 'put fro his prerogatyf, to shewe such mercy and grace as shall please his Highnes' to anyone named in the act.[240] This should not be

soveraigne lorde of his blessed conversacion ys of his owne noble disposicion as gracieuxle aplied to the seid comone wele ... as ene prince cristen' (BL Add. MS 48031(A), fol. 137v, and see below, p. 352).

235 *PPC*, III, p. 297.

236 *PPC*, IV, pp. 287–8: as the mirrors implied, this prevented him from judging what was good for the people and what was not. See above, p. 24, and below, p. 122. Note also the words reputedly spoken by York at St Albans: 'beseching to our soveraigne Criste Jesus ... to yeve the vertu of prudence and ... geve you verray knowlege of oure trowthes' (BL Add. MS 48031(A), fol. 127v; cf. *PL*, III, p. 26).

237 *RP*, V, p. 200. For Justice as a personal quality of the king, see below, p. 60.

238 *RP*, V, p. 217. See also *PL*, II, p. 207, in which Judge Yelverton told the chancellor that the gentry of Suffolk would pay no taxes if the king pardoned Heydon and Tuddenham.

239 *RP*, V, p. 348. Fortitude, or at least *magnanimitas*, was evoked by scattered references to the king's 'knyghtly corage', and his 'so witty, so knyghtly, so manly' address to his forces: *ibid.*, pp. 346, 348.

240 *Ibid.*, p. 350.

seen as testimony to the particular gentleness of Henry of Windsor: the king's Mercy was known to fulfil a constitutional function in the common interest. Only a few months before, the Yorkists had observed that the 'ryghtwysnesse [i.e. justice]' of the king's grace was to 'repute and accepte youre trew and lowly sugettys': he was obliged by his office to look kindly on all who were not proven traitors.[241] In 1458, according to the attainder bill, the king had preferred 'Mercy bifore Justice, for pacification of youre Roialme', by granting the Yorkist lords protection to come to arbitration.[242] Evidently, in this formulation 'Justice' is meant in the harshest sense of the word, but it is significant that the king and his advisers – for whom 'pacification' was the aim of government, because peace was the basis of the common weal – offered Mercy in 1458 and, to a lesser extent, 1459.[243] Normally, of course, kings were expected, and able, to offer an amalgam of Mercy and Justice: a just condemnation of the crime, but another chance for the criminal under most circumstances.[244]

If the political significance of the various royal virtues seems to have been widely understood, so also was their relationship with 'drede'. According to the advice-books, the love and 'drede' which guaranteed the king's security arose from the virtuous fulfilment of his duty to the common interest. In 1455, the commons argued that the ability of past kings to fund their households out of their own resources, thus preserving the common weal of their subjects, was a major reason why other kings held England in 'grete drede'.[245] Similarly, the Yorkists pointed out that because the king's laws were 'parcially and unrightfully guyded', 'no manne dredethe to offende ayenst' them.[246] Of the two, the Yorkist statement is the more significant, with its implication that society was held in place by the protection of mutual interest, that once authority departed from this, then obedience – on the ground, if not at the centre – would be withheld. In a sense, of course, both comments miss out a stage in the argument. It was not precisely the king's performance of his duties which induced 'drede', but the reserves of loyalty which rightful rule created. This loyalty was felt both positively and negatively: the individual enjoyed the fruits of good rule, and that was one source of

---

[241] *English Chron.*, p. 82. In this context, 'grace' means something very close to 'office'.

[242] *RP*, V, p. 347.   [243] See below, pp. 343ff.

[244] For these views in the advice-literature, see e.g. 'Tractatus', p. 50; 'Three Consideracions', p. 200. Such principles were applied in the loveday document of 1458, which referred to the 'obviationem et insultationem' done at St Albans (*Registrum Whethamstede*, I, p. 299) and implicitly placed the burden of guilt upon the Yorkists. The sense of a crime was thus conveyed, but mercy was nonetheless forthcoming, in the interests of *unitas* (e.g. pp. 298, 301). See below, pp. 343–5, for a discussion of the loveday.

[245] *RP*, V, p. 300.

[246] *English Chron.*, p. 86, and see BL Add. MS 48031(A), fol. 137v.

obedience; but he was also aware of the loyalty of everyone else, and that was another.[247]

Meanwhile, even as the nobility recognised the utilitarian and, in a sense, conditional basis of the king's authority, their every use of it reaffirmed his pre-eminence, which in turn increased its stature. It was by this means that the *servus servorum Dei* came to look more like *deus* than *servus*. A host of miscellaneous examples demonstrate that royal sovereignty was recognised and cherished. In 1426, the lords made reference to 'the grettest auctorite ... in this lande, that is to say Kyng and souverain lorde'.[248] In 1435, Sir John Fastolf observed that the king 'hathe no souverayne in erthe that may be his juge' unless it be 'at his owne pleasure and wille'.[249] The ruling of the justices in the parliament of 1425 that only the king could make peerage creations and the declaration of the councillors in 1434 that only the king could alienate his patrimony, are both good examples of how the vesting of certain powers in a higher authority was seen as essential to the operation of the body politic.[250] Lastly, that the king was held to 'command' where nobles, even when addressing their own men, were more likely to 'desire' shows a neat distinction between the power of the *communitas* vested in the king, and the power of the individual represented by one nobleman.[251]

In the crisis of 1459, the importance attached to the pre-eminence of this power was demonstrated. At Ludlow, the Yorkist lords beseeched the king not to subordinate 'youre sayde blessednesse, ne the grete ryghtewysnesse and equite wherinne God hathe ever endowed youre hyghe nobeley' to the malice of those who 'procede under the shadow of youre hyghe myghte and presence to oure destruccione'.[252] It is the king's independence from his subjects which justifies his possession of the jurisdiction expressed in the words 'ryghtewysnesse and equite'. The lords made this clearer still in 1460, condemning those who had the 'guydyng' about the king's person 'whos hyghenes they have restrayned

---

[247] Note that those whose loyalty did not arise from the king's performance of his communal duties were open to criticism on the grounds that they did not have the king's interests at heart and were thus motivated by 'covetise'. See above, pp. 40–2, and *CSP Venice*, I, pp. 89–90, where Coppini makes a distinction between the (attainted) Yorkist lords who were loyal to the king and 'desirous to maintain and augment the commonweal of the kingdom' and the lords about the king 'who profess themselves devoted to you and are not'.

[248] *PPC*, III, p. 185. See also McKenna 1979: pp. 481–4.

[249] *Letters and Papers*, II, ii, p. 578.   [250] *RP*, IV, p. 274; *PPC*, IV, p. 246.

[251] Bedford pointed out in 1433 that the king's 'prayer and wille is unto me a commaundement' (*RP*, IV, p. 424). The distinction emerges clearly in a letter of 1471 from the earl of Oxford: 'in the kyngs name, ... I straitly charge and command you, and in my owne byhalf hertly desire and pray you' (*PL*, V, p. 96). In a sense, of course, noblemen exercised more than purely individual power: see below, p. 73.

[252] *English Chron.*, p. 82.

and kept from the liberte and fredom that bylongethe to his seyde astate' and who would not let the king receive the lords 'as he wolde have done, yet [i.e. 'if'] he myghte have had his owne wylle'.[253] They justified their invasion on the grounds of duty not only to the king, but to 'hys estate, prerogatyf and preemynence, and to th'asuerte of hys most noble persone'.[254] The king's pre-eminence was the perfect counterpart to his responsiveness and receptiveness. He could operate for all only by remaining above all. It was in these ways that a utilitarian conception of kingship could function in tandem with a sense of the king's independent and exalted status. This status was reinforced through the concept of the dignity royal and the 'drede' which it evoked.

Finally, there is every reason to suppose that counsel was as dominant in noble expectations of rule as it was in the advice-books. As Archbishop Stafford pointed out in a letter to the king, 'every reame and lordship wel ruled is goeverned by grete forsight and good and sad policye and advisinesse of counsail'.[255] Its vital function in bringing to the king's attention the needs of the *communitas* was evidently understood.[256] This is implicit in the charges against the duke of Suffolk in 1450, which varied between casting his counsel as bad or untrue and accusing him of inducing the king to pursue various policies 'withoute deliberation and avyse of youre Counseill'.[257] Where the advice-books generally commended the advice of the wise and the good, politicians tended to call for the advice of the lords.[258] There is no contradiction here: as is well known, aristocracy, goodness and wisdom were anciently associated,[259] and – given the functional nature of virtue – it is clear that the association had some real meaning. Lords were good and wise counsellors because they spoke for large numbers of men, because they had the 'politik rule' of the regions and because (having so much already) they were thought to be resistant to the temptations of 'covetise'.[260]

At the same time, there was some understanding of the subtle balance required between counsel and will in the process of decision making. A distinction seems to have been made between 'counsel', which, being

---

[253] *Ibid.*, p. 88.
[254] *Ibid.*, p. 89. This is an instance of the dual allegiance – to king and common weal – familiarly adopted by York: see ch. 7.
[255] *PPC*, VI, pp. 338–9. See also *ibid.*, p. 319, for the familiar view that many heads were better than one.
[256] E.g. the claim made in 1455 that the king's councillors 'knowe the direction to be had moost expedient for the sadde and politique reule of this his land': *RP*, V, p. 290.
[257] *Ibid.*, pp. 179–81: the quotation is from p. 180. See below, pp. 249–50.
[258] E.g. Gloucester's articles of 1440 (*Letters and Papers*, II, ii, pp. 441–3, 445), York's articles of 1454 and 1455 (*RP*, V, pp. 242, 286) and the lords' declaration in 1427 (*PPC*, III, pp. 231–4).
[259] Keen 1984: chs. 8 and 9; Watts 1991: p. 280 and n. 5.   [260] Above, p. 41.

given freely and without expectations, deferred to the lord's will, and 'stirring' or 'moving', which involved unacceptable pressure and so, in a sense, usurped the lord's right of judgement. For example, the lords of the parliament of 1428 marvelled that Gloucester, having agreed to the 1422 settlement, should now 'in any wyse be steryd or moeved noght to contente yow therwith'.[261] The suggestion, owing much to the *politesse* of the lords, is that the duke was not wholly responsible for this behaviour. Similarly, in 1427, Bedford, having heard the lords' view on the proper distribution of authority during the king's minority, 'of his free wille withouten that eny other persone stured or moeved him thereto' swore to stand by their proposals.[262] Bedford accepted full responsibility for his actions, but could hardly have claimed that he had not been counselled by the lords to this end, especially as they had openly asked him to say whether his view of matters was the same as theirs.[263]

At times, the distinction could be very important. In the 1445–6 parliament, for example, the chancellor declared on behalf of the lords that only God 'hath liked to ster and meve' the king to make peace with France, 'withoute that any of the Lordes or other of your suggettes ... in any wise have stered or meved you soo to doo'. A few lines later, he added that the lords would do and had done all they could for the accomplishment of the king's 'blissid entent'.[264] It is as if the lords, as counsellors, recognised their duty to *execute* the king's policy, but accepted no responsibility for the authorisation of that policy, even though it is inconceivable that they, or some of them, did not advise it.[265] The king's actions were ultimately his alone: only thus could they be consonant with the wishes of the *communitas*, because only in him did it find full representation. The importance of counsel in the effective operation of the body politic meant that issues of responsibility were complex and potentially dangerous. Normally, the independence of the person receiving counsel protected the counsellor from the consequences of his advice being taken. In cases of stirring and moving, on the other hand, it was the recipient of counsel, not the giver, who was absolved from responsibility.[266] It was thus in the personal interest of counsellors, as well

---

[261] *RP*, V, p. 327. 'Steryd' could be 'steered', not 'stirred', I suppose.

[262] *PPC*, III, p. 235.   [263] *Ibid.*, p. 234.   [264] *RP*, V, p. 102.

[265] See below, pp. 180ff, 221ff, for the relationship between the king, his counsellors and the peace policy.

[266] An exception, which shows that a distinction between counsel and stirring was not always invoked, is Viscount Beaumont's declaration on behalf of the lords that the king's decision not to try Suffolk 'proceded not by their advis and councell, but was doon by the kynges owne demeanance and rule' (*RP*, V, p. 183). Evidently, in the tense circumstances of March 1450, it would have been dangerous for any lord to be thought to have suggested that Suffolk should be released, let alone 'stirred' or 'moved' it. See below, pp. 247–8, for an account of the political context.

as the general interest of the realm, that they should accept, and even emphasise, the authority of the king to make what he chose of their advice.

Short as this survey has been, it does suggest that the framework of political relations described in the theoretical material was influential, at least as theory, in the political transactions of the nobility on the national stage. What we must now consider is how this theoretical model was reconciled with actual practice or, rather, what were the practical manifestations of this net of principles. For the nobility, the practice of government was normally dominated by the task of mediating between centre and locality. In the section which follows, we shall consider the mores of local lordship, as expressed in the correspondences. The aim will be to discover whether its values were essentially similar to those of royal lordship as represented by the mirrors and, if so, how they were affected by differences in the circumstances of kings and noblemen.

. . .

The political world evoked by the major gentry correspondences – the Paston, Stonor and Plumpton letters – is rather different from the 'public' and national stage upon which mirrors for princes, constitutional analyses and, until recently, political histories have been focused. Here, it is practical concerns which are paramount: in essence, it seems, the experience and exercise of lordship, which meant the local execution of the law, the defence of peace and the maintenance of an affinity which made the fulfilment of these aims possible.[267] As a consequence, statements of principle and theory are few. Most of the letters do not engage with the systems of lordship and clientage which appear to have characterised local government: they are internal to them. Even so, the hierarchical nature of medieval politics and the ingrained habit of appealing to the authorities of custom, right and reason ensure that enough of the assumptions of local politics are exposed for some sort of discussion to be possible.

A good place to begin an examination of these assumptions is perhaps the concept of 'rule'. Even in its sense of direction or government, the word bore several meanings in the fifteenth century. At times, it plainly meant much as it does today, as when Edward IV told William Brandon that 'he knew well inow that he myght reauyll my Lord of Norffolk as he

---

[267] In the following pages, it is assumed that noble lordship was the recognised and normal structure of social and political organisation in the counties. This has become a controversial assumption to make, but it does seem to be borne out by the sources examined here. See ch. 3, below, for a defence of this way of approaching fifteenth-century local rule and a discussion of some of the secondary literature on the topic.

wold'.[268] The word was also used to express ideas of order and self-restraint, as in 'the Shirereve of the Shire ... wilbe at Caster ... to se that goode rule be kept', or 'a worchepeffull man and a well rulede'.[269] In these more abstract usages, 'rule' was evidently a force, moral or actual, which directed behaviour. At the same time, it was recognised that the 'rule' of the shires belonged, in general, to the nobility.[270] But this 'rule' was, like the king's, highly complex: a power mediated through others, responsive to local pressures and, more than anything else, associated with the preservation of harmony and its familiar end, the common interest. An investigation of the 'rule' of the dukes of Norfolk in East Anglia may serve to illustrate this proposition.

Let us begin with a proclamation which the third duke made to the men of Norfolk some time in the early 1450s.[271] Coming 'in to this contre' to restore order, the duke had heard that

> serteyne servaunts of the Lord Scales schulde in his name manasse and put men in feer and drede to compleyne to us at this tyme of the seide hurts and greves, seynge that we wolde abyde but a schort tyme her, and aftir our departynge he wolde have the rewle and governaunce as he hath had affore tyme. We lete yow wete that nexst the kynge our soverayn Lord, be his good grace and lycence, we woll have the princypall rewle and governance throwh all this schir, of whishe we ber our name whyls that we be lyvynge, as ferre as reson and lawe requyrith ...

and that Lord Scales and his men should know that 'thowh our persone be not dayly her, they schal fynde our power her at all tymes to do the kynge our soverayn Lord servyse, and to support and mayntene yow alle in your right that ben the kyngs trewe lige men'.

It is interesting to note that the duke's attitude to the shire 'of whishe we ber our name' was strikingly similar to the attitude the king was expected to have towards his realm. By claiming the authority to redress

---

[268] *PL*, V, p. 31.

[269] *Ibid.*, p. 24; *Stonor*, I, p. 70. The word 'governed' is used in a similar way, as in the promise of Thomas Daniel that, during his stay in Norfolk, he would be 'wel governed', *PL*, II, p. 138. 'Misrule' was also a word in contemporary usage: for example, a royal letter to the mayor of Exeter in 1455 recited the 'trouble, outragious governaunce and mysreul' in the county (E28/87/22); another, written in January 1461, recited the coming of 'mysruled and outeragious people' from the North (BL, Cotton MS Vesp. C xiv, fol. 239).

[270] See e.g. *PL*, II, pp. 87, 111–12, 254–5; III, pp. 19–21; *Plumpton*, pp. 31–3. Evidence that this was also the crown view is to be found in letters to members of the nobility written in the 1450s, urging them to recognise, typically, that their status was given to them 'to the service and supportacion of us in keping of our pees and of our lawes' (1453 letter to the earls of Northumberland and Salisbury: *PPC*, VI, pp. 159–61; see also *ibid.*, pp. 147–8, 161–3; E28/84/41 (to the earl of Devon); and Rawcliffe, 'Richard Duke of York', pp. 238–9 (to the duke of Exeter)).

[271] *PL*, II, p. 259. Gairdner proposes April 1452 as a dating, but Storey 1966: p. 248 n. 20, suggests February 1451.

the grievances of the people of the shire and undertaking to support and maintain all true subjects in their right, Norfolk echoed the royal commitment to uphold the common weal through the maintenance of right and justice.[272] There is, indeed, a sense in which the lord's 'country', an area roughly defined by the recognition of his lordship, was a microcosm of the kingdom.[273] If this threatened to raise the problem of contending jurisdictions – both king and duke seeking to guarantee the interests of local men – it seems that resolution was at hand. Norfolk was prepared to acknowledge that he ruled the shire by royal 'grace and lycence', maintaining the rights of men who were not simply his own, but the true lieges of the king. In return, the king gave lordship (in this case, in the quite specific and formal shape of a commission of oyer and terminer) to the pre-eminent local figure, the man who bore the name of the shire and whose 'power' was, independently of royal support, 'her at all tymes'.[274] Jurisdictional conflict, then, was unnecessary: king and lord could each take account of the other. The king had a general right and duty to rule and the duke a local one. As the part is subordinate to the whole,[275] so the duke was subordinate to the king. But the parts were, in certain ways, more real than the whole. Whatever the duke's authority derived from his role in the royal service, it also came from the influence he wielded over local society. The sources of this influence were diverse – land, money, status all played a part – but, in the end, it was a matter of men.[276] The 'power' of which Norfolk spoke was essentially that of his affinity.[277]

Pursuing this point, the analogy between lordship and kingship can be taken a stage further. In some respects, it was understood that the king's power was that of his nobility, just as Norfolk's, in real terms, was that of

---

[272] Something of this is evoked by Gilbert Hay's 1456 translation of Lull (see above, p. 34): 'a man is not a lord suppose he have never so much of worldly goods: but he is a lord that has seignory and jurisdiction upon other men, to govern them and hold law and justice upon them when they trespass' (Ferguson 1960: p. 117). Note, too, Edward IV's promise to John Paston that, regarding Paston's claim to the manor of Dedham, 'he wold be your good Lord therin as he wold be to the porest man in Inglond. He wold hold with yowe in yowr rygth': *PL*, III, p. 302.

[273] This area was not necessarily a county: see Carpenter 1992: pp. 33, 290–1, 312–21, 340–4, 347–8 (although cf. e.g. Virgoe 1990).

[274] Something of the naturalness of Norfolk's authority is implicit, perhaps, in the use of the word 'lycence' alongside 'grace'.

[275] See e.g. *Aquinas*, p. 83.

[276] This is nicely illustrated by an indictment describing the malicious wounding of one John Wattes, gentleman, at Hawkhurst, Kent. He was attacked by a yeoman who had raised a number of local people saying 'quod ipse haberet plures homines ... quam predictus Johannes Wattes haberet cum omnibus bonis suis'. In the end, it was force which counted (KB9/47/1, m. 31). Note also *Regement*, line 463: 'What is a lord withouten his meynee?'.

[277] 'Power' could literally mean a force of men in fifteenth-century English (e.g. *Town Chrons.*, p. 123).

his local following.[278] But the parallel is not an exact one, because the king had a very considerable advantage in being unique.[279] There was rarely a viable alternative to his rule and this meant that his power was not normally in question, regardless of its quality. The nobility who maintained it were not a 'party', but the members of an estate: the king's leading servants, dealing with each other and their underlings in the king's name, furthering his interests – rule, peace, justice – automatically, because these interests were, in a general sense, theirs. The 'constructed' nature of royal power was thus disguised by the fact that there was only one possible object of allegiance. This was not the case for the nobility when they sought to exercise lordship: the rule of the counties was open to competitive tender.[280] Despite Norfolk's romantic notions concerning the name of his dukedom, the rule which he claimed would rest more than anything else on the local following he was able to maintain, whilst his capacity to maintain it would depend quite directly on the might of his affinity, his ability to protect the interests of the majority of local worthies and his ability to keep the peace which permitted all to flourish. Like most noblemen, he faced competition. If Scales' claim that he would rule in Norfolk's absence was true, then the duke's lordship must have been deficient. A lord had to be able to guarantee the rights of his men and their friends fairly consistently or his clients would take their loyalty elsewhere. While there was a sense in which both royal and local rule depended on the defence of a related common weal, it is clear that the local lord was much more directly accountable to his constituents than the national one. This meant real differences in the immediacy of force in the two structures and also in the nature of the common weal which that force upheld. The common weal of the realm was as strong and confident as its stewardship was uncontested. The common weal of the lordship was frequently embattled: much more crudely and closely, then, did it resemble the interests of those wielding an uncertain majority of local power.

This much is apparent from the earl of Oxford's intervention in the sessions of oyer and terminer held in Norfolk in January 1451. The earl commented that only 'the pupplyk wele of all the shire' justified holding sessions in the middle of parliament, and, quoting reports that the sheriff was not showing 'trow favour' to those who wished to indict certain persons, threatened to withdraw his support from the sessions if this were

---

[278] This is implied in *Secreta*, pp. 214–15, and, more vaguely, in all the body politic thinking. See, in particular, Denholm-Young (ed.), *Vita Edwardi Secundi*, pp. 28, 33, 36 etc.

[279] See above, p. 19, and note Carpenter 1992: p. 354.

[280] See McFarlane 1981c for the classic exposition of this point.

so.[281] We know from other evidence that Oxford himself wanted to secure the indictment of those being protected by the sheriff, even though it was the common interest he claimed to stand for.[282] But can we make a valid distinction between Oxford's wishes and the common interest of the locality? Inasmuch as the earl represented the controlling group, he did represent the common weal. This may seem rather casuistical, but it is worth remembering that among the reasons why Oxford and others wanted to remove the old De La Pole affinity from power was the widespread support that such a move appeared to command in the county. Like the king, lords were means for the representation and realisation of interests. They achieved comprehensive control through comprehensive representation and vice versa. If Oxford possessed this kind of authority, then his view of the common weal was, and is, difficult to quarrel with.[283]

So it was that lords were often concerned to exercise 'rule' – not only as force, but also as representation – beyond, as well as within, their own affinities. The dream of every nobleman was surely the unchallenged rule of the locality, in which case everybody would be, in some sense, a part of his following, because everybody would look to him for justice. Such a lord would indeed have the 'princypall rewle and governance', next to the king, and the distinction between the affinity and the local *communitas* would all but disappear.[284] Normally, however, the common weal of a lordship closely reflected the interests of the lord's own particular supporters, on whom his power was immediately founded. How did lords reconcile this state of dependence with the preservation of their authority, on the one hand, and the more widely representative rule which befitted their status, on the other? These are the questions we shall be considering in the remainder of this section.

Justice – alongside peace, the richest fruit of lordship – often, of course,

[281] *PL,* II, pp. 203–4. The association of 'truth' and 'favour', qualities usually regarded as antithetical, is enlightening.

[282] Those who should have been indicted were the members of the old Suffolk affinity. Oxford was among those who had requested a commission to deal with them (*PL,* I, p. 90).

[283] A similar example comes from the elections of autumn 1450, at which time Norfolk wrote to tell Paston which two knights he and York thought 'convenient and necessarie for the welfare of the said shire': *PL,* II, p. 184. Once again, had Norfolk's rule been influential, it is hard to imagine that the election of alternative candidates could have conduced to the common weal of the shire. The fact that only one of Norfolk's choices was actually elected – even in the circumstances of 1450 – is indicative of the tenuousness of his control: see McFarlane 1981e: p. 5.

[284] This seems to have been the state of affairs prevailing in Warwickshire under Richard Beauchamp, for example, or in Richmondshire under Richard Neville: see Carpenter 1992: ch. 10; Pollard 1979; and below, p. 97.

meant justice as it appeared to the client.[285] It was results, after all, that men were seeking. As Lord Strange said in 1478 of his lord, the duke of Gloucester, 'I trust in all thinge he woll defend me and my tenauntes, and I am frendid so to help my self.'[286] The delicate balance of interests between lord and suitor is widely illustrated in the correspondences. Many letters emphasise the mutual advantage of this sort of associa-tion.[287] However, the sense of an equal exchange of services was not allowed to appear too blatant, at least as far as the lord's contribution is concerned, and this is important. Lords found ways of emphasising that whatever they did for their followers was done as a matter of grace. One way of doing this was to be unspecific about what might be done in return for a particular service, promising, instead, a general gratitude or 'remem-brance'.[288] At times, they could go further and simply invoke the 'reverence' due to them or hint at the uncertainty of future favour.[289] Formulae such as these preserved the lord's initiative in granting reward, particularly when accompanied by the odd put-down to make sure that suitors did not become too presumptuous.[290] Obviously, the extent to which lords could assert themselves in this way was modified by the extent of their control over local affairs, but it seems that they were generally at pains to mystify the process of service and reward so as to emphasise the fact that it was they who ruled, and not their men.[291]

[285] For examples of this attitude, see *PL*, IV, pp. 7–9; *Letters of Margaret*, pp. 107–8. In a striking extension of the concept, Edward IV requested the men summoned to escort his sister to Flanders not to fail in this 'as ye intend to do us justys': *PL*, IV, p. 297.

[286] *Stonor*, II, p. 70.

[287] E.g. *PL*, II, pp. 117 (Warwick to Tuddenham: 'as we may do for you in tym for to com'), 140; *Plumpton*, p. 27.

[288] E.g. 'to have you therfor in right tendre remembrance of oure good grace in tyme comyng': *Letters of Margaret*, p. 94 (and see *ibid.*, pp. 90, 97–8, and *PL*, VI, p. 72). Another formula was to promise that 'ye shal therin deserve of us right good and especial thanke': *Letters of Margaret*, p. 90; *PL*, II, pp. 144, 171–2.

[289] 'Reverence' was invoked by Oxford and York, for example: *ibid.*, pp. 144, 331. Richard of Gloucester took the point a step further, asking Sir William Plumpton to show a man of his favour 'the rather att the instance of this our letters' (*Plumpton*, p. 26; also *ibid.*, p. 27). See *Letters of Margaret*, p. 121, for the more threatening 'as ye desire to stande in the favor of oure good grace in tyme commynge'. Note Glanvill on homage: 'The bond of trust arising from lordship and homage should be mutual ... save only reverence' (quoted by Hanson 1970: p. 16).

[290] In 1478, Sir William Stonor was brought up short by Lord Strange when he impertinently requested payment for a service done: 'as for my graunt of a fee, I wold ye thowght yf ye do me servyce, as the wrytinge is, I woll dele more largly with yow, but I woll not be ovirmastred with none of my feed men ... yf ye dele as ye owght, I wolbe your goode lorde, and eke I dare better displese yow than ye me': *Stonor*, II, p. 70.

[291] Moreover, it was evidently assumed by lords that their suitors would feel beholden to them for the rewards they received: note Godfrey Grene's comment that the earl of Northumberland would have 'no deputie but such as shall please him, and kan him thank for the gift thereof, and no man els, and also doe him servise next the king' (*Plumpton*, p. 32). If lords were successful in shifting the balance of gratitude on to their men, then this was another factor in substantiating noble 'rule'.

In this, they employed many of the same techniques as kings and could, to some extent, exploit the same underlying verities which made these successful. If the nobility were to preserve their rule of the shires, they had to some extent to be a separate and superior caste, ensuring that members of local society looked to them for direction, instead of to each other.[292] Superiority was maintained partly, as above, by ensuring that the contractual elements of the lord–servant bond were sublimated, and partly by a separateness emphasised by frequent absences at court and in the king's wars, by the right to counsel the king, by a seat in the House of Lords, by ancient wealth and long heredity, by extra-regional land-holding, by manners of dress and speech.[293] If lords lacked uniqueness, they did possess distinction. It was for them to exercise lordship and for their underlings to consume it.[294] While the gentry were often in a position to exploit competition between lords – sometimes to the point where they gathered quasi-independent followings themselves – territorial rule generally remained the prerogative of members of the nobility.[295] Like the king, in the realm, the lord spoke to each man in his affinity with the authority conferred by the loyalty of the remainder: this did not give him freedom to ignore the *common* interest of his men, but it did mean that he had a certain licence where the *individual* interest of a follower was concerned. Moreover, since changes in the prevailing structure of lord-ship were rarely achieved without periods of strife in which gentry protagonists would be among the main losers, there were powerful incentives in favour of acceptance and inertia: the 'free market' of lordship was not, perhaps, as free as it may look.

This, then, was the essence of lordship: the organisation of potentially 'free' local power around the 'reverence' of the lord. This 'reverence' was based in the first instance upon inherited authority and its trappings; was modified by additional authority bestowed by the crown, distant guar-antor of peace and justice; and was converted into power by the

---

[292] A good example of this is the firmly defended concept of 'lordes maters'. See e.g. *PL*, III, p. 46, and also *Plumpton*, p. 33, for a most illuminating example, in which an attempt by Plumpton to labour the lord chamberlain directly, instead of through the normal offices of the earl of Northumberland (his lord), was firmly rebuffed with a warning which Plumpton's agent took as a 'watche word for medling betwixt Lords'. See also McFarlane 1973: pp. 124–5.

[293] The duke of Norfolk's sententious listing of his titles and offices in a safe-conduct for John Paston in 1469 conveys something of this: 'John, Duke of Norffolk, Erle Marshall, of Sussex, Surrey, and of Nottyngham, Marshall of Inglonde, Lorde Mowbray of Segreve, Bromfelde and Yalle, to al our frendes, servauntes, and othir Crystyne people, gretyng' (*PL*, V, p. 56).

[294] This is not to say that there were not gradations among the nobility themselves: for an example of the earl of Oxford addressing the duke of Norfolk as 'ryght high and myghty Prynce and my right good Lord', see *PL*, II, p. 165.

[295] See below, pp. 91–7.

acceptance of its claims on the part of the leading men of the region, who, in seeking the benefits of lordship, created its substance. More even than kingship, lordship was 'politic' rule, in which authority was recognised on account of its representativeness and in which the lord was the corporation of his men. Even so, as we have seen, the mantle of representativeness gave the lord some freedom of initiative.[296] He could afford to expect obedience first and think about reward afterwards, provided that, like a king, he kept an eye on the common interest of his 'country'.

The means by which this common interest was thought to be maintained, its rhetorics and its overtones were very similar to those apparent in the larger sphere of the realm. We have seen that just as the peace of subjects arose from the king's protection, so the peace – or 'rule', in both senses – of the shires depended on the organised power represented by local noblemen. Once again, a substantial part of this power was created by the 'drede' which arose from the lord's good rule and the following which he acquired through it. Anticipating the arrival in Norfolk of the courtier Thomas Daniel, Lord Scales pronounced that if he wished to wrong 'the lesse gentilman in the chirre, it shal not lye in his pouer be the grace of God'.[297] Not only did this evoke the comprehensiveness of Scales' lordship, it also presupposed that such mastery would have a deterrent effect: Daniel would be unable to act. Peace reigned because the lord took over the defensive powers of the men in his jurisdiction and exercised them communally.[298]

Once it is understood that a lordship was like a small realm, the ready identification of justice with what suited the lord and his men becomes more acceptable. It is thus difficult to distinguish 'maintenance' – the lord's pursuit of his subject's right – from justice, its more exalted cousin.[299] In the shire, the force which underpinned the exercise of justice was all too obvious. As a consequence, the dialectic of justice tempered by mercy, which predominated in the realm, was replaced in the locality by the more evidently utilitarian, but not actually dissimilar, modifiers of 'love', 'reason', 'friendship' and 'welfare', which are discussed below.[300] All were forces which mitigated absolute right in the interests of the social reality. This reminds us that, in certain ways, local justice was conceived

---

[296] Just as it did the king: above, p. 18.   [297] *PL*, II, p. 138.

[298] The Hobbesian parallel is obvious. The *Book of Fayttes of Armes*, ed. Byles, p. 11, hinted at the same idea with the argument that lordship was provided for the protection of the subject, that this might mean a duty to take up arms on the subject's behalf and finally that 'therfor oweth the subgette to resorte to the lorde as to his refuge'. See also Kemp's address to the parliament of 1427: *RP*, IV, p. 316.

[299] McFarlane 1973: pp. 114–16; Carpenter 1983b: pp. 214–15. The acceptability of maintenance under certain circumstances is shown by its periodic inclusion in the conditions of brotherhood in arms: Keen 1962: p. 10.

[300] See above, pp. 24–5, for justice and mercy.

in terms of the local common weal, just as in the national context: the difference is that county notables knew that any kind of local community was purchased at a price; it was a rougher, less equitable, phenomenon.

The idea of 'love' as an antithesis of 'law' has been examined by Michael Clanchy in a famous essay.[301] 'Love' was, in essence, the justice of the common weal: right adjudicated with reference to social force, rather than abstract principle. As such, the justice of 'love' reflected the local balance of power.[302] 'Reason', linked with 'equity', seems to have had a similar meaning. In one example, Brian Roclife reported back to Sir William Plumpton that he had told an agent of the treasurer, who was at pains to reconcile Plumpton to the escheator he had chosen for the county, that 'ye would agree to all reason'.[303] The implication is surely that what was 'reasonable' to Plumpton was the best approximation to his interests that prevailing power structures would allow.[304] If this sounds rather squalid, we should bear in mind that what enabled the king's justice to rise to something like the moral heights implicit in the term was his unchallenged position at the pinnacle of national society. An impartial, or adverse, judgement was generally unlikely to damage the king's authority: there was nowhere else to turn for redress. The position of the lord, as we have seen, was rather different.

The relationship between the lord's justice and the common weal of his 'country' was held together, just as in the realm, by counsel. It came from both inside and outside the affinity,[305] but it was the lord's regular counsellors who were expected to have the most profound influence on his policies: in 1452, for example, the Pastons were anxious to discover 'under hos rule that the gode lord is at this day, and whiche be of his new cownseyll'.[306] In fact, the only detailed account we possess of counsel being given to a duke of Norfolk suggests that it was probably the duke who 'ruled' and not his advisers. In September 1472, John Paston, acting for his brother, put a proposal to the duke's councillors. They read it and

---

[301] Clanchy 1983a.

[302] *Ibid.*, pp. 60–5, deals with the resultant weaknesses of the justice of 'love'.

[303] *Plumpton*, p. 6. For other examples of the use of this term, see *ibid.*, p. 25, and *PL*, II, p. 320 (Lord Scales to John Paston about a distraint he had made at the expense of one of his tenants: 'all that reson or lawe wyll, I wyll be right glad ze have, and otherwise I trowe ze wold not desire').

[304] A discussion of 'reason' and other features of local justice, 'legitimate' and 'illegitimate' appears in Carpenter 1983b: sections i and iv; and see also 1992: p. 623. For a similar use of 'reason' in the context of diplomatic negotiations between England and France, see Palmer 1971: pp. 52, 57.

[305] In August 1450, for example, the duke of Norfolk was visited by a number of local notables 'to have comonyngs with youre good Lordshep for the sad rule and govern-aunce of this counte'. The earl of Oxford, who could not attend, urged the duke to 'comon with the seyd knyghtes and squyers as with your feytfull servaunts': *PL*, II, pp. 165–6.

[306] *Ibid.*, II, p. 273.

showed it to the duchess, who, when laboured by Paston, agreed to support the proposal if it was first endorsed by the council. Paston returned to the council and made various offers. The council agreed to 'meve my Lord with it, and so they dyd, but then the tempest aros, and he gave hem syche an answer that non of hem all wold tell it me'. Even so, some of the councillors did tell Paston that, if he could get some greater men or lords to labour the duke, he could have his wish.[307] Although on this occasion the lord chose to ignore the advice of the council, the basic principles underlying its existence are affirmed: the duchess recognised its authority with her refusal to act except with its prior approval; the duke would give way if weightier men supported Paston's proposal. At the same time, as in the matter of reward, the lord preserved a limited area for the exercise of grace. Despite the obvious political necessity of taking counsel, he, like the king, could in practice invoke a higher prudence to justify its repudiation. Lords retained the power of direction, and were expected to exercise it.[308] Even if the expectation was that they would normally do so in accordance with 'reason' (what counsel enjoined and power permitted) they were still regarded as more than executives: as we saw earlier, Edward IV plainly felt the influence of Sir William Brandon over the duke of Norfolk to be unusual and disproportionate.[309]

Appropriately enough for a means of transmitting the common weal, the baronial council operated in a more than purely advisory capacity.[310] This was because lords, no less than kings, had their *consiliarii nati*: men whose local influence and loyal service demanded their participation in the lord's counsels and rule.[311] Advice, representation and administration overlapped. A letter from the duke of Norfolk to John Paston the youngest reveals the pyramidal nature of the affinity. Paston, one of the duke's leading men and hence a counsellor, was asked to attend upon the duke at his coming of age in London and 'also that ye doo warne owr ffeede men and servaunts, suche as be nye too yow, that they be ther thann in owr leverey'.[312] Even if 'nye' is meant literally and not as an indication of

---

[307] *Ibid.*, V, pp. 150–1.

[308] For example, after Sir William Plumpton's men had complained to Northumberland's council about his treatment, the council told the earl and he agreed to speak to them himself, telling them that he had postponed the court of the sheriff's tourn 'unto time he might come into the country and se a derection betwixt' Plumpton and Gascoigne (*Plumpton*, p. 32). It was the lord who took action: the council was simply intermediary.

[309] The king concluded that if the duke did anything illegal, 'he knew well inow that it was by no bodys menys but by hys', which surely suggests that the degree of influence wielded by Brandon was felt to be improper (*PL*, V, p. 31).

[310] It would be better to talk of baronial 'counsel' since the council acting for and advising the lord varied from area to area, and perhaps from day to day: Ramsay 1985: pp. 107–9.

[311] The role of the council at the centre of the management of the estate and to some extent of the affinity is discussed in Rawcliffe and Flower 1986.

[312] *PL*, IV, pp. 200–1.

political ties, this demonstrates how the greater members of the affinity were expected to organise the lesser.[313] It is easy to see from this how lords' councillors bound and represented the localities in just the same way as knights and burgesses of the king's parliament were held to do.[314] Conciliar structures empowered the lord as much as his men.

It seems then that, in the shires, notions of the common interest were closely bound up with a recognition of the interests of controlling lords; provided that it is recognised that by 'lord' is meant a combination of will, counsel and power that operated in one man's name. The lordly *persona* was all but as complex as the king's, a point which we must bear in mind when assessing the superficially 'personal' jealousies and conflicts of the fifteenth-century nobility. Personal authority, as we have already seen in the case of the king, could also mean public authority and public responsibility. The representative concentration of rule in each lord guaranteed peace and justice in exactly the same way as the rule of the king: it was rendered to all within the lordship, provided they accepted the lordship. At the risk of repetition, it must therefore be clear that the quality of rule depended on the security of the ruler. When we read the words of Lord Moleyns to the tenants of the Paston manor of Gresham, which he had recently seized –

> Trusty and welbeloved frendys, I grete yowe well, and putte yowe all owte of doute for all that ye have doon for me; and the money that ye pay to my welbeloved servaunt … I will be your warant as for your discharge, and save yowe harmeles ayenst all thoo that wold greve yowe, to my power. And as hertly as I can, I thanke yow of the gud wyl ye have had, and have, toward me[315]

– we are inclined to feel at once that we are reading about the worst kind of gangsterism. Moleyns shamelessly thanks the tenants for the money he has extorted from them and offers them protection in return. But who provides warrants for discharge in lordships but the lord, be he king, earl or baron? Who is the defender of peace, but the lord? Who is the guarantor of justice and the common weal? The reductiveness of Moleyns' message – money for protection – is explained by the 'war' situation. At other times, under a less immediately challenged lordship, a more complex and benign distribution of both power and interest was possible. The only difference between the political morality of the realm and that of the shire was that the latter was at the sharp end, the place where political decisions were executed, justice administered and, most

---

[313] For good examples of Sir William Plumpton mediating Northumberland's rule to lesser men, 'for asmuch as ye have the rule ther under me', see *Plumpton*, pp. 74–6.

[314] Harriss 1975: p. 47 and ch. II in general; Cam 1962b: especially pp. 166–75.

[315] *PL*, II, p. 99.

importantly, lordship erected. This demanded a more immediate under-standing of what ideas like justice and the common weal amounted to, but this is not to say that something significantly different was meant by these terms in the regions. Nor is there anything to suggest that these principles were not right at the centre of local politics and ideology, just as they were on the national stage. Lordship, like kingship, was a composite political force, responding to and ordained for – and also determining and consuming – the common weal.

Nonetheless, as we have seen, an important practical difference remains in that it was necessary for local lords to assert their lordship. Everyone, under normal circumstances, held the crown aloft, but the nobility were forced to establish and then to justify their rule, by a mixture of responsiveness to the common good (taking counsel, giving reward, attending to the 'reason' of power) and self-assertion (inspiring 'drede', preserving apartness, pursuing martial honour). Assertiveness involved a measure of violence and *realpolitik* of a kind largely absent from the central political stage, though it has been shown that its absence depended on there being one focus for the national political community. When kingship was in competition, as during the 1460s and 1480s, kings got a taste of what politics could be like in the counties.[316] Normally, however, it was the duty of the king to help the lords in the establishment of local 'rule' by adjudicating between them, by drawing them to 'oonhede'. In the local realm, no less than in the kingdom proper, the peace and justice of the common weal depended on the existence of a stable and recognised structure of authority. In, and only in, such a structure could the common weal be realised and loyalty assumed. Where unchallenged lordship was established in the localities, it would have required no more than the now familiar balance of will and counsel to keep it in place, except that the accidents of heredity, personality and socio-economic change ensured that rule was rarely unchallenged forever. For this reason, in fact, royal intervention was ever necessary, but very much as a response to the demands of the common weal which lordship guaranteed. How this was expected to be done is the stuff of the next section.

. . .

The intimate relationship between the authority of the lord and the common weal of those who formed his lordship, which we established with regard to the king by the mirrors for princes and other works of theory, has been shown to be the conceptual basis for 'rule' in the localities, albeit modified in practice by the continually contested nature

---

[316] Above, pp. 50–1.

of local lordship. It remains to explore the practical manifestations of the model in the national sphere and, particularly, to establish how the two separate structures of lordship – local and national, each with its own 'common interest' – were reconciled. Although the principle of unity on which medieval monarchy rested demanded that jurisdictions were encapsulated hierarchically, and the prevailing imagery of the body politic and of the organic state has suggested that this was possible, it is nonetheless obvious that the reconciliation of many interests, each with its own representatives, in one grand common interest cannot have been entirely straightforward.

As we have seen, it was only when periods of crisis threatened the total subversion of the polity that the crown was able to invoke the exclusive, and, in a sense, convenient, dependence of the common weal on the recognition of its own authority. Clearly enough, the common weal for which royal policy provided in such desperate circumstances more closely resembled the lowest common denominator of need than the best interests of the people. Normally, however, it was the king's anticipated capacity to deliver a maximal satisfaction of interests which produced the fund of loving loyalties on which his 'drede' depended. The Thomist dictum that 'whoever promotes the common welfare of the community promotes his own welfare at the same time' was supposed to be brought home to each subject in his direct experience of rule, both local and national.[317] Because such an ambitious representation of interests was intrinsic to the success of the monarchical state, it comes as no surprise to find that effective personal rule was not a purely personal matter. Systemic arrangements were made for its achievement. These arrangements, though simple for the user, are far from obvious to the analyst. In the next few pages, an attempt will be made to identify them.

In many ways, it was locally that the most direct representation of the people took place, and the agency of this crucial function, central to the realisation of the all-important common weal, was local lordship. Parliament, of course, provided an important link between centre and locality, but neither its elections nor its sessions were altogether free of the nets of lordship, and, the granting of petitions apart, the tools of its trade were too general in scope – even when the community succeeded in wresting the use of them from the crown – to effect significant improvements in the local sphere.[318] Noblemen, on the other hand, derived a great part of

---

[317] *Aquinas*, p. 81.
[318] For discussions of the associations between parliament and lordship, see McFarlane 1981e; Maddicott 1981; and Jalland 1972. A good example of the inadequacy of parliamentary solutions to the problems of local society is provided by the legislation on livery and maintenance: see Carpenter 1983b for a discussion.

their power and status from their capacity to serve their inferiors, and it was the immediacy of their task of representation which introduced frictions in their dealings with each other and with the king above them. The royal preoccupation with the common interest of the realm meant that the king could not always meet the common interest which each lord represented, just as he could not always meet the interest of each individual subject. This was easily accepted in principle – the more so, in fact, because the nobility were often at work on 'the great business of the realm', in which individual concerns were sublimated to national ones – but it was harder to accept in practice on account of the hard fact that, unlike the king, the nobility needed to satisfy a significant proportion of small-scale interests in their 'countries' in order to maintain themselves, because their lordship was always subject to competition. There was thus a continual potential for divergence between the king and individual members of the nobility arising from the practicalities of the related processes of representation and reconciliation. How, in practice, was this resolved?

It will be clear at once that the key to the resolution of differing interests lay more in the directive power of lordship (in this case, royal lordship) than in the consultative power of counsel. This is worth exploring at some length, because it is of enormous importance in explaining why the monarchy we have described, a system founded above all on representative authority, did not make more use of representative institutions. We have seen that the common weal, which the king was sworn to defend, seemed to leading subjects, such as noblemen and parliamentary knights and burgesses, to possess a measurable identity, quite distinct from royal policy.[319] It was this separate identity which provided the nobility, in particular, as the principal and continual mediators between the king and his subjects, with a basis for criticism of the crown. Did it also provide them with a basis for authority? Given the role of counsel as the principal means by which the common weal was transmitted, were not the nobility in a position to establish a self-sufficient regime, based on their corporate counsel, and so capable of governing in the common interest?

This was indeed the assumption on which the various representative councils and reformist movements of the later middle ages were founded, and it was an important and pervasive one; but, all the same, it was riven with flaws. Some of these were conceptual: medieval theory placed a premium on the representation of the whole body of subjects, but it was impossible to obtain the counsel of each individual; partly as a result, ideas of counsel always presupposed the existence of a superior who

[319] Above, pp. 35–6, 57.

made a final assessment on the basis of what he had heard – theorists, as we have seen, authorised rulers, not counsellors. But there were also practical problems. The satisfaction of the common interest meant the reduction of diverse advice to a single policy. In a society which did not, for the most part, accept the majority principle, this could not easily be done by a committee.[320] Few powerful men, particularly if they were *consiliarii* of the king, were prepared to accept anything less than the unanimous judgement of their peers unless it suited them. Meanwhile, the fact that it was conventional for a king to decide policy and, moreover, to execute it through his officers, meant that governing councils were continually aware of their own abnormality: the traditional distribution of authority continued to exercise its charm, even in the depths of division, and these rather contrived unities tended to disintegrate.

On all these grounds, a higher authority was necessary for the transformation of advice into policy: to supplement the limited representativeness of counsellors; to arbitrate between their counsels; to enforce decisions. This was acknowledged by Henry VI's subjects as – through force of circumstance – they set up councils to govern in his name. Even though the members of these councils frequently obtained the right to 'conclude' and 'spede' matters, they normally claimed that they had nothing more than the 'execucion' of the king's authority and the right to counsel it, not its possession, even for short periods.[321] In practice, as we shall see, their modesty was justified: the king's authority, his authorising power, was exceedingly difficult to detach from his person. *Faute de mieux*, a council could possess an interim legitimacy and standing; it could even achieve certain things which a delinquent or ineffectual king could not; but it could not hold out for long against royal authority: the pull of lordship was simply too strong.

It was, then, the king – almost alone – who provided the single will essential for the formation of common policy. This explains why the importance of having unity among the lords was particularly emphasised in periods where there was no 'natural unity' above them.[322] It was

---

[320] For the majority principle, see Reynolds 1984: pp. 30–1, 247 and elsewhere; Edwards 1964.

[321] See below, pp. 113–15, for the declarations of 1427. In 1455, the lords found themselves 'takyng uppon [themselves] th'exercise of his auctorite': *RP*, V, p. 286 (see also p. 290). Note that the lords of the minority council were not always so precise: in the course of the same meeting, they made reference to 'oure soverein lordes name, whos auctorite we have' (*PPC*, III, p. 239). Even so, it seems fairly clear that the lords did recognise that some power, intrinsic to the king, was beyond their grasp.

[322] For the king as a natural unity, see above, p. 19. Bishop Stafford, in 1433, identified 'Pax, Unitas, et vera Concordia' as the triple *virtus politica* of the lords (*RP*, IV, p. 419), while Bishop Russell, in 1483, talked of the lords, 'in whoos sure and concord demenynge restithe the wele of alle the commen' (Chrimes 1936: p. 171). In 1425, it was declared that, in the king's nonage, peace lay in 'the good oonhede and accord

usually enough for the lords to present their counsels and have the king judge between them. Without a functioning king, they had to perform the process of judgement themselves, hence the particular need to avoid division.[323] Obviously, unity among the lords was always desirable, but it was usually encouraged by a common focus upon the king and to some extent compelled by the process of 'drede'. Under other circumstances, this unity was difficult to achieve, a fact implicit in the unstated dependence of the minority council on the overlordship of the duke of Bedford,[324] and the telling demand of the commons of 1455 that 'there must be a persone to whom the people of this lande may have recours to sue to for remedy of their injuries'.[325] Without such a person, there was nothing to put an end to division except peer pressure, which, once separated from the superior jurisdiction with reference to which it usually operated, did not necessarily encourage stability. As the account of the later 1450s will show, it was rarely clear whether unity was better served by indulging those who rocked the boat or excluding them. A single authority was needed to judge matters of this kind, but it was nearly impossible to erect from within. The counsel of the lords could not keep the peace and protect the common interest by itself. The common weal depended on the action of counsel upon a superior and independent will.

The necessary pre-eminence of the king's will dictated a freedom of access to it, so that it could be as fully informed as possible. To deny another person access to the king was, in fact, to assert control over the king: the familiar act of 'accroachment of the royal power'; a terrible crime not only because of the offence to royal dignity, but also because of the instability it created.[326] For most, access was achieved by representation, but for the nobility, who led and spoke for the local communities, it had to be direct.[327] This was a significant reason why conciliar authorities were incompatible with monarchy: they restricted free access to the highest source of judgement, but the provision of this judgement was the

among the Lordes' (*RP*, V, p. 407). In 1455, the chief aim of parliament was 'to sette a parfite love and rest amonge the Lordes of this lande, to th'entent that they mowe drawe directly togidres in oon union and accorde' (*ibid.*, p. 279).

[323] This is partly evoked by Russell's distinction between the 'true justice' which the lords used to rule the commons and the 'lovynge tretie' by which, with the king's aid, they ruled themselves (Chrimes 1936: pp. 172–3).

[324] See below, pp. 116, 120–1.   [325] *RP*, V, p. 285.

[326] Note the declaration made by the lords, in January 1426, that it was not fitting for the king 'to weyve the presence of any of his lige men, nor to lymitte him who shal be or not be in his presence' (*PPC*, III, p. 183). For anyone else to dictate to the king whom he could have as an officer of his, they added, showed 'to grete a takynge ... upon the K. and upon his freedome' (*ibid.*, p. 186).

[327] As Bishop Russell observed, 'the peuple must stond a forr, and not passe the lymittes; ye speke with the prince, whyche is quasi deus noster in terris' (Chrimes 1936: p. 173).

king's central service to his people.[328] Ideally, but surely also in typical practice, there was a personal link between everyone who exercised significant local lordship and the king. It was through links of this kind that the myriad and conflicting individual interests which went to make up an effective common interest, were satisfied. Through a direct – and, in a sense, private – relationship with the sovereign, lords could discharge their representative function, achieving as much as possible for themselves and their men.

The king was not expected to indulge each suit put to him by members of the nobility: he had to reconcile one request with another and to consider circumstantial details if his duty to the common interest was to be fulfilled. But as long as the power of final satisfaction – or 'grace' – was vested in a free individual, who followed the regimes of mercy, justice, humility and magnanimity prescribed by advice-literature, the possibility of obtaining it was always there and this was enough.[329] Private dialogues, conducted in an informal environment, were the key vehicle for the synthesis of counsel and judgement upon which the common weal of kingdom and country and the lordship of king and nobility depended. The kings may, at times, have needed extraordinary devices to assist the working of these dialogues – displays of affection or of *ira et malevolentia*, the gathering of more formal counsel to impress upon suitors the fact that there were other interests to be considered – but they were, in themselves, the perfect combination of force and attentiveness, of the single good and the common weal. Private and personal methods, in an informal and confidential environment, were thus a central means of achieving the common and public interest. When Fortescue complained of how the lords of Henry VI's council concerned themselves only with their own matters and those of their men, he was actually condemning the very essence of later medieval government.[330]

Laws and organised councils were not sufficient means of government in a society founded on lordship. Because the nobility depended on representation for their power, they required a more flexible and precisely responsive structure for the defence of their interests.[331] Only the king,

---

[328] This was captured perfectly by Cade's rebels, with their demand that, contrary to practice under the rule of Suffolk, 'every mane myghte have his dewe comynge in dewe tyme to hyme [the king] to aske justyse or grace as the cause requirethe' (Harvey 1991: p. 189).

[329] Note, for example, the petition of a suspected Lollard to Henry V, asking for power to sue to the king alone 'in youre owne solempne propre personne, withouten any other Juge' (*Letters of Margaret*, p. 26).

[330] *Governance*, p. 145.

[331] This was implicit in, for example, the king's reply to the 1456 resumption bill, in which, contrary to the terms of the bill, he exempted a large number of individuals.

who alone had *jurisdictio*[332] – the speaking of the law and thus the power of defining the common weal – could respond to the individual as well as to the mass. Guided by virtue, assisted by counsel, surrounded by the demands of the *communitas*, he was the common interest activated:[333] his judgements might be inscrutable, even idiosyncratic, in practice, but there was a usable justice in their ultimate independence of inferior wills. In the person of the virtuous king, law and grace, justice and mercy converged free from binding force: the force exerted by favourites, ministers or councillors against the community; the force exerted by communal representatives against the individual and those he or she stood for.[334] Only in the unity presented by an individual could the variable, but broadly predictable, reconciliation of these properties take place. Opposition which stopped short of proposing a substitute monarch was, in the end, doomed to failure: laws and councils would not work. Nothing short of the suspension of the polity in civil war was sufficient to reform a king who would not reform himself. The events of Henry VI's reign were to bring these verities to light.

His defence was 'the egalte and reason' that he ought to do to his people: *RP*, V, p. 303. This usage of 'reason' (and of 'equity') tallies with the meaning proposed above: see p. 71.

[332] Jolliffe 1955: pp. 5, 32–49.

[333] In a sense, a later incarnation of the twelfth-century idea of the king as *lex animata*: see e.g. Kantorowicz 1957: pp. 127–9 (and chs. IV and V for the shift from what Kantorowicz called 'law-centred' to 'polity-centred' kingship).

[334] Note the view of Serjeant Billing, in 1469, that 'to every king by reason of his office, it belongs to do justice and grace: justice in executing the laws, etc., and grace to grant pardon to felons' (quoted by Doe 1990: p. 85).

3

GOVERNMENT

N OW THAT SOME of the concepts which shaped and sustained the
government of fifteenth-century England have been explored, the
time has come to examine the means by which they were normally put
into effect. Since the birth of 'administrative history', the discussion of
government has been more or less dominated by the examination of
institutions.[1] At first, this was because the institutions of the royal
administration were believed to be the real venue for the struggle between
royal and 'constitutionalist' forces which earlier generations of historians
had located in parliament. More recently, that point of view has been
abandoned, but the institutional approach has, broadly speaking, been
retained. By those who discuss it in detail, government tends to be seen as
an essentially uncontroversial and bureaucratic exercise, carried out to a
large extent by professional administrators under the king's general
command.[2] While this way of looking at government certainly avoids the
'excessive addiction to constitutional issues' which vitiated earlier accounts – and, indeed, reflects the important perception that, in the later
middle ages, consensus over the management of affairs was more normal
than division – it does raise certain problems.[3] For one thing, it may, as
we shall see, go rather too far in playing down the constitutional
implications of governmental forms: administrative convenience was not
the only factor shaping the development of institutions. A second
problem is that the continuing emphasis on institutional and 'official'
structures for the expression of royal authority can lead to a sense that
'unofficial' organisations of power were antithetical, or at least extrinsic,
to royal ones; that they were not part of the enterprise of government.
This has had a significant impact on the analysis of both local and

---

[1] For administrative history and its assumptions, see Tout 1937: I, pp. 1–9. See, more
recently, the observations of Chrimes 1963: p. 19 and Brown 1989: introduction (notably
the comment, 'This is a book about the "governance of England" . . . a personal impression
of how government worked within a framework of description of institutions', on p. 4).
[2] E.g. Brown 1989: pp. 42, 52.   [3] Quotation from McFarlane 1973: p. 2.

national politics. The tendency, for example, to promote the chain of royal administrative and judicial offices as the main point of contact between 'centre' and 'locality' can make informal bodies such as magnate affinities or other gentry groupings into alien forces whom the crown must either seduce or destroy.[4] In a like way, there remains a sense in quite a lot of writing that the (official) 'council' was somehow a more proper forum for the expression of the will of central government than the (unofficial) 'court'.[5] Finally, the persisting focus on the administration of policy at the expense of its formation tends to understate the important political functions which contemporaries expected the king to fulfil as part of his duty of government. In doing so, it helps to confirm the divorce between the 'personal', on the one hand, and the 'public' and 'constitutional', on the other, which is beginning to emerge as a misleading feature of the historiography of this period.[6]

It will now be clear that, to the later medieval nobility, the essence of rule was the making of authoritative decisions, a process in which, as we have seen, the role of the king was both pre-eminent and fundamental. In this chapter, therefore, we shall regard government as primarily a political exercise, intrinsic to the personal lordship of the king over his greater subjects. What follows, then, is not an account of the secretarial and financial offices which made up the bureaucracy of the late medieval crown, but, instead, an analysis of the way in which its more obviously political structures – in the centre, the organs of counsel and, in the provinces, the media of royal justice – provided for the seminal task of government: the representation of the common weal. Parliament, which also, in a sense, fulfilled this function, is not considered here. It was not strictly part of the government and its representativeness was highly formal and specialised. It was not, moreover, a forum in which king and lords normally or continuously dealt with each other: rather, it was where they confronted directly and *en masse* the wider constituency of the realm.[7]

NATIONAL GOVERNMENT

According to the constitutional framework established in the preceding chapter, the king's government required a free environment for the

---

[4] See e.g. Kaeuper 1988: pp. 5, 179–80. Cf. Harriss 1993: pp. 28–9, 32–3.
[5] See e.g. Wolffe 1981: ch. 6.   [6] Above, pp. 9, 14, 38–9.
[7] This is not to suggest that the king and lords necessarily acted as a united body before the commons, but that their behaviour in parliament was conditioned by the extraordinary, if regular, circumstance of the communities speaking for themselves. Parliamentary affairs are not explored at length in this book. Even so, the emergence of discrepancies between the common weal the nobility were striving to achieve and the common weal as perceived by the commons in parliament is an important feature of the later 1440s: the problems this caused and the issues it raises are discussed in ch. 6, below.

making of decisions: no law or institution could constrain the exercise of royal will. It has been suggested that the defence of the common weal depended on the availability of access to the king for all those exercising lordship immediately beneath him. In most historical accounts of the period, however, a body known as 'the king's council' appears at the centre of the polity. Typically bearing a fixed membership and meeting regularly, its task is to aid the king in the making of decisions and to assist him in carrying out the minutiae of government.[8] In the light of the ideas we have investigated, such a body must seem rather anomalous. An advisory institution of this kind might reasonably be expected to exercise some sort of monopoly over counsel, but this would involve a tacit accroachment of the king's power to consult whomsoever he chose. It would condemn him to a rigidity in decision making which ill suited his comprehensive authority. It would have grave consequences for the exercise of lordship by those noblemen who were not among its members. It could even seem to offer a continual and constitutional check upon the free action of the royal will: something which has been shown to be utterly against the grain of the monarchical system. Was there such a disjunction between ideas and institutions at the centre of the later medieval state, or was 'the kinges counsail', which is so widely featured in the records of government, something other than its place in our histories would suggest?[9]

The problem is, above all, one of terminology, both medieval and modern. *Consilium* and its French and English analogues had a variety of meanings: not only counsel or advice itself, but also the men who gave this counsel and, by association, an assembly of men charged with the making or executing of decisions. The potential for confusion has been widely noted and some commentators have been at pains to stress the interpretative problems which result.[10] Broadly speaking, the difficulty for historians of government lies in determining which form of 'consilium' it was that appears to have become institutionalised in the course of the fourteenth and early fifteenth centuries: decision making, advice or administration. Nineteenth-century historians took the Lancastrian council to be the forerunner of the modern cabinet, a body fulfilling all

---

[8] E.g. Virgoe 1970: p. 155 and *passim*; Lander 1958: p. 46 and *passim*; Storey 1966: pp. 35–6, 39–40; Griffiths 1981: ch. 12; Wolffe 1981: pp. 102–4; Wilkinson 1964: p. 219. The classic treatment of 'the king's council' remains Baldwin 1913, but see the works of Brown listed in the bibliography for a series of important revisions.

[9] This matter is discussed in Watts 1991. Here, for reasons of space, I present only the conclusions of my article and such amendments as have become necessary.

[10] E.g. Baldwin 1913: p. 104; Quillet 1988: pp. 520, 547; Ramsay 1985: pp. 106–7. Note that another meaning of *consilium*, not considered here, was secret matters: the king's *consilium* could thus be those who knew his mind on certain topics, or were charged with carrying out his will; an ever-varying and scarcely homogeneous group, in other words.

three roles and dominating the government of the realm in every sense.[11] Since Plucknett's essay of 1918, it has instead been common to stress the indefinite and protean nature of the later medieval council: at times, it could be a large body of named men assembled to advise on a particular topic; at other times, it might be a small group of administrators meeting regularly to despatch mundane business.[12] More recently, the picture has become rather confused. Historians have argued both that 'the king himself governed the kingdom' and that 'the council', an advisory and executive body, was becoming a fixed and established part of a more and more 'bureaucratic and professional government': government, then, was 'both thoroughly royal and thoroughly conciliar'.[13] The paradox contained in these claims is mostly resolved by allowing readers to assume that issues of government had no constitutional dimension; that, as in Fortescue's *Governance*, kings and councils were fundamentally compatible. In fact, at a fundamental level, they were incompatible, and only a particular kind of council could have existed on a continual basis.

If any kind of council became a normal and everyday part of the king's government in the later middle ages – and there can be no certainty on this point – it can only have been an administrative body made up of the king's leading clerical and financial officers, afforced by a few other men, often expert in law or diplomacy, often especially trusted by the king.[14] When councils of this kind were in operation – in the early years of Henry IV's reign, for example – their business was mundane and politically insignificant, too boring or time-consuming for the king himself, or, indeed, for the lay nobility, who scarcely featured in them.[15] They could have been a useful tool of management, particularly in periods of great activity or financial stress, but there is no evidence that they were normally regarded as an essential part of the king's administrative equipment or even that their activities were always thought worth recording.[16] Contemporaries were principally interested in the quality of

---

[11] E.g. Stubbs 1875–8: III, pp. 247, 252, etc.

[12] Plucknett 1918: pp. 162, 173–5; McFarlane 1972: pp. 82–3.

[13] Quotations from Brown 1989: pp. 240–1, 52, 23, respectively.

[14] See *ibid.*, pp. 37–41, for the most up-to-date description of this sort of council and *RP*, II, p. 322, for a reference to 'le Conseil notre sieur le roy' which appears to mean nothing more than 'les officers q'ont este acustumez d'estre en couste le roy' (1376). The idea of the council as a group of particularly trusted men – 'de consilio nostro seu familia nostra', as Edward I put it (Petit-Dutaillis and Lefebvre (eds.), 1929: p. 417) – was also an important theme in advice-literature: e.g. *Secreta*, pp. 210–11.

[15] The low level of noble involvement in this sort of council is a major theme of Brown 1969b. See *idem* 1989: pp. 38–9 for some comments on typical business and *PPC*, I, for examples.

[16] Note that under Edward IV, the activities of this kind of council went largely unrecorded: indeed, it was not even thought necessary to indicate, in endorsements and notes of warranty, that such a council had played any part in the formation of policy, even when it apparently had (Lander 1958).

government, and only when this deteriorated did they concern themselves with its form; as a rule, a fairly vague sense that the king was surrounded by 'good and wise counsel' was sufficient.[17]

This 'administrative' council was not important as a source of advice, except in matters of detail or bureaucratic practice. Whilst its members often were important advisers of the king, this was either on their own account or because of the offices they held, not because of their membership of a council. Meanwhile, counsel in the sense of advice and information reached the king by a number of other means. One was the receipt of petitions, oral or written, from his subjects: kings were bombarded with requests for action, attention and judgement, and we may fairly assume that applications from subjects played an important part in the day-to-day formation of royal policy.[18] A second means of obtaining advice and information was the summoning of temporary councils for the discussion of particular issues.[19] These varied in size and solemnity from parliaments and great councils to emergency gatherings hastily assembled from whoever was at hand. A third means was the informal dialogue between the king and his greater subjects, a phenomenon which has begun to emerge as the key to reconciling the common interest of each and all.[20] This dialogue may have been the most significant avenue of counsel in political and constitutional terms, but it is the least well documented, with the result that although its importance is often acknowledged, it barely features in accounts of 'the king's council'.[21]

In periods when relations between the king and the rest of the political community had broken down or been suspended, another form of council emerged: bodies, characteristically dominated by magnates, but also containing administrators, ordained, usually at the wish of the commons in parliament, to assist the king in the tasks of government which, through illness or absence, youth or incapacity, he could not perform satisfactorily by himself.[22] These bodies were not only administrative, but also advisory and, indeed, virtually adjudicatory. Assisting the king in this way effectively meant replacing him: the freedom of action which was the normal corollary of his office was denied; the threads of counsel ended in the council, not the king, who was obliged to authorise whatever the council

---

[17] See e.g. Harriss 1975: pp. 302–4; Brown 1981: pp. 134–5ff.
[18] Brown 1989: pp. 19–20; 1964a: pp. 148–9, 154–5; Hicks 1991d: pp. 61–2.
[19] Baldwin 1913: pp. 106–8.   [20] See above, p. 79.
[21] The existence of this sort of counsel is acknowledged by e.g. Condon 1986: p. 231; Catto 1985a: p. 83; Brown 1989: pp. 30, 36–7.
[22] Examples are those of 1341 and 1376, the councils of Richard II's childhood and the bodies imposed by the parliaments of 1386 and 1388, 1401, 1404 and 1406: see Harriss 1975: ch. XIII; Holmes 1975: p. 158; Baldwin 1913: ch. VI; Brown 1964b.

proposed.[23] Councils of this kind became quite common in the period of recurrent crisis which ran from the 1370s to the early 1400s, but they continued to be at odds with the norms of authority. While they accurately reflected the representative power of the nobility, and (at times) provided a basic measure of political or fiscal order, they were unrealistic in other ways. Apart from being offensive to royal dignity, they lacked fully effective means of decision making. As we have seen, the rule of majority was generally regarded with distaste in medieval England and the consensual judgements which were preferred usually required definition and backing from a higher source.[24] More importantly, these councils disrupted the free and open relationship of king and lords which was one of the most basic features of the polity.[25] As a result of these flaws, they were almost always short-lived. They represent a traditional, but desperate, solution to governmental crises. At other times, they had no place in the apparatus of government.

If it is accepted that counsel was not normally transmitted through a separate and specific institution, then an alternative venue for the political interaction of king and nobility must be sought. The court seems a likely answer, but first of all we need to establish what is meant by this term.[26] Defining the court was a problem which baffled even medieval analysts: as Walter Map, writing in the twelfth century, commented, 'I can say that I am in the court, and speak of the court, and know not – God alone knows – what the court is.'[27] By the fifteenth century, the word seems to have fallen out of common use, at least in this context: in the debates of Henry VI's parliaments, for example, it almost never appears; instead, the word 'household' predominates, except, curiously enough, in the famous bill for the removal of certain persons 'mysbehavyng aboute youre Roiall persone'.[28] This was perhaps because public discussion of the king's domestic establishment was almost invariably focused on its financial and institutional aspects – more appropriately represented by the term 'house-

---

[23] Rather as in Fortescue's model: see above, pp. 47ff.

[24] See above, p. 77, and note Archbishop Chichele's disapproval of the system of one man, one vote, adopted at Basle (Jacob 1953: p. 55). For some interesting anthropological insights on decision making by majority or consensus, see Bailey 1965.

[25] Above, pp. 74–80.

[26] A problem noted by e.g. Asch 1991: pp. 8–9 and explored at some length by Griffiths 1991b (esp. pp. 12–15).

[27] From 'De Nugis Curialium', quoted in J. A. Burrow's introduction to Scattergood and Sherborne (eds.) 1983: p. ix.

[28] RP, v, pp. 216–17. The king's includes a promise to remove some of these people from him and his 'court'. In Edward IV's Black Book, 'household' or 'house' appear much more frequently than 'court', though the terms do seem to be interchangeable (e.g. 'this royal court to stond after thies apoyntmentz that folowe after', 'this honorable houshold and lantern of Inglond': Myers, 1959: pp. 87, 89). Griffiths 1991b: pp. 12–13 notes the propensity of medieval historians to talk about 'household', rather than 'court'.

hold'[29] – and, in fact, chiefly upon its solvency and cost. It is undoubtedly true that issues of funding were indeed the most common cause for public concern about the court,[30] but where it received a more theoretical or political consideration, for example in the advice-literature, the term 'household' still predominated.[31] It has also been suggested that court self-consciousness did not develop until the 1480s, though this is not to say that what came to be called 'the court' did not exist before.[32] It is as if contemporaries were no clearer than historians about how the area about the king's person, which seemed to contain the central elements of rule, should be defined and described.

In the historiography of government, the court has had a bumpy ride. The complex circumstances of the royal household, where public and private converged more obviously than in other branches of the royal administration, evoked a certain distaste from the scholars of the nineteenth century. 'Household' government was frequently contrasted with the more 'constitutional' forms of rule associated with parliament, the council and the offices of state.[33] A passage from Baldwin's history of 'the king's council' exemplifies this view: following Stubbs, he claimed that the great issue of the Lancastrian period was 'whether the council should be maintained as a department of the royal household in the interests of the monarchy, or whether it should be like the parliament, a body representative of the estates of the realm'.[34] The inappropriateness of this antithesis – private household versus public parliament – has now been demonstrated,[35] but only recently have historians begun to examine the consequences for our ideas about the court. On the one hand, it must be accepted that certain vital functions of government remained in the royal household, and on the other it must be realised that this body comprehended public, as well as private, elements, despite its focus on the person of the king and its truly informal nature.[36] As we have seen, the king himself was both private and public person: it should

---

[29] G. R. Elton, for example, calls the royal household, 'the one formal, almost professional, component of the Court': Elton 1983: p. 41. See also Griffiths 1991b: p. 15. Cf. Given-Wilson 1986: p. 2, where the distinction between *domus* (the domestic establishment of the household) and *familia* (the household expanded) is discussed. Dr Given-Wilson concludes that only the *domus* is precisely definable, but suggests that 'household' comprises both aspects.

[30] Given-Wilson 1986: pp. 12–14.

[31] 'Household' is the preferred term in the *Three Consideracions*, for example (Genet (ed.), *Political Tracts*, pp. 184–5, 204), and in *Governance* (p. 122, ch. XVII).

[32] Morgan 1987: pp. 68–70.   [33] Harriss 1975: pp. 208–9.

[34] Baldwin 1913: p. 147. See Guy 1986 for a view of early sixteenth-century counsel which is in some respects parallel.

[35] Harriss 1975: ch. IX; Starkey 1987a: pp. 10–21.

[36] See Starkey 1981: pp. 261–3 for an interesting discussion of the interplay between what he calls the 'formal' and 'informal' structures of government. See also Griffiths 1991b: p. 24.

not surprise us that his house possessed the same mixed quality. Perhaps we might usefully take 'the court' to be 'the household' in its more public aspect.[37]

As is often noted, the forms of later medieval government originated in the more or less undifferentiated *curia* of the Anglo-Norman kings.[38] What is less commonly emphasised is how much of government actually remained in a curial setting and how little this undermined its public quality. The *curia* seems to have provided for three main functions: government (counsel and judgement); defence; and the king's domestic life.[39] Clearly enough, even in the twelfth century, each of these had both public and private aspects, deriving from a combination of Anglo-Saxon and classical political ideas and the king's slightly schizophrenic position as supreme feudal lord, which made him simultaneously lord of a baronial following and lord of all.[40] As a result, the *curia* was both the king's house and the meeting-place of the leading men of the realm. Within it, every private place, man or function had the potential to acquire public significance. In a way, this was recognised by the physical removal of some of the functions of the developing administration from the im-mediate environment of the peripatetic king.[41] But this process, by which 'offices' were established 'out of court', does not mean that what remained at the king's side was necessarily private. As David Starkey has pointed out, 'other branches of the court stepped forward to duplicate the work of the departments of state'.[42] Since most government required the king's active involvement, or at least intervention, the chain of command between the stationary offices and the mobile court could not be broken. At the same time, all government depended on counsel of some kind, with the result that access to the king's presence remained a tacit and general right for leading subjects. 'Household government' was thus the norm, in the sense that the king lived in a public, as much as a private, place.[43] Whilst it may be right to posit 'a kind of debate or dialectic between "household" and "bureaucratic" forms of government' (at least at a conceptual level), it is important to understand that, except at periods of unusual tension between the king and the political nation, both forms were equally acceptable to, and usable by, all.[44] In certain respects, therefore, the later medieval court was the true heir of the *curia regis*: the

---

[37] This is captured by Elton 1983: p. 39 – 'the sort of court that Elizabeth queened it in, that stage of all public life, social and cultural and political'.

[38] E.g. Warren 1987: pp. 78–80.

[39] Green 1986: pp. 19–20. Chris Given-Wilson identifies the same basic functions as the role of the medieval king's household servants, and adds a fourth: finance (1986: p. 1).

[40] For this view of the king's position, see Jolliffe 1955: chs. I.i and I.ii.

[41] Brown 1989: pp. 23–4.   [42] Starkey 1973: p. 299.

[43] Note the comments of Given-Wilson 1986: p. 260.

[44] The phrase is David Starkey's (1973: p. 300).

central components of government – counsel and the judgement of matters of equity, as represented by responses to petitions and by the formation of policy – continued to repose in the undefined, informal environment of the king's house, because the king was there.[45] 'Where', asked Bishop Russell, 'ys the wombe of thys grete publick body of Englonde but that and there where the kyng ys hym self, hys court and hys counselle?'[46]

A distinction between public government and private domesticity was to some extent reflected in the physical division of the royal apartments into hall and chamber.[47] Even so, for the same reasons that it was impossible to separate government and administration from the king's person, a wholly private royal refuge was difficult to preserve. By degrees, the chamber, though supposedly the centre of the king's private life, became 'the principal reception room of the palace'.[48] As a result, it had become subdivided, by 1471, into 'upper', 'middle' and 'inner' chambers. The last, and supposedly most private, of these became the 'privy chamber', which has been shown to be a major centre of Henry VIII's government.[49] Notwithstanding this almost inevitable development, the advice-literature seems to have expected the household to provide for the king's private life as well as for public hospitality. In it, ran one mirror, there should be some 'pryve trew Pepill amonge whom he may glad him'.[50] These people should be young and a source of solace, but they should also be quite separate from the king's counsellors.[51] Ideas of this sort formed the basis of expectations concerning the actual staff of the household: its most intimate officers were supposed to be its least 'political'. Private domestic functions had to be provided as cheaply as possible and by 'privy' men, unconnected with politics.[52] Even so, nothing in the structure or institutions of the household clearly delimited the private from the public: it was for the king and the leaders of the polity to

---

[45] See Brown 1989: pp. 23, 28–9; Given-Wilson 1987a: pp. 176–7; and especially Horrox 1989: p. 251 – 'it is inevitable that in a personal monarchy any attempt to define the court turns into a definition of government'.

[46] Chrimes 1936: p. 175.   [47] Starkey 1973: pp. 1–2; Given-Wilson 1986: p. 29.

[48] Starkey 1973: p. 2.   [49] Starkey 1987b: pp. 73–4 and *passim*.

[50] *Secreta*, p. 140.

[51] Fortescue makes the point quite explicitly in his 'Articles to Warrewic', saying that the king should not be counselled by men of the chamber or others 'which can not counsele hym' (*Governance*, p. 350). See also 'Three Consideracions', p. 192. A parallel is provided by the role intended to be played by the queen: *ibid.*, pp. 204–5. Note Gascoigne's criticism of Henry VI's 'iuvenibus consilariis': the men he was describing were not, in fact, young, but they were officers of the household (*Loci e Libro*, p. 189).

[52] The situation in the departments of state was analogous. Whilst political involvement was acceptable in their heads, who were well known, public and accountable figures, it was unacceptable among their staff. The clerks of the chancery, the courts and the privy seal lived apart from other society in hostels kept by their seniors (Catto 1985a: pp. 76–8).

agree where affairs were to be conducted. By their disciplined behaviour, some princes were able to convince their subjects that nothing
but royal prudence would be at work behind closed doors.[53] Those
who were unable to achieve this faced bitter protests.[54]

It seems reasonable to conclude, then, that government had to be,
and under normal circumstances was, 'public', no matter where it was
located. Even if a lot of acts were done, in an immediate sense, in a
'private' environment – by the king and his secretary alone, by the king
in his chamber, and so on – this was more in the manner of delegated
public jurisdiction, a concept familiar to lords and office-holders, than
private, independent action. It is worth noting that when, in the later
1450s, Henry VI seemed to withdraw into the company of his domestic
servants and feed men, a chronicler remarked that he 'helde no householde': the very opposite of what historians haunted by the spectre of
'household government' might have expected to be said.[55] Private as it
was, the household was also public. A king who failed to realise that,
even in his home, he was the centre of a public sphere brought the
polity crashing down about his head. Formal councils might be one
way of preserving the public character of government, but they were an
inadequate one. In the 'political' monarchy of the English, everything
depended on the king. If he resisted counsel, it failed. If he accepted
the counsel of a defined group and no other, then important interests
were certain to be excluded. The subtly extensive, yet absolutely
necessary, form of representation which normal counsel provided could
only be maintained by the king himself. Only through the personal
application of the political virtues prescribed by the advice-literature
could he guarantee public government with the private forms at his
disposal.

---

[53] A good example is provided by Elizabeth I, whose major household officers were
members of the privy council and openly participated in politics, while the women of the
privy chamber were able to use their access to the sovereign only for the prosecution of
minor suits: 'the influence of the privy chamber could be discounted by the queen's
leading ministers, confident that their monopoly over the conduct of affairs of state
would be upheld' (Adams 1984: pp. 62–3, 73–4). Edward II is perhaps the most obvious
counter-example.

[54] A major cause of the row of 1376 was the king's withdrawal into a 'privata familia'
separate from the household (though in fact composed of intimates from the chamber),
during the 1370s (Given-Wilson 1986: pp. 33–4). The object of opposition was not,
therefore, the household, nor even the chamber, but the fact that a clique monopolised
the king's attentions.

[55] *English Chron.*, p. 79 (it is not the truth of the observation which matters here, but the
view that what we would tend to regard as a household *coterie* was presented as 'no
householde'). In a like way, the similar withdrawal of Edward III in the 1370s robbed the
household of 'much of its political importance' (Given-Wilson 1986: p. 34). See *ibid.*, p.
260, for an assault on the concept of 'household government'.

LOCAL GOVERNMENT

The rule of the shires was a matter of common, national and, therefore, royal as well as local concern. This was clearly reflected in the array of formal agencies of justice and administration which brought royal government into the localities, but it was also borne out through the working of more informal enterprises, in which the public and the private were, at all levels, more subtly intertwined. These enterprises were governmental, in that they turned on the representation of interests, involved the formation and execution of decisions and were geared to the preservation of order and harmony. They were also royal, inasmuch as they were conducted in the interests of the king and under his sympathetic direction. Nonetheless, these enterprises were composed of people whose power was partly independent and partly negotiated, people who were not, in any simple sense, the king's employees. These people were the nobility and gentry of England, characteristically organised in structures of lordship which reached upwards from the shires to the royal court. In this section, the aim will be to discuss how the informal dealings of king and nobility at the centre combined with the formal framework of the royal administration to produce a workable and representative form of justice in the localities. First of all, however, it will be necessary to consider whether the view that noble lordship was the normal form of local rule is justified. Although it has been presented as a central implication of the material discussed in chapter 2, this view commands neither unconditional nor universal assent among historians.[56]

Debate centres on two inter-related questions: whether magnate lordship – conceived as a vertical system – was actually more prevalent in England than 'independent gentry establishments', in which the dominant bonds were horizontal ones;[57] and whether it was normal for the crown to attempt to supplement its political resources with the direct exercise of local lordship via the medium of a 'royal affinity'.[58] The near-inevitability of the 'county study' as a medium for the examination of local society has to some extent influenced the responses of historians

---

[56] What follows is not intended to be a contribution to a debate in which this author is ill-qualified to participate. The aim is the more limited one of establishing the assumptions underlying the present study and, in some measure, defending them. As this is intended to be a brief survey, supporting material has been kept to a minimum and placed mostly in the notes. As a consequence, some of these are longer than would otherwise be desirable.

[57] This antithesis is posed in e.g. Payling 1991: pp. 87–8, 105–8. See also Saul (who coined the term in 1981: e.g. pp. 260–1) 1986: pp. 56–7; Walker 1990: pp. 3–4.

[58] See e.g. Starkey 1981: pp. 268–9 for a distinction between the 'presidential' method of rule adopted by Edward III and Henry V and the policy of royal retaining pursued by Richard II, which he finds 'more usual'.

to both questions.[59] Those who have analysed counties where there was no dominant lord, or where seigneurial landholdings were minimal, or where the crown itself was a major landowner have tended to emphasise the independence of the gentry and also to focus on direct royal rule rather than magnate lordship.[60] On the other hand, Simon Walker's recent study of John of Gaunt's affinity argues that even in the counties of greatest Lancastrian influence, Gaunt's lordship was never all-embracing or particularly effective.[61] Must we accept, therefore, that magnate lordship was a social norm only in a limited number of areas – Martin Cherry's Devonshire, Christine Carpenter's 'Greater Warwickshire', and so on – and that even where it was present, it may have been less significant than has been imagined?[62]

Part of the problem lies in how we interpret a term like 'lordship'. If it were a purely private and autonomous force, expressed through the paid-up followings of rich landowners, then there would be every reason to doubt the scale, or indeed value, of its impact upon the gentry societies of later medieval England. But there is no more reason to assume a natural separation of lordship from community, or indeed an opposition between them, than there is to assume that the king was fully separable from, and antithetical to, the realm.[63] Lordship was not a simple exercise in private domination, but a private and public agency for the satisfaction of shared interests, in which, as has been suggested, a small number of individuals

---

[59] Payling 1991: p. 105. Note that some studies of local politics have focused on magnates and their affinities, rather than counties (e.g. Rawcliffe 1978; Woodger 1974). This would tend to encourage an emphasis on lordship, though cf. Walker 1990.

[60] E.g. Payling 1991: chs. 1–2 (Nottinghamshire: and see p. 219 for the connection between 'independent gentry' and 'royal affinity'); Wright 1983: pp. 12–14, 60–6 (Derbyshire); Bennett 1983: ch. 2 (Cheshire and Lancashire). Cf. Pollard 1979, which deals with a community of substantial gentry in an area dominated by royal lands which was nonetheless under the lordship of the Nevilles of Middleham (Richmondshire). A similar situation obtained in the central West Riding, where the Percies ruled: Arnold 1984: pp. 113–14, 374; Pollard 1979: p. 52.

[61] Walker 1990: chs. 5.3 and 6.2.

[62] Cherry 1979: especially pp. 75–6; Carpenter 1992: chs. 2 and 9; 1980: pp. 514–15. For other examples of areas dominated by magnate lordship in this period, see Rowney 1983 (Staffordshire); Pollard 1990: chs. 4–6 (the North-East); 1968: p. 227ff (Shropshire).

[63] It is interesting to reflect that while few would now deduce the existence of a long-term 'constitutional' conflict over the role of (say) the royal household from the well-known series of clashes and crises on this issue which marked the politics of the thirteenth, fourteenth and fifteenth centuries, there is still a readiness to assume that the expression of grievances about the practices of lordship – maintenance, retaining and so on – reflects a fundamental opposition, notably on the part of men putatively 'outside the embrace of bastard feudalism' (e.g. Saul 1981: pp. 102–3, 165–6; Walker 1990: pp. 255–6). But are these sets of responses not analogous and, if they are, does this not mean that protests against the practices of lordship should be read as protests against a malfunctioning institution and not against the institution itself? See Carpenter 1983b for an interpretation of commons petitions against magnate abuses which does not rest on the promotion of these criticisms by 'independent gentry'.

acted for a larger number.[64] It did not demand the 'subservience' of the gentry to the nobility, merely a degree of deference proportionate to its satisfaction of gentry interests.[65] Moreover, once it is accepted that it was the more complex results of good lordship – protection, or advancement, or even harmony – which were most important to the gentry, it seems unwise for historians to focus too closely on the documentation of fees and indentures for evidence of its workings: these documents may indicate connections, but their absence indicates nothing; it may have been the most nebulous associations which were the most important.[66] Nor did 'vertical' relationships in local society necessarily clash with 'horizontal' ones: connections of gentry, even local communities, could co-exist with the presidency of a lord, affirming and extending his influence even as they expressed their own.[67]

It is certainly important to stress that lordly power had to be negotiated and that where lords had minimal landholdings their position was weaker – sometimes to the point where alternative means of representation and organisation would have to be devised – but it is equally important to realise that the existence of a spectrum of potential did not necessarily undermine the claim of lordship, as a system, on the imagination of most of the gentry.[68] It is striking that whenever effective lordship became available, the gentry made use of it.[69] If noble power was unavailing, they

[64] See e.g. McFarlane 1981c; Harriss 1981: pp. xvii–xviii; Carpenter 1980: esp. p. 525; above, pp. 65–74.

[65] Cf. the implication of Payling 1991: pp. 105, 107. Note the comments of Carpenter 1992: p. 618 and n. 7 and of Horrox 1992: pp. 394–5.

[66] See e.g. Pollard 1990: pp. 121–3, 129; Walker 1990: p. 124 (though cf. p. 254); Saul 1981: pp. 73–5, 90–1, 100; Hicks 1991c: pp. 32–3; Carpenter 1992: pp. 284–7 and *passim*. Bean 1958: pp. 95–7 shows that it was not Northumberland's retainers and annuitants that turned out to help him in 1453, but his officers and other well-willers. All this must cast doubt on recent attempts to assess the prevalence of lordship by counting retainers and feed men (e.g. Saul 1981: pp. 97ff; Payling 1991: pp. 106–7, with reservations; Walker 1990: p. 254). Walker 1990: pp. 248–9 makes an interesting distinction between the sort of affinity which was an effective agency of local lordship and the sort of affinity possessed by Gaunt which existed for other purposes than local rule and was characterised by large numbers of indentured retainers and other feed men.

[67] Carpenter 1992: ch. 9; Pollard 1979; Hicks 1991c: p. 24.

[68] Walker 1990: pp. 141, 229, 233 seems to acknowledge the resort to lordship as a normal reflex among the gentry. See also Carpenter 1992: pp. 287–8 (and *passim*); Hicks 1991c: pp. 24–5.

[69] Carpenter 1992: p. 288. A number of examples will help to prove this point. The Lancastrian affinity was the greatest single power in Staffordshire under Henry IV at least partly because of minorities among the principal magnate houses (Stafford, Audley – Powell 1989: pp. 208–9 and n. 88). The power of this virtually unsupervised affinity was vigorously resisted by the non-Lancastrian gentry, headed by the families of Mynors and Erdswick, leading to several years of feuding and disorder. Henry V imposed a direct royal lordship over the county by drawing the leading disputants into his service, but it is interesting to note that the Erdswick following, which was broadly victorious in the disputes of *c.* 1410–15, went into the affinity of Humphrey, earl of Stafford, when he came of age in 1423 (*ibid.*, pp. 214–16). Stafford was later able to annexe much of the

found leaders among themselves, or looked in desperation to the king.[70] It
was natural for medieval men and women to expect their affairs to be
governed by superiors, even if the essence of this government was the
representation of their own interests and its means were provided by
themselves.[71] If the power of individual lords was often temporary and
vulnerable, resort to lordship continued to be a natural response, rather as
kingship remained the natural system of national rule despite the fact that,
in the period c.1370–1500, successful lordship from the crown was also
temporary and often vulnerable.[72]

Where noble lordship was at its thinnest, it was often because the
crown was the major landowner.[73] The extent of royal landholding
progressed by leaps and bounds during the middle ages, and this
expansion played an important part in the development of more direct
and interventionist forms of local government by the Yorkist and early
Tudor kings.[74] This development seems to have encouraged the view that
the way forward for medieval rulers was to attempt to exercise local
authority themselves, notably through the agency of a royal affinity of
knights and esquires, ideally drawn from areas where the crown had a
landed presence, but typically maintained through membership of the

---

Ferrers of Chartley following, which had opposed Erdswick, and by the 1440s, his own
affinity dominated the county (Rowney 1983: pp. 49–51 and *passim*). In the case of
Derbyshire, meanwhile, the death of Richard Beauchamp freed Humphrey Stafford's
hands and he rapidly obtained the exercise of lordship in the county, pulling in the
affinities of the only indigenous lord of any significance, Grey of Codnor, and the leading
gentleman, Sir Richard Vernon: Wright 1983: pp. 68–9. Note that Stafford lordship
began to collapse in the later 1440s as Buckingham found himself resisted in Warwickshire: competition amongst peers destroyed the charms of lordship (for details, see *ibid.*,
pp. 69ff). Finally, in Nottinghamshire, home of 'a wealthy, independent gentry establishment', Ralph, Lord Cromwell seems to have exercised an increasingly dominant lordship
from the early 1430s to his death in 1456 (Payling 1991: pp. 10, 92, 96–8, 102–5, 140ff,
166–7, 195–8, 207ff).

[70] In Nottinghamshire, it appears that royal lordship required a local intermediary for
effective operation: until 1406, this was Sir Thomas Rempston, replaced by William
Rigmayden after his death (Payling 1991: pp. 121–4, 130–5). These two certainly owed
their position to the patronage of the crown, but the fact that it was channelled through
them suggests that local lordship was favoured by those in authority as a medium of
social order. Meanwhile, in Derbyshire, there are grounds for seeing Sir Richard Vernon
as something of a lord over other gentlemen in the 1430s: Wright 1983: pp. 66–8.

[71] See above, ch. 2, generally. Note that even 'peerage' theories of the origins of authority
envisaged its exercise by a lord: Whitaker (ed.), *Mirror of Justices*, p. 6; *Governance*, p.
112.

[72] See esp. Gillingham 1987 for the persisting strength of kingship.

[73] E.g. Hicks 1991c: p. 25. This was true of many of the areas in n. 60, above. Staffordshire,
Derbyshire and West Yorkshire contained large tracts of land belonging to the duchy of
Lancaster (Rowney 1981: pp. 50–1; Wright 1983: pp. 12, 83–5; Arnold 1984: pp. 16–
21). Other major tracts of royal land included Cornwall, Cheshire, Lancashire, Pembro-
keshire and the lordship of Richmond: as a rule, therefore, lordship exercised in these
areas was operating by the licence of the crown.

[74] Goodman 1988: p. 53. See Carpenter 1992: pp. 633–5 for a discussion of the relative
importance of this factor.

household or tenure of royal and local offices.[75] However, few later medieval kings seem to have shared this perception. Although they were often prepared to exercise a degree of direct rule in the counties where they were the principal lords, they hardly seem to have relished the task,[76] and only Richard II made real efforts to extend this sort of authority to other areas, with disastrous consequences for himself and his realm.[77]

Evidently, there were differences between the form taken by royal lordship when its constituency was local and populated by the gentry, rather than national and populated chiefly by the nobility, but there is no sense in which the direct rule of the crown in the areas where it held the most land was a blueprint for its normal role in the government of the localities.[78] This, even so, is what the concept of a 'royal affinity' seems to imply. The problem here is perhaps terminological: told, as a general principle, that the affinity is 'the most important political grouping in medieval society', and that we are about to explore 'the extent, structure and *raison d'être* of the greatest of all these affinities, that of the king', we might expect to encounter something claiming to be the chief organ of national rule.[79] In fact, except during the atypical reigns of Richard II and Henry IV, the 'royal affinity' was something very much less. The crown did not normally need a private army to govern its kingdom, but it did require servants for the exercise of a wide range of functions, most of them mundane and uncontroversial.[80] These servants, though they may have felt a special loyalty to the king, were not continuously discrete from the more immediate structures of authority in the shires.[81]

---

[75] See e.g. Starkey 1981: pp. 269ff; Guy 1988: p. 165; Barron 1985; 1990: p. 145; Given-Wilson 1987b.

[76] By the latter part of Henry IV's reign, for example, many of the counties where he was the major landowner were in a state of considerable disorder: Payling 1991: pp. 130–2, 135, 189–93 (Notts. and Derbs); Powell 1989: pp. 208–16, 224–8 (Staffs. and Notts.).

[77] Given-Wilson 1986: p. 266. Similar claims have been made for Henry VI (e.g. Jeffs 1960: pp. 148–9, 153, 218–20, 256), but Rosemary Horrox is surely right to suggest that the expansion of the household in this period was not a matter of royal policy (1989: p. 228). See below, pp. 172–6, 218–21.

[78] It is extremely unlikely that the king would have been able to exercise direct power where alternative, and more immediate, sources of lordship existed. For a particularly dramatic example of susceptibility to local rule, note the case of Sir William Clifford, who was made king's knight in 1399, but continued to dabble with the king's principal enemies, the Percies, who were far and away the greatest source of local lordship, until 1408. Henry IV knew of this and, each time, forgave him (Given-Wilson 1986: p. 229; Ross 1951: pp. 278–9).

[79] Quotations from Given-Wilson 1986: p. 203. The significant differences between these two forms of 'affinity' are not made clear. See also Pugh 1972: p. 108 ('After 1399, the crown was the centre of bastard feudalism because the king's own affinity was far greater and stronger than that of any other subject'); Payling 1991: pp. 219–20.

[80] These functions, mostly related to court display and the minutiae of an embryonic civil service, are detailed in Given-Wilson 1986: pp. 210–12, 219–21, 226, 246–54.

[81] Horrox 1989: introduction and ch. 5, especially pp. 16–22, 268–9.

These issues are relevant in the assessment of the 'Lancastrian' affinity, which was the core of the 'royal' affinity in the early fifteenth century.[82] From 1399, there was, in the areas dominated by the lands of the duchy of Lancaster, a reservoir of particular loyalty to the king as duke, which it was open to him to exploit in return for the provision of the normal services of direct lordship. Even so, as has been said, what made this lordship possible (and, indeed, necessary) was the concentration of land in royal hands in these areas. It is not clear what part this apparently anomalous following was intended to play in the wider government of the realm once the Lancastrian crown was fully established, but it is difficult to believe that the special authority which kings enjoyed in duchy areas would have been acceptable anywhere else.[83] The decline of the Lancastrian affinity during Henry VI's reign may not have been a matter of more than local significance.[84] It may even have been a natural process, as the coup of 1399 receded and the Lancastrians came to possess the immemorial authority of kings of England. In any event, that Henry came to need a retinue to defend him at the end of his reign is testimony only to the destructive nature of his kingship: it has nothing whatsoever to do with his abandonment of the following which had brought his grandfather to power.[85]

Normally then (and bearing in mind the representative implications of the term), the rule of the localities was in the hands of the nobility; with the result that it was they who formed the principal constituency and agency of the crown's overall jurisdiction. This had significant implications for the working of this jurisdiction, and notably for the formal institutions at its disposal: the common law, its courts and its personnel; the local administration of sheriff, escheator, coroner and so on.[86] It was essential that those who worked these institutions – especially the sheriffs,

---

[82] Lancastrian support had been important in military and administrative service to the crown in the 1390s: Goodman 1986: p. 85.

[83] See the comments in Horrox 1989: p. 269. These issues receive a full-length treatment in Castor 1993.

[84] It seems that it was during Henry VI's majority that the decline of the affinity was most marked: Carpenter 1992: ch. 12; Pugh 1972: p. 108; Payling 1991: pp. 142ff. The process is shown partly by the decline in connections between local gentry and the royal household (e.g. in Staffordshire and the West Riding: Rowney 1983: pp. 61–2; Arnold 1984: pp. 41, 113, 116, 122). Another important indicator is the transfer of the major duchy offices to the hands of nearby members of the territorial nobility and their followers. For full details, see below, pp. 172–4.

[85] Cf. Jeffs 1960: p. 256 – 'the disintegration of a retinue had been one of the causes of a dynasty's fall'. Note that Queen Margaret's affinity, built up in the mid- to late 1450s, was partly based on duchy lands in the Midlands, but this was chiefly because they were in her hands and those of her chief supporters than because of any lasting 'Lancastrian' interest: see below, pp. 337–40.

[86] For analyses of appointments to office-holding, see e.g. Carpenter 1992: ch. 8; Saul 1981: ch. 4.

juries and justices of the peace – reflected the local balance of power.[87] Only thus could they exercise governmental force without provoking violence or open disobedience.[88] Authority, as we have seen, rested principally on the 'drede' which local lords inspired.[89] So it was that the 'infiltration' of crown offices by the nobility and their gentry supporters and associates, long regarded as an instance of corruption typical of the later middle ages, was fundamental to the operation of royal justice in both practice and theory.[90]

Even so, the process required a degree of regulation. To represent the common interest, it was not sufficient simply to hand over the public agencies of justice to the most powerful magnate in the locality. Few counties were entirely represented by one lord, so that there were always other interests to be considered; interests which were characteristically looked after by other lords.[91] While local societies did possess their own means of reconciling competing lordships, some of these, such as outright war, could involve unacceptable levels of disorder or violence; while others, such as arbitration, were not always effective without external pressure.[92] The inability of local societies perpetually to regulate themselves meant that royal intervention, beyond the provision of a framework of laws and courts, was often necessary. This intervention took a number of forms, which may be gathered under two heads: 'prescriptive' (or patronal) and 'restorative' (or judicial).

Prescriptive measures included taking care in the making of local appointments to strike a balance between the representation of majority and minority interests: the effectiveness of a commission of the peace, for example, would depend in part on its capacity to satisfy the leading local interest group, but it would also depend on retaining the respect and obedience of the county as a whole by taking account of other groups and interests.[93] Another way in which the crown could intervene

---

[87] Jurors were not, of course, officers of the crown in any strict sense, but they were a fundamental agency of justice and, as such, did the crown's work at a local level. See Powell 1989: ch. 3; and Chrimes 1972: pp. 155, 187 for Henry VII's efforts to control their behaviour.

[88] See e.g. Clanchy 1974; Carpenter 1992: p. 349.   [89] Above, p. 70.

[90] Contrast, for example, Virgoe 1981 (especially p. 73) with Plummer's 1885 introduction to the *Governance*, pp. 19–24.

[91] See e.g. Carpenter 1980 and 1992: ch. 10 for the diverse sources of lordship in Warwickshire. As Richard Beauchamp's power advanced, other interest-groups did not so much disappear as become subsidiary to his own.

[92] For examples of ineffective arbitration, see Maddern 1992: pp. 16, 194ff; Payling 1991: pp. 192–4 (eventually resolved following royal intervention). See Powell 1989: p. 100 for comment.

[93] The commission of the peace in Bedfordshire in the 1430s, for example, where Lord Grey of Ruthin was the leading landowner, was dominated by his followers, but it – and, more particularly, local juries – also included two or three of those of Lord Fanhope, his leading rival: Maddern 1992: pp. 208, 214–15, 217 and note *CPR, 1436–41*, p. 578, for

prescriptively was by granting rights, fees, custodies and offices which could alter the pattern of lordship so as to encourage harmony.[94] This was perhaps the most important role for royal 'patronage' in the later medieval polity: not as a means of reward, still less a means of purchasing loyalty, but rather as a device for modifying the natural pattern of lordship to suit the vagaries of the common interest. As has been said, this device was under the king's control, but was exercised as part of a dialogue with the nobility and other local leaders.[95]

The forms of restorative intervention open to the crown are much more familiar. The king could resolve disputes informally by dealing directly with the participants or by summoning them before his council, where they would receive a form of arbitrative justice by advice of their peers.[96] He could attempt to resolve them more formally by an array of judicial commissions ranging in importance from the regular visitations of justices of gaol delivery and assize, to extraordinary commissions of oyer and terminer or inquiry and, if necessary, peregrinations of the king's bench.[97] Whether these commissions were obtained by the plaintiff or despatched on royal initiative (and the difference may be less than is sometimes imagined), their make-up was a matter of considerable importance. Apart from assize and gaol delivery,[98] they were generally a demonstration that the normal structure of local lordship and justice had failed in its duty to protect the common weal of the shire: interests which were too powerful to be overlooked had not received the representation they merited; peace had broken down as a result.[99] The aim of judicial commissions was thus to intrude, to upset, and so to redress, the local equilibrium, partly by offering a voice to the disenfranchised,[100] but above all by asserting the king's supreme authority, which was in fact the authority of everyone else,

the addition of another man of his, William Pekke, just before the affray between the two lords at Silsoe.

[94] This policy was particularly evident in areas where the crown was a major landowner: see e.g. Carpenter 1992: pp. 366–9 (Midlands); Griffiths 1991c (Wales); Morgan 1973 and Ross 1974: ch. 4 (various parts of England under Edward IV). Even so, note, for example, the grants of the custody of Nottingham Castle and Sherwood Forest to successive leaders of Nottinghamshire society under the Lancastrians (Payling 1991: pp. 91, 97, 121). See below, pp. 172–3, for the pursuit of these ends with respect to the duchy of Lancaster offices under Henry VI.

[95] See above, pp. 78–9, 85.

[96] A brief introduction to conciliar justice appears in Leadam and Baldwin (eds.), *Cases before the King's Council.*

[97] See Powell 1989: pp. 62–4 for an introduction.

[98] These commissions were regularly issued and became closely associated with the commissions of the peace: Powell 1989: pp. 56–9, 89.

[99] Avrutick 1967: pp. 13, 332; Powell 1989: ch. 7. See Wright 1983: pp. 127–36; Payling 1991: pp. 190–200 for oyer and terminer commissions in practice.

[100] Juries were often more willing to indict members of the local elite before visiting commissions: see e.g. Payling 1991: pp. 189–90, 193. For royal justice as a disruptive, but also productive, force, see Powell 1989: pp. 87–91 and Carpenter 1992: pp. 235–6.

underdogs and neutrals.[101] They were therefore often dominated by men outside the normal structures of power and, as a result, needed the 'drede' inspired by the personal backing of the king to be effective.[102]

The crown's right to intervene directly, which was also its duty, was based, then, on the failure of local lordship to protect the local common weal: this could be because of a conflict of lords in a broader locality which ran across county boundaries, or it could be because the body claiming lordship within a particular county was incompetent to exercise that lordship.[103] In either case, violence or disruption was the inevitable result. This violence could ultimately be contained because a superior authority existed to judge the lord: this authority was the king, and this was the essence of his role in the locality. He was to reconcile the exercise of lordship with the defence of the common weal – in practice, harmony[104] – whenever they patently diverged. His normal posture was thus responsive, rather than initiatory. This was always the case, whether he was employing the prescriptive means of appointment to office and other items of patronage, or the restorative ones of judgement and arbitration. In the fulfilment of the latter function, a temporary resumption of delegated lordship was permitted. This was already implicit in the visitation of royal justices, or the summoning of miscreants to Westminster, which involved the direct application of royal rule. It could also emerge in practice in the – often temporary – appointment of men from

---

[101] This is neatly demonstrated by the comment of William Pekke, one of Lord Fanhope's supporters, who sat in a commission of enquiry which Fanhope had acquired as a means of redressing the local balance of power in his favour (see n. 93, above). In response to an allegation that he had advised Fanhope to hold the sessions in the town of Silsoe in order to undermine the rule of Lord Grey, he observed that 'it was the K's matier and noon other and for him it was sette there' (*PPC*, V, p. 36, and see pp. 35–41, generally). See above, pp. 59–60, for the nature of the king's authority.

[102] In the above example, it proved to be too dangerous to proceed: no sessions were held 'consideryng the perill that was lyke for to have fallen'. However, the fact that royal justice had been effectively countered was no small matter: the council launched an enquiry into what had happened.

[103] Cross-boundary disputes tended to require royal intervention because, while local judicial agencies were organised on a county basis, magnate networks were not (e.g. Harriss 1981: p. xv). This meant that lords who were quite powerful in one area could be denied access to power in a neighbouring one. Lady Bergavenny, for example, a major landowner in Leicestershire, was quite unable to obtain justice in Warwickshire during the rule of Richard Beauchamp, even though she had interests and supporters in the county. She managed to enlist the aid of the crown in 1427: Carpenter 1980: pp. 527ff. The more common problem of a disjuncture between the established lordship in a county and growing interests which it refused to accommodate was a feature of the disturbances in Bedfordshire, discussed above (see nn. 93, 101). Other examples from Henry VI's reign, prompting royal intervention of one kind or another, are the dispute between Ormond and Tiptoft in Cambridgeshire (Virgoe 1973) and, most famously, the Courtenay–Bonville dispute for the rule of Devonshire (see Cherry 1979 and 1981a, and below, pp. 204, 239–40).

[104] Above, pp. 19, 24, 56–7.

the king's household to judicial commissions, including that of the peace, and to the shrievalty.[105] Such measures might be less for the exercise of direct control than for the interpolation of neutrals, though there is a sense in which this came to the same thing. This illustrates another important point about royal intervention: it had to be manifestly independent. Obviously, it depended on the prompting of petitions and other forms of counsel which were likely to be partisan, but if it was to preserve the respect of all parties, it had to be exercised free from the interference of the local – and malfunctioning – power structure.[106]

What local rule depended on, therefore, was a combination of resolution and reconciliation: justice and mercy, in other words, just like national rule. If this could be achieved in the locality itself, so much the better. If not, then – and only then – the king was expected to provide it.[107] Certainly the king was to bear in mind the need to preserve the common weal in his intervention, but this was the point at which the task of representation meant more than the satisfaction of demands from lesser representatives: the action of independent will was required. It could be guided by prudence and assisted by the counsel of the parties, but its absolute independence was essential. It was for this reason that the personal will of the king was ultimately necessary for the operation of local as well as national government. For mediation and arbitration to be successful, they had to be 'an assertion of the king's authority, not an admission of weakness'.[108] This authority arose not from force – which accrued to anyone possessing lordship naturally, provided that he had the most minimal resources of personality – but on the convincing freedom of the king's judgement, so that the outcome of an invocation of actual royal justice was final, binding and, in the last resort, dependent on the king's grace.

It is thus clear that the local government of the realm, which was integral to the preservation of the common weal, did indeed rely on the free access of lords, as representatives, to the person of the king. Royal intervention in local government, both prescriptive and judicial, was to a large extent personal, therefore, and its forum was the court. As we shall see, it was not possible for a council to discharge the king's functions in

---

[105] The addition of the courtiers Suffolk and Sir Henry Brounflete to the Bedfordshire bench in the tense year of 1437 would seem to be an attempt to restore some neutrality to its composition: *CPR, 1436–41*, p. 578. Similar motives were behind the composition of the household-dominated oyer and terminer commission to Nottinghamshire in 1414 (Powell 1989: p. 225; Payling 1991: p. 193). The appointment of household sheriffs need not be seen as an assertion of co-ordinated royal power (see above, n. 77).

[106] Evidently, all the parties concerned sought to influence the personnel and activities of royal commissions (see *PL*, II, pp. 162, 166–7, 168, 182, for examples), but unless they were recognised to be reasonably independent, they were unable to operate effectively.

[107] See also Powell 1989: pp. 240–1.   [108] *Ibid.*, p. 230 (and ch. 9 generally).

this area, except when there was no choice, and then rather inade-quately.[109] A council could give disputants a chance to air their grievances in public and this may have encouraged them to desist from violence (at least in the short term), but it could not provide for the private expression of their concerns; it could not issue binding judge-ments unless backed by the crown; and it had no final means of healing its own divisions. These factors made the settlement of all disputes difficult. So it was that in practice, as well as in theory, the governance of England was carried out via a sophisticated system of representation, achieved through the informal mediation of the nobility, as counsellors of the realm and rulers of the shires, but ultimately dependent on the existence of a right and independent will in the king. No effective alternatives existed. If it was possible, in circumstances of necessity, for the nobility to take up a corporate rule themselves, then it was only the presence of necessity which made it so. Conciliar rule was a poor imitation of normal royal authority: it could not effectively reconcile the disparate elements of royal representativeness, and so stimulate the loyalty which made the king's public authority so irresistible. No king, or other lord, ruled his followers without their counsel, in the manifold senses of the word, but he, not his counsellors, was the locus of their government.

[109] This is not to say that a council of the kind described above, p. 84, could not *assist* the king in the task of judgement, by advising on matters of law and precedent, despatching matters of limited political importance, and so on: see e.g. Brown 1989: pp. 37–8.

4

FEATURES OF HENRY VI'S POLITY

I N THE PRECEDING chapters, we have been concerned with some of the general conditions of later medieval monarchy, the ideological and institutional frameworks which influenced the language, and perhaps the behaviour, of the king and other leading politicians. For much of what follows, we shall be looking at the ways in which these conditions affected the politics of Henry VI's reign; but as we make our descent from the general to the specific, there are other circumstantial factors to be considered. K. B. McFarlane once observed that the character of politics in the forty years after Henry V's death was largely governed by the fact that the crown descended 'upon the head of a baby who grew up an imbecile'.[1] Not everyone would agree that this is a sufficient explanation for the disturbances of the period, or even a fair assessment of Henry VI's abilities, but it is clear that both the king's personality and his long minority must have played some part in shaping the rule of England during his lifetime. In order to gain a realistic sense of what part this was, we need to explore these factors in relation to the scheme of common values and practices we have so far been investigating: we need to know how a group of men who believed in a representative but independent monarchy, and were familiar with its modes of operation, might respond to the challenge of an infant king, or indeed an idiot one. First of all, however, it will be necessary to tackle a difficulty which has arisen since McFarlane wrote. While no one can deny that Henry VI was a baby when he became king, historians have come to doubt that, in his adolescence and adulthood, he was as 'inane' as traditional accounts proposed.[2] Clearly enough, we have to know what kind of a king we are dealing with if we are to assess his political impact. We must therefore begin by taking a look at the debate over Henry VI's personality.

---

[1] McFarlane 1981c: p. 42.
[2] This was McFarlane's neat description of Henry's capacities: 1981f: p. 240.

THE PROBLEM OF THE KING'S PERSONALITY

Until 1981, there was a fair degree of scholarly consensus on the character of Henry VI. If some writers depicted a saint and others a weakling, it is clear that they had more or less the same array of personal qualities in mind: as J. W. McKenna has pointed out, in political terms, there is little to choose between the fool evoked by Henry's detractors and the monk evoked by his friends; J. R. Lander's epithet, 'saintly muff', seems to capture this fusion perfectly.[3] The comments of Henry VI's contemporaries appeared to provide a firm basis for views of this kind: chroniclers wrote of 'simplicity', pliability, even idiocy; subjects called the king 'a sheep', 'a natural fool', a 'lunatic' and commented on his childlike appearance for years into his adulthood.[4] Even Henry's admiring biographer, John Blacman, did not attempt to hide the king's disengagement from the world of politics: as Roger Lovatt has shown, he composed, from close quarters, a portrait of Henry as *imitator Christi* which presented his public inadequacies as signs of a deep personal devotion.[5] A decade or so ago, however, the authors of the two most recent histories of the reign, B. P. Wolffe and R. A. Griffiths, raised doubts about the value of contemporary evidence, arguing that much of it was distorted by the political demands of the Wars of the Roses.[6] To separate the man from the myth, Wolffe argued, historians would have to study the king 'through

---

[3] McKenna 1974: esp. pp. 78–9; Lander 1969: p. 68. Contemporaries hinted at this: note esp. the comments of Whethamstede ('in verbis Rex mitis, Rex pietatis, / Attamen in factis nimiae, vir simplicitatis': *Registrum Whethamstede*, I, pp. 414–15) and Rous ('Deo et beate virgini Mariae devotissimus, sed mundo et mundanis operibus minime deditus': Rous, *Historia Regum Angliae*, p. 210).

[4] See, for contemporary views in general, Wolffe 1981: ch. 1; Storey 1966: pp. 32–5 (esp. for the comments of subjects); Griffiths 1981: introduction and pp. 240–2, 248–54. For a sense of the views of contemporary chroniclers, many of whom had met the king or knew people who had, see *English Chron.*, p. 79; *Chrons. of London*, p. 184; *Collections*, pp. 208, 209; de Waurin, *Croniques*, IV, p. 350; Ellis, (ed.), *Chronicle of John Hardyng*, p. 396. Even in 1450, it was possible for an apparently disinterested eye-witness to describe the twenty-nine-year-old king as 'very young and inexperienced' (Griffiths 1981: p. 254).

[5] Lovatt 1981, esp. p. 435 (and see also Lovatt 1984: especially p. 182). For a typical example of the content of this work, note the protest allegedly made by Henry to Blacman at Eltham Palace when 'a certain mighty duke' disturbed his studies: 'they do so interrupt me that by day or night I can hardly snatch a moment to be refreshed by reading of any holy teaching without disturbance': James, *Blacman*, p. 38. Another enlightening biography written by a contemporary is the brief account in John Capgrave's *Liber de Illustribus Henricis*, discussed by Wolffe 1981: pp. 15–16.

[6] Wolffe 1981: ch. 1; Griffiths 1981: pp. 2–6, 241–2. This does not lead Griffiths to discard this evidence, however: he notes the impressive sources at Blacman's disposal (pp. 3–4), for example, and subsequently uses 'a revealing episode' or two from his memoir (pp. 249–50). See Lovatt 1984: pp. 176–7 for the useful point that material written after 1461, even for political purposes, cannot be dismissed out of hand.

his actions, through what was done in his name and the consequences thereof.[7]

But the study of Henry's actions is not a straightforward matter. Certainly, there are a number of eye-witness accounts of the king's activities; and most of them, in fact, convey a similar picture to that of the chronicles.[8] To Piero da Monte, for example, the fifteen-year-old king spoke wisely and well, but had a mild, rather saturnine air.[9] Eight years later, in 1445, a visiting French embassy found Henry behaving less gravely but scarcely more impressively: during the sessions he attended, the king seems to have done little more than stand about in a variety of opulent costumes, grinning broadly and crying 'Saint Jehan, grant mercis!' when Charles VII's name was mentioned.[10] In his *Loci e Libro Veritatum*, Thomas Gascoigne records how the fully grown Henry turned to him one day and asked him why he was not a bishop.[11] Finally, the report of a royal visit late in the reign to Westminster Abbey shows the king to be almost speechless and barely conscious of those around him.[12] Although Wolffe and Griffiths tend to suggest otherwise, there seems to be little sign in these accounts that Henry VI possessed much political sense or personal force;[13] but perhaps we should not place too much reliance on them in any case, since few observers recorded their impressions disinterestedly, and it was rare indeed to encounter the king in

---

[7] Wolffe 1981: p. 21. Note that Wolffe seems to have missed McKenna's point about the basic homogeneity of contemporary comment: he writes as if the critical views of Henry's subjects cancel out the approving ones of Blacman, leaving us with nothing.

[8] Blacman's Life is also full of what appear to be eye-witness accounts, of course: see Lovatt 1984: pp. 176, 184–9.

[9] He talks of 'an old man's sense, prudence and gravity', of a man 'mild gentle and calm ... less like a king or secular prince than a monk': Schofield 1973: pp. 93–4. Piero's view that Henry answered visitors 'wisely' may be a response to the brevity of his responses: consider Blacman's comment that Henry 'used very brief speech' (James, *Blacman*, p. 37) and the view of the *Secreta Secretorum* that kings should say little (*Secreta*, p. 139).

[10] *Letters and Papers*, I, pp. 110, 123, 146.   [11] *Loci e Libro*, pp. 176–7.

[12] Stanley, *Historical Memorials of Westminster Abbey*, pp. 600–8. The counsellors proposed a number of suitable places for the king's tomb, but most of the time Henry 'gave them noone answere' (pp. 600–1, the fullest of several accounts of the episode).

[13] For example, the report of the French ambassadors is used to show how vigorous Henry was capable of being (Griffiths 1981: pp. 252, 491; Wolffe 1981: p. 185), but it is plain that the diplomatic exchanges were stage-managed by his ministers, whilst the king's rather *gauche* interventions, whether unreflecting or contrived for diplomatic purposes, can hardly be used as evidence of political intelligence or prowess. Suffolk's dominance in the proceedings is obvious (see *Letters and Papers*, I, pp. 96, 102, 105, 106, 112, 114, 115, 121–3 etc. for examples) and the fact that when the ambassadors attempted to leave, the king said, '"No" and detained them, and he appeared to be much pleased to see them, but he did not speak otherwise to them' (p. 124) cannot have inspired much confidence in his capacities. Henry's beaming smiles might have appeared rather peculiar: see e.g. *Secreta*, p. 141, on the importance of behaving demurely and not laughing too much.

private.[14] Clearly enough, the king's public behaviour is unlikely to have been the simple product of his private self.

This, of course, is the heart of the problem, and the issue becomes even more acute when administrative and political records are used to throw light on the king's personality. Among the reasons why Wolffe and Griffiths were moved to question the traditional portrait of the king was presumably the fact that there is such copious evidence of his activity in government.[15] In the Public Record Office lie mounds of documents, many of them bearing the royal signature, all of them claiming to be issued (one way or another) at the royal will. In addition to these, there are other sources – letters, manifestoes, even narratives – which declare that the king himself was the author of particular policies or acts of government. This material presents rather a different picture from the *fainéant* king depicted in the chronicles and it is difficult not to be swayed by it, particularly as it has traditionally been believed that there were some areas of royal policy – such as the foundation of the colleges at Cambridge and Eton – which did reflect the king's personal interests.[16] Victorian scholars, working largely from chronicles and making familiar assumptions about the division of private and public business, typically assigned responsibility for the foundations to the king and responsibility for other matters to his ministers.[17] Modern historians, working from a wider range of evidence and recognising the control a king might wield over all areas of policy, have generally been more consistent. McFarlane apart, they have portrayed a much more

[14] Piero, for example, was at pains both to impress his English hosts and to assure the pope that his embassy was making progress (Griffiths 1981: p. 235). Meanwhile, Gascoigne, who probably thought he ought to be a bishop, might have invented his exchange with the king (though see Wolffe 1981: p. 108 for a famous case in which the king's control of episcopal appointment seems very tenuous indeed).

[15] This seems to be implicit in their treatments: see especially Wolffe 1972: pp. 30–1, 35 and, in fact, generally.

[16] The royal foundations are discussed at length below, pp. 167–71, but see the note which follows.

[17] Stubbs, for example, took Henry to have been personally responsible for the foundation of the colleges, but traced the peace policy to the influence of Beaufort, Suffolk and the court, and the cession of Maine to Suffolk alone (1875–8: III, pp. 129, 131–3, 140–1). He blamed Somerset for the executions following Cade's rebellion (*ibid.*, p. 130 n. 1). Ramsay followed a similar path, making Henry responsible for the colleges (1892: II, p. 49) and saying 'that Henry himself wished for peace, we may be sure', but accusing Suffolk of surrendering Anjou and Maine in 1444 (pp. 25, 62). All these things were recorded as having been done on royal authority (below, pp. 169, 225, 290), but the chronicles typically ascribed much of the impetus behind foreign policy to Henry's advisers. The king's decision not to marry the daughter of the count of Armagnac in 1442, for example, is often put down to the earl of Suffolk (*Chrons. of London*, p. 155; Leland, *De Rebus*, p. 493; *Brut*, p. 509). As for the cession of Maine, the 'Great Chronicle of London' has it being agreed by the king and 'the more part of his counsayll' after the 1445 marriage (*Great Chron.*, pp. 176–7), while Gascoigne traces it to pressure from the queen, acting 'per instanciam ... ducis Suthfolchiae' (*Loci e Libro*, p. 221).

active king.[18] In the most recent works, the king has become a significant promoter of the policy of peace with France and, in Wolffe's account, if not also in Griffiths', he is the conscious (if ineffective) director of domestic affairs.[19] Far from being a cypher, then, Henry emerges as 'capable of taking a sustained, positive, sometimes intelligent and constructive, interest in affairs, provided they were to his liking': indeed, to Wolffe, the king's 'perverse wilfulness' lay behind every action of his government.[20]

What these deductions may overlook is that, as the preceding chapters have argued, the king was not simply a man, a private person; but the fundamental agency of public government, a person both private and public. His publicly declared will was not his private property alone, but also the public property of the realm: the king spoke for others as well as himself.[21] This means that, while Henry's acts of government can (as Wolffe proposed), tell us a great deal about his kingship and its results, they cannot necessarily tell us much about his private beliefs and interests. The institutional and conceptual conditions of kingship conspired to make Henry VI formally responsible for everything done in his name, and it is often the case that all we may legitimately deduce from the evidence of his public initiatives is the existence of these conditions: we cannot know whether the stuff of policy comes from without or within.

One way of illustrating this is to look again at the view that the king was a major source of inspiration for the peace policy. The case seems to rest on two main foundations: the existence of a series of declarations, mostly made in the king's name, that the inspiration behind the policy was his alone; and the fact that the king's words in speeches and letters appear to reveal a profound inner conviction. As far as the declarations are concerned, the fact that they were issued in response to actual or anticipated criticism means that we cannot be sure that they are true. Indeed, when it is considered that policy was conventionally assumed to be authorised by the king, the decision of the government to emphasise his involvement – and to deny that decisions had been made out 'of symplesse, ne of self wille' – invites the suspicion that the real situation

[18] McFarlane put the peace policy down to Suffolk and the cession of Maine to the queen: 1936: pp. 399–403. See also 1981f: p. 240 and 1973: pp. 284, respectively, for his famous comments about Henry's 'inanity' and the 'forty years of virtual minority' during his reign.

[19] For Henry as the author of the peace policy, see Griffiths 1981: pp. 235–6, 252 etc.; Wolffe 1981: pp. 146, 157–8, 174 etc.; Harriss 1988: pp. 295, 316–17. For the king's domestic role, see Griffiths 1981: pp. 248–54 and *passim* and Wolffe 1972 and 1981.

[20] Griffiths 1981: p. 250; Wolffe 1972: p. 44; 1981: p. 332.

[21] See above, pp. 28–30, 73. Many of the points in this paragraph are also made by Harriss 1982.

was much more complex.[22] Similarly, the real significance of the king's words cannot be easily grasped. For obvious reasons, extravagant and committed language was far from unusual in diplomatic or political exchanges. It was not only Henry VI who addressed Charles VII in intimate terms, for example: one of James II's letters declared that 'the said king of Scotland loves the king, his brother and ally, as cordially and entirely ... as if he were his own father'.[23] Meanwhile, a professed concern to halt bloodshed was surely a staple feature of the language in which peace was discussed and cannot easily be used as evidence of a 'sincere, Christian revulsion' on Henry's part.[24] Nor, finally, is it only matters of public policy which were shaped by counsel as well as will. There was, as we have seen, no purely private zone in English kingship: royal marriage, religious worship, even the enterprise of founding colleges – all these were public, as well as private, works.[25] They were authorised in exactly the same way as every other product of government: Henry willed them to happen, and if ever this fact was particularly emphasised, that may tell us more about the public needs of the moment than the private interests of the king. It was precisely because 'a fifteenth-century English king both reigned and ruled', as Wolffe put it, that what we would call his 'personality' remains unidentifiable from the content of his public deeds.[26]

In a sense, this does not matter very much because it is not actually the king's private wishes and interests which are important, if we want to understand Henry's role in the politics of his reign, but his capacity for transforming wishes and interests – those of other people as well as his own – into coherent policy. It is the king's public character with which we are concerned, and whilst this was unquestionably rooted in his private character, the latter is only dimly perceptible in the former and only some parts of it have any significance. Indeed, it is tempting to suggest that the only thing it is necessary to know about the private person of a medieval ruler is the quality of his will: was the king virtuously responsive to counsel, as the system demanded? Was his will flexible at the point of

---

[22] Quotation from the declaration concerning the release of the duke of Orléans, 1440 (*Letters and Papers*, II, ii, p. 452). Griffiths took this document to be 'the clearest revelation of the king's feelings' on the matter of the release of Orléans and of peace in general (1981: p. 443), but William of Worcester described it as 'a playne declaracion made by the lordes of the kynges counsaille of the causes that the kyng was moeved by' (*Letters and Papers*, II, ii, p. 451) and Harriss 1982: p. 842 suggests that it 'carries indications of Beaufort's authorship' (although cf. his views in 1988: pp. 316–17). See below, pp. 187–8, for more on this matter.

[23] *Letters and Papers*, I, pp. 334–5.

[24] Cf. Griffiths 1981: p. 443. A speech to be made by Beaufort at the Oye meeting used similar language, for example: *PPC*, V, pp. 356–7.

[25] See below, pp. 167–71 (foundations), 192–5 (marriage). [26] Wolffe 1981: p. 25.

consultation, wise at the point of decision, and firm at the point of execution? If not, was it too strong, or too weak, or too little guided by virtue? What courses of corrective action were open to leading subjects? If we approach the question of Henry VI's character in this way, some surprising points emerge about current perceptions of the king. From this perspective, there is rather less to choose between the 'inanity' of McFarlane's Henry and the malleable capriciousness of Wolffe's: neither would be able to make decisions adequately, or keep to them consistently; each would be vulnerable to the charge that others directed policy.[27] On the other hand, the king depicted by Griffiths and Harriss – generally rather mild, but determined to obtain peace, or to protect his favourites, or (for a time) to resist the duke of York – is as much an active and autonomous figure in politics as the king imagined by Wolffe: in some areas, at least, he is shown to have possessed the resources of will necessary to sustain and order policy; there would be no denying his fundamental, personal, responsibility for at least some of what was done in his name.[28] Whatever Henry's private nature, the really important question about his kingship is whether or not he possessed sufficient independence of will to wield authority properly. In recent years, the consensus seems to have been that he did. If he did not, then it is clear that the politics of the reign must be understood very differently. The authorisation of common policy was perhaps the most important personal service expected of a king: if Henry was fulfilling this service, then, plainly, we must look elsewhere for the causes of the political disorders which marked his reign; if he was not, then we may agree with Wolffe that it was indeed the king who 'dissolved the unity and purpose of the realm, and made all his advisers seem like knaves or fools or both'.[29] The question is: how would a deficiency in the royal will affect the workings of the polity?

It has been shown that the realisation of the common interest of the people, on which royal authority fundamentally depended, was achieved

[27] Wolffe saw this parallel himself: 1972: p. 44. It is striking how often it is a *lack* of will which seems to characterise the king's performance in his account. Wolffe writes of a 'dangerous compound of forcefulness and weakness' (1981: p. 133); a 'lack of judgement' (p. 107); 'vacillation' (p. 108); 'failure ... to stand up to ... unscrupulous pressure' (p. 109). He identifies an 'open-handedness' in the distribution of patronage and observes that 'it is hard to believe that in the 1440s Henry weighed the consequences of granting any petition which reached him, or refused it': pp. 106, 113.

[28] See above, nn. 19, 22. Griffiths holds the king responsible for the downfalls of Eleanor Cobham in 1441 and of Gloucester in 1447, and for the punishment of the rebels in 1450–1, though he also describes how Henry's long experience of tutelage, his limited powers of judgement and his lack of interest in some important areas of responsibility opened the way for others to shape policy in various ways: 1981: pp. 231, 234, 242, 250, 253–4.

[29] Wolffe 1972: p. 44.

through the action of representative counsel upon the will of the king. To this extent, a limited personal will on the part of the king might seem to be ideal: his public acts would be full of the advice of his counsellors and empty of his own private – and hence potentially tyrannous – concerns.[30] But to take this view would be to overlook the crucial point that because no counsel was adequately representative, the king's will had to be stronger than those of his counsellors. In other words, counsel was very important, but what ultimately guaranteed the common weal was the king's lordship: his freedom to make what he would of what he was advised. This means, as we have seen, that the virtuous condition of the king's will – the extent of its Prudence, its Justice, its Temperance and Fortitude – was of enormous importance, both in preserving the independence of that will and in ensuring its deployment in the common interest. If anything, the first of these two concerns was the more important, since good counsel was widely available to aid the king in the task of determining the common interest, but he alone would have to find the strength of will to arbitrate between conflicting counsels. Without a modicum of virtuous, but wilful, resistance in the king, the common weal could not be guaranteed: indeed, the 'natural unity' which monarchy so neatly supplied for its fulfilment would not exist. The king would continue to operate as a fulcrum of counsel – greatly to the satisfaction of his counsellors, in fact, since he would never deny their advice – but he would be unable to perform his fundamental function of reconciling counsel in the common interest. Conciliar bodies could go some way towards relieving him of this task, but they raised as many problems as they solved. Would the counsellors of an undiscriminating king be aware of his deficiency as he readily endorsed the good advice they singly gave him? Even if they were, would they be willing to establish a council? How could they ensure its control of the administration without damaging the freedom of the king? And how would they overcome its systemic inability to make binding and representative judgements? Finally, was this kind of united action really possible in the midst of a situation which was certain to produce division?

Evidently the removal from the monarchical system of that normal degree of private will on the part of the king which it presupposed would be sufficient to cause profound and complex dysfunction. Does this mean that the instillation of self-will should actually have been more of a priority for mirrors for princes and other didactic sources than the instillation of virtue; that, in fact, will was more important than virtue in the rule of the realm? Leaving aside the fact that medieval writers simply assumed that

---

[30] For meanings of tyranny, see above, pp. 19, 20 n. 32.

their princely readers were, like everyone else, wilful and selfish – that the urgent importance of the interests of others, and, notably, those of the whole *communitas*, had to be taught and learned – it is clear that in prescribing the political virtues, rather than, for example, the theological ones, they were encouraging the exercise of will at the same time as defining its proper ends. The exercise of Prudence, Justice, Temperance and Fortitude meant having the will to listen and think, to insist on right and mercy, to hold to a course of action in the face of ill-judged opposition. If Henry VI could not do these things, he was not a virtuous prince in the sense that advice-writers understood the term; hence there may be no mystery in the dismal results of his rule, and the familiar deduction that virtue was of little use in the governance of England may not be justified. The advice-literature of the age is scattered with observations that clearly indict the sort of behaviour typically associated with Henry's adult rule. On the subject of piety, Christine de Pisan told her readers that the king's service to God was not a matter of 'long lyyng in his orysons' but 'rather to serve him with good dedis'.[31] On patronage, the 'Three Consideracions' warned the ruler to make grants considerately: 'and who that othir wyse yiveth ... he ne is no liberalle yiver, but rathir a verry sparpoyler and wastoure by foole largesse'.[32] Elsewhere, its author noted that 'mercy with oute justise is no verrey mercy, but rathir it may be seid folye and symplesse' and that 'to ben inconstaunt ... is a signe of little wytte or noon and of [little] hardyesse, and ... suche a prince is nat estable ne ferme ne for to be allowed'.[33] What does this imply about the king's notorious readiness to award pardons and to change his mind about grants and policies?[34] It is not impossible that Henry got the wrong idea of what kingship involved from the largely conventional material placed before him – Whethamstede certainly thought so – but if he did, this was more a matter of his own inadequacy than that of the advice-literature and the modes of behaviour it proposed.[35]

Returning to the histories of Henry VI's reign, it is clear that in all of them, Wolffe included, there is evidence to suggest that the adult king

---

[31] *Livre du Corps de Policie*, p. 50.   [32] Genet (ed.), *Political Tracts*, p. 186.

[33] *Ibid.*, pp. 200, 202.

[34] For pardons, see Storey 1966: app. ii; and for inconstancy, see below, p. 253.

[35] Something of this problem emerges in Whethamstede's account of how, as it seemed, the king was led astray by his counsellors: 'Suggesserunt utique ipsi sibi decere regem largum esse, et liberalem, neminique quicquam dedicere, qui vellet ab ipso aliquid, per viam supplicationis, humiliter postulare; asserentes liberalitatem virtutem esse illam, quae non minus quam justitia, confirmat regis solium': *Registrum Whethamstede*, I, pp. 248–9. Some interesting work has been done on the one mirror which shows signs of having been tailored to Henry's personal requirements, the 'Tractatus de Regimine Principum ad Regem Henricum Sextum', printed by Genet: see Wolffe 1981: pp. 14–15; Griffiths 1981: pp. 239–40; Kekewich 1987: pp. 54–63; and Lovatt 1984: 184–5.

was a man of little will and little judgement: enough evidence, indeed, to invite the suspicion that the few decisive policies of the period were the work of Henry's counsellors, temporarily permitted (or driven) by circumstances to act firmly and unitedly in the king's name. If the private nature of the king's personality must remain an open question, it is hard to deny that, as the following chapters will show, the politics of the reign were marked by a deep and lasting problem of authority. Contemporaries could not be sure that responsibility for policy lay, as it ought to have lain, with the king, the only man who spoke for all of them. At times, indeed, they knew that this was not the case. The periods of royal minority and madness show the leading lords bonding together to produce a usable authority, linked to the king's person and using his name but receiving absolutely no guidance from his supine will. We must accept that, in a modified form, similar processes may have been at work in Henry's adulthood. The same impulse to preserve the common interest which drove the nobility together to restrain strong-willed kings would have driven them together to assist and afforce weak-willed ones. At the same time, a shared sense that only in the free and independent person of a king could the common interest be properly advanced would have drawn the nobility away from the necessary devices. Plainly, the rule of a 'weak king' was not a simple matter.

THE MINORITY AND ITS LEGACY

This Star of England. Fortune made his sword,
By which the world's best garden he achieved,
And of it left his son imperial lord.
Henry the Sixth, in infant bands crowned King
Of France and England, did this king succeed;
Whose state so many had the managing
That they lost France and made his England bleed.

William Shakespeare, *Henry V*, epilogue, lines 6–12

To Elizabethans, probably to some contemporaries, it seemed that the wheel of fortune had never turned so sharply as at the death of Henry V. It is no surprise that a number of historians have made it the turning-point of Lancastrian fortunes, taking the inheritance by a baby king of an occupied but undefeated France to be the underlying cause of subsequent downfall.[36] More recently, however, the years of Henry VI's minority have been portrayed as an interval between the startling successes of his father's rule, and the equally startling failures of his own, a period of competent management, in which the king's estate was preserved and his

---

[36] Wylie and Waugh 1929: p. 423; Chrimes 1964: pp. 52–3.

conquest in France initially, at least, extended.[37] Not until Henry VI took up his sceptre himself, it is argued, did the Lancastrian polity begin to fall apart.

There is much to recommend this view. In many practical respects the minority represents a *post mortem* extension of the reign of Henry V. The unity he had created was largely maintained, his achievements were mostly perpetuated and the commitments he imposed accepted. However, the fact that 1422 was also the beginning of a new reign cannot be overlooked. In an important sense, Henry VI's 'personal rule' began at the moment of his accession. This was more than just a legal nicety, it was a conceptual and political necessity. If there was no royal *persona publica*, there could be no body politic. So it was that the lords of 1422 set out not only to provide counsel, but also to establish an artificial royal authority as the basis of the governmental will which they needed to be able to exercise. The effective operation of this demanding but essential contrivance depended on the absence of alternative claimants to the execution of royal will; claimants who, from 1432, included the youthful king himself. In this respect, the minority period had a considerable influence over the politics which followed it.

As recent studies of his reign have shown, the conquest of Normandy and the Ile-de-France was by no means the limit of Henry V's achievement: his successes in the government of England were quite as significant.[38] It was under the second Henry that the house of Lancaster was truly established, as the king drew the heirs of his father's opponents into an ever-widening circle of favour and succeeded in effecting the transformation from duke of Lancaster to king of England which had (in part) eluded the usurper.[39] He did this through the impartial and firm imposition of justice as well as by enlisting the aid of the landowning classes in a great national enterprise to reconquer France, and he framed these measures with a telling emphasis on the reciprocal nature of king and realm. Not only did Henry govern successfully, but he made explicit connections between his own deeds and the traditional expectations of kingship. If he was indeed 'the exemplar of kingship', as G. L. Harriss has

---

[37] Wolffe 1981: chs. 2–4, especially p. 27. Allmand 1983: pp. 26–32, remarks upon the military successes of 1422–8, but identifies 1428–31 as 'the major crisis and turning-point in the war' (p. 36). However, see Jones 1989b: pp. 116–17 for a view that the English did not believe the situation to be lost even in the later 1430s and p. 104 for the (missed) opportunities of 1441.

[38] See, in particular, Harriss (ed.) 1985 and Powell 1989.

[39] The process of restoration was not entirely complete – Mowbray and Holland had to wait until Henry VI's reign for a chance to get back their ducal titles and a certain amount of land confiscated from the Percies and others remained in trusted hands – but there is no question that these families were fully reconciled to Lancastrian rule: Harriss 1985b, especially pp. 35–6, 38–40.

proposed, this was partly, it seems, by design.[40] The sense of common purpose between king, nobility and, through the latter, the entire realm – whether in parliament, or in the counties, or fighting in the war – was perhaps never stronger. This powerful consensus may have been of decisive importance in the sudden crisis of September 1422. Faced with a nine-month-old claimant, the lords seem to have accepted his succession without demur: they gathered together at the new king's side and, resisting proposals for a regency, set up a council to help him to govern.[41]

The basic principle of the minority – that the rule of Henry VI had already begun – was made clear at almost every opportunity. Within weeks of his accession, Henry received in person the great seal from his father's last chancellor.[42] At the age of three, he presided over the opening of parliament, and so removed the need for a parliamentary lieutenant.[43] When he was five, the lords of the council recognised that, in Henry VI, they had a king 'whom and noone other they knowe' and declared that, 'How be it that the king as now be of tendre eage nevere the lesse the same autoritee resteth and is at this day in his persone that shal be in him at eny tyme hereafter whan he shal come withe Goddes grace to yeers of discrecion.'[44] As may be imagined, the blandness of this statement masked a considerable complexity in practice. The assertion of a model closely resembling normal government – royal authority, representative counsel – was accompanied by a number of artificial expedients and restrictions designed to take account of the inescapable fact that the king was a small child and unable to wield his authority in the normal way. Characteristic of this was the appointment of the king's uncles to attend to the protection and defence of realm and church in the king's stead and also to be chief counsellors.[45] It is worth noting that, in a sense, the two appointments are different in kind. The former reflects an aspect of the kingship which Henry was in no way able to fulfil, later defined as 'a personell duetee of entendance to the actuell defense of the land': it invites the dukes to represent, or replace, the king.[46] The latter, on the other hand, makes them Henry's servants: the post of counsellor, even

---

[40] Harriss 1985a; Powell 1989: pp. 125–34.

[41] Some of the lords gathered at Windsor on 28 September (*CClR, 1422–9*, p. 46) and sent out writs for a parliament the following day (pp. 43–4), in which Gloucester was summoned by name and not as *custos*. This suggests either that he had not yet formulated his regency plan, or that the lords had already resolved to resist it, as they did on 5 November and during the parliament: *PPC*, III, pp. 6–7; *RP*, IV, p. 326; Roskell 1953, *passim*. Note that much of the rest of this chapter is a revised version of Watts 1994.

[42] *CClR, 1422–9*, p. 46. Henry received the seal from Langley and then, by Gloucester's hands, presented it to Simon Gaunstede. By July 1424, the king, then two and a half, was able not only to receive the seal, but also to give it to Beaufort himself 'by advice and assent of the council' (*ibid.*, p. 154).

[43] *RP*, IV, p. 261; *Chrons. of London*, p. 285.   [44] *PPC*, III, p. 233.

[45] *RP*, IV, pp. 174–5.   [46] *Ibid.*, p. 326.

chief counsellor, presupposes a figure of authority to whom counsel is offered.[47]

This ambivalence was reflected in the other arrangements for government made in 1422. Various men were named 'pur Conseillers assistentz a la governance'.[48] They were to counsel the king as if he were an adult, but, because he was not, they were also to 'assist' in government. The king's rule was expressed through his own public will, as was normal, but, in view of his inability to contribute personally to the making of decisions, the process was managed by his counsellors, who devised various artificial means to this end. The 'lords of the council' were a fixed, named group: the king could not take counsel from just anybody, even any lord.[49] They were, in themselves, as representative a group as could be devised.[50] A sufficient number of them had to attend before acts could be considered 'doon by Counseill'.[51] In a significant shift from the norm, decisions were to be made according to majority support and not through the exercise of lordship.[52] Most importantly, the councillors were held responsible for what they advised, which is to say that, while formal authority for their actions lay with the king, their power as 'assistants' was recognised.[53] In other words, because the king's contribution to the process of government was so insubstantial, he could not, as was usual, release his advisers from responsibility. At the same time, therefore, the councillors denied themselves the exercise of some aspects of the king's grace, notably the power to reward good service. Items of patronage, such as offices and casualties, were regarded in purely utilitarian terms: the first to be filled as uncon-

---

[47] Above, pp. 62, 77. Even so, it may be argued that the notion of a 'chief' counsellor was anomalous: note, for example, the comment in the king's second letter to York in 1450 that 'in counsales, grettest and the leste, the riche and the power, in liberte, vertu and effecte of your voices ben equale' (Griffiths 1991e: pp. 303–4). It was for the king to decide which counsels should prevail.

[48] RP, IV, p. 175. The question of who appointed the counsellors is neatly avoided in the roll by the use of the passive form ('furent . . . nomez'). In this way, the gap between the theory (the king appointed them) and the reality (the lords, or some of them, chose them) was bridged.

[49] This was implicit in the publications of lists of councillors' names in the 1422 and 1423–4 parliaments, in the ordinances which accompanied them and in the practice of swearing in new members (RP, IV, pp. 175–6, 201; PPC, III, 22–3, 147). The ordinances read at Reading in 1426 and agreed in the parliament of 1429–30 made it quite explicit that no one 'of what degree or condition that he be of' was to be present when the council debated, apart from councillors and people specially invited by authority of the council (RP, IV, p. 343; RP, V, p. 408).

[50] Baldwin 1913: pp. 170–1.

[51] RP, IV, pp. 176 (1422), 201 (1423–4), 343 (1429–30).

[52] See the ordinances of 1422, 1423–4 and 1429–30: RP, IV, pp. 176, 201, 343. Special arrangements were devised to take account of the higher status of Bedford and Gloucester. See above, p. 77, for the normal avoidance of decision making by majority.

[53] In the 1422 ordinances, it was declared that names of those present should be taken 'to see what, howe and by whom, eny thyng passeth': RP, IV, p. 176. See also ibid., pp. 201 (1423–4) and 343 (1429–30).

troversially as possible; the second to be used for finance.[54] As much as possible, the king's estate was to remain untouched, while those parts of it which were immediately necessary to the most minimal rule of the realm were usurped corporately by the council. This is what the lords meant in 1427 when they declared that 'the ... counsail, the king being in suche tendrenesse of age, represente his persone as toward execucion of the saide pollitique rule and governaille'.[55]

So it was that the minority regime rested on a certain paradox. Bedford, Gloucester and the lords of the council served the infant sovereign, but they also represented him. He ruled, but the lords executed his rule. They counselled him, but equally, they, not he, were the recipients of this counsel. This description may seem needlessly elaborate, but it is worth recalling that a peculiar compromise of this kind was the only feasible answer to a grave situation. As we have seen, the only source of fully legitimate authority was the will of the king, but this was rooted in his own person and thus unobtainable in 1422. In establishing the forms of government, the lords could turn for guidance to a number of sources – the testament of the dead king, the principles of inheritance and the counsel of the realm in parliament – but they could only do so amid a vigorous assertion of the rule of Henry VI if they were to avoid open divisions; particularly when Gloucester, and then Bedford, set out their claims to regency.[56] Under these circumstances, it is not hard to see that the attribution of authority to the infant king was the obvious, indeed inescapable, solution, and that this, in turn, necessitated the ambiguous council.[57]

King and counsel, then, was the nature of the minority settlement, defended systematically by the lords against the assaults of Gloucester in

---

[54] *Ibid.*, pp. 175–6. Offices were to be filled when necessary and according to the advice of the council (with certain unimportant exceptions in favour of the chancellor, treasurer and protectors). Casualties were to be sold to the highest bidder. See Griffiths 1981: pp. 83–106, for what actually became of royal patronage in this period.

[55] *PPC*, III, p. 233.

[56] It was on these grounds that the regency claims of the duke of Gloucester could not be admitted (see Harriss 1988: pp. 115–17; Chrimes, 'Pretensions of the Duke of Gloucester'; Roskell 1953). Part of the problem with Gloucester's claim was Bedford's superior hereditary interest, which he soon asserted: see Sharpe 1894–5: III, pp. 367–8. In addition, any kind of regency threatened to accroach the royal power in a potentially damaging way: note the disapproval voiced by the lords in January 1427 (*PPC*, III, pp. 232–4), specifically the comment that no one single person may 'ascribe unto himself the [king's] said rule and governaille' (p. 234).

[57] This solution had, in a sense, already been reached. The writs for the 1422 parliament were sent out in the new king's name by a group of peers meeting in his presence (*CClR, 1422–9*, p. 43). As the lords were to point out in 1428, Gloucester's acceptance of his summons sealed the fate of his proposed regency (*RP*, IV, p. 326). Once the king's authority was recognised in this way, the organisation of means of counsel around it was probably inevitable.

1422, 1425–6 and 1428.[58] The paramountcy of the king's authority was
upheld on a daily basis by the council, but it was given practical assistance
by the lords in parliament, from whom it was acknowledged to be a
delegation.[59] In an effort to keep the peace, oaths not to act upon
grievances or maintain peacebreakers were sworn.[60] By inducing the
nobility to bind themselves together and recognise their corporate responsibility, these helped to realise royal authority and the common interest
which it protected. In addition, the protector himself, as intended,
provided for the personal expression of royal authority in the localities
whenever necessary, though the power he wielded on these occasions was
as much conciliar as royal and he could not extend its use to the sphere of
central government.[61] Only after Beaufort and Gloucester took up arms
in the autumn of 1425 did the conciliar principle waver. Unable to resolve
this serious crisis by any other means, the lords appealed to the duke of
Bedford, who came home and took control, exercising an authority which
appears to have been personal and intrinsic, rather than delegated, and
certainly more considerable than any enjoyed by Gloucester.[62] Although
it was parliament which brought Beaufort and Gloucester to terms, it was
Bedford's superior status which made this possible, and it meant that the
forces of counsel gathered temporarily about him, rather than the king.[63]
Even so, this was not a distinction which Bedford, or anyone else, would

[58]   In January 1426, for example, Gloucester was told that the king, at barely four years of
age, charged him upon his love to come and discuss his ill-will towards Beaufort and
offered him a just and reasonable consideration of his heaviness. Should the duke protest
against the presence of Beaufort at such a meeting, he was to be told that it was not fitting
for the king 'to weyve the presence of any of his lige men nor to lymitte him who shal be
or not be in his presence' (*PPC*, III, pp. 183–4).

[59]   According to the statement of January 1427: *ibid.*, p. 233. Note the role of parliament in
the settlement of some of the more important noble disputes: e.g. Talbot–Ormond, 1423
(*RP*, IV, pp. 198–9), Fitzhugh–Scrope, 1424 (*ibid.*, pp. 212–13), Warwick–Marshal,
1425 (*ibid.*, pp. 262–75), Gloucester–Burgundy (*ibid.*, p. 277), Gloucester–Beaufort,
1426 (*ibid.*, pp. 296–9), Norfolk–Arundel (*ibid.*, pp. 441–3). This was a role which, in
fact, it continued to play during Henry's adulthood, though this was not always recorded
on the roll (see below, pp. 184, 197).

[60]   E.g. *RP*, V, pp. 406–7 (1425); *ibid.*, p. 408 (1426); *RP*, IV, p. 344 (1429–30); *ibid.*,
pp. 421–2 (1433).

[61]   For examples from 1427 and 1428, see Harris (ed.), *Coventry Leet Book*, pp. 111–12
(with Gloucester summoning the town corporation 'and in my lordes name and ouris')
and Roskell 1954: p. 18 n. 5, respectively.

[62]   Note, for example, the terms of Bedford's commission as parliamentary lieutenant,
which was made 'de avisamento consilii', but which does not otherwise mention the
council. Most striking is the absence of the 'de assensu' rubric, which had so enraged
Gloucester in 1422 (*RP*, IV, p. 296; *PPC*, III, pp. 6–7). See Wolffe 1981: pp. 43–4, 79
for some shrewd comments on Bedford's abilities and his role in the crisis of 1425–6.

[63]   Bedford was not among the arbitrators in the 1426 parliament: rather, he presided over
their award. He had come, as Chichele declared, to work for a solution to the great
dispute and, when Beaufort made his declaration, it was Bedford, by advice and assent of
the councillors, who announced that the king had understood him and was willing to
declare him true (*RP*, IV, p. 298).

have cared to make. Before his departure, the duke was explicitly asked to acknowledge the king's authority and to recognise its 'execucion' by the council: he did so willingly.[64]

Among the concepts employed to support the power of the governing council was the expectation that the king would authorise its deeds when he came of age. The lords declared this in 1427, but found that the principle was used against them by Gloucester.[65] The duke replied, as he apparently had before, that if he had 'doon eny thing that touched the king his soverain lordes estat, therof wolde he not answere unto no persone on lyve, save oonly unto the King whan he come to his eage'.[66] If the king was not physically competent to rule in person, then his authority could not be presumed upon. In effect, the duke was repudiating the council's right to govern by asserting the inseparability of the king's private and public *personae*. This had always been implicit in Gloucester's position: if the king could not rule in his private person in 1422, then he could not rule in his public person either and a regency was therefore necessary. The exchanges of 1427 reveal the precarious nature of the council's position. Its right to exercise the king's public powers depended not only on the idea that public and private could be separated, but also on a widespread acceptance that Henry was incompetent to express his own will. This acceptance was easily obtained while the king was an infant, but it would become less so as time went by, even if it were true. When the king was old enough to license the deeds of the council, he would also be able to license the deeds of others. In 1427, the lords were able to compel the duke to agree to be 'ruled and governed' by them because, with no authority to be had from the king's private will, they represented the greatest accumulation of power and their claims to 'execucion' stuck. But the king was getting older all the time and the council's argument of 1428 – that it could not allow Gloucester greater powers because the king would shortly be able to exercise them himself – undermined, rather than strengthened, its position.[67]

In the event, the council sealed its fate with the coronations of 1429 and 1431.[68] Within weeks of the first of these, the protectorate was ended on the grounds that Henry had now personally undertaken the protection and defence of realm and church. Gloucester was left with the rather empty title of chief counsellor, during the king's pleasure.[69] In this way the private and public *personae* of the king were moved a step closer

---

[64] *PPC*, III, pp. 231–42.   [65] *Ibid.*, pp. 232, 238.
[66] *Ibid.*, p. 241.   [67] *RP*, IV, p. 327.
[68] These were a response to the victories of Joan of Arc, notably her triumphant crowning of Charles VII: see Harriss 1988: p. 191; Griffiths 1981: p. 189.
[69] *RP*, IV, pp. 336–7.

together, yet the council still claimed the 'execucion' of the latter in practice. In recognition of the new distribution of power, it was decided that Bedford's title of regent should cease when the king arrived in France.[70] When the royal party reached Rouen, Bedford duly surrendered his authority and government devolved upon the Grand Conseil afforced by an English delegation, headed by Beaufort.[71] He was less willing to accept the royal commission to govern France in the king's absence which was delivered to him at Rouen in October 1431. Having refused such commissions in the past, Bedford now protested that by his acceptance he should not be held to have abandoned his natural right to the regency, if any such right existed.[72] In fact, however, he was able to go on exercising quasi-regal powers, while Gloucester lost almost all of his already minimal pre-eminence.[73] This may be testimony to the younger brother's disruptive handling of his status as protector, but it also shows the growing impact of the king's personal authority on the politics of the minority in England itself.

Gloucester responded to the changes of 1429–31 with a move which shows that he understood their implications. At the end of January 1432, he presided at a meeting which licensed changes to the council ordinances: changes which were more attuned to the circumstances of a ruling king, and which he used to remove the three great officers within weeks of Henry's return.[74] A few days later, new household officers were appointed, the king's secretary was dismissed and his signet deposited in the treasury with Gloucester's own.[75] These measures directly reflect the increased significance of the king's personal authority. Gloucester took no action until Henry had returned, implicitly invoking the direct authority of the crown against the assumed authority of the

[70] *PPC*, IV, p. 37. In February 1427, Bedford had said that he had interpreted the dying words of Henry V to mean that he was to have regent powers in France until his son should come of age and this had been endorsed by the council (*PPC*, III, p. 248). The fact that his regency was now being undermined would seem to confirm the sense that the coronation was understood to indicate some real change in the king's status.

[71] Harriss 1988: p. 202.   [72] *PPC*, IV, p. 95; Harriss 1988: p. 208.

[73] Rowe 1934: p. 227 and *passim*.

[74] These almost unnoticed changes to the council ordinances, dated Canterbury, 28 January 1432, before the king's return, were the necessary precursor to Gloucester's famous coup of February/March (for which, see Harriss 1988: ch. 11). They abolished the quorum, but at the same time provided for matters within the competence of the chancellor and treasurer to be dealt with in the presence of at least one of them (*RP*, V, p. 433). This made it easier to get rid of the current officers, but it also anticipated the demise of conciliar rule, since a 'council' (really a bureau) composed chiefly of the three officers would be more like normal royal government (see above, pp. 84–5). More discussion of Gloucester's actions appears in the next chapter, below, pp. 155–8.

[75] *PPC*, IV, p. 110; *CPR, 1429–36*, p. 196; Griffiths 1981: pp. 58–9 for details. Some use of the king's signet had been made during the coronation expedition, presumably without consultation (e.g. C81/1367/1, dated 18 Jan. 1432). It does not seem that Gloucester made use of the signet himself: perhaps his seizure of it was purely precautionary.

councillors.[76] Had he changed the officers while the king was still in France, he would not only have breached the ordinances of April 1430, but would also, as in the 1420s, have appeared to be acting against both king and council, rather than with the king against some of the councillors – a subtle, but important, political difference.[77] The fact that he found it necessary to make changes in the household is highly illuminating. It had become important to have influence about the king's person, sure evidence that the 1422 council's monopoly of the 'execucion' of royal authority was already weakening.[78]

Gloucester's coup failed because Beaufort, the great defender of the 1422 settlement which protected him and his interests above all, was not destroyed.[79] Even so, Duke Humphrey continued to use the king to subvert the power of the council, and this is surely what prompted the protest of the earl of Warwick, the king's tutor, in November 1432.[80] Warwick claimed that his powers about the king's person no longer sufficed, but what he really needed was an assurance that they still applied.[81] It was no longer clear whether Henry was to be treated as a child or as a ruler, or even whether this was a valid distinction. It is this uncertainty, more than any important insight into the king's character,[82] which is revealed by Warwick's fears regarding the king's growing resistance to punishment. Behind his various requests – that Gloucester and the councillors should help chastise the king, that they should tell Henry that they had all agreed that he should be punished for bad behaviour and that they should persuade him from any indignation against the earl – lies an evident fear that the king's personal wishes might become the recognised basis of royal will in the near future. In Warwick's absence, the king had been taken aside from his studies and told of matters 'not behovefull'. The earl's response was to try to restrict private access to the king: exactly what the conciliar regime demanded. Gloucester retaliated by invoking his closeness in blood, and so retained the right to see the king alone.[83]

The duke had changed the basis of his campaign against the defenders

---

[76] Harriss 1988: p. 217.

[77] *PPC*, IV, pp. 37–8. It should not be overlooked that it was, in practical terms, control of the council which enabled Gloucester to reappoint the officers.

[78] It is interesting to note that Burgundian ambassadors, visiting in 1430, were given letters of credence not only for Gloucester, Beaufort and the king (i.e. council), but also for Warwick, as Henry's guardian (*Letters and Papers*, II, i, p. 165).

[79] Harriss 1988: pp. 220–2 and also pp. 118, 132, 144.   [80] *PPC*, IV, pp. 132–7.

[81] For example, Warwick already possessed, under the terms of his 1428 appointment, the power to remove anyone whom he suspected of 'mysgovernance', pending reference to Gloucester and the council (*PPC*, III, p. 300). If he was having to ask for it again in 1432, it was surely because it had been challenged, presumably on the grounds that it was for the king to decide the company he kept. See also Griffiths 1981: p. 59.

[82] Cf. Wolffe 1981: pp. 13, 69.   [83] *PPC*, IV, p. 136.

of the minority council and, in doing so, he had inaugurated a new politics. It was he, not Beaufort or Suffolk, who first exploited the dependence of the monarchical system upon the private person of the king. It would be easy to see the duke's behaviour as a species of opportunistic manipulation, but this may be unfair. The termination of the English protectorate and French regency, the re-emergence of the signet and the short series of grants made by the king as he prepared to return to England may have been part and parcel of Henry's admission to the powers celebrated at his coronation.[84] We do not know when late medieval men and women expected child kings to come of age: perhaps it was as young as ten.[85] At such an age, Henry should have been capable of rational judgement and susceptible to guidance. He could be allowed to feel his way into his task while the experienced counsellors around him supplemented his deficiencies.

Laden with the erroneous assumption that any lingering insufficiency in the king posed problems which were purely practical and not political, the ruling elite was probably almost ready to make a tacit transition from the orderly but limited rule of a council to the potentially disorderly and unlimited rule of an incompletely prepared king. Doubtless eager to revive royal government, the lords may have overlooked the fact that, in moving the king to the centre of affairs, they would forfeit the corporate control of his actions which seemed the best guarantee of prudent rule. The answerability of an adult king to the peers of the realm was at most general and theoretical, never specific. Of course, a significant part of the lords' desire to permit the king's accession to his powers must be traced to their need for an arbiter to assist them in the direction of their affairs, both local and national. Such a person, as we have seen, required absolute powers of dispensation, or grace: his exercise of them could not be constrained.[86] Did Henry VI yet have the combination of virtue and will necessary for the proper operation of this grace? Probably not, but one thing is certain: the question could not easily be tackled once Henry had begun to rule. With the king in full possession of the power to execute his authority, the distinction between legitimate counsel and 'stirring and moving' would be a difficult one to make.

Interestingly enough, the behaviour of the lords during Bedford's second visit suggests that they may have got cold feet. The power

[84] A large number of grants of French land were apparently made by the king at Dieppe (Rowe 1934: p. 225).

[85] As in the case of Richard II, perhaps. See Tuck 1985: p. 175 and also Horrox 1989: pp. 93–4 for some interesting comments on the problems posed by Edward V's age at his accession. See also Wood 1988: ch. 2 for a general treatment of the problems of minority which makes some similar points to those made here and in ch. 5, below.

[86] Above, pp. 78–80.

concentrated in the hands of the duke during the parliament of 1433–4 appears to have been meant as a check to the uneasy drift of attention towards the king's private person: a halting of the trend towards royal rule and, as such, a corporate act of self-denial on the part of the lords. On the advice of some of the peers in parliament, the king asked Bedford to remain in England and he agreed, subject to various articles making his 'advis' a precondition for changes in the council, offices of state, household and duchy, for calling parliament and for making appointments to vacant sees.[87] The dominant group on the council was reasserting a conciliar monopoly of 'execucion' via the paradoxical expedient of increasing the powers of the king's elder uncle.[88] No longer was it necessary to assert the king's rule against a bid for autonomy from the royal dukes. What had instead become important was to preserve the separation between the king's *persona publica*, which was in public hands, and his *persona privata* which still could not look after itself. The lords openly revived the council – described as 'prius existente', interestingly[89] – and focused it on a proven arbiter and defender of the peace. They explicitly acknowledged Bedford's protection, calling him, 'oure right worthi and ful noble lord' and referring to themselves as 'your servantes the consaillers of the kyng'.[90] All in all, the events of November 1433 involved a deliberate repudiation of the king's personal exercise of his powers in the interests of political harmony at the centre, the essence of the common good.[91] It is significant that, as in the appointment of the 1437 council – in many ways a parallel development – this repudiation came ostensibly from the king in person: the defenders of *public* 'execucion' of the king's authority needed a mascot too.[92]

Once Bedford had returned to France, his brother again attempted to

---

[87] *RP*, IV, p. 424. Note that it was only Bedford's 'advis' and not his assent which was to be sought. In practice, the two may have been much the same, but the former avoided raising the constitutional issue.

[88] Roger Hunt, who, as speaker, presented the commons' request, had been speaker under Bedford in 1420 and had led the commons deputation to him in 1426 (Harriss 1988: p. 151; *RP*, IV, p. 296), but was also associated with Beaufort (*CPR, 1436–41*, p. 219; Harriss 1988: pp. 151, 194, 203) and his ally Tiptoft (Roskell 1965: p. 208). It seems fair, therefore, to see the defenders of the council behind these events.

[89] *RP*, IV, p. 446. It is as if the council had indeed ceased to exist (at least in its earlier form) following the king's return from France.

[90] E28/55/8 Nov. 1434, a letter dealing with the council's advice on the promotion of Thomas Brouns to Rochester.

[91] Note, in this connection, the councillors' refusal to endorse Bedford's petition for lands in Guyenne on the grounds that they dared not give away the king's inheritance in his nonage: *PPC*, IV, pp. 246–7 (June 1434). This may be contrasted with the grants of lands in France made by the king's authority at Dieppe in 1432: see n. 84, above.

[92] *RP*, IV, p. 423. Note that when the king's lordship was invoked to end the quarrel of his uncles at the great council of spring 1434, Henry acted 'de ipsius consilii voluntate et assensu' (*PPC*, IV, p. 211: the emphasis that the king was acting at the will of the council is unusual and rather anomalous). See below, pp. 133ff for the arrangements of 1437.

transfer power to the king's private person. The resultant confrontation at Cirencester in November 1434 inevitably focused on Henry's capacity to execute his authority himself.[93] The same lords who had wheeled the king on to arbitrate between his uncles earlier that year were now in the difficult position of telling him to his face that his attempt to assume the execution of his authority himself was not in his own interests.[94] The episode has been used as evidence of the king's precocity, but only negatively, in fact, does it reflect upon Henry's personality: the lords were evidently not convinced that the king could absorb counsel with the necessary discretion.[95] At this time, they were able to take action to prevent the establishment of royal rule because the king was not quite thirteen and could still pass for a child and because the transfer of power was supported only by Gloucester. In later years, it would not be this simple.

As we shall see, the Rubicon was finally crossed when the political nation was united by the threat posed to Calais by the perfidy of the duke of Burgundy. With Bedford dead, the treasury empty and England's most precious possession on the continent about to be lost, the moment had come when a unanimous recognition of royal power was both necessary and possible. At Canterbury, in July 1436, in the presence of Beaufort, Gloucester and the other leading magnates, Henry VI began to exercise his grace on his sole, though scarcely independent, authority.[96] But this development did not vanquish the problems apparent since the coronations. Just as in 1422, or at any time since, the over-riding concern of the lords was that the king should be adequately representative. Besides deference, counsel was the only medium they could employ to achieve this. Its provision was quite as important now that the king was almost an adult as it had been when he was a baby: in fact, more so. Now that application could be made directly to the king for grace, the possibility of drawing him away from representative advice became more real than before. The varying responses of the nobility to this problem in the years after 1435 are documented in the following chapters.

[93] *PPC*, IV, pp. 287–8. Gloucester was absent from the meeting which took place in the heart of his 'contree' between the king and nearly all the other councillors. The inference that he had taken the king away from Westminster and the council in order to commence personal rule seems inescapable (see Harriss 1988: p. 242).

[94] The lords' unease is reflected in the elaborate form of authentication for their declaration: 'de advisamento, consensu et mandato dominorum de consilio ... et per eundem dominum Regem gratanter admissus et acceptatus' (*PPC*, IV, p. 288).

[95] Cf. Wolffe 1981: pp. 79–80; Griffiths 1981: p. 231.

[96] See below, p. 129.

5

THE YEARS OF TRANSITION, 1435–1445

THE TEN-YEAR period from 1435 to 1445 saw the establishment of what has been called the 'personal rule' of Henry VI. It began with the first successful moves to shift the exercise of power towards the youthful monarch himself, and ended in his marriage, arguably the most meaningful signal to political society that the minority and the forms of government associated with it were at an end. In most of the literature on this period, the story of these years is a fairly simple one. The minority comes to an end between 1435 and 1437, and the king, now effectively an adult, proceeds to rule in a more-or-less normal way until he falls under the influence of Suffolk and his faction round about the mid-1440s. To a large extent, the pace of change in the 1430s is set by Henry himself: already conscious of his high estate in 1432, he strains on the leash of conciliar power in 1434 and begins to assert control over royal patronage in 1436. In November 1437, a council is appointed to rule with the king along broadly traditional lines. Its demise, between about 1444 and 1447, is treated as one of the main indications and, indeed, features of the curial takeover which was to play such an important part in causing the crisis of 1450.[1]

In this chapter and the next, I shall be arguing for an alternative version of events. There seems to me to be little evidence that Henry himself was the author of his slow and halting progression to something resembling full authority: indeed, the fact that it *was* so slow and, in certain ways, incomplete tends to suggest the opposite. We have seen that the establishment of personal rule was the aim of others besides the king. To some extent, of course, it was the aim of everyone. The action of counsel upon a free and independent royal will was known to be the best means for achieving the common weal of the realm. Even from the start of his reign, Henry had been recognised to possess, in person, every bit of the

---

[1] See e.g. Griffiths 1981: pp. 231–6, 275–8, 284–6; Wolffe 1981: pp. 65, 87–92; Virgoe 1970: pp. 143–6.

authority he would wield as an adult, and his subjects began to draw on this authority as soon as the coronations of 1429 and 1431 gave them a public licence to do so. As the king grew older, and the employment of his authorising power by individuals grew less questionable, the pressure for 'personal rule' must have become irresistible, whatever Henry's personal aptitudes or interests. The real questions thrown up by the political and institutional history of the 1430s and 1440s, therefore, are not, why – or even how – did the king obtain power, but why was this process so elaborate, so publicly managed and so frequently thwarted? Why did a group of men who appear to have believed in, and indeed to have promoted, the almost absolute monarchy typical of English rulers also take steps which limited the king's freedom of action? Why did Henry VI continue to govern with the aid of a highly authoritative council until he was in his early twenties, when this appears to have contravened the normal principles of royal government? And finally – perhaps most importantly – what did this peculiar distribution of authority mean for the conduct of high politics in these years?

These are among the questions we shall be exploring in the following pages. To answer them, we shall begin by looking in close detail at the changing pattern of government in the decade 1435–45, trying to gain a sense of what was happening and of what this tells us about the king himself and about the problems faced by his leading subjects.[2] Then, having established a chronological and structural framework for the history of government in this period, we shall move on to explore the formation of a politically effective regime based in the household. This, it emerges, was the necessary precursor to the peaceful transfer of authority from artificial council to (in effect) artificial king. An informal and potentially unstable power structure had to be made acceptable to the territorial lords whose interests had, for the most part, been represented by the minority council and its successors. A discussion of how this acceptance was achieved forms the second part of the middle section of the chapter. And then, finally, we shall consider the central question: how the whole process of transferring power from council to court both conditioned, and was itself conditioned by, the politics of the 1430s and 1440s.

THE CHANGING FORMS OF GOVERNMENT

The long survival of a council with a significant role in government is, in certain ways, a godsend for historians of Henry VI's reign. Because kings were the only legitimate source of authority in their realms, all power

---

[2]   A certain amount of this section revises material which appears in either Watts 1991 or Watts 1994.

which was not directly exercised by them required both description and justification. As a result, the activities of councils and ministers tend to be better documented than the activities of kings, and we thus have more detailed evidence for the internal operations of Henry's government than we do for those of most earlier and many later kings.[3] This evidence – minutes, ordinances, memoranda and warrants – has been widely used in past accounts, principally to trace the development of public policy. Here, it will be used to a slightly different end: namely, to determine the means by which policy was authorised, with a view to understanding the distribution of power and authority in the middle years of Henry's reign.[4]

As several commentators have remarked, however, the internal records of later medieval government are not easy to interpret.[5] Perhaps the greatest problem is that we have very little idea what proportion of these records have survived, which means that we cannot be sure that what appear to be patterns or changes in the way acts of government were authorised are not simply mirages caused by a random rate of loss and destruction.[6] Conclusions about the fluctuating importance of Henry VI's council which are based on the evidence of warrants may be particularly shaky: an unknown, but possibly high, proportion of warrants issued by the council must have gone up in smoke in the Privy Seal Office fire of 1619; if this fire had not happened, we might have a very different picture of the institution's nature and significance.[7] On the other hand, it is possible that Sir Robert Cotton's collection of conciliar memoranda, pillaged mostly from the Privy Seal Office in the later sixteenth century, and printed by Nicolas as the *Proceedings and Ordinances of the Privy Council*, is a fair sweep of the more meaningful kind of council record: minutes of meetings and decisions; ordinances and other more substantial

---

3   The major collection is, of course, *PPC*, III–VI, which contains a mixture of minutes – some original, some seventeenth-century copies – and miscellaneous documents involving king and council. The collection gives a specious appearance of uniformity to what was often an *ad hoc* body: as Margaret Condon has commented, there is no certainty that council registers were regularly kept before 1485 (1986: p. 228). The rest of the relevant material is scattered through a number of different classes of documents in the PRO – some of them quite as artificial as *PPC* – Exchequer, Treasury of Receipt, Council and Privy Seal (E28), Chancery, Warrants for the Great Seal (C81), Privy Seal Office, Warrants for the Privy Seal (PSO1), Chancery, Council and Parliament (C49) and elsewhere.

4   The various means which medieval governments used to attach and record authority are dealt with at length by Maxwell-Lyte 1926 and Brown 1964a. Storey 1966: p. 31 shows how records of authorisation might be used to illustrate changes in the pattern of authority under Henry VI.

5   Brown 1969a provides the fullest discussion.

6   Brown 1969a: pp. 2–3, argues that warrants collected in chancery have survived reasonably well, whilst those collected in the privy seal office have not. Note that a proportion of warrants were oral ones, often recorded in the latter office but not in the former (Brown 1964a: p. 144).

7   Brown 1969a: p. 3 and 1954: pp. 7–11.

materials.[8] If it is accepted that the making and preservation of records such as these was a sign of unusual prominence for the council in the government of the realm,[9] it may be possible to make judgements about the relative strength of the institution from the materials which we possess; and this is even more the case when their content, together with evidence drawn from other sources, seems to bear this out. Certainly, the documents I have consulted do not betray much sense of a lost continent of council records and the story of institutional change presented here appears to be corroborated by the account of politics which appears later in the chapter.

Before embarking on this story, it may be helpful to discuss some of the ways in which the records of government can be used to show changes in the pattern of authority. In many ways, the best sources for a study of this kind are the various means used to 'authenticate', or authorise, issues of government. As has been said, the purpose of authentication was principally to attach the will of the sovereign to orders written by his servants and, to this end, endorsements of various kinds were written on warrants and bills to indicate the way in which the royal will had been transmitted. These endorsements can be used in a number of ways. On the one hand, they cast light on the changing status of formal and informal methods of counsel during this period of transition. On the other, they offer a more general insight into the peculiarities of Henry VI's rule. Although the majority of Henry's adult acts of government are warranted in a normal, and entirely opaque, way, there are also a substantial number of abnormal warrants, often revealing who, other than the king, was involved in, and took some responsibility for, the formulation and exercise of royal will. It is, of course, important to recognise that normal kinds of warrant existed under Henry VI, and necessary to conclude from this that the king's authority was generally, for one reason or another, effective within the administration at least.[10] But, at the same time, it is reasonable to focus attention on the latter types – the oddities – because they alone can help us to resolve the hoary question of who held the pen.

Individual means of authentication are examined in the course of the account below, but it may be helpful to introduce here some of the general principles which have been applied to their analysis. The practice of signing warrants issued by the council, which was carried out during the minority and protectorates, can be taken as a direct admission of responsibility on the part of those who signed.[11] It was part and parcel of

---

[8] Brown 1954: p. 8 and n. 11.   [9] Cf. above, p. 84.

[10] Note that some royal warrants were questioned, however (below, p. 137).

[11] This practice had been ordained by the council in November 1426 (*RP*, V, p. 408), but seems to have begun in 1424: Brown 1969a: p. 22 and n. 2.

the creation of an artificial royal will in periods when the king could exercise no will in person.[12] When these signatures came to be replaced by notes of who was present, the degree of practical responsibility for decisions made by those who were party to them may not have been affected, but a changed perception of where formal responsibility lay does seem to be indicated. Meanwhile, from about 1439, it became unusual for the surviving council to describe its deeds in ways which straightforwardly declared its activity. Instead of notes of endorsement like 'Concordatus est per dominos de consilio', the formula 'Rex de avisamento consilii' was used. Conciliar participation is still indicated, but authority is now plainly with the king. Moreover, we know that it is 'the council' which is meant by 'consilii' and not simply 'counsel' from evidence of who was present and from the existence of an alternative formula, 'Rex apud ... concessit ..., praesentibus ...', to indicate the presence of advisers who were not, for the time being, acting as councillors. Why it was necessary to indicate the presence of anyone about the king when he was making grants which it was clearly within his authority to make is an interesting question, and one to be considered below. Meanwhile, let us return to the circumstances of the mid-1430s.

. . .

The principles which had seemed so convenient at the establishment of Henry VI's minority government placed the lords in a difficult position as the king began to grow up. Inevitably, the council's claims to the 'execucion' of royal sovereignty wavered as it began to look as if Henry might be able to exercise it himself. By the mid-1430s, most leading subjects must have been keen for the king to take up the reins of government and restore good rule. Conciliar government was time-consuming, unrewarding, artificial, offensive to the claims of monarchy and possibly even a liability in foreign affairs.[13] At the same time, however, the lords wanted to hand over power to a man who could be trusted to arbitrate prudently, to resist importunity and to tread the difficult path between constancy and flexibility, between law and grace, at his own judgement. Up till now, as we have seen, the councillors had done what they could to provide prudent, representative and authoritative

---

[12] Above, pp. 113–15.

[13] The arrival of the *Tract of Self-Defence*, which Pope Eugenius circulated to princes in June 1436 as a warning of the threat which the Basle Council posed to monarchical authority, might have reminded the councillors of the undesirable constitutional implications of their power (Black 1970: pp. 88–9). Meanwhile, it is interesting to note that Hue de Lannoy's famous letter of advice to Philip of Burgundy, written in September 1436, made much of the fact that the English king is too young to rule and that the French king 'does not himself rule, but is ruled' (Vaughan 1970: pp. 104–5).

government themselves. To some extent, they could go on doing so, but only if the integrity of the council and its effective monopoly of state affairs could be maintained. As a consequence, the lords found themselves pursuing conflicting aims: both the promotion of the king, as the best source of rule, and the preservation of the council as the most reliable one. This confusion of interests overshadowed central politics throughout the king's slow transition from manifest infancy to manifest adulthood. Until the day arrived when Henry gave unmistakable signs that he was ready and able to take the lead, the lords would be forced to muddle through, tacitly assessing whether or not he was capable of ruling, and trying to organise themselves and their affairs accordingly.

It was in the atmosphere of crisis created by the death of Bedford and the defection of Burgundy that the first decisive, and probably corporate, moves to admit the king to the exercise of his powers were made.[14] On 1 October 1435, apparently for the first time, Henry attended a meeting of the council. In his presence, a new lieutenant of Calais was appointed: an important act, because the town was believed to be under threat and the new appointee would therefore bear a particularly heavy responsibility.[15] In the following weeks and months, the king was often present at council meetings and, from early 1436, this was acknowledged in its issues and minutes, as the phrase 'Rex de avisamento consilii ...' began to take its place as a note of authorisation alongside older formulae such as 'Concordatus est per dominos de consilio.'[16] Despite these developments, several indicators suggest that the business of government, and to some extent even the authority to govern, remained with the council for the time being: acts were still mostly authenticated by the signatures of lords; Westminster, where the council met, remained the seat of command; and, as yet, the king expressed his authority only in association with council and parliament.[17] Even so, major changes were patently anticipated.

---

[14] See Harriss 1988: pp. 250–5 for these events. Bedford died on 15 September 1435. As the English ambassadors returning from the Congress of Arras had feared, Burgundy signed a treaty with the French king six days later.

[15] C81/1545/55 (Richard Woodville was the appointee). The connection between the crisis in Flanders and the king's emergence is also evoked by the request which Henry made in person to the lords in the 1435 parliament to lend their support for a rescue expedition (see *PPC*, IV, p. 352c).

[16] E.g. E28/56/20, 22 Feb., 9 Mar., 27 and 30 Apr. 1436. In most of these cases, the lords of the council appended their signatures: a sign of the real location of authority. Endorsements denoting conciliar authority continued to be used: *e.g.* E28/56/5 Feb., 11 Mar., 18 Apr. 1436 (signatures); E28/56/7 Mar. 1436 (a note that the lords of the council made the grant). Note that on one occasion when the king was present, the signatures of the councillors were the only endorsement (E28/56/19 Jan. 1436).

[17] The vast majority of surviving government instruments were dated at Westminster, and most of those at the Star Chamber: E28/56, 57 *passim*; *PPC*, IV pp. 308–44 *passim*. In April, a privy seal letter was despatched from Eltham and so, probably, from the king and from those around him (E28/56/10 Apr.: and see Wolffe 1981: p. 81 for another,

Whatever the cessation of the fourteen year 'Book of the Council' in the summer of 1435 owes to the retirement of Richard Caudray from the clerkship, it must also reflect a sense that the minority councillors' period of account was drawing to a close: no longer was there any need for such extensive records of what they had done; the king was now of an age to hear of their deeds and deliberations as these took place.[18] Efforts were made to publicise his increasing activity. A letter to the Norman council, for example, told of Henry's regular attention to affairs.[19] Another letter, written in March 1436 to Cardinal Orsini, looked forward to the day, now close at hand, when the king would take up the reins of power and reward those who had served him so well in his infancy.[20] Two months later, the councillors discharged the king's tutor, the earl of Warwick.[21] His childhood was at an end.

As is now well known, the next important step in the king's advance to power came at Canterbury in late July 1436, as a royal army prepared to assist the beleaguered garrison at Calais. By making a series of grants of lands and money on the sole authority of his signature, the king began to exercise a power which was, to all intents and purposes, independent of his subjects.[22] This was royal grace: the right to dispense, to pardon, to grant. In many ways, its reappearance marked the full return of monarchy to England. There is, even so, no need to assume that Henry himself was behind this new departure. Rather as in the previous October, the main reason for the king's empowerment at this time seems to have lain in the demands of public policy. Raising two armies, one to protect the Ile-de-France, the other to rescue Calais, stretched the fiscal and political resources of Henry's government to the limits.[23] Bringing the king into

more suggestive, example). Later that month the council twice met in the king's chamber at Westminster, presumably in his presence (E28/56/27 Apr. (two)).

[18] See Brown 1969a: pp. 25–6 for the role of these considerations in the production of the book.

[19] Wolffe 1981: p. 88.

[20] E28/56/20 Mar. 1436. I am most grateful to Dr G. L. Harriss for his advice regarding the authorship of this letter and to Dr A. Sapir Abulafia for helping me with the tortuous Latin.

[21] E28/57/19 May 1436; CPR, 1429–36, p. 589.

[22] The best known of these is the grant of Canford and Poole to Cardinal Beaufort on 28 July, which was made 'de mero motu nostro' and signed with his own hand (E28/57/28 July 1436: note that whose 'motion' lay behind an act was a matter of some significance – above, p. 62). It was not the first, however. On 26 July, Henry released to Gloucester the 5,000 marks which he owed to the crown, signifying his will by the sign manual and the endorsement, 'of [the king's] grace especiale and by thadvis of his counseil' (BL, Cotton MS Vespasian F xiii, fol. 79; cf. Griffiths 1981: pp. 231–2 and Harriss 1988: p. 275). The same day, Henry granted on his own authority ('it is granted by the kyng') a petition from the earl of Salisbury for the forfeited lands of a French rebel, but in this case authentication seems to have been provided by the signatures of those councillors present (E28/57/wrongly dated 26 June).

[23] Harriss 1988: pp. 256ff.

play – as titular captain of the Calais force, and good lord to all his people – could significantly extend the regime's claim on the support of its subjects.[24] Royal headship promised unity of direction, full backing for those who took up arms and, perhaps above all, the promise of reward and a redistribution of offices and perquisites.[25]

In the ensuing weeks, therefore, the king began to rule, but the way in which he did so was far from typical. Henry had had greatness thrust upon him, and its architects appear to have been his councillors. Whatever the initiative of individual suitors in putting up their bills to him from late July onwards, there is much to suggest that the king's accession to power was, as far as possible, managed publicly by his leading subjects.[26] The exercise of royal grace developed in measured stages: from grants made by king and council in 1435–6;[27] to grants made by the king alone but only during pleasure in 1436–7;[28] and finally to grants made for life from the spring of 1437 onwards.[29]

[24] The (short-lived) plan to place the king at the head of the Calais army is revealed by a letter to the abbot of Bury St Edmunds, dated 16 June: BL, Add. MS 14,848, fol. 191v. I am very grateful to Dr Michael K. Jones for bringing this source to my attention. Note that, shortly before he became king, the ten-year-old Richard II had been set to lead an expedition to France with John of Gaunt (Goodman 1992: pp. 63–4).

[25] Something of the king's new importance is conveyed by the comment of the *Great Chronicle*: 'the kyng herd his conseill atte Caunterbury with grete partie of his lordes' (p. 172). See also Sharpe (ed.), *Calendar of the Letter Books ... of the City of London... I*, p. 206.

[26] Harriss 1988: p. 275 suggests that Beaufort led the king into making grants on his sole authority behind the council's back, but, since Gloucester and others were able to obtain them as well, perhaps they were a natural development of the leadership increasingly accorded to Henry at this time.

[27] The existence of a trend is suggested by the fact that on 30 June 1436, for example, the lords of the council had taken the trouble to obtain the king's advice before granting a petition of Sir Thomas Rempston concerning the duchy of Lancaster (E28/56/as dated). Confusion over the boundaries of royal and conciliar authority is apparent in a number of the endorsements of summer 1436: four grants made on 26 July, for example, were recorded as granted by the king (which suggests independent royal authority), but were also signed by councillors (E28/57/26 July 1436 and see n. 22, above). Interestingly, the last warrant signed by councillors which I have been able to find before the 1450s was endorsed as granted by the king's command (E28/57/17 Aug. 1436), which suggests that, by then, the royal command had become a crucial component. Note that there are a very small number of earlier grants which may have been made by the king alone: e.g. one of July 1435 in favour of the king's clerk John Bathe, on which only the chancery memorandum 'concessa est per dominum regem' appears (C81/1424/1); one of April 1436 in favour of William Ayscough (Wolffe 1981: p. 81 – a privy seal writ, the warrant for which is unknown).

[28] Henry seems to have made one more grant during the summer (5 August: *PPC*, IV, p. 345). There was then a pause until after the meeting of a great council in late October to early November (E28/58; note that no letters patent based on royal grants were issued between 1 September and 31 October 1436). On 1 November, the first of a long series of patents was issued upon a warrant under the sign manual (*ibid.*/as dated; *CPR, 1436–41*, pp. 20–91, *passim*). With the exception of the grants mentioned in n. 22, above, all the grants made up to the end of January 1437 were during pleasure only.

[29] From January to the end of March, there was only one life-grant: the appointment of a

Although this pattern could be explained by the steadily diminishing uncertainty of petitioners regarding the extent to which the young king's personal authority had become effective, it may also be traceable to a process of public consultation and recognition directed by the councillors. Each new power was taken up during a great council, and it seems possible that the agreement of the lords was sought on each occasion.[30] Whilst no one could actually deny the king the right to act as he pleased once it was understood that he was no longer an infant, the corporate judgements and mutual self-restraint of leaders of society could govern the activities of suitors: to some extent, the exercise of royal will could be modified externally, so long as this was agreed among the political elite.

The arrangements made for government during the fifteenth year (1436-7) set precedents which were to endure for some time. The king went on dispensing patronage, mostly upon application and, apart from one or two deferential interventions from his councillors, on his own sole authority.[31] The council, meanwhile, managed the great bulk of public affairs and presented all but the most routine matters to the king for judgement.[32] By April 1437, Cardinal Beaufort felt able to remark that Henry was now of such an age 'that he [Beaufort] may the better absente him': the days of conciliar rule, it seemed, were drawing to a close. It is likely, however, that if the cardinal's confidence was genuine,

serjeant-at-arms (*CPR, 1436-41*, p. 47). In April alone, there were eleven such grants, and a further thirty-two during the rest of the regnal year (data from *CPR, 1436-41*). This move could, perhaps, have been prompted by a petition to parliament from the servants of the king's person during his tender age to have their grants confirmed for life: SC8/142/7053 (dated 22 March, probably 1437).

[30] Harriss 1988: p. 275 proposes that the king's power to make grants was confirmed at the great council of autumn 1436. Since another great council met in April 1437, it is possible that it made some formal recognition of the validity of *life*-grants: *PPC*, V, pp. 6-15 (from 7 April, at the latest, to 17 April). The 1437 parliament saw the first granting of a general pardon since the reign had begun (*RP*, IV, pp. 504-5). This was doubtless another signal to political society that the king had come of age: it was granted by the king's special grace, though, significantly, with the assent of the lords.

[31] Whilst the councillors generally deferred to the king in this area, they kept an eye on matters. It was they, for example, who assessed petitions left over from the 1437 parliament, albeit adding the rubric 'as long as it shal lyke the kyng': *RP*, IV, pp. 506-8. They intervened to amend the king's grant of a petition from the earl of Warwick and it is clear that Lord Willoughby's petition for pardon came first to them (*PPC*, V, pp. 28-9, 40-1). On 21 November 1436, for example, they resolved to warn the king to 'yeve offices to such persones as thoffices wer convenient to': *PPC*, V, p. 3.

[32] The council continued to meet fairly regularly at Westminster and to make decisions, apparently by itself and often on its own authority: e.g. 13-28 November 1436 (E28/58/ as dated and *PPC*, V, pp. 3-4), 26 April-1 May 1437 (E28/58/as dated and *PPC*, V, pp. 17-22), most of June 1437 (*PPC*, V, pp. 27-41). Even so, king and council often met together: e.g. 6 and 11 May 1437 (*PPC*, V, pp. 23-4, 25), 16 June 1437 (*ibid.*, pp. 33-4) and for much of July 1437 (*ibid.*, pp. 42-50). One decision, made apparently by king and council, records not only the 'advice', but also the 'assent' of the councillors: *PPC*, V, p. 10.

it was misplaced.[33] There is not much to suggest that the king's well-documented role in authorising the council's deeds was more than formal. Except in matters of grace, where the substance as well as the authorising of decisions was apparently left to his discretion, Henry seems to have done little more than lend unquestioning endorsement to conciliar recommendations.[34] There is even some evidence to suggest that the government's clerks sought to indicate Henry's activity because they had to rather than because it was truly forthcoming.[35] This state of affairs may not be particularly surprising, given the king's relative youth and inexperience, but we should not mistake it for the normal pattern of government. Perhaps the most important thing to emphasise is the developing rift between matters of grace and affairs of state. Under normal circumstances, as we have seen, it was through the exercise of grace that kings discharged much of the business of state – most notably, of course, in the sphere of justice.[36] Grace flowed through every element in the governmental machine: law, counsel and administrative routine played their parts within its bounds, not as part of a separate public enterprise. There may have been every reason to assume that the king would soon begin to use his grace in this way, to involve himself more fully in the more complex business of government. Certainly, there is something optimistic in the council's persistent submission of administrative matters to his attention. Instead, however, things took a different tack. In November 1437, the divorce between 'grace' and 'state' was to be accepted and institutionalised.

Before we consider this important development, it might be helpful to pause and take stock of what we have seen so far. On the whole, there seems to be plenty to suggest that Henry, at least at this stage, was not the initiator of his so-called 'personal rule'. If he had been behind the events of 1436, the whole tiresome process of recognition, definition and tentative restriction could have been avoided. The king would simply have begun to exercise his free will over the full range of royal responsibility, while counsellors, those of 1422 and others, advised him. Instead, he made no move to exploit the councillors' recognition of his adulthood.

---

[33] *PPC*, V, p. 9. This statement should not, of course, be taken too literally: Beaufort wanted to leave and the lords were bent on restraining him from doing so (*ibid.*; Harriss 1988: p. 276).

[34] See n. 32, above.

[35] The minutes of 6 May 1437 appear to have been altered to state that the king rather than the council decided the matter in hand (presumably because it concerned the king's grace): *PPC*, V, pp. 23–4. Similarly, four days later, the councillors resolved to make an act to borrow money, but the terminology of the act, which appears later in the minute, runs 'The Kyng, consideryng...' (*ibid.*, p. 24). See also Harriss 1988: p. 294.

[36] Above, pp. 79–80, 97–8, 100–1. This finds a natural corollary in the continuing, if respectful, interference of the council in matters of grace: see n. 31, above, and n. 54, below.

The impetus for royal activity came not from within, but from below, with the result that it was for the councillors, who could bind the political community, if they could not bind the king, to define and govern the exercise of royal power. This is how that power came, in practice, to be focused on relatively minor matters of grace. Because more overtly public political activity often required the aid of assembled counsel, it was easier for the councillors to exercise a corporate control over it. Patronage, normally administered in private, was beyond their reach. They might still be able to issue general guidelines or to intervene in certain specific cases, but it was difficult to stop the initiative falling to individual petitioners, among whom, of course, they themselves were numbered. At the same time, the unmanaged disposal of this sort of patronage created few political problems (at least in the short term): faced with an open-handed king, suitors were more or less guaranteed satisfaction. Matters of governance, on the other hand, and especially of justice, meant the reconciliation of divergent interests, many of them absent from the scene of decision. The settlement of such matters demanded reflection, representation and, often, the use of will. If a council possessed rather less of these qualities than a fully functioning king and his advisers, it possessed rather more of them than Henry VI.

The tendencies of the previous couple of years were crystallised in the formal reappointment of the council, which took place in yet another assembly of the lords, sitting at Clerkenwell from 9 November 1437.[37] This episode marked the final stage in the process of publicly defining the king's new powers. On 12 November, the existing councillors and four new men were formally appointed to be 'of counsailx' and were granted powers according to a lengthy schedule included in the minutes of the following day.[38] On the 14th, conciliar wages were reorganised and, on the 15th, the date for beginning the term was fixed upon.[39] The peculiarity of these measures has been underplayed in most modern treatments: partly, perhaps, because older ideas of 'constitutional conflict' between kings and councils have been too hastily rejected.[40] Never before had what was ostensibly the transfer of governmental control been achieved in such a legalistic setting: earlier kings had simply seized power when they felt themselves to be of age.[41] The very fact that such a natural

---

[37] This seems to be the council which met with the king at Sheen on 21 October 1437 and moved with him to Clerkenwell: *PPC*, V, pp. 64–73, 90.

[38] *PPC*, V, p. 71; *PPC*, VI, pp. 312–15.   [39] *PPC*, V, pp. 72–3.

[40] Wolffe 1972: p. 45 and Griffiths 1981: pp. 275–8 provide convincing correctives to the arguments of the 'constitutional historians', but there *is* something of a tension between 'royal' and 'conciliar' forms of authority: see above, pp. 83–4. Brown 1969b: p. 111, on the other hand, argues for a reluctance to hand over power to the young king.

[41] Consider Edward III's coup in 1330, for example (McKisack 1959: pp. 101–2, 152). Richard II declared himself of age in 1389, and sacked a number of councillors and

and flexible process as the taking of counsel had to be expressed and ordained in such a formal way seems to indicate that the initiative for change came from the lords themselves. Far from being 'the king's declaration',[42] the schedule of November 1437 was the latest response of the councillors to their continuing, but still rather obscure, predicament.[43]

In consequence, the document did little more than emphasise the formal subordination of the existing council to the will of the king. Henry's over-riding authority and the powers of 'grace' which went with it were explicitly recognised,[44] but it was also made clear that the king needed to be 'supported' by councillors, rather than simply advised by them, because 'he shal not mowe attende to [the great labours of government] in his owne persone as oft as he wold'.[45] The arrangements may indeed, as Ralph Griffiths argues, have been envisaged as a temporary measure to take account of the king's youth – though Henry, now almost sixteen, was not particularly 'young' by medieval standards – but there is no getting away from the fact that they provided for control of affairs to remain in the hands of the council for the time being.[46] The council was to discuss and conclude 'suche matiers as shal happen for to be moved among hem', but there is no clear indication that it was the king who would move them, indeed quite the reverse: great matters which the council discussed were not to be concluded without the king's 'advis' being first taken. This is the exact opposite of the traditional format of counsel discussed in earlier chapters: the council has replaced the king as recipient of advice and maker of decisions.[47] Only when the councillors were significantly divided was the king to be informed of the matters

---

leading officers to prove the point. He had plainly been making efforts to obtain power long before this (*ibid.*, pp. 463–4 and ch. XIV, generally). Even Henry III declared himself of age when he was twenty (in 1227): Carpenter 1990: p. 389.

[42] Griffiths 1981: p. 275.

[43] In this regard, it is perhaps significant that none of the existing councillors was removed: note the laconic comment in the record of the 12 November meeting ('Thei that wer of counsailx befor beth appointed to be of counsailx now', the passive form perhaps suggesting that the appointment of councillors was, as in 1422, made by the lords, albeit with the king's assent). A deleted passage from the note about the council's new powers ('And the K' to graunte us now': *PPC*, V, p. 71) tends to reinforce the sense that the councillors were the authors of the new arrangement.

[44] That is to say the power to appoint to offices, grant pardons and 'other thynges that stond in grace', which Henry had been exercising since July 1436. These were to be 'reserved' to him and were not to be a part of the councillors' business. Note that a few days later, on 17 November, regular arrangements for the payment of the king's personal expenses were first instituted: Johnson 1981: p. 206 (E404/54/130).

[45] *PPC*, VI, p. 313. This phrase was copied from the provisions of 1406, on which the schedule was based (see Wolffe 1972: p. 45). The term 'supported' evokes the duty of the 1422 councillors not only to counsel, but also to 'assist': see above, p. 114.

[46] Griffiths 1981: pp. 275–6; also Harriss 1988: p. 292, where the unusually wide responsibilities of the council are noted.

[47] See above, pp. 26–8.

under discussion, and of the diversity of opinions, so that he could make a decision himself.[48] It was, of course, the ever-present danger of division, particularly in matters of local government, which made personal rule not only desirable and natural, but ultimately necessary. It is not surprising that in this matter the framers of the 1437 'declaration' appointed the king to make decisions: no other sufficient authority existed, as the experience of the minority had begun to show. Nor is it clear that what the schedule provided was in any way an extension of the role as final arbiter which Henry had been playing in a formal sense since at least 1434.[49] Only the king in person could reveal the difference between licensing the decisions of others and deciding for himself.

By no means, then, was this the 're-establishment ... of traditional royal rule in which the king's councillors had an acknowledged part'.[50] Rather, it was an attempt to create a satisfactory basis for government which took account both of the authority now recognised to lie in the king and of his continuing insufficiency in its 'execucion'. If anything, it was more an extension than a suspension of the minority: no less than in 1422, the councillors were trying to realise the pressing need for royal leadership by using the tools available to them. They sought on the one hand to bow to royal authority and on the other to provide a means through which it could be encouraged, expressed and yet contained: it is small wonder that the result of their exertions possesses such a bewildering, schizophrenic quality. The lords could not make the king into an effective ruler: they could either accept that he was one, or not. In 1437, they made a corporate decision that he was not, enlisting, as they did so, the co-operation of a number of the men about him in his household; men who were otherwise in a position to subvert this settlement by inducing the king to exercise his power directly.[51] If the lords did not admit to these concerns, and if they left the king with independent powers of grace which were integral to the task of government, this was because they were bound, as they had always been bound, to observe in every public act the 'exceeding authority' rooted in the king's person. The separation of matters of 'grace' from matters of 'state' was a compromise: a convenient, if ultimately problematic, response to the insubstantial nature of Henry's character.

Over the following two years, very little changed. Henry continued to dispense grace, while the council continued to meet, on much the same

---

[48] *PPC*, VI, p. 314.   [49] See above, p. 121 n. 92.   [50] Griffiths 1981: p. 277.
[51] Three of the new councillors, Bishop Rudbourne, Sir John Stourton and the wardrober, Robert Rolleston, were influential in the household or chapel: *ibid.*, p. 278. The other was the cardinal's nephew, the earl of Salisbury.

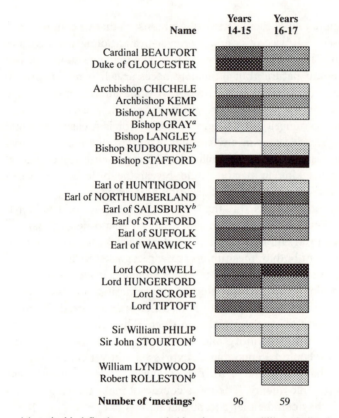

Name	Years 14-15	Years 16-17

Cardinal BEAUFORT
Duke of GLOUCESTER

Archbishop CHICHELE
Archbishop KEMP
Bishop ALNWICK
Bishop GRAY[a]
Bishop LANGLEY
Bishop RUDBOURNE[b]
Bishop STAFFORD

Earl of HUNTINGDON
Earl of NORTHUMBERLAND
Earl of SALISBURY[b]
Earl of STAFFORD
Earl of SUFFOLK
Earl of WARWICK[c]

Lord CROMWELL
Lord HUNGERFORD
Lord SCROPE
Lord TIPTOFT

Sir William PHILIP
Sir John STOURTON[b]

William LYNDWOOD
Robert ROLLESTON[b]

Number of 'meetings'   96   59

A 'meeting' is defined as an act made 'de avisamento consilii', or similar, for which the names of those present at its making are recorded. If a councillor attended more than one 'meeting' in the space of a particular day, this has been counted as one 'meeting' only. Great councils have not been included. No one not formally appointed to the council attended during this period. Henry VI's regnal year ran from 1 September to 31 August: year 14 began in 1435.

Key: percentage of meetings attended
Not a councillor   (blank space)

☐ None   ▨ 1-20%   ▨ 21-40%   ▨ 41-60%   ▨ 61-80%   ■ 81-100%

[a] Died February 1436.   [b] Joined the council in November 1437.   [c] Became lieutenant of France in July 1437 and died April 1439.

Figure 1   Attendance at the council, 1435–9

lines as before, to direct affairs of state.[52] While it often gathered 'in presencia Regis', we cannot be sure that any real interaction between king and council took place at these meetings; and equally often, in fact, the council assembled by itself.[53] The king did not, of course, have to be present at council meetings to be aware of their proceedings, but, unless he was, he could take no part in the discussions which preceded its decisions, decisions to which he readily gave assent. Meanwhile, the councillors became, if anything, less uneasy about interfering with the king's administration of royal grace, notwithstanding the terms of 1437. Apart from openly participating in decisions about major items of patronage, they also intervened in specific cases where the king had exercised his grace imprudently.[54] The tone of conciliar interference was certainly deferential and it stopped short of outright resistance to the king's expressed wishes, but this is symptomatic of the councillors' position: they wanted Henry to manage affairs efficiently by himself, and, if he did not, it was because he could not, which meant that the object of their criticism was not properly the king, but rather those members of the political community who made inconvenient applications for his grace.[55]

[52] Simple notes of who was present and endorsements such as 'granted by the lords of the council' returned to use: e.g. 16–29 November (*PPC*, V, pp. 73–82, C81/1545/64, 66), 7, 14, 16 February (E28/59/as dated), 5–7 May (*PPC*, V, pp. 93–5). Attendance was high, though apparently not regular. The records suggest that the council met intermittently, rather than continuously, but that when it met, large numbers of councillors attended. No one who had not been appointed to the council in November 1437 came to its meetings until at least the summer of 1439. See figure 1 for details of attendance.

[53] It met without the king throughout November 1437 and most of February 1438: *PPC*, V, pp. 73–82, 87–93; C81/1545/64, 66, 69; E28/59/as dated. It met with the king on a few occasions in May 1438, May 1439 and July 1439: *PPC*, V, pp. 95, 98–9; E28/60/6 (two), 7(two), 8, 21, 22 May; E28/62/11, 12, 13 (three) July.

[54] The council probably oversaw the notorious sale of Chirk, for example: although the original warrant uses the 'Rex apud ... concessit ...', praesentibus' formula (E28/60/25 May 1439: see p. 138, below, for what this means), all those present were councillors and the Beaufort proviso to the 1449–50 act of resumption insisted that the grant had been made by advice of the council: *RP*, V, p. 187. A like example is the grant of the disputed lordship of Holderness to the earl of Stafford, made by the king at Windsor with 'all' the councillors present: E28/62/19 Aug. 1439. Other examples, this time concerned with territorial patronage, arise from a meeting organised by the council with the marcher lords in late April 1438 (*PPC*, V, p. 92). Among these appear to be a life-grant to Edmund Beaufort of the various duchy offices he held during pleasure in South Wales (29 April) and a release to Richard of York of the whole farm he paid for Montgomery and part of that paid for Builth (30 April): Somerville 1953: pp. 640, 647; *CPR, 1436–41*, pp. 167–8. For corrective interventions on the part of the council, see *PPC*, V, pp. 88–9, 90 (11 and 12 February 1438).

[55] There are several instances of deference to the king in matters of both grace and state in this period. On 10 February 1438, for example, the lords agreed to a petition for payment from the duke of York, offering him certain jewels as securities if this should please the king. Thirteen days later, the king at Windsor, in the presence of Suffolk and the chancellor, commanded that this should indeed be done (E28/59/10 Feb. 1438). In May 1438, while the council alone drew up plans for an embassy to the emperor and the Council of Basle and made arrangements for transporting Dorset's army to France, it

All the same, the business of applying for grace was made smoother by the revival of some of the more familiar means of authenticating royal grants in the wake of the 1437 declaration. The unwieldy 'RH nous avons graunté', which Henry had been writing at the top of bills he approved, was reduced to a simple 'RH'.[56] The traditional practice of obtaining endorsement from the chamberlain on the king's behalf was revived in February 1438 and, in the same month, the first references to a secretary appear, betokening the re-emergence of the signet.[57] In response to these measures, which made it easier for comparatively unimportant and unrepresentative men about the king to exercise influence, the council seems to have extended its surveillance of the king's grace via a novel expedient involving its clerk, Adam Moleyns.[58] From the spring of 1438, Moleyns began to write endorsements on a significant proportion of the instruments issued by the king, as well as on those issued by the council. In them, he recorded the names of those present when the king made grants, whether or not they were councillors.[59] The resulting formula, 'Rex apud ... concessit ..., praesentibus ...', rapidly became a common way of recording grants made by the king without the council.[60] This rather extraordinary extension of the scope of conciliar interest has received little attention, but it draws attention to some of the problems faced by the hybrid regime of these years.[61] If the council wished to maintain practical control of its own sphere of influence, it needed to know what was going on at Henry's side. After all, there was, in theory, nothing to stop suitors from seeking his judgement on political matters as well as on patronal ones. As we have seen, the line between the zones of 'grace' and 'state' was a highly artificial one, and the councillors found that they had to keep an eye on both; although it is significant that, as

obtained the presence of the king for the appointment of ambassadors to treat for peace and new war-leaders: *PPC*, V, pp. 95–102.

[56] E.g. E28/59/20 and 26 Feb. 1438; E28/60/7 May 1439; E28/62/11 July 1439.

[57] For endorsement by the chamberlain, see E28/59/10 Feb. 1438. The first reference to the secretary is a patent letter dated 13 February 1438 (grant to Thomas Beckington, king's secretary – *CPR, 1436–41*, p. 134). The signet seems to have been in fairly regular use from January 1437, however (PSO1/5) and one signet warrant for the great seal survives from May 1436 (C81/1367/2).

[58] As Moleyns was continually in transit between king and council, bearing messages and advice from the one and responses from the other (e.g. *PPC*, V, pp. 123–4, 175–6, 234–5, 250), this was not difficult to orchestrate.

[59] See e.g. E28/59/28 May 1438 (Windsor: Sir William Philip, John Hampton and Robert Felton present).

[60] A similar formula was used by the king's secretary, Thomas Beckington (e.g. C81/1425/17, 18, 25 and see Maxwell-Lyte 1926: pp. 154–5; n. 63, below). It should be noted that there are plenty of surviving signet warrants, signs manual and chamberlain's endorsements which, as emphasised in 1444 (*CPR, 1441–6*, pp. 312–13), were perfectly valid without the clerk of the council's endorsement.

[61] Only McFarlane 1936: p. 399 and Brown 1969a: pp. 32–3 have really attached much significance to this strange development.

before, they tackled problems with Henry's performance by taking steps which might restrain his subjects rather than the king himself.

In many ways, of course, the larger question raised by Moleyns' endorsements is why, during Henry's reign, the traditional royal forms of authentication were not always considered sufficient by themselves. In earlier reigns, it had been quite normal for the king to make grants of patronage simply by handling petitions to the chancellor, whose clerks recorded the transaction on the document soon after.[62] Under Henry VI, this became comparatively unusual, even when the king and the chancellor were in the same place. Extra tokens of the king's will were commonly provided: normally a sign-manual; quite often an endorsement written either by the king's secretary, or another signet clerk, or – as we have seen – the clerk of the council.[63] Do these elaborations suggest a particular need to emphasise what ought to have been obvious: namely, that the king had willed something to happen? Do they suggest doubts about the care with which the king gave his authorisation? Perhaps by encouraging him to sign his issues, his advisers hoped to encourage him to think more carefully about them. Perhaps fearing that Henry was unduly vulnerable to persuasion, they ordered his clerks to record the circumstances of his grants so that they knew that he had truly made them, and in whose presence. Perhaps it was not the king's advisers, but his suitors, who requested these measures, knowing that his ministers were concerned about the ease with which the royal will could be turned to private advantage and fearful that their grants would be held up or even rejected unless the king's 'mere motion' was as fully expressed as possible. In any event, it is difficult to avoid the conclusion that the councillors still had little faith in the independence of the king's will. If it remained important for them to know who was present when the king made grants, this surely indicates that the king's private person was recognised to be as susceptible to the control of others as his *persona publica*.[64] A power which was supposed to be free and independent was actually nothing of the kind.

---

[62] Maxwell-Lyte 1926: p. 141; Brown 1964a: p. 141.

[63] See, for example, C81/1425/17, dated 5 March 1440, a warrant which contained, in addition to a note written in chancery to record what had happened, the king's sign-manual *and* a note by the secretary, Beckington, to the effect that 'the kyng hath graunted [the bill] in the palais at Canterbury'. The chancellor seems to have been present, or at least in Canterbury, at the time (*CPR, 1436–41*, p. 384). Note that there are also a fair number of these 'direct warrants' which were completely conventional (i.e. neither signed by the king nor endorsed by officers outside the chancery).

[64] The naming of those present gave them an equivalent responsibility for the acts done by the king under these circumstances to that of the councillors recorded as present at acts done 'de avisamento consilii'. Note that not all Moleyns' endorsements on royal grants indicate who was present at their making.

In practice, even so, the councillors appear to have made little use of the knowledge which this arrangement, and other similar ones, gave them. Apart from the series of ordinances on making grants which Nicolas dated to 1444, but which may actually date from later, there is no evidence of their attempting significant intervention.[65]

The first real changes to the position of the council came in the year 1439. From 14 March, its issues were almost exclusively endorsed with the 'Rex de avisamento consilii' formula, whether or not the king was present.[66] The purpose seems to have been to advertise the royal authority behind governmental actions now that Henry was in his eighteenth year.[67] Small as the semantic change was, it may have been part and parcel of a real shift in the balance of power, away from the council and towards the king and those generally around him. The politics of this transition are discussed in the next section, but it is worth noting here that no more than before was it necessarily the work of Henry himself; nor, it should be emphasised, was this a case of one faction displacing another – the men around the king were often councillors.[68] What was happening, rather, was a change in the format of rule, a change which matters because it altered the institutional and conceptual environment in which leading figures had to operate. Other evidence seems to suggest that such a change was indeed taking place. By the latter part of the year, the

[65] This document is discussed below, pp. 255–6. The councillors did make some minor interventions during these years: see e.g. E28/60/21 May 1439. In early 1441, it briefly became common to record who had solicited particular bills (see *PPC*, V, E28/66–72, C81/1545, *passim*). Once again, this suggests surveillance rather than intervention. The practice was petering out by the middle of the year, though stray examples are to be found before and after. Note too that a letter from Beckington and the ambassadors in Guyenne in October 1442 asks the king 'not lightly to passe upon suche grauntes of your demaynes or other lands, rents or revenues here, as peraventure shal be axed of your said Highnesse, but that hit please your Mageste t'abide th'advisement of your said counseille' (Nicolas, (ed.), *Journal of Beckington*, p. 52).

[66] E28/59/14 Mar. 1439. On that day, for example, he was at Canterbury, while the councillors were at Westminster. Note that this form of words (or the equivalent 'de mandato regis per avisamentum consilii') continued to be used throughout the reign whenever the council was active – even during the king's madness when he himself can have played no part: see E28/84, *passim*.

[67] Occasionally, this process can be illustrated. For example, on 10 June 1439, two documents arising from a council meeting at St Mary Overeys, at which the king was not present, bore different endorsements. One, an order to deliver the muniments of Chirk to Cardinal Beaufort was recorded as granted by the lords of the council. The other, a grant to Lord Tiptoft accessory to the lease of the Richmond lands already given him, was allegedly made by the king by advice of his council (E28/61/10 June 1439). It seems that an act involving the alienation of the royal estate specifically required the royal imprimatur. Meanwhile, a decision of August 1439 to summon Sir Robert Ogle before the council was made 'per dominos de consilio', but the resulting letter was endorsed 'Rex de avisamento consilii', presumably in an effort to secure obedience (E28/62/Aug.? 1439).

[68] See table 1.

Table 1   *Access to king and council of selected figures*

Name	With king	With council
Beaufort	7	36
Cromwell	29	77
Gloucester	15	23
Kemp	3	33
Moleyns	126	89
Stafford	58	89
Suffolk	40	29

The table records the number of occasions on which certain key individuals were recorded as being present at decisions made by the king independently ('With king') and at decisions made by advice of the council ('With council'). Data from 15 November 1437 to 31 August 1441 (for sources, see n. 3, above).

council seems to have met more rarely and it was not always noted who was present.[69] More and more did the councillors join with the king for the settlement of important business.[70] When they acted alone in the years around 1440, their business was usually small scale – grants of safe conducts, payments to messengers and officers and so on – or contingent upon broad lines of policy decided in parliament or in the king's presence.[71] In short, the council was ceasing to be the governmental organisation it had been since 1422, and becoming a source of purely administrative assistance.

Meanwhile, the king and those at his side were beginning to handle not only routine matters and petty issues of grace, but also, increasingly, policy initiatives. Chief among these were the foundations of the colleges

---

[69] For example, a warrant of 13 July 1439 merely records that the king made a grant 'in his ful consail' (E28/62). Cf. E28/63/19 (1 December 1439) – 'in pleno consilio'; E28/63/30 (11 December 1439) – 'praesentibus dominos de consilio'. The information that the full council was present is not to be taken literally: in the first case mentioned above, several of its members were at Calais.

[70] It is not always easy to tell whether the king was present or not, on account of the use of the problematic 'Rex de avisamento consilii' formula. However, examples of business apparently carried out by king and council together include: the provision made in June 1440 for the household in accordance with a parliamentary appointment (issued to the council alone, in fact: *RP*, V, p. 7; E28/63/76); letters sent to the earls of Salisbury and Westmorland naming arbitrators to settle their dispute (E28/64/8 Oct. 1440); arrangements made in February 1441 to divide £1,000 among the Calais soldiers (E28/66/55); arrangements made in May 1441 to transfer York's army to France (E28/68/10).

[71] For examples of small-scale business, see E28/58/14 Mar. 1439, E28/65/8. For activity pursuant to earlier orders, see E28/61/10 June 1439 (instructions for the earl of Huntingdon's musters) and E28/68/30 (orders to York to hurry across to France). Some important matters were still handled by the council, apparently: it seems to have appointed Sir Thomas Kyriell lieutenant of Calais in December 1439, for example (E28/63/33).

and the release of the duke of Orléans, but there were others as well.[72] On 18 February 1441, for example, the king made a series of new appointments at Calais and Guisnes by direct command to the chancellor and in conditions of great secrecy.[73] On this occasion, no record of who else was present was made: an important indication that the king took full responsibility for what was decided. In the following March, Henry issued a letter to Lord Grey of Codnor telling him to keep the peace and in April he arranged instructions for the ambassadors going to Calais.[74] Many of these personal initiatives were carried out by the king in the presence of his associates, whether household men, courtiers, magnates or, in fact, councillors. As Moleyns' endorsements show, the king had, since early 1438, been counselled in various matters by men who were not members of the 1437 council,[75] but this does not mean that the councillors were in any way excluded from his presence.[76]

By 1440, then, counsel – even in matters of state – was no longer monopolised by the 1437 council. In itself, this was not a cause for concern. The fact that certain household men – notably the chamberlain Sir Ralph Butler, the carvers Sir John Beauchamp and Sir Edmund Hungerford, the confessor William Ayscough and Lord Beaumont – came to enjoy a disproportionate influence in the king's counsels was merely a reflection of Henry's lack of prudence.[77] The dominance of household men was not the inevitable corollary of non-conciliar rule and

---

[72] See C81/1425/32–6 for the September 1440 grants concerning Eton. For other foundations business handled without the council, see E28/65/4, 28, E28/67/61–2. For further discussion, see below, pp. 167–71, 186–8.

[73] E28/66/68.

[74] E28/67/20 (cf. a similar letter to the earl of Devon, which was sent on 9 November 1440 by the council: E28/65/19); *PPC*, V, pp. 139–40.

[75] When the council was present *en bloc*, Moleyns recorded the fact by using the 'Rex de avisamento consilii' formula: e.g. 8–18 May 1439 (E28/60/as dated), 20 and 28 April 1440 (E28/63/61, 65) and very many other occasions.

[76] For example, on 22 May 1441, the king granted a petition of Lord Bourgchier regarding the captaincy of Crotoy, in the presence of Gloucester, Stafford (bishop), Huntingdon, Stafford (earl), Cromwell and Bardolf, all of whom were councillors, yet the 'Rex apud ... concessit ..., praesentibus ...' formula was used (E28/68/32). See also table 1.

[77] For examples of occasions when these men were present when the king acted, see E28/60/1 May 1439 (Beaumont, Ayscough, James Fiennes); E28/60/7 May 1439 (Beaumont and Ayscough); E28/60/20 May 1439 (Ayscough); E28/60/25 and 26 May 1439 (Ayscough); E28/62/2 July 1439 (Ayscough and Butler); E28/62/10 July 1439 (Butler); E28/64/16 Sept. 1440 (Beauchamp); E28/64/13 Oct. 1440 (Beauchamp); E28/66/2 (1 December 1440 – Hungerford); E28/66/84 (19 February 1441 – Beauchamp). Virgoe 1970 counts these as council meetings, but the existence of a separate endorsement for meetings of the council and Virgoe's own willingness to exclude documents endorsed with the 'Rex apud ... concessit ..., praesentibus ...' formula when the king's companions were men such as John Hampton, James Fiennes and so on, suggest that he is wrong to do so. This means that his dates for the first attendances at the council of Ayscough, Beaumont, Fanhope and Sudeley are all too early (p. 157 n. 2), though, clearly enough, the distinction between 'councillor' and 'counsellor' was losing importance at this time.

certainly not its intended consequence. Continuous proximity was indeed the key to influence over Henry VI, but it should not have been: as we have seen, kings were expected to maintain the public quality of their rule even in their most private surroundings. Nonetheless, Henry's inability to manage the media of government did not prevent the re-establishment of informal modes of rule. For a variety of reasons, there was a growing disposition to look to the king for governance as he reached his late teens. The moment was finally ripe for the royal takeover which had been anticipated in 1436 or 1437. The politics of this transition are discussed in the following section, but here it is sufficient to emphasise that, in principle, there was nothing alarming or unnatural about the decline of the council in this period. Persuaded that it was safe to do so and spurred on by the trend of events, the lords were simply abandoning the artificial mechanisms reaffirmed in 1437 and drifting towards what was ostensibly normal royal government, even though it was really something rather different.

The sense of change is reflected in a number of manifestoes produced during the dispute over the release of the duke of Orléans in 1440.[78] Although these were written with specific political aims in mind, they can be used to illustrate common attitudes to counsel and to provide some insights into the organisation of government in this obscure period. In his famous 'Appeal' against the cardinal, Gloucester argued that Beaufort should not be a member of 'youre counsaille, as be alle other lordes spirituell and temporell at the parlements and greet counsailles, whan youre liste is to calle hem'. This proposition – that all the lords were properly the king's counsellors – was borne out by other points made by the duke: that lords 'of youre kyn' should not be excluded from 'knouleche of eny grete matires that might touche youre high estate, or other of youre royaume';[79] that being 'of blood' and 'of counsel' were synonymous;[80] that 'of right', the archbishop of Canterbury should be the

---

[78] See below, pp. 186–8. The three documents considered here are: [1] Gloucester's 'Appeal' against Beaufort and others, which should probably be dated to early 1440 (*Letters and Papers*, II, ii, pp. 440–51; see Harriss 1988: p. 308 and n. 9 for dating); [2] Gloucester's 'Advys and Oppinion' against the release, published on 2 June 1440 (*Foedera*, V, i, pp. 76–7); [3] The 'playne Declaracion' made by the lords who advised his release, which has been dated to late October 1440 by Dr Harriss (1988: p. 315 n. 29; *Letters and Papers*, II, ii, pp. 451–60).

[79] For this and the previous quotation, see *Letters and Papers*, II, ii, p. 442. Note also *Brut*, p. 488, which recorded that the 1445–6 parliament was adjourned by the king 'and his Consayle of his lordes of the parlement'.

[80] For references to 'lordes of youre bloode and counsaille' (sometimes 'your kyn and counsaille'), see *Letters and Papers*, II, ii, pp. 445–6 . Archbishop Stafford gave the same emphasis to the advice of the 'lordes of his [the king's] blood and counsail' in his letter discussed below, pp. 207–8. See also Kempe, *Historical Notices of ... St Martin-le-Grand*, p. 132, for a case heard in Star Chamber by 'the Lordes of his counsail and

'chief counsaillier' among the lords spiritual.[81] Against the representative counsel of the whole body of the lords, Gloucester set the malign influence of the 'prive counsaille' given by Beaufort and Kemp; men who had been, in many ways, the dominant figures in the council appointed in 1437.[82]

Implicit in the duke's attacks was a sense that this council had ceased to play an appropriate role in the government of the realm. It was for the king to govern. He would receive formal counsel from full assemblies of the lords. Informal counsel he might take as he chose, though it would be assumed by his subjects that he was consulting 'sad and substantial' men, such as Gloucester himself.[83] The possibility that a formally-appointed council should continue in existence to administer affairs of state was, moreover, condemned in a reference to the French king who 'neither hath wisdom nor discretion to governe himselfe, but must be led, for defaut of naturell raison, aftur th'entent of theym that have hym for the tyme in governance'.[84] In a normal polity, it seems, the king's control over policy, and his freedom to consult representatively, would be plain. Significantly, the duke's opponents appear to have taken a similar view. In the 'Playne Declaracion' concerning the release of Orléans, which the government issued in 1441, it was made perfectly clear that responsibility for the move lay with the king: he had been 'moeved and stured' to act not by Beaufort and Kemp, as Gloucester claimed, nor by any tacitly governing body such as the council of 1437, but by 'God and ... raison' alone.[85]

Taken together with the evidence of attendance and endorsement, these documents suggest that, by the summer of 1441, the formal role of the 1437 council in the government was much reduced. The king, or those around him, attended both to matters of grace and to matters of

bloode' (all of whom, bar Lord Fanhope, were actually men appointed councillors in 1437).

[81] *Letters and Papers*, II, ii, p. 442.

[82] *Ibid.*, this could mean 'privy council' rather than 'private counsels', but if so, Gloucester plainly meant a cabal dominated by the cardinal by the term and not the king's advisers – or perhaps the 1437 council, of which Gloucester was a member – as a whole (see p. 450).

[83] Note the 'Advys': 'a gret part of this roialme paraventure wold ymagyn or thynk that the deliverance ... of the said duc, which that toucheth soe nygh my lord and his roialmes, wold not be doon, assentid, nor concluded withoutyn myn advis, conseil or consent' (*Foedera*, V, i, p. 77).

[84] *Ibid.*, p. 76.

[85] *Letters and Papers*, II, ii, p. 452. There is one explicit reference to the king's 'counsaille contynuel' in this document, but it comes in the middle of a historical survey of English toil in France and may well refer to that of the minority (p. 455). The question of whether or not to release Orléans had actually been debated by a council, but it seems fairly clear from Gloucester's 'Advys' that this was not the 1437 body: the duke talked of 'certein lords of [the king's] counseil' being appointed to discuss the matter: *Foedera*, V, i, p. 76.

state, taking counsel on an informal basis when this was necessary. This situation was recognised by the lords as essentially normal, though Henry's failure to lead actively meant that not everyone could rely on either of the compensating alternatives of good government or a word in the king's ear, a factor which helped to provoke Gloucester's criticisms. The council seems to have withered, meeting with more or less the same membership and form, but increasingly peripheral to the developing royal government.[86] It declined because the lords deserted it, willing now, as they had not been before, to see government managed in the comparatively informal surroundings of the court.

Within a few months, however, this decline was suddenly arrested. The autumn of 1441 witnessed a remarkable revival of conciliar activity which was sustained until the beginning of 1444.[87] On 15 November, the council met at the Star Chamber and minutes of its deliberations were taken under a new format.[88] Headed by the date and place and then by a simple list of lords, the minutes, though in draft form, are, in both their detail and the language used, reminiscent of the minority. This format proved to be the general rule for the next twenty months. In the first instance, as A. L. Brown has noted, the new records must be associated with the work of the acting clerk of the council, Henry Benet.[89] Even so, it seems unlikely that all we are witnessing is a development in clerical practice or a new man's enthusiasm for record keeping. Benet's minutes reflect a new vigour in the council. Notes of attendance were assiduously kept. The simple formulae for recording who was present – sometimes just a list, sometimes 'present my lordes ...' – imply the return of a council of fixed membership. In this respect, the minutes of 28 November 1441 are particularly interesting, the names

---

[86] On 20 March 1441, all the 1437 councillors still living were summoned to discuss certain matters, with the exception of Bishop Rudbourne (who may have been visiting his distant see of St David's), the keeper, Lyndwood, and Lord Bardolf, who are both likely to have been at court anyway. The only new councillor summoned was Lord Fanhope, who did not begin to attend regularly until the autumn of that year (E28/67/26). This would therefore seem to be a specially summoned council rather than the start of a new term for the old continual council. Such an explanation is corroborated by the fact that the draft summons to Gloucester speaks of the lords of 'notre counsail' being assembled 'acommuniquer avec vous sur certaines matiers'.

[87] A good set of council minutes survives for November 1441 to at least July 1443: *PPC*, V, pp. 153–311.

[88] *PPC*, V, p. 157.

[89] The style and handwriting of these minutes are distinctive and all but uniform. They can be ascribed to Benet by his note of a command to 'me Benet' which appears in the minutes of 29 August 1442: *PPC*, V, pp. 207–9. Benet was not the clerk of the council, but the minutes we have seem to be coterminous with the period in which he is known to have been active (Brown 1969a: pp. 30–2). He stood in for Moleyns from November 1441 and was more or less replaced by Thomas Kent (appointed clerk of the council in November 1443: E28/72/88) during the winter of 1443–4.

of Chichele, (Bishop) Stafford, Lyndwood, (the earl of) Stafford, Suffolk, Beaumont, Scrope and Fanhope being followed by the word 'counsaillers', whilst Warwick, Dorset, the secretary and Moleyns are recorded simply as being present.[90] This restriction of the right to give counsel was mirrored by the addition of new councillors, most of them men with influence about the king's person.[91] No less than in 1437, when a number of courtiers had been added to the council, the creation of an artificial governing institution required the co-operation of those about the natural seat of government, Henry VI himself. Although 'Rex de avisamento consilii' remained the usual formula for council warrants, the language of the minutes takes the reader back to the minority period: 'it was advised', 'be there made ...', 'it was assented' and so on.[92] Moreover, the pattern of minutes seems more or less to correspond to the old council term-times, especially between 25 February and 13 July 1443, when there was a meeting nearly every day except during the Easter and Whit breaks.[93]

The existence of a fixed council meeting regularly with its deeds recorded was, however, more than a matter of form. The content of its business – major items of defence and diplomatic policy; the management of justice and the arranging of finance – reflects a real return to the situation of the mid-1430s, in which the council was the main source of government.[94] Much of this work seems to have been carried out in the king's absence, although contact between king and council was common, if perfunctory. It is clear that, even when he did attend, Henry's role was once again little more than formal. The meeting of 28 November 1441, at which Devon and Bonville were brought to arbitration in the king's presence, is a classic example. Benet records that 'it was reherced by my

---

[90] *PPC*, V, p. 173.

[91] On 14 October, Viscount Beaumont, Lords Fanhope and Sudeley and Bishop Ayscough all attended for the first time, at a council meeting in the king's presence (*PPC*, V, p. 153: cf. n. 77, above). Fanhope actually attended a council meeting for the first time on 8 May 1440 (E28/63/69), but it is likely that this was in order to obtain payment for keeping the duke of Orléans, since there is a warrant to this effect bearing that date (E404/56/258).

[92] Benet's surviving council warrants are always endorsed 'Rex de avisamento consilii', except for 19 April 1442. Where minutes and instruments can be matched directly, we can see how Benet translated council meetings at which only the lords were present into warrants bearing this formula. An example is 25 November 1441 (E28/69/59 and *PPC*, V, p. 169).

[93] *PPC*, V, pp. 224–308.

[94] For examples of conciliar business in this period, note the following: arrangements to pay the duke of York, as lieutenant in France (*PPC*, V, pp. 155–6); discussion of articles from York, from Guyenne and from Calais (*ibid.*, p. 159); arrangements to repay a £10,000 loan and instructions to the lieutenants of various castles in Normandy (*ibid.*, pp. 163–5); business concerning the feud between the earl of Devon and Lord Bonville (*ibid.*, pp. 158, 160, 166: and see next note).

Lord Chaunceller ~~be therle of~~ [*sic*] by the kynges commandement' how the king was displeased by Devon's behaviour.[95] It seems likely that the deletion is an attempt to disguise the fact that someone else, probably Suffolk, inaugurated the proceedings, whilst the king simply sat in silence. That it was the chancellor who berated Devon may simply be in line with court protocol, but it is hard to imagine a vigorous king remaining silent under these circumstances.[96] Meanwhile, although the events of the meeting are recorded in the past tense, the actions ascribed to the king are mostly in the present – 'the K wol' and so on – implying that these are no more than formal orders, reminiscent, perhaps, of the sentences of a court.[97]

Whilst the councillors continued to emphasise the king's independence, they seem to have had a highly pragmatic sense of how his authority should be employed. At times, they seem to have proceeded much as they did during the minority, when their counsel was the sole constituent of an imaginary, but authoritative, royal person. A particularly elaborate example of this was their observation to ambassadors from Guyenne, in November 1441, that, regarding a post in the administration there, 'it was not the kynges counsaill part to graunte any such thing for it lay but oonly to the kyng and to noon other persone'. However, they went on, 'it was semed at that tyme to the said lordes of the K' consail that it was most fittyng that an Englishman occupied the said office'.[98] Sometimes, the councillors simply claimed the authority of royal will for their independent actions, deploying the means of his personal authority as if that authority were theirs.[99] At other times, they routinely approached others who could declare the king's will, notably

---

[95] *PPC*, V, p. 173.

[96] Compare, for example, Edward IV's handling of allegations made against the duke of Norfolk by Sir William Brandon: *PL*, V, p. 240.

[97] A similar picture is evoked by the responses to articles committed by the duke of Somerset to Yerde and Eltonhede 'to seye unto the K and my lordes of his counsail'. On 9 July 1443, the councillors answered the articles one by one in a form which revealed that they alone were responsible for what was said: *PPC*, V, p. 303. Even so, the schedule given to the men to take back to Somerset claims that these are answers 'yeven by the King oure souverain lord': *ibid.*, pp. 409–14. Compare too the articles from the Irish, answered by the council alone on 4 July 1443, each answer beginning 'The K wol ...' (*ibid.*, p. 297).

[98] *PPC*, V, p. 161.

[99] For example, a minute of 8 October 1442 records simply 'the kyng to commande...' (this was in his presence: *PPC*, V, p. 211); while on 14 March 1443 'my lordes of his counsail by the kynges licence charged' John Seintlo to go and raise loans in Bristol even though the king had, the previous day, requested that he be 'forboren to go' (*ibid.*, pp. 242–4.). On 4 June, they made a memorandum to speak to the king to send a warrant for the payment of Somerset's ordnance (*ibid.*, p. 284). On 21 June they ordered, 'be ther maad a lettre under the Ks signet' – supposedly a seal under his personal control (*ibid.*, pp. 288–9); on 13 July, they themselves appointed that the king 'wolde delivere [military equipment] unto hem and satisfie the partie therfor' (*ibid.*, p. 307); whilst on 2

Suffolk and Beaufort, even when Henry himself was close at hand.[100]
Not surprisingly, the new distribution of power achieved a certain
amount of contemporary recognition, with the corporation of London,
for example, approaching the council in March 1443 to ask that if
anything was sued to the king against their wishes concerning the
Hansards, 'that it be not entended unto'.[101]

Henry himself played no meaningful part in the creation of government policy at this time. Even when he was involved directly in decision
making, he seems merely to have supplied bland approbation.[102] It may,
indeed, seem strange that the councillors bothered to consult the king at
all, but it should be remembered that royal will, in which an apparently
normal adult king would be expected to have the controlling share,
remained the only legitimate basis for public action.[103] Even if its
exercise by the king was at this time purely formulaic, it was not possible
for the councillors to discard him altogether. It is, in any case, unlikely
that the councillors had entirely abandoned the hope that the king, now
at the normal age of majority, would begin to exert himself more
effectively. For various reasons, which will be discussed in the following
section, they had decided in 1441 that, as in 1437, Henry still needed
the support of a formal council if government was to be managed
successfully: this was, let us remember, the only tool they possessed to
improve the quality of government. All the same, as before, their
decision remained continuously open to reassessment. As soon as the
king appeared to be able to manage alone, or, alternatively, as soon as
they found themselves united by their need for an adult king – as in

---

December, they alone wrote to the duke of Brittany, apparently on their own authority
(*PPC*, VI, p. 16).

[100] On 18 October 1442, for example, it was decided to send messengers to Cardinal
Beaufort, who would declare 'the Kynges entent' in the matter of assignments to
creditors on the lay subsidy: this decision was made by a council gathered in the Great
Chamber at Eltham, presumably within yards of the king himself (*ibid.*, pp. 220–1;
Henry's presence at Eltham is shown by Wolffe 1981: p. 363). There are lots of other
examples: see *PPC*, V, p. 250, for an occasion when the chancellor and Adam Moleyns
'commanded for the K' in Henry's presence that certain letters should not pass; *ibid.*, p.
259, for an example of Suffolk, Moleyns and the chancellor granting petitions at
Suffolk's house; *ibid.*, p. 248, for an order to Benet to 'be with my Lord of Suffolk at the
kynges hous with a note of a lettre to therle of Ormond and to therchebisshop of
Dyvelyng'.

[101] *PPC*, V, pp. 233–4. This time, the councillors did not bother putting them right about
the division of powers.

[102] On the evening of 11 May 1443, for example, when Stafford and others reported the
day's activities to the king in his secret chamber, he simply commanded them to be done
'as is befor writen' (*PPC*, V, p. 271). On 13 December 1443, Moleyns reported that
when he had told the king of all the matters currently before the council, Henry 'thanked
theim of their laboures and helde their advisementes good and commandeth theim to be
don' (*PPC* VI, pp. 18–19).

[103] Cf. Storey 1966: p. 36.

1436 and, in a sense, 1439–40 – they would abandon the demeaning and inconvenient conciliar format in favour of a more traditional relationship with the sovereign.[104]

This is what began to happen towards the end of 1443. In many respects, the pattern of 1439–41 was repeated. Attendance records show a steady decline in interest from 1442 onwards on the part of all but the officers.[105] While in November 1443, there were apparently more appointments – Lord Dudley and probably Bishops Lowe and Brouns – this seems to have been part and parcel of the merger of court and council which was taking place at the time.[106] Late in the same year, Thomas Kent began to take over as clerk and Benet's minutes, though not his endorsements, became few and far between. Although the king was apparently not often present at the council,[107] his personal activity seems to have increased, as those who had flirted with the revived council drifted back to a more direct control of affairs through the king. Very few warrants have survived for the second half of 1444,[108] but the evidence of early 1445 tells the same story: more activity by the king, less by the council; and king and council apart until the opening of parliament at the end of February. In the wider sphere of politics, Suffolk had, by the latter part of 1443, succeeded in drawing the court – both household and

---

[104] The reasons why the lords may have wished to advance the king to power in 1439–40 are discussed below, pp. 180–8.

[105] See figure 2.

[106] Dudley was appointed and sworn in on 3 November 1443 (E404/61/114). He actually began to attend in January 1444. Bishops Lowe and Brouns first attended on 13 and 31 January respectively (E28/71/29, 53). The bishops would not appear amongst the warrants for issues, since clerics were not paid for their attendance at the council after 1437, apart from Beaufort and the officers (*PPC*, V, p. 72). It seems reasonable to assume that Brouns and Lowe were added to the council at about the same time as Dudley. The marquis of Dorset first attended a council meeting on 14 November 1443 (E28/71/27), so perhaps he too was part of a new intake.

[107] For example, the king was at Sheen for most of February and early March 1444, while the council met chiefly at Westminster. Sheen was, of course, well within a day's journey of Westminster, but since the councillors could (and did – e.g. 11 February) travel to be with the king, it is safe to assume that if they met at Westminster, they did so in his absence. In April and May, the council remained there, while the king roved around higher up the Thames Valley (E28/72, 73 *passim*).

[108] There were meetings, however. On 13 January 1445, the lords were reminded of an act of the council made on 12 September 1444 to settle the feud between the earl of Shrewsbury and Lord Berkeley (E28/74/10). This could have been an *ad hoc* council, assembled for the purpose, but note also Meekings 1975: p. 332, where it appears that indictments against Thomas Kerver, drawn up in August 1444, refer to 'the king and the lords spiritual and temporal of his council, existing for the peace and good of the realm'. This seems to evoke a public perception that the king was still assisted by a formal council. There is some evidence that MPs went on believing this right up to 1450 (below, pp. 249–50). If this does not prove that a council like that of 1437 did still exist, it does suggest that – at some level – such a body would have been regarded as acceptable.

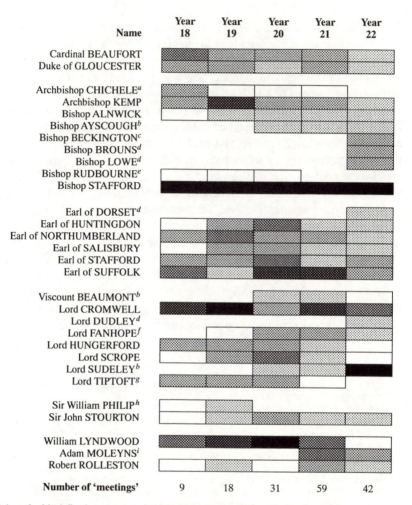

A 'meeting' is defined as an act made 'de avisamento consilii', or similar, for which the names of those present at its making are recorded. If a councillor attended more than one 'meeting' in the space of a particular day, this has been counted as one 'meeting' only. Great councils have not been included. No one not formally appointed to the council attended during this period. Henry VI's regnal year ran from 1 September to 31 August: year 18 began in 1439.

Key: percentage of meetings attended

Not a councillor   (blank space)

☐ None   ▨ 1-20%   ▨ 21-40%   ▨ 41-60%   ■ 61-80%   ■ 81-100%

[a] Died April 1443.   [b] Joined the council in October 1441.   [c] Became keeper of the privy seal in July 1443, and attended the council thereafter.   [d] Joined the council in November 1443, though Dudley attended one meeting in Year 20 and Lowe and Brouns may not have joined until early 1444.   [e] Dead by July 1442.   [f] Died December 1443.   [g] Died January 1443.   [h] Died June 1441.   [i] Councillor by February 1443. Became keeper of the privy seal in February 1444.

Figure 2   Attendance at the council, 1439–44

nobility – together.[109] In the ensuing year, amid moves to obtain a royal marriage and a final settlement of the problem of Lancastrian France, the king was placed once again at the centre of government and the lords returned to a more traditional posture of informal and non-exclusive counsel. In 1445, therefore, an adult, married king sat on the throne and political society ranged itself about him accordingly. The long-enduring council, a symptom of the king's mysterious inadequacy, had finally been laid to rest, or at least moved to the sidelines. Suffolk had succeeded in persuading the lords that the king, in the court, could cater for their interests, both individual and collective. How he achieved this is the subject of the next section.

THE FORMATION OF A ROYAL REGIME

The convention that royal authority was bestowed by God and not by man had a solid practical basis. As we have seen, it was the king's ultimate independence of communal, or 'political', power that enabled him to rule and represent his people: his right was both inherent and overwhelming. This was, of course, the fundamental problem facing the *communitas* in all cases of royal incapacity – periods of minority, illness or insanity as much as the more familiar example of misrule: human agency could not easily create the independent power on which human government ultimately depended. For this reason as much as any other, the process of transferring power to kings who came to the throne in childhood or adolescence was an unnatural one, never achieved without some disruption. The artificial measures devised by the leaders of society to provide a fair standard of rule in the absence of normal kingship were fundamentally at odds with royal authority, both institutionally and constitutionally, yet they guaranteed certain political goods to at least a part of the elite: a reasonable source of representative judgement, an orderly administration, and so on. The rule of the king offered much more, but gave no such guarantees, particularly to individuals: no nobleman, then, can be blamed for hesitating as the time to hand over drew near. Was the king old enough? Was he wise enough? Could his sympathy be counted on?

Few kings left the nobility to make these difficult judgements undisturbed. Edward III rapidly convinced his leading subjects that he could govern them properly.[110] Richard II rapidly convinced his that he could

---

[109] See below, pp. 172ff. Gerald Harriss settles upon the latter half of 1444 as the moment when the direction of policy finally shifted to the household (1988: p. 349). See Griffiths 1981: pp. 281–2, for something of the same view.

[110] This has not been the view of some recent accounts (e.g. Ormrod 1990: ch. 1), but cf. e.g. McKisack 1959: pp. 152–4; Nicholson 1965.

not: as the king expressed his will with the resources available in the royal household, leading noblemen struggled to retain a measure of control over government through parliamentary, conciliar and administrative means.[111] Only Henry VI succeeded to power without a significant degree of friction or abruptness and this is highly illuminating. If we approach the question of authority structurally, there is little to choose between Henry's position in the mid-1430s and that of Richard II in the early 1380s: in each case, the king had full authority to rule, but was unable to inspire sufficient confidence among the nobility for them fully to surrender the corporate direction of policy which they had exercised during his infancy. Under Richard, this state of affairs produced a bitter and rapidly escalating conflict between the king and his chamber intimates, on the one hand, and leading members of the territorial nobility, on the other. Why did no similar conflict emerge under Henry VI?

One answer can be rapidly discarded: the possibility that, as the councillors had hoped, effective rule began with the king's first personal exercise of power in the summer of 1436. This was plainly not the case. The king did not, as was normal, begin to discharge the full range of affairs of state, grace and justice from a royal court located in the household and composed of noblemen and other notables. By November 1437, the minority council had been authoritatively re-established and it continued to exercise a varying degree of control over government until the mid-1440s. Whilst this state of affairs was an important factor in the enduring conflict between Cardinal Beaufort and Humphrey, duke of Gloucester, it did not divide the king from the lords, nor the household from the council, nor the rest of the lords from one another. To some extent, perhaps, this lack of division can be explained by the sense of common purpose which the inspiring rule of Henry V had bequeathed to the leading men of the period. It might also owe something to the fact that there was always good reason for the lords to avoid division, although, given the diverse pressures upon them, this underlying concern was not normally sufficient to preserve harmony by itself.

Paradoxically, the principal reason for the absence of division in these years of ineffective royal authority may have been the failure of the king to assert himself: the same feature, in fact, which created that ineffectiveness. Henry's inertia removed the possibility of conflict between leading councillors and any hypothetical household clique with a greater stake in the establishment of purely royal power, because there was no unmistakable, independent and over-riding royal will on which such power could

---

[111] For details of the early years of Richard II's reign, see Tuck 1973: chs. 2–4 (esp. pp. 33–4) and Chrimes 1956.

be based. Household men, who could activate the king and who might otherwise have formed the nub of a royal party in this period of divided jurisdiction, were forced to negotiate the power which was both his and theirs (and, indeed, the access on which it depended) with the men in the council.

All the same, the situation was not a static one. A number of factors conspired to produce a trend in favour of the establishment of royal rule, among them, of course, the king's progression towards adulthood. This has generally been given a pre-eminent role in explaining the politics of this period, but given that we may not assume any commensurate growth in the king's will-power and that, as we have seen, 'youth' was by no means a simple impediment to royal authority, it may deserve a different kind of emphasis. The king's age mattered because, as time went by, it made conciliar rule look more anomalous and appeals to royal judgement look more plausible: it did not really affect the fundamental problem facing Henry's subjects, except, perhaps, by making it easier to perceive. Just as important in determining the pace and direction of governmental change were the demands of circumstance, both general and specific. On the one hand, the inadequacies of conciliar government were tiresomely familiar, and this disposed political society as a whole to long for royal direction. On the other hand, as we shall see, the policies required by the worsening situation in France in the later 1430s and 1440s needed a king to authorise them. At the same time, only peer-pressure and self-discipline existed to restrain the leading members of a naturally hierarchical society from invoking a higher lordship to satisfy their individual interests. No matter how much reason there was to doubt the credibility of his judgements, the temptation to turn to the king must have been great and it was surely made greater by the sense that one's peers were doing so: once the common front behind the council was broken, its disintegration was rapid, even if concern at the shortcomings of a more purely royal authority could, at times, provoke its subsequent restoration. Peer-pressure alone was not, therefore, a notably stabilising force.

In the period of this chapter, then, politics contained the ingredients of anarchy, if not those of division. Yet a fairly smooth transition was achieved from a system of government by council to a system of royal rule in the court. This was, to a large extent, the work of the earl of Suffolk and it is with his policy and its impact that the rest of the chapter will be mostly concerned. By establishing a workable lordship in the royal household and by making it acceptable to the major temporal lords of the council, the earl did much to satisfy the natural trend towards royal government, despite the unnatural weakness of the royal person. In the sections which follow, we shall consider first the earl's creation of an effective authority in the household and second the means by which this authority was extended into the rule of the realm.

The underlying cause of 'policy' in the household and self-denial among the lords was the lack of firmness, resistance, prudence in the young king. Looking at Henry's administration of his powers following the summer of 1436, it is difficult to escape the conclusion that he simply endorsed all requests put before him. This was certainly the implication of various conciliar initiatives to stem the flood of royal generosity.[112] It is also suggested by the preponderance of grants to those enjoying most continuous access to the king,[113] by the tendency for grants to particular people to be concentrated on occasions when we know them to have been at Henry's side,[114] by the notorious royal propensity for granting the same thing more than once[115] and by the developing practice of granting reversions once the original stock of patronage was exhausted.[116] There is no reason to suppose that this was a consistent policy of generosity on the part of the king: far more closely does it resemble 'foole largesse' than the quality of 'fraunchise' admired by commentators.[117] The satisfaction of suitors, and the political benefits which the crown derived as a consequence, can only have been individual and temporary. The long-term costs, on the other hand, were wide-ranging, public and enduring. Throughout his youth and for most of his adulthood, Henry's patronage

---

[112] See above, pp. 131, 137–9, and below, pp. 212–15, 255–6.

[113] In the fifteenth year (1436–7), for example, there were upwards of 150 grants to men in the household (including members of the nobility such as Gloucester and Suffolk): *CPR, 1436–41*, pp. 1–91, *passim*.

[114] For example, on 20 September 1437, the earl of Salisbury received a series of life-grants of major territorial offices from the king and an important lease from his mother, the countess of Westmorland (see below, p. 173, n. 202). All this was presumably arranged in London, where Salisbury seems to have been. He was certainly there for the great council of October/November, at which he was made a councillor and doubtless assisted in the subsequent promotion of his brother to the see of Durham (*PPC*, V, pp. 64–73; Davies 1974: p. 408; *CFR, 1437–45*, p. 18; and see Somerville 1953: p. 500, for the insertion of Salisbury into Sir John Stanley's stewardship of Blackburn on 7 November 1437).

[115] The most famous example is, of course, the grant to both Devon and Bonville of the stewardship of the duchy of Cornwall lands in Cornwall (*CPR, 1436–41*, pp. 133, 532), but note also the grant of the stewardship of Wallingford to Philip whilst Suffolk was survivor (below, p. 159). See *CPR, 1446–52*, p. 79, and Wedgwood 1936: p. 638 for other examples. When Thomas Daniel told the king in February 1447 that the grant he had secured of a fine to be paid by the founder of a chantry was valueless because the same had already been granted to Sir Edmund Hungerford, he was able to get a privy seal reimbursing him from the exchequer to the tune of £100 (E404/63/22)! That this problem was not unusual under Henry is implied by clauses 5 and 6 of the ordinances on royal grants usually dated to 1444 (*PPC*, VI, p. 318).

[116] See nn. 221 and 321 for examples of the resulting problems, and also below, p. 217, n. 50.

[117] Above, p. 25. The king's noted mercy was of a similar kind: above, p. 110.

was a barely organised rout in which the pattern of royal activity was determined mostly by the applicants for grace. While efforts were apparently made to manage their activities, the only final limitation on suitors was their own discretion.

This state of affairs reminds us that the mere act of recognising the king's possession of authority did not in itself enable him – or others – to use it effectively, even within the household. If the king's will floated freely in his presence, anyone with access to him could make use of it: the lowliest groom as much as the highest duke. No less than the other political enterprises of Henry VI's reign, therefore, the household required organisation if it was to fulfil any governmental function: this, it seems, was a king for whom even purely royal power had to be artificially constituted. Normally, of course, it was the will of the ruler which held in place the structure of personal and public authority based in the household.[118] Henry's courtiers had to find alternative means for the creation and preservation of this structure. If the king himself could not exercise his lordship – first over the household, the lair of his *persona privata*; second over the realm itself, where royal rule was so fundamentally necessary – they would have to set it up themselves and exercise it through him. This, in effect, was the basis of household organisation. It had to be twofold: internal, in that its members had to recognise their common interest and pull together; and external, in that its leaders needed the sympathy of at least a proportion of the magnates if they were to succeed in exercising real power. In the 1430s and early 1440s, these aims were steadily fulfilled. This was the earl of Suffolk's great achievement.[119] During the rest of this section, we shall be exploring how Suffolk came to stand in for the king as lord of the household and how he extended this lordship into the realm itself. For comparative purposes, it may be useful to begin with another look at an earlier attempt to achieve similar objectives: Gloucester's failed coup of 1432.[120]

Gloucester's action neatly illustrates the difficulties involved in any attempt to change the distribution of authority. It had three main strands, each of them full of relevance for the later period: first, the creation and

---

[118] See above, pp. 89–90.

[119] It has been argued by Morgan 1987 that the household of Henry VI was by no means a monolithic institution, even at its zenith in the later 1440s. He comments that 'its incoherence is its dominant feature' (pp. 38–41). This is an important insight and fits the later 1440s particularly well, but, at the same time, it seems hard to deny that a household connection of some kind was the only possible basis of Suffolk's power: even he could not be with the king all the time, yet he still enjoyed a measure of continuous authority. Dr Morgan notes Suffolk's paramountcy (*ibid.*, pp. 39, 40–1) and observes that it did not rest on an influx of new men (p. 41), but does not seem to offer any alternative explanation of where it came from.

[120] See also above, pp. 118–20.

maintenance of support in the council, as the existing centre of authority; second, the attempted transfer of government from council to court; and, third, the creation and maintenance of support in the household, as the institutional base of this new court. The principal men replaced by Gloucester in 1432 – Kemp, Hungerford, Alnwick, Cromwell and Tiptoft – were plainly associated with Beaufort.[121] They had also been among the leading attenders at the minority council and, naturally enough, the two facts are far from unrelated: the council was the basis of Beaufort's power and the source of Gloucester's exclusion. Even so, it is clear that the cardinal's control of the body was not total, since Gloucester could hardly have got as far as he did without at least some conciliar backing.[122]

The duke was certainly aware of the importance of this. He had already taken steps to recruit possible supporters to the council – Suffolk among them – and proceeded with this in mind when appointing new officers in February and March.[123] Scrope, the new treasurer, was a councillor who had shown support for Gloucester in the past.[124] Other new men were associates of Archbishop Chichele, perhaps the most important of the councillors outside the Beaufort orbit and probably a friend of Gloucester.[125] The new chamberlain and steward, Sir William Philip and Sir Robert Babthorp, who had not been members of the council, were soon added to it.[126] The duke's ultimate aim, as we have seen, was probably to supplant the council altogether, but in the meantime he needed to prevent it from uniting against him as it often had before. His alteration of its

---

[121] Harriss 1988: p. 217.

[122] See above, p. 118, n. 74, and Harriss 1988: ch. 11, where Gloucester's support on the council is discussed extensively. The January 1432 changes to the council ordinances were agreed by Gloucester himself, Bishop Stafford and Lord Scrope (who were shortly to benefit from them), Archbishop Chichele, Bishops Morgan, Gray and Langdon, the duke of Norfolk, the earls of Huntingdon and Suffolk and, curiously, Lord Hungerford. This was a very similar group to those appointed to try petitions in the 1432 parliament, an assembly dominated by Gloucester and intended to be the scene of Beaufort's destruction (Harriss 1988: p. 218; *RP*, IV, pp. 388–9). Gray and Huntingdon, who were not among the triers, were witnesses to the transfer of the great seal to Stafford on 25 February (*CCIR, 1429–35*, p. 181).

[123] Suffolk was appointed on 28 November 1431 at a meeting from which Kemp and Hungerford were absent: *PPC*, IV, p. 108. Owing to the absence of so many councillors in France, Suffolk's appointment was, in effect, made by Gloucester, Chichele, Gray, Morgan, Stafford (bishop), Norfolk and Scrope, substantially the same group who were to agree the new articles two months later.

[124] E.g. *PPC*, IV, pp. 8, 104–5.

[125] For Chichele's connections with the new chancellor (Stafford), keeper of the privy seal (Wm Lyndwood) and almoner (Robt Felton), see Jacob 1967: pp. 26–8 and 1962: pp. 1, 3; Griffiths 1981: p. 59. For connections with Gloucester, see Jacob 1967: p. 107.

[126] Philip joined in May 1432: *PPC*, IV, pp. 113–14. There is less evidence for Babthorp, but he seems to have become a councillor, being present on 23 and 24 May 1433, just after Gloucester's return from Calais (C81/1545/41–2).

personnel demonstrates the political necessity of retaining the support of the existing institutions of power, a necessity which was quite as pressing later on. At the same time, Gloucester seems to have taken similar care with the new court, attempting, perhaps, to recreate the martial *ambiance* of Henry V's establishment with his appointments[127] and seizing the opportunity to draw the household together with some financial incentives.[128] By these means, he might create a united body capable of steering the king towards the martial policies he claimed to favour and sustaining his own political position as it did so.[129]

In its immediate political objectives, Gloucester's coup was, of course, a failure.[130] His opponents responded by taking refuge in the authority of Bedford and by refocusing politics on the council under his protection. Even so, once it had been established by Gloucester as a political interest group, the court developed a momentum of its own. From this time forward, the council was no longer so free to dictate the composition of the household: in the reaction of 1433, for example, Gloucester's appointee, Sir William Philip, remained as chamberlain,[131] while Suffolk, who replaced Babthorp as steward, was probably as acceptable to the duke as he was to his opponents.[132] When Gloucester again attempted to transfer power to the king in 1434, the council was, admittedly, still able to stop him, but an important reason for this was that the dominant

---

[127] Several of the 'new' men had been part of Henry V's court: Stafford had been keeper of the privy seal from February 1421 until the king's death (Jacob 1962: p. 4); Babthorp had been controller of the old king's household and Philip its treasurer (*CPR, 1429–36*, p. 254: note that Babthorp had also been steward of the household from the end of September 1421 (when Gloucester was *custos*) until April 1424: *HBC*, p. 77). Suffolk, the new steward, had no particular connection with Henry V, but he was, by 1432, something of an experienced, if rather unsuccessful, old soldier: see Kingsford 1925: pp. 147–8. Some of the men Gloucester removed were also courtiers of Henry V, of course (note especially Hungerford, Henry V's steward and one of the dead king's chosen companions for his son: Strong and Strong, 'Will of Henry V', pp. 84–5), but their subsequent association with Beaufort doubtless made them unattractive to the duke.

[128] In October 1432, Philip and Babthorp, together with Hungerford, were commissioned to divide among the old king's servants the £4,000 willed to them (*CPR, 1429–36*, p. 254). At about the same time, it was decided to pay the king's carvers, appointed in 1430, but unpaid since then, £40 a year (*PPC*, IV, p. 128).

[129] Gloucester's concern at the progress of the war was to be aired openly at the great council of April–May 1434, though Bedford's speech to parliament on 13 July 1433 suggests that criticisms had already emerged by then (*PPC*, IV, pp. 210ff; *RP*, IV, p. 420).

[130] Harriss 1988: ch. 11, *passim*. The turning-point was the conference at Calais in April and May 1433 (*ibid.*, p. 228).

[131] Cromwell could not get back the chamberlainship (see *RP*, IV, p. 392), despite his attendance at the Calais conference. There may even have been arguments about his appointment as treasurer (see *PPC*, IV, p. 175, and Harriss 1988: p. 230).

[132] Suffolk almost certainly became steward in the wake of the Calais conference (see Griffiths 1981: p. 49 n. 76 and *Letters and Papers*, II, i, p. 222). Babthorp's surrender of the stewardship of Kenilworth on 18 July 1433 seems to corroborate this (Somerville 1953: p. 560).

figures in the household were faced with a choice of two avenues of power. The courtier-councillors, Suffolk and Philip, were well placed to benefit from a slow change in the source of authority: their position in the household would later give them access to the personal authority of the monarch, but this authority was not yet fully accepted. They could succeed where Gloucester had failed by adopting a more judicious and co-operative approach to the matter of transferring authority. For this may actually be the key to Gloucester's failure in 1432: the fact that he was trying to use important changes in the structure of government as a tool in his struggle against the cardinal. Despite its significance as a spur to the establishment of personal rule, division among the elite was not at all a sound basis for the exercise of such an insecure authority. As yet, the personal rule of Henry VI could only be a factitious affair: its establishment would have to rest upon consensus. Suffolk perceived this and the attention which, as a result, he gave to preserving the unity of the governing group brought him considerable success.

The simple basis of Suffolk's power was the office of steward of the household, which bestowed upon him a valuable mixture of proximity to Henry and authority within the household. Through these means, he was able to exert a measure of surveillance, and indeed control, over the exercise of royal will. However, there must have been more to Suffolk's hegemony than this. For one thing, Sir William Philip's post of chamberlain placed him in a similarly privileged position.[133] For another, as we have seen, the importance of household offices depended on the validity and effectiveness of the king's *persona privata*. Clearly, the hegemony of Suffolk, over Philip and other courtiers as much as over the realm at large, also depended on extra-curial sources of power. For Suffolk, like most members of the nobility, who were both lords of the land and the king's servants, these sources were of two distinct, but inter-related kinds: local and territorial; and national and 'political'.

Suffolk's lands were concentrated in two main areas: Norfolk and Suffolk, which by now formed the heartland of the De La Pole patrimony; and the Thames Valley, where the earl acquired the Chaucer lands soon after his marriage to the heiress, Alice, dowager countess of Salisbury, in late 1430.[134] In both areas, his estates brought him useful connections. In

---

[133]   These offices governed access to the king's person, subject only to royal control. Given-Wilson 1986: pp. 72–4; Myers 1959: pp. 104–5, 142–3.

[134]   For Suffolk's lands, see James 1979: pp. 231–4, 239–40, and note his suggestion that Suffolk may have resided mostly at his wife's manor of Ewelme, Oxon. (p. 240). For the Chaucer lands, see *CIPM*, IV, 13 Hen. VI, no. 35. The De La Pole family had held no lands in the Thames Valley: *ibid.*, 3 Hen. V, nos. 48a&b. For Suffolk's marriage, see *CPR, 1429–36*, p. 86. Helen Castor has taken the investigation of Suffolk's power in

East Anglia, the most valuable of these was Sir William Philip himself. Philip, a Norfolk and Suffolk landowner of some substance,[135] had had the custody of the earl's lands during his three-year wardship.[136] This proved to be the basis of a close and enduring relationship, as Suffolk rapidly filled the vacuum of lordship in the area created by the deaths of Philip's lord, the Beaufort duke of Exeter (1426), and of the Mowbray duke of Norfolk (1432).[137] The development is evident in the appearance of a number of men hitherto associated with Exeter and/or Philip in the earl's service. These included some of Suffolk's leading supporters: men like Sir Thomas Hoo, Sir Thomas Tuddenham and John Heydon.[138]

The importance of the relationship between Suffolk and Philip was demonstrated when the king's admission to his powers and the coincidental deaths of the queens dowager presented those in the household with opportunities for rich reward. In January 1437, Philip seems to have seized the chance to acquire from the king the stewardship of Queen Katherine's honour of Wallingford, an office which Suffolk had held as survivor to Chaucer during the last years of the queen's life.[139] Seven

East Anglia much further since this rather sketchy account was written. See Castor 1993.

[135] His inquisition *post mortem* records seven manors in Suffolk and twelve in Norfolk: *CIPM*, IV, 19 Hen. VI, no. 30.

[136] *CPR, 1413–16*, pp. 383–4. Philip continued to receive an annuity of £50 from Suffolk's sister-in-law, Elizabeth, widow of Michael De La Pole the younger (Elder 1964: p. 133).

[137] Exeter had been granted custody of the Bardolf lands from 1405 and those of the De Vere earls of Oxford from about 1417, and as a result, had quite a following in East Anglia (see Elder 1964: pp. 133–4; *GEC*, X, p. 260). Philip was a member of Exeter's household, and it was doubtless to him that he owed his marriage to Joan Bardolf, from which he was later to take his title (*GEC*, I, p. 420 n. 'd'). He was the leading executor of the duke (Nichols, *Wills of the Kings and Queens*, pp. 258–9; *CPR 1422–9*, p. 518, and see *CCIR, 1429–35*, pp. 228–9, for a 1432 transaction also involving Suffolk). For the abeyance of Mowbray power from 1432, see James 1979: pp. 236, 240, 271 and Archer 1984b: pp. 24–5, 28–9.

[138] Hoo: Exeter connection – Nichols, *Wills of the Kings and Queens*, p. 262; Suffolk connections – E163/7/31/1; *DKR*, XLVIII, p. 313; James 1979: p. 46; *CAD*, V, no. A.10892; *CFR, 1430–7*, p. 60; *CPR, 1429–36*, p. 346; *CCIR, 1429–35*, p. 361. Heydon: Philip connections – *CFR, 1430–7*, pp. 59–60, 86–7, 314–15, 336; Somerville 1953: p. 430; Jacob, *Reg. Chichele*, II, pp. 598, 602; connection with Suffolk began in Wingfield–Lyston dispute of summer 1440 – James 1979: p. 262. Tuddenham: Exeter connection – below, this note; connections with Suffolk's men – *CFR, 1430–7*, pp. 121, 337; connections with Suffolk – *CCIR, 1429–35*, p. 361; *CCIR, 1435–41*, p. 62. Note that in Harvey (ed.), *Worcestre: Itineraries*, pp. 355–7, there is a list of figures in Exeter's household, which includes Sir John Shardelowe, Sir William Philip, Sir Thomas Tuddenham, Sir William Calthorp, Sir Robert Clifton, Sir William Wolf and others. Most of these later became De La Pole connections (see Griffiths 1981: p. 336 for Calthorpe; Maddern 1992: pp. 161–2, for Wolf; *CFR, 1430–7*, p. 33, *CAD*, V, no. A.10892 for Shardelowe).

[139] At Queen Katherine's death, Suffolk held this office during pleasure: *CPR, 1429–36*, pp. 346–7. Philip obtained his grant the day after the queen died: *CPR, 1436–41*, p. 32. A possible explanation for Philip's provocative behaviour is that he was seeking to put pressure on Suffolk to come to some arrangement regarding the manor of Wormegay

weeks later, the office was regranted: this time to Philip and Suffolk together, in survivorship.[140] The episode perfectly illustrates two things: both the way in which Henry's apparently unreflecting treatment of petitions could be a potential source of friction among his leading subjects; and also how outright division could be, and had to be, resolved through their own efforts at negotiation and compromise. It is likely that part of this process was the acceptance by Philip of Suffolk's superiority: it was, as we shall see, the earl who had the broader basis of support and it is a matter of some significance that the second of the two grants above was made by deliberation of the council, while the first had been made by the king alone. When the opportunity to reshape the entire duchy of Lancaster establishment arose a few months later, Philip adopted a more co-operative path.[141] The major duchy offices, both central and East Anglian, were shared between himself and Suffolk, despite Philip's prior ascendancy in 'Lancastrian' circles.[142] An equivalence in access to the central, but only partially realised, source of power – the king – was gradually being resolved into a co-operative relationship in which Suffolk enjoyed pre-eminence.

The earl owed his second area of territorial dominance to his marriage, which made him the heir of Thomas Chaucer, one of the leading landowners in Oxfordshire. Stepping into Chaucer's shoes, he acquired a ready-made following in an area highly convenient for anyone planning to spend a lot of time at court.[143] In June 1434, Chaucer surrendered his

---

and other Bardolf lands in East Anglia which were in the earl's keeping. It seems that Henry IV had not intended the 1405 forfeiture of Bardolf's lands, to which Philip's wife was a coheiress, to be permanent (see e.g. *CPR, 1405–8*, pp. 448–9). Wormegay *et al.* had been farmed by Exeter (during which time we might imagine Philip to have enjoyed the use of them) and were farmed by Suffolk from February 1431: *CFR, 1430–7*, p. 33. The earl's farm was renewed as late as 15 July 1437, but, four months later, he surrendered his patent and the lands were granted to Philip: *CPR, 1436–41*, pp. 117–18. It is probably from this time that Philip became known as Lord Bardolf, since Wormegay was the nucleus of his wife's patrimony. He cannot seriously have expected to be able to operate as steward of Wallingford without Suffolk's approval: see next paragraph for the earl's influence in the area.

[140] *CPR, 1436–41*, p. 44.

[141] On 23 April 1437, Suffolk was appointed, during pleasure, chief steward of the north parts of the duchy: Somerville 1953: p. 420. On 11 May, the feoffees made the earl chief steward for life in their lands in the north parts and Philip chief steward for life in their lands in the south parts: *ibid.*, pp. 420, 428. Philip was appointed chief steward in the king's lands in the south parts the following day (*ibid.*).

[142] Henry V's feoffees had already appointed him steward of Norfolk, Suffolk and Cambridgeshire in their lands, while Sir Thomas Tuddenham was steward in those of the king (Somerville 1953: p. 594). Philip's servant, John Puttock, was made feodary in Norfolk in February 1437 (*ibid.*, p. 598), though he himself had to surrender his stewardship of the feoffees' lands for Sir Thomas Tuddenham in November 1437 (*ibid.*, p. 594). The relationship between Suffolk, Philip and the duchy establishment in East Anglia receives much fuller attention in Castor 1993.

[143] A Berkshire oyer and terminer commission, issued in August 1432 (by Suffolk himself,

sole right in the stewardship and constableship of the queen's castle and honour of Wallingford, so that it could be regranted to him and Suffolk together.[144] Not only was this the perfect complement to the Chaucer lands,[145] it also provided a link with Queen Katherine and her entourage which may have been useful in helping to create for Suffolk the network of household connections which would come to prove the basis of his rule.[146] Nor was this all. The Chaucers were also close associates of the Beauforts,[147] a happy position which had brought advantage not only to themselves,[148] but also to those like the Montagues, and now William De La Pole, who married into the family.[149]

Whether or not it was the Chaucer connection which created links

together with Gloucester and Hungerford: BL, Add. MS 19,398, fol. 25), shows the extent to which the earl was integrated into local society even before Chaucer's death. It comprised Suffolk, Chaucer himself, John Cotesmore, John Golafre, Robert Danvers and Andrew Sperlyng (*CPR, 1429–36*, p. 218). Golafre, a Chaucer feoffee (*CCIR, 1422–9*, p. 446; *CPR, 1436–41*, pp. 448–9, 451; *CCIR, 1447–54*, p. 342 – with Sperlyng), had also gone into Salisbury's service during the period of Alice's marriage (*CPR, 1422–9*, p. 474; Jacob, *Reg. Chichele*, II, pp. 394–5) and the queen's service, surely as a result of Chaucer's lordship (E163/7/31/2). Together with Sperlyng and Danvers, he was acting for Suffolk by the end of 1430 (*CAD*, V, A.10892) and continued to be a close associate of the earl: *CPR, 1436–41*, pp. 307, 309; Roskell 1954: p. 186. Sperlyng ended up in the duchy, almost certainly thanks to Suffolk (see *CPR, 1429–36*, p. 346; Somerville 1953: p. 425). Other Chaucer/Montague connections entering Suffolk's service were Richard Alred (Jacob, *Reg. Chichele*, II, p. 394; *CAD*, I, B.57; *CPR, 1429–36*, p. 429; *CPR, 1436–41*, p. 47; Somerville 1953: pp. 398–9, 607); Henry Somer (*CPR, 1436–41*, pp. 448–9; later involved in the foundations – see n. 193, below); and the related families of Stonor and Hampden (McFarlane 1981d: p. 99 n. 76; *CCIR, 1422–9*, p. 446; *CCIR, 1429–35*, pp. 448–9, 451; *Stonor*, I, pp. xix–xx, xxii–iii, xxvi; *CAD*, I, C.401, C.1229, C.1482; II, C.2793, C.2794 (also involving Cotesmore); VI, C.6160; *CPR, 1429–36*, pp. 346, 444). See *CCIR, 1447–54*, pp. 209–14, for more dealings of Suffolk, Sperlyng, Golafre and the Hampdens.

[144]   See *CPR, 1429–36*, pp. 346–7 and n. 139, above. Chaucer died soon after. Suffolk appears as steward and constable of Wallingford in the queen's tax-return of 1436: E163/7/31/2.

[145]   A large amount of land in Bedfordshire, Berkshire and Buckinghamshire was held of the honour: *Feudal Aids*, I, pp. 8–128, *passim*.

[146]   Among the other annuitants of Queen Katherine recorded in 1436 were Bishop Lumley, Sir Roland Lenthale, Sir John Stewart, Sir John Pelham, John Hotoft, William Scarlet, John Golafre and arguably Jenkin Stanley (his name is readable, but deleted): E163/7/31/2. Many of these men retained links with both the royal service and the earl of Suffolk. Lumley, at this time a close ally of Beaufort, was in 1448 to be sponsored by Suffolk for the vacant see of London against Thomas Kemp (Wolffe 1981: p. 108). Stewart was master of the king's horse by the late 1430s (E101/409/2, fol. 37v). Scarlet and Stanley were esquires of the hall (E101/408/25, fol. 8r; E101/409/9, fol. 37r). Lenthale was a king's knight (*CPR, 1422–9*, p. 450). For Golafre, see above.

[147]   For the close links between Chaucer and Henry Beaufort, in particular, see McFarlane 1981d: especially pp. 101–2; Harriss 1988: pp. 67, 97–9, 108n, 117–18, 120 etc.

[148]   See Roskell 1965: pp. 149–50.

[149]   Alice's Beaufort connections had already been influential in the career of her first husband, Thomas Montague, earl of Salisbury, and his associates. The cardinal had been a Montague feoffee on several occasions (*CPR, 1422–9*, pp. 474, 477, 504, 541; *CPR, 1429–36*, p. 49) including for the performance of his will, of which he was not, perhaps oddly, a beneficiary (Jacob, *Reg. Chichele*, pp. 394–5). Dr Harriss suggests that

between Suffolk and the cardinal, these plainly existed by the later 1430s.[150] The earl worked alongside Beaufort in the council of 1437–9 and, in all probability, lent support to his foreign policy.[151] In return, the cardinal made Suffolk one of his feoffees in the mixture of former Montague and crown lands which he purchased in May 1439.[152] As long as Beaufort dominated the council and the council dominated the realm, it was essential to be on good terms with him. Even so, Suffolk was no lackey of the cardinal. Far from blind to the possibilities of his own position, he seems also to have retained the good relations with Gloucester which had provided him with his first opportunity.[153] This association may have been a factor in the many successes which came Suffolk's way in the year 1436, when Duke Humphrey apparently enjoyed a temporary dominance.[154] It certainly enabled the earl to exploit the rivalry between Beaufort and Gloucester when this rose to the surface again in 1439–40.[155] As the friend of both the great disputants, the earl was nicely positioned to advance his own interests: those of the king and the court, which eventually displaced both Beaufort and Gloucester and made their feud irrelevant.[156]

Drawing all this together, it is clear that the earl was the obvious person to exercise lordship about the person of Henry VI. His position in the

Beaufort may have helped to bring the marriage off in the first place (1988: pp. 129–30).

[150] Links with the family had already been established by Suffolk's efforts, following his capture at Jargeau, to obtain the release of the cardinal's nephews, who had been in French hands since 1421: Allmand 1983: p. 33; Jones 1982: pp. 27, 31. The result was a close connection with the junior Beauforts which was to endure for some time: *ibid.*, pp. 37, 46–52.

[151] Suffolk was, for example, a frequent attender at meetings held in the cardinal's chapel at St Mary Overeys: E28/59/24, 28 Mar. 1438; E28/61/10 June 1439. Suffolk and Stafford were alone with the king, when he granted Beaufort's petition for licence to take gold and silver to Oye 'in as special wise as it couth be': E28/60/ 21 May 1439. Note that the earl had been part of the embassy at Arras in 1435: Griffiths 1981: p. 199.

[152] *CPR, 1436–41*, pp. 276, 311. Suffolk seems to have entered some sort of agreement with Beaufort regarding the dower portions of the Montague lands. Although he and his wife were granted compensation for surrendering them in November 1440 (*ibid.*, p. 480), the earl's willingness to accept money in place of land – and that after a considerable interval – may suggest a fairly strong bond between him and the cardinal. As a feoffee in Chirk, Suffolk was permitted to appoint its constable: E28/62/13 July 1439.

[153] For Gloucester's probable role in the earl's appointment to the council, see above, p. 156. A connection between the two men is suggested by the transfer of the duke of Orléans to Suffolk's custody in July/August 1432, a period in which Gloucester was still in the ascendant (*PPC*, IV, pp. 124, 182). Note that Suffolk had fought under Gloucester in 1417: Kingsford 1925: p. 147.

[154] See below, next paragraph.   [155] See below, pp. 185–6.

[156] A nice demonstration of Suffolk's standing with these two bitter enemies is provided by a charter of July 1435 establishing Alice's jointure in a large number of De La Pole manors: Beaufort and Gloucester, acting as feoffees, head the list of grantors (BL, Add. Ch. 2016).

household was underpinned by valuable connections, acquired both locally and nationally, which gave him real political credibility among his peers. The extent to which Suffolk had already arrived by the crucial year of 1436 is shown by the extraordinary series of preferments and grants he received in return for his agreement to serve once again in France. Most significant among them is perhaps his acquisition of patents granting that in his absence he would not be removed from his office 'in the household and about the king's person' and that at the end of it he would be received back by the king with the same favour.[157] At the same time, he obtained a breathtaking series of rewards, repayments and privileges, including the right to declare his attendance at the council on oath rather than by submitting records.[158] If the earl's claim that he was absent for only fifty days between joining the council in November 1431 and the date of account in February 1436 was true, it suggests that he was quite aware that a high profile amongst the lords was as important politically as proximity to the king.[159] By the time of the king's first decisive emergence in politics, Suffolk was in the happy position of both councillor and counsellor. Such influence as he possessed was rooted in the 'real' politics of the community of lords as much as in the potential power inherent in access to the king. However, as has been suggested, the realisation of this potential depended in the first instance upon the organisation of the household: its constituents had to look towards a single head. Although there was much to recommend Suffolk for this position, he would none-

---

[157] *CPR, 1429–36*, pp. 514, 590. These were dated 20 March 1436. An interesting parallel is Sir Ralph Butler's patent for the office of butler, which he received in January 1435. It emphasised how he had surrendered a large number of French captaincies in order to serve about the king's person (*ibid.*, p. 447). See also *CPR, 1436–41*, p. 140, for Lord Welles' 1438 appointment as lieutenant of Ireland, which promised that he would not be removed from the household in the meantime.

[158] Grants to Suffolk of various kinds appear in E159/212, *br.*, Hil., mm. 20r, 24r, 24v, 26r, 27v, 29v. Note especially the pardon of 20 February 1436 for crown jewels allegedly paid to Suffolk and his brothers which the earl claimed neither received (m. 24r: an entry in m. 1 of the Easter *communia* section shows that Suffolk *had* received these; they were worth nearly £900 and he kept them in return for releasing the king from an equivalent amount of outstanding debt – one is reminded of the episode which preoccupied Beaufort on his deathbed: McFarlane 1981b) and the 20 March waiver of £96 13s 4d overpaid to Suffolk for his costs at Arras only two weeks before (mm. 24v, 29v). Other privileges included grants that Suffolk and his wife could alienate up to £400 worth of land without having to apply for licences and that he would not have to repay any wages if he should die before his term was complete (*CPR, 1429–36*, pp. 508, 509). Even more remarkable is the annual pension of 5,000 livres which Suffolk obtained from the king on 22 November 1436 (Johnson 1981: p. 59). For the right to declare council attendance, see E159/212, *br.*, Hil., m. 26v.

[159] E159/212, *br.*, Hil., mm. 26v and 29r. Note that Suffolk's petition had claimed that his absences were not recorded 'in the Recordes of oure seid counseil' (E404/52/210), which does suggest that some records, which we may tend to think of as lost, were actually never kept (above, p. 126).

theless have to offer and exercise some sort of lordship. The rest of this section is concerned with how he did so.

We should remind ourselves first of all that lordship was the natural system for the representation and realisation of interests: all that was unnatural about Suffolk's lordship of the household was that it ought to have been the king's. Once the earl's primacy was established, as it surely was by 1436, other interests in the household would naturally tend to coalesce about his leadership, as long as he retained pre-eminence.[160] Some of these other interests were represented by powerful men, like Sir Ralph Butler,[161] Sir John Beauchamp of Powick[162] and James Fiennes,[163] who did not in any way owe their household position to Suffolk's influence and who came to enjoy the same proximity to the king. Towards men like these, the earl needed to be especially responsive and co-operative, but this did not rob him of superiority. Pre-eminence was self-perpetuating: competent lordship could not but expand within the confines set by time and nature, because hierarchy was the key to the informal representation of interests which dominated medieval politics. Outside these structures, anarchy, recognised to be in the interests of nobody, prevailed. These were

[160] Suffolk was perhaps able to further his power in the household by drawing into it men with whom he had local connections in order to create a core of loyal followers. This was, of course, an essential feature in his relationship with Philip (see above, pp. 159–60), but it may also explain the entry to the household of, among others, Edmund Hampden (see above, n. 143, and E101/409/2, fol. 35r), Richard Alred (see above, n. 143), Edmund Clere (to judge by his connections in 1454 – PL, II, p. 307; E101/408/25, fol. 8r), and William Calthorp (*ibid.* and see above, n. 143, for a possible connection with Suffolk).

[161] Butler was Bedford's chief chamberlain (*Letters and Papers*, II, ii, p. 434) and this connection may have been instrumental in his appointment to the vacancy among the knights of the body in February 1430, though as the son of the king's nurse, Butler may have been no stranger to the household (Griffiths 1981: p. 57). It was probably also Bedford who secured Butler's appointment to the stewardship of Kenilworth in July 1433 (Somerville 1953: p. 560). An interesting deed of 1427 has Butler a feoffee in an Essex manor together with Bedford and a group of Beaufort associates such as Alnwick, Kemp and Salisbury (Montague), as well as Chaucer and his man Thomas Haseley (*CClR, 1422–9*, p. 383). Butler acquired Chaucer's office of king's butler in January 1435 (*CPR, 1429–36*, p. 447).

[162] Beauchamp was also one of Bedford's counsellors (*Letters and Papers*, II, ii, p. 434) and household men (Harvey (ed.), *Worcestre: Itineraries*, p. 339). He had apparently long been in the king's service by October 1432, when arrangements were made to pay him as a carver (*PPC*, IV, p. 128). This means that he was settled in the household before Suffolk. The influential position of Sir John Beauchamp and Sir William Beauchamp of St Amand, who may have owed his *entrée* to Gloucester (Griffiths 1981: p. 65 n. 45), is also noted by Morgan 1987: p. 42 and n. 47.

[163] Fiennes presumably owed his introduction to the household to his brother, Sir Roger, who had been a king's knight since Henry V's time (*CPR, 1416–22*, p. 54) and was soon to be treasurer of the household (Griffiths 1981: p. 302). Jeffs 1960: pp. 154–6 seems to regard the Fiennes connection in household and locality as separate from Suffolk's own. See also below, p. 176.

powerful reasons for the acceptance of De La Pole leadership during the construction of court rule.[164]

Given the continuing importance of the council, it is evident that control of its channels of communication with the king would be a prerequisite for influence in the household. Here, again, Suffolk was well placed. By 1438, a year in which the council still prevailed, he had established himself as the principal conduit between it and the king.[165] Evidence survives to show the earl conveying both conciliar advice to the king and royal authorisation to the council.[166] This gave his opinion a particular significance: on 17 July 1439, for example, an endorsement to a petition records that 'my lord of Suff halde wele with your coment as touching the lettre that is nowe seeld upon this bill';[167] on 8 February 1441, the earl went so far as to order the despatch of a warrant on the authority of his own signature.[168] Suffolk did not have a monopoly of the king's company at this time: others, notably Gloucester, played a similar role on occasion.[169] Even so, no individual was present under such repeatedly intimate circumstances as often as he was and no one else enjoyed the same broad base of power: an influence in the household, which created power in the council; and an influence in the council which preserved power in the household.[170] This influence endured even during

---

[164] Note that some threats to Suffolk's leadership of the household probably did develop in the early 1440s, however: see below, p. 196.

[165] In fact, Suffolk may already have been in this position before Moleyns' endorsements begin to give us information about activity around the king (May 1438). On 23 February that year, Suffolk and the chancellor were present when the king, in his secret chamber at Windsor, made various grants, including a confirmation of a conciliar decision (E28/59/10 and 23 Feb. 1438). As early as January 1436, the earl was conveying the views of ambassadors from the French council to the king: E28/56/28 Jan. 1436.

[166] E.g. C81/1367/8 (Dec. 1438); E28/60/20 May 1439; E28/61/10 June 1439.

[167] E28/62/17 July 1439. Since we know that even at this time, Suffolk could be instrumental in obtaining the royal imprimatur (e.g. E28/62/22 Aug. 1439), this is not surprising.

[168] E28/66/29. Suffolk had no formal authority to do this. The warrant in question concerned a fairly routine administrative matter, but the fact that the earl's name could expedite it is nonetheless significant.

[169] For a grant made by the king in Gloucester's presence and handed to Moleyns by the duke himself for expedition, see E28/60/25 May 1439. Gloucester not infrequently endorsed royal grants in his capacity as chamberlain of England; sometimes under circumstances when, it seems, he may have been influential (e.g. E28/61/24 June 1439 – a petition from an Oxford scholar). It was also common for the great officers to be about the king, sometimes alone, both in and out of council.

[170] For example, Stafford and Suffolk were the only ones present at decisions made by the king on 21 May 1439 and 28 November 1440 (E28/60/as dated; E28/64/22 Oct. 1440). Grants were made by the king in Suffolk's presence alone on 5 December 1439 and with Moleyns also present on 26 October and 2 and 3 November 1440 (E28/63/27; E28/64/26 Oct. 1440; E28/65/1–2). In early February 1441, when evidence begins to appear of who solicited bills, Suffolk emerges as particularly active: he alone solicited a bill for Cromwell on 2 February (E28/66/28); on 13 February, he solicited two bills, one

the period of revived conciliar rule which began in late 1441.[171] Suffolk, together with Moleyns, apparently continued to be integral to the necessary business of obtaining the royal agreement to policy.[172]

A further source of influence for Suffolk was the duchy of Lancaster establishment, which underwent a series of changes, beginning in 1437. The matter of the chief stewardships, to which Suffolk and Philip succeeded in 1437, has already been touched upon. This was, arguably, the crucial step, permitting the household connection an official and enduring role in the making of duchy appointments.[173] As a result, household men were soon advanced to the central offices of the duchy administration.[174] Once a curial presence was established, it was self-perpetuating: when Sir William Philip died, in the summer of 1441, his replacement as chief steward, in the lands of both king and feoffees, was Sir Roger Fiennes, treasurer of the household and brother of James, one of Suffolk's leading associates.[175] In a sense, the pattern of earlier Lancastrian kingship was reproduced: the duchy provided a structure for the realisation of a household *nexus*.[176]

  with Sir John Beauchamp (E28/66/46, 51); on the 14th he solicited the grant of a wardship to himself (E28/66/58). See also Griffiths 1981: p. 281.

[171] On 28 November 1441, for example, five meetings were held in the king's chamber at Westminster with only Suffolk and Bishop Stafford present, and several more in which the two were joined by unspecified 'aliis' (probably minor figures): E28/69/60–73. Among the results of this activity, incidentally, may have been Suffolk's grant of the reversion of the New Forest, currently in Gloucester's hands. The importance of this grant is discussed below: see p. 189, n. 287.

[172] See above, p. 148 and n. 100.

[173] Interestingly, this was as much the case in the enfeoffed parts of the duchy as in the areas under the direct rule of the crown: Somerville 1953: pp. 202–3.

[174] Richard Alred (an associate of Suffolk's, see n. 143, above, who became receiver-general of Queen Katherine's lands on 27 February 1437 – five days after Suffolk's position at Wallingford was confirmed) was appointed receiver-general of the duchy (Somerville 1953: pp. 398–9, 607). Walter Shirington, a connection of Gloucester's (Otway-Ruthven 1939: p. 183) and probably first appointed to the office of chancellor by the duke (on 16 February 1431), was given this office for life in July 1437, which would seem to suggest that he was regarded as favourable to the court and its designs (Somerville 1953: pp. 389–90 and *ibid.*, p. 476 for his appointment to William Troutbek's office of chancellor of the county palatine in May 1439; see also *CPR, 1436–41*, p. 172, for a grant of two prebends and the designation 'king's clerk' in June 1438). In 1442, the reversion of his office (and the chancellorship of the county palatine) was granted to William Tresham, a household squire and already a feoffee on behalf of the royal foundation at Eton (Somerville 1953: pp. 390, 476). When Sir Walter Hungerford finally relinquished the chamberlainship of the duchy in 1441, it was to a leading figure in the household – his younger son, Sir Edmund Hungerford, the king's carver: *ibid.*, p. 417.

[175] Somerville 1953: p. 428. See Harriss 1953: pp. 43, 51 for the household domination of offices in the duchy. See Griffiths 1991c: pp. 174ff for parallel developments in the Principality of Wales, this time dating from the early 1430s and Suffolk's appointment as steward of the household.

[176] See above, p. 96. Note that similar developments to those described above took place in the territorial offices of the duchy. Since these relate to the external position of the household, they are discussed below, pp. 172–4.

So far, the treatment of the court has been almost entirely secular, but, as the broad sweep of Gloucester's changes in 1432 demonstrates, there was also a very significant religious element.[177] In the absence of the firm, martial leadership of an adult king, there was, perhaps, a greater role for the higher clergy in the polity of the 1420s, 1430s and 1440s than was usual. Positions characteristically dominated by clerics – chancellor, keeper of the privy seal, secretary – acquired a greater significance when there was no single controlling will behind them: no longer mere executives, such men might become mandarins. Meanwhile, the holders of the spiritual offices of the household enjoyed the same potential advantage arising from proximity to the person of the king as their secular counterparts. Any attempt to capture and shape the house-hold interest would thus need to represent religious as well as secular interests. Just such an opportunity arose in the enterprise of the royal foundations.

The part played by Suffolk and the developing community of the household in the foundation of the royal colleges deserves more con-sideration than it has usually received. While historians have often been prepared to recognise the earl's initiative in matters of public policy, even when the king's own interest was explicitly alleged, it has been widely assumed that Henry himself was behind the foundation of Eton and King's.[178] This is certainly a possibility, but the fact remains that the institutional and constitutional environment in which the foundation of the colleges was carried out was essentially the same as that in which more explicitly political decisions were made. The role of petition and counsel was quite as significant in this area as in others and the particular problems faced by the founders of ecclesiastical institutions ensured that royal approbation, and perhaps even patronage, were likely to be sought for projects in which the king had no significant personal stake.[179] A number of Henry's courtiers, of course, were founders themselves and some of them, notably Archbishop Chichele, seem to have enlisted the king as co-founder with the aim of protecting or advancing the interests of

---

[177] The duke replaced the king's confessor, his almoner and the dean of the chapel royal, as well as the secular officers: *PPC*, IV, p. 110; *CPR, 1429–36*, p. 196.

[178] See above, p. 105; and Wolffe 1981: ch. 8; Griffiths 1981: pp. 242–8 for the foundations.

[179] See Jacob 1968 for the various dealings of founders with the crown, which could vary from applications for licences (p. 155), to outright invitations for patronage in the interests of protecting the endowment (p. 158). A comment in the will of Sir John Fastolf neatly illustrates the pragmatic way in which some founders sought and deployed royal favour: 'sithe I have ordeyned to make the Kyng founder ... me thinketh I shuld not be denyed of my desire, but the rather to be remembrid and spedde' (*PL*, III, p. 111).

their houses.[180] Were such men the real driving force behind the foundations at Eton and Cambridge?

The establishment of major religious and educational enterprises by the crown was hardly a novel policy. Jeremy Catto has argued that Henry V's double foundation at Sheen and Syon was the centrepiece of a confident reassertion of national and orthodox devotion.[181] Perhaps in religion, as in other areas, the policies of the dead king were perpetuated by the political establishment which outlived him. This is almost certainly true of the universities founded in the name of Henry VI at Caen (in 1432–7) and Bordeaux (in 1441), and, indeed, no one has ever suggested that the young king was a source of inspiration for these foundations.[182] Are there not grounds for a similar scepticism concerning Eton and King's? John Langton, whose 'instancias ... et labores speciales' were thought to have procured the latter foundation;[183] Andrew Doket, who played a dominant role in the foundation of Queens';[184] Thomas Beckington, who was archdeacon of Buckingham, and thus concerned with Eton from the start;[185] and William Waynflete, who was head master at Winchester and may have promoted the idea of a dual foundation on Wykehamist lines[186] – all these men have good claims to be considered the true originators of

[180] Among the founders in Henry's immediate circle were Suffolk (Ewelme, 1439), Kemp (Wye, 1439), Walter Hungerford (Heytesbury, various, 1415–40s) and Chichele (Higham Ferrers, 1425, and All Souls, Oxford, 1437): see Leach 1908: pp. 150–1; Hicks 1991e: pp. 86–7 and Davis 1987: p. 44. In the case of his Oxford foundation, All Souls, Chichele incorporated the king as co-founder little more than a year after first obtaining the licence (*CPR, 1436–41*, pp. 45–6, 172–3). He was then able to use this appointment to obtain the college's exemption from clerical taxation in October 1439 (*ibid.*, p. 341; Chichele's petition for this has survived: E28/63/7). William Bingham, founder of Godshouse, Cambridge, had incorporated Henry as co-founder by 1448, perhaps to protect his foundation (first licensed in 1439) from total submersion by the new royal college. See Leader 1988: pp. 225–6.

[181] Catto 1985b: esp. pp. 106–7, 110–11. Note that a later fifteenth-century source reports that Henry V had intended to found a college at Oxford using alien priory land (Leach 1908: p. 150). See also Rosenthal 1987.

[182] Leach 1908: p. 151 suggests that Chichele and Beckington (see below, n. 185) were the prime movers.

[183] Langton was the master of Pembroke, Cambridge, at the time: see Saltmarsh 1959: p. 376 for his role in the foundation of King's. The quotation is from an early list of King's benefactors (*ibid.*). While the idea of a dual foundation on the Wykehamist model only seems to have developed in 1443, land for a royal college at Cambridge was being acquired only two days after the transfer of the advowson at Eton in October 1440 (*ibid.*, pp. 376–7).

[184] Queens' was founded by the king in 1446 and 1447, and refounded by the queen in 1448: see Laffan 1959: pp. 408–9 and Twigg 1987: pp. 3, 5–6 for Doket.

[185] Leach 1908: pp. 151–2 and Judd 1961: ch. II, esp. pp. 48–51, provide information on Beckington's crucial role in the early stages of the college. See also below, n. 192, and elsewhere.

[186] Waynflete became involved in the Eton project following the king's visit to Winchester College, where he was head master, in July 1441 (Davis 1987: p. 44). He is likely to have been the chief influence behind the 1443 transformation of Eton (and King's) along Wykehamist lines (*ibid.*, pp. 45–6). Note that a fair number of other Wykehamists

various plans put forward in the king's name. A host of other interested men – Chichele, Richard Andrewe, John Somerset, William Alnwick, William Ayscough and the earl of Suffolk himself – could have provided them with the political and administrative means to see their designs effected.[187]

We must accept that it is impossible to know how eagerly Henry seized upon the proposals he almost certainly received from these men. Clearly enough, part of the point of encouraging the king to found colleges was to gain access to the huge resources at royal disposal and this, in turn, demanded that Henry's personal determination to part with his quasi-public resources be clearly demonstrated to outsiders.[188] This means that the several tokens of the king's enthusiastic will are rather meaningless as guides to his personal inclination. Blacman's assertions of Henry's commitment to Eton can hardly be counted disinterested, for example.[189] Much more suggestive, on the contrary, is the evidence of wavering – changes of plan, fluctuations of interest, and so on:[190] these are the normal hallmarks of personal authority in the reign of Henry VI, an authority which was always more formal than real. The king *may* have been the motivating force behind the foundations, but it is at least as likely that there are other explanations. Most important from the point of view of the issues considered in this chapter is the fact that the project was an ideal vehicle for drawing together lay and clerical members of the household and involving them in the corporate deployment of the personal power of the king.

As an example of the way in which the foundations encouraged co-operative action among leading figures in the household, the body of men appointed to receive the alien priory lands with which Eton was to

were involved in the foundations at various times, including Beckington, William Say, Richard Andrewe and Andrew Holes (Leach 1908: p. 151).

[187] See below, n. 192, and note the presence of many of these men about the king when business concerning Eton, King's and other colleges came before him: All Souls (E28/60/20 May 1439: present Suffolk and Ayscough); Oriel, in November 1440 (E28/65/54, 49, 51: present Suffolk, Fiennes, Moleyns and perhaps Beckington). Suffolk was particularly energetic on 25 and 26 March 1441, when the patents for the endowment of Eton were issued (*CPR, 1436–41*, p. 556; E28/67/28–43, *passim*). Suffolk, Fiennes and John Somerset were all busy about the king in mid-February 1441, when the patents for the foundation of King's were issued (*CPR, 1436–41*, pp. 521–3; E28/66/29–67, *passim*).

[188] The money came from two main sources. The colleges, Eton in particular, were endowed from the lands of alien priories, resumed by Henry V in 1414 (Keen 1973: pp. 215–16; see Leach 1908: pp. 150–1 for other founders, including Wykeham, Chichele and Beaufort, using alien priory lands which they had bought to endow their houses). Building works were funded by a series of enfeoffments of duchy land made between 1443 and 1445 (Somerville 1953: pp. 210, 221): see below, p. 185, for more details.

[189] Blacman had enjoyed close links with the college (Lovatt 1981: pp. 419–22).

[190] Wolffe 1981: pp. 139–45 emphasises this feature of the foundations, but puts it down to the king's capriciousness.

be endowed is typical. These were Archbishop Chichele, Bishops Stafford, Lowe and Ayscough, the earl of Suffolk, John Somerset, Thomas Beckington, Richard Andrewe, Adam Moleyns, John Hampton, James Fiennes and William Tresham.[191] The extent to which these men were representative of the household in its religious and secular aspects is striking: most of them were often to be found at the king's side.[192] Almost all of them were associated with Suffolk, who, himself, played a substantial part in the work of the foundations, opening Eton with Bishop Beckington and standing in for Henry at the laying of the first stone of King's chapel.[193] Even after the 1440 feoffment was ended, these men, and others who joined them, continued to work together in a variety of ways,[194] and notably in the several feoffments of duchy lands

---

[191] *CPR, 1436–41*, pp. 454, 471 (Moleyns, Andrewe and Tresham were appointed nine days after the others).

[192] Andrewe was the first warden of All Souls, and later became the king's secretary (Jacob 1967: p. 28). Beckington was the king's secretary and soon to become keeper of the privy seal (Griffiths 1981: pp. 232, 281). Both of these men had been members of Chichele's entourage and it is interesting that Andrewe succeeded Beckington as archdeacon of Bucks.: Jacob 1967: pp. 27–8; Leach 1908: p. 151. Bishop Lowe had been appointed king's confessor in the coup of 1432, a position also held for a time by Alnwick, who was also involved in the foundations, but now filled by Ayscough (Griffiths 1981: pp. 59, 72, 244; and see figure 2 for Lowe's appearance on the council). Fiennes and Hampton were members of the household, frequently to be found about the king (for Fiennes, see below, p. 176; for Hampton see *CPR, 1436–41*, pp. 45, 76, 221, 232, 285 and *passim*). Moleyns was the clerk of the council, already fulfilling an expanded role as recorder of royal decisions made in its absence (above, p. 138). John Somerset was chancellor of the exchequer and the king's doctor and teacher (Emden 1957–9: III, pp. 1727–8). As of January 1441, he was also king's almoner (E28/66/18–19). He and John Langton were described as 'in familia regis' in August 1441 (Cambridge, UL, MS Ee.iii.61, fol. 175v). For the importance of William Tresham, another household man, see below, p. 185 n. 265.

[193] Maxwell-Lyte 1899: p. 20; Saltmarsh 1959: p. 378 and n. 32. Suffolk also headed the group of bishops who brought the royal statutes to King's in 1447 (*ibid.*) and the list of those appointed to hear the oath of the first provost in 1446 (C81/1370/32). A number of Suffolk's personal – as distinct from household – connections were also actively involved in the foundations: John Ulveston, his steward, was receiver of Eton's revenues (James 1979: p. 12); Henry Somer, a Thames Valley associate of the earl's (see n. 143, above), was one of the royal agents in the foundation of King's (Saltmarsh 1959: p. 379).

[194] E.g. *CPR, 1441–6*, p. 35 (23 January 1442 – Ayscough, Beckington and John Hampton receive a forfeiture for the building of Eton); 32, 50 (27 January 1442 – Ayscough, Suffolk, Beckington, Henry Sever, provost of Eton, John Carpenter (later bishop of Worcester) and Hampton receive all taxes to be paid by Cheshire for three years (worth 3,000 marks) and a fine to be paid by the duchess of Norfolk); p. 54 (16 February 1442 – Suffolk, Ayscough, Beckington, Sever, Carpenter and Hampton receive farms paid by the earl of Devon and others for the keeping of the Bodrugan heir); p. 316 (19 December 1444 – Suffolk, William Waynflete, now provost, and Hampton get the wardship and marriage of the Speke heir and a fine to be paid by the widow). Instances exist of members of this group working together on projects not associated with the foundations. An example is the October 1441 foundation of a gild by Ayscough, Suffolk, Beckington, Golafre, Noreys and others for the purpose of repairing the road from Abingdon to Dorchester (Oxon.): *CPR, 1441–6*, pp. 36–7.

which were made in 1443–5 to pay for the building works at the two colleges.[195] As a result, bonds of real affection, strengthened by corporate commitment to this inspiring enterprise, may have begun to grow among them.[196]

What are we to conclude from all this? Certainly, if the king was the real author of the foundations project, its results could have been the same. There is no knowing the truth of the matter, but the convenience of the foundations to the needs of all concerned is rather striking, to say the least. In the letters patent of 14 October 1440, signifying the foundation of Eton, Henry asserted that he had now undertaken the governance of his realms in person.[197] It is in this sense that the later reference to the colleges as the 'primer notable werkes' of his reign should be understood: the foundations marked the start – in the event, a false start – of full royal rule.[198] Within weeks of this patent, the king was to release the duke of Orléans: another decisive assertion of the power of the renascent crown to direct policy.[199] In relation to this refocusing of government on the king's person, the bonds created by the foundations may have been very important. The satisfying experience of working together under royal headship was exactly what royal military enterprise characteristically achieved in the martial culture of the nobility. The foundations, as the focus of what was almost a 'gild' of the king's courtiers, fulfilled the same function in the domestic and clerical atmosphere of the royal household.[200] So it was that the development of Henry VI's 'personal' projects and the rise of a new form of 'personal' rule went hand in glove: either the king was genuinely the initiator of these enterprises, and of the rule which underlay them, or, as the evidence of the changing structures of politics seems to suggest, a *familia* was developing to act in his name.

. . .

[195] The new body of feoffees contained all those of 1440–1 except Chichele, who had died, and John Lowe, who was soon to be bishop of Rochester: *RP*, V, pp. 70–1. There were twenty-one new feoffees as well: see below, p. 194.

[196] This can be illustrated from the career of Thomas Beckington. He chose to be consecrated bishop of Bath and Wells at Eton in 1443 (Maxwell-Lyte 1899: pp. 19–20: with Alnwick and Ayscough among the officiating prelates). Before leaving for Guyenne in 1442, he especially asked Suffolk to commend him to the provost and scholars (*Letters of Margaret*, pp. 78–9; it is perhaps significant that almost all the letters written by Beckington in that collection were to people who were either feoffees for Eton in 1440–1 or for both colleges in 1443–9: *ibid.*, nos. xliii to lv).

[197] *RP*, V, p. 46.   [198] See e.g. Davis 1987: p. 43; Rosenthal 1987: p. 172.

[199] Below, p. 187.

[200] In this respect, the 1445 petition of King's for the parliamentary ratification of its various patents is interesting: an ornate introduction contrasted Wisdom with Power as properties necessary for the government of kingdoms, concluding that military power, which always required the direction of wisdom, would flourish 'ubi studium scientarum et sapientia plus invaluit' (*RP*, V, p. 87).

The coalescing of household interests was only part of the process of transferring power. Equally important was the matter of convincing the nobility, as lords of the shires and tutors of the realm, to transfer their attention from council to king. As the king grew, this should have happened naturally, but the confusions created by Henry's mildness and the pre-existence of a reasonable structure of artificial rule in the shape of the council meant that the nobility needed to be persuaded that the king was old enough and good enough before they would make a united transition to the normal forms of government. A tacit acceptance of royal rule in 1439–41, for example, was not enough to erase their attachment to conciliar forms. Only in an atmosphere of unity, focused on the king and encompassing both household and realm, could the transition to royal rule, in the court, be effectively made. This was not finally achieved until the middle of the decade.

Suffolk's efforts to organise the household had been conducted with considerable sensitivity. Whatever else may be laid against the earl, he was aware of the necessity for consultation, co-operation and appeasement which a shaky jurisdiction imposed. This emerges as a constant theme in his dealings with the nobility. The price of the transition to royal rule was a willingness to represent the same interests that the council had represented (and to do so, in fact, in a similar way). In the event, this was also the key to the weakness of the Suffolk regime: an impersonation of royal power which actually offered no more to its noble constituency than the system it superseded. Even so, the likelihood is that if it had not been prepared to satisfy dominant interests, the rule of the court could not have been established in the first place.

The responsiveness of the regime is exemplified by the prevailing pattern of local rule under Henry VI, in which a series of leading noblemen were apparently able to develop or perpetuate regional hege- monies with the assistance of the crown. It may seem appropriate to represent these men as courtiers, but they were rarely permanent members of the household. The basis of their influence at the centre and of their general access to royal favour was their prior possession and exercise of territorial lordship. On the face of it, then, the government of the localities under Henry VI was carried out according to the normal configuration of royal and landed authority: the architects of household power were apparently not concerned to create a royal following in the provinces. Their intentions are evident in the appointments to the territorial offices of the duchy of Lancaster and other royal lands, which followed the king's first admission to his powers.[201] For example, in the

---

[201] The key offices were the stewardships of the various honours: see Somerville 1953: pp. 111–12.

autumn of 1437, the earl of Salisbury received life-grants of the steward-ships of a corpus of duchy and other crown lands in Yorkshire and Lancashire,[202] which, together with his existing estates and offices and further marks of royal favour,[203] gave him a comprehensive influence in the North approaching that of Richard of Gloucester in the 1470s.[204] At about the same time, the earl of Stafford was given life office in a complex of duchy lands in Lancashire, Staffordshire and Derbyshire. Once again, it was a move which reflected and extended his own territorial interests.[205] In a similar way, Lord Beaumont, [206] Lord Cromwell[207] and others[208]

---

[202] See Somerville 1953: pp. 500, 507, 514 and *CPR, 1436–41*, p. 96 (Richmondshire and the forests beyond Trent). On the very same day that most of these grants were made and possibly at the behest of the government, the earl was granted by his mother a lease of the lordship of Middleham, which complemented the Richmond lands perfectly and was the basis of the Neville hegemony in north Yorkshire (*CClR, 1435–41*, pp. 157–8; Pollard 1979: pp. 42, 52). See also Pollard 1990: pp. 249–50.

[203] The earl's main holdings were in north Yorkshire, Westmorland and county Durham: Pollard 1990: pp. 91–5, 246. In November 1437, Salisbury was appointed to the council (above, p. 135, n. 51) and it was doubtless through his influence that, soon after, his brother Robert became bishop of Durham, a development which greatly assisted the earl's lordship in that county (Davies 1974: p. 408; Storey 1966: p. 115; Pollard 1990: pp. 267–8; *PPC*, V, p. 80). See Horrox 1989: ch. 2 for Gloucester in the 1470s.

[204] Pollard 1990: p. 402. Salisbury was already life-steward of the duchy honour of Tickhill since November 1432 (Somerville 1953: p. 528). He was not warden of the West March between 1435 and 1443, but this may have been by choice and he had the reversion of the office from 1439: Storey 1957: pp. 604–5, 613–14.

[205] Somerville 1953: pp. 511, 540, 557. Although Stafford did not have a significant landed stake in Derbyshire, he was interested in extending his lordship there and it was natural for him to do so, given the close interaction of political society in Staffs., Derb. and north Warws.: Wright 1983: pp. 66–8; Carpenter 1992: pp. 27–8, 392–3 etc. See Rowney 1983: pp. 49–51, for Stafford's lands.

[206] In 1437–8, Beaumont received the life stewardship of the honour of Leicester, including the Northampton lands, and of Castle Donnington (Leics.) (Somerville 1953: pp. 563, 573) and, in May 1440, the (duchy) stewardship of Bolingbroke (Lincs.) and the (crown) stewardship of the town of Boston and the Richmond lands in the county (*ibid.*, p. 576; *CPR, 1436–41*, p. 401). Beaumont had significant estates in each county: Storey 1970: p. 68; Acheson 1992: pp. 20–1.

[207] Cromwell took over as life-steward of Pickering (north-east Yorks.) in June 1437 (Somerville 1953: p. 533). His wife held a number of manors in the county (*CIPM*, IV, p. 266). For examples of Cromwell's involvement in East Riding politics before the time of this grant, see *CAD*, IV, A.6967; *CFR, 1422–30*, pp. 101, 102–3, 166–7. In the course of 1437, he was confirmed for life in the crown offices of steward of Sherwood Forest and constable of Nottingham Castle (*CPR, 1436–41*, pp. 19, 73). These were of considerable importance in his expansion (from a small, but expanding, territorial base) in Nottinghamshire: Payling 1991: p. 97.

[208] E.g. Suffolk and Philip, already discussed above (pp. 159–60). Tuddenham's life-stewardship of the duchy lands in Norfolk and Suffolk reflected and extended De La Pole lordship in the area (of which Philip was a part): Somerville 1953: p. 594. Note also the life-stewardship of the duchy lands in Oxon., Bucks., and Berks. – the other main area of De La Pole lordship – granted to Suffolk and Philip in April 1437 (*ibid.*, p. 622: as with the stewardship of Wallingford, Philip had secured this for himself in January 1437, only to admit Suffolk three months later – cf. above, p. 159 n. 139).

were granted royal stewardships which bolstered their existing landed influence.

To some extent, this pattern of appointments reflected the disposal of office made during the minority.[209] No less than existing local elites,[210] the newcomers were men with influential friends in the council, notably the cardinal.[211] A fairly direct link between power in the localities and power in the representative council continued to exist, therefore; unaffected, at first, by the king's emergence. This is not simply because the council continued to rule, but also because those who were in a position to exercise some guidance over the king's grace – notably Suffolk and Philip, as leaders of the household and chief stewards of the duchy – saw the wisdom of working within the structure of power which obtained in 1436–7 and which had grown out of the long period of conciliar rule. Because this had also been a long period of Beaufort hegemony, the inherited power structure, now perpetuated by the common alignment of court and conciliar interests, was largely composed of the allies and satellites of Cardinal Beaufort, many of whom were directly represented in the council. As a result, the question of whether the structure was prescribed by those dominant at the centre or demanded by those dominant in the localities does not arise: the two forces were in equilibrium. The power of the council at the centre was backed by the power of its members and satellites in the provinces and vice versa, but the court could become the dominant jurisdiction if it took over the council's task of representation.

That the lords of the household recognised this is suggested by the treatment of the territorial nobility during periods in which rule was focused more on the person of the king, which is to say, briefly, in 1440–1 and then, more enduringly, from the summer of 1443 onwards. Grants of important marks of favour and, notably, of titles, were concentrated in

---

[209] Stafford and Salisbury, for example, had held many of their offices since the mid-1430s (though, admittedly, only during pleasure).

[210] Salisbury was Beaufort's nephew, whilst Stafford, who was Salisbury's brother-in-law, seems to have been associated with the cardinal on the minority council (e.g. Harriss 1988: pp. 182, 194). Meanwhile, Edmund Beaufort doubtless had his uncle to thank for the complex of duchy and royal offices in South Wales which he was given in 1433–5 (Somerville 1953: pp. 640, 647 and *CPR, 1429–36*, pp. 286, 498 for details). These were regranted for life in April 1438: Somerville 1953: pp. 640, 647; *CPR, 1436–41*, p. 188.

[211] Beaumont had been Beaufort's ward (*CPR, 1422–9*, pp. 524–5). He joined the council in 1441 (above, p. 146). Cromwell was an important colleague on the council and among those appointed by the cardinal to receive his goods in 1432 (*CClR, 1429–35*, p. 234). Beaufort assisted him in the foundation of Tattershall (*CPR, 1422–9*, p. 212; *CPR, 1436–41*, p. 292). See also Harriss 1988: p. 252. For Suffolk's associations with Beaufort, see above, p. 162.

these periods. The most important recipients – for example, Huntingdon, Salisbury, Stafford, Shrewsbury, Dorset, York, Cromwell, Beaumont – were already powerful men.[212] The purpose of this patronage was surely to demonstrate the continuity, or even expansion, of fortune which they could expect under the emergent rule of the king. A similar aim may have lain behind the creations, although they also emphasised the king's majesty and, as Ralph Griffiths has argued, strengthened his dynasty.[213] There is no need, even so, to see these as a policy emanating from the king personally: on the one hand, councillors were perfectly capable of recommending such marks of honour;[214] on the other, the tendency for the 'new' titles to be either restorations,[215] or simple promotions of earls to marquisates or dukedoms,[216] may suggest that they were simply petitioned for, just like everything else.[217] It seems almost certain that rewards to some would inspire others to make demands, a suggestion to some extent borne out by the series of precedence disputes which dogged the later 1440s.[218]

It seems, then, that the leaders of the household were perfectly content for territorial power to remain with the major landowning families. There was no 'court–country' conflict, no nation-wide royal affinity besides the established nobility. There is only one clear example in the reign of a

---

[212] See Appendix A, at the end of this chapter, for details.   [213] Griffiths 1991i.

[214] The creations of Norfolk (1425), Fanhope (1432) and Arundel (1433) were manifestly ordained by the council, even though in the case of Norfolk, it was emphasised that only the king could bestow such honours: *RP*, IV, pp. 274–5, 400–1, 443. Given the dominance of the council in 1442, Talbot may well have owed his title of earl of Shrewsbury to its advice (see below, Appendix A). Six days before the creation, the council was arranging his musters (*PPC*, V, pp. 186–7; *CPR, 1441–6*, p. 106). At the time, Shrewsbury was in England raising reinforcements for York. An earldom may have seemed appropriate to Talbot's position as captain of Rouen and lieutenant-general under York (see Pollard 1983: p. 58). A parallel with the elevation of Somerset to his dukedom in 1443 begins to suggest itself (see n. 217, below).

[215] For example, the titles of Norfolk to John Mowbray in 1425, Dorset to Edmund Beaufort in 1442, Buckingham to Humphrey Stafford in 1441 and Exeter to John Holland in 1444 (*HBC*, pp. 473, 460, 453, 462).

[216] E.g. Dorset and Somerset in 1443, Suffolk and Buckingham in 1444: *HBC*, pp. 484, 460, 482, 453.

[217] It is difficult to believe that Somerset's dukedom, for example, was not requested by him. Its announcement came at the end of a series of royal replies to petitionary articles of service. The announcement was not couched in terms which suggest that it was a direct reply to a direct question, but the duke's immediate request for 1,000 marks worth of land to support the title suggests a certain amount of prearrangement (*PPC*, V, pp. 252–3). The lords' refusal to advise the king 'to depart from suche livelode ne to opon their mouthes in suche matiers' (p. 253) is an instructive reminder of the need for direct royal authority in matters of grace. An example of a petition concerning a matter of this kind is Beaumont's request for recognition that his viscountcy took precedence over all others, made in March 1445 (*CPR, 1441–6*, p. 348; E28/75/19).

[218] E.g. Buckingham–Warwick in the parliament of 1445–6 (C49/26/14); Arundel–Devon at the same time and in 1449 (*RP*, V, p. 148; BL Lansdowne MS 229, fols. 17v, 162v–163r).

territorial lordship manufactured by royal patronage alone: that of James Fiennes, Lord Saye and Sele. Beginning life as a younger son and minor member of the South Coast squirearchy,[219] Fiennes was granted, between 1437 and 1443, a whole string of lands and territorial offices concentrated in Kent and Sussex.[220] At the same time, he also received a series of annuities and grants of central office and became involved in the foundations project from its inception in 1440.[221] What permitted this meteoric rise to power is not entirely clear, though a vacuum of lordship in Sussex resulting from the ineffectiveness of William, earl of Arundel, might be part of the reason.[222] Fiennes could be comparatively easily sustained in his 'country' by the proximity of the court: this would be quite impossible at a greater range.[223] In any event, his case is unique. Normally, the crown restricted itself to supplementing, not creating, the landed resources of territorial lords whether they were in the household or not.

If the crown's territorial 'patronage' responded chiefly to the interests of the leading magnates, its judicial arrangements were of a similar kind.[224] In the later 1430s, the settlement of disputes and the regulation of local rule remained in the hands of the council along with other matters of governance.[225] The amount of judicial business handled by the king and his immediate entourage was very negligible, even during the period

[219] Fiennes probably owed his introduction to the household to his older brother: see above, n. 163; Griffiths 1981: p. 301; *CClR, 1435–41*, p. 123. He was an esquire of the household by 1439: E101/408/25, fol. 8r, and had a £50 annuity from the exchequer by a grant of October 1438: James 1979: p. 16 n. 3.

[220] For details, see *CPR, 1436–41*, pp. 77–8, 309, 383, 471; *CPR, 1441–6*, pp. 83, 140, 160, 169; E28/65/60–1 (the manors of Thorne and Tracy, Kent: 1440); Somerville 1953: p. 616. Apparently in response to a royal suggestion, Fiennes was appointed steward of all the estates of the see of Canterbury by Archbishop Stafford in 1443: Sheppard (ed.), *Literae Cantuarienses*, III, no. 1024.

[221] E.g. *CPR, 1436–41*, pp. 414, 423 (reversion of chamberlain of Receipt of Exchequer, which was actually usurped by Cromwell in November 1442 – *CPR, 1441–6*, p. 158), 470–1; *CPR, 1441–6*, pp. 133, 296, 401. See above, pp. 167ff, for the foundations.

[222] In 1415, the Arundel earldom had been divided and the Warenne lands lost to co-heirs: this must explain the relative feebleness of the fifteenth-century earls, who inherited only the core of the old estate (*GEC*, I, p. 246; McFarlane 1973: p. 136). In addition, the long survival of one Fitzalan dowager (Eleanor, wife of Walter, Lord Hungerford: d. 1455) may have robbed William of some of his inheritance, and a substantial part of the rest of it seems to have been granted to feoffees in July 1447 under terms which were not clearly in Arundel's own interests (see *CClR, 1454–61*, pp. 87–90; E28/77/26).

[223] Fiennes' need for support might explain the large numbers of household men apparently active in Kent in the late 1440s: see below, p. 220, n. 59.

[224] See above, p. 97, for a distinction between the 'prescriptive' and 'restorative' measures typically employed by kings in the administration of justice.

[225] Harriss 1988: p. 294. For examples since the end of the minority, consider: the hearings of the witnesses to the Bedford riot of January 1439 (Leadam and Baldwin (eds.), *Cases Before the King's Council*, pp. 104–6); a summons in October 1439 to Sir Thomas Neville and Sir Thomas Lumley following a petition of the countess of Cambridge (E28/63/5); a summons in April 1440 to various people to be before the council (E28/

of Henry's emergence.[226] Even so, the extent to which the king's participation in judicial affairs could be restrained was limited by his power of pardon, which was soon put to extensive use.[227] The situation was thus an ambiguous one, but there were good reasons for maintaining it: whilst pressure for individual dispensation could, in the short term, at least, be met relatively harmlessly by an inexperienced king, judicial (which is to say political) decisions required more substantial treatment, which in effect meant conciliar intervention, as long as the council remained the dominant representative body. At the same time, however, the council's capacity to govern, or indeed to do justice, depended directly on the preservation of its unity. If divisions broke out among its membership, its already tenuous hold on authority was likely to collapse: warring parties would tend to seek the lordship of the king, regardless of its overall quality. As a result, achieving and maintaining unity was an over-riding concern for the councillors. Where a king, with his ultimately independent authority and his capacity both to punish and to reconcile, could provide unity through acts of judgement, a council, whose powers were all too obviously derived from its members, could not afford to distribute its favours unequally among them.[228] As a result, it was reduced to providing rather feeble arbitration, proceeding with force only against those who were already the underdogs. It is thus highly significant – both for what it reveals about Henry VI and for the results it produced – that throughout the transition period, and even after it, those acting for the king continued to employ 'conciliar' rather than 'royal' means of dispute settlement. Let us take a closer look at what this meant.[229]

63/68); letters to the earls of Devon, Westmorland and Salisbury, telling them to keep the peace (E28/64/19 and 28 Oct. 1440).

[226] For example, a letter sent – apparently under Suffolk's influence – to the justices of Lancashire to stay proceedings against John Troutbek (E28/62/17 July 1439); a summons to Ralph Grey in August 1439, which may have been for judicial reasons (E28/62/as dated: note that at the same time the councillors summoned another northern knight, Sir Robert Ogle); an order to Sir Thomas Brown to reply to proceedings against him (E28/63/35: since Beaufort and Lyndwood were both present with the king, this may have been a conciliar decision anyway).

[227] Above, p. 134, n. 44; Storey 1966: appendix II. A nice example of the inconvenience caused by Henry's vapid use of his power to pardon is provided by a report of August 1442 that the king had released, presumably upon petition, two servants of Robert Whitingham whom the council had imprisoned as part of its corruption investigations concerning the ex-treasurer of Calais: *PPC*, V, pp. 194–5.

[228] See above, p. 101.

[229] The question is, of course, affected by the extent to which it was normal for arbitrative justice among the nobility to be handled by a council, a matter which has never been properly examined for this period. Most surviving examples of this sort of activity show a council of some kind in action, but most surviving examples are also from periods like Henry VI's reign when formal councils frequently existed. Councils could only perform these tasks successfully in tandem with an actively interested monarch, who would provide final judgement. It seems clear that Henry V's personal arbitration was a central

In practice, conciliar justice meant either the protection of the ambitions of the dominant party, which usually enjoyed representation in the council; or, if neither or both disputants enjoyed such representation, weak, indecisive and last-minute intervention. There are countless examples of the former tendency, which incidentally emphasise the predictable dominance of Beaufort and De La Pole interests among the lords: in the disputes between the junior and senior Nevilles (1430–43), between Scrope and Fitzhugh (1438–42), between Cromwell and Grey of Codnor (1440–1), between Northumberland's men and Kemp (1441–3), and between Norfolk and Wingfield (1443–4) those who were better connected to Suffolk and the cardinal were every time triumphant.[230] Usually, the defeated parties were cowed by the superior power and influence of their opponents, though this was not always the case: the Berkeleys, for example, used their local predominance in Gloucestershire to keep up a long resistance to the Beauchamps and their Talbot, Beaufort and Neville heirs, opponents who had far greater landed resources and enjoyed the consistent support of the government.[231] If the practice of supporting the stronger party created fewer immediate difficulties for a weak central authority, it was scarcely the sort of responsive justice the localities required. Some landowners must have become convinced that they could not expect to obtain justice from Henry VI: a particularly disturbing conclusion for men like Northumberland and Scrope who were members of the council and who, in the former case, at least, had previously enjoyed good relations with the Beaufort interest.[232]

However, it was scarcely 'justice' that disputants who had not run foul of leading interests received from the government either. The crown's treatment of the Fanhope–Grey dispute (1437–9) and, more notoriously, the Courtenay–Bonville dispute, reveals that it was quite unable to impose any sort of workable settlement between 'neutral' parties who were evenly matched.[233] Through the application of palliatives, the government, conciliar in form if not in name, was generally able to smother conflicts in

element in the 1414 settlement of the Talbot–Arundel dispute, for example: Powell 1989: pp. 222–4. It should also be noted that a king who maintained good channels of communication with his leading subjects ought to have been able to pre-empt conflicts in an informal way which would leave few traces in the records.

[230] See Appendix B, below, under the heading 'Disputes involving associates of Beaufort or Suffolk', for details and references.

[231] Pollard 1968: pp. 39–51. Note that Gloucestershire juries repeatedly refused to recognise the Talbot (Beauchamp) claim to Berkeley Castle (p. 51). See also Sinclair 1987, which stresses that the arbitration of 1425, which went rather against the Beauchamp interest, successfully kept the peace for more than a decade (p. 46).

[232] It was, for example, 'by the meane' of the cardinal that Northumberland obtained the hand of the Poynings heiress for his eldest son: *Cartularium Abbatiae de Whiteby*, II, p. 695.

[233] See Appendix B, under the heading 'Disputes involving neutrals only'.

the hope that fate would save the day.[234] But this way of proceeding offered nothing more than a façade of representation without the real satisfaction of interests. If, in the short term, it proved possible to prevent crises created by the pressures of local rule from affecting stability at the centre, over a longer term the government's measures must have inspired a loss of confidence in royal justice. Whether one was favoured, or excluded, or neutral, the message was much the same: application to the centre was ultimately pointless. Even so, it took time to undo the long built-up habits of deference to royal judgement and, in the meantime, conciliar and pseudo-conciliar arbitration, though inadequate, at least tended to reflect some sort of balance of power.

As a result of the readiness of Suffolk and other champions of royal power to defer in all important respects to the power structures established in association with the minority council, it is difficult to find evidence – or even grounds – for serious dissatisfaction on the part of most of the territorial nobility with the treatment which they, as individuals, received from the government. Major offices tended to remain in the same hands for long periods of time after the partial shake-up of the late 1430s.[235] If some lords were particularly well rewarded with fees, lands and offices in support of their private holdings, most of the rest were not badly treated, if they were men of any standing. The earl of Northumberland, for example, was able to regain a certain amount of his forfeited patrimony following the death of Bedford.[236] The earl of Huntingdon, though traditionally associated with Gloucester, received major commands in 1438 and 1439 and did very nicely in the 1440s.[237] All in all, it seems that a large group of territorially powerful noblemen were held together in the later 1430s: in the following decade, with the

---

[234] It seems that in the case of the Fanhope–Grey dispute, it was largely the deaths of the major protagonists (in 1443 and 1440, respectively) which forestalled more serious and prolonged disorder. The dispute between Lord Talbot and the earl of Ormond, which began during the minority, actually ran on into the 1440s before being settled through the arbitration not of the king, but, significantly, of the duke of York (Pollard 1968: pp. 129–34; and see Griffith 1940–1).

[235] For example, Lord Poynings had the wardenship of the East March from 1440 and the earl of Salisbury the West March from 1443, in each case until more or less the end of the reign (Storey 1957: p. 614); Huntingdon was admiral from 1435 until his death in 1447 (CPR, 1429–36, p. 488); most of the offices in the duchy, the Richmond lands and the principality of Wales remained in the same hands undisturbed. Storey 1966: p. 38 discusses the same tendency in the offices of state.

[236] CPR, 1429–36, pp. 531–2; Bean 1958: p. 72. Sir William Plumpton, who was backed by Northumberland, remained in office as steward of Knaresborough from 1439 to 1461, despite trouble with Kemp in 1441 (Somerville 1953: p. 524; see above, p. 178).

[237] See Harriss 1988: pp. 141, 168, 214 etc., for the connection with Gloucester and DKR, XLVIII, p. 322 and Stansfield 1987: pp. 211–26. Perhaps Gloucester was instrumental in obtaining a royal grant of the lordship of Lesparre to Huntingdon in February 1440 (E28/63/55). See also Appendix A, below.

superimposition of a self-limiting royal power, they would become the court.[238]

In matters of local rule, therefore, Henry VI's household, not unlike the crown in the thirteenth and fourteenth centuries, extended its jurisdiction by recognising, and co-operating with, subject power structures. This was, as we shall see, mirrored by its attitude to the formation of national policy. The transfer of control to the king and such counsels as were gathered around him was not accompanied by any repudiation of the council or even any formal declaration of majority.[239] This meant that the possibility of conciliar government was never entirely repressed, as the events of 1441 and, to some extent, those of 1449–50, demonstrate.[240] Although this state of affairs introduced qualifications to the corporate loyalty felt for the king as independent ruler, it did, for the nobility, remove a considerable amount of risk from the acceptance of royal rule. This risk was minimised still further by the willingness of Suffolk and others to continue to provide for consultation and to do what they could to regulate the king's exercise of grace.[241]

AUTHORITY AND POLITICS, 1439–1445

The politics of the 1430s and 1440s were overshadowed by the need to protect Lancastrian France, but this does not mean that defence was the only factor affecting public affairs. Policy, whether it favoured war or peace, was certainly directed towards this all-important end, but the politics of this period were concerned with more than policy, or the content of policy: they were also concerned with authority; the authority which selected and licensed policy and made it work; the will which guaranteed that counsel was representative and effective. While it is likely that the circumstances in which the king was edged towards power were affected by disagreements over policy in France, it seems almost certain that the debate over French policy was itself influenced by the political and institutional ramifications of Henry's emergence. These, as we have seen, were complex, and they were complex because the forces which governed this emergence seem to have been external to the king. Percep-tions of Henry's advancing age, the activity of his advisers and intimates, the need for a ruler: these forces were apparently unmatched by any drive from within the king to express his personal will. If we assume, as has

---

[238] A similar point has recently been made by Ralph Griffiths (1991b: p. 31).
[239] Compare Richard II's dramatic, but necessary and unresisted, declaration of majority, which ushered in several years of normal rule: above, p. 133 n. 41.
[240] See above and below, pp. 145ff, 242–8.
[241] See above generally, and below, pp. 187ff and ch. 6.

become conventional, that Henry had his own ideas about the protection of his lands and title in France and that these were an important conditioning factor in the politics of this period, we invoke a completely different framework for that politics from the one proposed here.[242] Instead of crippling uncertainty over the location of authority, we have a fully active king, one with whom it would have been possible to quarrel, as with Richard II, but one who would more probably have been obeyed and whose personal will would have brought direction to the polity.

But there are few signs that this was the situation Henry's advisers faced. As he embarked on his eighteenth year as king, commentators were still remarking on Henry's youth in terms that suggest it was an impediment to his exercise of rule.[243] His father had fought his first battle, at Shrewsbury, when he was sixteen and there is every reason to find the fact that the relatively supine Henry VI's youthfulness was still a matter of note suggestive. When the duke of Gloucester raised the question of evil counsel, in the winter of 1439–40, it is rather striking that he did not for a moment suggest that the eighteen-year-old king was in any way its conscious accessory, and no one, then or afterwards, appears to have believed such a thing.[244] Indeed, it may have been the problems of managing decision making around a somewhat infantile king which had prompted Gloucester's assault on Henry's advisers, and not the hawkishness for which the duke has been so famous. As Maurice Keen has recently remarked, historians have typically seen this period in terms of clashes between a peace party and a war party, but this may be rather misleading.[245] Is it not possible that tensions over policy had other causes, that it was the absence of an effective means of authorising decisions that created the impression of deep divisions over what ought to be done? The tendency of recent accounts to focus on the military, diplomatic and fiscal dilemmas facing Henry VI's regime, or on the distribution of its patronage, has meant that the question of how it obtained the authority to act in any of these spheres has been overlooked. To some extent, of course, the issue is covered by assuming that, after about 1436 or 1437,

---

[242] See above, p. 106 n. 19 (and also Harriss 1988: p. 303, for the suggestion that the king was determined to protect his French title).

[243] Note, for example, the submission from (perhaps) the Norman council concerning the 1439 truce proposals, which talked openly of the king's 'jonesse' and implied that he was little disposed to take action in defence of his French lands: Allmand, 'Documents of 1439', p. 141. Thomas Gascoigne remembered that the king had given the alien priories to his colleges 'in juventute sua' (Loci e Libro, p. 219: actually in 1440–1). Giles, Chronicon, p. 30, refers to the king as being, in 1441, young in years and in nature.

[244] Compare the criticisms which Richard II, at the same age, allegedly elicited from Gaunt: Hector and Harvey (eds.), Westminster Chron., p. 115. These included the accusation that the king should not have surrounded himself with such bad counsellors. See also pp. 54–5.

[245] Keen 1989: pp. 308–10.

the king himself authorised both the government and its policy; but, as I have suggested, it is precisely that assumption that we may not make.[246] Henry's leading subjects may have disagreed about the conduct of the war, and they may not have done. They may have cared passionately about the plight of Lancastrian France, or they may simply have done their duty of defence and given priority to domestic affairs. Whatever their private beliefs and aspirations, however, one factor above all shaped the environment in which they had to seek satisfaction: the nature and authority of Henry VI's government. It is with this factor, and its role in politics, that the following account is principally concerned.

In the mid-1430s, the need for royal direction was greater than ever before. Bedford's death had removed the only intermediate authority competent to co-ordinate the prosecution of the war. He had no obvious successor: the king was not about to assume direct command; and Gloucester, next highest in blood, had little martial experience and did not command the loyalties of the conciliar establishment.[247] At the same time, the deteriorating fortunes of Lancastrian France made central direction and backing all the more important for the military classes. The greater likelihood of failure and the real losses which could now be expected to arise from it placed captains in an extremely vulnerable position: only a king's support could rescue them from the charges of incompetence, negligence or even treason which were sure to follow any setbacks. War, then, was becoming very difficult; but peace was scarcely a more straightforward option. Diplomacy raised the issue of authority quite as pressingly as warfare did.[248] There could be no peace unless the English king was prepared to surrender his title to the French crown, and this was something which Henry VI alone could do and which no one could afford to be thought to have advised until the king was of an age – or of a will – sufficient to take full responsibility for his actions.[249] Moreover, as the French made clear at Arras, in 1435, and again at Oye, in 1439, even a truce, or a 'half-peace', would have to be purchased by concessions of some kind, and these too would require Henry's personal authorisation.[250] Counsellors who urged the unformed king to controversial action ran the risk of allegations that they had 'stirred' or 'moved' him

---

[246] See above, p. 106.   [247] Harriss 1988: pp. 254–5.

[248] This is nicely illustrated by the request for a clearer commission made by Thomas Beckington, head of the envoys negotiating with the count of Armagnac in 1442. His reason was that 'in matiers of so grete weight as this is, furst men wol look that our auctorite and pouaire be suffisaint': Nicolas (ed.), *Journal of Beckington*, p. 8.

[249] The problems created by the king's youth were noted by the French ambassadors at Arras, in 1435: *Letters and Papers*, I, p. 60.

[250] See Palmer 1971: esp. pp. 51–4, for the general context of negotiations.

to do what he had done. As the events of 1450 were later to demonstrate, responsibility for deeds which could be seen to have diminished the crown could be placed upon the shoulders of the king's advisers, making them little more than traitors. In the sphere of peace no less than in the sphere of war, therefore, the probity and competence of Henry's agents was established by nothing more secure than public debate and public judgement: the king himself was, as yet, unable to license them. Creative policy of any kind, therefore, demanded the establishment of royal rule, but how was this to be achieved when the king gave no clear lead?

The council's direction of government, and the ascendancy of Cardinal Beaufort which generally went with it, had been little shaken by the crisis over Calais in 1436 and the king's admission to power which it necessitated.[251] If Gloucester had seen in the latter development an opportunity to assert himself at the cardinal's expense, he was mistaken. At this stage, as we have seen, Henry's rule amounted to nothing more than the dispersal of royal patronage: the council remained the agency of government and, in the later 1430s, it was effectively Beaufort who presided, and his policy of pursuing a negotiated peace or truce via Burgundian mediation which commanded the support of the lords.[252] In the summer of 1439, however, this policy began to come unstuck, as it became clear that no agreement at all could be reached with the French unless the king were prepared to surrender his sovereignty for a time, restore French landowners to their lands in Normandy and Guyenne and release the duke of Orléans without ransom.[253]

These exacting terms, gamely put by Kemp to an assembly at Windsor in August which roundly rejected them, exposed the weaknesses in Beaufort's position.[254] They were almost certain to be unacceptable to

---

[251] Above, pp. 129ff; Harriss 1988: pp. 293–4. Note that Beaufort shared with Gloucester the commons' thanks for victory in the 1437 parliament (*RP*, IV, pp. 502–3), while the central role of his nephew Edmund in the defeat of the Burgundians was widely acknowledged at the time (Jones 1982: p. 96).

[252] The cardinal's headship was manifested in various ways: the refusal of the lords to permit him to go abroad (to Rome in April 1437 and Basle in February 1438: *PPC*, V, pp. 9, 93); the particular significance attached to his advice (*ibid.*, p. 27); his apparently independent conduct of certain business (*ibid.*, pp. 81–2); the holding of meetings at his church of St Mary Overeys (e.g. E28/59/14 Feb., 24 & 28 Mar. 1438; E28/61/6, 10 & 12 June 1439); and the fact that his salary, for services done 'in assistendo consiliis nostris', was increased from December 1437 to £400 (PSO1/5/280; *CPR, 1436–41*, p. 126). Note that Gloucester's title of principal councillor seems to have lapsed by the mid-1430s. Beaufort's policy is discussed in Harriss 1988: pp. 295–305, esp. p. 303.

[253] See Allmand 1967: esp. p. 22 and *PPC*, V, pp. 378–9. Harriss 1988: p. 301 notes that the final French proposal waived the sovereignty issue.

[254] For the meeting at Windsor, we only have Gloucester's account: *Letters and Papers*, II, ii, p. 446. It led to a series of counter-proposals, issued at Langley on 30 August, which the French would never have accepted: *PPC*, V, pp. 388–91; Harriss 1988: p. 302; Ferguson 1972: p. 23.

a group of lords invited to give public judgement on such compromising matters in front of one another and in the presence of the youthful king, yet it was on the effective support of a public body of this kind that Beaufort's power rested. If it rejected his policy and did so, moreover, partly because it could not authorise the necessary action, the cardinal had nowhere else to turn.[255] While he had supposedly been briefed by the king on the matter of his title and was, in some sense, his plenipotentiary, he was evidently unable to use royal power to make the sort of concessions necessary to halt the war.[256] It was becoming clear that there was insufficient authority, either in the body of the lords, or in a king still effectively subordinate to the council, to meet the demands of policy. In a sense, therefore, the conciliar compromise had proved ineffective and the failure of the Oye conference led to changes in the structure of power.[257]

These began with the famous attack on the cardinal and his policies made by the duke of Gloucester, probably in the second session of the 1439–40 parliament.[258] What is particularly interesting about the duke's 'Appeal' is that the major constitutional charge laid against Beaufort – that, abetted by Kemp, he had got at the king behind the backs of his natural counsellors among the lords – does not make much sense if taken at face value.[259] As we have seen, Beaufort's power had rested fairly and squarely upon the avowedly representative and formally established council: it was this body, not the king, that Gloucester had so far been unable to influence.[260] The collapse of its policy provided the duke with an opportunity to strike both at the cardinal and, less explicitly, at the council. Gloucester must have hoped that his suggestion that Henry's power had been accroached by some of his councillors would encourage the establishment of normal royal rule, in which counsel would be informal and king-centred, rather than formal and

---

[255] There were sound reasons for rejecting the French proposals (see Allmand, 'Documents of 1439', pp. 80–1; *PPC*, V, pp. 392–5; Harriss 1988: pp. 302–3), but, it may be suggested, none so compelling that royal authority could not have overcome them, if it sincerely wished to obtain a truce.

[256] *PPC*, V, p. 361.

[257] See Harriss 1988: pp. 303, 306, for the effects of the failure of the conference on Beaufort's standing.

[258] *Chrons. of London*, p. 153; Harriss 1988: p. 308 n. 9.

[259] See particularly articles III (*Letters and Papers*, II, ii, pp. 442–3), X (p. 445), XIII (pp. 446–7), XIV (p. 447) and in XXII (p. 451).

[260] This is tacitly admitted in some of Gloucester's charges, notably article XVII, in which Beaufort is accused of accroaching the royal estate by calling the king's 'counsaille' to his own house (p. 449). Note that Gloucester had been present at a number of council meetings at which decisions concerning Oye were made: e.g. those of 8 May 1439, when the ambassadors were chosen (E28/60/as dated) and 22 May 1439, when Beaufort's wages were fixed (E28/60/as dated).

Beaufort-dominated.[261] With government transferred to the court, his voice might carry more weight than it had in recent years.

If this was Gloucester's aim, it is not difficult to see how neatly it fitted with the interests of Suffolk and his following in the household. It is worth noting that this group drew no criticism from the duke, despite the fact that they were surely best-placed to exercise the sort of private influence over the king which he appeared to be condemning. It is much more likely that Gloucester saw Suffolk as an ally than as a threat: the duke had his own place and, perhaps, his own connections in the household;[262] he had provided Suffolk with his first political opportunities and seems – albeit on fragmentary evidence – to have remained on good terms with the earl.[263] Under these circumstances, there is, as Gerald Harriss has suggested, every reason to see a connection between Gloucester's attack on the cardinal and the other main business of the 1439–40 parliament, the attempt to terminate Henry V's duchy feoffment in the interests of the household.[264]

The move against Henry V's feoffees, of whom only Beaufort, Chichele and Hungerford remained, was apparently conducted by Suffolk with the enthusiastic support of the commons. Its aim was to regain the enfeoffed lands under the guise of stabilising household funding. But in fact, as Gerald Harriss has demonstrated, the household was already enjoying sound financial provision, and there seems little doubt that Suffolk's real intention was to use the enfeoffed estates of the duchy in the foundations project.[265] Almost as soon as the feoffees had surrendered their trust, in May 1443, a valuation was begun in preparation for a new feoffment, which was made in four instalments between November 1443 and June 1445.[266] The purpose of this feoffment was entirely concealed until 1445

---

[261] See above, pp. 143–4.

[262] See table 1. Thomas Beckington, the king's secretary, John Somerset, his almoner, and Walter Shirington, the chancellor of the duchy of Lancaster, were one-time servants of Gloucester (see p. 166 n. 174; Griffiths 1981: pp. 309, 347) and the duke might have believed them to be his men.

[263] The two men exchanged their offices of justice of North Wales (Gloucester to Suffolk) and justice of South Wales (Suffolk to Gloucester) on 19 February 1440 (*CPR, 1436–41*, p. 376). This move could have been contrived for Gloucester's benefit as much as Suffolk's (cf. Griffiths 1991c: p. 175): Duke Humphrey was also earl of Pembroke, while Suffolk's interest in the posts must have been more patronal than territorial. See above, pp. 156, 162, for Gloucester's earlier relations with the earl.

[264] Harriss 1988: pp. 308–9; *RP*, V, pp. 8–9.

[265] Harriss 1953: pp. 33–68 and 1988: pp. 307–8, 323–4. The government's intentions became clearer in the parliament of 1442, which heard a petition for the termination of the feoffment in order that its revenues could be used to meet a variety of expenses including, alongside the household, the king's works: *RP* V, pp. 56–9. Note that William Tresham, one of the feoffees' officers, but also a household man (receiving robes by 1441: E101/409/9, fol. 37r) and soon involved in the foundations project, was speaker in both parliaments (Roskell 1965: pp. 219–23; above, p. 170).

[266] Somerville 1953: pp. 206, 210; Harriss 1953: p. 67.

and even then blandly declared to be the fulfilment of the king's 'voluntas'.[267] It turned out to be a means of paying for the building of the royal colleges.[268] Given the importance of the foundations in creating coherence among the major figures of the household and in signalling the king's accession to power, it seems possible to suggest an alignment of interest between Suffolk and Gloucester at this time: both wished to see the cardinal's power, and its bases in council and duchy, undermined in favour of royal rule.

This, however, was the limit of Suffolk's interest in proceeding against Beaufort.[269] There was nothing to be gained by forcing him to answer Gloucester's charges and it is hard to believe that such a measure would have found much support. The cardinal's political activities had been endorsed by the only authority available until recent years: that of the council. Beaufort was distinguished from the other councillors only by his leadership: there is little to suggest that his aims or activities were particularly controversial.[270] Moreover, he was at the centre of a network of territorial rule, which, for Suffolk's assertion of a new authority to work, needed to be eased into the court, not blown apart by a direct attack. It seems very likely that Gloucester was persuaded to abandon his more serious charges against the cardinal in favour of wider consultation over the immediate problems of foreign policy.[271] At first sight, this solution may seem an odd one, given that the accent of Gloucester's demands had been on more royal rule rather than more consultation, but, of course, the two properties were closely associated: the virtue of making the king, rather than the council, the centre of decision making was that it promised to extend the sources of counsel. So it was that the lords seem to have resolved the crisis by focusing attention on the matter of releasing the duke of Orléans – which was hardly the centre of the duke's charges[272] – and removing it from the direct control of the cardinal by

---

[267] *RP*, V, p. 73.

[268] In December 1444, granted £1,000 a year to each college out of named duchy lands. In July 1446, the terms were revised to provide an extra 400 marks a year for Eton and an extra £400 for King's: Somerville 1953: p. 221 and n. 6.

[269] See also Harriss 1988: p. 309.

[270] The degree of endorsement for the cardinal's activities is nicely illustrated by the dealings over Chirk, which Gloucester had condemned (*Letters and Papers*, II, ii, p. 448). Gloucester himself (as he acknowledged), Suffolk, (Bishop) Stafford, Northumberland, Salisbury, Cromwell and other lords were present at the making of the king's grant of the property: although technically the king acted on his own authority, these men can hardly have dissented (E28/60/25 May 1439).

[271] Although chronicle evidence suggests that the duke's charges were made in parliament (above, n. 258), the silence of the roll seems to suggest that the matter was swiftly buried. It is possible that a grant of the lieutenancy of France also played a part in appeasing the duke: see below.

[272] This may explain why such a wide-ranging body of accusations against Beaufort came to be labelled by its fifteenth-century editor as 'the declaracone ... ayeinst thenlargisse-

submitting it to the counsel of a different group of lords.[273] At the same time, Orléans himself was removed from the keeping of Sir John Stourton, probably a close associate of Beaufort's, and placed in the hands of the more neutral Lord Fanhope.[274]

The possibility of handing over Orléans, which had been an element in English diplomacy for some years, had not been entirely discounted by the lords in the wake of the Oye conference.[275] It is thus perfectly possible that the king's decision to release him, which came a few weeks later, was indeed made with the advice of the counsellors to whom the matter was committed: the crucial new ingredient was royal authorisation, which alone could license such a step.[276] As we have seen, the implementation of royal rule did not necessarily mean that policy making was to be less representative, only that it was to be more authoritative. There is nothing to justify the familiar assumption that the emergence of the king disguised the takeover of comparatively private and unaccountable interests. On the contrary, Henry was being brought forward in order to satisfy a common

ment ... of Charles, duc of Orliaunce' (*Letters and Papers*, II, ii, pp. 440–1). Gloucester's own text begins with a much more accurate heading: here, he declared, was a list of things done in the king's tender age and still done 'into derogacion of your noble estate, and hurte of bothe your royaumes' (p. 441). The only chronicle to mention the episode refers only to articles against Beaufort being presented by Gloucester: *Chrons. of London*, p. 153.

[273] Above, p. 144 n. 85 (the identity of these men is unknown: they *could* all have been members of the council appointed in 1437, but Gloucester – and almost certainly Beaufort – were not among them).

[274] E404/56/259 (29 January 1440). Orléans had earlier been transferred to Stourton's keeping from that of Sir Reginald Cobham, Gloucester's father-in-law, on 15 July 1438, two days before a preliminary agreement to release Orléans was made (see E404/53/128; E404/55/128; *Foedera*, V, i, p. 54). This, together with the fact that Stourton had joined the council in 1437 (*PPC*, V, p. 71) and served in the embassy at Oye (*ibid.*, p. 334), may suggest that he was connected with the cardinal (see also Harriss 1988: pp. 151, 356). Fanhope had kept Orléans and other French prisoners in the 1420s (*RP*, IV, pp. 338–9; Champion 1911: pp. 106, 195).

[275] For schemes from the years 1437–9 which involved the possibility of releasing Orléans, primarily to act as a mediator in peace negotiations, see *PPC*, V, pp. 64–9; *Foedera*, V, i, p. 54; Allmand 1967: p. 2. By August 1439, the government's position was that Orléans would be permitted to return to France to negotiate a peace and would only have to return if he was unsuccessful (*PPC*, V, p. 391). Although this linked the duke's release to the concrete results which were expected to arise from it, it did not prevent it from taking place and was not actually very different from the terms to which Orléans swore in July 1440 (see Griffiths 1981: p. 453, for details).

[276] See above, p. 144, n. 85, for commission of the matter to counsellors. Maurice Keen has suggested another reason why returning the duke to France might have appealed to a broad spectrum of opinion: below, p. 192, n. 302. The need for royal authorisation of the move was surely underlined by the fact that in his will of June 1421, Henry V had distinguished Orléans and the count of Eu from the other prisoners in royal custody, stipulating that they should remain in the keeping of his successor for as long as was convenient to the good of his two realms (Strong and Strong, 'Will of Henry V', p. 92). Eu had been released in 1436 and, interestingly enough, it had been necessary to involve the king personally in the process (Jones 1982: p. 41). I am most grateful to Dr Michael K. Jones for discussing this matter with me.

and public need: in fact, to break a real deadlock over policy. As such, this particular assertion of royal power was very much in key with other developments of the turn of the decade, such as the decline of the 1437 council and the genesis of the foundations. Accordingly, the king's personal responsibility for the release of Orléans was made absolutely clear in the document of justification which emerged later in 1440.[277] The first paragraph established that the king had freed the duke 'of hymself'.[278] The second emphasised that the king 'wol not that eny charge shulde be layde therfore at eny tymes herafter upon eny othr personne'.[279] This does not preclude the possibility that the measure had been widely, if tacitly, recommended by leading men. To use the declaration as evidence of the king's genuine personal commitment to peace at all costs misses the point that this is exactly what it was supposed to demonstrate, in order to justify and, indeed, permit the exercise of power by his agents and advisers.[280] In the same way, there is no reason to see Suffolk as the single architect of the king's policy.[281] He was the creator of royal authority, not its director. Given his continual attention to the realities of noble power and opinion, it seems unwise to assume that he went beyond the provision of a means for the fulfilment of a common aim.[282]

In the event, therefore, the displacement of Beaufort and the council did not produce dramatic changes in either the personnel of government or the trend of policy. If Gloucester had intended to increase his own influence over affairs, then he had failed. The lieutenancy of France, which he seems finally to have secured in the wake of Beaufort's failure, was lost to the rising duke of York.[283] His advice concerning Orléans had not prevailed. It is difficult to know how much this mattered to him. Although he has always been presented as a hawk, the broader aims behind Gloucester's career are actually rather uncertain: it seems likely that he saw himself as a military leader in the mould of his brothers,[284]

---

[277] *Letters and Papers*, II, ii, pp. 451–60.   [278] *Ibid.*, pp. 451–2.

[279] *Ibid.*, p. 452.   [280] See above, p. 107 n. 22.

[281] Cf. Harriss 1988: p. 317.

[282] The matter had, as above, been committed to counsel, which would have made it difficult for Suffolk, even armed with the nascent royal authority, to pursue an independent and contradictory policy. Moreover, 'all the Lordes, except my Lord of Gloucestre' were apparently present when, in October 1440, Orléans took his oath to the king before departing (*PL*, II, p. 46).

[283] See Jones 1982: pp. 109–10, 123–6, for this obscure episode. Harriss 1988: pp. 312–13 convincingly suggests that it was Beaufort's continuing hold over the royal finances which prevented Gloucester from realising his opportunity.

[284] The poem *Humfroidos*, which Gloucester seems to have commissioned (alongside the *Vita Henrici Quinti*) in the wake of the Calais campaign of 1436, presented the duke as continuing Henry V's martial achievements, and even enlarging upon them by fighting Burgundy as well as France: Weiss 1957: pp. 221–5.

but this does not mean that he was inevitably or irrationally hostile to the cause of peace.[285] The scheme of 1444–5, for example, seems to have received his full and public support.[286] His bitter opposition to the release of Orléans in particular may have arisen as much from exasperation at his inability to influence a government of questionable authority as from his own personal conviction. Gloucester may have expected the devolution of full power to the king to introduce changes in the political landscape: if so, the limited consequences of the demise of the council must have surprised and nonplussed him, but it is difficult to see what he could have done about this. The directing power of the crown which he had helped to invoke was difficult to resist. While the fact that it worked in favour of policies closely resembling those of the old conciliar elite *may* have led Gloucester to doubt the independence of the royal judgement, there is no evidence to this effect and nothing to suggest that he took any action against what the king had willed. In the end, if there is a single theme in the duke's career, it is one of obedience to Henry's personal authority, something which was gaining definition only at this time. The king's new prominence must play an important part in explaining his acquiescence during the years which followed. Faced with the destruction of his wife, a series of threats to his property and, finally, a thoroughly dubious charge of treason, Gloucester was unresisting.[287] Was this because he accepted the central pretension of Suffolk's rule, that it was backed by the will of the king?

If so, he was surely mistaken. The roots of this new rule lay, just as before, in the will of the lords. The changes of 1439–41 had, in a sense, been more superficial than real: although, as we have seen, the emergence of the king extended the range of policy options, it did not affect the

---

[285] Gloucester had accepted, as early as 1431, that neither England, nor the occupied portion of France, could support the costs of continual war (*PPC*, IV, p. 96). At the same time, he agreed to a truce, if one could be arranged, provided that no way of pursuing the war more profitably should arise (*ibid.*, p. 95). On 22 February 1432, immediately prior to the duke's coup and surely with his agreement, arrangements were made to pay his chancellor, Thomas Beckington and others, who were off to negotiate with Charles VII (*ibid.*, p. 109).

[286] Gloucester's delight in the arrival of a queen was noted by one chronicler (*Chrons. of London*, p. 156) and his readiness to endorse Suffolk's work at Tours appears in the roll of the 1445 parliament (*RP*, V, p. 73).

[287] An alarming series of grants of the reversions of Gloucester's holdings upon the death of – or even, as in the following case, 'cession' by – the duke began in November 1441: *CPR, 1441–6*, p. 63 (this was the wardenship of the New Forest, and Suffolk was to be the beneficiary). From the following summer, the government began to interfere with Gloucester's tenure of his lands. On 14 August, a Wiltshire manor of his was granted to one of the king's esquires, the duke receiving an annual rent in return (*CPR, 1441–6*, pp. 102–3). A few months later, some alien priory lands, worth £370 17s 2d, were resumed from the duke. Once again, he was compensated, but only with monetary incomes (E28/71/4, 10).

government's dependence on the approval of the lords. By giving some substance to the fiction of royal decision the regime had gathered enough power to license – and therefore to effect – policy, but not enough to defend itself from public criticism. In this vulnerability lay the roots of the familiar hostility shown by Henry VI's principal ministers and intimates to anyone who possessed independent public standing and seemed likely to use it to inaugurate public debate over policy. Not only did such debate threaten the lives and livelihoods of the king's advisers, it also threatened the fragmentation of the government and, therefore, the subversion of royal rule and of the common weal which it protected. This explains why those lords whose direct involvement in the regime was more limited still regarded troublemakers with distaste and why, despite the government's fears to the contrary, they tended to put loyalty first. These were the preconditions for Gloucester's decline into impotence and ignominy as the rule of Suffolk and the king developed. The duke had a long career of wild schemes and disruptive appeals to public opinion behind him: he simply could not be trusted by Henry's leading agents and this, in itself, denied him the sympathy of even relatively uncommitted lords. Arguably the first sign of hostility from the governing circle was the removal of Gloucester from the captaincy of Calais in February 1441.[288] The act was made on royal authority alone, in circumstances of some secrecy,[289] but, if the government feared the consequences of moving against the king's remaining uncle, the events of the summer were soon to reveal the indifference of the lords to his demise.

While the lords had acquiesced in the direct exercise of royal power over the matter of Orléans and a number of more minor issues, they were also prepared to see the restoration of conciliar government in the autumn of 1441. An important element in this change of heart may have been the scandal which brought about the fall of Eleanor Cobham, duchess of Gloucester, during the summer. This episode has been treated as part of the reduction of the duke of Gloucester by a faction headed by Beaufort and Suffolk, but it may be that deeper dynamics were involved.[290] There seems to have been a general presumption that

---

[288] E28/66/68; *DKR*, XLVIII, p. 347. Gloucester's captaincy might have lapsed some time before this: note the existence of uncertainty as to the identity of the captain as early as November 1437 (*PPC*, V, p. 75: so dated by Nicolas) and the observation made by the treasurer of Calais, in September 1439, that there was neither captain nor lieutenant: *ibid.*, p. 400. Even so, it is unquestionably on this occasion that he was removed from the lordship of Guisnes, which was given, tellingly, to Suffolk.

[289] The decision, made by the king at Windsor, was endorsed 'The K commaundith that no thing ... passe in contenye of this but that this be spedde after the acte here ... in alle commodious hast and in secrete wise.'

[290] See Griffiths 1991j, though note his important point that no contemporary chronicler saw the attack as politically motivated (*ibid.*, p. 237). The second (Yorkist) version of

Eleanor was at least guilty of imagining the king's death and commissioning horoscopes, which is far from impossible, given the contemporary interest in astrological matters.[291] If the lords believed this, then the affair could have served more than anything else to remind them of the vulnerability of the king and his government to manipulation, or even violence, from within the royal household.[292] This can hardly have been in Suffolk's interests, even if it did, perhaps, serve those of Beaufort, the doyen of conciliar rule. For this is a striking feature of the crisis: although household men were involved in the trial and imprisonment of Eleanor, the most prominent role was played by the 1437 councillors, both individually and corporately.[293] Beaufort and Kemp returned to the centre of affairs, sitting on the clerical panel which examined the duchess and joining other lords to witness the recantation of Roger Bultingbroke.[294] The earls of Huntingdon and Stafford and Lords Cromwell, Fanhope and Hungerford – all but Fanhope members of the 1437 council – were similarly involved in proceedings,[295] and the many references to the 'Kynges consayl' in the Brut chronicle account may reflect a sense that this body had, in the midst of the crisis, resumed its old importance and formal shape.[296]

Faced with a major threat to the king's security, therefore, the lords abandoned their flirtation with personal government and resorted to the firmer ground of their own institutionalised counsel. In the ensuing months, the council, afforced by new members from the wider court,

---

Hardyng's chronicle is the only source I have found which relates the episode to the decline of Gloucester and even he does not suggest that charges against Eleanor were manufactured: Ellis, *Chronicle of John Hardyng*, p. 400. Note that, of the many chroniclers who entertained suspicions about Gloucester's death in 1447, not one made any connection with the Cobham affair.

[291] See, most recently, Carey 1992, esp. ch. 8.

[292] This is what the account in Giles, *Chronicon*, pp. 30–1, evokes: following Bedford's death, Eleanor, aware of the king's youth and meekness, set out to rule him according to her own will and desire.

[293] Suffolk was among those ordered to investigate sorceries and treasons against the king (*English Chron.*, p. 58) and, on 11 August, Eleanor was placed in the keeping of Sir John Stewart and Sir William Wolff, both of whom were associates of his (*Brut*, p. 479; see pp. 161 n. 146; 159 n. 138, above). Even so, the prominence of other councillors, beside the earl, is noted by Griffiths 1991j: p. 250 and Harriss 1988: p. 322.

[294] *Brut*, pp. 478–9; although Harriss argues that Beaufort kept a low profile (1988: pp. 322–3).

[295] Huntingdon and Stafford were also on Suffolk's commission: see n. 293, above. On 25 July, the king sent these three earls, together with Cromwell, Fanhope and Hungerford and others to 'fele and see' what could be done to save king and realm: *Brut*, p. 479. Note that Fanhope was soon to join the council (below, n. 297).

[296] E.g. Eleanor's fate was to be decided by 'the kyng, with his Consayll'; she was to be kept at Leeds 'unto the wille of the kyng and of his Consayle'; and was to be brought from there to London by the commandment of the king 'and his Consayl' (*Brut*, pp. 477–81, *passim*). 'Consayl(le)' could, of course, just mean 'counsel', but it is perhaps rather odd that it is not simply the king who is recorded as making these decisions.

regained something of its old dominance in affairs.[297] There was, it seems, a tacit understanding that the king was not yet ready to rule in the normal way. Clearly enough, it would be too much to attribute the refoundation of the council solely to this one unfortunate event: affairs in Normandy,[298] doubts about the king's credibility and a need to dance to the cardinal's tune in return for his financial support[299] must all have played a part. Even so, it is perfectly possible that the Cobham episode tipped the balance, edging the lords from one uncertain authority to another. Neither king nor council answered all the needs of the political elite, but with the council once again made representative of the leaders of the household as well as of the lords at large, the compromise of the later 1430s was to a large extent revived.

To some extent, the restoration of the council meant the restoration of Cardinal Beaufort, but this development did not lead to major changes of policy, nor did it mean that the court lost all its earlier importance.[300] Ultimately, it was still on royal authority that government turned and this authority had to be obtained. The principal broker in obtaining it was, inevitably, Suffolk, aided by Adam Moleyns, the council's clerk.[301] In particular, a number of diplomatic initiatives required the king's personal attention. For a few months in 1441–2, the activities of the freed duke of Orléans seemed to offer the English a chance of resisting Charles VII with the help of a league of French princes.[302] The government responded enthusiastically to the possibility of a marriage alliance with the dissident count of Armagnac, but it could do so only with the participation of the king.[303] So it was that, in the early 1440s, Suffolk and other figures in the

---

[297] See above, pp. 145–6. The new members were Bishop Ayscough, Viscount Beaumont, Lord Fanhope and Lord Sudeley, the new chamberlain.

[298] In the summer of 1441 the king received a letter from the Norman council, still waiting for a lieutenant, which depicted the situation in the duchy in the most alarmist terms: 'signifying that our malady is akin to death or exile; and, as regards your sovereign power, very close upon total ruin' (*Letters and Papers*, II, ii, p. 604).

[299] Harriss 1988: pp. 324–5.

[300] Once again, the cardinal played a somewhat presidential role in the council. For example, in meetings of 12 and 18 October 1442 his advice seems to have carried particular weight even though he was in a minority of two on the first occasion (*PPC*, V, pp. 216, 220). On the latter occasion, Beaufort was expected to declare the king's will (*ibid.*, pp. 220–1). On 8 July 1443, an act made for the keeping of the sea was put before him (*ibid.*, p. 302). On 13 December 1443, his advice was specifically sought and reported back to the council (*PPC*, VI, pp. 18–19). See also Harriss 1988: pp. 332–4.

[301] See above, p. 148, and also figure 2 for the regular attendance of Suffolk at the council.

[302] Ferguson 1972: pp. 25–6. Keen 1989: p. 308 makes the interesting suggestion that Orléans had been released with this in mind.

[303] The commission sent to Gascony to negotiate the Armagnac marriage was issued by the king, or rather, 'in our presence', and subsequent instructions were said to proceed solely 'of our owne mocion' and were signed with the sign manual, 'the whiche as ye wote well, we be not muche accustumed for to do in other caas': Nicolas (ed.), *Journal of Beckington*, p. 6. Note that the French ambassadors at Arras had calculated that, in

household remained prominent in the formation and execution of policy and it is interesting to see them at work, in the king's name, on more aggressive policies than those for which both they and their master are usually remembered.[304] In the event, the plan came to nothing as the French king amassed an army and marched off to strike at Armagnac, creating consternation among the allies. This setback had two major consequences: a low-key, and presumably rather half-hearted, resumption of peace negotiations with King Charles;[305] and, in the summer of 1443, the despatch of a major expedition to distract the French from the vulnerable duchy of Gascony and restore English military fortunes.[306] The expedition was to be funded by Beaufort money and led by the cardinal's nephew, John, duke of Somerset. Despite its explicit royal backing, it seems to have been seen as the flagship of Beaufort ambitions and, as such, its disappointing performance was partly responsible for further changes in the pattern of rule.[307]

If Suffolk's rule had been undermined by the Cobham scandal of 1441 and the failure of the Armagnac plan, the shambolic progress of the Somerset expedition seems to have weakened the cardinal and permitted the revival of a modified form of household power. In July 1443, as John Beaufort repeatedly failed to muster, household men moved into the offices of state. Lord Cromwell, one of the mainstays of the old council, was replaced as treasurer by the chamberlain, Lord Sudeley, whilst Thomas Beckington, soon to be elected bishop of Bath and Wells, took over as keeper of the privy seal.[308] From this time onwards, as we have

---

1442, Henry would be 'aagé' and thus competent to take counsel and deliberate fully upon marriage, the surrender of territory and other ingredients of Anglo-French diplomacy (*Letters and Papers*, I, p. 60).

[304] For example, in the early spring of 1442, the duchess of Burgundy, who was involved in the Orleanist league, sent messengers to both Beaufort and Suffolk (Ferguson 1972: p. 26). The commissioners who went to Gascony were all household men: Thomas Beckington (see above, pp. 168–70, nn.), Sir Robert Roos, one of the king's carvers (*PPC*, IV, p. 128) and apparently a close associate of Suffolk (co-feoffee with Tuddenham in October 1438 and with Philip and Suffolk some time before June 1441: *CPR, 1436–41*, p. 221; *CPR, 1441–6*, p. 183), and Edward Hull, an esquire of the household from at least 1439 (E101/408/25, fol. 8r) and later a duchy feoffee and member of Queen Margaret's household (Lewis 1985b: pp. 217–18). Many of Beckington's letters regarding the expedition were to prominent courtiers (*Letters of Margaret*, nos. xliii–lv), but others make it clear that the council was also involved (*ibid.*, pp. 81, 82, 85–6). Suffolk's influence remained general: Beckington mentioned a series of high-level discussions with the earl about the provision of an army to defend Guyenne in the spring and summer of 1442: Nicolas (ed.), *Journal of Beckington*, p. 5.

[305] An embassy was appointed on 9 October 1442: *PPC*, V, pp. 212–13.

[306] Jones 1981.

[307] See Harriss 1988: pp. 349–50.

[308] For Sudeley's appointment as treasurer (7 July), see *CPR, 1441–6*, p. 180. Beckington became keeper on 18 July and was provided to Bath and Wells six days later (*HBC*, pp. 95, 228). Cromwell's departure from office might have been voluntary: he was discharged upon his own petition, although his elaborate articles and the insistence of

seen, the council began to subside: fewer meetings were held and record keeping seems to have declined.[309] Meanwhile, court preoccupations, most notably the matter of the royal foundations, began to come to the fore again. The college in Cambridge was ambitiously remodelled in new letters patent of 10 July 1443 and four months later the process of enfeoffing portions of the duchy of Lancaster to meet the costs of the foundations began.[310] The new feoffees included, in addition to an expanded group from the household and duchy establishments,[311] a number of lords familiarly associated with Beaufort power and with the council: Archbishop Kemp, the earl of Northumberland, Viscount Beaumont and Lords Cromwell and Hungerford.[312] Similarly, in December 1443, as the Beaufort expedition began to show signs of failure, Suffolk and Sudeley made efforts to accommodate the duke of York, who had been alienated by the redirection of resources and attention to Somerset since late 1442.[313] Once again, Suffolk took advantage of the cardinal's discomfiture to edge the king and his household to the centre of the political stage. Once again, he did so without destroying the cardinal's dominant constituency among the lords, making it his own by aping conciliar representativeness with the various means open to the manager of the court.

By the early 1440s there was, in many ways, little to choose between the rule of a council which did what it could to represent the household and defer to the king and the rule of a royal household which strove to accommodate the lords. This, more than anything, must explain the ease with which the nobility shifted allegiance from one to the other. That it was the household which triumphed is not at all surprising: if the lordship of Suffolk and that of Beaufort had a sort of equivalence, only the former could orchestrate the superior lordship of the king, which, whatever Henry's personal contribution, was the only proper and effective form of authority as his adulthood became undeniable. In the latter part of 1443,

the formal record that it was for illness and 'noon other cause' that he had sought discharge invites suspicion (*PPC*, V, pp. 298–9). Lord Dudley, a member of the household fraternity, and recently awarded a £100 annuity (*CPR, 1441–6*, p. 207) became a councillor in late 1443 (above, p. 149).

[309] Above, pp. 149–51.   [310] Above, p. 185.

[311] *RP*, V, pp. 70–1. These included, *inter alia*, Sudeley, Sir John Beauchamp of Powick and John Noreys: it is tempting to suggest that this may have been related to their association with the nascent, and potentially divisive, Beauchamp interest in the household. See below, p. 196.

[312] See above, pp. 156, 173–4, 178, for the associations of these men. Note that Kemp was also appointed one of the conservators of the lands of King's College (Saltmarsh 1959: p. 377). Bishop Gilbert of London, another feoffee, was a friend of Kemp's: Griffiths 1981: p. 66 n. 53. Northumberland had been in trouble earlier in 1443 (above, p. 178): his inclusion in the feoffment may have been intended as part of a rehabilitation.

[313] They revived the payment of his wages, for example: Harriss 1988: p. 347. See also Appendix A and, for York and Somerset, below, p. 197.

negotiations with the French were revived, their tempo quickening soon after Somerset arrived back in England, in disgrace, in January 1444.[314] On 1 February, Suffolk gained the necessary authority – in the shape of a command from both king and lords – for an embassy to cross to France and negotiate a peace and a marriage.[315] Although the episode reflects the earl's victory over the council and his decisive emergence as the director of English foreign policy, it also shows the ambivalent position of the king. Even now, public and conciliar support was required for the royal word to be sufficient to authorise Suffolk's activities.[316] All the same, the outward pattern of government had changed, bringing with it a new politics and, though this was unrealised as yet, a new array of problems. In the course of the following year, the court – now comprising king, household and peers of the realm – came, as was proper, to provide the only venue for politics. With the marriage to Margaret of Anjou in April 1445, the personal rule of Henry VI took on a more traditional appearance.[317]

CONCLUSION

By 1445, the transition from conciliar government to royal rule in the court had more or less been made. Suffolk had created a coherent base in the household and drawn the dominant following among the lords into its ambit. Even so, the limitations of this achievement, which became all too obvious in the later 1440s, are perceptible even at this time and so deserve a preliminary discussion here. The loyalty felt by lords to the personal rule of Henry VI can perhaps be characterised as the willing suspension of disbelief. There is no reason to assume that the nobility were now convinced, as they had not been in 1432 or 1434 or 1437, or even 1441, that their king was a substantial figure with an independent will. This does not mean that they were not persuaded, or even constrained, to behave as if this was the case: disobedience was still treason, and, while the rest of the seigneurial body did its business in the court, the individual lord had no choice but to do the same. The long shadow of Henry V may

---

[314] Harriss 1988: pp. 343–4; Jones 1981: p. 96. By the end of August 1443, arrangements had been made to pay Suffolk, Ayscough and John Wenlock for an embassy to France.

[315] *PPC*, VI, pp. 33–5; *Foedera*, V, i, p. 130.

[316] Suffolk's patent, granted in the 1 February meeting, attempted to make royal responsibility for the embassy quite clear: 'Stricte praecipimus praefato consanguineo nostro [i.e. Suffolk] curam eiusdem ambassiate nostrae et onus in se suscipere.' It was, even so, said to be issued 'de auctoritate parliamenti', which suggests that these events took place in a great council, rather than in a meeting of the council of 1437/41. Note that the earl once again requested (and was granted) guarantees that, if the mission were unsuccessful, he should not be put out of favour: *PPC*, VI, pp. 34–5.

[317] The foreign policy of 1444–5 is discussed in the following chapter.

still have held many of the lords together in a corporate and unreflecting loyalty to his son, especially as some of the old king's associates – notably Beaufort and Gloucester – retained some degree of public prominence into the 1440s. The self-motivated loyalties of the nobility were, however, a profoundly different basis for the exercise of authority from that which normally obtained in the English polity. Conventional royal lordship derived, in the last resort, from the king's independent will, which was subject only to God. The royal lordship of Henry VI, which seems in fact to have been that of Suffolk, derived solely from the support of its own immediate constituency among the lords. It was not directed by an independent will and so it had no independent base: the earl was able to exercise authority only with the direct assent of the leading magnates.

Although there is every reason to believe that the magnates were willing to give this assent in the mid-1440s, the absence of an effective royal will is profoundly significant in explaining the nature of Henry VI's polity. Royal power, even now that it was located in the court, was essentially conciliar: oligarchical, not monarchical. Conciliar governments, as we have seen, had two great weaknesses: first, they could not offer the comprehensive representation of interests which the crown provided, with the result that 'public' authority – which was thus not truly public – was steadily undermined; second, they could not easily resolve divisions among their own number, but, by attempting to satisfy intermittently conflicting interests, they caused such divisions. A collapse of public authority did not strike Henry VI's government until 1450, but the dangers posed by divisions among the governing group can be illustrated by two instances from the middle years of the reign in which only the intervention of fate averted disaster.

The first of these is constituted by the career of Henry Beauchamp, earl and duke of Warwick, who came to a rapid and disruptive prominence in 1444. Beauchamp had grown up in the royal household, where his father had been the king's guardian and still seems to have resided there as the king's ward in the early 1440s.[318] There he became the focus for a developing network of court figures, headed by Lords Sudeley and Beauchamp of Powick, who shared both in the custody of the comital lands during Henry's minority and in the renascence of Beauchamp lordship in about 1444.[319] It was doubtless the backing of

---

[318] Griffiths 1981: pp. 298, 315.

[319] See above, p. 164, for the position of Sudeley (Sir Ralph Butler) and Beauchamp in the household. Sudeley, Beauchamp, Sir William Mountford, John Noreys, John Nanfan and others were appointed keepers of the dowager countess's lands from late 1439 (*CPR, 1436–41*, pp. 359, 360; the last three were among her executors – Furnivall (ed.), *Fifty Earliest English Wills*, p. 119). Beauchamp and Noreys were also guardians of the earl's lands: *CPR, 1436–41*, p. 279. For the place of Sudeley and Beauchamp in the

these courtiers that secured for Henry a series of remarkable grants: the titles, successively, of premier earl, and then duke of Warwick;[320] and the stewardship of the duchy lordship of Tutbury in tail male.[321] Conversely, as a long-term associate of the king, a member of the ancient nobility and a source of local lordship, he offered the likes of Sudeley and Beauchamp of Powick a more direct representation of their interests than Suffolk did.[322] Warwick and his eager supporters threatened to create an alternative source of lordship in the household, which could have had profoundly divisive and destructive consequences.[323] The new duke's ascendancy was already beginning to disrupt the Beaufort-focused equilibrium among the nobility, with trouble breaking out in Warwickshire and the duke of Buckingham, threatened there and in Staffordshire, contesting in parliament his cousin's newly acquired precedence.[324] If the duke had not died suddenly three months after his twenty-first birthday, the chances of preventing a multi-faceted division among lords and courtiers could have been slim.

Another potentially serious division arose in 1443 with the Beaufort expedition, which, whatever its strategic justifications, redirected resources and attention from the duke of York, as lieutenant of France, to the new duke of Somerset.[325] Resistance from York was plainly anticipated when the plans were being drawn up, and some seems to have arrived, in the shape of a deputation enquiring about Somerset's powers.[326] That there were no more profound consequences is almost certainly due to the widely perceived failure of the expedition and the

household, see above. Noreys and Sudeley had the captaincy of Conway jointly for a year from December 1440 (*CPR, 1436–41*, p. 497). Noreys and Nanfan were esquires of the household by this time, and Noreys, like Sudeley, enjoyed a position in the duchy honour of Leicester, which held lands in Warwickshire: E101/408/25, fol. 8r.; Somerville 1953: pp. 569, 571; *CPR, 1436–41*, pp. 309–10. He acted as a feoffee for the Catesbys and Treshams, other men with duchy and Beauchamp connections (Griffiths 1981: p. 303). For the role of Sudeley, Beauchamp and the household interest in Warwickshire in the 1440s, see Carpenter 1992: ch. 11. Note that influence worked both ways: Mountford, in many ways the lynchpin of the Beauchamp connection, was a king's knight by the early 1440s (Carpenter 1992: pp. 408–9).

[320] *CChR, 1427–1516*, pp. 41, 50.

[321] Castor 1995 shows that this grant, made in October 1444, was actually a grant of the reversion, so that Humphrey Stafford's tenure of the office was not directly threatened (cf. Somerville 1953: p. 540).

[322] Note that Beauchamp was involved in the endowment of Eton, surrendering lands to that end and receiving others in return: Ross (ed.), *Rous Roll*, no. 54.

[323] It is possible that Beauchamp and Sudeley were taking advantage of Suffolk's long absences in 1444–5 to undermine his position.

[324] See Carpenter 1992: pp. 412–20; and C49/26/14 for the precedence dispute. Control of Tutbury was essential to Buckingham's lordship in Staffordshire: Carpenter 1992: pp. 392, 400, 412.

[325] For the threat to York's leadership, see Johnson 1988: pp. 42–3. For the effect on wage payments to the duke, see *ibid.*, p. 56. For the strategy, see Jones 1981: pp. 85–6.

[326] *PPC*, V, pp. 251–2, 259–64, 290.

disgrace and death of Somerset which followed soon after.[327] Had
Somerset been successful, it is difficult to see how York could have been
so easily reconciled in the absence of a single central authority.[328] Whilst
it often needed to bow to the demands of the cardinal, the court could not
afford to alienate its leading noblemen, yet this is what its need to satisfy
the present interest could sometimes require.

This version of events has significant implications for the most historio-
graphically prominent division of Henry's early years: the quarrel
between the cardinal and the duke of Gloucester. Although it provided a
stimulus to changes in the pattern of authority in 1432–3 and 1439–40,
this conflict was not threatening to the developing consensus in the court.
By the late 1430s, if not before, Gloucester had no real constituency
among the Beaufort-focused community of lords whom Suffolk made it
his business to represent. If there was intermittent sympathy among them
for his views on particular issues – as, perhaps, in the debates over peace
policy in 1439 – there was no real commitment to his lordship, and it was
lordship that counted. The duke's fall from grace had no significant
repercussions in political society: the myth of Good Duke Humphrey
only developed in the 1450s, when Henry VI's government faced the
scrutiny of a different, wider, public.[329]

Drawing this together, it is clear that although Suffolk, following
Beaufort, had kept in being a united and broadly representative following
among the lords, he never acquired the wherewithal to regulate it. It was
not enough to establish a series of regional lordships and protect them
with a restricted representation at the centre. A free lordship over this elite
was necessary: there was no adequate replacement for normal royal
authority. This made Suffolk himself acutely vulnerable. If, in reality, his
power rested on his capacity to satisfy the interests of this dominant elite,
in public terms it rested on the personal authority of the king, based in the
household. Suffolk had, in a sense, accroached the royal power, though it
is difficult to see what royal power there could have been without his
efforts or those of someone like him; as it was, there was precious little
even for him to use. If he could not meet the needs of his noble
constituency, he faced disaster. If, in trying to perform this feat, he
neglected interests which were not directly represented – those of
alienated noblemen who deserted the public machinery of justice; those of
the realm at large expressed in military success, local order and an
appropriate level of taxation – he again faced disaster, though the dangers

---

[327] Johnson 1988: p. 45.
[328] Disagreements could have been avoided from the start, of course, if the king had led the
expedition.
[329] The events of 1447 are discussed in the following chapter: pp. 228–32.

in this second area were less immediately pressing. Because the earl worked at the construction and leadership of an affinity centred in the household, there is no need to see him as either a diabolic genius or a greedy courtier: he simply responded in a logical way to both the demands and the opportunities placed before him as a noble servant of Henry VI.[330] Some of the nobility were in a position to exploit proximity to the king and others were not. Is there a significant moral difference between Suffolk, who drew the rewards which control of the royal person brought, and, say, Beaufort, who derived parallel benefits from his preeminent position in the council of lords?[331] Both attempted to serve the Lancastrian crown and both found that their service to Henry VI involved them in the exercise of a lordship which was properly his. Government meant making decisions. As the king grew, these decisions needed the endorsement of his royal person, and this person was largely in Suffolk's hands. The real problem of Henry's reign was not venal courtiers, though this was the only obvious way to formulate it in 1450, but the absence of an independent royal will.

[330] For the meaning of service, see Horrox 1989: introduction. For a discussion of the greed of the lesser men of the household, see below, pp. 216ff.

[331] Although attention to the context of Suffolk's rule immediately demands a more sympathetic appraisal of the duke's career, it must be said that his concern to further his own interests was, at the very least, indiscreet. The acquisition of the heiresses of Beauchamp and Beaufort and of the earldom of Pembroke and even Suffolk's elevation to a dukedom were and are difficult to justify on any public grounds (*CPR, 1441–6*, pp. 198, 283; *CPR, 1446–52*, p. 1; *HBC*, p. 484). It may be said in Suffolk's defence that the extent of his service justified the extent of his reward, but in the absence of any real authority other than his own which could make such a judgement, his self-promotion was unwise. A distinction should be made between the above grants and Suffolk's acquisition of other offices – such as chamberlain of England, the chief stewardships of both parts of the duchy and even the headship of the Staple – which enabled him to exercise a necessary political control (*CPR, 1446–52*, p. 45; Somerville 1953: pp. 421, 428; Harriss 1986: p. 162). As for Beaufort, see McFarlane 1981b for the view that the cardinal was far from blind to his own interests and drew profit not only from the service he gave the Lancastrian crown, but also from the power he exercised under its last incumbent. Harriss 1988: pp. 147–8, 291, 390 offers a more sympathetic, but not dissimilar, view.

Appendix A

DETAILS OF GRANTS TO CERTAIN LEADING TERRITORIAL LORDS DURING PERIODS IN WHICH ROYAL POWER WAS APPARENTLY IN THE ASCENDANT (1440–1, 1443–5)

Beaumont

Beaumont received a whole series of territorial grants in May 1440 (see above, p. 173 n. 206), shortly after his elevation to a viscountcy. In August 1441, he was granted the reversion of four Bardolf manors which would otherwise have gone to the crown (*CPR, 1436–41,* p. 558). In August 1443, he and his wife were granted a fifty mark heritable annuity (E159/221, comm., Trin., m. 1).

Cromwell

In February 1440, Cromwell's life-grant of two-thirds of the manors of Wressle (Yorks.), Burwell and Leadenham (Lincs.) etc. was changed into a grant in fee simple, together with the reversions of the remaining thirds (*CPR, 1436–41,* p. 384). He received the custody of – rather surprisingly – an alien priory at a 1d rent that July (*ibid.,* p. 435).

Huntingdon/Exeter

Huntingdon is something of an oddity within this group, since he did not possess any significant territorial lordship. Instead, he owed his political importance to his family's long association with the royal family, his military service and his position on the council (see Stansfield 1987 for details). On 4 February 1440, Huntingdon was granted the lordship of Lesparre in Guyenne (E28/63/55). In July 1441, he was awarded 500 marks per year on the customs in respect of his lost patrimony (*CPR, 1436–41,* p. 565). It may be illuminating that this grant was reissued in late November 1443, when conciliar influence was again waning (*CPR, 1441–6,* p. 242). In the ensuing few months, Huntingdon was given custody of the royal castle and lordship of Berkhamsted, surely a post of court significance, created duke of Exeter and granted a series of forfeited Holland manors in Cornwall (*ibid.,* pp. 228, 267; *HBC,* p. 462).

Mortain/Dorset

In December 1443, the marquis of Dorset was given £224 6s. 8d. per year until he could be given suitable lands: *CPR, 1441–6*, p. 277.

Salisbury

In July 1443, the earl of Salisbury was granted a hereditary estate as justice of the forests beyond Trent: *CPR, 1441–6*, p. 191.

Shrewsbury

Shrewsbury's elevation to the higher nobility came at the strange moment of May 1442, when the council was certainly dominant. The timing is perhaps explained by his continuous residence in France until that year (Pollard 1968: pp. 184–5), though see also above, p. 175 n. 214. At any rate, efforts were made to pay his arrears in December 1443 (*CPR, 1441–6*, pp. 227–8) and he was granted a £100 annuity in March 1444 (*ibid.*, p. 235).

Stafford/Buckingham

On 1 December 1440, Stafford seems to have made some progress towards regaining the disputed appurtenances of the lordship of Brecon (*CPR, 1436–41*, p. 491; E28/66/1). Soon after, he began to use, surely by royal permission, the title of earl of Buckingham, which emphasised his descent through the female line from Edward III's youngest son, Thomas of Woodstock (the first occasion seems to have been 26 May 1441: E28/68/36). In February 1441, the king appointed him captain of Calais under highly secretive circumstances at Windsor: E28/66/68.

York

In February 1444, serious attempts were made to recommence wage-payments to the duke of York: *CPR, 1441–6*, p. 242. In December of that year, he was granted a major appanage in southern Normandy: Jones 1989a: pp. 289–90.

Appendix B

DETAILS OF MAJOR DISPUTES INVOLVING THE NOBILITY DURING THE PERIOD *C*.1435–45

Disputes involving associates of Beaufort or Suffolk

Berkeley vs. Beauchamp Coheirs

This dispute is referred to in the text. See Pollard 1968 and Sinclair 1987 for accounts.

Cromwell vs. Grey of Codnor

For details of this dispute, see Payling 1991: pp. 92–3, 97–8, 195–8. Cromwell was able to use the formal means of royal jurisdiction, in the shape of an oyer and terminer commission, to destroy Grey's influence in Nottinghamshire. It is interesting to note that Grey received some backing from Gloucester: E28/67/6–8.

Norfolk vs. Sir Robert Wingfield

Wingfield had been one of Norfolk's men and a servant of his father: see *PPC*, IV, pp. 300–1; *DKR*, XLVIII, p. 328; *CPR*, *1436–41*, p. 24; Archer 1984a: p. 279. As recently as 1440, he had benefited from the duke's protection in a dispute with one of Suffolk's men (see *PL*, II, p. 47, for details and note that this episode probably resulted in Norfolk's imprisonment and certainly led to the imposition of humiliating conditions and a bond of 10,000 marks: Storey 1966: p. 226; *CClR*, *1435–41*, p. 381). At some point in the ensuing few years, however, Wingfield seems to have decided that De La Pole offered the best local lordship and defected to his following, inspiring Norfolk to seize the manor of Hoo, which his father had given to the faithless knight: E28/82/70; Storey 1966: pp. 226–7 (where cause and effect are the other way round). It might be felt that Norfolk had some justification for his actions, but he was bound in £2,000 to appear before king and council (*CClR*, *1441–7*, p. 196), made to appoint Wingfield chief steward of all his lands in Suffolk (*ibid.*, p. 213) and obliged to hand over a Hertfordshire manor of his to a group of Wingfield's feoffees, including Suffolk, in compensation for Hoo (*ibid.*, p. 215; E28/82/70). Small wonder that, two years later, the duke was petitioning for licence to go abroad on pilgrimage: C81/1370/38.

Northumberland vs. Cardinal Kemp

This seems to have begun as a jurisdictional dispute between the men of the honour of Knaresborough, headed by Northumberland's retainer Sir William Plumpton and those of the archbishop's towns of Ripon and Otley (*Plumpton*, pp. liii–lxi). In May 1443, Kemp presented a letter written by Northumberland (presumably to raise his men) to a great council, whereupon Hungerford, Sudeley, Beaumont, Suffolk and Salisbury agreed that he should be brought to answer: *PPC*, V, pp. 273–4. Two days later, he did so and was ordered to surrender himself to the Tower (*ibid.*, p. 275; *CClR, 1441–7*, p. 98). The earl was later released under humiliating terms, having given security for himself and his men (*ibid.*, pp. 136, 144, 149). Soon after, an award was made very much in Kemp's favour (*PPC*, V, p. 309).

Scrope vs. Fitzhugh

In 1425, Scrope had regained from the Fitzhughs a large number of the lands forfeited by his elder brother Henry, at the time of the Southampton Plot of 1415 (*CClR, 1422–9*, pp. 224–5). The main reason for Scrope's success was probably less the sponsorship of Gloucester (it was Beaufort, as chancellor, who was empowered to make the decision: *RP*, IV, pp. 287–8) than the fact that Henry Lord Fitzhugh had died in 1424, leaving a minor heir who was unable to defend the family interests (see e.g. *RP*, IV, pp. 288–9). By 1438, the heir, William, had come of age and, increasingly enjoying the lordship of the earl of Salisbury (Ross 1951: pp. 267–9; *CFR, 1437–45*, pp. 185–6), felt strong enough to reopen the matter. Scrope had powerful backers (the earl of Stafford and Bishop Alnwick were his choices as arbitrators, and he seems to have had the support of Cromwell and Northumberland: *CClR, 1435–41*, pp. 316–17, 323–4, 358; *CPR, 1436–41*, pp. 271–2, 292, 446), but Fitzhugh's were stronger (not only Salisbury, but also Bishop Ayscough and Suffolk himself: *CClR, 1435–41*, pp. 358, 373). Suffolk may have become involved because he had a claim to Scrope's manor of Faxflete (*CPR, 1446–52*, pp. 17–18), but, in any event, his intervention surely resolved what could otherwise have been a difficult dispute among members of the Beaufort interest (Cromwell, Stafford, Salisbury and, to a lesser extent, Northumberland). In 1442, in a series of conveyances, Scrope surrendered a number of the disputed lands to Fitzhugh (*CClR, 1441–7*, pp. 74–5).

Senior Nevilles (Westmorland) vs. junior Nevilles (Salisbury)

The junior Nevilles, sons of Joan Beaufort, were consistently successful in this famous dispute: Westmorland was forced to undertake extra-legal activities in his attempt to regain what he regarded as his rightful inheritance (Ross 1951: p. 57); Salisbury was able to insist on securities from his opponent before agreeing to be warden of the West March in 1431 (*ibid.*, p. 52; *CClR, 1429–35*, p. 125) and before consenting to serve in France in 1436 (Leadam and Baldwin (eds.), *Cases before the King's Council*, pp. 101–2: remarkably, these securities were not to be cancelled 'at any tyme with oute the assent' of Salisbury, his mother or their executors!). Salisbury himself seems to have been under no pressure to settle affairs. When he did so, he got very much the best of the bargain: Westmorland succeeded to only a small part of the inheritance, for which he had to pay rents totalling £450 p.a. to Salisbury and his brothers (Ross 1951: p. 58).

Disputes involving 'neutrals' only

Courtenay vs. Bonville

For a published account of the whole dispute, see Cherry 1981a. See below, pp. 239–40, for more details. The crown's response to the dispute was characterised by efforts to indulge the disputants rather than to compel them to behave themselves. Its judicial activity does not seem to have extended much beyond a series of angry letters, summonses and bonds which had little impact on the situation 200 miles away in the West Country (see e.g. E28/64/19 Oct. 1440; E28/65/19; E28/68/22; E28/70/48; *CCIR, 1435–41*, p. 396). The inappropriateness of the 'indulgence' policy is pleasingly demonstrated by the violent consequences of the grant to Devon of the stewardship of the duchy of Cornwall lands: see above, p. 154 n. 115. The only way that the government was able to produce a brief period of peace was by inducing Lord Bonville to go and serve in Aquitaine: an almost parodic example of the supposedly pacifying effects of military service! See Storey 1966: p. 88, for details.

Fanhope vs. Grey

For details, see Maddern 1992: pp. 206–25, and above, pp. 97–100 nn. 93, 101, 103, 105. In 1437, the crown seems to have checked Grey power by issuing an inquiry commission to Fanhope's supporters (*ibid.*, pp. 213–14), before proceeding, after trouble had broken out, to strengthen Grey's hand on the commission of the peace (*CPR, 1436–41*, p. 578). After renewed violence, in 1439, Fanhope received the better treatment, but Grey had not been personally involved and was soon to die (see *CPR, 1436–41*, pp. 246–7, for Fanhope's pardon and E404/55/151 for his release from most of the fine levied for it). Both Fanhope and Edmund Grey, who succeeded Lord Reginald in 1440, were associated with the court (for Fanhope, see above, p. 146; for Grey, see *CPR, 1436–41*, pp. 468–9). There seems to have been a renewal of trouble in 1442 (*PPC*, V, p. 192) and it is significant that Grey was personally involved in deals concerning the Fanhope lands after the baron's death in 1443, finally obtaining them himself in the later 1450s (*CCIR, 1441–7*, pp. 222–3; Payling 1989: p. 903).

6

THE RULE OF THE COURT, 1445–1550

T HE CRISIS OF 1450 entirely changed the nature of Henry VI's polity. So broad and so deep was the failure of the government that the authority of king and lords momentarily, but entirely, collapsed. Into the breach stepped the commons of England, both the people themselves and their *soi-disant* representatives in parliament. For the next year or two, it was they who dictated the political agenda, leaving the nobility little choice but to represent them and to respond to their concerns. This transformed the way in which government was perceived, redefining the arena of political activity and driving the nobility into a partial abandonment of the informal relationships with the crown and each other which had been the hallmark of Suffolk's court. Inevitably, the recent past became a matter of intense public interest, and an authoritative version of events was rapidly established and publicised. By almost all commentators, the period of Henry's personal rule, from the Truce of Tours in 1444 to the attack on Fougères in 1449, was depicted as a series of betrayals and derelictions of duty on the part of the king's household intimates: five years of corruption in government, which led inexorably to the loss of France and the destruction of England.[1]

This familiar critique has had a significant impact on modern accounts of the later 1440s. Most historians write of a narrowing household clique which dominated the government, pursued muddled and defeatist policies in France and sponsored the interests of their lawless clients in the countryside, while the tide of criticism which would eventually engulf them rose all around.[2] The myths of 1450 have hardened into facts, it seems, but everything we have seen so far suggests that the true political situation of the later 1440s was probably rather different. The triumph of Suffolk's

---

[1] In contrast, political and narrative sources discuss most of the events of 1422–45 without much of a gloss (noted by Wolffe 1972: p. 39).

[2] See e.g. Storey 1966: pp. 47–8; Griffiths 1981: pp. 284–8, 362–7, 676–8; Keen 1973: pp. 399–401, 423, 427, 430–1; Tuck 1985: pp. 284, 286.

policy had been the creation of an effective royal court, which was indeed centred in the household, but which was also responsive to the views and interests of a significant majority of noblemen. Whatever their doubts about Henry's personal credibility, the greatest of his subjects were, by the mid-1440s, willing to see the business of government managed through the private and informal mechanisms which normally characterised royal rule. They were confident that this transition, which entailed the final abandonment of the minority council, would enhance, and not curtail, the representative dialogue between authority and community which was the essence of kingship. In the event, their confidence was not misplaced. A detailed study of the government in the later 1440s will reveal there is no evidence to suggest that Suffolk and other leading figures in the household seduced the king away from his natural counsellors among the lords: on the contrary, the magnates were involved in all the major policy initiatives of the period. If the crown had lost touch with the common weal, this was not at all for the reasons identified by its critics at the end of the decade. The task of public representation was, after all, the inalienable duty of the king. If we want to find the reasons for the disasters of 1450, therefore, perhaps we should start with Henry VI himself.

THE WORKINGS OF THE `PERSONAL RULE´

As has been suggested, the 'personal rule' of Henry VI was more a matter of form than content: the royal and curial power managed by Suffolk had no real means of support beyond the counsel and consent of the lords. Even so, the change of form had significant effects. As we shall see, counsel came to be given through a continuous, but informal, dialogue with the king in the court, supplemented by a series of intermittent, but comparatively formal, gatherings of leading men. Inevitably, this pattern introduced a certain distinction between the executive and advisory parts of government, a distinction absolutely characteristic of the rule of a king, but not, of course, of the rule of a council. Normally, this distinction was of negligible importance. It was, after all, in the person of the king that the crucial link between advice and action was made. In a strict sense, indeed, he alone was the government, his agents in the departments of state and household merely the vessels of his will and his counsellors little more than extensions of his senses. Authority was thus absolutely centralised: provided that they did not 'stir and move' the king, his advisers and executives were free of responsibility for what was done in his name.

Under Henry VI, the situation was rather different. Throughout the period of his personal rule, it was – and is – possible to distinguish the existence of a sort of government; a group of men 'dayly and nyghtely abowte his hyghnesse' as Cade's rebels were to put it.[3] This body was regarded as separate from both the king himself and from the 'lordes of his counseil'. It was seen to be made up principally of household men and headed by Suffolk, though it also contained the great officers and other bureaucrats. It was thought to have manipulated the king and, as a result, it was held responsible for the fiscal, judicial, diplomatic and military failures which were exposed in 1449–50.[4] We have seen that such a government did indeed exist: it had been composed by Suffolk and others in order to manage a royal authority which did not seem to be able to look after itself. Try as they might, of course, these men could not rule in the king's name: they could not make fully authoritative decisions without his active and emphatic support. But the important thing to note is that they really did try, that within the normal mechanisms of royal power, Suffolk and his associates did what they could to channel the royal authority in their hands along representative lines. For a few years, they actually succeeded, though in the wake of their subsequent failure, it was in the interests of no one but themselves to advertise the fact.

Predictably, this version of events is difficult to demonstrate from the evidence. As we have seen, the public and internal records of the administration were made with the express purpose of showing that, one way or another, Henry VI was the author of every act of government. While these records cannot be used to prove that policy was (either always or sometimes) essentially the king's, nor can they be used to prove that it was not. Even so, there are good grounds for suspecting that Henry's 'personal rule' was really nothing of the kind. On the one hand, as will appear, there is plenty of evidence to show that not everyone found expressions of the royal will convincing. On the other, we have already seen how both the fundamental structures of royal authority and the specific arrangements made by Suffolk encouraged Henry's leading subjects to behave as if nothing was amiss. Once it is accepted that what was in many ways a conciliar regime could masquerade as a royal one, it becomes legitimate to doubt the power of Henry's will. In the following pages, we shall be taking a closer look at the artful mechanisms of the 'personal rule' and discussing why it was the king, and not his ministers, who must bear responsibility for its failure.

. . .

The arrangements made for counsel in the later 1440s are neatly captured in a letter written by the chancellor, Archbishop Stafford, around the middle of the decade:[5]

---

[3] Harvey 1991: p. 189.   [4] Below, pp. 240ff.

[5] *PPC*, VI, pp. 337–9. The letter cannot be firmly dated (cf. Watts 1991: pp. 293–4,

Also yif it lyke unto the kynges hieghnesse it semeth unto my said lord
chainceller that there as every reame and lordship wel ruled is goeverned by
grete forsight and good and sad policye and advisinesse of Counsail, and
that, as him semeth, such thinges as that oughte to be doon now in haste
and also wer necessari and behoveful to be doon in the begynnyng of the
next somer seson, oughten now in haste to be wel and advisely beten and
laboured by his consail, that therfor it wolde lyke unto the K' hieghnesse to
do calle his counsail, such as that him shal lyke, to assemble at such tyme
[and] place as also him shal lyke, whenne and wher shal be shewed unto
hem by my said Lord Chaunceller, in alle that he can remembr him, such
thinges as that the K hath to do, the which as him semeth beth many and of
grete weight.

Stafford's words reveal how the pattern of government had changed: no
longer was there a continual council in charge of affairs; instead, Henry
and those about him directed policy on the normal model. From time to
time, as on this particular occasion, matters of 'grete weight' or difficulty
would arise and the king would supplement the conventional dialogue
with his subjects by summoning his counsellors to debate them and help
him to reach a representative judgement.[6] It seems clear that what
Stafford meant by 'counsail' was not a consistent body of fixed appointment, like the old minority council, but a group of men to be assembled at
the king's wish: these men might be described as 'his counsail' because
they were typically his advisers, not because they were the members of a
defined group. Significantly, this 'counsail' was to be chosen by Henry
himself, rather as Gloucester had proposed in 1440: in theory, at least, the
representativeness of the king's person exceeded that of any artificial
body of his subjects.[7]

It seems to have been about the time of the royal wedding that the formal
and continual council of the period 1420s, 1430s and 1440s finally
subsided.[8] The 'personal rule' had begun in earnest, and, from 1446, a
new and more appropriate pattern of government becomes visible in the
records. In mid-July of that year, a temporary council met for several days

where the autumn of 1446 is declared to be its date. There are insufficient grounds for
this conclusion. The letter was written in the autumn, but any year from 1443 to 1446
would fit with the content. In some ways, indeed, the autumn of 1443 fits better: see
Ferguson 1972: p. 212).

[6] Griffiths 1981: pp. 284–5 interprets this letter differently.

[7] Above, p. 144.

[8] Although see above, pp. 149, 151 nn. 108, 109, and note that on 27 April 1445, a week
after Henry's wedding, Thomas Kent, clerk of the council, was paid for riding between it
and the king since November 1444 (E28/75/55): I have found no evidence of similar
payments thereafter. Because there is much less evidence for the working of the
administration in the later 1440s, the conclusions reached in this chapter are rather
provisional. On the other hand, the relative dearth of such material seems to bear out the
suggestion that formal counsel, well-documented before this date, had been abandoned:
see above, p. 151 and below, at n. 15.

to discuss a limited number of matters: the raising of loans for the king's proposed expedition to France; arrangements for the embassy of Moleyns and Dudley; the punishment of the earl of Ormond; and some other bits of business.[9] It seems to have set the pattern for the succeeding years, with short-term councils apparently meeting in December 1446,[10] January, April/May, July and November 1447,[11] and January and May 1448,[12] though, in the absence of more explicit record material, it is difficult to be certain.[13] Sometimes, these councils were specially summoned.[14] On other occasions, perhaps, they were simply composed from those present at court. They have left few records and this, in itself, is likely to be a reflection of their subordinate position in the hierarchy of government.[15] The names of those who attended were often left unrecorded, because now that the king's adult authority was uncontested, it was technically unnecessary to know who had given counsel and to what effect.[16] On similar grounds, the distinction between conciliar and non-conciliar modes of authentication weakened: the issues of these councils are generally endorsed with the 'Rex, apud ... concessit ..., praesentibus' formula;[17] and until the

[9] *PPC*, VI, pp. 51–4.

[10] This was mostly held at Sheen: see Harriss 1986: pp. 151–2; C81/1546/18; E28/77/13–15; *PPC*, VI, pp. 57–8.

[11] The January 1447 council was summoned in December 1446 (see below, n. 104, for its summons; E404/63/28 for evidence that it met; and E28/77/19 for a record of its activities). It was described as a great council, but this is more likely to mean that it had been specially summoned than that all the lords were present: Baldwin 1913: pp. 106–10. In March 1447, it was decided to summon a number of counsellors to assemble at the start of the next term (about the end of April): *PPC*, VI, pp. 60–1. These may have been the men who publicly exonerated Suffolk on 25 May: *CPR, 1446–52*, p. 78. A council seems to have met in late July to discuss compensation for Maine: although this could simply have been a gathering of lords already at court (C81/1546/20 and see below, p. 232). Various council meetings took place in November and December 1447, including one at which the compensation for Maine was finally fixed: below, p. 234; C81/1546/22–5.

[12] See C81/1546/26–7 for council meetings in January 1448. For May 1448, see E28/77/45–51.

[13] These are occasions on which councils are known to have been held and/or periods in which documents attested by fair numbers of noblemen are bunched together, but there are stray issues either endorsed 'de avisamento consilii' or witnessed by significant numbers of lords dotted throughout the period 1446–8 (e.g. on 17 June 1447 a group advising the king at Westminster included York, Buckingham and Dorset, among others – C81/1546/19). This may simply reflect the frequent appearance of a proportion of the nobility at Westminster and the court in these years.

[14] Two notes of summons survive: E28/77/3 (25 September 1446) and E28/77/15 (17 December 1446).

[15] Reasonably formal minutes survive only for the meetings of July 1446, for example: *PPC*, VI, pp. 46–54.

[16] The practice did not altogether die out, however: e.g. 16 November 1446 (*PPC*, VI, p. 56), 14 and 21 December 1446 (*ibid.*, p. 57, E28/77/16), 26 February 1447 (E28/77/20), at least nine occasions in 1448 and eight in 1449. A possible reason for this is discussed below, p. 213.

[17] For the normal meaning of this formula, see above, p. 138. For examples of its use in connection with the councils of the later 1440s, see e.g. C81/1546/18, E28/77/14

'personal rule' began to subside in the autumn of 1448, reference to 'avisamentum consilii' was only made when the king was absent from the scene of deliberations – this may even have been the main reason for the use of the phrase at this time.[18]

In keeping with the new dispensation, it is doubtful that the term 'councillor' had much institutional significance in this period: certainly, the old distinction between those who counselled the king as members of a formal body and those who must also have counselled him, but who were not members of this body (and whose counsel therefore went unacknowledged), was ceasing to exist.[19] The 'consilium' in the now rather misleading phrase 'de avisamento consilii' was a widening group, including Bishops Lumley, Lyhert and Boulers from 1446[20] and Bishop Waynflete and the duke of York from 1447.[21] Even so, it appears that not everyone in the royal presence was considered to have given counsel, and this may explain the addition of 'et aliis' or 'et multis aliis' to attendance lists, which became common in these years.[22] Who these 'aliis' were is, of course, a mystery, but it is likely that they were minor figures, such as pages, clerks and grooms, who were present in a solely domestic or secretarial capacity.[23]

(December 1446); *Foedera*, V, i, p. 177 (May 1447); *Letters and Papers*, II, ii, pp. 643, 685 (July 1447).

[18] E.g. C81/1546/15–16 (23–4 November 1446: council at Westminster; king in Kent, though arriving at Westminster some time on the 24th), E28/77/19 (20 January 1447: council at Westminster; king at Southampton), E28/77/25 (29 April 1447: council at Westminster; king at Windsor); C81/1546/26–7 (27 and 30 January 1448: council at Westminster; king at Windsor). By the autumn of 1448, when a council seems to have been in fairly continuous existence once again, the term was probably in more straightforward use.

[19] There is no evidence of the formal appointment of councillors in this period, appropriately enough. The king, being advised on 8 February 1446 by the earls of Shrewsbury and Arundel and Bishop Bourgchier, none of whom had been councillors before 1444, was said to be in the presence of lords of the council: C81/1546/10. Bourgchier was, in fact, present at what appears to have been a meeting of the council in May 1445 (*PPC*, VI, p. 39), but had never attended before, and was not formally appointed. On the other hand, there is a proposal in a document of 19 March 1447 to summon 'the lordes of his [the king's] consail and such other as shall be thought gode to my Lorde Chancellor' (*PPC*, VI, pp. 60–1). Whilst this may at first seem to imply the existence of a defined body of councillors, it could be that the 'other' refers to men of lesser status, or perhaps to men who did not immediately spring to mind as the usual counsellors of the king, or to men who had not been appointed to the council of 1437 or that of the early 1440s.

[20] Boulers was first present at what appears to be a council meeting on 2 December 1445, but was then absent until 10 November 1446: E28/76/5, C81/1546/13. Lyhert had been summoned to the special council of autumn 1446, but the other two, both of whom attended on 10 November, had not.

[21] E.g. 25 November 1447, 27 and 30 January 1448 (Waynflete: C81/1546/24, 26–7); 17 June, 10, 12 and 18 October 1448 (York: C81/1546/19; E28/78/7, 9, 11).

[22] E.g. E28/75/34 (March 1445); C81/1546/5, 19, 26 (February 1446, June 1447 and January 1448).

[23] Virgoe 1970: p. 136 (and see *Foedera*, V, i, p. 177, for an instance which supports this suggestion).

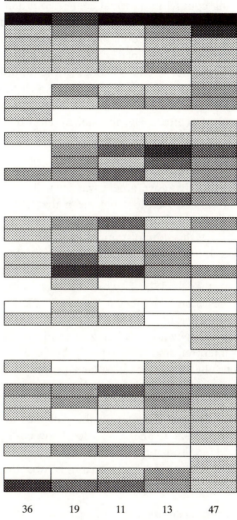

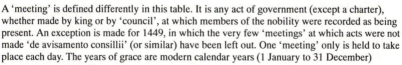

A 'meeting' is defined differently in this table. It is any act of government (except a charter), whether made by king or by 'council', at which members of the nobility were recorded as being present. An exception is made for 1449, in which the very few 'meetings' at which acts were not made 'de avisamento consilii' (or similar) have been left out. One 'meeting' only is held to take place each day. The years of grace are modern calendar years (1 January to 31 December)

Key: percentage of meetings attended
Not part of the government (blank space)

☐ None   ▨ 1-20%   ▨ 21-40%   ▨ 41-60%   ▨ 61-80%   ■ 81-100%

[a] Died February 1447.   [b] Died December 1445.   [c] Died August 1447.   [d] Of Powick.

Figure 3   Participation in the government, 1445–9

What these developments reveal is a blurring of the distinction between giving counsel in a formal context and doing so in the course of general participation in central government. This was the inevitable corollary of a single royal jurisdiction, and it is full of significance for the evaluation of Henry VI's kingship that this comparatively normal pattern of government did not obtain for long. In the autumn of 1448, recorded council meetings, dominated by bishops, began to increase in frequency as the regime's problems multiplied.[24] The structures of 'personal rule' were tacitly, but effectively, abandoned. How this came about we shall consider later in the chapter.

. . .

The fact that government was formally royal and not conciliar for a few years after 1445 does not mean that concern about the king's capacity to administer his powers had evaporated or, in fact, that measures to improve this administration could not be attempted. Indeed, it is likely that, by this time, leading figures in the government were a lot less optimistic about the chances of the king becoming a more effective ruler than they had been when he was younger.[25] There is evidence to suggest that a number of figures in the government were unsure about the independence of the king's will and about the extent to which he really knew what was being done in his name. This evidence is difficult to interpret, and that is partly because the sense that King Henry was not fully in control of affairs produced two apparently contradictory responses. On the one hand, the king's administrative officers seem to have sought assurances that Henry had truly willed what was put before them. This is reflected in the fact that, for example, a number of the signet letters to the chancellor between 1444 and 1448 are signed by the king, sometimes with the adjunct that by the sign manual, the chancellor would know that this was the king's 'ful wille' or 'hertly desire' and not, we may infer, the products of stirring.[26] In a like way,

---

[24] Attendance remained very wide and variable, however. In all, upwards of thirty different people attended council meetings between the autumn of 1448 and the end of 1449.

[25] This may be a factor in the regime's tendency to over-react to seditious speech in this period (notably, of course, to slurs that the king, now in his mid-twenties, was like a child): Wolffe 1981: pp. 128–9.

[26] For example, C81/1373/31; C81/1370/35, 52 and 68 ('to thentent that ye shal wele understande and knowe that this oure writing procedeth of our hertly desire'). A particularly interesting example is a letter dated 18 December, the year of which is unknown (1443–9). In it, the king refers to signet letters lately sent to the chancellor signifying the king's grant of the office of 'peyser' of the wools at Hull to John Penycook. The chancellor has refused to make letters for Penycook, so 'we write unto you yet eftsones inasmoch as our sayd graunt passed us by our mere deliberacion'. Henry adds his sign manual so that Stafford 'the more clerely mow understande that this is our ful wyl and entent': C81/1374/7. Note that there was not necessarily anything wrong with

two endorsements of September 1449 record royal orders as being given 'vive vocis': there was to be no question that the king had licensed these instructions.[27] At other times, however, Henry's officers were apparently anxious to know that the king had been guided by the right people. So it is that we encounter, in 1448 and 1449, a number of cases in which those present with the king when he made grants signed their names as an endorsement: one bill is signed by Suffolk and no one else; the others are also signed by Henry himself.[28] The practice of lords signing issues of government, abandoned at the end of the minority, unequivocally indicated the responsibility of the signatories for what was done.[29] It is therefore very strange to find it on what are ostensibly royal warrants.

If these measures seem rather at odds with the acceptance of free royal power which was implicit in the abandonment of conciliar government, much the same could be said of the interesting series of restraining ordinances which were devised in the mid- and later 1440s, as the consequences of Henry's largesse became apparent. The best known of these are probably the instructions concerning the making of royal grants which are usually dated to 1444.[30] These were an attempt to limit the uncounselled exercise of royal grace, principally by introducing a greater degree of bureaucratic (and, in a sense, conciliar) surveillance into the process. They were accompanied by other schemes of a similar kind. In 1445, for example, new ordinances for the household were drawn up which effectively prevented the king from adding to its personnel without the approval of the counting house: royal warrants which contravened the new rules were to be ignored.[31] Similarly, in the wake of the fiscal crisis of 1446, attempts were made to stop the king and his suitors from using special licences to disrupt either the payment of revenues into the exchequer or the associated embargo on assignments.[32] In November 1447, the chancellor and privy seal were empowered to defer, until the treasurer could advise, all grants which seemed to be made as a result of

---

signet warrants to the chancellor: Henry V used them indiscriminately (Otway-Ruthven 1939: p. 40; Brown 1954: pp. 139–41).

[27] E28/79/6, 12.

[28] 8 September 1448 (Wentworth, Ayscough and the king: E28/78/2); 13 December 1448 (Sir William Beauchamp and the king, twice: E28/78/38–9); 15 September 1449 (John Penycook and the king: E28/79/7); 26 October 1449 (a petition signed by Suffolk alone, without any clear indication that this is related to his office of chamberlain of England or other endorsement: E28/79/35).

[29] See above, p. 126.

[30] *PPC*, VI, pp. 316–20. See Watts 1991: pp. 295–8 for a lengthy, if rather inconclusive, discussion of the dating of this document, and below, Appendix A, for certain revisions.

[31] Myers 1959: pp. 65, 66–7.

[32] See below, p. 215, and Harriss 1986: pp. 150–6.

'importune labour and pursute' to the king and which infringed the preferment of the wardrobe.[33]

Part of the problem in interpreting these measures has been the assumption that they were imposed from outside the court regime.[34] But once it is accepted that the court had become, as was usual, the key institution of government, and that it was very much in the interests of Suffolk and his more substantial associates to preserve the stability on which its capacity rested, it becomes plausible to suggest that the marquis took these steps for himself. One possible indication that such measures did indeed come from the inner reaches of the court is the fact that similar restrictions are to be found in the royal 'will' of 1448. These prevented Henry from changing the provisions for the funding of the foundations at Eton and Cambridge, a project which, as we have seen, was dear to the hearts of the regime's leaders.[35] Even if the court was not the inspiration for these moves, it must have supported them. Restraints on the activity of the king in the household could only have been imposed with the agreement of Suffolk and others who could otherwise frustrate them. Whether or not it was, as Gerald Harriss suggests, Lord Cromwell and other sometime members of the minority council who arranged the appointment of the reforming Bishop Lumley as treasurer in 1446, there is little doubt that Suffolk endorsed his policies and gave him all possible backing in executing them.[36] Ensuring stable funding for the household was, indeed, among the new treasurer's chief priorities: fiscal order served the interests of everyone in government.[37]

The flaw in the policy of restraint, naturally enough, lay in its dependence on royal will, the sole source of authority in the land. In practice, of course, Henry was easily persuaded to depart from what he had formally ordained. Petitioners responded to general restrictions imposed at the king's will by demonstrating that the same will was now being shown on their behalf, sometimes by inducing Henry to sign the instruments they had composed, sometimes by including in them forceful *non obstante* clauses, and sometimes, as above, by obtaining signet letters

---

[33] C49/26/18 (dated by Harriss 1986: pp. 158–9).

[34] E.g. Otway-Ruthven 1939: pp. 36–7; Wolffe 1981: pp. 113–15. Note that Griffiths 1981: pp. 283–4 takes a different line.

[35] 'Alway foreseen that it be lawfull for me, dureing my life onely, by writing, to change this my will ... except such ordinances and appointments as belong and concerne unto my said colleges, which be above rehearsed': Nichols, *Wills of the Kings and Queens*, p. 310.

[36] Harriss 1986: pp. 152–3. Note that Suffolk attempted to obtain the see of London for Lumley in 1448 (Williams (ed.), *Correspondence of Bekynton*, I, p. 155). One chronicler thought that Suffolk was responsible for Lumley's promotion to Lincoln in early 1450: although this seems less likely, it may at least indicate that a close relationship between the two men was perceived to exist (*Letters and Papers*, II, ii, p. 766).

[37] Harriss 1986: *passim*.

ordering the chancellor to proceed. As a rule, the state of confusion which resulted tended to be resolved in favour of the individual suitor. It was always difficult, and often impossible, for the bureaucrats charged with executing royal instructions to resist this sort of pressure. Whatever doubts they may have harboured, they could scarcely disobey an order to ignore any restraint 'howe speciall ever it be', particularly when told 'that in noowise ye leve this'. Quite apart from the offence to royal majesty, there was the response of those for whom the king was acting to be considered.[38] For a short period of time, in fact, Lumley was able successfully to resist, or at least delay, a fair number of orders which had resulted from application to the king alone.[39] Similarly, to judge by the protests included in signet letters, Stafford seems on occasion to have exercised a restraining influence in the chancery.[40] This does suggest that royal officers enjoying the confidence of the community of lords had, as before, some latitude in their handling of the royal will.[41] Even so, resistance to the king's orders required the painstaking acquisition of corporate authorisation as well as a certain amount of courage or calculation in each individual case. The advantage definitely lay with the royal grace and its users, hence the reams of straightforward signet warrants and other conventional endorsements to be found alongside these curiosities.[42]

Henry's advisers and ministers were thus in an anomalous position. There was little choice about the acceptance of royal power. Conciliar government, an unattractive option at the best of times, was out of the question now that the king was a grown man and, in any case, it offered no more to the nobility, at least, than Suffolk's more informal and court-centred regime. Royal government, however, meant royal liberty and this, in practice, was easily exploited. With their eyes on the common interest, the lords could and did devise restraints and enforce them by political means, but they had no independent authority at their disposal. They could not contradict the royal will, yet this will was constantly being invoked against the restrictions they imposed. They themselves, indeed, used royal grace as a means of evading 'political' restraints, but before we condemn them for hypocrisy, or selfishness, or cynicism, we should remember that these evasions were quite legitimate in their way. The common interest was supposed to be an amalgam of particular interests: their own as much as (if not more than) those of others. It was up to the

---

[38] *Ibid.*, p. 155 (the creditor in this case was Moleyns and he prevailed).
[39] *Ibid.*, pp. 155–6.
[40] Though note that he caved in to repeated instructions, however these were issued: see Maxwell-Lyte 1926: p. 122.
[41] See above, pp. 147–8.   [42] See above, p. 126.

king to reconcile the claims of each and all. The lordship of Suffolk had seemed to offer a means for the prudent management of royal will in both common and individual interests. The creation of more formal devices to control this management suggests that the marquis was failing in his crucial task.

SUFFOLK AND THE HOUSEHOLD

In the previous chapter, it was shown how proximity to the king, combined with a pre-eminence conferred by his status and connections both inside and outside the household, enabled William de la Pole to establish his own single lordship in a court which came to include most of the nobility and thus became the natural centre of government. By building an artificial power structure so intimately connected to the royal person as to be virtually indistinguishable from it, Suffolk had, on the face of it, conquered the problem of an undirected royal authority. In fact, however, his achievement was both superficial and short-lived. No sooner was the court regime in operation than it began to run into trouble. The source of this trouble was not, as is usually suggested, among the lords, or even, at this stage, among the people: rather, it lay in the household, on the face of it the heartland of Suffolk's power.

While it is clear that the personal authority of Henry VI could only be made effective in the realm because of noble confidence in, and accep- tance of, Suffolk's lordship, this authority was the king's inalienable possession and, as such, was open to the use of any who could gain access to him. If noblemen and other members of the regime mostly saw the wisdom of approaching Henry through Suffolk's mediation, it is possible that the staff of the household did not. Unlike the nobility, these men had a simple means of getting at the king and less of a stake in the preservation of an effective governing consensus. While the growing recognition of personal royal authority placed greater responsibilities upon Suffolk, it actually freed his inferiors. The more fully this authority was established, the less such men had to fear immediate oversight by jurisdictions other than the one of which they formed a part. Suffolk's lordship of the household had partly rested on his ability to protect the interests of its complement in the long period when personal royal authority was controversial.[43] The need for such protection was now less obvious.

This situation had two results: one was that household men made less

---

[43] See above, pp. 162–6. Personal and territorial connections had also played a part, of course, but these only worked in Suffolk's favour when he had the upper hand at the centre (see above, pp. 159–60, for the case of Sir William Philip and the stewardship of Wallingford and below, p. 219, for Suffolk's later difficuties in East Anglia).

cautious use of their proximity to the king, helping themselves to unheard of honours with gay abandon; the other is that Suffolk's lordship of the household became less secure, as episodes such as the rise of Henry Beauchamp demonstrate.[44] Examples of the unedifying way in which some of the minor men about the king learnt to exploit his grace are not hard to find. It was probably about this time that Thomas Kent, clerk of the council, petitioned for, and got, a 50 per cent increase in his salary, partly on the rather insulting grounds that 'he hath left all services of other men to be occupied in [the king's] service'.[45] In 1447, Gilbert Parr and Sir Edmund Hungerford, seeing that the duke of Exeter was 'eithre dede or in point to dye' hastily petitioned Henry for his farm of the castle and lordship of Berkhamsted.[46] Meanwhile, in 1445, John Trevilian took advantage of the fact that the king was in his barge (and thus free, perhaps, from the usual extended coterie), to obtain his assent to a bill of John Say.[47] These instances were far from unusual: as the ordinances on grants declared, the king was overcome by huge numbers of importunate suits and apparently exercised no discretion in granting them.[48]

Paradoxically, the very fact that petitioners increasingly dictated the agenda of royal patronage undermined their long-term chances of satisfaction. For one thing, the activities of busy suitors about the king had severely depleted the stocks of what was available. This was the solemn reality which underlay the familiar hallmarks of Henry VI's 'foole largesse': the busy and growing trade in reversions; the accidental duplications of grants; the fierce competition for what was available.[49] Because the pressure on resources produced confusion and friction in the court, it did, to some extent, revive the demand for lordship, a demand which Suffolk, together with his colleagues in the administration, Moleyns, the keeper of the privy seal, and Stafford, the chancellor, attempted to exploit.[50] Even so, as we have seen, the licensing power of

---

[44] See above, pp. 196–7.

[45] SC8/248/12384. He also requested, and obtained, a life tenure in the office.

[46] C81/1370/50. The king signed the petition without knowing whether Exeter was dead or not, it appears.

[47] E28/75/14a.

[48] Nicolas has 'importante', but this must be a mistranscription. The routine nature of appeals to the royal grace is illustrated by a remark quoted by Morgan 1987: p. 40: 'thus my lord of Suffolk got the bill signed and so forth the patents ensealed'.

[49] See above, p. 154, and note the immediate and substantial redistribution of grants on the deaths of Warwick (1446) and Gloucester (1447): *CPR, 1441–6*, pp. 432–7; *CPR, 1446–52*, pp. 42–5.

[50] The situation is nicely captured in a letter of May 1445 (E28/75/61), in which John Hampton, one of the esquires of the body, asked Moleyns to prefer over any other a warrant which he had obtained from the king on behalf of his 'right welbeloved Thomas Burghill', because he had heard that 'Maister John Langton, Tresorer of Caleys, hath sewed for a man of his oune to have the same office, notwithstanding that he promised me afore tyme that my seid welbeloved shold have had hit'.

the king far exceeded the restraining influence which more contrived authorities could exert, and it is likely that suitors calculated that, if conflicts over their acquisitions were inevitable, a royal warrant would be a valuable weapon.

It is important to remember that it was the politically constructed nature of Suffolk's authority which was its great weakness. Faced with men who could not, or would not, be restrained, the marquis had no choice but to appease and accommodate them. This had already been the government's policy earlier in the decade, when rising figures of some status – Edmund Hungerford, Thomas Stanley, Thomas Tuddenham, for example – had been successfully incorporated in the duchy of Lancaster establishment.[51] It is likely that something similar was happening when the leading household offices were reshuffled in 1446–7, and room was found for Tuddenham, Stourton and James Fiennes alongside more established figures such as Sudeley and Suffolk himself.[52] There were, however, obvious limits to a policy of this kind. By the last years of the decade, it was becoming increasingly difficult to find ways of accommodating new men in the existing power structure. This meant disruption, as some earlier supporters lost their footing,[53] and a series of *parvenus* used their access to the king and their leverage over Suffolk to obtain prominence at the centre or opportunities in the localities.

There were quite a number of such men, but among the most notorious

[51] Edmund Hungerford became chamberlain of the duchy in succession to his father in 1441 (Somerville 1953: p. 417). Stanley became chief steward of the enfeoffed lands with Suffolk (*CPR, 1446–52*, p. 123) and joined him as chief steward of the south parts in 1450. He also became receiver-general of Lancashire in 1443. Tuddenham joined Suffolk as chief steward of the north parts in 1443: Somerville 1953: pp. 420–1, 428–9, 492, 494. More minor men were found placings in the duchy later in the 1440s, including Thomas Daniel (p. 504) and Philip Wentworth (p. 499): see below, for more on these two.

[52] Tuddenham became keeper of the great wardrobe on 26 October 1446: *CPR, 1446–52*, p. 4. Stourton became treasurer of the household on 15 November 1446: Harriss 1953: p. 397. James Fiennes, newly created Lord Saye and Sele, replaced Lord Sudeley as chamberlain some time before 9 March 1447: C53/189, no. 36. There is not much to suggest that these men were any more favoured, or more closely associated with the court than those they replaced (cf. Griffiths 1981: pp. 284–5): the ejected chamberlain, Sudeley, replaced Suffolk as steward of the household when the marquis took up Gloucester's place as chamberlain of England (*CPR, 1446–52*, p. 45; *HBC*, p. 77); Sir Roger Fiennes, who had been treasurer of the household, remained chief steward of the south parts of the duchy, though a lot of these lands were in the enfeoffed portion under Suffolk's and Stanley's control from 1447 (Somerville 1953: p. 428) and was still able to obtain a pardon of account from the king in March 1448 (C81/1370/68). John Noreys, who had been keeper of the great wardrobe, enjoyed several positions in Queen Margaret's service, including treasurer of her household: Myers, 'Household of Queen Margaret', p. 427; Harriss 1953: p. 399.

[53] For the exemplary case of John Somerset, the king's doctor and sometime almoner, who lost his reversion of the chancellorship of the exchequer to one John Lemanton, see Morgan 1987: pp. 39–40.

were Thomas Daniel, John Trevilian and William Tailboys. The first two had drawn enormous benefits from their place in the household during the 1440s: a string of fees, offices and other interests, both at the centre and in the royal domains of Cheshire and Cornwall, respectively.[54] By the end of the decade, they had turned to piracy on the high seas, apparently profiting from the confusion in government to capture the Bay Fleet of the Hansard merchants in 1449.[55] Just as damaging, and more important for our purposes, was their activity in the localities. Trevilian's expansion in Cornwall merely added to existing tensions in the South-West,[56] but Daniel's decision to involve himself in the politics of East Anglia from the later 1440s was a very alarming development for the region's lord, the duke of Suffolk. Daniel rapidly acquired importance in the area, even prompting a local suggestion that the rule of the De La Pole affinity was under threat.[57] This suggestion deserves more attention than it has usually received: what did Suffolk's power amount to, if it could be so easily challenged at a local level by a mere esquire? And is it not remarkable that Suffolk himself should find his local lordship undermined by household power? Perhaps the conventional interpretation of the riotous events in East Anglia in the later 1440s deserves to be revised. Far from being the co-ordinator of an empire of crime, Suffolk may have been the unwilling front-man for ungovernable underlings.[58]

It is possible that something similar was taking place in the other areas where the court was dominant; notably, of course, in Kent, where Lord Saye and Sele, demonised by Cade's rebels, may actually have been

---

[54] Daniel, a henchman by 1440 and king's esquire by 1444 (E101/409/6, fol. 16v) acquired a string of offices and fees mostly in Cheshire and the west Midlands in the mid-1440s (*CPR, 1441-6*, pp. 256, 328, 333, 399, 433, 440-1, 453). Trevilian was a serjeant by March 1441 and proceeded, in the following years, to obtain a similar array of grants, concentrated in Cornwall, but including offices at the exchequer and the royal palace of Eltham (*CPR, 1436-41*, p. 508; *CPR, 1441-6*, pp. 21, 95, 126, 134, 238, 322; *CPR, 1446-52*, pp. 60, 79, 80).

[55] Postan 1933: pp. 127-8; Harvey 1991: pp. 57-8; *PL*, II, pp. 103-5.

[56] See Cherry 1981a: p. 128.

[57] *PL*, II, nos. 69 and 75: it is quite clear from these that Daniel was not on Suffolk's side (see also *ibid.*, p. 150). In September 1448, Daniel petitioned for, and got, the reversion of Lord Cromwell's constableship of Castle Rising (Norf.): C81/1371/1-3; *CPR, 1446-52*, p. 203.

[58] See e.g. Smith 1984, Griffiths 1981: pp. 584-8, for accounts which give Suffolk absolute and malign power over the region in the later 1440s. It may be that the duke's maintenance of Wingfield against Norfolk (see above, p. 202), of Moleyns against the Pastons (Richmond 1990: pp. 47ff), of Hull and Wentworth against Fastolf (Lewis 1985b and Smith 1984) and, for that matter, of Harcourt against Stafford (Storey 1966: pp. 57-8) were forced upon him by the exigencies of his lordship in East Anglia and Oxfordshire, respectively. These, of course, are mere suggestions: the full-scale study of East Anglian politics undertaken by Helen Castor for her PhD thesis – and partly abstracted in a paper given at Manchester College in September 1992 – is certain to tell us a great deal more.

struggling to preserve control.[59] But this was not the limit of the problem. Just as damaging was the threat posed by the more irresponsible courtiers to the independent networks of noble lordship which Suffolk had so carefully nurtured. This is exemplified by the most famous instance of the subversion of local rule by the household: the case of William Tailboys, king's esquire, which bulked so large in the debates of the 1449–50 parliament.[60] The commons' view that this was an example of outrageous maintenance on the part of Suffolk has not been significantly challenged by historians.[61] In actual fact, Tailboys enjoyed the local protection of Viscount Beaumont,[62] a factor which Suffolk could scarcely afford to ignore, even though Tailboys' antics had offended others – Lords Welles and Cromwell – who were also important members of the court.[63] The government's response to this unappealing division among its constituents was not the unambiguous support of a household rogue, but a more characteristic hedging of bets: if Cromwell was not fully satisfied, at least Tailboys was brought to London to answer charges in the autumn of 1449.[64] Suffolk's proven involvement in the matter was minimal, and surely related to his pre-eminence in the government, not to any particular interest in the politics of Lincolnshire.[65]

What seems to have been happening in the later 1440s, therefore, was less a household tyranny than a household anarchy, with Suffolk, and perhaps other figures among its *senior et sanior pars*, struggling to retain, or regain, control of social inferiors who enjoyed an improper and

---

[59] This is sheer speculation, but note the appearance of John Trevilian and another household squire in Kent in 1447, for example (Harvey 1991: p. 36, where the 'rich pickings for such opportunists' are noted, but the possible consequences for Saye's lordship not explored).

[60] See Virgoe 1972–3 for the fullest account and e.g. E101/409/16, m. 35r, for Tailboys' connection with the household.

[61] E.g. Virgoe 1972–3; Griffiths 1981: p. 580.

[62] Noted in *ibid.* See *PL*, II, pp. 118–20, and *CPR, 1446–52*, pp. 201–2, for Beaumont's involvement. Note that his liberty of return of writs in his lands was granted the same day as Tailboys' pardon (8 November 1448: *ibid.*, and *CChR, 1427–1516*, pp. 102–4).

[63] For Cromwell's links with the court, see below, p. 257; for Welles', see Storey 1970: p. 68 and note that Welles was one of those named as potential feoffees for the colleges in the will of 1448: Nichols, *Wills of the Kings and Queens*, p. 311. Willoughby, the third member of the group opposing Tailboys, was linked by marriage to Welles (Storey 1970: p. 69) and his nephew was feed by Cromwell (Virgoe 1972–3: p. 464).

[64] See Virgoe 1972–3: pp. 465–6. It is worth remembering that Cromwell was able to obtain a commission made out to himself to investigate the matter in May 1448, even if this *was* soon superseded (*ibid.*, p. 464). A second commission against Tailboys was issued in July 1448, despite the fact that he was already bound over: *CPR, 1446–52*, pp. 189, 201–2. It was apparently weighted in Cromwell's favour, inasmuch as it was headed by Sir John Talbot and included John Portington, both leading allies of his (Pollard 1968: pp. 58, 71–2; Payling 1989: p. 890). It is plain that Cromwell and his supporters wielded almost as much influence as Beaumont and his.

[65] Suffolk, together with Beaumont, witnessed – and no doubt ordered – Dymoke's release of securities to Tailboys in September 1448 (*CPR, 1446–52*, pp. 201–2).

unusual access to power.[66] To some extent, then, the charges of the government's critics were correct: the king *was* surrounded by a group of self-interested courtiers blind to the interests of the community at large. It was in their assumption that this group was actively directed by Suffolk and other leading members of the court and household that these critics were mistaken. The duke, and those few others – Ayscough, Moleyns, Saye and Sele – who were so closely bound up with the management of curial power that they could not avoid association with its abuses, may have paid the price for an experiment in lordship which had failed. The mixture of indulgence and restraint with which they attempted to rein in their subordinates was quite inadequate. In the end, the disintegration of Suffolk's lordship is one more illustration of the fundamental truths of monarchy: no one but the king could maintain and exercise authority effectively. Henry VI's inadequacy doomed to failure all those public enterprises which in any way incorporated him (and, as we shall see in the next chapter, those which did not incorporate him were scarcely more successful). But this, perhaps, is to anticipate too much. In 1445, Suffolk had enjoyed the backing not only of the household, but also of the nobility: the next step must be to explore how that crucial relationship developed in the years that followed.

SUFFOLK'S POLICY AND THE NOBILITY, 1445–1448

Among the most important tasks facing the government in the later 1440s was, of course, the defence of the English holdings in France. As we have seen, under Henry VI, the management of policy in this area frequently involved problems of authority alongside the more typical considerations of diplomacy, finance and military strategy. In 1450, one of the major charges against Suffolk, Moleyns, Dudley and other men prominent in the administration of Anglo-French affairs was that they had used their undue influence about the king to effect secret and nationally disastrous policies in their own interests.[67] The 'lordes of the counseill', it was alleged, had not known what was afoot and would not have approved if they had. The line taken by modern accounts is not dissimilar: the major

---

[66] Anarchy in the ruling elite could, of course, appear tyrannous to subjects: see Lewis 1968: pp. 100–1, for parallels in France. It is possible that it was against men of the Daniel and Trevilian mould that the restraints described in the preceding section were particularly aimed. Note this interesting case in which a signet grant to Thomas Daniel was stalled by someone in the king's entourage (C81/1373/14: the letter was written between 1444 and 1449): referring to a grant of a tax on wine shipments from parts of Guyenne which were in rebellion, the king's letter ordered the chancellor to 'souffre not oure lettres patentes to passe you therupon withouten that ye shal have the contrary [i.e. further] commaundement of us hereafter'.

[67] See below, pp. 248ff.

difference is that the 'circle' discreetly pursuing unpopular policies is generally considered to have acted, at least in part, at Henry's inspiration or command.[68] In the light of what we have seen so far, we may doubt that the king's professed devotion to peace was ever a significant engine of policy: indeed, if it had been, Suffolk's position – both in 1450 and earlier – would have been a great deal stronger. Instead, as De La Pole was apparently aware, it was only the support of the nobility which made royal authorisation credible. This means that the policy pursued in the royal name is likely to have rested on a much broader base of support than the claims made in 1450 implied. Was this the case? Another look at the formation of policy and the activities of the lords in the mid-1440s may provide us with an answer.

The bitter recriminations which attended the failure of the policy begun at Tours in May 1444 make it easy to overlook the enthusiasm which it had excited at the outset. Suffolk was the undoubted hero of the 1445 parliament, receiving handsome thanks from the commons and a commendation from Gloucester and the rest of the lords.[69] The Anjou marriage, which he had negotiated at Tours, promised great benefits. The new queen's family were, at the time, the most influential princes at Charles VII's court, and it must have seemed likely that, through their intercession with a king notorious for his vulnerability to factional pressure, the deadlock of 1439 could be broken and more favourable peace terms extracted.[70] Even if peace proved elusive, an alliance with the Angevins would provide the English with welcome assistance along the vulnerable southern border of Normandy where the family's lands lay.[71]

---

[68]   See e.g. Griffiths 1981: chs. 12, 13 and 18; Wolffe 1981: chs. 7 and 11.

[69]   *RP*, V, p. 73. A London chronicler comments that the queen was received honourably by the lords 'and in especiall' by the duke of Gloucester: *Chrons. of London*, p. 156 (also *Brut*, p. 510).

[70]   For Angevin influence, see Vale 1974: pp. 22–3, 95, 97; Beaucourt 1881–91: IV, pp. 102–3. The fact that the principal French royal negotiator at Tours, Piers de Brézé, was an Angevin servant (Vale 1974: p. 93) may have helped to give the English a false impression of the extent of Angevin power. Improving the chances of peace was recognised to be the aim of the marriage policy by e.g. Giles, *Chronicon*, p. 32, and d'Escouchy, *Chronique*, p. 85 (see also Harriss 1988: pp. 345–6). As for Charles VII, it is important to remember that it was only in the wake of the conquests of 1449–53 that he came to be seen as 'le tresvictorieux' (Vale 1974: pp. 4, 70). There was no reason for the English to assume before this that the French king was much more in control of affairs – and notably of the great princes – than his father had been: see above, p. 144, for Gloucester's belief that Charles was a natural fool; and Vale 1974: ch. 4, pt 1 and pp. 84ff for his problems with the princes in the early 1440s.

[71]   It seems very likely that the plan for a twenty-year alliance with the Angevins, first recorded in Henry's letter of 22 December 1445 as the *quid pro quo* for ceding Maine (*Letters and Papers*, II, ii, p. 641) was – like the cession itself (see below) – hatched at Tours, when the marriage was negotiated, and not later. This seems to me to be the drift of Beaucourt 1881–91: IV, pp. 163–4, but cf. Ferguson 1972: pp. 28–9 and Griffiths 1981: pp. 494–5.

In this respect, it was very much of a piece with earlier diplomatic adventures in France, most notably the Armagnac marriage plan of 1442 and even the release of Orléans in 1440. Once again, the English were trying to forge links with a French princely house.[72] If the Valois kingdom should return to its familiar condition of anarchy, an Angevin alliance might even pave the way for English gains.[73]

While the specific terms of both the peace and the alliance were yet to be settled at the time of the royal wedding, in April 1445, few of Henry's leading subjects can have failed to realise what concessions might be necessary. It had been clear in 1439 that peace would be impossible while Henry continued to press his title to the crown of France;[74] and it was likely that Maine, openly claimed by Charles of Anjou and more or less on the table since the negotiations at Oye, would be the price of Angevin good will.[75] Under these circumstances, and given the general context of Henrician government, it seems more than likely that the stance adopted by English executives and negotiators – Suffolk, above all,[76] but also Moleyns, Dudley and, in a sense, the king – was based on wider counsels. While the evidence for participation and consultation is difficult to assess, since, as usual, the royal will was the only proper authorising force for public action, there is plenty to suggest that the lords, or many of them, were quite aware of what was being done and that, initially, at least, it was being done with their backing. If this was not openly declared at the time, it was probably for two reasons. First, just as in the case of the release of Orléans, no one but the king could be thought to have willed the surrender of royal property, whether titles, lands or prisoners: Henry had to take sole responsibility; no group of counsellors, even the broadest, would have wanted to risk accusations of stirring from those who stood outside the governing circle. It may have been this concern which, for example, prompted the lords to declare in parliament that only God had moved the king to seek a personal

---

[72] Above, p. 192. This point has recently been made by Keen 1989: pp. 308–9.

[73] There was nothing inevitable about the 'recovery' which France experienced under Charles VII and his successor: see Lewis 1968: ch. 1.

[74] Above, pp. 182ff.

[75] Maine was not among the lands demanded by the English in 1439: see above, p. 183, and Harriss 1988: p. 304. When the county was granted to Edmund Beaufort in July 1442, the grant included a clause allowing for the possibility that the king would surrender it to the French: Jones 1989a: p. 292 n. 4. Leguai 1967: p. 144, suggests that it was in order to regain the territory that the Angevins were pressing the cause of peace at the French court. Most of the chroniclers were convinced that the promise to cede Maine was made as part of the marriage negotiations: see e.g. *Chrons. of London*, p. 155; *Brut*, p. 511; d'Escouchy, *Chronique*, p. 128; *Three Chrons.*, p. 166; Basin, *Histoire*, p. 59 n. 4; Giles, *Chronicon*, p. 32; *Loci e Libro*, pp. 158, 190, 205, 219.

[76] Evidence of Suffolk's primacy in foreign affairs abounds: see e.g. Beaucourt 1881–91: IV, p. 289; Joubert 1880: p. 228 n. 2 for some telling examples.

convention with his uncle of France.[77] There is no evidence that they were actually hostile to the project, merely that they did not wish to take responsibility for it.[78] A second reason for not broadcasting noble support for the peace plan was that the matters under negotiation were initially being kept secret: not, as we shall see, from the king's high-born counsellors, but from a wider public which knew rather less about the strategic realities across the Channel. This does not mean that the king's advisers were conscious of pursuing an outrageous policy, merely that they did not wish to show their hand until the fruits of their efforts could be demonstrated.

Mindful of the need to secure full authority for any settlement with either Charles VII or Duke René and Count Charles, Suffolk seems to have done no more at Tours than indicate a willingness to surrender Maine to the Angevins and receive, without comment, what he took to be an offer from the French king to allow his nephew to keep Normandy, Gascony and Calais if he surrendered his claim to the crown.[79] It was further agreed that Henry VI, advised by such lords as he might call to him, would aim to conclude a peace treaty with Charles' representatives upon their arrival in London in July 1445. When negotiations with this embassy opened, however, English plans encountered their first setback. Normandy was no longer among the territories that Henry would be permitted to retain.[80] Astounded by what they evidently took to be a change of heart on the part of the French, the English negotiators were brought to agree to a proposal for a personal convention between Henry VI and Charles VII, at which this difficult matter could be dealt with and a final peace concluded.[81] At the same time, they probably gave further encouragement to the Angevins concerning Maine: after all, if Charles

---

[77] *RP*, V, p. 102.

[78] The editor's marginal note ('Protest against the peace with France') is highly misleading. The lords did not protest against the king's 'blissid entent': indeed, they declared that they had done all in their power to see to its fulfilment.

[79] For Suffolk's account of what he had done, see *RP*, V, p. 74. Beaucourt argues that no formal agreement to surrender Maine was made at Tours (e.g. 1881–91: IV, p. 284), but this does not preclude the exchange of informal understandings, and, indeed, he cites evidence that, following discussions at the city, the Angevins expected that the province would be handed over in September 1445, during Moleyns' embassy (viz. before Charles VII became clearly involved in the scheme and before Henry's letters formally appointing the surrender): *ibid.*, p. 284n. See also Harriss 1988: pp. 345–6. There are plenty of references to discussions – even the exchange of offers – at Tours in the record of the French embassy of July 1445: e.g. *Letters and Papers*, I, pp. 129–30, 132. These suggest, incidentally, that Suffolk had not included Maine among the territories to be retained by the English (it seems unlikely that the 'etc.' in Suffolk's defining comment 'cest assavoir Guienne et Normandie etc.' refers to Maine: where the English were prepared to argue, in July 1445, about the status of Normandy, they made no comment concerning Maine, which was also excluded from the French offer).

[80] *Letters and Papers*, I, pp. 131–5.   [81] *Ibid.*, pp. 141–7.

VII was going to be awkward, the help of this faction would be all the more valuable.[82]

It is almost certain that a number of leading noblemen knew what had happened and what was to be done next. Most of the dukes and a number of bishops, earls and barons participated in the formal sessions of the conference,[83] and Kemp and Buckingham joined Suffolk and Sudeley in the more detailed negotiations.[84] There is no reason to assume that these men were opposed to the possibility of surrendering the crown of France or to the convention plan, or that the latter was agreed by Suffolk and the king alone without their knowledge.[85] Similarly, when, in December 1445, Henry made a formal promise to surrender Maine to the Angevins, it is highly unlikely that this was anything but government policy, known to a fair number of important men, probably including York, and almost certainly agreed by them.[86] We should not be surprised

[82] See Wolffe 1981: p. 172 and note Kemp's announcement on 30 July 1445 that the king was been willing to employ a great part of his French inheritance in the achieving of peace (*Letters and Papers*, I, pp. 146–7).

[83] Gloucester, Exeter, Warwick (dukes), the marquis of Dorset, Salisbury, Shrewsbury and Ormond (earls), Lyhert, Bourgchier and Moleyns (bishops) and Lord Scales were noted by the French as present on one or more occasions: *ibid.*, pp. 87–159. The ambassadors also paid Cardinal Beaufort a visit on 21 July (p. 137). This means that apart from York, who was, of course, in France, Northumberland, Beaumont and Cromwell were the only lay lords of any prominence who were not apparently involved in the proceedings: even this may owe more to a failure to identify them on the part of the French than to their absence (Northumberland and Cromwell are listed among the witnesses to a royal charter granted on 29 July 1445, a day on which the king's counsellors were supposed to be meeting with him: C53/188, no. 24; *Letters and Papers*, I, p. 143).

[84] *Ibid.*, pp. 123, 138, 141. Note that Kemp and (Archbishop) Stafford seem to have been as integrally involved in the policy as Suffolk, to judge by the king's signals to them during the first formal meeting: *ibid.*, p. 110.

[85] Cf. Ferguson 1972: p. 28. The break in negotiations between 21 and 30 July was apparently to secure the agreement of the lords to the convention plan, as well as the all-important authority of the king (see esp. *Letters and Papers*, I, p. 143). The king's agreement to the scheme was conveyed by Kemp following what were presumably rather staged discussions between these two, Suffolk and Sudeley (p. 146). English readiness to surrender Henry's title, at least for a time, is plain from the trend of all the transactions during the embassy.

[86] The embassy of December 1445, at which Suffolk, Beaumont, Sudeley and Moleyns were the English negotiators, is certain to have discussed Maine along with business concerned with the truce (see *DKR*, XLVIII, p. 369, and Beaucourt 1881–91: IV, pp. 163–7, 284–5, for details; Kemp was about on the day the ambassadors were appointed: C81/1546/7). James Fiennes must also have known about the cession, since he was the queen's chamberlain and it is difficult to imagine her letters, promising to help in obtaining the cession, having been sent without his knowledge (C81/1370/25; see *Letters and Papers*, I, pp. 164–7, for Margaret's letters). York was in London at the same time as the ambassadors and was still pursuing, with Suffolk's encouragement, a marriage with the French royal family: his letter to Charles VII, dated 21 December 1445, the day before the royal letter authorising the cession, refers to a credence brought to him by Havart and Cousinot (*Letters and Papers*, I, pp. 168–70). Note that the king's letter of 22 December was not necessarily, as Wolffe 1981: pp. 185, 189 argues, issued under the signet. The 'seel de secret', referred to in the authorisation clause, could be the privy seal: see Otway-Ruthven 1939: pp. 20–2, 26, 53. Even if the letter was issued under the

at this: what the government proposed to do was entirely reasonable. By taking the cession of Maine a step further, the English hoped not only to appease Charles VII, who had begun to take a direct interest in the matter,[87] but also, no doubt, to provide the Angevins with an incentive to conclude the alliance and press the French king to look more sympathetically at the English position on Normandy.

If 1446 saw little progress in dealings with the French, this was not necessarily because the government was paralysed by fear of public opinion, nor because it was riven by internal disagreements, nor again because it was deliberately preserving a state of truce (in preference to contracting a full peace, which would release the *communitas* from its taxative obligations).[88] Henry VI's ministers may simply have done nothing because there was no reason to believe that, at this stage, further concessions would produce results.[89] Whether the English were aware that the Angevins had lost whatever power they may have possessed over Charles VII is not clear,[90] but there was little point in rushing ahead to stage the personal convention unless there were reasonable grounds for believing that it could have a successful outcome.[91] While the French king turned towards affairs in Italy, relations with Brittany and Burgundy – both of which received attention in this year – may have seemed more immediately important to Suffolk and his colleagues.[92] It was only when they tried to extend the truce with France and postpone the convention that the government's negotiators realised how gravely the situation had turned against them.[93] Charles VII's response

---

signet, this does not mean that it was necessarily personal and secret, as Wolffe claims. It was perfectly possible for the king and his advisers to express common policy through a signet letter, especially in the case of diplomatic correspondence.

[87] See Harriss 1988: p. 346 and Henry's letter of 22 December 1445: *Letters and Papers*, II, ii, pp. 639–42.

[88] For elements of the first two explanations, see Griffiths 1981: pp. 494–6 and Wolffe 1981: pp. 189–91. The third is suggested by Harriss 1986: p. 149.

[89] Maine was supposed to be surrendered on 30 April 1446 according to Henry's promise of December 1445, although the English failure to act seems to have gone officially unnoticed (Wolffe 1981: p. 190).

[90] The Angevins were ejected from Charles' court in the autumn of 1445 (Vale 1974: p. 97). Count Charles, at least, was back in favour by the autumn of 1446 and royal campaigns in Italy were conducted partly to suit his interests, but there is no sense that the king was under his thumb (*ibid.*, pp. 104–6).

[91] Encouraging letters were sent concerning the convention, which was scheduled for October 1446 (*Foedera*, XI, pp. 109, 114, 119) and some arrangements were set in train to find the money for it: *Letters and Papers*, I, pp. 183–6, and II, i, pp. 368–71; *PPC*, VI, pp. 46, 51; Beaucourt 1881–91: IV, p. 287.

[92] For Charles VII's Italian campaigns, see n. 90, above. For Brittany, see Wolffe 1981: pp. 200–2. We know nothing of the negotiations with the Burgundians, except that the truce of 1443 was extended for another four years (e.g. Ferguson 1972: p. 32).

[93] Moleyns and Dudley were appointed to go to France to negotiate this on 20 July 1446: *Foedera*, V, i, p. 163.

was to announce that he could not agree to either request unless Maine were surrendered first.[94]

At this point it must have become clear to the English that no advantage was to be derived from their link with the Angevins: evidently, René and Charles had thrown in their lot with the French king, concluding that they could obtain and hold Maine more easily from him than from Henry VI. Now, the government was faced with a stark choice: either it could recognise that its diplomacy had failed and prepare for the renewal of war at the expiry of the truce in April 1447; or it could continue negotiations over the cession and convention plans, in the hope that appeasement would win French co-operation over Normandy, or at least prolong the truce. Gerald Harriss has recently shown how the fiscal priorities of the regime – a large household, royal foundations, generous patronage – left no room for military expenditure.[95] As we have seen, Suffolk had little choice about these priorities: they were the unavoidable corollary of the exercise of royal authority under Henry VI. If in 1449 there was 'neither the money, nor the mechanism, nor the will to fight a war', this was no less the case in the autumn of 1446. Parliament had been dissolved only a few months before. The gentry, after granting two tenths and fifteenths, were anticipating a long release from taxation, and the exchequer was in the grip of a crisis of overassignment.[96] With war virtually unthinkable, the government was forced to consider appeasement; but, typically, Suffolk had no intention of considering it alone. The day before Charles VII delivered his final ultimatum, a council, comprising most of the leading lords with diplomatic and administrative experience, was summoned to Westminster.[97]

The events of this assembly, and of the next few months, are obscure. Even so, it is possible to make some rather provisional suggestions about what was happening. First of all, it is highly unlikely that Suffolk would have concealed the diplomatic situation from those summoned to the council of October 1446, most of whom continued to be involved in

---

[94] Beaucourt 1881–91: IV, pp. 288–9.   [95] Harriss 1986.

[96] *Ibid.*, pp. 171 (the quotation), pp. 150–1 (the crisis).

[97] E28/77/3 (25 September 1446: Moleyns and Dudley did not return with Charles' message until some time after 26 September, but they had been meeting with the king throughout August and had probably been able to send word to England of his attitude: Beaucourt 1881–91: IV, p. 288). The personal convention was named among the matters to be discussed at this council. The following were summoned: Kemp, Lyhert, Alnwick, Beckington, Lowe, Exeter, Buckingham, Dorset, Suffolk, Cromwell, Hungerford and Stourton. Of these, Kemp, Alnwick, Exeter, Dorset, Suffolk and Hungerford had been at Arras (*PPC*, IV, pp. 302, 305); Kemp, Buckingham, Hungerford, Stourton and Beckington had been at Oye (*PPC*, V, p. 334); Kemp, Buckingham, Suffolk and Lyhert had been involved in recent negotiations (see above). Only Cromwell and Lowe seem to have had no experience of dealing with the French. York is perhaps a surprising omission from the list of summons, Gloucester a less surprising one.

affairs during November and December.[98] Sooner or later, the government would have to act, and then the sympathy of men like these would
be crucial. It seems reasonable to conclude that the various steps which
were taken in the ensuing months towards arranging the convention and
paving the way for the cession of Maine were undertaken in the belief, if
not the direct knowledge, that leading men would find them acceptable.
On 10 December, a parliament was called for February 1447 at which
arrangements for the king's safety on his voyage and for the rule of
England in his absence were to be discussed.[99] A fortnight later, the
marquis of Dorset, governor of Maine, was given the lieutenancy of
France, presumably as a means of ensuring his co-operation in the
surrender of the county.[100] The day before, another embassy had been
sent to Charles VII: it can only have offered fresh guarantees concerning
Maine and the convention, since the French king agreed to its request for
a further prolongation of the truce.[101] During these difficult weeks, the
English front did not collapse completely: the new arrangements for the
surrender of Maine seem to have included demands for compensation,
demands to which the French were ultimately willing to bow.[102] Even so,
this small victory did nothing to disguise the new realities of English
policy: Henry VI was not conferring Maine upon a powerful French
vassal; he was giving it to the French king, in return for the gift of time
and the faint hope of peace. If it seems unlikely that the nobility could
have agreed to such a craven and uncertain policy, it is worth considering
their behaviour at the time of the Bury parliament and during the months
following.

It will have become clear that at the time of this assembly, so famously
overshadowed by the arrest and death of the duke of Gloucester, the

---

[98] Scattered records from November show Buckingham, Exeter, Suffolk, Dorset, Cromwell, Sudeley, Dudley and Scrope and a number of bishops to have been present on
more than one occasion (C81/1546/13–16; E28/77/9). The great council at Sheen in
December, during which (*inter alia*: see Harriss 1986: pp. 151–2) writs for a parliament
were sent out, meetings with French ambassadors were held and another English
embassy appointed (*CClR 1441–7*, p. 453; Beaucourt 1881–91: IV, pp. 289–90; *DKR*,
XLVIII, p. 372) involved at least York, Dorset, Suffolk, Dudley and Scrope among the
lay lords, and probably others (see C81/1546/18 and E28/77/14 for the rather limited
records).

[99] See *RP*, V, p. 128, for the point of the Bury parliament.

[100] This appointment was made on 24 December 1446. For the fullest analysis, see Jones
1989a: pp. 291–3.

[101] Ferguson 1972: p. 30 and Beaucourt 1881–91: IV, pp. 289–90.

[102] The government cannot have been blind to the issue of compensation, which had been
so prominent in 1439 (Harriss 1988: pp. 302–3). In the negotiations over Maine, it does
not seem to have been introduced until July 1447, however (*Letters and Papers*, II, ii, p.
643). Perhaps the English had been ready to meet the costs themselves until the
diplomatic situation went against them (Harriss 1988: p. 358, provides an alternative
explanation).

government was committed to major expenditures and concessions with no guarantee of positive returns. This was a thoroughly uneasy position from which to confront the broader public of taxpayers and local land-owners which parliament represented. Many of those in the know may have been prompted to question the wisdom of what had been under-taken, but they were quite aware that unless the war was to be resumed in a matter of weeks, there was not much room for manoeuvre.[103] The choice for responsible members of the regime was therefore clear: what-ever the weaknesses in government policy, there could be no change of direction. In the meantime, because these weaknesses were becoming apparent, there was every reason to stifle public discussion.[104]

These considerations set the scene for Gloucester's demise. Whether or not the duke intended, as he had done before, to exploit the difficulties of the governing group to gain advantage for himself or his policies cannot be known, but it seems likely that this is what Suffolk anticipated.[105] A typically public and populistic assault on the proposed convention – or on the cession of Maine, which Gloucester must have known about – could have been extremely damaging, especially as there was every reason to expect that, as in 1439–40, Gloucester would accompany his condemna-tion of the policy with criticism of the forms of its authorisation.[106] If, on the earlier occasion, Beaufort and Kemp had been vulnerable to charges that their 'prive counsaille' had stirred and moved the king against his proper interests and free regality, now, in 1447, Suffolk and his colleagues were scarcely better protected. What made their situation all the more unstable was the fact that the king's planned departure from the realm would probably mean the appointment of a *custos Anglie*, a post for which Gloucester was the obvious candidate. Given his past record of active and

---

[103] When parliament gathered, the date for the expiry of the truce was still 1 April 1447.

[104] Was this what lay behind the summons of most of the leading lords, including Gloucester, to a council due to convene at Westminster two weeks before the opening of parliament (E28/77/15)? Stafford's address to the parliament itself, with its condemna-tion of the counsel of the impious and reprobate and its association of good counsel with peace, seems full of significance (*RP*, V, p. 128).

[105] On 24 January 1447, the venue of the parliament was suddenly changed from Winchester (originally Cambridge, where there was found to be plague) to Bury St Edmunds, in the heart of Suffolk's 'country' (C81/1370/41). Tension had been building up for some weeks: over Christmas 1446, a great watch was kept at London (*Collections*, pp. 187–8), an area where Gloucester seems generally to have had some support, and it is interesting that the route taken by Henry on his way to the parliament was an indirect one, which avoided the city (see Wolffe 1981: p. 365).

[106] See above, p. 184, for the duke's earlier assault. The evidence of the chronicles is problematic, because they were written after 1450, but note claims that Gloucester was dealt with because he was likely to prevent the cession of Maine (Leland, *De Rebus*, p. 494) or because he knew that Henry was incompetent to govern by himself and thought that his principal advisers were drawing him into foolish policies (d'Escouchy, *Chronique*, pp. 115–16).

voluble opposition, and the likelihood that the government was now beginning to be nervous of popular dissent, it can scarcely have wanted to hand him such a major political opportunity, whether by appointing him to the post or denying him it.[107]

Although chroniclers and others characteristically traced Gloucester's destruction to the action of Suffolk and other prominent figures in the reviled household clique of 1450, it was the support of more substantial men which made the whole process possible.[108] While it was indeed household men who met the duke on his arrival at Bury and diverted him from the king's presence,[109] it was leading members of the nobility – Buckingham, Dorset, Salisbury, Beaumont (the constable) and Sudeley – who were sent to arrest him.[110] A number of other magnates, including York, and probably Exeter and Viscount Bourgchier, were present at the parliament itself.[111] Clearly enough, we cannot conclude that all, or any, of these lords had sought Gloucester's arrest, but it remains the case that they did not oppose it and some of them evidently condoned it.[112] This was surely not because they believed the duke to be guilty of the treason charges laid against him,[113] but rather because they did not want to see

[107] See *RP*, V, p. 128, for the need to make provision for the government of the realm in the king's absence.

[108] See e.g. *English Chron.*, p. 62 (Suffolk and James Fiennes); d'Escouchy, *Chronique*, pp. 115–16 (Suffolk and Moleyns); *Crowland*, p. 404; C47/14/6, no. 48 (Suffolk and Thomas Daniel). Cade's rebels implied that Suffolk alone was the cause (Harvey 1991: p. 189), while versions of the *Brut* accused the men who 'rulid a boute the king' in general (Leland, *De Rebus*, p. 494; *Brut*, p. 513).

[109] Sir John Stourton and Sir Thomas Stanley, according to what is probably the best source for the Bury parliament, the 1448 memorandum printed by Davies: *English Chron.*, pp. xv, 116. Soon after the parliament, Stourton received some offices and custodies in Wiltshire which may have been Gloucester's (*CPR, 1446–52*, pp. 35–6), whilst Stanley shared in the grant of the duke's goods (*ibid.*, p. 45).

[110] *English Chron.*, pp. 63, 117.

[111] York petitioned for Gloucester's manor of Great Wratting, which he claimed was his 'of right and inheritance', although it had actually escheated to the crown on the attainder of March in 1403. The grant was made just two days after Gloucester's death (Johnson 1988: p. 66 and n. 112; *CPR, 1446–52*, p. 43). Exeter and Bourgchier were recipients of grants made in the period of the parliament, albeit not from Gloucester's estates (*CPR 1446–52*, pp. 32, 46). Together with Buckingham, Dorset, Salisbury, Northumberland, Beaumont, Cromwell, Scrope, Kemp, Lumley, Beckington and Bishop Bourgchier, Exeter and York were named as triers of petitions and this makes it likely that they attended at least the opening few days of the parliament (*RP*, V, p. 129; Brown 1981: p. 122; Roskell 1956: p. 184).

[112] See above note. It was later reported that 'the duke of Exceter was comaundyd to arrest the duk of Gloucestr and he sayde that he wolde noght' (C47/14/6, no. 48). The story may be true since Exeter was apparently present at the parliament, yet was not recorded as one of those taking part in the arrest.

[113] Gloucester's men were supposed to have intended to make the duke king and to release his wife (KB9/255/2, m. 19). This move was apparently to be backed by a force or rising of Welshmen (*English Chron.*, p. 62; 'Benet's Chron.', pp. 192–3). We are in the unusual position of knowing something of Gloucester's movements in the autumn of 1446, when the duke might have been expected to be planning this wild scheme. He was

the governing body broken up by a major public debate about foreign policy and how it had been made. It is worth remembering with what reluctance the lords submitted to such an examination in 1450.[114] Their behaviour in 1447 was the first indication – and rather a chilling one – of how far they might be prepared to go to protect a workable regime from internal disruption or, worse, from exposure to the potentially hostile gaze of the parliamentary public. Good Duke Humphrey, hero of the 1450s, had no significant support among the magnates in the preceding decade: after twenty-five years of divisive interventions on behalf of a putative national interest, he, not Suffolk, appeared to be the chief enemy of the stability on which all depended.[115]

If this was indeed the lords' thinking, it testifies both to the success and to the weakness of the court jurisdiction which Suffolk had established: on the one hand, the magnates were ready to support a thoroughly dubious initiative in the interests of maintaining the consensus about the king; on the other, in doing so, they began to depart from the wider public they were supposed to represent. There seems little doubt that many people, town and country notables among them, were horrified by Gloucester's downfall.[116] The removal of the erstwhile protector may have reinforced a growing concern that all was not well in the government of the still rather insubstantial king, since, from this point onwards, instances of public criticism begin to multiply.[117] Even so, it was not until the end of

at Marlborough (Wilts.) on 30 August and Devizes (Wilts.) on 14 October and at Christmas 1446: E159/223, *comm.*, Mic., rot. 3; BL Add. Roll 8,500. This suggests that he was neither raising the Welsh, nor compassing the king's death with his men at Greenwich (although see Griffiths 1991d: p. 191). The likelihood that no one really believed in Gloucester's guilt is indicated by the pardon – obviously issued with Suffolk's agreement – which his men received even after juries had been found to convict them of these ludicrous crimes: Leland, *De Rebus*, p. 494. The oyer and terminer commission which heard the Kentish indictments of Gloucester's men in June 1447 was dominated by household men, notably those who had been involved in the duke's arrest: KB9/255/ 2, m. 6 (Suffolk, Saye, Stourton, Stanley, John Noreys, William Tresham and Thomas Browne *et al.*).

[114] See below, p. 247. [115] Note also Keen 1989: p. 309.

[116] Public opinion is more than usually difficult to assess in this period because of its shortness (*c.*1446–50) and the fact that the crisis in which it ended coloured almost all retrospective comment. Even allowing for hindsight, however, the insistence of many chronicles that Duke Humphrey's death unleashed a great deal of popular murmur seems convincing: e.g. *Town Chrons.*, p. 121; *Brut*, p. 513; Giles, *Chronicon*, p. 34. Contemporary support exists in the form of an indictment of the keeper of Gloucester Castle in June 1447, who was supposed to have said that the king had killed the duke and that it would have been better if the duke had killed the king instead: KB9/256, m. 13. Whethamstede claims that petitions were submitted to every parliament after 1447 calling for the duke's rehabilitation (*Registrum Whethamstede*, I, p. 181).

[117] It seems likely that, whatever Duke Humphrey's standing among his peers, he may well have been a symbol of responsible government to many of Henry's other subjects: see e.g. *Town Chrons.*, p. 121; Leland, *De Rebus*, p. 494; *Registrum Whethamstede*, I, p. 179. John Capgrave's *Liber de Illustribus Henricis*, written in late 1446 or early 1447 (preferring the datings of Hingeston (ed.), *Liber . . .*, p. xxv, and Gransden 1982: p. 389

1447 that this development seems to have driven the lords to reconsider their priorities. Until then, many of them continued to occupy themselves with the familiar problem of maintaining authority at the centre; for lying at the heart of the unsavoury scenes at Bury St Edmunds was, of course, the problem of Henry VI's inadequacy. Had the king been able to demonstrate that control of policy was his alone, criticism could have been confronted and absorbed; suppression, of this drastic kind, would not have been necessary.

During the ensuing months, leading noblemen gave more explicit support for the surrender of Maine as the policy became more widely known. In May 1447, a number of lords, including, notably, York and Cromwell, heard and endorsed Suffolk's protestation that, contrary to rumour, he had not acted 'infideliter' or 'contra coronam nostram' in this matter.[118] When, in July, a French embassy came to settle the issue of compensation, several major noblemen were probably on hand, and Buckingham and Scrope joined Suffolk, Moleyns and Dudley in the actual negotiations.[119] These men were thus party to the letters patent, issued on 27 July 1447, which promised that Maine would be in French hands by 1 November, in return for appropriate 'provisio' and the surrender of Charles VII's original licence for the Angevin alliance.[120] At this stage, then, it is quite clear that Suffolk's policy commanded the support of most, if not all, leading men. Whilst each of its parts – the marriage, the cession, the convention – was authorised by the explicitly independent power of the king, this authorisation was made meaningful by the recognition and consent of the magnates. As was evidently feared in 1446–7, it would have been possible for lords to make charges of false counsel against Suffolk and others close to the king had their exercise of power been seen as unacceptable. This did

over that of Wolffe 1981: p. 15 n. 18) makes several references to political dissent, both in London and elsewhere: Hingeston (ed.), *Liber* ..., pp. 4, 129–30, 134–5. For seditious comments about the king's advisers made in 1446, see KB9/996, m. 55, and KB9/260, m. 85. For evidence of government concern, note that the document exonerating Suffolk in May 1447 (below, n. 118) provided for measures to be taken against slanderers and that it was on the day after the record of this exoneration was exemplified under the great seal that the oyer and terminer commission against Gloucester's men was appointed (18 June 1447: above, n. 113).

[118] *Foedera*, V, i, pp. 176–7. Those present were Archbishop Stafford, Lumley, Lyhart, York, Buckingham, Cromwell, Sudeley, Saye and other servants, familiars and domestics.

[119] *Foedera*, V, i, p. 178; Beaucourt 1881–91: IV, pp. 290–4. See *Letters and Papers*, II, ii, pp. 679–80; *PPC*, VI, p. 60, for the likelihood that a number of other lords were also involved. Dorset was present to receive a promise of compensation on 27 July 1447, the day the patents for the cession were issued: *Letters and Papers*, II, ii, p. 685. York was present on that day as well (Jones 1982: p. 199). On 18 July, Archbishop Kemp lent the king £500 (E403/777, m. 3).

[120] *Letters and Papers*, II, ii, pp. 638–43.

not happen.[121] The surrender of Maine and the arrest of Gloucester were not the bitter fruits of improper influence, but the products of a policy both royal and public, guaranteed to be in the common interest by the sanction of the nobility.

The trouble was that, by the later 1440s, noble approbation was no longer living up to its claims. It did not confer a universal endorsement of policy. To some extent, perhaps, this was because the mechanisms of the 'personal rule' – geared to preserving a fictional royal authority whilst gaining consent from the small elite of powerful men – made the participation of the nobility insufficiently visible to the rest of political society. Those outside the corridors of power had a very different view of the political arrangements of Henry VI's court from the one depicted here. The wider *communitas* did not see a process by which Suffolk obtained corporate support for policy paraded under the king's name; they did not see that the court comprised leading magnates as well as clerks and grooms. What they saw instead was a clique of household men headed by a seemingly invincible favourite, drawing the king away from his good old council and inducing him to follow unprofitable policies. As the bankruptcy of these policies became clearer and as, in due course, the government realised it would have to turn to the country for aid, the communal perception of how affairs had been managed assumed greater and greater importance.

These are matters to be explored in the following section, but it is clear that the government was already running into problems with its wider constituency in the latter part of 1447. The transfer of Maine was proving difficult to effect. The immediate problem was the refusal of the French to pay any compensation until the territory was actually in their hands,[122] but this does not alter the fact that the English government was quite unable to compel its own servants to carry out its wishes. Part of the reason for this was probably continuing resistance from the marquis of Dorset,[123] but, even when he agreed to co-operate, it remained impossible to coerce local officers into handing over the fortresses until the arrival of a large army made it clear that the French were capable of taking them by force.[124] In

---

[121] False counsel was evidently the main theme of the slanders against which Suffolk defended himself in May 1447 (n. 118, above), but it is almost certain that these criticisms were popular ones. They were plainly not sustained by a significant proportion of the lords.

[122] The patent of July 1447 was rather ambiguous on the point: see *Letters and Papers*, II, ii, pp. 638, 643 and pp. 672–90, for the original order and the subsequent debates.

[123] See Jones 1989a: p. 293 and *Letters and Papers*, II, ii, pp. 692–6. The suspicion that Dorset refused to issue the letters of discharge which his officers demanded (*ibid.*, pp. 705ff) until his compensation was agreed is perhaps confirmed by York's version of events in his 1452 articles against the marquis (*PL*, I, pp. 107–8).

[124] See Griffiths 1981: pp. 501–3, for details.

fact, it may have been the embarrassing scenes which preceded and attended the actual surrender of Maine that first provoked the lords to reconsider their commitment to the government and its policies. As late as November 1447, several of them, including Buckingham, York and Cromwell, were still sufficiently interested in effecting the cession to help settle the matter of Dorset's compensation.[125] After this date, most of the nobility seem to have withdrawn from the centre until the gathering crisis forced them to return in the autumn of 1449.[126] It may be this factor, above all, which explains why a policy instituted (and, for a time, sustained) by many came to be regarded as the work of Suffolk, Moleyns and other executives alone.[127] There were some who could not escape responsibility for the king's actions.

. . .

The beguiling image of a court clique, unsupported by the mass of the nobility, dominating government around a pliable but conspiratorial king is thus shown to be rather wide of the mark. Most of the men one might expect to find involved in the work of proper consultative government were so involved. The sense that power was seized from the old noble council by a cabal of household men was illusory, manufactured even. If the regime of the mid-1440s had a somewhat flimsy appearance, this is mostly to be explained by the fact that it was in these years that the 'Establishment' of the 1410s and 1420s finally withered away. Between early 1443 and mid-1447, a large number of great men associated with the past governance of the realm either died or retired into obscurity.[128] This meant an inevitable transformation of the public scene, as new or newer men rose to take their places. At the same time, a number of the more prominent noble houses were without adult heads: Beaufort since 1444, Beauchamp after 1446, Holland after 1447. This too must have affected perceptions of the government, especially in the wake of Glou-

---

[125] Jones 1989a: p. 293 n. 5.   [126] See below, pp. 245ff.

[127] Compare, for example, the view of *Great Chron.*, pp. 176–7, that it was agreed by the king 'and the more part of his counsayll' that Maine should be surrendered, with *English Chron.*, pp. 68–9, which insists that the surrender had been arranged by Suffolk and Dorset without assent. Note too Suffolk's careful answer to the commons' charge that he had been the principal causer of the delivery of Maine: the policy had been made by other lords as well as himself; its delivery had been made by Bishop Moleyns (*RP*, V, pp. 178, 182). Similarly, the protests of the York–Fastolf circle in the years after 1450 focused on Dorset's compensation and the circumstances of the actual delivery, rather than on the principles implicit in the policy itself, which York and others had sanctioned: *PL*, I, pp. 107–8; also College of Arms, Arundel MS xlviii, fol. 325r–v.

[128] Lords Tiptoft and Fanhope, Archbishop Chichele, John Holland earl of Huntingdon and duke of Exeter, Cardinal Beaufort and Humphrey of Gloucester all died, whilst Lord Hungerford and Bishop Alnwick retired from affairs. Of the councillors of the 1420s, only Kemp, Stafford, Buckingham, Northumberland, Scrope and Cromwell remained.

cester's mysterious death.[129] It would not be surprising if these years were marked by a general sense that links with the glorious past of successful and equitable rule had been severed, or that royal counsel had taken on a rather insubstantial, youthful, or even malicious aspect.[130] Since it is also the case that Henry VI's lack of martiality meant that noblemen involved in the defence of his various realms were removed from affairs about the king, rather than being central to them, it is possible to suggest that English public life actually experienced a net loss of nobility in the later 1440s.[131] Nonetheless, the fact remains that almost all of those who were available to participate in government did so: only the unimportant were excluded.

As before, this was apparently the design of those around the king who, in the first instance, managed his power. The policy of representing and promoting the territorially powerful continued unaffected following the transition to court rule. These men were apparently involved in other aspects of government besides foreign policy. It is impossible, given the constraints of space, to go into details here, but it is clear that the surviving members of the Beaufort-focused group among the nobility – Buckingham, Salisbury, Cromwell, Beaumont and Dorset, joined in the early 1440s by Exeter, Shrewsbury, York – continued to play a part at the centre and to see their interests satisfied by it right up to 1448, when the regime began to disintegrate.[132] Even the earl of Northumberland, initially disadvantaged by the pre-eminence of Salisbury and the struggles of his own retainers with the men of Cardinal Kemp, seems to have found himself a place.[133] As generational change took its toll, moreover, new

---

[129] Note the view of Cade's rebels that not only Gloucester, but also Beaufort, Exeter, Somerset and Warwick had been murdered (Harvey 1991: p. 191).

[130] Beaufort's death prompted similar tributes (and putative forebodings for the future) to that of Gloucester: e.g. *Town Chrons.*, p. 104; Giles, *Chronicon*, p. 34. The latter – interestingly, given the broadly pro-government sympathies of its account of the 1450s – thought that Gloucester's death prepared the way for Suffolk and Saye to dominate the king's counsels. See *Loci e Libro*, p. 189, for a reference to the king's 'iuvenibus consiliariis' in 1450.

[131] Note 'Benet's Chron.', p. 195, where the rule of Suffolk is directly related to the absence of leading noblemen.

[132] See Appendix B, below, for supportive detail concerning those named here, except York, who is discussed on pp. 237–9.

[133] See above, pp. 179 and 203, for Northumberland's position in the early 1440s. It seems possible that his main role was as a bridge between the government, based in the South, and his important following in the North, which seems mostly to have been managed by his sons and leading retainers (Henry, his heir, was warden of the East March from 1440: Storey 1957: p. 614. Sir William Plumpton, a Percy retainer, was steward of the duchy honour of Knaresborough in the period 1439–61: Somerville 1953: p. 524; Bean 1958: p. 92 n. 1). The suggestion that the earl resided mostly in the South finds support from numerous pieces of evidence. There was, for example, a threefold increase in fees paid out of the Percies' Sussex estates during Henry VI's reign (*ibid.*, pp. 92–3) and the earl contracted a Sussex marriage for his eldest son, which brought with it a string of

magnates were successfully absorbed into this great network. The creation of three new earls in the west Midlands, for example – James Butler (Wiltshire), John Tiptoft (Worcester) and Richard Neville (Warwick) – was achieved without any serious friction.[134] If this owed something to the common association of the last two with the powerful Neville interest,[135] it also says much for the continued effectiveness of the Beaufort-De La Pole consensus among the lords.[136]

The inescapable conclusion to be drawn from all this is that Suffolk's court, at least until 1448, enjoyed a following among the nobility as great and as representative as that of any regime since 1422. Contrary to the traditional view, this was no narrow clique but a legitimate government, which emanated from the king in his household with the tacit, or even

properties in the county (above p. 178n). Interestingly, Northumberland was not among those asked to remain in the North instead of coming to parliament in February 1449: E28/78/49. He witnessed about a third of charters 1445–9, inclusive. SC1/43/178 has him bringing messages to London from the king. He was a trier of petitions in the parliament of 1447 (*RP*, V, p. 129) and came to be closely involved with the royal foundations (*ibid.*, pp. 70–1, 165–6; also *CPR, 1441–6*, p. 364). The fact that Northumberland's second son was able to petition for – and receive – the title of Lord Egremont in November 1449, on the basis of virtually no service, seems to indicate a good relationship with the court on the part of his father: E28/79/40; *PPC*, VI, p. 161.

[134] All three men became earls in July 1449, about the end of the Westminster/Winchester parliament (*HBC*, pp. 486, 487, 569; *CChR, 1427–1516*, p. 111). Tiptoft's advancement may have been related to his Neville associations. He had married Cicely, widow of Henry Beauchamp and daughter of the earl of Salisbury in April 1449 (*CPR, 1446–52*, p. 242), and the earldom of Worcester was an old Beauchamp title. Neville acquired the Warwick earldom in right of his wife and as part of a negotiated share of the Beauchamp inheritance (Carpenter 1992: p. 442 and n. 136, below). The patent drew attention to his long service in Scotland and, interestingly, about the king's person (*CPR, 1446–52*, pp. 235–6). Butler was closely associated with the court, being a member of the Sudeley–Beauchamp of Powick group which had obtained control of part of Warwickshire in the 1440s (Carpenter 1992: e.g. pp. 411, 413, 422) and having accompanied Suffolk's expedition to collect the queen in 1444–5 (*Letters and Papers*, I, p. 447). He was also associated with York, for whom he surrendered the justiceship of the forests south of Trent in September 1446 (Rosenthal 1965: p. 190; *CPR, 1446–52*, p. 83).

[135] Had his wife lived beyond 1450, Worcester could have been a very significant figure in the west Midlands, but his evident attachment to the Neville connection removed any dangers which might have arisen in the meantime. In May 1450, for example, he surrendered the keeping of the Beauchamp/Bergavenny lands, granted to him in June 1449, for Warwick's benefit: *CFR, 1445–52*, pp. 111, 157–8.

[136] It is a remarkable achievement of Suffolk's court that the partition of the Beauchamp inheritance among the Nevilles, Talbots, Beauforts and others was carried out with so little friction (Carpenter 1992: pp. 440–2). The problems which arose after 1450 must be related as much to the breakdown of government in that year as to deficiencies in the settlement. Note too that it was partly thanks to the reconciling lordship of the earl of Suffolk that the earldom of Warwick was even available. In November 1446, Lord Beauchamp of Powick, a leading figure both in the household and in Warwickshire, had put in a 'quite tenable' claim to the earldom. It was presumably to avoid trouble with the Nevilles and other interested parties that Suffolk, apparently pressed by Salisbury, intervened to persuade Beauchamp to withdraw his claim (C81/1546/14; Carpenter 1992: pp. 421, 442). See above, pp. 196–7, for more on Beauchamp.

active, support of the greater men of the kingdom, the majority of whom were themselves joined together in a series of overlapping networks. The model of 'ins' and 'outs', which has dominated explanations of the ensuing crisis, is simply not applicable. We can demonstrate this point by looking again at the relations between the regime and those who have been most famously identified as 'outs': the dukes of York and Norfolk, and the earl of Devon.[137]

That the crown preserved good relations with York right up to the moment of his return from Ireland is fast becoming the orthodoxy.[138] We have already seen that the duke was as ready as anyone else to give endorsement to the peace policy.[139] He was a significant participant in the government and certainly not regarded with suspicion or enmity.[140] The financial hardships which he experienced with regard to his military service were not proportionately greater than those of any other of Henry VI's accountants.[141] In fact, the government seems to have made a special effort to pay the duke's arrears, somewhat remarkably finding cash for him in the desperate circumstances of July 1449.[142] It is difficult to argue, even, that York's appointment as lieutenant of Ireland, in July 1447, was any kind of turning-point.[143]

[137] See e.g. Storey 1966: pp. 72–3, 78–9, 85–9.

[138] This view was first expounded in Pugh 1986a, though it is also implied in Johnson 1981 and developed by Jones 1989a: pp. 289–90, 294–5.

[139] See above, pp. 225, 232, 234, and also Harriss 1988: pp. 347–8. Johnson 1988: p. 70, has the duke certainly hostile to the government's plans for Maine, but there is no clear evidence to support this view.

[140] The duke attended meetings sporadically throughout the later 1440s (see figure 3). He was present at the Bury parliament and benefited from Gloucester's downfall (above, p. 230). In October 1446 (possibly 1447), he was despatched, on the king's behalf, to regain the lordship of Abergavenny from Edward Neville: C81/1370/56. He was a witness to more than 75 per cent of royal charters issued in the years 1446–8 inclusive (C53/189–90) and received a series of royal grants in 1446–7, including – in addition to the spoils from Gloucester (CPR, 1446–52, pp. 43, 79; Johnson 1988: p. 66) – the stewardship of the forests south of Trent (CPR, 1446–52, pp. 66, 83) and, albeit at a price, the wardship and marriage of the Holland heir (ibid., p. 86). In October 1447, he managed to secure a 125 mark annuity, with payment backdated to May 1433 (ibid., p. 117). Connections with the court are revealed by his choice of feoffees in 1448 (Stafford, Waynflete, Cromwell, Stourton, William Tresham and Sir Robert Roos: ibid., p. 124) and even 1449 (Alnwick, Beaumont, Sudeley, Cromwell, Hungerford and Tresham et al.: E28/79/3).

[141] See e.g. Pugh 1986a: pp. 125–6; Jones 1989a: p. 295; Bean 1984.

[142] Johnson 1988: pp. 57–8, 62; Harriss 1986: pp. 165, 169. York's success at the exchequer may be partly traceable to his feeing of the under-treasurer, Thomas Brown (Johnson 1988: p. 60).

[143] A point made by e.g. Pugh 1986a: p. 127. For the date of York's appointment (30 July) see Johnson 1988: p. 68. Note that York was granted custody of Henry Holland the same day (CPR, 1446–52, p. 86) and that he was reappointed to the lieutenancy in December 1447 when it was clear that Dorset would co-operate over Maine (ibid., p. 185; above, p. 234). The 'exile' idea comes originally from a comment in Gregory's chronicle which reads as if prompted by hindsight (Collections, p. 189: 'exsylyde in to Irlonde for hys rebellyon' in 27 Hen. VI). Even so, it has been followed by most

Whilst it is possible that, as Anne Curry has suggested, Duke Richard had envisaged a career in France as natural successor to Bedford, it is unlikely that he saw anything particularly dishonourable or second-best in taking up the rule of Ireland: it was, after all, a post which some of his greatest ancestors had held.[144] The duke's departure for the province in June 1449 was inspired less by resentment, perhaps, than by a desire to withdraw from the centre as the inevitable crisis approached. Ireland gave him a chance to perform effective military service to the crown, and to do so in circumstances altogether less dangerous than those in France.[145]

Before 1450, there is nothing to associate York with opposition, and, more particularly, very little to link him with the duke of Gloucester, whose final destruction at Bury York must have witnessed.[146] The setbacks in his career – the loss of the lieutenancy and the curious argument with Moleyns in 1446 – are not uncharacteristic of the problems faced by the nobility in their dealings with the consensual but inadequate regime: they need not have rankled with York especially.[147] If Dorset's appointment as lieutenant in 1446–7 upset York, it is worth noting that tensions also arose between Warwick and Bedford over the captaincy of Calais in 1428, and (in all probability) between the Beaufort

historians, including the most recent commentator on York (Johnson 1988: p. 70). Johnson himself cites York's power to appoint a deputy in Ireland as being 'at odds with any intention of banishment' (ibid.).

[144] Dr Curry's suggestion was made in an unpublished paper on the end of Lancastrian France, which was presented to Peter Lewis' seminar on Later Medieval France, at All Souls College, Oxford, in Hilary Term 1992. Lionel, duke of Clarence, source of the March/York claim to the throne, had served his father as lieutenant of Ireland (McKisack 1959: pp. 231–2).

[145] Note that the position of English lordship in Ireland looked particularly shaky in 1448–9 (Griffiths 1981: p. 420). This supplies a further reason why York should have chosen to go there in person.

[146] See CCIR, 1435–41, p. 376, and CFR, 1437–45, p. 69, for some minor land transactions involving Gloucester and York (or his men) in 1439–40. Little can be deduced from these and see Johnson 1988: pp. 32–3, for some persuasive comment about the meaning of Gloucester's reference to York, among others, in his articles against Beaufort. It is interesting to note that York was apparently considering buying Beaufort's manor of Canford at some point in 1444–5 (BL, Egerton Roll, 8782). This suggests that his relations with the cardinal were perfectly good at that time, and also that – unlike Gloucester – he was not concerned with the propriety of this famous alienation from the royal demesne: see Letters and Papers, II, ii, p. 448.

[147] If York was angered by the criticisms of his performance as lieutenant which he claimed had been made by Bishop Moleyns, the bishop, himself, as Wolffe 1972: p. 42 noted, was plainly the more unnerved party: BL, Harley MS 543, fols. 161–3. Even if this argument was a factor in York's loss of the lieutenancy (e.g. Griffiths 1981: p. 507), it is surely too much to see the episode as the beginning of York's alienation. It is interesting to note that, some time before October 1446, the marquis of Dorset was also apparently exposed to criticisms of his military performance (C81/1371/46, which can be dated from Northumberland's mainprise for Roger, Lord Camoys, who had made them: CCIR, 1441–7, p. 460).

brothers over the governance of Maine in 1443.[148] These tensions should not be overlooked, but their role in shaping national politics is not clear: none of these other men became opponents of the government as York was to do.

The exclusion of Devon and Norfolk, meanwhile, was manifested principally in their inability to obtain justice. This is important to note because, hard as it was for them, it implies that they lacked the might to force the regime to accommodate their interests. While Suffolk lived, they posed no threat to the government and, in fact, neither played any part in the duke's downfall.[149] It is, of course, true that Norfolk and his supporters offered vigorous support to Richard of York in the autumn of 1450, but this is explained by two factors: on the one hand, the fact that the De La Pole affinity, so long sustained by central as well as local power, was kept in being; and on the other, the fact that its sponsors were members of an unusually vulnerable government.[150] If Norfolk helped to sustain York's opposition, then York certainly sustained Norfolk's. Once a workable authority was re-established at the centre, Norfolk fell under its jurisdiction, still impotently struggling against the power of his dead opponent.[151]

Devon's situation was different again. Where Norfolk's alienation arose directly from the local supremacy of Suffolk, Devon's was caused by the judicial inadequacy of the regime, since both he and his opponents were to some extent backed by the centre.[152] Various pieces of evidence show the court attempting to maintain links with the earl, as well as with Lord Bonville, in the later 1440s.[153] More than this, it could

[148] *Letters of Margaret*, pp. 37–43; *PPC*, V, pp. 252, 255. I am most grateful to Dr Michael K. Jones for discussing his views of relations between the Beaufort brothers with me (see also Harriss 1988: pp. 336, 354–5). Note that Jones 1989a: pp. 294–5 doubts that there was any open breach between York and Somerset in the later 1440s.

[149] Norfolk was not even present at the duke's banishment, though Devon was (*RP*, V, p. 182). Both lords made loans of £100 to the crown in the autumn of 1449 and Devon actually took part in the government at that time (E403/777, mm. 4, 6; below, p. 243 n. 168). It is interesting to note that Suffolk voted for both Norfolk and Devon to join the knights of the garter in the 1445 chapter: Anstis (ed.), *Register of the Garter*, II, p. 130.

[150] The affinity was apparently kept in being by the duchess of Suffolk and Lord Scales. See *CFR, 1445–52*, pp. 154, 220; *PL*, II, pp. 176, 196, 206–8, 259 etc., and below, pp. 291 n. 134, 299 n. 163.

[151] Below, p. 291.   [152] Above, p. 204.

[153] It is therefore difficult to accept the model proposed by Cherry 1981a, viz. that Devon broadly enjoyed Beaufort support and Bonville broadly enjoyed De La Pole support. In general terms, there was no obvious divergence between 'Beaufort' and 'De La Pole' interests in the localities: see above, pp. 172ff. More specifically, the following connections between Devon and the court in the later 1440s can be noted: grants of the stewardship at the queen's coronation and the conservancy of the river Exe in 1445 (Cherry 1981b: p. 258); orders to various officers to see that Devon's £100 annuity was paid in autumn 1447 (*CCIR 1447–54*, pp. 3–4); Devon acting as a feoffee with Suffolk for Sir James Butler of Ormond in 1447 (Cherry, 1981a: p. 127); Devon's nomination as a future duchy feoffee in the 1448 will (Nichols, *Wills of the Kings and Queens*, p. 311); Devon's appointment to head a commission, including figures from the

scarcely be expected to do. Devon may have entertained designs of restoring the lost hegemony of his father's day, overturning the Bonville–Courtenay of Powderham alliance which had established rule in the South-West during his nonage, but it is not clear that the government was under any obligation to help him.[154] Its duty was to provide for local order and this would not necessarily have been better served by re-establishing comital rule in the county. There is no reason to assume that Devon harboured any special resentment against Suffolk's regime. He simply exploited the opportunities which the government's weakness left open to him. After 1450, these opportunities multiplied as the court disintegrated and the levels of local order declined. Rather as in the case of Norfolk, or, in fact, of York, Devon's 'opposition' had little to do with the rule of Suffolk and a great deal to do with the fact of its having collapsed.

That Suffolk's regime rested on the unspoken consent of the nobility is not, in the end, surprising. This is what had made it possible in the first place. The withdrawal of this consent presaged the downfall of the duke, but it did not cause it. It has already become evident that while the participation of the nobility was essential to the rule of the royal court, it did not necessarily make it strong. One reason for this has already received attention: the nobility could not effectively constitute royal power themselves. A second reason is that the essence of the normal contribution of the nobility to royal government was representation, but these lords – as they apparently began to realise in 1448 – were not representative. It would soon become clear that public opinion had diverged wildly from public policy, tearing the nobility in two and leading inexorably to the explosions of 1450. The time has come to discuss the final stages of Suffolk's uneasy rule and the birth of a dilemma which was to dog the lords throughout the ensuing decade.

THE DECLINE AND FALL OF SUFFOLK'S REGIME,
1448–1450

Towards the end of the decade, the court actually began to resemble the small body of household intimates and administrators depicted by its critics in 1450. During 1447 and 1448, the king roved about the realm,

exchequer and not Bonville, to act as assessors for all the lands of the duchy of Cornwall in Devon and Cornwall for twenty-one years from Michaelmas 1448 (*CPR, 1446–52*, p. 190: the matter of who was to enjoy influence over the local Duchy estates had been disputed between Bonville and the earl); Devon's numerous appearances at the council in 1449 (see figure 3).

[154] See Cherry 1979 and 1981a: pp. 125–9.

reaching as far north as Durham and as far west as Glastonbury, but spending only about a fifth of his time in or near London.[155] This new development may have any number of explanations: protecting the king from burgeoning discontent in the capital;[156] spreading the localised cost of victualling the household; exposing Henry and his queen to more of their subjects in the hope that this would dispel seditious talk;[157] warning the king of Scotland that he could not break the truce with impunity.[158] Its main result, however, may simply have been to reinforce a growing sense that royal authority was managed by a clique based in the household. Particularly in 1448, the king's itineration seems to have been accompanied by a decline in governmental activity and, more importantly, by a restriction of the governing circle. As ever, the absence of records makes judgements uncertain,[159] but it is interesting to note that in the handful of cases where we can see who was about the king in the spring and summer of 1448, it is household figures and especially those associated with the foundations project who predominate.[160] In fact, the foundations enjoyed something of a revival at this time and this may reflect an attempt to revive solidarity at the heart of the regime, or perhaps the retreat of king and household from public affairs.[161] Clearly enough, policy – notably over the problem of Brittany – continued to be made, but it seems legitimate to speculate that, at this stage, it was being made by a smaller number of men.[162]

[155] See Wolffe 1981: pp. 365–7 (cf. about 120 days in 1446 and upwards of 150 in 1445).

[156] See above, p. 231 n. 117 and Harvey 1991: pp. 30–2.

[157] Showing off the queen would have helped to lay to rest the possibly widespread idea that the king was either a born fool or still a child, as well as demonstrating the prospect of an heir: see Storey 1966: pp. 34–5 and KB9/997, m. 67 and 260, m. 85, for evidence of concern about the lack of an heir.

[158] Griffiths 1981: p. 409.

[159] A single file of 'Council and Privy Seal' material covers the period September 1446 to August 1448, for example (E28/77), and it is especially thin for 1448, mostly containing privy seal letters issued at Westminster with little evidence of how they were authorised. There is not much supplementary material in other sources: only in matters of grace was there much activity.

[160] E.g. the witnesses to a charter granting the king a garden in Cambridge, made by the prior of Anglesey Abbey (Cambs.) on 28 June, were the young duke of Exeter, Suffolk, Beaumont, Saye, Bishop Waynflete, Thomas Stanley and William Beauchamp (*CAD*, IV, A.6816). Exeter apart, these were all holders of household office or feoffees for the colleges. On 17 August, the king made a grant at Eton in the presence of Stafford, Beckington, Somerset (so in the document: he was actually in France), Suffolk, Stourton, Lyhart, Waynflete and Beauchamp of Powick (C266/60/59). All but Somerset and Stourton, treasurer of the household, were members of the Eton circle.

[161] Note that the king's 'will' (above, p. 214) was made in March 1448 (Nichols, *Wills of Kings and Queens*, p. 319) and that spending on the colleges revived in 1448–9 after a lull in 1445–7 (Knoop and Jones 1933: p. 78). See above, pp. 167ff for the significance of the foundations in general.

[162] See e.g. Wolffe 1981: pp. 199–209 and Keen and Daniel 1974 for accounts and explanations of English policy concerning France in 1448–9. Even at this stage, there is no need to assume that Suffolk and others were forming policies which were significantly

Contemporaries assumed that the new apartness of the court was the deliberate policy of its leaders,[163] but there are grounds for suggesting that it was actually the product of a voluntary and unlooked-for withdrawal on the part of leading noblemen. Personal abstention from national political activity was the characteristic way in which the late medieval nobility demonstrated disapproval of the government.[164] Although the lords had borne with the court for quite some time after the Tours policy had begun to show signs of failure, it is possible that the undignified events at Le Mans in early 1448 exhausted their patience. As troubles crowded in upon the regime during the rest of that year and the truce itself began to seem threatened, they were reluctant to get involved.[165] If war began again, it would be impossible to finance without recourse to parliament, and there was no reason to assume that that body would be sympathetic.

The abstention of the nobility can actually be demonstrated, because there are signs that, in the autumn of 1448, the remaining courtiers began to respond to the regime's worsening problems by taking steps to restore a more organised form of government. This meant an increase in records and, although these are difficult to interpret, it seems that a continual council was once again beginning to operate.[166] Predictably, there is no evidence of formal appointment: the last thing anyone wanted was a public measure which raised doubts about Henry's capacity to govern. The king went on answering requests for his grace much as before, and it seems possible that the more important policy initiatives, such as the assault on Fougères, were made according to the informal methods of recent years, but now without the support of noble counsel.[167] Low-key as this council may have been, its records do give us some insight into the personnel of government, and it is significant that, until the first session of

---

at variance with what other lords would have recommended. As Keen and Daniel demonstrate, the Fougères scheme was of a piece with earlier policy towards Brittany and the lords who attended parliament at Winchester knew of, and seemingly approved of, the assault on the town (pp. 382–3 and *passim*).

[163] Note Gascoigne's observation that at this time Lord Saye, the chamberlain, and others vetted all sermons to be preached before the king in order to ensure that they contained nothing derogatory to the king or his 'assistentes': *Loci e Libro*, p. 191. (The term 'assistentes' may evoke something of Henry's inadequacy, incidentally: above, p. 114.)

[164] Roskell 1956: pp. 189, 199 and generally.

[165] See above, pp. 233–4. For difficulties in Scotland and Ireland, see Griffiths 1981: pp. 409–10, 420–1. The deteriorating situation in France is discussed in *ibid.*, pp. 508–9.

[166] Much of its business was fiscal and judicial, but it seems also to have set about tackling the particular problems of the moment. See E28/77–8 generally (also for trouble in Wales in the latter part of 1448); and note E28/78/87 (appointment of sea-keepers against piracy); E28/78/103, 104, 106 (letters of 3 April 1449 to northern lords, the Calais garrison and those in the West Country who were to deal with the pirates).

[167] The king's grace continued to be subject to certain restraints, however: see above, p. 213.

Table 2   *Participation in the government, 1448–9*

	Attendance rates (man-days)
Autumn 1448[a]	
Bishops	42
Higher nobility	5
Barons and other laymen	15
Spring 1449[b]	
Bishops	72
Higher nobility	11
Barons and other laymen	16
Autumn 1449[c]	
Bishops	156
Higher nobility	31
Barons and other laymen	41

This table shows the rates of attendance of different groups of councillors in three periods drawn from the last years of Suffolk's regime.

[a] Data from 16 September to 10 December 1448 (ten 'council meetings' with records of attendance, where a 'council meeting' is defined as an occasion on which a decision is recorded as having been made 'per avisamentum consilii', or similar).

[b] Data from 27 January to 30 June 1449 (fifteen 'council meetings' with records of attendance).

[c] Data from 28 July to 20 December 1449 (thirty-nine 'council meetings' with records of attendance).

the 1449–50 parliament, members of the nobility were conspicuously absent.[168] In the meantime, more or less the only men prepared to take part in affairs were those who were so closely associated with the regime in the public imagination that it would have been impossible for them to avoid taking responsibility.[169] During the frantic spring and summer of

---

[168]   The fact that records of attendance were more assiduously kept may suggest that this council was regarded as a more important feature of the government than earlier gatherings of administrators. Figures for attendance are presented in tabular form in table 2. Note that if the duke of Suffolk is excluded, the attendance of the earls and dukes becomes even more disproportionately small: four, five and twenty man days, respectively. York, Buckingham and Salisbury were the only other men of this status to attend in the first two periods. Suffolk, Buckingham, Salisbury, Warwick, Wiltshire, Arundel and Devon were present in the third.

[169]   Most of the bishops who attended were notorious curialists and/or officers: Cardinal Kemp is the only major exception. Equally, if Dudley, Sudeley, Stourton, Saye, Thomas Stanley and John Say are removed from the figures for the barons and laymen, then the new figures for this group are seven, eight and seventeen, respectively, revealing that there was not much more commitment to the regime from among the lesser lay lords either.

1449, it was these men – the so-called clique of traitors, aided by Kemp and Cromwell – who struggled to meet the costs of defence as war first loomed and then became a reality.[170] They managed sessions of parliament; they despatched loan commissions to the provinces; they lent large sums of money themselves.[171] When, in mid-September 1449, Bishop Lumley left the treasury, he was succeeded by the chamberlain, James Fiennes, Lord Saye and Sele. This was perhaps because only someone from within the household could be induced to take the post at such an unpropitious moment.[172]

The parliament which met at Westminster and Winchester in the spring and summer of 1449 provided clear evidence of the widening gap between government and community. In response to requests for taxation, the commons pressed for a resumption of royal grants and made demands for better rule in all parts of the realm.[173] These postures can scarcely have encouraged the lords to resume their once-prominent role in Suffolk's regime. Most of them had, it is true, attended the parliament and taken part in discussions over policy, but this did not commit them in any way to what was decided.[174] Parliament, the solemn assembly of the kingdom's notables, provided a safe and public platform for intervention. No such freedom extended to normal government, where only the king's will bestowed public standing on his agents and advisers. The lords already knew how factitious was this will in reality. By 1449, they had made other unpleasant discoveries: chief among them, the fact that many in the realm believed that the king was in the thrall of advisers who sought only the satisfaction of their individual interests and not the common interest of the realm. The incidental accuracy of these perceptions may not have escaped the pillars of the Beaufort–De La Pole establishment as they reflected on the distribution of the king's judicial and material patronage: Henry had indeed been managed by a self-interested clique, albeit a clique headed by noblemen, public figures, whose corporate self-interest impersonated, if it did not represent, the common interest of the realm.[175] The point is that only part of this group – Suffolk, the

---

[170] See figure 3.   [171] Harriss 1986: pp. 167–9; *Town Chrons.*, pp. 124–5.
[172] Harriss 1986: p. 169.   [173] *RP*, V, p. 143; Harriss 1986: pp. 166–8.
[174] Present in the first session were Buckingham and Suffolk, Arundel, Devon, Salisbury and Oxford, Viscounts Bourgchier and Beaumont, Cromwell, Sudeley and eight other barons (evidence from Myers, 'Parliamentary Debate of 1449'; *RP*, V, p. 141). Present at the Winchester session were Suffolk, Warwick, Devon, Wiltshire and Worcester, Bourgchier and Beaumont, Cromwell, Sudeley and eight other barons (Griffiths, 'Winchester Session', p. 261n.).
[175] Note that of 169 recipients of grants of crown land, nine were great lords, seventy-four were full-time members of the household, fifteen were 'country' members of the household (king's esquires and so on) and twenty-two were crown officers of one kind or another (Wolffe 1971: pp. 107–9). This means that at least 120 out of the 169 were active participants in the administration.

household, and other prominent executives – had caught the public attention, because these were the men most continuously present about the king and active upon his behalf, especially in the period when the failure of the regime's policies was most clearly exposed. The lords' first response was to leave these men to face the music. They did not join the government. They refused both their money and their service as, in August 1449, Charles VII began his invasion of Normandy.[176]

We should not be too critical of the lords' behaviour. The approach of such a massive crisis was bound to have a paralysing effect, particularly as it was only by acting corporately to reform and support the government that the situation could be rescued. There was little to recommend or facilitate this sort of action: on the one hand, agreement over the best way to tackle the numerous problems facing the regime was unlikely; on the other, the whole point of court rule was that, whatever its compromises and half-truths, final responsibility for both policy and its execution was to lie with the king and the ministers he was thought to have appointed. It was probably becoming clear that Henry could not guarantee the safety of these men and, if this effectively invalidated the form of rule established (finally) in 1445, it scarcely created circumstances in which a new pattern of authority could be devised and imposed. Only when the bankruptcy of Suffolk's regime was absolutely plain was it possible, and indeed necessary, to build a government capable of deploying effective public authority in the changed environment of rule. In the event, as the next chapter will show, building such a government proved to be an impossible task, but the lords began to take up the challenge in the autumn of 1449.

The reasons for this change of heart are hard to fathom. Perhaps it was at this point that the plight of Henry's ministers had become too desperate to ignore. In any event, the lords' return to participation seems to have begun with a great council held at Sheen in late September.[177] This assembly is poorly documented, but, following it, a parliament was summoned and loan commissions were despatched to almost all the leading noblemen.[178] In the ensuing months, a number of lords beyond

---

[176] An intriguing anecdote included in Mathieu d'Escouchy's chronicle may represent, albeit in a somewhat stylised form, the mood of the nobility at this time (d'Escouchy, *Chronique*, pp. 299–300). It recounts how an earl, appointed to head an army going to the defence of Normandy, refuses to serve if he is only going to receive pay for three months instead of the normal twelve and tells the king so in front of Suffolk, adding that Henry should be careful as he is governed by traitors. See Griffiths 1981: pp. 514–20 for the problems experienced by the government in raising forces during 1449–50: no one of higher status than Lord Grey of Powys was prepared to go.

[177] According to Benet's Chronicle, this assembly was well attended and granted the king a large subsidy (p. 196). See Wolffe 1981: p. 368 and E404/66/172 for more information.

[178] *CClR, 1447–54*, pp. 160–1; *CPR, 1446–52*, pp. 297–9. The loan commissions were despatched to a broad group, including a number of figures whom historians have regarded as disaffected, such as Cromwell (Notts.), Norfolk (Norf.) and Devon (Devon

the immediate circle of government made loans to the crown and, from the opening of parliament in November, many of them attended council meetings.[179] The result was to transform the regime, tacitly replacing the rule of king and court with that of king and lords, the natural configuration of authority in a crisis.[180] If this transfer of government – in effect from household to council – raised questions about Henry VI's regality, these remained implicit: in part because the new form of rule was tentative and unannounced; in part because it coincided with parliament, in which the lords were normally and naturally prominent; and in part because the commons' diagnosis of the causes of misrule ignored the king altogether, focusing instead on the question of how he had been advised.

What position Suffolk held in the new government of late 1449 is far from clear, though we may be sure that the extent of his authority was determined by the lords alone and, indeed, by their perceptions of the broader political situation. Given the volatility of London in that terrible autumn, as Rouen fell to the French and the commons' schemes for fiscal reform made no progress, the lords' most pressing concern must have been the preservation of order and authority.[181] It was, as we shall see, something of an open question whether this was best achieved by repression or appeasement. It is likely that the commons and other figures claiming to represent *vox populi* were openly calling for justice upon Suffolk and other leading advisers, executives and members of the household.[182] Should they be given their way? Was there any choice? What would be the consequences of allowing parliament to scrutinise the recent

and Cornw.) and a large number of York's associates (e.g. William Browning (Dors.), William Ludlowe (Salop.), Sir John Scudamore, Sir John Barre and Thomas FitzHenry (Herefs.) etc.). The government plainly felt it could call upon the assistance of a wide spectrum of support (cf. Harriss 1986: p.169).

[179] For attendance at council meetings, see figure 3 and table 2, and n. 168, above. Examples of loans from lay noblemen include Sudeley and Arundel 100 marks each on 1 October (E403/777, m. 2), Wiltshire £100 on 16 October (m. 3), Grey of Ruthin 100 marks on 30 October (m. 3), Devon £100 on 18 November (m. 4), Norfolk £100 on 11 December (m. 6).

[180] For a contemporary reference to 'the rule of the lordes', see *Town Chrons.*, p. 128.

[181] *Town Chrons.*, pp. 125–6, 135. Note that it had been planned to hold the parliament in the Tower of London and, in the event, a great watch was kept in the city throughout its sessions: *ibid.*, pp. 105, 125; *Chrons. of London*, p. 158.

[182] Even before Cade's rebels and York popularised the idea of a clique of traitors, public opinion blamed misgovernment and defeat on a group of men and not Suffolk alone: e.g. Ayscough (Wright (ed.), *Political Poems*, II, p. 224, lines 11–12); Daniel, Noreys and Trevilian – the last of whom is identified as having a 'trayne' who blinded the king – (*ibid.*, p. 222, lines 13–14, p. 223, lines 1–2); Suffolk, Ayscough and Saye (*EHL*, p. 370); Thomas Kent, Saye, Daniel and Trevilian (Postan 1933: pp. 128 and 376–7 n. 60); Ayscough (KB9/996, m. 55, 260, m. 85); Ayscough, Saye, Dudley and Boulers (KB9/263, m. 64, KB27/755, m. 3). Bishop Moleyns, of course, was actually murdered before the attack on Suffolk began (9 January 1450: *English Chron.*, p. 64; *Collections*, p. 189). For the commons' attempts to indict other men besides Suffolk, see e.g. *Three Chrons.*, p. 66 (Saye and Daniel); Leland, *De Rebus*, p. 494 (all three 'and divers other').

workings of Henry's government? These questions are likely to have divided the lords, since not only were some probably more vulnerable to criticism than others, but there was also no obvious answer and no real source of lordship to impose agreement.[183] Even so, it was probably in the consciousness of a shared predicament that the lords acted. There is not much evidence of individual enmities and even less to suggest that it was these that prompted Suffolk's downfall.[184] In the circumstances of early 1450, even his closest friends were willing to desert him.[185]

We cannot know why the duke decided to confront the commons at the opening of the second session of parliament in January 1450. The murder of Bishop Moleyns two weeks earlier may have persuaded the government that a new initiative was necessary to contain a situation which was spiralling out of control, but whether Suffolk acted of his own volition or under pressure from his peers is not clear. In any event, the method he chose to defend himself from the comprehensive charges of the commons highlights the lords' dilemma. In the matter of ceding Maine, he said, 'other lordes were as privy therto as he': it was impossible for him to have done 'so grete thinges' without the co-operation of other men.[186] The truth of this is absolutely undeniable and, for the lords and other notables who had worked alongside Suffolk, his words must have been profoundly alarming, particularly as the duke appears to have been challenged to name the responsible parties if he wished to clear himself.[187] It was surely this consideration that disposed the lords to abandon the process of impeachment which the commons had demanded and, instead, to promote a settlement based on the king's grace.[188] The duke was to be

---

[183] It is unusual for anything less than unanimity to be recorded, but note, for example, that only 'the moost parte' of the lords agreed on 7 March that Suffolk should answer the commons' charges (*RP*, V, p. 179).

[184] Various lords have been named as particularly inimical to Suffolk: most famously Cromwell and Kemp, but also Sudeley and Beauchamp of Powick (see e.g. Storey 1966: pp. 47-8; Griffiths 1981: p. 286 for Cromwell, Kemp and Sudeley; Smith 1982: pp. 114-15 for Sudeley and Beauchamp). It is interesting to note that, at Winchester, in June 1449, Lords Sudeley and Cromwell had called for 'a goodd acord among the Lordes' (Griffiths, 'Winchester Session', p. 261), but it would be unwise to assume that this encouraged them to attack Suffolk. See above, p. 220, for the Tailboys affair, which is often supposed to have turned Cromwell against Suffolk. Wolffe 1981: pp. 222-3 provides some good reasons for not accepting the judgement of the pseudo-Worcester that the commons' attack on Suffolk was inspired and managed by Cromwell (*Letters and Papers*, II, ii, p. 766). Kemp may have been annoyed by the tussle over the see of London in 1448 (as suggested by Storey), but his nephew was victorious in this fairly typical case of Henry's muddled patronage (Wolffe 1981: p. 108) and there is nothing to suggest rancour in his behaviour towards Suffolk during the 1449-50 parliament.

[185] For example, Bishop Lyhert (see Griffiths 1981: p. 285 for Suffolk's role in his advancement) and Archbishop Stafford, who acted as arbitrators over Dedham between Suffolk and Fastolf in February 1450, and found for Fastolf: Smith 1984: p. 67.

[186] *RP*, V, p. 182.   [187] *HMC 3rd Rept, App.*, p. 279.

[188] The lords' reluctance to try Suffolk is suggested by various pieces of evidence: they were

banished untried, the 'misprisions' alleged against him, most of which dealt with matters of domestic government, left unanswered.[189] Damaging revelations were thus avoided by an intervention which could be laid on the shoulders of the king.[190] The statement that Henry had acted 'by his owne advis, and not reportyng hym to th'advis of his Lordes' should not, therefore, be taken as simple fact.[191] Once again, the lords were trying to hand the king a responsibility which was truly his. Once again, their efforts were only partially successful.[192] The people had already regarded Suffolk's transfer to custody in Westminster Palace as a release from confinement engineered by his affinity.[193] Now they continued proceedings against the duke and his allies outside parliament in the wave of risings and murders which marked the ensuing summer.[194] Popular support for 'punishing the traitors' provided a live constituency which York was able to exploit until 1452.

The crisis of 1450 exposed a complete divorce between, on the one hand, popular and 'communal', expectations of royal government – represented by the commons and the people of the towns and shires – and, on the other, the considerations which had, from the 1430s to about 1448, influenced the lords and others who had actually participated in that government. The principal concern of the commons was the familiar theme of the abuse of public money by the agents of the crown: specifically, a spoliation of the royal fisc which had led the king into an unjust dependence on taxation.[195] A second concern was the abuse of

unwilling to commit him to prison in the first place, though there is no question that they could have done so had they wished (*RP*, V, pp. 176–7); having heard his answers to the treason charges, they first postponed consideration of how to proceed for two days and even then 'was noo thyng doon in that matier' (*ibid.*, p. 182).

[189] *RP*, V, pp. 182–3. It seems likely that the account of Suffolk's replies to the commons' first bill in the roll of the parliament (13 March: p. 182) is highly abbreviated. The document in *HMC 3rd Rept, App.*, pp. 279–80, is a response to a lengthy refutation made by the duke (a 'booke', containing numbered articles). See Griffiths 1981: pp. 682–3 for more on this.

[190] This was emphasised in Beaumont's declaration: *RP*, V, p. 183, and above, p. 62, n. 266.

[191] Cf. e.g. Griffiths 1981: p. 682.   [192] See below, p. 253.

[193] See e.g. *English Chron.*, p. 69; *EHL*, p. 344; *PL*, II, p. 136.

[194] For the murders of Ayscough, Saye and Suffolk himself, the attacks on Boulers, Dudley, Beckington and Lyhert and the indictments of Kent and Edmund Grimston, see e.g. Harvey 1991: chs. 3–5. Note that 'proceedings' is hardly too forced a term in the light of the commissions demanded by Cade's rebels and the kangaroo court which tried the duke of Suffolk on board the Nicholas of the Tower: *ibid.*, pp. 92–3; Virgoe 1964–5.

[195] For the general context, see Harriss 1975: chs. VI and VII. Holmes 1975: pp. 63, 128 deals with the issue in the similar crisis of 1376. Its prominence in 1450 is shown by the explicit fiscal significance of all but three of the 'misprisions' of which Suffolk was accused, even those apparently designed to show treasonable dealings with the French (*RP*, V, pp. 179–81). The exceptions were arts. 15–17, which dealt with judicial matters: see next note. Storey 1966: p. 59 argues plausibly that the misprisions should

royal justice, which had produced a disrespect for the law and a consequent decline of public order.[196] In these areas, together with the all too obvious matter of the disasters in France, the government had failed in its duty to the *communitas regni*. It had done so, according to the commons' diagnosis, because of the comprehensive accroachment of royal power by the covetous duke of Suffolk and his train.[197]

This accroachment was the more easily identifiable because the commons appear to have believed that royal government ought to have been conducted in association with some sort of formal council. A central theme of their accusations is that Suffolk had time and again gone behind the backs of 'the Lordes of your Counseill' to 'stir and move' or otherwise 'cause' the king to do things according to his own particular will.[198] Two specific examples show the difference between the commons' perceptions regarding the distribution of power and what we know to have been the case. In article 6 (and implicitly in articles 4, 7 and 8), the duke was condemned for persuading the king to make grants of patronage in France and Normandy to unsuitable people 'withoute deliberation and avyse of youre Counseill', but since 1437, and by ancient tradition, such grants were conventionally expected to be made at the king's grace, *de mero motu suo*. Similarly, Suffolk was accused of having, in 1445, 'caused by his motion, withoute the knowyng or assent of the Lordes of your Counseill, the [French] Ambassatours to have a pryve communication with you oonly aparte, none of youre Counseillours save hym self therto assentyng' (article 9). In fact, this is unlikely to have been true, but, in any case, on what authority could the lords of the 'Counseill' have presumed to assent to a royal decision to meet the ambassadors alone? It is just possible that, by 'counseillours', the commons meant the sort of informal counsel a king was expected to take, but, if so, it is strange that they laid all the blame for the frustration of this dialogue on the duke, leaving the king himself unscathed. The otherwise comparable charges against Gaveston in 1308 leave the reader in no doubt as to the willing complicity of the king in the favourite's activities.[199] The impression created by the

---

be taken as a more significant revelation of the commons' concerns than the treason charges, which were drawn up to secure the duke's destruction if convicted.

[196] See arts. 15–17 for the duke's alleged manipulation of the agencies of justice and of the appointment of sheriffs (*RP*, V, p. 181) and the petition regarding the Tailboys case for a critique of the king's failure to keep peace and justice (*ibid.*, p. 200). Like finance, this issue had arisen in the spring parliament as well: see above, at n. 173.

[197] 'Covetise' was actually taken to be the main motive for Suffolk's treasons, interestingly: see arts. 1, 3 and 7 (*RP*, V, pp. 177–9) and above, pp. 40–2.

[198] E.g. art. 1 (*RP*, V, p. 179) and a host of instances of 'subtill Counseill, importune and unprofitable labour', 'sotill meanes and sinistre suggestions', 'untrue suytes and Counseill', 'excityng and false avertisment' on pp. 179–80.

[199] Wilkinson 1948–58: III, pp. 364–5.

assault on Suffolk is that Henry VI, for whatever reason, was expected to rule in association with a formal council and that the essence of the duke's crime, therefore, was the circumvention of this body.[200]

These perceptions were poles apart from those of the lords, with which we have been most concerned. The complexities of the transfer of jurisdictions which took place between 1435 and 1445 were invisible to the commons. They were used to dealing with a royal power mediated through ministers and noblemen: as Bishop Russell would later point out, it was not for them to deal with the king face to face.[201] The importance of the king's ultimate freedom from counsel, central to the informal and private structures of representation which dominated national politics while parliament was not in session, was lost on the gentry when they met together as representatives of the *communitas*: then, they asked only for economical, responsive and effective rule. The evidence of local disorder, military defeat and financial mayhem led them to believe that the king was not being properly counselled. In fact, as we have seen, this was not the case: until about 1448, at least, the king was being advised by the right people and in more or less the right way.

Two things made this invisible to the commons. The first was the fact that, from 1444–5 at the latest, government ostensibly proceeded from the king's personal will, located in his household where Suffolk all too obviously prevailed. The private means of the duke's authority were indefensible in the public context evoked by the commons. The court connection which he had built and maintained with such care over fifteen years as a means of translating royal authority into the irresistible action of government now appeared to be little more than a syndicate for the organised exploitation of the royal estates. We know that household power could not have been exercised without the consent of the nobility, but this was not obvious to MPs. In formal terms, the deeds of the king's servants, which had had such destructive results, had been authorised by Henry alone. When the king was not manifestly a man of strong character and the nobility, seeing the failure of policy, had withdrawn, Suffolk was left to take responsibility for what looked like an open-and-shut case of wicked counsel.

The second cause of the commons' misconceptions was the failure of the nobility to carry out their representative functions properly. Between parliaments – and even, to some extent, during them – the presentation of the counsel of the realm to the king was the task of the lords. It was

---

[200] As will be becoming clear, this well-publicised assumption has profoundly influenced historians' accounts of Henry VI's reign and, to some extent, of the later medieval political system.

[201] See above, p. 78, n. 327.

through their action that the protection of the interests of the *communitas regni* was normally achieved. Although the majority of lords had succeeded in protecting the interests of their followers and so, in an indirect way, guaranteed the peace and harmony of areas indisputably under their jurisdiction, this was not enough to prevent landowners in some parts of the country – East Anglia, the South-West, and now, notoriously, Kent and Lincolnshire – suffering unacceptable levels of injustice and disorder. Moreover, if judicial interests were partly met, then the less pressing concerns of the non-noble classes were disregarded: no voice was given to what must have been a mounting dissatisfaction with the composition of the government, with its policies and with its dubious use of public money. When the nobility became aware of this rising anger, Gloucester apart, their response was not to make the criticisms which their representativeness demanded, but to withdraw. If this seems a dereliction of duty, as York, quite hypocritically, was soon to suggest, it was not altogether an unjustified one.[202] What distracted the nobility from the fulfilment of their normal role was the highly abnormal and absorbing responsibility for creating and defending the authority of Henry VI which had fallen on their shoulders. This altered their priorities: after all, as we have seen, the preservation of the king's authority was the first and most basic interest of the *communitas regni*; if it was not upheld, no other interests could be truly satisfied.[203] As a result, the lords about the king had given the best part of their attention to the demanding procedures and principles which maintaining his authority required of them, hoping, all the time, that this would produce the good government the realm desired. No one can blame them for backing away when it became clear that the requirements of preserving the king and those of preserving the realm had sharply diverged. The real fault lay with King Henry, who alone could reconcile the will of government with the counsels of his people.

CONCLUSION

Once again, the fundamental problem in the polity of Henry VI can be shown to be one of authority. This was both the making of Suffolk's regime and the destruction of it. The duke was no invincible favourite, backed by royal wilfulness. Had he been, the circumstances of 1450 would have been much simpler and the position of the nobility totally different. The duke's power rested purely on the acceptance by a number of great men that, through his agency, Henry's personal rule could be made to work. So it was that, as the commons of 1450

202 BL Add. MS 48031A, fol. 126r (1450): see below, p. 273.
203 Above, pp. 43–6.

perceived, the fundamental commitment of Suffolk's regime was to keeping itself in being. In both financial and political terms this was costly: the distribution of Henry's patrimony among the men on whom his government relied consumed the fisc and, in the process, undermined the political estate of the crown and its agents; the foundations, which drew the administration together, were indeed 'over chargefull and noyus'; the arrangements at the exchequer which such a regime necessitated guaranteed disaster if war broke out anew; policies of restraint, finally, were doomed when it was the basis of the regime's power which they restrained.[204]

Suffolk's whole method of constituting rule was also, arguably, self-defeating. Medieval kings did not govern by appeasement. They maintained loyalty through the exercise of will in accordance with the simple framework of royal authority. Under Suffolk's direction Henry VI was effectively paying for what should have come to him freely. The prominence of patronage in the criticism of 1450 was not the consequence of its mismanagement by Suffolk, but testimony to the fact that, under him, royal lordship had finally amounted to little else. It should have been offering much more. The crisis of 1449–50 demonstrated forcibly the real, public, responsibilities of the regime and how they had not been met. Real government involved decisive intervention which could not but clash with the whole process of buying support. Real government was real patronage, because it was real lordship, which is to say it dealt with the individuals on whose support it depended with a perspective formed by the needs of society at large: it reconciled the individual interest with the common interest. 'Patronage', in the sense that it is normally meant by historians of the later middle ages, was not the basis of royal authority and it could not be: it did not confer real authority; it did not, as an approach to managing power, permit the exercise of governance. Suffolk's regime provides the perfect proof.

The problem with the government of the 1440s, therefore, was not Suffolk, but Henry. Throughout the decade, evidence accumulates to show that the king simply lacked the independence of will to make authoritative decisions and that this frustrated all forms of government which were focused upon him. Something of this is revealed by Sir John Fastolf's 'instructions' to Somerset, drafted in March 1448, shortly before the duke's departure to take up his lieutenancy.[205] What

---

[204] Quotation from *RP*, V, p. 218. Note that Lumley continued to give priority to the satisfaction of existing obligations (in order to restore exchequer credit and to maintain the political support of creditors) even when the military crisis demanded the wholesale redirection of funds: Harriss 1986: pp. 165–71.

[205] *Letters and Papers*, II, ii, pp. 592–4.

concerned the old soldier was not questions of strategy, but the importance of ensuring adequate support among the duke's friends remaining in England, 'that thei may, in youre absence, laboure and quyte hem truly unto you … in supportacion of the kingis righte and of youre trouthe, yff any charge in tyme comyng myghte be ymaginede ayenst you'. 'And,' he added, 'that ye purveie you of wise and sadde counseile in this royalme of soche as may, can or dare done for you in youre absence'.[206] Little, evidently, was to be expected from the constancy of Henry VI.

This preoccupation with matters which should have been wholly the concern of domestic government – really the basic duties owed by any lord to his servant – is very significant. The government did not, could not, protect its agents. No one embarked upon major military or governmental commissions without negotiating long and detailed articles of service.[207] Public acts of recognition were famously required in 1440, 1444, 1446, 1447, 1448 and 1450 in order to ensure that full responsibility for the authorised actions of his agents was bestowed upon the king.[208] Not one of these acts was entirely successful in this.[209] The duke of Somerset sent a credence to the spring parliament of 1449, warning the nation of the inevitability of defeat if the war should resume, fearing that his silence would lead to criticisms of him.[210] The duke of York, writing from Ireland, where he stood destitute of funds, asked the earl of Salisbury to have his letter published in parliament for his excuse in time to come.[211] None of this should have been necessary. The king should have been able to guarantee these men personally what they asked. Instead, they were reduced to the circumstances of the minority, without the benefits conferred by the patent emergency of an infant king: having to ensure maximum publicity for what they did and hoping that they could muster enough support to avoid criticism when things went

---

[206] *Ibid.*, p. 592.

[207] For examples, see *Letters and Papers*, II, i, pp. lxvi–lxxi (Warwick in 1437), ii, pp. 585–91 (York in 1441), pp. 592–4 (articles suggested by Fastolf for Somerset in 1448); *PPC*, V, pp. 251–6 (Somerset in 1443) and, for a comparison, *PPC*, V, pp. 299–300 (the terms set by Cromwell for resigning the treasurership!).

[208] These were, respectively, the declaration regarding the release of Orléans (above, p. 188), the appointment of Suffolk to the embassy of 1444 (p. 195), the declaration of the lords in the 1445–6 parliament (pp. 223–4), the declaration of Suffolk's probity concerning Maine (p. 232), letters patent for Matthew Gough and Fulk Eyton, retrospectively licensing their part in the surrender of Maine (*DKR*, XLVIII, p. 378) and Beaumont's declaration concerning Suffolk's banishment (p. 248).

[209] Suffolk was held responsible in every case by the commons of 1449–50, while Gough was murdered by Cade's rebels (Basin, *Histoire*, II, p. 169; *Brut*, p. 519).

[210] *RP*, V, pp.147–8. The petition of Richard Bokeland, treasurer of Calais until July 1436, to have it enacted of record that he persistently and dutifully petitioned the (infant) king to have repairs made to the fortifications provides a parallel: SC8/96/ 4768.

[211] Brewer and Bullen (eds.), *Cal. of Carew MSS*, VI, pp. 258–9.

wrong.[212] The combination of private means and public duties, which was the normal basis for the execution of later medieval government, could not function under these circumstances. The system demanded that there was no doubt about the downward flow of authority around which it was built. Suffolk's service, as what one might call 'lieutenant and governor general of England', was as vulnerable to this reality as anyone else's: the more so, because it was presented as resting on a private royal authority which did not actually exist.[213]

The events of 1450 must finally have convinced the lords of this. Henry VI, twenty-eight years old and married, could not bestir himself to save his kingdom of France, could not impose law upon his people, could not take responsibility for the authorised actions of his ministers and servants. The fall of Suffolk was also, in a sense, the fall of the king himself: the ending of the personal authority of the monarch as an effective source of jurisdiction, and the collapse of the court as a medium for its transmission. There was no going back to the solutions of the 1430s, however. Besides the interests of the king and the common interest of the lords, the two factors which had so far governed the manufacture of central authority, there was now a third factor to be considered: the common interest of the realm, brought to the fore in 1449–50 by dissidents, rebels, the commons in parliament and the duke of York. Ultimately, of course, it was for the king to represent the common weal, but this was no easy matter when the king himself required to be represented by the lords. It was no longer open to the nobility to make arrangements for the disposal of power among themselves and away from the public gaze: excluded interests had a broad new constituency to which they could appeal. Under these new conditions, the Beaufort–Suffolk consensus lost its territorial monopoly and fell in upon itself as the royal authority ceased to be concentrated in a manageable unity. The descent into anarchy began.

[212] Apart from the fact that they *acknowledged* the inability of the king to express his authority, there is not much to choose between the articles and disclaimers mentioned in nn. 207–11, above, and the public fabrications of rule in the parliaments of 1422, 1433 and, during the king's madness, 1454: *RP*, IV, pp. 174–6, 422–4; *RP*, V, pp. 240–3.

[213] It is interesting to see 'custodiam personae nostrae' listed among Suffolk's services in 1447 (*Foedera*, V, i, p. 177). This seems rather beyond the normal duties of a household officer under an adult king.

Appendix A

THE DATING OF THE '1444' ORDINANCES

I am now inclined to doubt whether the references to the 'kynges counsail' which appear in the document can be used, as I used them in Watts 1991, to limit the possible range of dates: as suggested above (n. 19), distinctions between lords of the 'counsail' and others may be harder to interpret than I had thought and do not necessarily indicate the existence of a council on the model of 1437–9 or 1441–4. It follows that these ordinances could have been drawn up at any time in the late 1430s or 1440s, with the result that more weight should probably be given to the cluster of evidence assembled in favour of 1444 (notably by Wolffe 1981: pp. 114–15) than I suggested in my article. Even so, the administrative evidence is far from clear. It is true that surviving royal letters to the chancellor sent under the signet in May and August 1444 and at various times in 1447–8 either suggest that the privy seal had, as the ordinances propose, become the normal warrant for the great seal in matters of grace or, at least, that the signet had become an unusual one (C81/1370/11, 13, 43, 50, 53, 55 etc., and note also a 1445 letter from a petitioner to the keeper of the privy seal, mentioned in n. 50, above: 'Uppon which I wold have sewed a secret lettre for your warant but the Secretarie is not here'). Even so, a letter of September 1444 has the chancellor dragging his feet over a warrant under the privy seal and yet this ought, according to the ordinances, have been perfectly sufficient (C81/1370/8). Similarly, all but two of the explicit references in signet letters to ordinances like those of 1444 (e.g. 'restraintes late made by thadvis of you and othere lordes of oure counseil' – C81/1370/17; October 1444) involve cases in which warrants under the privy seal were affected. These sources must therefore be referring to a different document, since the ordinances under discussion here did not affect privy seal warrants in any way. The two exceptions mentioned above are (1) an order of 19 March 1444 to accept a bill endorsed with the sign manual as a warrant, notwithstanding 'eny act restraint or commandement made or yeven by us or by oure counsail'

(C81/1373/10: this could refer to the content of the grant, which was to King's College, Cambridge, and not to the mode of authorisation); and (2) a signet warrant to the chancellor, dated 2 September 1448, which contains the words, 'make no difficulte or delay in thexpedicion of this matere notwithstanding that ye have no warant under oure prive seel therupon to you directed according to thappointment or act therupon late made' (C81/1371/1). This second example may mean a later dating for our ordinances, though the fact that the sentence continues with the words 'or any other appointement, ordinance or restreint into the contrary made in any wise', may invite the conclusion that measures of this kind were introduced on a number of occasions.

Appendix B

THE POSITIONS OF CERTAIN LEADING TERRITORIAL LORDS IN RELATION TO THE COURT

Beaumont

Chief steward of the queen's household from 1446 (Harriss 1953: p. 398), Beaumont was well placed in court circles. He received the joint custody of the Channel Islands with Sudeley on Gloucester's death (*CPR, 1446–52*, p. 42) and, upon his own petition in 1448, the remarkable liberty of return of writs on all his lands (E28/78/17). For the favourable treatment he received in the Tailboys dispute, see above, p. 220.

Buckingham

Humphrey Stafford seems to have spent a lot of time at court in this period (see figure 3). His captaincy of Calais does not seem to have absorbed his interests: he did not install his own supporters in the garrison (Rawcliffe 1978: p. 75), and may never have gone there (a stray account shows that he was not there during the entire year 1446–7, for example: E101/54/8). He made much use of his residence at Tonbridge and it is interesting to note that the lands he acquired on the death of Gloucester were also in Kent, conveniently situated for access to the court (Rawcliffe 1978: p. 67; *CPR, 1446–52*, pp. 45, 67). Buckingham was appointed trier of petitions in all three of the parliaments of 1447–9 (*RP*, V, pp. 129, 141, 171) and witnessed over 75% of royal charters issued during 1446–9, inclusive (see C53/189–90, *passim*, for all references to charter witness-lists in this note). He was not a major recipient of grants in this period, but his choice of associates for land conveyances suggests good relations with others in the court and household: *CPR, 1446–52*, pp. 78 (Dorset, Sudeley and Saye – 1447), 245 (Suffolk, Stafford, Alnwick, Lovell, Cromwell, Sudeley – 1447); *CClR, 1447–54*, pp. 51 (Sudeley and Beauchamp of Powick – 1448), 95–6, 110, 136–7 (Tresham, Suffolk, Tuddenham – 1448).

Cromwell

Lord Cromwell continued to be an important figure in court circles up to about 1448. He was a trier of petitions in all the parliaments 1445–49/50 (*RP*, V, pp. 67, 129, 141, 171). His removal from the treasury did not diminish his access to grants (e.g. *CPR, 1441–6*, pp. 325, 367, 461; *CFR, 1445–52*, pp. 11–12, 25). He was a feoffee for Arundel, York and Exeter (senior) between 1446 and 1449 (E28/77/26; *CPR, 1461–7*, pp. 44–5; *CPR, 1446–52*, p. 124; E28/79/3; *CPR, 1441–6*, p. 454). The alienation which may have sprung from Cromwell's difficulties with William Tailboys should not be antedated or overemphasised: see above, pp. 220, 247.

Dorset

For his participation in government in these years (especially in 1446), see figure 3. He was fairly well rewarded at home (Jones 1982: pp. 16–18; Harriss 1988: pp. 356–7), but his main interest and purpose at this time was in France, where he secured sizeable compensations for the loss of Maine, including, of course, the lieutenancy (Jones 1989a: pp. 291–4). In recognition of his service, Dorset was elevated to the dukedom of Somerset in March 1448 (*HBC*, p. 482).

Exeter

John Holland (d. 1447) was summoned to both the councils of autumn 1446 (E28/77/3 and 15) and was a trier of petitions in the parliaments of 1445–6 and 1447 (*RP*, V, pp. 67, 129). He was an occasional attender at councils, but a frequent charter witness (two-thirds of those issued in 1445 and 1446). The king was twice at Berkhamsted during his tenure of it (Wolffe 1981: pp. 364–5). Something of Exeter's favoured position emerges from the arrangements made for his son, Henry. In 1446 and 1447, he was included as survivor in his father's (life) offices of admiral and constable of the Tower (*CPR, 1441–6*, p. 405; *CPR, 1446–52*, p. 32). In September 1448, though still a minor, he was granted two-thirds of his father's 500 mark annuity on the customs: *CPR, 1446–52*, p. 201. For further information showing Exeter's rewards and associations with other leading members of the regime, see Stansfield 1987: pp. 220–5.

Salisbury

Richard Neville continued to prosper. In return for his surrender of grants of land made as recently in 1447, Salisbury was, in 1449, able to convert his life-stewardship of Richmondshire into a grant of the Yorkshire lands of the honour in tail male (*CPR, 1446–52*, pp. 281–2). It is surely a sign of Salisbury's influence that the lands he surrendered were promptly leased to his son for forty years (*CFR, 1445–52*, p. 131). The earl had also obtained control of the lands of his brother, George, Lord Latimer, as early as December 1449, even though a formal grant was not made until June 1451 (E159/227, comm., Mic., rot. 5; *CPR, 1446–52*, p. 430; Latimer was supposedly an idiot). Other grants included the keeping of parts of the lordship of Kendal in Westmorland in 1446 (*CFR, 1445–52*, pp. 14–15), a share in the Beauchamp wardship later in the year and various grants from the northern customs to secure the payment of his wages as warden of the West March, an office in which he was confirmed until the 1470s (*CPR, 1446–52*, pp. 1, 284, 184). Salisbury was a trier of petitions in 1445, 1447 and autumn

1449 (*RP*, V, pp. 67, 129, 171) and a witness to over 80% of charters in the years 1445–9. See also Pollard 1990: pp. 249–50.

Shrewsbury

Not a major participant in government because of his frequent absences, Shrewsbury was certainly associated with the regime. During his tenure of the lieutenancy of Ireland, to which he was promptly appointed following his return to England in the spring of 1445, he appointed Edmund Hampden and John Wenlock, both household men, constables of Dublin during his lieutenancy of Ireland (Pollard 1968: pp. 133, 135). He was named as a future feoffee for the colleges in 1448 (Nichols, *Wills of the Kings and Queens*, p. 311) and he was a witness to nearly every charter in 1446 (C53/189).

7

THE SEARCH FOR AUTHORITY, 1450–61

I N THE SUMMER OF 1436, when the English stronghold at Calais was threatened by the duke of Burgundy, Henry VI's government wrote to various notables that it would 'caste this lande oute of alle reputacion and in to perpetuelle reproche, vilonye and shame thorgh the world yf so fell – as with oure lordis mercy it never shall falle – that it were getyn by oure ennemys for lak of covenable defense in tyme'.[1] Exactly this fate descended upon the king's ministers in 1449–50 and for much the same reasons. Turning too late to the widest public forum for aid, the remaining participants in Henry VI's regime had opened the way for the expression of massive public resentment. As we have seen, the resulting crisis drew the lords back to the centre in a last-ditch effort to preserve public authority. Having accepted the presentation of charges against Suffolk and agreed to his removal, they then stood together to resist any further attempts at criticism or reform. For many of Henry's other subjects, however, this was not enough. The duke's escape without trial simply lent support to the widespread idea that the king was surrounded by wicked men who used his power to keep themselves beyond the reach of justice.[2] Popular anger exploded in the well-known wave of risings which swept across south-eastern England in the spring and summer of 1450 and went on unabated throughout the rest of the year.[3] More disconcertingly still, from the point of the view of the government, it emerged that landowners were not unsympathetic to the views of popular critics: as Somerset was to discover in the autumn of 1450, the *leitmotiv* of Cade's rebels – judgement on the clique of traitors in the royal household – found support among the commons in parliament.[4] So it was that, in

---

[1] BL, Add. MS 14,848, fol. 190r. The king's fears had been echoed by Somerset, with reference to Normandy, in 1449: *RP*, V, p. 148.

[2] See above, p. 248.

[3] Harvey 1991 supplies the fullest treatment.

[4] See *ibid.*, pp. 190–1, for the centrality of this theme in the rebellion, and below, pp. 273ff, for the parliament of 1450–1.

the succeeding years, the presence of a critical public became the over-whelming feature of high politics. The primary task for Henry VI's noble subjects remained, as it had always been, the creation of effective rule at both local and national levels, but this task was made far more difficult by the extensive loss of confidence in royal government, the associated problem of disorder and the emergence of divisions of opinion concerning the best way to rescue the situation.

Views on how to restore public authority had already begun to diverge by 1450. The implication of popular criticism, which had been steadily growing since the mid-1440s, was that just and lasting order could only be created by realigning the government with the common weal as it was identified and expressed by the *communitas* itself. After all, as one of Suffolk's murderers reputedly pointed out, 'crown' and 'communitas' were essentially the same thing.[5] The characteristic posture of the government itself, on the other hand, was that order, authority and therefore, in a sense, all public interests depended first and foremost on obedience to the king and his ministers. Clearly enough, both points of view had some degree of right on their side. Each gave emphasis to a different aspect of the royal office and this, in itself, draws attention to the fact that the lords should not have had to choose between one and the other. They were forced to consider doing so for two reasons. One is that the duke of York, backed by what appeared to be a significant public following, openly and forcefully took up the first of these positions, while the duke of Somerset, supported by the rump of Suffolk's regime, took up the second. The other reason is rather more complicated.

As we have seen, it was only in the person of a properly functioning king that the right to rule and the representation of the *communitas* could be fully reconciled. Henry VI, however, was unable to convince his subjects that the men who ruled in his name were doing so at his will, or, to put it another way, that the will which authorised government was in any way greater than the sum of the parts of that government. This explains why the myth of the 'traitors', once publicised, never went away: whatever their good intentions, all Henry's governments were indeed cliques manipulating the king; they really had, in the fourteenth-century phrase, 'accroached the royal power'.[6] At the same time, Henry's lack of will-power meant that any lord who professed loyalty to him, and who could gather behind him enough of the tokens of representativeness – above all, the backing of the nobility – could assert, and sometimes obtain, a greater authority than the king's ministers. These men, gathered about the king in the household and departments of state, might normally

---

[5] Virgoe 1964–5: p. 499; and see above, p. 22.
[6] See above, pp. 21, 78.

expect to have first claim on the execution of royal will; but as it came to be believed that there *was* no independent royal will, their claims faltered. For most of the 1450s, then, the rights of loyalist rebels and royalist ministers to execute the authority of Henry VI were approximately equal: only public support could determine who should rule. These were the parameters for the unstable politics of the decade: a persisting need to satisfy public opinion in order to secure authority; and a nobility who were united only by their common interest in the preservation of order and by their misplaced belief that allegiance to Henry VI was the only way of achieving it.

The price of this allegiance was the difficult task of incorporating the ineffectual king in the management of his polity. The fall of Suffolk was a dramatic demonstration of the inadequacy of Henry's personal authority. It drove leading men to accept that a regime deriving primarily from the person of the king and located in the royal household was unlikely to regain public confidence or to keep it for long. The explicit participation of the greater nobility in government was patently essential if the *communitas* was to be convinced that Henry was both properly counselled and free to make impartial judgements. In practice, this meant the restoration of some sort of council, as Henry's ministers conceded in September 1450.[7] However, while critical circumstances provided some justification for such a step, the fact remained that conciliar rule was difficult to reconcile with the natural authority of an adult king. A return to the extensive provisions of the 1420s and early 1430s would be a public recognition that Henry was incompetent to govern: a dangerous step to take in the midst of a crisis of public order. Such a move would also mean a major role for the duke of York, whose pre-eminent right in blood and landed power could scarcely be gainsaid. Even before his support for justice upon the 'traitors' made him unacceptable to many of those about the king, York was a doubtful choice for leadership of the king's government. The very factors which made him the most important person in Henry's battered polity made him the man most likely to try to end it.

Rather than risk further disruption, the obvious answer was to revert to a tacit compromise on the model of the early 1440s, with the king discharging 'grace' and a council attending to matters of state. This configuration was no more likely to create a platform for truly authoritative and effective government than it had ever been, but it had two advantages: it was familiar; and it was, after a fashion, already in being. Its disadvantages, even so, were many. It would not work without some sort of co-ordinating lordship, yet none was immediately available in the

---

[7]   Below, p. 272.

vacuum left by Suffolk. The commitment and participation of noblemen, though essential to the success of the system, was as unenforceable as ever: in periods of tension, as we have seen, the lords were apt to withdraw, leaving the regime's leaders and executives vulnerable. If too many lords gathered at the centre, on the other hand, the government's authority and integrity might be easily lost, as the corporate, but wavering, body of the peerage reabsorbed the power to execute the king's authority. Something of this kind had already happened in the autumn of 1449, leaving the crown almost helpless before the onslaughts of the following year. The pattern was to be repeated time and again in the ensuing decade. Meanwhile, because the balance between the conciliar and the royal had to be struck sufficiently in favour of the latter for a semblance of normality to be maintained, a government of the early 1440s kind continued to face the familiar problems stemming from active but incompetent kingship. Among the most crippling of these has already been mentioned: the fact that the authorising claim to be acting on the king's behalf was not restricted to the councillors. Anyone asserting a public interest could argue that he or she was acting for the king: it was the balance of political forces which, in every case, would determine who possessed the authority to speak for the crown. Another major difficulty was that the activation of the king meant, in effect, the activation of the household, whose members had the easiest access to the well-spring of authority. This was not, as we shall see, a wholly negative development, but, while the mood of 1450 persisted, it created a significant liability for any regime by undermining its professions of independence and propriety.

One way of resolving the quandary facing the lords would have been to remove Henry VI altogether. In the light of his conspicuous and repeated failure to fulfil even the most basic duties of his office, could he not have been deposed? As later events suggest, this was probably the only real solution to the problems facing the magnates; but a host of factors ruled it out of consideration at this time. Deposition was hard enough to effect and defend when the ruler was demonstrably violent or faithless like Edward II and Richard II. Henry VI could not be presented in these terms: even the victorious Edward IV barely attempted as much.[8] In any case, no grounds for deposition had been prepared. Little had been done to counter the public assumption that Suffolk and the traitors were responsible for the

---

[8]   The schedule which announced the new king's title in the parliament of 1461 focused on the disorder which England experienced under Henry's unrightful rule (e.g. *RP*, V, p. 464). Only in 1460 had the king himself been actively at fault, showing 'fraude and malicious disceit' in orchestrating York's destruction and having the duke 'tyrannously' murdered (*ibid.*, p. 466).

misrule of the 1440s and this perspective left the king unscathed, a helpless victim, like his subjects, of the men in his household. Abdication – in some ways an obvious answer for a king who, as John Rous put it, was 'little given to the world and its works'[9] – would surely have foundered on the familiar problem of Henry's overflexible will: until he died, it would always be in someone's interests to bring the king out of retirement.[10]

In many ways, drastic solutions were not the answer to the problems of 1450: despite the popular ferment, civil order had not entirely broken down among the landed classes and this must have inclined the lords to a more conservative range of solutions. They had enough to do without adding to their troubles by attempting to remove the divinely appointed head of the body politic. Later, as political control deteriorated and divisions hardened, more radical action became feasible, although – as we shall see – it was not until 1455, or even 1461, that the king himself was seriously challenged. One factor in this, which must also have borne upon the lords' thinking in 1450, was that no clear successor to Henry VI existed.[11] If, in the early years of the decade, Richard of York, grandson of Edmund of Langley, had the best claim to succeed Henry, he did not have the only one: Margaret Beaufort, the niece of the duke of Somerset, and Henry Holland, duke of Exeter, possessed titles likely to find some support.[12] These claims may have been outflanked by York's other, and more famous, title to the throne – through his descent from Lionel of Antwerp, Edward III's second son – but this, of course, raised other problems. Not only did it pass through a woman, but also, and more importantly, it directly challenged the legitimacy of the Lancastrian kings, who derived their title from Edward's third son. For this reason, it was quite unusable without placing the duke in conflict with the entire political

[9] Above, p. 103 n. 3.

[10] This was, of course, the major reason why 'the English killed their kings': see Lewis 1985c: pp. 191–2. It is worth remembering that Edward IV, who allowed King Henry to live on in retirement between 1465 and 1470, paid a heavy price for his leniency.

[11] A point made by Wolffe 1981: p. 219.

[12] See Griffiths 1991i for more on the various claims. Note that the argument in *ibid.*, pp. 89ff that York and his claim were deliberately set aside by the Lancastrian government has been questioned by e.g. Jones 1989a: pp. 289–90. It is interesting to note that in the copy of Christine de Pisan's treatise on chivalry which the earl of Shrewsbury presented to the queen in 1445, York is depicted together with Gloucester as joint supporters of a Lancastrian genealogical table: Byles (ed.), *Book of Fayttes of Armes*, p. xvii, and see Griffiths 1981: pl. 1, for an illustration. The Holland claim depended on the assumption that, following the precedent of 1377 (and not 1199), the succession ought to devolve upon the progeny of John of Gaunt before moving on towards Edward III's younger sons. Even so, it was rather weak: not only was it through a woman, but it ought to have taken second place to the claims of those descended from Henry IV's elder sister, namely, the kings of Portugal. The Beaufort claim had been mentioned (and denounced) in the 1449–50 parliament: *RP*, V, pp. 177, 182. Apart from the fact that it had been debarred in 1407 (see Griffiths 1991i: p. 89), it offered nothing more appealing than the succession of a little girl.

establishment. Only when public authority had totally collapsed could he even think of pressing such a claim. With no binding law on the matter, therefore, the succession could only be settled politically, a process which was certain to involve division and conflict, particularly once York had launched his campaign against the king's ministers.[13] Even when a direct heir was born, in October 1453, the prospects for deposition were scarcely any better: no one can have relished the thought of another long minority, in which the struggle for the crown might simply be transformed into a struggle for the regency or protectorate.

It is thus clear that, whatever their private feelings and attachments, the lords had no choice but to accept the continuing sovereignty of Henry VI. Conciliar expedients notwithstanding, this sovereignty was ultimately personal, so that – apart from the unique circumstances of the first protectorate – Henry's governments had always to contend with the two major problems introduced above: the existence of a royal power which could never be fully controlled by anyone other than its irresponsible possessor; and, in association, the continuing empowerment of the royal household, the venue of this power and, in some respects, almost as unmanageable as the king. If the first of these problems brought the regimes of the 1450s nothing but difficulties, the second brought them strengths as well as weaknesses. In the wake of Suffolk's fall, of course, household power was widely mistrusted and every government which incorporated and expressed it fell victim to the 'clique of traitors' charge. At the same time, however, the household furnished a supply of men who might be ready to take their chances with Henry VI and his ministers because (if for no other reason) they could not avoid association with their activities. The threatening circumstances of the 1450s seem to have brought an end to the anarchic household of the previous decade. Its members learned once again to offer loyal and co-ordinated support to those who made the king himself the ultimate basis of their authority.[14] So it was that, despite the crisis of 1450, many of the lords found themselves defending not only the king and those peers and other men of substance who were most deeply implicated in the activities of his court, but also the lesser men like Daniel and Trevilian, who had been the cause of so much inconvenience. So it was also that, in certain ways, the system established by Suffolk persisted into the 1450s, despite its proven inability to provide effective public government. As we shall see, this remarkable development owed much to the conflicts which broke out in the autumn of 1450. Division, and the fear of division, conspired to preserve the rule of Henry VI until the stitching of public authority had been entirely unpicked.

---

[13] Chrimes 1936: p. 22.   [14] Morgan 1987: pp. 49ff.

It emerges, then, that alongside the individual loyalties and interests which have loomed large in accounts of the politics of the 1450s, there were also a series of corporate structures, identities and problems created by the interplay of royal inadequacy and those patterns of authority which were intrinsic to the English polity or which had been built up steadily since 1422. It is on these more 'public' factors and on the ways in which they influenced the behaviour of the lords in particular that the following account focuses. Once again, it is by no means an exhaustive narrative: the aim is to extend what can be learned from other political histories by showing the working of political society at a public level and as a public organism.[15]

YORK AND THE COMMON VOICE, 1450–1452

Since the fifteenth century itself, comment on Richard of York's campaign against the ministers of Henry VI has neglected the public issues which it raised and focused instead on the personal motives and interests which might have led to dissidence.[16] Financial embarrassment, dynastic ambition, fear of exclusion and hostility to Somerset have bulked much larger in explanations of the duke's career than any concern for the welfare and tranquillity of the realm.[17] York's own account of his motives has persuaded almost nobody, and this, in turn, has encouraged the view that such abstract concepts as 'order' and 'the common welfare' were of little account in shaping fifteenth-century politics.[18] If political leaders

---

[15] The fullest account of the politics of this period appears in Griffiths 1981 (Wolffe 1981: chs. 13–16 is rather briefer). Johnson 1988 supplies a great deal of valuable information concerning York's activities. Storey 1966 provides detailed accounts of the main local disputes of the period. In this chapter, I have generally cited these and other secondary sources in preference to primary material, except where my interpretations significantly differ from those to be found in print or where I have new information to offer.

[16] E.g. York's 'diabolique unkyndnesse and wrecched envye' (*RP*, V, p. 347: 1459); his 'naturall disposicion to the restfull governaunce and pollicie of the ... Reame' (*ibid.*, p. 465: 1461); his 'aspiring to the crowne ... his pollicie tendyng to this ende, that by occasion of discorde amongst the commons he might procure himselfe authoritie' (Ellis (ed.), *Polydore Vergil's English History*, p. 84).

[17] Although Johnson 1988: p. 76 seems to suggest that York returned to England to obtain funds for his Irish service, it is now generally believed that financial concern was not a factor in York's return: see Bean 1984: p. 198 and *passim*; also Jones 1989a: p. 295 and Pugh 1986a: pp. 125–6 (although cf p. 128). The dynastic motive is rejected by Jones 1989a: pp. 289–90, but finds support from Griffiths 1991i: pp. 94–5 and Pugh 1986a: pp. 123–4, 129 and 1986b: p. 86. Hostility to, or rivalry with, Somerset emerges as an explanation of York's actions in e.g. Griffiths 1991e: pp. 289–90; Johnson 1988: pp. 89, 157; Storey 1966: pp. 73, 75; Jones 1989a: pp. 286–7, 303–7 (arguing that the origins of conflict between the two men lay in Somerset's surrender of Rouen).

[18] Even nineteenth-century historians were unwilling to place York alongside other baronial reformers, such as Montfort and Bolingbroke: see e.g. Stubbs 1875–8: III, pp. 155–6, though cf. Plummer, *Governance*, pp. 19, 33–5, Wilkinson 1964: pp. 88ff; and, more recently, Starkey 1986: p. 17.

were really pursuing personal ends, what possible relevance, it may be asked, can these public ideals have had? One answer to this question has already been proposed above: these and other concepts made up the common stock of political activity; whatever the private interests and beliefs of York and other politicians, their public transactions had to be performed in the prevailing currency, and this drove them to favour some policies and avoid others.[19] We do not have to believe that York was a spotless and devoted reformer, therefore, to place his professed defence of the common weal at the centre of an account of his activities. Not only was the range of options made available by political discourse a limited one, but the duke's freedom to choose from it was probably restricted. Like any public figure, York was subject to a host of external, as well as internal, influences: among them not only 'accepted principles', but also the institutional structures and practices which derived from these; not only the views and actions of his associates, but also those of his peers and, indeed, those of a wider public.[20] These external influences supplied the context – and, arguably, much of the content – of York's activism. Like the king, or any other lord, the duke was both private and public person: in the assessment of his activities in politics, the latter may deserve more attention than the former.

In the turbulent weeks before York returned to England, an expectation that he would undertake the stewardship of the popular cause became widespread. Of all the 'trewe lordes' supposedly driven out by Suffolk and his covetous 'trayne', Duke Richard was the greatest: leading prince of the blood royal, holder of lands in two dozen counties, it seemed that he had been exiled to Ireland so that the sale of France and the rape of England could be carried out undisturbed; now, surely, he would return to do justice upon the traitors and take up some prominent place in the government of the realm.[21] Up to the moment of his arrival in London, in September 1450, it seems that York played no active part in the fabrication of this mythology, but it is likely that he knew of it and clear that he was forced to take account of it.[22] The question of whether to

---

[19] See above, pp. 6–7.

[20] This is not, therefore, to suggest, as Johnson 1988 appears to do (see pp. 89, 114 and, more clearly, 224), that York was, as a man, particularly vulnerable to the advice of his counsellors. My point is the more general one that the representative aspects of lordship need to be considered alongside the personal ones: see above, pp. 73, 106.

[21] For details of the popular presentation of York before his return, see Griffiths 1991e: pp. 281–3 and Johnson 1988: pp. 79–81. For strictly contemporary allegations that York had been exiled, see *Collections*, p. 189; Harvey 1991: p. 191 (and for the belief that he would return and do justice upon the 'traitors': *EHL*, p. 371).

[22] Of the various bills York presented to Henry VI in 1450, the first referred to dangerous language concerning himself of which he had been informed since reaching Ireland (Griffiths 1991e: p. 299. I have followed the revised numbering in Johnson 1988: pp. 104–5, and the timings he proposes). The second bill claimed that he had returned

agree or to refuse to play a role in which circumstances had already cast him may have been a finely balanced one, but the hostile treatment which the duke received from royal agents when he landed in North Wales posed it in a particularly acute way.[23] On the one hand, the episode revealed that the government took the popular view of the duke seriously: a factor which must have increased his sense of both opportunity and danger.[24] On the other hand, it may have lent a certain credibility to the 'clique of traitors' idea, for who but such men had reason to fear the return of the king's cousin? York knew, of course, from his own experiences of government in the 1440s, that Henry had indeed been managed by a group of his subjects. He knew how vulnerable that made the regime in the circumstances of 1450. In the light of Gloucester's downfall, he also knew how vulnerable it made himself as he emerged, regardless of his own actions, as a serious inconvenience to the men immediately about the king. His first response to this delicate situation was to make an ambivalent protest about his treatment, insisting on his loyalty to date, but making no promises about the future.[25] At this stage, then, the duke was hedging his bets, but more decisive moves followed soon after. Ignoring the assurances of good will despatched by the government,[26] he proceeded to London, where he promptly fulfilled the hopes of the commons by demanding action against the men accused of treason and offering his help in the execution of justice.[27]

We cannot know why York jumped one way and not the other: fear,

---

to England to clear his name in person (Griffiths 1991e: pp. 299–300). See *ibid.*, p. 290, for details of communication between York and the mainland during his time in Ireland and *ibid.*, pp. 283–4, and Johnson 1988: p. 82 for scepticism over the possibility that York was actively involved in the stimulation of popular dissent during his absence.

[23] See Griffiths 1991h for details.

[24] The government's attitude to popular feeling about York is revealed indirectly by Cade's articles (Harvey 1991: p. 189) and directly by the first royal reply to the duke's bills (Griffiths 1991e: p. 301).

[25] Printed in Griffiths 1991e: pp. 299–300. Note the ominous words which close the petition: 'ffor myn entent is fully to persewe to your highnesse for conclusion of thees maters'.

[26] 'Henry VI's answer to the duke's first bill', printed in *ibid.*, p. 301.

[27] This was the fourth (third surviving) bill: see *ibid.*, pp. 302–3, for the text and *PL*, II, pp. 174, 177, and (perhaps) *Collections*, p. 195, for evidence of its dissemination. In it, York called for justice upon those indicted of treason and on others 'openly noysed of the same'. This was essentially the cry of the commons in 1449–50 (above, p. 246), of Cade's rebels (above, p. 260) and of the king's mutinous army in Kent on 18 June (*Three Chrons.*, p. 67). Note that the reference to 'those endited' was highly controversial, since the only known treason indictments against members of the court group were those made before the commissioners of July 1450, who had been appointed under pressure from Cade's rebels (cf. Griffiths 1991e: pp. 293–4). These indictments mirrored the charges made against Suffolk in parliament (see KB9/265, m. 145, for the charges against Thomas Kent). Not everyone followed York in regarding these indictments as authoritative: see e.g. *Letters and Papers*, II, ii, p. 770, and *RP*, V, p. 265, and note that those tried by York in 1450–1 were all acquitted (below, p. 277).

grievance, a sense of his own right, or honour, or greatness could all have played a part. What deserves more recognition, perhaps, is the extent to which York's subsequent actions were shaped and limited by the choice he had made: the popular constituency was well established when its chosen lord arrived to lead it; its critique was fully developed and, if York was to retain control of the situation in which his acceptance had placed both himself and the entire political community, he had little option but to give it public voice.[28] This may account for a great deal of the duke's rather sudden hostility to the regime and its personnel: far from being personally motivated, as most historians have assumed, it could have been manufactured to suit the circumstances of 1450. We might bear this possibility in mind when we look at the relationship between York and Somerset, which – in a certain sense – dominated the politics of the early 1450s. Whatever the personal feelings of the two men, the decision of the former to endorse the popular and communal critique and the acceptance by the latter of a leading role in the king's government placed them in direct opposition to one another.

As the king's lieutenant in France when English power collapsed, Somerset was already in some danger of public condemnation. While his absence from the court in 1448–50 may have saved him from immediate and damaging identification with the clique of traitors about the king, the spreading belief in a great conspiracy and the return to England of disgruntled and impoverished soldiers with first-hand accounts of the fall of France combined to make this fate more likely.[29] The duke's emergence as the king's chief minister within a few weeks of his return must have confirmed public impressions of a link between domestic corruption and defeat in France. It could only have been Suffolk's associates, known to be still powerful about the king, who contrived Somerset's restoration. He, it followed, must be one of them.[30] It was not York, therefore, who implanted in the common mind a connection between Somerset and the discredited men in the royal household, but Duke Edmund himself.[31] Once this connection was widely made, York was more or less forced to

---

[28] For an interesting treatment of the role of 'the popular element' in shaping 'Yorkism', see McCulloch and Jones 1983.

[29] It is possible that the 'Somerset' who appears among the list of traitors in the 'dirge' of Cade's rebels is Edmund Beaufort, and not the king's doctor. His is the final name, which may imply a certain importance, and the context – 'Where is Somerset? whi aperes he not here' – fits neatly with the circumstances of the absent duke. See Wright (ed.), *Political Poems*, II, p. 234, lines 19–20, and cf. Griffiths 1981: p. 662 n. 209.

[30] See the following section for Somerset's part in the formation of a new government.

[31] This much is acknowledged by Johnson 1988: p. 83, though on pp. 91–2 he is critical of Somerset's inclusion in the 1450–1 bill for the removal of persons about the king (see below, p. 275), calling the result a 'clumsy composite' and arguing that 'Somerset's fate was largely of interest to old soldiers'.

attack the duke if he wished to retain his footing in a politics dominated by popular and 'communal' perceptions.

This more public consideration is quite as likely to have shaped Duke Richard's behaviour as comparatively private factors such as rivalry, honour, or pressure from the old soldiers on his council.[32] The fact that he and his supporters used Somerset's performance in France as a weapon to beat the duke does not necessarily disclose their motive for attacking him. Whatever their intrinsic importance to the men most directly involved, the disasters in Normandy were also grist to the mill of domestic politics and it is interesting to note that some of the central themes of this politics – favouritism, injustice and, above all, 'covetise' – were recurrently invoked in Yorkist criticism of Somerset's performance as lieutenant.[33] Meanwhile, if contemporaries were often inclined to interpret the politics of the early 1450s in terms of a personal feud between the two dukes, this says as much about the norms of power under Henry VI as it does about the true preoccupations of York and Somerset.[34] For one thing, most political enterprises were personal in this age of lordship; although, as we have seen, the 'personal' was normally also political, public and representative. For another, if York caught the eye because he stood outside and, to some extent, against the king's government, Somerset (like Suffolk before him) attained a similar prominence because of the widespread belief that Henry was under his influence. The king's inability to convince his subjects of his independence from ministers and counsellors was the real reason why competing approaches to the problem of order and authority came to dominate the political scene in the wake of 1450 and, indeed, a major reason why

[32] Cf. Johnson 1988: pp. 89–92; Jones 1989a: pp. 285–6, 303–7. One might have expected grievances based on honour to have been settled by personal combat, but (as far as we know) this was never proposed by either duke (cf. Tuck 1985: pp. 299–300).

[33] See e.g. the articles in *PL*, I, esp. pp. 104, 107 (Somerset already possessed a reputation for avarice interestingly: see Jones 1989a: p. 300). The view that York's assault on Somerset's performance in Normandy was factitious gains support from the fact that York's only known reference to the loss of France before he returned to England in September 1450 was a comparatively mild one: urging the earl of Salisbury, in June, to obtain payment of his wages, he drew attention to the 'inconvenience' which could follow inadequate funding, adding that 'I have example in other places, more pity it is, for to dread shame' (Brewer and Bullen, (eds.), *Cal. of the Carew MSS*, VI, p. 258).

[34] Most chroniclers did make the Somerset-York feud the centre of their accounts of this period, as noted by Jones 1989a: pp. 285–6 (see e.g. *Registrum Whethamstede*, I, pp. 159–67; Basin, *Histoire*, II, pp. 171–5). Even so, some commentators emphasised other themes. For example, d'Escouchy, *Chronique*, pp. 301–2, has York, in the name of justice, opposing the king's 'petit gouvernement' of household men and, in time, receiving the rule of the realm himself, while the king is 'mis en tutelle' by parliament. Although this account is patently confused, it does not relate York's actions to Somerset in any way. See also *Crowland*, pp. 418–19, and note *English Chron.*, pp. 69–71, which talks of the enmity between York and Somerset, but also indicates a wider context for this enmity: York's populism and the support it elicited; Somerset's power about the king.

these approaches – each fundamentally rational and each backed by significant public support – have come to be seen in principally personal terms.

The famous bill calling for justice upon the traitors, which York presented to Henry at the end of September, was an ingenious document serving a number of different ends.[35] First, as has been said, it was a public statement that the duke endorsed the commons' cry against the 'traitors': he would personally assist the king in bringing them to justice. At the same time, it sought to establish that, despite his large forces, York was not in rebellion. Like Jack Cade before him, he was a 'public petitioner', looking for 'public justice' to be done.[36] This concern was part and parcel of York's allegiance to Henry VI: the duke was acting, he said, as the king's 'humble sugett and lyge man'.[37] This assertion of loyalty was to be a crucial element in York's position. On the one hand it was a licence for action against the government, a group of men who, to judge by their actions, were not at all devoted to the interests of king and realm.[38] On the other, it served as an assurance that the duke had no designs upon the throne.[39] Both of these claims could be countered, but York's professions of allegiance – though ultimately self-defeating and, in the end, abandoned – were indispensable both to his intermittent success and to his long-term survival. The duke's peers needed to be sure that he was with them and with the king whose feeble person was the focus of their unity.

York's appeal was directed less to the government than to its constituencies, both the immediate one of the lords and the broader one of the *communitas*.[40] Broadly speaking, he needed the support of the latter to obtain the support of the former and the support of the former to put his demands into effect. The 'comouns', both gentle and popular, probably gave an enthusiastic welcome to what were, after all, their own desires.[41] The feelings of the lords are unknown, but it is not at all unlikely that they were prepared to endorse the response to York which emerged from within the regime. This was, in effect, to call the duke's bluff with a public

---

[35] Griffiths 1991e: pp. 302-3.

[36] For these phrases, see *Loci e Libro*, p. 189. For York's forces, see e.g. 'Benet's Chron.', p. 202.

[37] Griffiths 1991e: p. 302.

[38] This was a key strand in their 'treason', of course: above, p. 41.

[39] Such an assurance was probably necessary: in the reply to York's second bill, the government had somewhat disingenuously confessed its alarm at rumours 'that ye schulde take upon you that that ye nothir aught nor as we doutenat ye wole not attempte' (Griffiths 1991e: p. 301).

[40] See below, pp. 282ff, for what this government amounted to.

[41] Note e.g. *PL*, II, p. 174.

letter of similar ingenuity to his own.[42] This well-known document
sidestepped York's call for justice by addressing the larger issue of
counsel. The king, it said, was soon to be advised by a substantial – that
is, lordly – council, in which the alleged treasons and other matters could
be discussed. Whatever grounds for criticism there may have been in the
past, the future was to be different: the king was to be better governed. As
it made these concessions, the royal letter also reasserted Henry's personal
authority. It suggested that the king alone would speak for the *communitas*,
assisted by the counsel of voices which were equal in 'liberte, vertu and
effecte', for it was not 'accustumed nor expedient to take a conclusion or
a conducte be avise or consaile of on person be hym selfe'.[43] Within this
council, then, the individual pre-eminence which York had assumed
would be swiftly dissolved: he was simply one more lord, valuable in
assuring the representativeness of royal government, but scarcely qualified to head it. Evidently, the duke had misjudged the depth of resolve at
the heart of Somerset's embryonic government. The men who authorised
this letter were not persuaded that further concessions to popular
criticism were necessary. They saw no grounds for handing over power to
York, but nor did they wish to exclude him altogether. Just as in the
minority, the obvious way to counter division and disorder was to stress
the authority of the king and to make discreet arrangements for its
inclusive and corporate execution.[44] The lords, once again under Beaufort presidency, responded to York as they and their predecessors had
responded to Gloucester: by upholding the common rule of the peers
against a more individual authority resting on a mixture of royal blood
and popular agitation.

York did not give up. We now know that he returned to the fray with
another bill, addressed, this time, not only to Henry, but also to the 'trewe
lordes of the kinges counsele'.[45] Though its message was essentially the
same,[46] this bill differed from its predecessor in a number of ways. First
of all, it seems to have been intended for the relatively private consumption of York's peers in the council: its language was more forthright and

---

[42] Griffiths 1991e: pp. 303–4. The terms of this reply were apparently widely known: see
e.g. *RP*, V, p. 346, and Giles, *Chronicon*, p. 42. Note that rejected petitions did not
usually receive replies at all: this was clearly a piece of propaganda.

[43] The point is not, of course, that all counsellors were considered equal, but rather that the
absolute power of the lord to decide what to do with their counsel had an equalising
effect: above, pp. 25ff.

[44] See above, pp. 115–16.

[45] BL Add. MS 48031A, fol. 126r–v. The timing proposed here is rather conjectural. For
further details, see my contributions to the volume concerning this manuscript which is
currently in preparation under the general editorship of Dr Margaret Kekewich.

[46] On this occasion York tacitly replaced his offer of personal assistance in the trials of the
'traitors' with a request that 'honorable knightes and Juges undefouled' be appointed to
handle the matter (fol. 126r).

more rhetorical than that of the duke's public manifestoes and it made a serious attempt to argue a case. The duke provided a firmer conceptual basis for the 'traitors' charge: the men under attack were guilty of treason because they had destroyed the king's capacity to keep the law – the very basis of his right and power – and, in doing so, had placed him at odds with his people, dishonouring him and making the realm ungovernable.[47] The duty owed to the king by 'trewe lordes' was clear: to vanquish the 'traitors' (now identified, using exactly the words of Cade's rebels, as men 'I-broughte up of noughte'),[48] and give true counsel to the king.[49] York's point was a persuasive one: the magnates could and should detach themselves from the tainted men about the court and act, like the duke himself, as stewards of the common interest. They themselves were not the 'traitors' – there was to be no doubt of that – but they should realise that they would pay a heavy price for defending them: justice would have to be done 'yif ye luste sette the king and you bothe in the surete of his comons'.[50]

Vox populi was, of course, the strongest weapon in York's armoury and it was shown to powerful effect in the parliament of 1450–1. This assembly had been summoned in early September as one of a series of measures intended to restore control.[51] Even two months later, at its opening, the government seems to have hoped that it would be possible to hold the line against further criticism.[52] It soon became clear, however, that the public mood was much as it had been earlier in the year. The

[47] E.g. 'for lawe causith the king Inheritable to the Croune … and the king is sworne to his lawe and to defende his people. And so … hit is conseyved who that subvertith … the lawe, it is the moste threason on erthe that can be thoughte' (fol. 126r); 'And thise causis have caused our soveraigne lorde to lyve in acontrarie, The whiche is the mooste threason that may be done tany prince' (fol. 126v).

[48] See art. 1 of the 'Magdalen' manifesto (Harvey 1991: p. 189). Compare also art. 2 of this manifesto with the extracts quoted in the note above.

[49] E.g. 'ye gracieux trewe lordes of the kinges counsele … thinkth on your othe that ye owe to our souveraigne lorde and lyve not in periurie, but yeve trewe counseile and dredeth the punisshing of god and yeveth and maketh trewe counseile withoute fere' (fol. 126v).

[50] Fol. 126r.

[51] On the same day that parliament was summoned (5 September: *CCIR, 1447–54*, pp. 225–7), commissions were issued against rebels in London and Cambridgeshire, and three days later Somerset was sent into Kent against revived insurgency there: *CPR, 1446–52*, p. 431. See the next section for the nature and aims of the government at this time.

[52] The causes of summons read by the chancellor included measures to pacify, punish and resist rioters and rebels gathering in various parts of the realm: *RP*, V, p. 210. York was not made a trier of petitions. Those appointed were representative of the lords who had governed since 1449: Buckingham, Somerset, Arundel, Salisbury, Devon, Wiltshire, Beaumont, Bourgchier, Cromwell, Welles, Roos, Lisle and Ferrers of Groby, Sir John Fortescue and a predictable array of bishops (*ibid.*). Discussion of matters at issue between the lords was forbidden by proclamation at the opening of parliament (*Town Chrons.*, p. 136) and one chronicler recorded the commons' irritation that neither the king nor 'his' lords made any reference to the 'traitors' ('Benet's Chron.', p. 203).

commons elected Sir William Oldhall, York's chamberlain, as their speaker and promptly introduced a bill requesting that the duke of Gloucester be proclaimed a true knight. The implications of these moves are not hard to assess: Gloucester stood for good rule by the princes of the blood and for resistance to the 'traitors' in the interests of the common weal; these claims had now devolved upon York.[53] By calling parliament – and, in effect, reopening the public forum – Somerset and the king's other ministers and advisers had inadvertently restored the circumstances which attended Suffolk's fall: gathered together as an estate of the realm, the lords were forced to take account of communal feeling. As a result, the government was not afforced by their presence, but dissolved; in fact, paralysed. The initiative moved to York, who was away attracting support in East Anglia. The other peers waited for him to come and declare his hand.[54]

When he finally arrived at parliament, on 23 November with his sword borne before and a large retinue at his back,[55] both York's intention to sustain the common critique and his capacity to do so were unmistakable. In parliament, on 30 November, the duke's supporters called for justice upon the 'traitors' responsible for the corruption and shame of the preceding years.[56] In the city, a mob of soldiers, lords' men and Londoners rioted through the homes of prominent courtiers, providing York with a pretext to arrest Somerset, who was then brought into parliament and charged with the culpable loss of Normandy before being taken to the Tower of London.[57] If this episode is placed alongside others

[53] *RP*, V, pp. 210–11; *Town Chrons.*, p. 137. The bill on behalf of Gloucester may be C49/ 30/19, which is rubricated and differs from the bill passed in 1455. Its themes included Gloucester's royal blood, his honourable military service and the effective rule of his protectorate. A reference to Gloucester's keeping of 'the kinges livelode unto his owne [i.e. Henry's] use and prouffit' raises the fiscal issue and may also suggest a 1450 dating. The commons also submitted a bill to attaint Suffolk: *RP*, V, p. 226. It contained, for the first time, charges of labouring Gloucester's downfall and death. Similar charges were made against Heydon and Tuddenham by a Norwich jury on 26 November, interestingly: KB9/272, m. 3.

[54] One indication of the government's paralysis is the fact that the appointment of sheriffs was delayed, pending York's arrival: *PL*, II, p. 186.

[55] See e.g. Johnson 1988: p. 88. Note that many lords brought large retinues to the parliament: *Town Chrons.*, p. 137; *Chrons. of London*, p. 162.

[56] The chroniclers make it clear that it was lords' men – presumably York's – who called for this: 'Benet's Chron.', p. 203; *Town Chrons.*, p. 137 (which alleges that the commons of parliament joined in the call). Note that their words echoed those of Cade's rebels.

[57] For attacks on the property of Somerset, Tuddenham and Sir Thomas Hoo, see Jones 1989a: pp. 287–8; *Collections*, p. 196. For Somerset's appearance in parliament, see *EHL*, p. 372. There must be some doubt as to whether this took place: no other primary (or, to my knowledge, secondary) source mentions it. It was perhaps for an attempt to try Somerset that Fastolf's articles in College of Arms, Arundel MS xlviii, fols. 324r– 325v, were prepared: note the opening ('Memor, savyng youre good correccion that it is right necessarie amonges othir of my lordes articlis that there be desired...'): see Jones 1989a: p. 288 and n. 5.

from the parliament, it becomes clear that, under York's *aegis*, the programme devised or supported by the various opponents of the government since the beginning of the year was actually put into effect. A bill was submitted for the removal of the 'traitors' from the person of the king.[58] There was pressure for a second resumption.[59] And a series of major state trials – of the duchess of Suffolk, Bishop Boulers, Lord Dudley, Thomas Daniel, John Trevilian, John Say, Edward Grimston and John Gargrave – appears to have been inaugurated.[60]

During this *bouleversement*, Duke Richard acquired a significant, if ultimately temporary, following among the more important lords. In particular, Norfolk, Devon, Warwick and Salisbury seem to have been fairly closely associated with his activities at this time.[61] An even larger

[58] *RP*, V, pp. 216–17. The bill charged the twenty-nine named persons (most of them familiar from earlier popular accusations – see Johnson 1988: pp. 91–2) with the main theme of the 'misprisions' alleged against Suffolk: their 'undue meanes' had led to the diminution of the royal patrimony, the suspension of the laws and the disturbance of the peace.

[59] The resumption bill, probably introduced in the first session of the parliament, was a key part of the communal programme, of course: Harvey 1991: p. 191; Wolffe 1958: p. 604. York may have been fairly directly involved in its progress: see e.g. Anstey (ed.), *Epist. Acad. Oxon.*, I, no. 206, and BL, Sloane MS 428, fol. 120v, which opens 'The puyntys that my lorde of yorke pootte to the consel', and continues, 'For thys materys thys present parlement ys ordaynyd to amende defawtes that byt in thys reeme. On ys that the kyngys dettes mythe be payde.' This does not appear to be a faithful account of York's own words, but it may genuinely reflect action on the duke's part. I am very grateful to Dr Rosemary Horrox for bringing this item to my attention.

[60] These trials – apparently for treason – have received little attention from historians, but they must have been eye-catching at the time. If the sources are so thin, it is perhaps because of the turn of the political tide, discussed below, which assured the acquittal of all concerned. We know of the trials from two chronicles, which refer to the acquittals of Dudley and Boulers and the duchess of Suffolk by the lords, and of Thomas Daniel, John Trevilian and John Say by the Londoners ('Benet's Chron.', p. 205; *Letters and Papers*, II, ii, p. 770) and from a letter dated 13 March 1451, which refers to the duchess of Suffolk and Bishop Boulers being acquitted 'be the lorde of y...', while '...y' (Say?) had been 'arayned yn the gyldhall and this day was delyvert and aquyt be worthymen of the Cytee and ... th... parlement of treson' (SC1/51/59). The letter also mentions the release of Gargrave, keeper of the writs in king's bench. It is possible that all these people had been indicted by the Londoners in July (Daniel, Say, Trevilian and Grimston certainly had and the duchess may have been: *CPR, 1446–52*, pp. 443–5 and 532; *Letters and Papers*, II, ii, pp. 768, 770). York's arrival, with Boulers, Dudley and Gargrave in his custody, of course (*EHL*, p. 297; 'Benet's Chron.', p. 202), would have permitted the indictments to take effect. It was perhaps under York's auspices that Sir Thomas Hoo, Lord Hastings, the late chancellor of Normandy, was appointed to be tried for undue retention of soldiers' wages in February 1451: *CPR, 1446–52*, pp. 439, 444. He too had probably been in the duke's custody since September (*PL*, II, p. 175). Among those commissioned to try him were York's man Thomas Palmer (Johnson 1988: p. 236 for the connection). The trials of Trevilian, Say and Grimston, which do not seem to have begun until March and April 1451 (*CPR, 1446–52*, pp. 443–5), may have been set in motion by the court, as well as (or instead of) by York: see below, p. 289.

[61] For Norfolk, see e.g. Johnson 1988: pp. 85, 88–9; *EHL*, p. 297; *Town Chrons.*, p. 157. For Devon, see Griffiths 1981: p. 691. Warwick arrived in London two days after York: *Town Chrons.*, p. 137. He was confirmed in possession of the Beauchamp chamberlainship of the exchequer, disputed with Somerset and the other Beauchamp coheirs, on

group, including Buckingham, Wiltshire, Worcester and Arundel took part in the royal procession of 3 December, which provided York with an opportunity to demonstrate his power, his concern for order and his intimacy with, and loyalty to, the king and his leading subjects.[62] While a number of noblemen probably saw individual advantage in the disruption of Somerset's nascent authority,[63] the duke's supporters were not all, or not only, self-interested: broader dynamics, working on the nobility as a whole, were surely an important factor in determining both the coming of York's hegemony and its subsequent demise. Regardless of what part he may have played in the making of it, the duke obviously enjoyed massive public support.[64] With parliament in session, the immediacy and authority of this support were all the greater and, with no countervailing authority to be had from the king – except through the utterly discredited filter of the household – the regime was forced to defer to York. The preservation of order and the effective execution of the royal will depended on the acceptance of his lordship, an acceptance which the duke made easier by his emphatic loyalty to the king and, we may assume, by a readiness to work consultatively and co-operatively with at least the noble members of Somerset's government. From early December, York was apparently able to affect the working of the royal administration.[65] A new form of rule seemed to be in prospect.

In the event, it never materialised. When the parliamentary recess arrived, and the duke was shorn of the visible support of his public

---

6 December: *CPR, 1446–52*, p. 409. Possibly in response to pressure from York, he was appointed to try various Norman captains in February 1451 (see preceding note) and, together with Salisbury, he headed an oyer and terminer commission which heard indictments regarding the spoliation of Somerset's goods (*Town Chrons.*, p. 138; *CPR, 1446–52*, p. 438). A thief who was caught was handed over to the earl of Salisbury for execution: 'Benet's Chron.', p. 203. Note that a German, present in London at the time, identified Salisbury, Warwick, Exeter, Arundel and Northumberland as York's supporters: Griffiths 1981: pp. 707 n. 108 and 708 n. 118.

[62] See e.g. 'Benet's Chron.', pp. 203–4.

[63] Examples may include those whose lordship had earlier been ineffective, such as Norfolk, Devon (above, pp. 239–40) and, in a different way, Exeter (see *CFR, 1445–52*, pp. 182–3, for his reward and Stansfield 1987: pp. 228–38 for his difficult position). Warwick's support derived in part from a desire to increase his share of the Beauchamp inheritance, notably at Somerset's expense: Carpenter 1992: p. 458; above, n. 61.

[64] Johnson 1988: pp. 87–8, 105–6.

[65] One possible indication of this is the fact that on 1 December, the day of Somerset's arrest, a prior order to take £3,000 from the Calais part of the customs for the expenses of the household was rescinded: E404/67/97. Note also the grant of the Beauchamp chamberlainship on 6 December (above, n. 61) and the appointment of sheriffs on 3 December (*CFR, 1445–52*, pp. 186–7; the fact that many of those appointed were established royal servants does not necessarily mean that York had failed to influence the process: cf. Jeffs 1960: pp. 171–2; Johnson 1988: pp. 92–3). Johnson 1988: p. 95 and Wolffe 1971: p. 131 suggest that some sort of council was created under York's direction: there is no evidence for this (see below, p. 286) and it seems to me more likely that the duke simply put pressure on existing administrative structures.

constituency, control of government began to drift back towards its natural centre about the king – in effect, towards the household and the supporters of Somerset, who was free again by Christmas.[66] London remained disorderly and York's opponents trod carefully – Tuddenham lost his office at the king's wardrobe in late December, for example[67] – but it is clear that the alliance of household and executive was gathering strength and beginning once again to exert a kind of gravitational force upon the lords.[68] This force was redoubled when, instead of returning to parliament in January, the court removed to Kent to suppress the rising of Stephen Christmas.[69] Away from London and the corroding effect of public criticism, different perspectives and a different politics were possible. Faced with a popular disturbance which seemed to give the lie to York's claims that indulging the commons would restore order, Somerset was able to draw enough of the nobility behind the king, the household and the pursuit of authoritarian policy to regain the initiative.[70] The absence of the king and many of the lords left York and the commons high and dry: if Duke Richard was still able to exert some pressure upon the writing offices and to continue his campaign of public justice for a few weeks more, his position was becoming more and more untenable.[71] When Henry and his entourage returned to London, on 23 February, there was no doubt about the credibility of Somerset's regime: it was the authentic voice of king and lords.[72] The convulsion was over. In the ensuing weeks, the courtiers being tried were acquitted and, once the

[66] 'Benet's Chron.', p. 204. See also *Letters and Papers*, II, ii, p. 770. The knights made by the king at Christmas include some politic choices, such as Salisbury's younger sons and William Herbert (*ibid.*): it is tempting to suggest that this was an attempt by Somerset, or others in the household, to draw support away from York.

[67] This happened shortly before 21 December: BL Cotton Charter iv/15. See *PL*, II, pp. 207–8, for the context. At the turn of the year, Sir John Fortescue, who had been condemned by Cade's rebels (*Three Chrons.*, p. 98; *EHL*, p. 365), was still barricading himself in his house: *PL*, II, p. 205.

[68] For an excellent reconstruction of the events of the ensuing few months, see Johnson 1988: pp. 94–8.

[69] Parliament was expected to reassemble on 20 January 1451 (*RP*, V, p. 213), but it is not clear that it did so. The king seems to have gone into Kent on 28 January (*Chrons. of London*: p. 162–3).

[70] It is actually more likely that Christmas' rising was stimulated by a sense that the tide was already turning against York and that repression was on the way. See Harvey 1991: p. 152. The impressive array of lords commissioned to accompany Henry included several – Exeter, Arundel, Worcester and Wiltshire – who may have flirted with York during December, as well as those more closely associated with the household, such as Sudeley, St Amand, Cromwell and, of course, Somerset himself (*CPR*, *1446–52*, p. 442). Not all of these men necessarily went (see e.g. 'Benet's Chron.', p. 204).

[71] For signs of York's continuing influence, see Johnson 1988: p. 96. For trials of Norman captains beginning in January and February, see n. 60, above and C253/32/162, 169 (subpoenas); *CPR*, *1446–52*, pp. 435–6, 439, 444 (commissions).

[72] Note that the king's return was accompanied by another procession, in many ways the obverse of that of 3 December: *Chrons. of London*, pp. 162–3

majority of the commons had been bought off with an agreement on the resumption, further criticism was easily stifled.[73] York's hegemony had collapsed as quickly as it had arisen. How was this possible?

It emerges that once the government had begun to rally, its success was more or less assured. Many of its problems stemmed from its inability to convince the lords that it was worth defending: as more and more of them were gathered into its ambit in the early months of 1451, so others followed suit and, by degrees, it became what it professed to be: a substantial body of the king's true lieges. On this basis, it could effectively negotiate with the commons and suppress rebellion: these were tokens of good governance which silenced public criticism and left York's opposition baseless. Really and truly, the duke failed because he had not gone far enough. His unwillingness to repudiate the rule of Henry VI meant that the king and his intimates continued to be a source of authority which it was difficult for York to contest openly or continuously. To maintain himself, he needed to develop and implement some alternative conception of government which gave institutional backing to the sources of his power: namely, his blood and the support of the *communitas*. In effect, he had either to claim the throne or to establish a protectorate of some kind. York did neither. He (and, indeed, others) may not have realised at first what radical steps his opposition demanded. Perhaps anxious to preserve credit with his peers – men with whom he had worked throughout the 1430s and 1440s when the crimes he now condemned had been committed – he erred on the side of caution and, as a result, lost his footing when circumstances returned to something more like normal. Even so, there are signs that he may have realised his mistake.

As the popular ferment of 1450 receded, York seems to have tried to regain his fading advantage by seeking public recognition as heir presumptive.[74] He may have hoped that this would endow him with a lasting primacy in government, or at least a platform for public criticism, on the model of the dukes of Bedford and Gloucester.[75] The enterprise did not,

---

[73] See above, n. 60, for the acquittals. For the appeasing effect of the resumption, see 'Benet's Chron.', p. 204: most of the lords and commons apparently left the parliament once it was certain to be granted (see *PL*, II, p. 243, for Norfolk's apparently premature departure), so that few were left to resist the order to disperse which was the royal response to Younge's bill (below, n. 74).

[74] Through Younge's bill: see *Letters and Papers*, II, ii, p. 770, and Johnson 1988: pp. 98–9.

[75] See above, n. 53, for the association between York and Gloucester which may already have been developing in the public imagination. York may have hoped to reinforce this by taking steps to acquire the earldom of Pembroke, which Gloucester had held (*CPR, 1446–52*, p. 445; Johnson 1988: p. 97). It is interesting to note that in an indictment of 1453, Oldhall and others were accused of attempting to make York 'king and governor' of the realm in 1450 (KB9/118/1, m. 30). Since 'king' alone would have sufficed to indicate treason, the inclusion of 'governor' may suggest that it was known that York had sought a loyal regency of some kind in the course of his first assault on the king's government.

could not, work.[76] Once again, it went too far without going far enough. York's identification with the burgeoning myth of Good Duke Humphrey may have brought him support among the commons – indeed, it may have originated with them – but to his peers, still mindful of Gloucester's disruptive role in the politics of the 1420s, 1430s and 1440s, it simply underlined the anomaly of his position. The king alone had the right to act for the public good. If he was unable to do so, the right reverted – but tacitly – to the body of the lords.[77] Nothing but the brief subversion of the political order and the temporary backing of some of his peers had delivered any right to York. When, in September 1451, the duke took action reminiscent of Gloucester's protectorate, and set off to heal the disorder in the West Country, the government made it clear that it viewed his exercise of public authority as a usurpation.[78] So it was that, with Henry's ministers strong enough to make convincing claims to the exercise of royal authority, and the duke continuing to behave as if this were not the case, the stage was set for a confrontation.

It began in late November with a move against Sir William Oldhall, who promptly fled into sanctuary and was declared a traitor.[79] York, damned by association, retaliated by appealing to the public on essentially the same platform as in 1450. Just as before, he issued declarations of loyalty to Henry VI and, in accordance with the duty implicit in his allegiance, called for action against the king's traitorous government.[80] By early 1452, however, circumstances were no longer so favourable to such a policy. Popular discontent had been effectively quelled, with two major results. The first of these was a restoration of the government's public credibility, which removed the excuse for initiatives which it had not authorised. As the crown was soon to insist, no one was to proceed by

---

[76] The government responded by dissolving parliament (Griffiths 1981: p. 692).

[77] Above, pp. 76–7, 114–15, 191–2.

[78] Devon had raised an army and led it against Lord Bonville and the earl of Wiltshire: see Storey 1966: ch. V for this dispute. York, who had also raised large forces, imposed some sort of settlement upon the warring parties (as even the indictments of Devon acknowledged: KB9/267, m. 42b): see esp. Wolffe 1981: pp. 250–2 for details of this episode. It was presumably in order to overawe the combatants that York had gathered his army (cf. Johnson 1988: p. 102).

[79] Kempe, *Historical Notices of St Martin-le-Grand*, pp. 138–41. It is difficult to be sure who were the real protagonists in this conflict – the government or York and his men. This account assumes the former (see also below, pp. 295–8). For an interpretation which assumes the latter – that the goverment was reacting to the fact that Oldhall had spent the late summer engaging in seditious activity – see Johnson 1988: pp. 101, 103–4.

[80] York declared his loyalty in a manifesto issued at Ludlow on 9 January 1452: *PL*, I, p. 96. In a letter sent to a number of towns in early February, of which one example survives, he drew attention to his 'liegeance' and 'true acquittal': *ibid.*, pp. 97–8. It was this, he suggested, which had led him to return to England in 1450 and put forward various articles 'right necessary' to the king. Equally, it was his hatred of York's allegiance to the king and favour to the realm which had led Somerset to lay these articles aside and turn upon the duke.

'way of fayt': aggrieved subjects, York included, were to sue to the king for redress.[81] The second result was that the duke himself had to play a larger part in creating the grounds for an unauthorised intervention at the very time when such activity was most likely to elicit criticism from his peers. With rousing letters to a number of towns, York attempted to return public attention to the theme of evil courtiers and the loss of Normandy.[82] At the same time, he narrowed the focus of his attack to the duke of Somerset alone.[83] Far from being a display of personal spite, this is likely to have been a matter of calculation: by identifying a single villain, he could hope to take action against the government without drawing accusations of treason and without uniting the rest of the lords against him; if he cast Somerset as a second Suffolk, there was a chance that peers and people would follow the same course that they had followed before.

Although some were apparently prepared to recognise York's all-important distinction between an attack on Somerset and an attack on royal authority,[84] it does not seem to have influenced the actions of the nobility on this occasion. They rallied to the government's aid.[85] For them, political options were increasingly crystalline: as the chaos of 1450 abated and the lords placed a growing confidence in Somerset's regime, York's assaults became rebellions in all but name.[86] His attempts to discredit those in control began to look as inconvenient and unwarranted as those of Gloucester, as the public forum of politics once again

---

[81] Below, p. 281.

[82] Johnson 1988: pp. 108–9 and n. 10. Note that the loss of Bordeaux and Bayonne in the summer of 1451 (Griffiths 1981: pp. 529–30) may have brought some of the heat back to the theme of defeat: see *PL*, I, pp. 97 and 105, for York's attempts to exploit it in 1452.

[83] Where the January manifesto refers to 'mine enemies', the letter sent to the towns holds Somerset alone responsible for the loss of France and the frustration of York's beneficial proposals of 1450: *PL*, I, pp. 96–8.

[84] For example, 'Benet's Chron.', p. 206, has York replying to royal orders not to rebel with an assurance that he would never rise against the king, but would always obey him: his insurrection was against Somerset and 'pro bono Anglie' and not against Henry. See also e.g. *Three Chrons.*, p. 149; *EHL*, p. 297; *English Chron.*, p. 69. Only Giles, *Chronicon*, p. 43, seems to regard York's enterprise as a straightforward rebellion.

[85] The lords' attitude had already been indicated by their decision, on 1 February, to despatch Thomas Kent to see York: E404/68/79 (sent 'by the commaundement of the lordes of oure counsaille'). A large number of them joined the royal expedition which left London on 16 February to confront the duke (*Chrons. of London*, p. 163). These included Exeter, Buckingham, Norfolk, Salisbury, Shrewsbury, Worcester, Wiltshire, Beaumont, Lisle, Grey of Ruthin, Clifford, Egremont, Moleyns, Stourton, Camoys and Beauchamp of Powick (*EHL*, p. 373), Viscount Bourgchier ('Benet's Chron.', p. 206), Lord Rivers (*Registrum Whethamstede*, I, p. 162) and the earl of Warwick (*Brut*, p. 520; *CPR, 1446–52*, pp. 523–4). See also Harvey (ed.), *Worcestre: Itineraries*, p. 345, for a list of those against York at Welling, a few miles west of Dartford. The list includes many of the above.

[86] This is exactly what the government later tried to suggest: see below, pp. 296–8.

narrowed to exclude the *communitas*. From the very fact that the government felt strong enough to move against him, York must have deduced
that both his position and his constituency had weakened, but it is difficult
to see what else he could do but try to recreate the instability of 1450 in
order to profit from it. If he and his men were to be cast as rebels anyway,
there was not much to lose by attempting to destroy the regime's
jurisdiction.[87] Ignoring royal instructions to lay down his arms and attend
a council at Coventry, York and his army, which included the earl of
Devon and Lord Cobham, set off for London, doubtless intending to
raise the city.[88] His attempts to obtain local support, there and, later, in
Kent, met with disappointment and this can only have confirmed the
lords in their resolve to support Somerset and the royal public body
which he and they had come to constitute.[89] They turned out in force to
confront York near Dartford.

It was surely as a consequence of this display of seigneurial unity that
the duke, whose forces were probably equivalent and whose strategic
position was good, was induced to negotiate: he had intended to overawe,
not to fight, but his bluff had been called.[90] He had little choice but to
surrender and to hope that his articles would receive a sympathetic
hearing from the lords.[91] In the event, they must have decided to treat
York's dispute with Somerset as a purely personal one, to put it aside for
future adjudication and to deal in the meantime with the fact of York's
having risen in arms.[92] Without the anticipated uprising of the *communitas*, the narrowing of York's attack to Somerset alone did not work: it
turned a public enterprise into a private quarrel, leaving the regime intact
and able to impose the traditional machinery of dispute settlement, which,
in turn, bolstered its own authority. The oath of obedience sworn by the
duke at St Paul's demonstrated, with perfect clarity, the consequences
which followed from the restoration of effective royal government.[93]
Aggrieved subjects, such as York, should apply to the king for satisfaction: he, his ministers and his law would defend his people and judge

---

[87] The letter to Shrewsbury records Somerset's labours to 'disinherit me and my heirs, and
such persons as be about me, without any desert or cause done or attempted, on my part
or theirs' (*PL*, I, p. 97). York had been placed in a similar position in September 1450, of
course: see above, p. 268.

[88] See Goodman 1981: pp. 19–22 for a clear account of the Dartford campaign. For the
involvement of Devon and Cobham, see below, p. 299. Note that York was obviously
not heading towards the king, who may have been *en route* for Coventry ('Benet's
Chron.', p. 206; Giles, *Chronicon*, p. 43).

[89] For the lack of popular support for York, see *EHL*, p. 297; *English Chron.*, p. 70.

[90] 'Benet's Chron.', p. 206, suggests that York's army was for his own protection.

[91] See Johnson 1988: p. 112 and *PL*, I, pp. 103–8, for what appear to be the articles
mentioned in e.g. 'Benet's Chron.', p. 207.

[92] Below, p. 296.

[93] *RP*, V, pp. 346–7.

between them. No one but Henry VI and the men he appointed spoke and acted for the common weal: there was no room in the polity for another regent, steward or protector. It may seem rather remarkable that the crown had re-established this degree of authority so soon after the nadir of 1450. How this was achieved is the subject of the following section.

SOMERSET AND THE RESTORATION OF GOVERNMENT, 1450–1453

The crisis which overtook Suffolk's regime in the autumn of 1449 forced the nobility to return to the centre of affairs, but this, as we have seen, did little to improve the position of the king's ministers and intimates. The intermittent participation of parliamentary peers in conciliar deliberations and public acts might have rescued the king and prevented anarchy, but it did not create a firm basis for authority and it did not alter the public perception that an inner ring of 'traitors', mostly from the household, remained in control of the executive.[94] In fact, this perception was not entirely inaccurate: the undesirability of making formal changes to the regime in the midst of crisis, and the unwillingness of all but a few lords to commit themselves to a sustained and prominent role in government, meant that in the weeks following Suffolk's removal, the day-to-day management of grace and state appear to have remained in much the same hands as before.[95] For the most part, it was men closely connected with the dead duke who, in the spring of 1450, took decisions, filled offices left vacant by the crisis and put the king's case to the commons at Leicester.[96] Many of them were prominent in the household, but it was

---

[94] Note that periods of conciliar activity appear to correlate with sessions of parliament. For example, a series of meetings running from 3 May to 29 May 1450 coincided with the Leicester session, which was attended by several lords (see *PL*, II, p. 148). Note too that several warrants of February 1450 are endorsed as made by advice of the lords of parliament (E28/80/6, 9, 11).

[95] It is difficult to say much with certainty about the composition of the government in the early part of 1450, since few records showing who attended its decisions have survived (only nine for the period February–July inclusive). What records do exist show the principal participants to be the prelates Kemp (the chancellor), Stafford, Waynflete, and Bourgchier and the Lords Cromwell and Dudley. The earls of Worcester and Warwick, Lord Scales and Sir John Fastolf attended one recorded meeting each. Ayscough and Saye and Sele attended before their deaths. This was substantially the same group of men who had been taking part in affairs during 1449 and, in many cases, before.

[96] Note, for example, the distribution of Suffolk's offices in the summer of 1450: Thomas Daniel (not a friend, but certainly a member of the household), Tuddenham and Stanley replaced him in the duchy (*PL*, II, p. 150; Somerville 1953: pp. 420, 428 – in both cases as his survivors); Beaumont became chamberlain of England (*CPR, 1446–52*, p. 329); Beauchamp of Powick became keeper of the New Forest and, more significantly, of the earldom of Pembroke (*CPR, 1446–52*, p. 326; *CFR, 1445–52*, pp. 150–1); Stanley was justice of North Wales by July 1452 (and probably from Suffolk's death, since he was

not proximity to the king which placed them in charge. What had happened, rather, was that the *grande peur* had thinned the ranks of the administration to those whose links with the condemned regime were difficult to disguise.[97] Apart from a handful of bishops and sometime councillors like Kemp and Cromwell, the lords without curial associations remained on the sidelines.[98] Only when Cade's rebellion seemed to threaten the whole structure of authority did the greater nobility take decisive action, and even then they were uncertain allies for the government: the lords would protect the king and themselves, but they could not be counted upon to save the 'traitors' as well.[99]

This pattern began to change in early August 1450, when, the vacation notwithstanding, king and lords gathered in London and began to respond to some of the immediate problems facing them with a new

already chamberlain: *CPR, 1446–52*, p. 581); Sudeley became keeper of Cornbury Park on 17 August (*ibid.*, p. 403); Lord Lovell, almost certainly a member of Suffolk's Thames Valley connection, was made steward of Wallingford on 11 August (*ibid.*, p. 333). The defence of Calais, the captaincy of which Buckingham had resigned, was entrusted to the same sort of men: Wiltshire, Bourgchier, Sudeley, Stourton, Stanley and Sir Thomas Rempston, appointed wardens on 2 April 1450 (*DKR*, XLVIII, p. 382). When the mutiny of the lords' men meant that a new treasurer had to be appointed in place of Saye, the choice fell on another curialist – Beauchamp of Powick, master of the king's horse (*CPR, 1446–52*, p. 330; *PPC*, VI, pp. 87–8, and note also the appointment of Beauchamp and the courtier St Amand as chancellor of the exchequer in October 1449: *CPR, 1446–52*, p. 311). One chronicler thought that Daniel had great rule about the king at the time of Cade's rebellion (*Town Chrons.*, p. 131) and another mentioned the activity of the king's 'iuvenibus consiliariis' – almost certainly household types – at Leicester (*Loci e Libro*, p. 189; and note the existence of a single proviso exempting all grants to Beaumont, Cromwell, Sudeley, Beauchamp, Saye, Stourton, St Amand, Sir Edmund Hungerford and Sir Thomas Stanley from the Resumption – *RP*, V, pp. 189–90 – could these have been the king's counsellors at Leicester?).

[97] This may also explain why attendance at decisions made 'per avisamentum consilii' in this period (e.g. at Leicester 3–29 May: E28/80/45–57) was so rarely recorded. Lords thought to be shielding the traitors were in danger, of course: note especially the threats made by mutinous retainers during Cade's rebellion (e.g. 'Benet's Chron.', p. 199).

[98] See n. 95, above. Cromwell seems to have become very influential indeed in 1450–1. He became chamberlain sometime before March 1451 (C53/190, no. 35) and was soon after accorded a dominant position in the duchy (Somerville 1953: pp. 421, 428–9, 492). Kemp, who had probably been appointed chancellor by the lords, seems to have played a role in government reminiscent of Cardinal Beaufort. An order to pay a messenger in February 1450 is endorsed 'de mandato cancellarii' (E28/80/7) and a bill of April 1450 requesting a reduction in a county farm was passed by the king 'yf [it] be thought resounable unto my lord chancellr . . . and elles not' (E28/80/42).

[99] During Cade's rebellion, the government evidently felt it could rely on the assistance of a number of important lords beyond its immediate circle: see *CPR, 1446–52*, p. 385, and C81/1371/23 for commissions to Buckingham, Oxford, Devon, Arundel, Scales, Salisbury, Greystoke, Northumberland and Clifford among others. Buckingham, in particular, took a leading part in confronting the rebels (*Great Chron.*, pp. 182–3) and a number of other lords, including Exeter, Northumberland, Lisle, Scales and perhaps others also turned out (*Town Chrons.*, pp. 130–1). The uncertain quality of their support is demonstrated by e.g. Exeter's refusal to release Lord Saye, the chamberlain, from the Tower of London ('Benet's Chron.', p. 199) and see *Town Chrons.*, p. 154, for similar attitudes on the part of Buckingham.

vigour.[100] Arrangements were made to restore order to the provinces by coupling repressive measures with the investigation of grievances.[101] Money was provided for the returning soldiers who were a source of disorder in the capital.[102] A formal council of peers met at the end of the month and may have agreed to call a parliament.[103] Finally, when the potentially rebellious duke of York arrived in North Wales a few days later, the government was sufficiently well organised to resist him.[104] The origin of these displays of energy and efficiency almost certainly lay in the sudden ascendancy of the duke of Somerset, who had arrived in London at the beginning of August and was taking part in government within a fortnight.[105] These were the opening stages of a three-year campaign to restore and maintain a measure of authority at the centre of Henry VI's polity. How Somerset achieved this, and with what results, are the issues which this section aims to address.

Edmund Beaufort's rapid advance to head the disparate group which comprised the government requires some explanation. Not surprisingly, given the scale of the disaster over which he had presided, he returned from Normandy under a cloud and may even have been imprisoned briefly.[106] What did he have to offer the lords that persuaded them to

---

[100] A council apparently met at St Albans on 24 July: its members may have gone with the king to London on the 28th (Wolffe 1981: p. 239).

[101] Commissions of inquiry, aimed at the alleged extortions of Suffolk's supporters were issued on 1 August for Kent and East Anglia: *CPR, 1446–52*, p. 388. At about the same time, other commissions, judicial and military, were sent to deal with continuing disturbances in London and the south: *ibid.*, pp. 431–3.

[102] E404/66/205, 215; E28/80/83; Griffiths 1981: pp. 645–6. Other financial arrangements were made at about the same time, including, on 14 August, orders to regain all the king's jewels currently in use as securities for loans and reuse them as pledges to raise money elsewhere (E28/80/78).

[103] The council, which was evidently quite a major affair, met on about 24 or 25 August (*PL*, II, pp. 162, 164–5; E28/80/83–6). Summonses to a parliament were despatched on 5 September (*CClR, 1447–54*, pp. 225–7).

[104] Griffiths 1991h. The question of what to do about York may have been discussed at the council of late August. Lord Lisle, who went, on royal orders, to intercept York in September, was present on 27 August (*ibid.*, p. 271; E28/80/86).

[105] Storey 1966: p. 75.

[106] Something of Somerset's disgrace is shown by the loss of his main West Country estates in the resumption of 1449–50 and the grant (in June 1450) of their custody to the young duke of Exeter (*CFR, 1445–52*, p. 175). Some of the French chronicles have Somerset being imprisoned on his arrival and then questioned by the lords about his conduct in Normandy, before being excused: e.g. d'Escouchy, *Chronique*, pp. 314–15; de Waurin, *Croniques*, V, pp. 261, 264. This could be the result of confusion with the events of December (though de Waurin does have the duke being imprisoned twice in 1450: see p. 265). Even so, a series of questions to be put to Somerset has survived: *Letters and Papers*, II, ii, pp. 718–22. They deal with the events of 1449 and 1450 only, which may rule out any later dating. They are worded in a hostile way and include explicit reference to, for example, the embezzlement of compensation for Maine. It may be that the duke was examined at the council held at St Albans on 24 July 1450 (n. 100, above; he left Normandy in mid-July: Jones 1982: p. 277). If so, he must have been promptly exonerated (as in d'Escouchy, above).

overlook his involvement in the humiliating defeats of the preceding year and to raise him above other leading figures, such as Kemp and Buckingham, who could otherwise have taken the lead? One possibility, raised by Michael Jones' research on his long career in France, is that he was a forceful, competent and ambitious man: this in itself could have enabled him to seize the initiative at a time when most others were happy to surrender it.[107] Another factor to consider is his Beaufort blood, which could have conferred on him a certificate of loyalty to the shaky dynasty and also, perhaps, given him precedence, even among the royal dukes.[108] His lack of regional lordship, which in some respects might seem to undermine his claims to a directing role, made him in other ways an ideal candidate: territorial lords would not have wanted to become embroiled in the court when the business of local rule required their attention in the provinces.[109] Finally, unlike York, who was in so many respects fitted for the leadership of lords and realm, Somerset was not about to endorse the public cry for justice upon the 'traitors': he himself was too deeply implicated.[110] The household needed protection and the nobility needed inspiration and a pole to gather around. Somerset could, and did, provide all this. Once his lordship had been sought and accepted, it grew in strength as the conflict with York unfolded.[111]

Somerset's government was, in reality, something very different from the band of impregnable courtiers, clamped like leeches on the royal person, which York and others disingenuously depicted. Far from being the latest favourite of a resurgent king, or the new lord of an indestructible court affinity, Duke Edmund was the manager of a discreetly consultative and representative regime, which – not unlike Suffolk's before it – succeeded in bringing together king, lords, household and bureaucracy to suit the demands of a complex situation. It was a difficult, almost self-contradictory, task which Beaufort faced. First of all, he had to reassert the king's right to personal control of the government, because it was only on the assumption that Henry was competent to govern that he and other royal ministers and servants were empowered to express his will. There was not much to justify this assumption in 1450 – and Somerset, as we

---

[107] See Jones 1982: esp. pp. 93–6, 213–14, 220–67 (a necessarily abbreviated version appears in Jones 1989a: pp. 299–300). Before the defeat, his military reputation was very high indeed, certainly higher than York's according to Jones 1982: p. 149.

[108] Griffiths 1991i: p. 90.

[109] For Somerset's lack of landed power, see Jones 1982: pp. 14, 19. Cf. the convenient position of Suffolk's more ample estates: above, p. 160.

[110] Above, p. 269.

[111] Somerset played a leading role in the suppression of disorder in Kent during September and October and was appointed constable on 11 September, presumably as a token of his pre-eminence and martial activity (Jones 1989a: p. 287; Griffiths 1981: p. 648; CPR, 1446–52, p. 401).

shall see, had to take action accordingly – but, if the alternative perception triumphed, the future for the duke, the 'traitors', and perhaps the house of Lancaster itself, looked grim. At the same time, it was essential to make visible improvements to the representativeness and competence of Henry's regime. The commons had to be persuaded that the king was well-advised: that the message of 1449–50 had got through; that finances were soundly administered; and that the government enjoyed the confidence and participation of great lords. The obvious answer was the restoration of some form of organised counsel, but, as has been said, this had somehow to be made compatible both with Somerset's own retention of overall direction and with the transmission of a sense that the king himself was directing affairs. Meanwhile, the duke faced both a short-term and a long-term challenge. The first was to create a regime sufficiently convincing to attract the loyalties of lords and commons and end the 'troubleus tyme' of 1450.[112] The second was to retain and manage these loyalties – in short, to govern – when the sense of crisis had evaporated and a measure of normality returned.

In the short period before York's return and the parliament of November 1450, there were few changes to the form of the government;[113] but, when Somerset regained power after the Yorkist interlude, in the spring of 1451, he seems to have set about building an executive council.[114] Key aspects of formalised counsel are certainly lacking from its records: membership, though increasingly settled, was apparently not fixed; minutes, if they were taken, have not, except in one case, survived; forms of endorsement reflecting conciliar autonomy were almost never used; no ordinances governing the council's work seem to have been drawn up. Even so, the survival of many instruments endorsed 'de mandato regis per avisamentum consilii', and the range of business covered by them, suggest that a reasonably formal body was at work restoring order to the royal finances and dealing with other administrative problems which arose.[115] Following the affirmation of Somerset's leadership at Dartford, moreover, a further reshaping of government may have

---

[112] Quotation from E28/81/4. See also E404/68/103 for a similar description of the period around 1450.

[113] Somerset's colleagues in government between the beginning of August and end of October 1450 were much the same men as those in power before, if it is safe to draw any conclusions from the minimal evidence (just eight documents: E28/80/79–86, *passim*; C81/1546/54–5). The men concerned were Archbishops Kemp and Stafford (particularly), Buckingham, Sudeley, Beauchamp, St Amand, Waynflete, Bishop Kemp of London, Boulers, Lowe, Rivers, Lisle and, additionally, Lord Welles.

[114] See E28/81, which covers the period May to August 1451. It seems likely that the many references to 'lords of the council' in contemporary sources for the summer and autumn of 1450 (see e.g. *PL*, II, pp. 164, 165, 182, 197, 200, 204) reflect the prominence of the peers at this time, rather than any more organised conciliar structure (cf. above, p. 282).

[115] The king was fairly often absent from the making of these decisions, almost all of which

taken place. Lord Beauchamp of Powick was replaced as treasurer by the earl of Worcester, for example, and it is possible that behind this manoeuvre was an intention to emphasise the regime's independence from the household.[116] In addition, the appointment of a new keeper of the privy seal seems to have been associated with the continuing development of this administrative council, although the limitations of the records make it hard to be sure.[117] Curiously, almost no recorded meetings took place in late 1452 and early 1453 – partly, perhaps, because of the parliament – but in the summer of that year, a small body, resembling a modern cabinet, met regularly until the king's collapse and dealt with business both routine and political.[118] As the council became more defined, so magnate participation diminished, but this is not necessarily because of declining confidence in the government.[119] The important

concern fiscal matters. A similar series, including some minor judicial business, exists for the early part of 1452 (E28/82/*passim*).

[116] One chronicler states that Beauchamp was 'expulsus' from the treasury (*Letters and Papers*, II, ii, p. 770), but, if this was indeed the case, he does not seem to have been out of favour, since he recieved a payment of £400 in respect of his good service: E404/68/103. Similar changes of office include Cromwell replacing Daniel and Tuddenham or Stanley in the chief stewardships of the duchy in the spring of 1451 (Somerville 1953: pp. 421, 428–9; *PL*, II, p. 150) and Somerset replacing Wiltshire, Bourgchier, Sudeley, Stourton, Stanley and Rempston as captain of Calais the following September (Harriss 1960: p. 31).

[117] The change of keeper may have been part of a deliberate revival of the council, since, from the day of Lisieux's appointment as keeper of the privy seal (15 May 1452: *HBC*, p. 95), notes of attendance are much more frequently kept. Evidence of reasonably regular council meetings exists for May, June and July 1452, but there is almost nothing after that until March 1453. Other evidence of conciliar vigour in the period 1452–3 includes a bill actually signed by a number of lords (BL, Add. MS 21,505, fol. 2: almost unique between 1436 and 1454), three instances of the council dealing with matters of grace (C81/1371/26, 37; C81/1546/64–5), the appointment of new keepers of Roxburgh while the king was away in Surrey (E404/69/64); a signet letter with a note of the lords witnessing it (PSO1/19/995); and even one formal appointment of a councillor (E404/69/190: this was Lord Dudley, in November 1452 – perhaps best understood as part of a process of restoration after his trial in 1450–1).

[118] A great council met from late November to late December 1452, although we have no record of its work (E404/70/2/52). See E28/83 and *PPC*, VI, *passim*, for summer 1453. During this period, names were nearly always recorded and actual minutes seem to have been taken on 23 May, including the phrase 'Be ther maad', which is reminiscent of earlier periods of conciliar rule, although the king's sign manual appears at the top (*ibid.*, p. 133; see also E28/83/31 for a usage of the conciliar endorsement 'it was commanded'). It seems likely that most of the July meetings and all those of August were held in the king's absence, though the council did meet with the king at Sheen on 21 July (E28/83/41). The membership was increasingly compact in July and August: dominated by Bishop Waynflete, the duke of Somerset, the prior of St Johns and the dean of St Severin's, Lord Dudley, Thomas Thorpe and the three great officers. Others termed as councillors at this time include Sir Thomas Tyrell and Sir William Lucy (*PPC*, VI, pp. 147–8, 163–4) and Thomas Browne, the under-treasurer, who was actually 'licensed' to be absent from the council for a time, which may imply that a formalised body was meeting (E28/83/48).

[119] This was typical: see Brown 1969b: p. 117. Figure 4 shows the changing pattern of attendance.

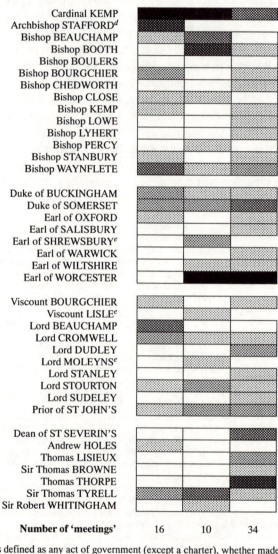

Name	1451[a]	1452[b]	1453[c]

Cardinal KEMP
Archbishop STAFFORD[d]
Bishop BEAUCHAMP
Bishop BOOTH
Bishop BOULERS
Bishop BOURGCHIER
Bishop CHEDWORTH
Bishop CLOSE
Bishop KEMP
Bishop LOWE
Bishop LYHERT
Bishop PERCY
Bishop STANBURY
Bishop WAYNFLETE

Duke of BUCKINGHAM
Duke of SOMERSET
Earl of OXFORD
Earl of SALISBURY
Earl of SHREWSBURY[e]
Earl of WARWICK
Earl of WILTSHIRE
Earl of WORCESTER

Viscount BOURGCHIER
Viscount LISLE[e]
Lord BEAUCHAMP
Lord CROMWELL
Lord DUDLEY
Lord MOLEYNS[e]
Lord STANLEY
Lord STOURTON
Lord SUDELEY
Prior of ST JOHN'S

Dean of ST SEVERIN'S
Andrew HOLES
Thomas LISIEUX
Sir Thomas BROWNE
Thomas THORPE
Sir Thomas TYRELL
Sir Robert WHITINGHAM

| Number of 'meetings' | 16 | 10 | 34 |

A 'meeting' is defined as any act of government (except a charter), whether made by king or by 'council', at which members of the nobility were recorded as being present.

Key: percentage of meetings attended
Not part of the government (blank space)

☐ None   ▦ 1–20%   ▦ 21–40%   ▦ 41–60%   ■ 61–80%   ☐ 81–100%

[a] 1 May–7 December 1451.   [b] 12 April–22 December 1452.   [c] 3 March–29 August 1453.
[d] Died May 1452.   [e] In France from autumn 1452 (Shrewsbury) or early 1453 (Lisle, Moleyns).

Figure 4   Participation in the government, 1451–3

point is that Somerset seems to have created a competent executive, capable of acting independently of the royal person and altogether better suited to the complexities of crown authority after 1450 than any alternative.

In this, as in other areas, Somerset and his supporters were responsive to the criticisms levelled at the government in 1449–50. Certainly, they rejected parliamentary demands for a council to scrutinise royal grants and they did nothing to incorporate York in a 'substancial' council bearing any 'more ample auctorite' than the body hastily put together in 1449, but they were by no means hostile to reform.[120] The fiscal provisions of 1450 were discreetly put into effect.[121] The possibility of pruning the household may have been floated.[122] Allegations of detention of war wages made against Sir Thomas Hoo and Sir Andrew Ogard received a hearing in early 1452[123] and the trials of the more notorious figures in the Suffolk regime – Daniel, Trevilian and Say, for example[124] – were allowed to continue after York's influence subsided. Although these and other so-called 'traitors' were acquitted, they were not restored to obvious favour for some time.[125] The crown was putting its house in

---

[120] *RP*, V, p. 218; Griffiths 1981: p. 288.

[121] For the effectiveness of the 1450–1 resumption, see Wolffe 1971: pp. 133–4. The 1449–50 provisions for the household were kept until 1452, at least: Harriss 1953: pp. 141–2. In January 1451, efforts were made to prevent debtors from using royal pardons to avoid exchequer process (*PPC*, VI, p. 104, and Griffiths 1981: p. 289). These should be read less as a move against the council, perhaps – (cf. Johnson 1988: p. 95 and Wolffe 1981: pp. 244–5 – than as an attempt to forestall any surcease of process, no matter how authorised. I am most grateful to Dr G. L. Harriss for his help with this obscurely worded document).

[122] See *PPC*, VI, p. 221.

[123] *CPR, 1446–52*, p. 537. Ogard was actually summoned to answer by letters of 15 May: E28/82/34. It is fairly certain that he was no longer an associate of York by this time, incidentally: he was not among those indicted for their activities in February 1452 and even figured on at least one of the indicting juries in February 1453 (KB9/85/1, m. 10). He was one of Queen Margaret's carvers by Michaelmas 1452: Myers, 'Household of Queen Margaret', p. 403.

[124] Above, p. 275 n. 60. Note that Daniel was ordered to be tried again in October 1451, at which point York had no influence over policy at all (*CPR, 1446–52*, p. 532). The fact that Daniel was reputedly in Somerset's favour at the time of the commission (*PL*, II, p. 255) did not prevent this instance of justice being seen to be done. To a similar end, perhaps, he had been pressed to surrender his office of remembrancer of the exchequer before the opening of the 1450–1 parliament: *CPR, 1446–52*, p. 405. He was in trouble again in January 1452: see C253/33/18.

[125] The duchess of Suffolk was allowed to keep her husband's lands, but she was made to pay for the privilege, advancing 3,500 marks out of the proceeds before 8 October 1450: *CPR, 1446–52*, p. 431. Although the evidence is sketchy, it seems that Bishop Boulers did not reappear at the council during 1451, whilst Lord Dudley was – or had to be – formally reappointed to it in November 1452 (see n. 117, above). John Trevilian had to wait until March and October 1452 to regain his losses from the resumptions: *CPR, 1446–52*, pp. 513, 526; *CPR, 1452–61*, p. 50. Bishop Lyhert, who faced no accusations, but was known to have been closely associated with Suffolk, seems to have stayed away from the government until the spring of 1453.

order, but it was doing so apparently at its own will and without resorting to extraordinary measures that undermined its authority.

Similar considerations influenced other policies. In order to restore an authority focused on Henry's person, without reviving the sense that government was being usurped by household men, Somerset and his colleagues launched a series of judicial and military initiatives in which the king could be seen to be performing his traditional duties with the wholehearted support of his true nobility. So successful was this enterprise that it has led to speculation that the crisis of 1450 elicited a new vigour from Henry VI.[126] This seems unlikely: the king himself was soon to plumb new depths of personal inactivity and, as we have seen, every previous display of royal firmness can be related to common or individual political needs and fairly presented as the work of others. After the humiliations of 1449–50, the time was ripe for ministerial action to advance the royal reputation.

The doing of justice was concentrated in three great tourns, headed by the king and including large numbers of magnates, the first of which – to Kent, in January 1451 – was, as we have seen, a basis for the restoration of royal authority after the Yorkist assault of the previous November.[127] Meanwhile, in April 1452, a general pardon was made available to all except the murderers of the curial bishops.[128] Grace of this kind was, of course, the corollary of justice and, in its way, quite as demonstrative of royal authority. On this occasion, it must have signalled the end of the period of chaos and division, awakening hopes of a return to order. It is not difficult to see how important these measures were in undermining York. Against the suggestion that disorder could only be met by reforms of various kinds, Somerset was appearing to show that firm royal justice, casting criticism as rebellion and ignoring its content, could work just as well. In a sense, the men who rose up in the wake of Cade presented the regime with a golden opportunity: a threat to order and property from outside the aristocracy, which, once effectively resisted, drew almost all landowners together, including the parliamentary knights of the shires.

---

[126] See e.g. Griffiths 1981: p. 253; Wolffe 1981: pp. 264, 267. Interestingly, the equivalent crisis of summer 1453 is often alleged to have produced not vigour, but stupor in the king: *ibid.*, p. 270; Griffiths 1981: p. 715.

[127] See above, pp. 276–7. Henry was accompanied by many of the lords who had taken part in the government of summer 1450, viz. Somerset, Exeter, Arundel, Shrewsbury, Wiltshire, Worcester, Bourgchier, Roos, Cromwell, Sudeley and St Amand: *CPR, 1446–52*, p. 442. The ensuing progresses were in the summers of 1451 and 1452: for the commissions accompanying the king, see *CPR, 1446–52*, pp. 477, 580–1; *CPR, 1452–61*, p. 54. They contained a total of four dukes (all except York), six earls (all the southern earls except Devon), Viscount Bourgchier and a dozen barons. For illustrations of the king's prominence in these proceedings, see e.g. Harvey 1991: p. 152; *Town Chrons.*, p. 107.

[128] Storey 1966: p. 101.

This enabled the quasi-conciliar government to do justice effectively, and so to advance its claims to sole defence of the peace and sole representation of the *communitas*, without creating tensions or divisions within the body of lords on whom much of its power actually depended.

Not only in the sphere of justice, but also in the other great area of kingly duty – the prosecution of war – did Somerset make important moves. Although plans to rescue Gascony in 1451 foundered amid the usual problem of lack of cash, the government regained the initiative with a well-publicised scheme to send the king to the defence of Calais in early 1452.[129] Although, as in 1436, Henry did not actually go, the parallels with the earlier expedition are clear and instructive: through the agency of an active adult king, a corporate commitment among the nobility could be inspired.[130] By chance, in fact, the episode coincided with York's rising, and this must have brought Somerset additional advantage by casting doubt on Duke Richard's claim to be opposing the government on behalf of the national interest.[131] Meanwhile, a second expedition to Gascony in the autumn of 1452 was much more successful than the first.[132] Shrewsbury's reconquest of Bordeaux provided the background to the triumphant parliament of 1453, in which the government demonstrated the fact that it had recaptured the confidence of the commons by launching a decisive attack on those who had dabbled in insurrection in the preceding few years.[133]

The visible participation of the nobility was, of course, as integral to the success of Somerset's regime as the visible participation of the king. Besides providing the lords with opportunities to serve a more active and effective royal power, the duke seems to have taken some more direct steps to secure the support of key figures. There is some evidence to suggest that Somerset set out to woo the duke of Norfolk[134] and the earls

---

[129] The expedition to Gascony may have been Somerset's idea, since it seems that plans were first drawn up in August 1450 and resumed at Christmas of that year, when Somerset was again at liberty (Griffiths 1981: p. 529; *CPR, 1446–52*, p. 437). The duke lent some of his own plate to help pay for the expedition (*EHL*, p. 372), but to no avail: Bordeaux and Bayonne were lost by the time adequate funding arrived (Griffiths 1981: p. 530). For the Calais initiative, see e.g. Wolffe 1981: pp. 256–7.

[130] Above, pp. 129–30.

[131] His specific accusations concerning Somerset's captaincy of Calais (*PL*, I, pp. 106–7) – e.g. that he would 'bylike sotill meanes contrive and ymagyn the losse and amission of youre said Toun of Cales' – must also have fallen rather flat.

[132] Griffiths 1981: pp. 530–2.

[133] Below, pp. 294ff.

[134] Somerset may have been involved in the creation of Norfolk's son as earl of Surrey and Warenne on 24 March 1451 (*CChR*, VI, p. 114: the measure is likely to have required royal participation, although the presence of York and Warwick on the witness-list (C53/190/33) may mean that it was a measure promoted by the peers in parliament rather than those about the king). Norfolk probably brought a contingent to the royal host at Dartford: he was certainly at the council at Dunstable (above, p. 280 n. 85) and

of Salisbury[135] and Warwick,[136] for example; men who had gone further towards York than some of their peers during the early stages of the 1450–1 parliament.[137] As has been seen, the capacity of the peerage to resist York's lordship when circumstances favoured him was rather restricted and Somerset's main hope of success lay in making sure that such circumstances did not arise again. Patronage could help to soothe specific grievances or to create limited bonds of association against an outsider, but it was on the regime's ability to provide both its noble constituents and the *communitas* at large with adequate rule that its survival would ultimately depend.[138] In the short term, however, what mattered most was to gather a convincing body of lords behind king and government. Here, Somerset was plainly successful. Although we can be fairly sure that it was indeed Beaufort who was the principal figure co-ordinating the regime, it is interesting that some contemporaries identified a number of substantial men – Kemp and Buckingham, for example, as much as Somerset himself – as Henry's leading advisers at this time.[139]

received a large reward for recent service in May (E404/68/129 – though this may have been for service done in suppressing riots in Norfolk in April: *PL*, II, pp. 258–9). He received a pardon of all financial abuses on 20 March 1452: *CPR, 1446–52*, p. 530. At the same time, the government seems to have been willing to show Norfolk some sympathy in the rule of East Anglia. In 1452, it was noted that the duke was co-operating with Thomas Daniel, apparently in response to pressure from Somerset (*PL*, II, pp. 273–4, 254–5, and see Harvey, *Worcestre: Itineraries*, p. 253). When Norfolk found himself in conflict with the resurgent De La Pole affinity (under Scales) in 1452–3, the government was not unfavourable to him. Signet letters of February and April 1453 ordered that no exigent should be had against any of the duke's servants indicted that year (KB9/118/2, mm. 163–4). Many of them were pardoned, including even William Ashton, who had been accused of high treason (*ibid.*, m. 241).

135 Salisbury's sons were knighted at Christmas 1450 (above, p. 277 n. 66). In June 1451 Salisbury's *de facto* control of the lands of his idiot brother, Lord Latimer, was recognised by a patent (*CPR, 1446–52*, p. 430) and three months later, the earl brought troops to the king's side at Coventry (Wolffe 1981: p. 252). On 14 February 1452, as the government's showdown with York approached, Salisbury was granted a series of lands and rents in tail male to hold as a fee for the wardenship of the forests beyond Trent and regranted various items lost in the resumptions (*ibid.*, pp. 566–7). He was summoned to join the king with an army in the autumn of 1451 and was later rewarded for remaining, in arms, with the court until after the encounter at Dartford: E404/68/96. Finally, when a new earl of Richmond was created in 1453, Salisbury's possession of the Yorkshire honour continued undisturbed: below, pp. 294–5.

136 Warwick's 'restoration' seems to have waited until after he had proved himself by joining the king at Dartford. On 17 March, he was pardoned all unlicensed entries and, more significantly, intrusions, into his wife's inheritance and granted £300 for his recent service (*CPR, 1446–52*, pp. 523–4). Nine days later, he received a regrant of various lands – including the barony of Egremont – which had been in his keeping before the resumptions (*CFR, 1445–52*, p. 268).

137 See above, p. 275 n. 61. Note that Warwick and Salisbury were the two lords temporal appointed to negotiate with York at Dartford, which may suggest that they were thought to have preserved credibility with the duke: *Chrons. of London*, p. 163.

138 Cf. above, p. 252.

139 For example, an October 1453 indictment for seditious words claimed that some men of Southwark wanted the heads of Somerset, Kemp and Buckingham (KB9/273, m. 103),

As the Dartford episode illustrates, Edmund Beaufort had secured the backing of almost all the leading noblemen. Whether their support was any less provisional (if more prolonged) than that accorded to York in December 1450, however, remains to be seen.

In order, meanwhile, to make use of the royal person in the way that he did, Somerset needed a measure of control over the household: and the more so, perhaps, because he had no official position there himself.[140] This, in turn, is partly explained by the important consideration that, after 1450, it was essential that the axis of power should be seen to lie between the king and the nobility, not, as under Suffolk (particularly in his later years), between the king and the household-dominated court. The tone of Somerset's regime was, as we have seen, more conciliar than curial, but even so, various factors disposed the household to support the duke. For one, it was already well represented in the body of men he took over in 1450.[141] More importantly, it seems possible that the household had learnt its lesson from the events of that convulsive year. Its members were not free to do as they pleased: only a slender authority protected them from York and the howling mob, and that authority was not Henry VI himself, but the manager of his public government, Somerset. As in the 1430s, the household drew together to accept the lordship of someone other than the king, providing him with a secure platform for the management of royal rule. Because of the changed nature of Henry's personal authority, the household's loyalty to Somerset is shown less by its participation in government and more by the assistance it must have given the duke in 1450 and 1455, when he had temporarily lost his following among the lords.[142] In return, and notwithstanding the competing interests of the *communitas*, the government did what it could to indulge this crucial base of support: expenditure was allowed to rise from 1452 and almost nothing was done to check the freedom of at least the greater men of the household to apply to the king for grace.[143]

---

while the pseudo-Worcester noted that the realm was governed by Somerset 'et alios duces adhaerentes': *Letters and Papers*, II, ii, p. 770. Some, of course, presented Somerset as a curial bogeyman on the Suffolk model: e.g. *English Chron.*, p. 71.

[140] Note the intriguing comment of the pseudo-Worcester that although it was Cromwell who was chamberlain, Somerset was 'familiarissimus' with the king and it was he and his supporters that governed: *Letters and Papers*, II, ii, p. 770. A Paston letter tellingly describes the king as having written to the duke of Norfolk 'by the meanes' of Somerset (*PL*, III, p. 4). On 10 December 1451, a grant made and signed by the king was also signed by Somerset, a measure which evokes the rule of Suffolk and, at the very least, proves that the duke was busy about the royal person: C81/1461/47.

[141] See above, pp. 282–3.

[142] Above, p. 277; below, pp. 312–13.

[143] For the pattern of household finance in this period, see Harriss 1953: pp. 115, 129, 134ff. For examples of the fairly lavish grace shown to the more important household men during Somerset's rule, note the grant of 100 marks to Richard Tunstall for service

Another route to influence over both king and household was Somerset's connection with the queen, who paid the duke an annuity of 100 marks from the autumn of 1451.[144] Now in her twenties, Margaret was about to make what appear to be her first independent moves in the field of politics.[145] Apparently a person of some will, she wielded a connection of her own which extended throughout household and realm.[146] Not only this, but a certain capacity to speak for, and through, the king, must have made her a valuable ally to Somerset, enabling him to extend his control over the royal component in his power in a manner unlikely to damage his public standing. This is rather interesting, because it draws attention to the fact that at the heart of Somerset's primarily noble regime, the framework of later Lancastrian rule – focused, amid circumstances of more open division, upon the queen and the household – was already beginning to develop. Despite the prominent public components of the duke's authority, the household was its citadel. The support of the lords could go either way, as the events of 1450–1, 1453–4 and the later 1450s demonstrated, but the household remained loyal to Somerset and the subsequent defenders of the king's immediate interest. There was a good reason for this. Ultimately, as we have seen, the king and his household could not be separated: Somerset had to play the courtier whether he wanted to or not; and York was eventually to find that he could not oppose the curial establishment and remain within the limits of his allegiance to the king.

The high point of Somerset's power was reached in late 1452 and early 1453. Buoyed up by victory over the rebels at home and over the French in Guyenne, the duke put the finishing touches to his refurbishment of the royal estate in November 1452, with the creation of the king's half-brothers, Edmund and Jasper, as earls of Richmond and Pembroke respectively.[147] Endowed with resumed lands, many of them once held

---

done and to be done on 11 August 1451 (E404/67/238) and the payment of £60 'arrears' of resumed annuity to Sir Richard Roos (E404/68/116).

[144] Myers, 'Household of Queen Margaret', p. 418. Note that one chronicler was convinced that Somerset's hegemony rested on the favour of the queen (de Waurin, *Croniques*, V, pp. 264–6), although this view could have been inspired by hindsight. Interestingly, Suffolk's wife had been stationed about the queen in 1446, if not later (E404/63/14) and his confessor, Walter Lyhert, was also hers (*Foedera*, V, I, p. 177).

[145] Most notably the submission of regency plans in the winter of 1453–4: see below, p. 305. Another early political intervention from the queen is a letter she wrote to the duke of Norfolk at some time between 1452 and 1454 telling him that he would not be trusted by the king while he had Richard Southwell in his service (*PL*, III, p. 4).

[146] Leading members at about this time included Viscount Beaumont, the wives of Lords Scales, Grey, Roos and Dacre (all men coming to some prominence in the early 1450s), Sir Edward Hull, Sir Edmund Hungerford, and the clerics William and Laurence Booth and Walter Lyhert (see Myers, 'Household of Queen Margaret', *passim*; *CPR, 1446–52*, pp. 55, 143; *Loci e Libro*, p. 40; Harriss 1953: p. 240).

[147] Griffiths 1981: p. 698.

by Bedford and Gloucester, these two were intended both to increase the royal presence among the peerage and to act as utterly reliable regional powers in the manner of the Beauforts earlier in the century.[148] At the same time, a parliament was summoned which was intended to publicise the achievements of the regime and make a decisive break from the troubled period of the beginning of the decade.[149] This enterprise was to some extent qualified by the government's financial embarrassment, which resulted in the attachment of conditions to the tax-grant, and by its promise – presumably made under pressure – to establish a strong council, but Somerset's success was clear.[150] With Henry himself a prominent feature of the proceedings, large tax-grants and an absence of criticism demonstrated that the king and his ministers had regained the confidence of the wider public represented by the commons.[151]

Somerset had decisively dislodged York from the representation of the national constituency. He pressed this home with uncompromising measures against those who had been involved in the insurrections of 1450–2, including the attainders of Jack Cade and Sir William Oldhall and, it appears, an act of resumption against those who had risen at Dartford.[152] The preamble to the latter referred to those who had been

---

[148] See Thomas 1971: pp. 31ff, 38ff. Typically, the honour of Richmond was already in the hands of the earl of Salisbury, where political realities dictated that it would have to remain (e.g. *CPR, 1446–52*, pp. 566–7; *RP*, V, p. 251). For the Beauforts under Henry IV, see Harriss 1988: pp. 42–3.

[149] *CClR, 1447–54*, pp. 394–6. Various details strongly suggest that the government hoped to obtain particular political dividends from this parliament: Bale's chronicle claimed that it was packed (*Town Chrons.*, pp. 139–40) and certainly the commons included more household men than ever (Wolffe 1981: p. 263); Thomas Thorpe, the speaker, and already a member of the governing council, received £200 by way of reward a week or so after the end of the second session: E404/69/179.

[150] *RP*, V, pp. 228, 240.

[151] Henry thanked the commons in person twice: *ibid.*, pp. 231, 236. Other references to his personal activity included the respiting of the grant of archers until the king chose to 'labore in his Royall person for the defence aforesaide' (p. 233) and the prorogation of parliament in July with a promise that the king proposed to go in person to confront the continuing disorder (p. 236). The various sizeable grants of men and money appear on pp. 228–33, 236.

[152] *RP* V, pp. 265, 266, 329. Cade had already been attainted in the parliament of 1450–1 (*ibid.*, p. 224) and the aim of this second attainder was primarily to damage York and Oldhall by association. Cade was condemned for his pretence of acting on behalf of 'justice and reformation of youre lawes' and for disseminating 'fals and untrue articles and petitions'. Oldhall was accused of giving advice to Cade – an implication which the Tudors were to reproduce as fact – that York had provoked the rebellion (see e.g. Ellis (ed.), *Hall's Chronicle*, pp. 219–20). We know of the resumption only from its subsequent repeal, though it is possible that it may have served as a pretext for grants of York's lieutenancy of Ireland to Wiltshire (*CPR, 1452–61*, p. 102) and his life office of justice of the forests south of Trent to Somerset (*ibid.*, p. 88) and, perhaps, for Thomas Thorpe's alleged confiscation of property belonging to York from the house of the bishop of Durham (*RP*, V, p. 239). All of these appropriations took place in the spring of 1453.

against the king, his weal and the weal of the realm, a perspective which entirely ignored the distinction York and others had drawn between loyalty to the king and common weal, on the one hand, and obedience to his corrupt ministers, on the other. On the basis of its strength in 1453, the government was able to rewrite the history of the opening of the decade. The shame of 1450 had been effaced. The total lack of public confidence in a government which had had no strong claims to authority could now be overlooked. The simple logic of monarchical authority was reinvoked and projected backwards: those outside the court who had taken action to make the crown face up to its public responsibilities were now recast as rebels. From the second half of 1452, these men were hunted down and indicted for their participation in what was now presented as a sustained campaign of opposition, stemming, in the case of Oldhall, from Cade's rebellion itself.[153]

At the time of Dartford, of course, the picture had been more confused. Although the government had brought York, Devon and Cobham to heel, it had not charged them with the treason it was now suggesting they had committed.[154] The lords had even given a partial endorsement to York's actions by making arrangements for arbitration between him and Somerset.[155] Even some months later, most of them showed a marked reluctance to sit in judgement upon his men.[156] The implications of all

---

[153] Avrutick 1967: pp. 118–29. It was in October and November 1452, for example, that the raising of York's retinue for the 1450–1 parliament was portrayed as a series of risings to assist the duke in his evil purposes: KB9/65A, mm. 19, 36; 94/1, m. 5; 7/1, m. 10; 26/1, m. 28. For other indictments of 1452–3 alleging dissidence in 1451, see KB9/65A, m. 1; 85/1, m. 10; 118/1, m. 30; 40/1, m. 5; Johnson 1988: p. 101. York's intervention in the South-West in September 1451 – indeed, even the troubles there, which had a long and independent history – was presented as part of a plot which came to a head at Dartford the following spring (see Johnson 1988: pp. 101–4, where the government's version of events finds a certain acceptance). Note that because Devon and Cobham had risen up in York's train in February 1452, it was easy enough to claim afterwards that they had also done so the preceding September. Similarly, the coincidence between the dates of the south-western riots and the date on which Oldhall was supposed to have planned to seize the king may reflect nothing but the government's ingenuity in creating a plausible tale of intrigue (cf. p. 101).

[154] The oaths sworn by the lords at St Paul's (*ibid.*, pp. 346–7) make no explicit reference to rebellion or treason, although this is clearly implicit. Note that all three oaths were exactly the same (E163/8/19–21).

[155] *CClR, 1447–54*, pp. 327, 334. It may be significant that Somerset was bound in the same large sum (£20,000) as York, despite the fact that he had not at any time resorted to violence.

[156] All the lords appointed to the royal judicial commission of 1451 actually took part in the tourn which followed, but this was not the case in 1452, when it was the South-West and the lands of Richard of York which were the focus of the king's attentions. The commission appointed on 6 July 1452 included Buckingham, Cromwell, Sudeley and Beauchamp, who are not known to have taken part, as well as Somerset, Warwick, Wiltshire, Worcester, Lisle, Moleyns, Hungerford, Stourton, St Amand and Bonville, who did (*CPR, 1446–52*, pp. 580–1). It may be significant that only Wiltshire, together with the justices, seems to have dared to attend sessions in Shropshire, the heartland of

this are important: in a sense, if there had been no rebellion, then there had been nothing to rebel against; the government which York had opposed had not been fully authorised by the king. Had this been true then York's activities were fundamentally justifiable. Even in 1453, as it moved against his men, the government was not prepared to charge the duke himself with treason. While this was perhaps a political calculation, a preference for mercy over justice in the management of a powerful magnate, it was also a tacit admission of the continuing fragility of royal authority. Apparently, the crown could not count on the loyalty of its subjects, common and perhaps even noble,[157] if it tried to deal with York as it had earlier dealt with Gloucester.[158] However inconvenient the duke's behaviour, it was evidently not entirely illegitimate, and this provides a fascinating insight on the problem of authority in Henry VI's last decade. Even as political circumstances dictated that York's assaults on the king's ministers would not succeed, they also protected the duke from total failure. The very fact that it was a political and not a legal problem which York posed and that the crushing logic of monarchy – offering only obedience or treason as political options for the subject – could not be invoked against him, demonstrates that the crown was actually no stronger under Somerset than it had been under Suffolk, or during the minority. Its power was as factitious as it had ever been. Moreover, since it seems that a crucial element in this power was, just as in 1449–50, the existence of an external threat to political order, it becomes especially interesting to explore what happened in 1453 when

York's power: KB9/270, m. 34; 103/1, mm. 9, 22; 270A, m. 77a. There certainly seems to have been some reluctance to endorse the judicial suppression of what was tacitly being cast as a rebellion by York. Warwick, St Amand and Worcester attended none of the sittings in York's towns. A second commission was issued on 28 September 1452 to cover the October progress through the eastern counties: this contained Exeter, Norfolk, Oxford, Worcester, Bourgchier, Roos, Beauchamp, Scales, Sudeley and Stourton who do not seem to have taken part, in addition to Somerset, Wiltshire, Beaumont and others, who did (*CPR, 1452–61*, p. 54). The fact that many of York's more senior followers were exempted from prosecution by signet letters (Johnson 1988: p. 118) may reflect a degree of support for the duke among the lords.

[157] In 1455, it was claimed that the act of resumption and its implicit assault on the probity of York and others had 'set greet and perilouse division amonge many Lordes' (*RP*, V, p. 330), although this may not be true. On the other hand, note the well-known comment of Gregory's chronicle on the mood of the king's thirty-first year: although it had been 'competent welle and pessabylle', the people regretted the passing of Gloucester, and 'sum sayde that the Duke of Yorke hadde grete wronge, but what wronge there was noo man that darste say, but sum grounyd and sum lowryd and hadde dysdayne of othyr and c.': *Collections*, pp. 197–8.

[158] Johnson 1988: p. 120 n. 97 notes that there were no attacks on York's property during his period of disgrace (in contrast to the experiences of Somerset). This must surely reflect a realisation that York could not be made a pariah in the way that Suffolk or Somerset had been, but that he would always represent a power at least sufficient to defend himself and that his rehabilitation thus remained a possibility. This too damaged the government's hopes of crushing the duke decisively.

this threat abated. With York quiescent, and popular dissent quelled, how would Somerset's authority, forged in crisis, manage the peace?

THE DEMISE OF THE KING, 1453-1456

One of the most striking features of high politics in the period of crisis which ran from 1449 to about 1452 is the fact that the division between government and *communitas* did not, at first, produce a corresponding division among the nobility. If most of the lords hesitated to give their support to the various regimes of the period, almost none of them joined in York's call for justice upon the traitors.[159] Only when his power was briefly insurmountable, in November and December 1450, did a significant proportion of the nobility gather behind the duke.[160] It may be, however, that the loyalty of the rest of the lords to Somerset's ministry is less to be explained by its positive capacity to satisfy their interests than by the negative factor of a serious threat to authority. Throughout the so-called 'troubleus tyme', the lords' principal concern appears to have been the preservation of order. For the most part, this led them to act corporately and to support the king; which in turn meant that they supported the government, provided that it could plausibly be presented as the expression of a royal and public will. Because it possessed the same virtues as the councils of the 1420s, 1430s and early 1440s, the Beaufort regime was able to project this image, to obtain credit with the parliamentary commons and to bring the riotous populace under control. Unfortunately, however, it also possessed the same vices as its predecessors. Above all, it could do little to assist the nobility in the rule of the localities.

We have already seen that conciliar, or quasi-conciliar, authorities were unable to impersonate the royal capacity for doing justice among the landed classes.[161] Somerset's government was no exception: indeed, in this respect, it was probably weaker than its predecessors. Earlier regimes had sometimes achieved a limited success by siding with the stronger or better-represented party, but Somerset could not even do this, because, amid the instability of the early 1450s, he could not afford to alienate anyone who might flout, and thus weaken, the fragile authority of his government.[162] The newly emphasised royal justice was, it appeared, effective only against rebels: Somerset, like Suffolk before him, was virtually unable to rule the loyal constitutents of his government. So it was that, in these years, judicial provision at the highest level of society amounted to little more than appeasement, on the one hand, and the

---

[159] As noted by e.g. Storey 1966: pp. 78, 103–4; Griffiths 1981: pp. 695, 700.
[160] Above, pp. 275–6.
[161] Above, pp. 100–1, 176–9, 239–40.   [162] Cf. above, pp. 251–2.

despatch of pleas to behave peaceably, on the other. In East Anglia, for example, the duke seems to have backed all the competing factions at once, a policy which made lordship of any kind impossible, creating confusion and prolonging disorder.[163] In the South-West, he did much the same, until Devon and Cobham opened themselves up to attack by supporting York at Dartford. If this freed the government to give more support to the Bonville group, and so to restore a measure of peace, it seems that success was more a result of luck than good judgement.[164] As much as anything, it was the crown's long-term and continuing failure to provide justice which had inspired Devon to join York's venture.[165] If the Dartford episode had ended differently, it would have been been an early illustration of the dangers inherent in the mismanagement of the localities.

As it was, Beaufort's inability to rule the noble constituents of his government may have begun to become clear in the summer of 1452, with the dispute between the duke of Exeter and Lord Cromwell – both of them important participants in the regime – over the Fanhope properties in Bedfordshire. Exeter's opportunistic entry, the bizarre allegations of treason against Cromwell and the inability of the government to impose any settlement must have advertised the weakness of central control.[166]

---

[163] Somerset seems to have been conciliating not only the Mowbray interests old and new (i.e. pre-Daniel and post-Daniel), but also the De La Pole interest, now mostly under the local direction of Lord Scales: see above, n. 134 and p. 239, and n. 150; *PL*, II, p. 255; *CPR, 1446–52*, p. 577, and *CPR, 1452–61*, pp. 55, 58, for commissions to Scales in Norfolk (the last of which included Norfolk and Oxford alongside Heydon and Tuddenham!); *CFR, 1445–52*, p. 220, for Scales' keeping of the De La Pole lands; *PL*, II, p. 259, for Mowbray's enmity to Scales.

[164] See Storey 1966: ch. V and above, p. 279, for the government's ineffectiveness in 1451. In the wake of Dartford, Bonville's hand was strengthened, and this seems to have been the right solution, to judge by the defection of the more substantial gentry from the earl's following (Cherry 1981a : pp. 132–3).

[165] Above, pp. 239–40.

[166] See Payling 1989 for this dispute. Exeter's importance to the government is shown by his appointment to a large number of the major judicial commissions of 1450–3 (*CPR, 1446–52*, pp. 442, 444–5, 532, 585; *CPR, 1452–61*, pp. 54, 60) and by various custodies of land, granted during the same period (*CFR, 1445–52*, pp. 179, 180, 182–3, 238, 241–2). There is not much to suggest that Cromwell was not similarly favoured, or at odds with Somerset, or associated with York's opposition until the Ampthill dispute. He was, for example, chief of the feoffees in the manor of West Deeping, Lincs., for Margaret, dowager duchess of Somerset (KB9/269, m. 62). This was where Somerset took up residence on his return from France according to *Crowland*, I, p. 398. Cromwell was first placed in control of the duchy of Lancaster in April 1451, by which time Somerset was almost certainly back in power (above, p. 283 and n. 98; although note that in June 1452 Somerset became surveyor and chief councillor of the duchy, perhaps as a check to Cromwell). His feoffees in Ampthill in 1453 were headed by Fortescue and Dudley, men of unquestionable influence in the regime (Payling 1989: p. 894; see *ibid.*, pp. 885–6 for a different view of Cromwell's standing with the regime). Note that both men were appointed to one of the major judicial commissions of July 1452, seven weeks after trouble began in Bedfordshire (*CPR, 1446–52*, p. 585).

No less than in 1449, it seemed to the commons in parliament that 'lakke of execucion of justice' threatened to destroy the realm, and, in March 1453, the government was sufficiently concerned about public opinion to promise the appointment of a substantial council 'for mynistring of justice, equite and rightwesnesse'.[167] In practice, however, Somerset pressed ahead with less drastic solutions, doubtless hoping that with the exemplary treatment of Yorkist dissidents still fresh in every mind, calls for unity and discipline might have some effect.[168] Unity and discipline, however, required a sovereign lordship to maintain them, and this, all too obviously, did not exist, whatever the fictions of Beaufort's power. Unless the king was able to give optimal and committed protection to the interests of all his subjects, local rule became a matter of immediate and divisive significance for members of the nobility.[169] It was impossible for them not to proceed by 'way of fayt', because there was no real higher resort. If they took direct action, however, they revoked – whether tacitly or openly – the public authority of the crown. Because, by this time, royal authority rested on not much more than their complaisance, the results of this revocation were to be dramatic.

The decisive demonstration of the government's impotence came, of course, in the summer of 1453, when a feud in Yorkshire between Sir John Neville and Thomas Percy, Lord Egremont rapidly engulfed the leading magnate families of the North.[170] The participants simply ignored the stream of privy seals summoning them to come and answer before the council, remaining in arms and apparently moving towards open conflict.[171] Incapable of pursuing a strong and independent course, the government combined empty posturing with tacit support for the Nevilles, but this was not enough.[172] Short of raising an army and heading north with the king, Somerset's regime could do nothing to impose its lordship at this stage, whether in favour of the Nevilles or not.

---

[167] RP, V, pp. 183, 240.

[168] At some point in the early sessions of the parliament, the lords were roundly warned that they should not proceed against each other in arms, but instead submit their grievances in writing: PPC, VI, p. 160. For the attack on York, see above, pp. 295–6.

[169] Above, pp. 74, 97. Note also McFarlane 1981f: pp. 247–8 and Wolffe 1981: p. 274.

[170] See Griffiths 1991f; Storey 1966: chs. VII and VIII; Pollard 1990: pp. 254–65.

[171] PPC, VI, pp. 140–63, passim.

[172] Not until the end of June did the government respond to the activities of Salisbury's son (ibid., pp. 141–2), and the first oyer and terminer commission, despatched on 12 July 1453, was certainly weighted in favour of the Nevilles (Griffiths 1991f: pp. 326–7). Note that it was reissued on 25 July, two days before the less partisan commission under William Lucy (CPR, 1452–61, pp. 123, 122). It seems likely that exasperation with persistent governmental preference for the Nevilles was a factor in Percy agitation: Pollard 1990: p. 254. It was presumably this which encouraged Percy tenants at Topcliffe to claim that royal officers should have no jurisdiction in the Percy lands: Griffiths 1991f: p. 324.

Oyer and terminer commissions to local notables were entirely ineffective as a means of asserting central authority: most of the commissioners with muscle were already belligerents; those without were soon drawn in.[173] Forced to act for themselves, then, both sets of disputants continued to ignore the forms of politic rule, raising damaging questions about the validity of royal authority as the violence mounted.

These trends were soon exacerbated by the onset of the king's madness, news of which may have opened the way for the first real battle in the war in the North: the Percy attack on the Cromwell–Neville wedding party at Heworth on 24 August.[174] The removal of the king only emphasised what was already becoming obvious: application to the centre for justice could safely be abandoned; greater risks could be, indeed had to be, taken. Already, in June and July, other contending lords – Exeter and Cromwell in London; Warwick and, possibly, Somerset in Glamorgan – had begun to use force beyond what were taken to be the proper limits.[175] The results of this alarming state of affairs were somewhat paradoxical, as some of the nobility addressed their immediate responsibilities and others looked after their common ones. In the North, the disputants prepared for war. By 20 October, most of the baronage of Yorkshire stood ranged in two opposing armies.[176] Within the same week, however, another group of lords, meeting as a great council at Westminster 'to sette rest and union betwixt the lordes of this lande', despatched a letter to the duke of York, inviting him to attend their deliberations.[177] This was no factional measure: the men who summoned the duke were not associates of his.[178] Their act was a recognition that royal power had collapsed; that only a representative assembly of lords possessed the authority to restore order; and that York must therefore play a part, if not a leading part, in such a body.

Undoubtedly, Henry's illness was an important factor in moving the lords at the centre to take the action they did, but it was not the only one.

[173] Lucy, for example (see above note), was later accused of joining the Percies in their attack on the Neville wedding party: Griffiths 1991f: p. 332. Beaumont was more or less the only powerful neutral on the commissions of 12/25 July. By the end of the year, he had joined the Percies (*ibid.*, p. 337), but political conditions were rather different then.

[174] *Ibid.*, p. 329. It seems fairly likely that news of the king's collapse escaped quite rapidly. An indictment of 3 October 1453 has men of Southwark speaking 'contumelious and irreverent' words about the king on 1 August (KB9/273, m. 103): the indicting jury's choice of date may mean that it was soon widely known that this was the day on which the king had fallen ill (see also 'Benet's Chron.', p. 210). Members of the nobility probably knew what had happened by the end of August.

[175] Payling 1989: pp. 892–3; Storey 1966: p. 135.

[176] Griffiths 1991f: pp. 336–7. Only the intervention of Westmorland and the northern diocesans prevented a battle (*ibid.*, p. 342).

[177] PPC, VI, pp. 163–4. It seems almost certain that the government had not, as it claimed, sent York a summons to this assembly at the outset.

[178] Johnson 1988: p. 125 names and discusses them.

Confidence in Somerset's regime was already collapsing.[179] The events in the North had proved it to be unequal to the task of government. On the one hand, its association with the king's personal authority had been a failure. Even with the support of organised counsel and the regular participation of the lords, Henry VI could not provide effective rule. Now that the king had sunk into stupor, there was absolutely no hope of improvement: even shows of authority such as the tourns of 1451–3 were out of the question. At the same time, the conciliar element in Somerset's authority was also failing: regular participation in government had dwindled to office-holders and bureaucrats: a perfectly natural development, but an unhelpful one for a regime which, now above all, needed to demonstrate substantial support.[180] While the duke had probably summoned the Westminster council as a means of afforcing his authority in the act of imposing a consultative settlement on the powerful disputants, the effect of including York in its composition was to transform a judicial body into a constituent assembly.[181] It is not unlikely that the lords who issued York's invitation realised that this would be its result. The time had come to devise a new, more sufficient, authority, and, in many ways, the nullification of the king created the perfect opportunity.[182] In contrast to the circumstances of 1450, the distraction of a royal power which had to be rooted in Henry's provenly useless person could be swept aside. All the same, it seems clear that the claims of royal government were wavering before the demise of the king, and that the principal cause of this was the failure of royal justice.

The autumn and winter of 1453–4, during which the new authority haltingly emerged, was a tense and complex period. At first, it appeared that York might carry all before him. The duke seems to have timed his arrival at the council to coincide with the reassembly of parliament at Reading, perhaps in the hope that the coup of 1450 could be repeated.[183] He spoke of attending not only to the immediate business before the lords, but to 'all that sholde or might be to the welfare of the king and of his subgettes', a possible indication that he had in mind larger plans

---

[179] The view that, by late 1453, the lords' sympathy for Somerset had evaporated appears in 'Benet's Chron.', p. 210; *English Chron.*, p. 78; and even Giles, *Chronicon*, p. 44.

[180] Above, p. 287; Johnson 1988: pp. 122–3.

[181] York was summoned to discuss his 'variance' with certain unnamed lords (*ibid.*), but many must have realised, as the duke himself did, that his attendance would have broader consequences. See below.

[182] This is not to suggest that, on this occasion, the king's illness was factitious: see e.g. Wolffe 1981: pp. 270–3 for a discussion of the evidence and *PL*, II, pp. 295–6, for an example.

[183] 12 November 1453: 'Benet's Chron.', p. 210; *RP*, V, p. 238. Kemp's immediate prorogation of the parliament may have been intended to prevent such a repetition. York had not brought large forces with him on this occasion.

beyond the pacification of disputes.[184] He requested, and was granted, the restoration of his advisers; and this, of course, amounted to a discreet assault on the claims of the previous regime, which had condemned them as traitors.[185] York's earlier identification with Gloucester seemed to be on the point of paying dividends. With the king's personal agency in abeyance, his royal blood, extensive power and professed concern for the common weal lost much of their threatening quality and became purely positive attributes. No longer did he have to bend over backwards to reconcile his allegiance with his assaults on Henry's ministers: his loyalty could now be expressed in simple terms. Provided that he treated the vacant king with appropriate deference and showed a readiness to absorb the counsel of the lords, there was much to justify the replacement of the existing ministry with a body operating under York's protection. It was presumably in this spirit that, on about 23 November, a number – probably a large number – of lords bowed to the duke of Norfolk's demands for the imprisonment of Somerset pending charges of treason.[186] Within a fortnight, York and the lords had begun the process of vesting authority in a council.[187]

If, as seems likely, it was Duke Richard who was behind Norfolk's attack on Somerset, it should not be accounted mere vindictiveness. As we have seen, the conflict between York and Somerset was not (or not inherently) personal, but public, and, in a sense, national; the contest of two forms of authority and two structures of power more than that of two men.[188] It was important for York to establish his priority over Somerset, and useful if this could be done by reinforcing the position he had

---

[184] CPR, 1452–61, pp. 143–4.

[185] Johnson 1988: p. 126.

[186] 'Benet's Chron.', p. 210. Note that Thomas Thorpe, speaker of the parliament and a supporter of Beaufort, came under attack at about the same time: he made a gift of all his goods to a group of courtiers on 25 November (CCIR, 1447–54, p. 484) and was soon in prison (Johnson 1988: pp. 130–1).

[187] Griffiths, 'King's Council', pp. 315–17. Note that significant numbers of peers were involved in these decisions: forty-six on 30 November, and twenty-four on 5 December, neither of them a partisan group, although as Griffiths notes (pp. 311–12), ten lords, some of them closely linked to the former regime, do not appear to have signed the second document. From that day, for virtually the first time since the minority, the signatures of lords, together with the formula 'it was avysed, assented and ordeyned by my lordes of the Kynges Counsell' were used as a means of authorisation, betokening the recognition of a new source of government: PPC, VI, p. 164. The decisions of the lords, once parliament had reassembled in February, were almost all described in these terms, often with the addition of 'praesentibus et se subscribentibus': e.g. E28/84/1, 2; C81/1546/74, 78–80; BL, Add. MS 19398, fol. 27.

[188] The fact that it was Norfolk, not York, who attacked Somerset and that the themes which dominated the attack were clearly public – the loss of Normandy and Guyenne; the assumption of 'over grete autoritee' – meant that this episode can hardly be accounted a part of the dispute settlement for which the council was originally convened (see also Johnson 1988: pp. 124–6).

advanced in 1450–2: that it was his predecessor, and not himself, who had been a traitor to king and realm. In 1453, York was not visibly backed by the *communitas* and did not claim to be its representative. The only source of authority to which he could pretend was the still uncertain confidence of the lords. This meant that, in a sense, he had little structural advantage over Somerset: only the relative, and perhaps temporary, ignominy of Duke Edmund made York a more appropriate choice for the post of chief counsellor to the redundant king. Meanwhile, much as Somerset had lost control of the assembled lords, his stock had not entirely collapsed. He continued to enjoy the backing of Cardinal Kemp, who, as chancellor, exercised a certain control over the execution of government.[189] He was also probably supported by many in the household, who faced an uncertain future at the hands of York and the lords. The collapse of the king ought to have robbed these men of most of their significance, but fate had intervened on their behalf: one important ingredient in the politics of this period which we have not yet considered is the fact that a male heir was born to the king and queen on 13 October 1453.[190]

This event made the transfer of lordship to a council headed by York rather more problematic. The birth of an heir had introduced an alternative, and, in terms of blood, higher, power to set against that of the duke. Over Prince Edward, York had the capacity to offer adult lordship and the basis of a following among the lords, but his advantage over Somerset in these respects was much narrower. Even if there was a degree of dissatisfaction with Somerset's rule in the autumn of 1453, it was nonetheless possible that, as in the winter of 1450–1, the superior claims of the blood royal, enlivened by loyalists in the administration and household, could have effected his restoration, particularly if it seemed that the dynasty was under threat. Duke Edmund's past career, his Beaufort blood, his status as a godfather to the prince, made him an obvious choice if men of this kind chose to sponsor their own candidate for the rule of the realm during the king's illness.[191] Such a move may

---

[189] See 'Benet's Chron.', p. 211; *Loci e Libro*, p. 37. It appears from Norfolk's petition against the duke of Somerset (*PL*, II, p. 290) and Giles, *Chronicon*, pp. 44–5, that Kemp had tried to resist any judicial process against Somerset. For his prompt prorogation of the parliament, see n. 183, above. He may have delayed the sealing of the act permitting York's servants to resort to him, since this was not exemplified, as the duke had successfully requested, until 6 December (*CPR, 1452–61*, pp. 143–4). This was the day after the lords agreed to establish a form of rule during the king's illness and it may be that Kemp was waiting for a decision of this kind before assisting the duke. The cardinal may also have been behind the binding over of Norfolk in the massive sum of £12,000 on 11 December 1453 (*CCIR, 1447–54*, p. 476). Note also Johnson 1988: pp. 129–30, 132.

[190] See e.g. Griffiths 1981: pp. 718–19 for details.

[191] The other godparents were Cardinal Kemp and the duchess of Buckingham (Griffiths 1981: p. 719).

have seemed unlikely in the weeks immediately following the prince's birth, and this may explain why an apparently disinterested body of lords was prepared to imprison Somerset and move towards a conciliar authority headed by York. Later in the year, however, the household seems to have rallied. At some point in December or January, the queen presented her famous request for regency powers and a group of household men petitioned for a garrison to protect the king and prince.[192] While these proposals are likely to have been unacceptable in themselves, they served as a statement to the lords that there were conflicting interests to be satisfied and that a negotiated settlement, preserving noble unity via a governing council, was not necessarily to be relied upon.[193] If the tense atmosphere were to deteriorate further and war actually break out among the peers, Prince Edward's friends would be in a powerful position: York's posture as the loyal servant of the house of Lancaster would cease to convince; he would begin to look like a contending dynast. A state of deadlock ensued as the lords, uncertain of how to proceed, abandoned the task of constructing authority and waited for a solution to present itself.[194]

One of the reasons why war might have seemed a possibility was the well-known development, over the turn of the year, of alliances among the lords; each of them linked in some way to either York or Somerset. A number of accounts have placed this phenomenon at the centre of explanations of this period: the Nevilles, it is said, offended by Somerset's handling of their interests in Wales and the North, swung their weight behind York instead, a move which paved the way for the protectorate, determined its allegiances and set the pattern of politics throughout the rest of the decade.[195] It is perfectly true that Warwick, at least, had personal grounds for resentment against Somerset, and that both Neville earls, together with the rest of the English nobility, had an interest in

[192] *PL,* II,, pp. 296–7.

[193] The powers the queen proposed to exercise were awesomely wide and she made no apparent commitment to take the counsel of the lords, something which it would surely have been important to emphasise at that time (*PL,* II, p. 297). See above, pp. 113, 115, for reactions to Gloucester's regency proposals in the not dissimilar circumstances of 1422. The only lord who was in the end prepared to desert the rest on the strength of an allegiance to the queen was Viscount Beaumont: Griffiths, 'King's Council', p. 319. He had attended none of the recorded meetings of late 1453. Lord Scales, another connection of the queen, was prepared to join the protectorate council, though he rarely attended its meetings: *ibid.*; Myers, 'Household of Queen Margaret', pp. 404, 426.

[194] This doubtless explains the open-endedness of the arrangements of 5 December: the lords were apparently going to do the minimum demanded by 'veary nesestye' until their powers could be fixed and declared 'by awtoryty' (Griffiths, 'King's Council', p. 317). See also Johnson 1988: pp. 126–9.

[195] E.g. Storey 1966: pp. 193–4; Ross 1974: pp. 14–16. See also Pollard 1990: pp. 245, 266; Payling 1989: pp. 881, 907. Cf. McFarlane 1981f: pp. 247–8; Griffiths 1991f: pp. 363–4.

building a more effective authority at the centre which could protect and assist their local lordship.[196] Even so, to conclude that they, their allies and their opponents largely dictated the agenda of politics in 1453–4 is to overlook both the complex framework of considerations discussed above and the existence of a large number of influential 'neutrals' among the lords. Neville opposition may have played a part in persuading the rest of the nobility to jettison Somerset in favour of York, but it is important not to put the cart before the horse. Why did the Nevilles assume they would get better justice from York than Somerset, unless they believed that Duke Richard offered some more effective jurisdiction? In response to the failure of the first conciliar initiatives to provide a workable authority, the Nevilles, together with Cromwell, Devon, Norfolk and, possibly, the earls of Pembroke and Richmond seem to have decided to nail their colours to York's mast and force the creation of a single leadership.[197] At the same time, the various opponents of this group drew together into an equivalent alliance, focused, it seems, on Kemp, Somerset, the household and, arguably, Buckingham.[198]

As a result of this development, the lords returned to London for the reopening of parliament in an atmosphere of extreme unease. There is evidence to suggest that, sometime in early February and presumably through *force majeure*, York and his supporters were able, for a time at least, to overmaster Kemp and gain control of the government.[199] The council records for this period suggest a much more partisan body than that of the previous autumn and most of the business transacted concerned the interests of either York or the Nevilles.[200] It was as a result

[196] For the various disputes over the division of the Beauchamp inheritance, in which both Warwick and Somerset had an interest, see Storey 1966: pp. 239–40; Pugh (ed.) 1971: pp. 193–6 and Carpenter 1992: pp. 446, 458, 463–6. Violence erupted when, on 15 June 1453, Somerset obtained a grant of the custody of the Despenser lordship of Glamorgan (then in Warwick's keeping). The duke may have realised the enormity of what he was doing, since on 20 June 1453 an order was despatched to the treasurer to pay Warwick the arrears of incomes from the Beauchamp chamberlainship of the exchequer since 6 December 1450, the date when, under York's influence, the office had first been granted to him: E404/69/160 (see above, n. 61).

[197] *PL*, II, pp. 297–9; 'Benet's Chron.', p. 211. See Carpenter 1992: pp. 466, 469 and Thomas 1971: pp. 150–65 for the surprising position of the Tudors. For Cromwell, see n. 200, below, and Payling 1989: p. 882.

[198] This connection comprised Exeter, the Percies, Beaumont, Wiltshire and Bonville: *PL*, II, pp. 296–7, 299.

[199] Cf. the similar circumstances of December 1450: above, pp. 274–6.

[200] See Johnson 1988: pp. 127–8. The attendance at the meeting which appointed York parliamentary lieutenant was typical (C81/1546/76). Apart from a large number of bishops, including Kemp and more neutral figures, the lords present can be divided into four groups: (1) a Neville bloc, comprising Warwick, Salisbury, Greystoke, Fitzhugh and Scrope of Bolton (see Griffiths 1991f: p. 337 for Fitzhugh and Scrope, and Storey 1966: p. 123 for Greystoke); (2) the enemies of Exeter, viz. Cromwell and Grey of Ruthin (see Payling 1989: p. 889; Somerset's government had turned on Grey,

of this coup that the 'Yorkists' were able to bring the parliament back from Reading and make the duke its lieutenant, an appointment which surely pointed the way towards the establishment of a protectorate.[201] Even so, it is important to note that this factional triumph does not seem to have inspired much confidence among the political community as a whole. For a month following the reassembly of parliament, very little business was apparently transacted, either there or within the administration.[202] Behind this inactivity, it seems reasonable to imagine a period of intense negotiation. Although York headed a body of support sufficient to gain the advantage at the centre, this was not an adequate basis for a public authority which could command the allegiance of the rest of the nobility. The successes of early February may well have inspired resistance, as the uncommitted began to question whether party rule really measured up to the public responsibilities of government. In this, they would almost certainly have received endorsement from the parliamentary commons, who, apart from being concerned to resist a Yorkist takeover, were anxious to see a workable – and therefore representative – authority established, so that the good and politic rule of the land could be restored.[203] York could only acquire sufficient jurisdiction to satisfy the Nevilles and others by representing the needs of a wider body, and this must have limited the significance of noble faction in determining events.

A settlement seems to have emerged in mid-March. It was marked by a

presumably as a maintainer of Cromwell's dispute, summoning him to answer charges under a £2,000 recognisance in September 1452 – CCIR, 1447–54, p. 398; on 23 February 1454, an oyer and terminer commission headed by Edward Neville, Lord Bergavenny, was despatched against the priest who had accused Cromwell of treason in 1452 – CPR, 1452–61, p. 171); (3) possible supporters of York, viz. Devon and Clinton (latter fought for York at St Albans: PL, III, p. 30); and (4) neutrals, courtiers and members of the preceding regime, comprising Worcester, Oxford, Shrewsbury, the prior of St John's, Dudley, Fitzwarin and Stourton. This makes the neutrals the largest group numerically, but it is not difficult to see how they could have been swayed by the committed and coherent force of those now fully behind York. Worcester, at least, was probably sympathetic to York: the same day that he was appointed to prorogue the parliament, he assisted in York's attempt to regain the lieutenancy of Ireland (RP, V, pp. 238–9; C81/1546/73). Buckingham, Pembroke, Richmond, Wiltshire, Sudeley and Scales attended none of these meetings, though Beaumont was, strangely enough, present on 9 and 13 February.

201 Johnson 1988: pp. 129–30.
202 There are virtually no council records between mid-February and mid-March (only C81/1546/77 (2 March), which, significantly, was agreed by the lords in parliament) and very few patent letters.
203 The commons' perspective is clear from their demand for adequate government, the main thrust of which was less that a council should be established than that the lords should concern themselves with bringing peace to the land (RP, V, p. 240). It may be that the arrangements for punishing lords who had not come to parliament, which focused on the period 14–28 February, were actually devised not by York, but by the commons, as a means of assisting the creation of a broadly based authority: ibid., p. 248.

series of demonstrations of loyalty from York, of which by far the most important was his recognition of Prince Edward, who was finally created prince of Wales and earl of Chester by patents dated on the 15th.[204] Perhaps in return, the earl of Devon was (somewhat stagily) tried and acquitted for his insurrection in 1452, an occasion which provided York with a chance to have his own probity publicly acknowledged.[205] At about the same time, those outside the immediate York–Neville–Cromwell circle returned to the council.[206] It seems that, at a stroke, the duke had removed all grounds for doubt about the propriety of his intentions and bound himself and his supporters to the exceeding lordship of the Lancastrian heir. By doing so, he annexed to himself the greater part of the prince's constituency. Just as in 1422, the power to execute royal authority devolved upon the lords in the absence of a functioning king.[207] York's acknowledgement that that authority lay in the monarch (or, more immediately in this case, his progeny), was a small price to pay in order to deny power and principle to the 'royalist' resistance based in the household.[208]

After this, events moved quickly. It is very likely that even before the death of the still-resisting Kemp on 22 March, the broad lines of the new government had been fixed.[209] Within a week, York was offered the post of protector. In order to preserve the newly established consensus, which was clearly the only basis for a restored central authority, the duke declared that he would only accept the post if the lords undertook to give him counsel and assistance, particularly those who had recently been

---

[204] Johnson 1988: p. 133.

[205] *Ibid.* and see Cherry 1981a: p. 133. The likelihood that this was a charade is signalled by the fact that Devon had evidently been at large for some months. He had even been appointed a trier of petitions at the opening of parliament (*RP*, V, p. 227).

[206] Council meetings in March, for which we have records of attendance on seven occasions (C81/1546/78–80; *PPC*, VI, pp. 166, 167, 169; BL Add. MS 19,398, fol. 27) characteristically involved a wider group of lords. Alongside many of those listed in n. 200, above, Viscount Bourgchier attended on six occasions, Buckingham and Wiltshire attended on five, Beaumont and Pembroke on four, Lord Willoughby on three and Lord Scales twice. Willoughby's allegiances are a mystery: he was the son of Lord Welles, Somerset's lieutenant at Calais (Storey 1970: pp. 68–9), but his wife's mother – the Cromwell co-heir – had married Salisbury's son, Sir Thomas Neville in 1453: *CPR, 1452–61*, p. 64.

[207] York was soon to recognise this explicitly: *RP*, V, p. 242.

[208] The household remained with the king at Windsor and was, as a bloc, similarly inert during the ensuing year. The collapse of its power was doubtless a factor in encouraging some, Wiltshire, for example, to come to terms with York's regime. Although the earl lost the lieutenancy of Ireland, there are other signs that he had become accommodated to the regime. He got custody of a wardship in February/May 1454 (*CFR, 1452–61*, pp. 73, 89) and was among those appointed to keep the sea: *RP*, V, p. 244.

[209] According to Worcestre's *Itineraries*, ed. Harvey, p. 153, Kemp died very soon after Norfolk began moves to achieve his dismissal. The names of councillors had already been fixed upon before the meeting with the king which took place two days later (*RP*, V, pp. 240–2).

named councillors.[210] Meanwhile, Prince Edward was appointed to succeed York in the protectorate as soon as he reached the years of discretion.[211] It was almost as if the duke and the other lords were bound together to constitute the *persona publica* of the infant prince and not that of his idiot father, an impression which is underlined by the fact that those commissioned, on 13 April, to carry out the prince's creation, were exactly the same men who were summoned to the protectorate council three days later.[212]

The creation of the protectorate was not, therefore, the simple work of a pre-eminent faction.[213] York's authority explicitly and truly rested on the representation of a wider constituency, a property which was vested not only in himself, but also in a broadly based council. If anything, this suited what may be imagined to be York's interests – a form of national lordship exercised by himself – rather more than the immediate interests of his principal followers. At the same time, of course, it began to answer the common interest of landed society as a whole by providing a more adequate central authority to which judicial resort could be made. All this deserves to be borne in mind when the well-documented events and policies of the protectorate are considered. If it is accepted that York was simply trying to govern the country, then it is clear that he had much of the normal political apparatus to do so and that he broadly achieved his ends. Yet the work of the protectorate government has often been interpreted in terms of a factional struggle in which York, the Nevilles and Cromwell were either more or less successful in defeating their enemies or in acquiring political assets to use against them in the future.[214] This view is evident from the tenor of accounts of some of the leading initiatives of the protectorate government: the settlement of the disputes in the North; the appointment of York as captain of Calais; and the reduction in the size of the household, for example.[215] It has meant that, by association, instances

---

[210] *RP*, V, p. 242, arts. 2 and 5. The meeting at which those named councillors considered their responses is that of 3 April 1454, printed by Griffiths, 'King's Council', pp. 317–20. York's patents were presumably issued after the meeting: *RP*, V, pp. 242–3.

[211] *Ibid.*: that this had already been agreed is shown by its implicit inclusion in the responses to York's articles of 28 March (*ibid.*, p. 242, art. 3).

[212] *CPR, 1452–61*, pp. 171–2; *PPC*, VI, p. 175. These were Archbishop Booth, Bishops Waynflete, Bourgchier, Lyhert, Boulers, Chedworth, the dukes of York, Norfolk and Buckingham, the earls of Warwick, Oxford, Salisbury, Worcester and Shrewsbury, Viscounts Beaumont and Bourgchier, the prior of St John's and Lords Cromwell, Scales, Sudeley, Dudley and Stourton.

[213] See also Griffiths, 'King's Council', p. 315.

[214] See e.g. Griffiths 1981: pp. 725–38 (esp. pp. 735–6); Harriss 1960: pp. 30, 34ff; Storey 1966: pp. 139–41.

[215] For the North, see Griffiths1991f: pp. 342, 352, 355; Payling 1989: p. 881; Storey 1966: chs. IX and X. For Calais, see Harriss 1960: pp. 34–9; Storey 1966: p. 140; Griffiths 1981: p. 730. For the household, see Wolffe 1981: pp. 282–4.

of the exercise of non-partisan rule tend to be put down to the limitations placed upon York's actions by the counsel of lords (which he so consistently sought),[216] or by the fragile circumstances of his authority.[217]

All this may be a little misleading. First of all, there are grounds for suggesting that York's power as protector was rather greater than that of Gloucester in the 1420s: in contrast to Duke Humphrey, he may have won the confidence of many of the lords through his willing recognition of their corporate authority; and, with Somerset out of the way, there was no counterweight to his rule within the government; York was Bedford, Gloucester and the cardinal rolled into one.[218] Second, there is no reason to assume that lordship and counsel were necessarily incompatible, that York would have wished to do anything other than represent the constituency which accepted his rule. While he had, like any lord, to look to the foundations of his power, it is important to remember that those foundations were public as well as private, that lords derived a substantial part of their authority from addressing the needs of community as well as those of party. Indeed, these needs merged. Much that satisfied the private interests of York and his closest supporters also satisfied the common interest of the realm: Neville rule, for example, may well have been the most natural and appropriate means of governing the fifteenth-century North.[219] At the same time, measures which showed a statesman-like concern for the common well-being – such as the restrained, and broadly equitable, distribution of patronage; or the modest changes to the household – increased the standing of the duke and the security of those who participated in his regime.[220] There were, of course, limits to what

---

[216] See *PPC*, VI, pp. 185–6, 214–16, for the summoning of great councils; E28/85/1, C81/1546/82, *PPC*, VI, pp. 216–17 and Roskell 1956: pp. 190–2 for York's efforts to secure attendance at them.

[217] See e.g. Johnson 1988: p. 149; Storey 1966: pp. 141, 147.

[218] Technically, the position of the two protectors was exactly the same, of course (*RP*, V, pp. 242–4; Roskell 1953: pp. 226–7). York's emphatic demands for the 'harty favours, tendre zele and sad advises' of other lords and for the agreement of those named councillors to accept the charge must have struck the right note (*RP*, V, p. 242). More than simply a matter of his 'discharge', the duke's acknowledgement of the importance of noble counsel and noble unity can only have strengthened his hand (see also n. 216, above).

[219] See Weiss 1976 and Pollard 1990: part 2, esp. p. 402, for the general pre-eminence of the Nevilles over the Percies.

[220] As has been noted (e.g. Johnson 1988: p. 149), hardly any grants were made during the protectorate and almost all of them were custodies or offices. York and the Nevilles rewarded themselves modestly (York resuming his lieutenancy of Ireland, becoming captain of Calais and taking over the lease of the gold and silver mines (*CPR 1452–61*, pp. 202, 158; *RP*, V, pp. 254ff); Salisbury obtaining the keeping of Porchester Castle, the fee-farm of Carlisle and the custody of some lands in Norfolk (*CPR 1452–61*, p. 208; *CFR 1452–61*, pp. 98, 112) and Warwick receiving nothing at all). Other recipients of grants were a catholic group: Beaumont (*CPR 1452–61*, p. 213) Buckingham and the Bourgchiers (*ibid.*, p. 154), Dudley (*CFR 1452–61*, pp. 82, 86), Queen

York could achieve, particularly in the sphere of justice: he was not the king; he had no fully independent power; he possessed only part of the public authority which a monarch naturally attracted. But his instincts, in the handling of the troubles in Devonshire, the Midlands and the North seem to have been correct. In every case, he sought to uphold effective agencies of rule while attempting to reconcile their opponents.[221] Against this background, the refusal of the Nevilles' enemies either to participate in the creation of the government or to accept its jurisdiction, which was sanctified by the weightiest forms available, appears self-determined and self-destructive. York's government was surely entitled to invoke the hard logic of royal authority against those in the North who resisted the operation of the king's justice, and particularly against Exeter, who openly rebelled against the publicly appointed executive of the crown.[222] We may sympathise with the refusal of the Percies to turn to central government for justice after decades of exclusion by pro-Neville regimes, but it is important to realise that it was this refusal which shaped their fate.[223]

Margaret (ibid., pp. 111–12), Pembroke and Richmond (ibid., pp. 112, 113), and, rather remarkably, Henry Percy, Lord Poynings (ibid., p. 113). This last was a grant of the custody of lands in Durham, forfeited by the Percies in 1405. Even though the rent was unreasonably high (Bean 1958: p. 75), this was a significant concession. For the household reforms, see Morgan 1987: pp. 48–9; Johnson 1988: p. 148. Note that those appointed to remain in the household included Beaumont, the Beauchamps, Sir Edmund Hungerford, Sir Philip Wentworth, John Say, John Noreys, John Penycoke, John Stanley and other well-known members of the pre-1454 establishment (PPC, VI, pp. 220–33).

[221] For the protector's even-handed and effective performance in Warwickshire, see Carpenter 1992: pp. 468–73. For Devonshire, where the regime attempted to restrain both Devon and Bonville, whilst offering a certain amount of support for the latter, see Storey 1966: pp. 165–6. Here, this impartial approach was not terribly effective (see Cherry 1981a : pp. 133–4) – chiefly, perhaps, because the protector was unable to back his policy with the necessary force – but both lords did appear before the council in February 1455, as they had been bound to do. As far as the North is concerned, note that Yorkist action – however sympathetic to the Nevilles – seems to have rested on a broad base of support: Viscount Beaumont and Lord Clifford were apparently drawn away from the Percy bloc, the latter even to sit in sessions at York alongside the protector in June (see Griffiths 1991f: pp. 337–8; CPR, 1452–61, p. 177; PPC, VI, pp. 194–5; KB9/149/1, mm. 39, 64, 69); and the participation of the earl of Shrewsbury in the same sessions may suggest that York's venture won the sympathy of lords not directly involved in the Percy–Neville dispute. For York's efforts to accommodate the vanquished Percies, see above, n. 200, and Johnson 1988: pp. 144–5, 147.

[222] For Exeter's rebellion, see esp. Griffiths 1991f: pp. 343–9; Johnson 1988: pp. 142–3. Note that most of the lords had sworn in November 1453 to obey the orders of the king's council as if they bore full royal authority: Griffiths, 'King's Council', pp. 315–16. It may have been a wish to emphasise the fully legitimate nature of his authority that inspired York to request the power to distribute the king's livery of collars to eighty gentlemen before returning to the north at the end of July 1454 (PPC, VI, pp. 209–10).

[223] Note that apart from Bishop Percy and Sir William Lucy, not a single figure in the family's orbit attended the meeting of 30 November 1453 at which the oaths to recognise the council's issues were sworn (see above note).

Percy recalcitrance played a significant part in making central authority the friend of the Nevilles: York was not the tool of faction.

It is significant that, on the contrary, the only area in which York's activities seem to have caused contemporaneous alarm was in the matter of his treatment of Somerset, who lingered untried in the Tower, an unpleasant reminder of the limits to York's concern with unity.[224] The essence of the duke's continuing hostility to Somerset was surely not the matter of the war, which was as inconvenient in its general divisiveness as it was fruitful for anti-Beaufort allegations, but rather the problem that York had no independent basis for his authority.[225] Duke Richard must have feared that Somerset, at liberty, would organise some form of resistance to his rule, yet this was not a case he could make publicly. He tried to proceed against Beaufort judicially, but the effort failed in the face of a withdrawal of noble commitment.[226] In a sense, the refusal of the lords to permit the destruction of Somerset – mirror image of their earlier refusal to permit the destruction of York – justified Duke Richard's paranoid treatment of his opponent. The corporate rule of the nobility was insufficient to give its leader, whether York, or, in fact, Somerset, full justice against his most important enemy. Despite an extensive and often effective invocation of the common interest and responsibility of the lords, York was unable to settle the most profound division of the early years of the decade. The result was that it emerged anew when the duke's provisional authority was trumped by that of the reviving king.

Henry VI's recovery of his sanity, at Christmas 1454, was the principal cause of the end of the protectorate and of the subsequent transition of leadership from York back to Somerset, but it was by no means the only one. Had York dealt with Somerset successfully during the protectorate, it might have been possible to maintain a common front among the lords when the king returned to health, and this could, in turn, have minimised the consequences of that event. As it was, the unreconciled Duke Edmund provided an obvious focus of attention and loyalty both for those immediately about the king's person, who had regained their source of power, and for the victims of York's government, who were eager to

---

[224] Johnson 1988: pp. 143–4.

[225] Note that the protectorate council included Bishop Boulers and Lord Dudley, two men whom York had apparently regarded as traitors in 1450: above, p. 275.

[226] See Johnson 1988: p. 144. Note that almost all the lords were summoned to attend the council of late June at which the trial was to be held (even Exeter, for example, though not Egremont, or, more surprisingly, Westmorland: *PPC*, VI, pp. 184–6, 206–7) and see E28/85/8 for the government's insistence that the business of the council required 'the presence advis and entendance of greet nombre of lordes'. York patently did not plan some hole-in-the-corner affair, and the letter he wrote to Norfolk six days after the trial had been postponed suggests that he *was* anxious to see the case settled (*ibid.*, pp. 218–19).

exploit it.[227] These two groups soon set about the restoration of the old royal regime; pressing, rather as in 1451, for Somerset's release from prison and persuading the council of lords to recognise the changing basis of power. Their efforts took time to bear fruit. Although the lords were prepared to release Somerset in early February, they did so under stringent conditions, which were not lifted until a month later.[228] Similarly, while the protectorate was brought to an end on 9 February, decisive moves against York, Salisbury and others were not made until after 4 March, when Somerset was fully restored.[229] The hiatus is probably explained by the time it took for the less committed lords, in whom reposed the balance of power, to come to terms with the change of jurisdiction.[230] When they did, York was not entirely reduced to the

[227] Although some of those associated with the royal household decided to co-operate with York during the period of the king's nullity (see n. 208, above, for one example), others, such as Beauchamp of Powick, St Amand and the earl of Richmond, for example, took no part in the protectorate. Beauchamp of Powick seems to have joined the council in February or March 1455 (E404/71/3/32), the very time at which Somerset's control was reviving. The first clear sign that York was losing control appears to be a privy seal writ, signed by the king and ordering the transfer of the duke of Exeter, which was despatched on 3 February (PPC, VI, p. 234). The sign manual reveals the household connection and it is hardly likely that the Yorkist government would have issued this order, since Salisbury later had to be compelled to obey it with a large bond (Payling 1989: p. 904). Exeter's release can only have appealed to those with revenge on their minds.

[228] For these conditions, see Griffiths 1981: p. 739. Note that Somerset's mainpernors were bound body for body, which suggests that either the treason charges or the restrictions on his person were taken seriously by the lords (CClR, 1454–61, p. 44). This is echoed by suggestions in the chronicles that the subsequent breaking of promises regarding Somerset made in February were a cause of unease and defection in the government: Chrons. of London, p. 165; Great Chron., p. 187.

[229] We know about the end of the protectorate from an unpublished proceeding of the 1455 parliament relating to York's arrears of pay: C49/69/4. Somerset was vindicated on 4 March (CPR, 1452–61, p. 226). York was discharged from Calais on 6 March, though this had been anticipated two days before (DKR, XLVIII, p. 404; C81/769/9967). Salisbury resigned the great seal on 7 March. York and Salisbury may have left the court at about this point. Warwick had probably done so already (absent from meetings of 25 February and 4 March). On 13 March Salisbury was ordered under a 10,000 mark pain to release Exeter from Pontefract (Payling 1989: p. 904). On 15 March, Wiltshire replaced Worcester as treasurer (CPR, 1452–61, p. 229). Salisbury lost Porchester Castle on, or before, 16 March (ibid., p. 217) and on 23 March York lost the lease of the mines (CFR, 1452–61, pp. 217, 218). On 31 March, Somerset had the events of 4 March exemplified under the great seal (CPR, 1452–61, p. 226).

[230] The changing composition of the council between early February and early March deserves mention. The 5 February meeting was joined by ten lords who had not been present before. These included two of Somerset's mainpernors, Roos and Fitzwarin, and Viscount Beaumont, but also the earl of Devon and Lord Greystoke, who need not be expected to owe Somerset any particular sympathy. On 4 March, a more committed group of fifteen extra lords were present, including Beaumont, Roos and Fitzwarin again, and also Scales, Northumberland, Clifford and Beauchamp of Powick, who are likely to have been supporters of Somerset by this time. After this point, as unity receded, the size of the council dwindled. Consider, for example, the much reduced group who attended the transfer of the great seal from Salisbury to Archbishop Bourgchier on 7 March: Buckingham, Somerset, Northumberland and Wiltshire,

circumstances of 1451: the involvement of the Nevilles' enemies in the restoration of royal authority brought him the support of Warwick and Salisbury. Even so, this was precious little to set against the organised power of the household and the queen, and also, of course, against the irreducible authority of king and prince, which enabled this formidable array of opponents to lay charges of treason upon any who resisted them. Given that the over-riding aim of the majority of lords was the maintenance of workable authority, it is not at all surprising that almost all of them accommodated themselves to this new regime as they had to its predecessor.[231] York and the Nevilles had no choice but to do as the Percies and Exeter had done before them and withdraw.

Once this withdrawal had taken place, some sort of confrontation was inevitable. Somerset's hostility to York and Salisbury, if not to Warwick, was absolutely plain and the summonses for a pseudo-parliament at Leicester, sent out in mid-April, strongly suggested that a judicial showdown was planned.[232] There is, of course, no reason to condemn Somerset for the combative line he took: it was as important for him to neutralise York as it had been for York to neutralise him; neither duke could form a fully authoritative government if the other was still at large. The trouble was that York was no readier to submit to justice in 1455 than he had been in 1452 and was now in a better position to resist.[233] He and the Nevilles gathered in arms, probably at Middleham, and marched south towards the king.[234] It is not clear, however, that the duke and his allies had as much to fear as they seem to have thought. Had the council taken place, Somerset may well have found that the backing he received from the large and disparate body of lords which set out with the king to meet the Yorkists extended only to an arbitrative settlement of out-

Viscount Bourgchier, Beaumont, Clifford, Scales, Fitzwarin, Berners and Bishop Percy: *PPC*, VI, pp. 358–9.

[231] Of the twenty-four lords (including bishops) present at one or both of the meetings of 21 November 1453, who may be considered likely to be a group similar to those who imprisoned Somerset on the 23rd, as many as seventeen were present at the meeting of 5 February which authorised the duke's release and eighteen at the meeting of 4 March which abolished the bails (*CPR, 1452–61*, p. 143; C81/1546/71; *CClR, 1454–61*, p. 9; C81/1546/99).

[232] For the Leicester council, see *PPC*, VI, pp. 339–42; Armstrong 1960: pp. 13, 15. The inclusion of 'our lordeshipp' among the items to be discussed may be a further indication of the charges of shattered fealty likely to be made: *PPC*, VI, p. 340 (though see Johnson 1988: p. 155, for an alternative suggestion). Note also an intriguing warrant for issue from December 1455 concerning guns provided for the king's last going to his parliament at Leicester (E404/70/3/34). This may refer to the later sessions of the 1449–50 parliament, but, given the timing of the payment, it seems more likely that the 1455 assembly is meant (also called a parliament in *EHL*, p.345).

[233] For the council summoned to Coventry in the weeks preceding York's rising of 1452, see above, p. 281.

[234] See Goodman 1981: pp. 22–5 for details of the campaign.

standing disputes and not to the delivery of punitive justice.[235] The lords as a whole had no case to press against York and the Nevilles. This was damaging, because it was the support of the larger body of lords which gave Somerset his power, and not the authority of the king, which he and the Percies attempted to invoke against the Yorkists.[236] These realities were clearly demonstrated when Buckingham replaced Somerset at the head of the king's army as the possibility of conflict loomed. The lords, it seems, were prepared to defend the king, and willing to protect Somerset, but only insofar as this accorded with the immediate interests of noble unity.[237] The government no longer had the power to sponsor acts of justice commensurate with the requirements of the two leading magnates. Whereas in 1452 York had come to claim a public authority which the lords were determined to deny him, in 1455 he and the Nevilles came to remove their most hard-bitten opponents, knowing that arbitration could solve nothing and that if they were victorious in battle they need not fear the resistance of the remainder of the lords: the experience of the protectorate had revealed how readily the community of lords coalesced around an effective authority.

The battle of St Albans was, in many respects, the first effective public act of judgement in Henry VI's reign, and certainly the culmination of York's long campaign for 'justice upon the traitors' which had begun in 1450.[238] As such, it had paradoxical results: on the one hand, it was an authoritative resolution of the divisions of the preceding years, clearing the way

[235] A fairly impartial panel had been appointed to arbitrate between York and Somerset on the day that the latter effectively resumed control (4 March 1455: see Griffiths 1981: p. 739). Although this damaged York, inasmuch as it reduced his avowedly public campaign to a private quarrel, it suggests that, as a body, the lords were not about to condemn the duke for treason.

[236] Note that, according to the most detailed and reliable account of the negotiations which took place before the battle, the king was barely involved in what went on, having allegedly delegated control to Buckingham (the 'Fastolf relation', printed in Armstrong 1960: pp. 65–7).

[237] Ibid., pp. 21–3. Buckingham apparently expected that the Yorkist lords could be persuaded towards peace and unity through his mediation and, according to the Fastolf relation, he emphasised that he and the other lords had come with the king to do their duty to him and not to support any other person or cause (ibid.). Since the royal army included figures such as Lords Fauconberg and Berners, who were very unlikely to have been hostile to the Yorkists, this seems a sensible assessment (ibid., p. 24).

[238] Some of the major concerns of 1450 apparently re-emerged at St Albans, where, according to Whethamstede, the Yorkists accused Somerset of losing Normandy, neglecting Gascony and reducing England to a miserable state: Registrum, I, p. 167. It was also echoed in the lords' request to Archbishop Bourchier to impose the censures of the church on all those who 'entende any untrouth, prejudice, hurt or derogation ayenst th'estate, prosperite and welfare' of the king or his land, a demand conceptually related to the accusations of treason against men who had been (at least superficially) loyal to the king himself: RP, V, p. 281.

for a new form of government;[239] on the other, it brought instability by exposing, more clearly than ever before, the destitution of Henry VI's authority, and by laying the foundations of a blood feud, the scope of which went far beyond the York–Somerset quarrel of the early years of the decade.[240] In a sense, therefore, York's consistent demand for justice was to some extent vindicated: it did provide a platform for authority, and this was implicit in the propaganda which the Yorkists produced to justify their act of war against the king. Not only did they argue that they had to resort to arms to defend themselves; they also laid claim to an independent right to seek and do justice, and even took account of the repudiation of royal authority which was implicit in this assertion: if the king would not 'be reformed at [their] besechyng', the Yorkist lords would have to act, 'consederyng yn what peryle Inglonde stondes inne at thys owre'.[241] As in 1450 and 1452, York's position was rather more than simple retaliation against the undue power of enemies about the king: he and the Nevilles emphasised their self-appointed responsibility to reform the king and improve the quality of government for the common weal, a responsibility which briefly exceeded their duty of obedience.[242] Having visited justice upon their enemies, they attempted to close the door on past divisions which could be conveniently – and, in many ways,

[239] There is evidence to suggest that at least some contemporaries did see the battle as a form of resolution. Note, for example, *Town Chrons.*, p. 142: 'which bataill the comones trusted brake moch inconvenience and hurt that shuld have fall'. Even the more negative inflection of Gregory's chronicle – 'hyt was noo seson to trete of pesse, for sum were welle contente and sum evylle plesyd' (*Collections*, p. 198) – seems to endorse the view that the time for negotiation was past: action and constraint were required to obtain obedience.

[240] This should not, even so, be overdone as an explanation of the problems of the later 1450s and 1460s. See below, pp. 343–4, for the context in which the feud was revived in 1458. Note that the 'mortalle and extreme enemyes' identified by the Yorkists in 1460 were not the heirs of Somerset, Northumberland and Clifford, but the earls of Shrews-bury and Wiltshire and Viscount Beaumont, among whom only Wiltshire was certainly present at the battle. Buckingham, who was wounded in the face at St Albans (*PL*, III, p. 28) seems to have been willing to co-operate with the Yorkists until at least 1458.

[241] Quotation from *PL*, III, p. 27. The actual demand made by the Yorkists at St Albans was that the king should recognise their 'ryghtwesnesse' and hand over to them all those whom they should accuse: *ibid.*, p. 26. They themselves would punish the shameful men 'whych hav deserved deth': royal promises to attend to the matter would not be acceptable, because they had been broken before (*ibid.*).

[242] Besides their need to defend themselves from enemies abiding 'under the whyng of your Magestee Royall' (*ibid.*, p. 23; and see *RP*, V, p. 280), the Yorkists pointed out that these same men had not applied themselves to work for the advancement and honour of the king and the realm. They themselves, conversely, had come to draw together those who were concerned for the quality of government and, proceeding upon their advice, to provide for the same, their loyalty to Henry VI unspotted (*ibid.* and p. 281). This loyalty was, just as it had been earlier in York's career (above, p. 271), a sophisticated affair: before the battle, York had promised to do whatever the king should command 'yf yt be his [i.e Henry's] worsship, kepyng right of the Croune and welffare of the londe' (*PL*, III, p. 26).

rightly – cast as symptomatic of the inadequacy of royal authority. This prepared the ground for a new and authoritative unity, the basis of a new government.

In the short term, however, the focus of Yorkist unity was to be nothing more novel than Henry VI himself, now bearing an arrow wound in the neck. As soon as Somerset, Northumberland and (perhaps incidentally) Clifford, lay dead upon the field, the Yorkists ended the fighting and submitted handsomely to Henry, leading him to London 'as kynge and not as a presener'.[243] This was no surrender: the victorious lords retained the initiative, keeping tight control of the king's person, remaining in arms and binding over a number of their peers.[244] At the same time, they sent positive signals to political society by holding a series of council meetings at which members of the old protectorate council attended.[245] The aim must have been to project a sense of continuity with the consultative traditions of the last regime in which York and the Nevilles had played a part; but, even so, just as in the autumn of 1450, or the winter of 1453–4, fears regarding Duke Richard's intentions must have been widespread.[246] In the event, however, all became clear in the parliament, which opened on 9 July 1455. The recent battle was blamed on the activities of the duke of Somerset, Thomas Thorpe and William Joseph: a device which drew attention away from the more damaging matter of rifts between the magnates by presenting division as a natural consequence of misgovern-

[243] Quotation from *Collections*, p. 198. See Armstrong 1960: pp. 49ff.

[244] Henry was carefully controlled. Initially, he remained in the city, staying at the bishop of London's palace ('Benet's Chron.', p. 215). It seems likely that the king was deliberately kept away from Westminster, where he made only the briefest of stops (Wolffe 1981: p. 370), in order to separate him from the household. A London chronicle records that in 1455 'all suche persons were voydid that afore tyme had rule abowte the kyng' (*Chrons. of London*, p. 165), which is partly reflected by the precautionary appointment of Lords Fauconberg and Berners to replace Somerset as constables of Windsor Castle (*CPR, 1452–61*, p. 243). At some point in June, the king was transferred to Hertford Castle, which belonged to the queen, who joined him there with the prince (*PL*, III, p. 32; Somerville 1953: p. 340). The Yorkist lords were close at hand however and Hertfordshire was a county where York had influence (*PL*, III, p. 32; Armstrong 1960: pp. 25–6). Before the parliament opened, the king stayed, perhaps for some time, at Waltham Abbey, which had been assigned to York for his sustenance on visiting London about a decade before (E28/86/26; *CPR, 1446–52*, p. 43). See *PL*, III, p. 44, for the Yorkists in arms and *ibid.*, pp. 32–3, for their handling of Buckingham, the Bourgchiers, Wiltshire, Dudley and Somerset's heir.

[245] The Yorkists assembled a council almost as soon as they arrived in London ('Benet's Chron.', p. 215). It doubtless authorised the despatch of writs for parliament on 26 May and the appointment of Viscount Bourgchier as treasurer on 29 May (*CCIR, 1454–61*, pp. 25–7; *CPR, 1452–61*, p. 242), although we have no records of its activities until 4 June. The meetings of the next few days were attended by more than a dozen lords, most of whom had been on the protectorate council: E28/86/7, 11 and 12. In their decisions, they referred to themselves as 'the lords of the council' and on two of these occasions they agreed to petitions placed before them if it should please the king.

[246] Note that Queen Margaret, doubtless with the prince, had been sheltering in the Tower of London on 23 May 1455: E159/232, comm., Mic., rot. 3.

ment and by lending support to York's old theme that England's troubles since 1450 could all be traced to the malign influence of a clique of 'traitors' about the throne.[247] Now, the troubled times were over: St Albans was no more to be spoken of, and a new unity was to arise among the lords.[248] It was to be achieved in two main ways. As a matter of priority, the quality of government was to be improved by a consultative and wide-ranging settlement of immediate problems.[249] This lent credence to the idea that it was to save the realm as much as themselves that the Yorkists had resorted to arms in the first place. Misrule had caused division: reform would restore unity. Meanwhile, Yorkist commitment to the crown of Henry VI was solemnly demonstrated with a parliamentary oath of allegiance.[250] This was far from being a sign that direct royal rule was about to be restored, but it did declare, perhaps more finally than York realised, that the royal duke was not attempting to make himself king.[251] There was to be a single community of lords, with a single sovereign: 'oonhede' in every sense. The crucial question of how, and by whom, this sovereignty was to be translated into rule could be left open for the time being; though, in the weeks following the parliament, the

[247] *RP*, V, pp. 280–2. The undignified quarrel between Cromwell and Warwick over the former's responsibility for St Albans (reported in *PL*, III, p. 44) reveals how important it was to distract attention from the barely resolved disputes between magnates by blaming the violence on the failure of government. It is interesting that the 'men brought up of nought' who fell with Somerset were bureaucrats as much as, if not more than, domestics (Thorpe had been chancellor of the exchequer and Joseph was a clerk of the signet). The distinction between these categories cannot be pressed too far, but it may say something about the more conciliar flavour of the regime which followed Suffolk's. See Armstrong 1960: pp. 57–8 for more on these two men.

[248] The Yorkist lords were recognised as true subjects, legal action relating to the events at St Albans was banned and a general pardon was issued for all crimes against the king (only) before the opening of parliament (*RP*, V, pp. 282, 283). The pardon excluded 'magnos computantes nostros' regarding the issues of their offices: a measure of the proposed restoration of good rule in fiscal matters. Contemporary references to a 'grete parlyament' (*Chrons. of London*, p. 165) may suggest that the 1455 assembly was perceived as something of a watershed.

[249] See *RP*, V, p. 280, and Johnson 1988: p. 162 for a brief discussion of the parliamentary arrangements. The new committees of lords were balanced and representative (e.g. the household committee included Beaumont, Sudeley, Stanley and the household officers) to consider each of them. It may be significant that York was not a member of any of these committees, except as a marcher lord (see below).

[250] *RP*, V, pp. 282–3.

[251] The lords swore to do all they could for the welfare, honour and safeguard of the king's person, his royal estate, pre-eminence and prerogative and to consent to nothing that might prejudice his person, dignity, crown or estate. This could be read as a promise to do nothing which might damage Henry's personal authority, but the honour, estate, crown and dignity of the king can also be taken to relate to his public attributes, permitting a wide variety of reforms, many of which could minimise the king's personal involvement in government. The role played by York in the royal procession at Whitsun was another demonstration that he had no designs on the crown: 'Benet's Chron.', p. 214.

business of government seems to have been carried out by the rump of the protectorate council.[252]

Moves to establish a new authority began in November, when the king did not return to parliament and the commons began the session by requesting the appointment of a protector. This was the fruition of another strand in York's five-year campaign. Although the business of the 1455 parliament had so far been weighted towards the reuniting of the lords, the associated theme of good government had provided the duke with an opportunity to resume his former mantle of public representation by furthering the designs of the commons. Earlier in the decade, the non-noble *communitas* had been York's principal constituency, and it was a valuable one: it permitted the duke to question the claims of the king's ministers; and, more importantly in the context of the mid-1450s, it gave him a measure of independence in his dealings with other lords. We have seen how easily and rapidly power shifted between Somerset and York when all that either duke could reasonably claim as the basis for his rule was the complaisance of his peers. It is possible that, as he moved to create a new regime in the aftermath of St Albans, York sought to increase his security by reviving something of his older posture as the vehicle of the 'comouns desyre'.[253] In the first session of the 1455 parliament, and presumably with York's encouragement, the commons had introduced plans for a new and far-reaching resumption.[254] They had also petitioned for the rehabilitation of the duke of Gloucester, model for the sort of loyal but populistic regency to which York had apparently aspired in 1450.[255] Now, quite probably at Duke Richard's inspiration, the commons invited him to resume the post of protector on the grounds of evident necessity.[256]

Although Henry VI's incapacity was a feature of this necessity, there is

---

[252] The records for 6–9 August show Booth, Waynflete, Thomas Kemp, Salisbury, Warwick and Worcester, the dean of St Severin's, the prior of St John's, Viscount Bourgchier, Stanley and Say to have been in attendance (E28/86/34–8; *PPC*, VI, pp. 257–8). All of these had been members of the 1454 council except for Kemp, who had attended during great councils. It seems that the Yorkist lords were still at pains to show the association of their power with that of the king, since the issues of council meetings early in August, endorsed 'Rex de avisamento consilii', were actually signed by Henry. The king also granted petitions himself on 2 and 5 August (*PPC*, VI, p. 255).

[253] Quotation from *PL*, II, p. 174 (1450).

[254] *RP*, V, pp. 301ff: see Johnson 1988: pp. 172–3, for dating. See below, for more on this particularly interesting bill.

[255] *RP*, V, p. 335. See Watts 1990: p. 260 (also for how the restoration of Gloucester encouraged the idea, raised by the Yorkists at St Albans, that no one could traduce the king by protecting the common interest on his behalf).

[256] See Johnson 1988: pp. 168–9 for details of what happened. The particular issue which the commons raised was, of course, the riotous situation in the South-West, but their requests imply a general inadequacy on the part of royal justice, much as in 1453 (see above, p. 300).

very little to suggest that he had lapsed back into the insanity of 1453–4.[257] Rather, it seems that, in 1455, the political community came nearer than ever before to taking corporate action to confront and resolve its fundamental problem: the inadequacy of its king. The solution was a revived protectorate, requested by the commons, as petitioners for the nation, and granted by the lords, as executors of the king's authority in its abeyance.[258] Alongside the protector, a governing council, reminiscent of 1422 or 1437, was appointed.[259] Together, protector and council proceeded to take up the rule of the realm. Although the fundamental inalienability of the king's powers was borne out in a few instances during the succeeding months,[260] it remains the case that York had more or less succeeded in creating the new, and potentially revolutionary, basis of authority which had long been implicit in his stewardship of the popular cause. The lords were on the brink of transferring their allegiance and service to a man whose pre-eminence rested not on divine appointment, but on common approval. Even so, it was still in the hands of the peerage that the duke's future rested.[261] If York's reviving popularity among the commons gave him the basis of an alternative authority, it was only the support of the lords, as he well knew, which made it usable. For the time being, this

---

[257] Lander 1960–1: pp. 50–4. The way in which the protectorate was established strongly suggests that something novel was being attempted: Watts 1990: pp. 259–60.

[258] It was officially the king who appointed York protector: *RP*, V, p. 288. However, the duke's articles noted that the lords were 'takyng uppon you th'exercise of his auctorite, for such urgent, necessary and reasonable causes, as move you so to take uppon you' (p. 286: the comparison with 1454, in which it was a case of 'you the Perage of this lande, in whom by th'occasion of th'enfirmite of our said Souveraine Lord restethe th'exercise of his auctoritee', is enlightening: *RP*, V, p. 242). Note that Thomas Gascoigne, writing soon after these events, twice observed that 'parliamentum Londoniis' had given York his protectorate: *Loci e Libro*, p. 204.

[259] *RP*, V, pp. 289–90. The membership seems to have been virtually the same as in 1454.

[260] There is a royal sign manual on a petition from the grooms of the chamber, passed 'Rex de avisamento consilii' on 12 December: E28/87/16 (mentioned by Lander 1960–1: p. 53 n. 3). Could it be that the grooms had cannily presented their petition to the king and got it signed, thereby presenting the council with a *fait accompli*? According to the arrangements of 22 November, the council would have been perfectly qualified to decide such a matter itself. Note that the councillors present did not sign this warrant, though they signed another (unsigned by the king) on the same day (E28/87/17).

[261] This is plain from the novel conditions on which the protectorate was to be terminated. The duke was to hold the office until he should be discharged by the king, by advice and assent of the lords in parliament: *RP*, V, p. 287. This was in place of the 'during pleasure' rubric in the grant of 1454. The change strongly suggests that the king was not incapable in 1455. The lords' fear (for it was they who made the change) was either that with Henry under Yorkist control, the free operation of his 'pleasure' could not be guaranteed or, conversely, that the protectorate was vulnerable to being terminated by the intervention of York's enemies in the household, rather as in 1451 or early 1455. Which concern was uppermost rather depends on which lords were present at the making of this decision and how closely the Yorkists were able to control the king. We cannot be sure of either. Note that the lords reaffirmed their authority in December by issuing York with letters patent to prorogue parliament for Christmas, even though he had already been empowered to do this as lieutenant: *RP*, V, pp. 453–4.

support was readily given, and it is not hard to see why. The first protectorate had shown that York was capable of working consultatively and that he was more concerned to promote unity than division: this must have commended him to the lords. In the wake of St Albans, moreover, he and the Nevilles unquestionably had the initiative. Finally, there was, as in 1453, a pressing need for both judicial authority and competent government, and, especially with Somerset dead, no one else to direct affairs.[262]

In accordance with the novel basis of his authority, York seems to have introduced some significant changes to the practice of government. A particular emphasis on consultation was not surprising under the circumstances,[263] but the tentative formalisation of a judicial role for the council was perhaps a new development.[264] The centrepiece of the regime's measures for sound and politic rule, however, was surely the proposed resumption.[265] This was built up into a coherent and far-reaching plan to provide for adequate funding, closely resembling Fortescue's plans outlined in the 'Governance of England' some time later.[266] It aimed not only at a comprehensive restoration of the king's patrimony, but at its protection in the future through bureaucratic improvements and the imposition of tight fiscal controls.[267] It invoked, in fact, a completely different system

---

[262] While it is certainly true that York did not intervene in the South-West in time to prevent a serious escalation of disorder, culminating in the battle at Clyst, it should be noted that, when he did take action, Devon was sufficiently struck by the duke's authority to capitulate at once, bringing the period of open warfare in the region to an end (Storey 1966: pp. 170–3).

[263] This is not to deny that York's efforts to induce the lords to take part were, as in 1454, impressive: see, for example, the letter of 15 December 1455 to the very large number of lords who had failed their 'dutee' in not coming to the autumn session of the parliament, threatening them with fines if they did not attend in January (*PPC*, VI, pp. 279–82). Note that eighteen lords (seven bishops, six higher lords, five barons) attended half or more of the meetings of the council in the autumn of 1455. A further ten lay lords attended at least one meeting in addition to a number of bishops (records for seventeen meetings from late October to the end of December: C81/1546; E28/87; *PPC*, VI, *passim*).

[264] In November, a council meeting ordained that privy seal summonses would be despatched automatically to offenders upon complaints of robberies or riots made to the council: E28/87/6. Arrangements for the automatic respiting of homage were made at the same meeting.

[265] York's power was closely associated with the progress of the resumption bill by one contemporary (*PL*, III, p. 75) and there is much to suggest that it was the product of official sponsorship. See Wolffe 1971: pp. 138–9, and note that Bale's chronicle says that the resumption was *granted* by the commons, which may mean that it was not put forward by them (*Town Chrons.*, p. 143).

[266] See above, pp. 47–50; Wolffe 1971: pp. 137–9; Starkey 1986: pp. 16–17. See next note for some of the bill's provisions.

[267] The duchy feoffments (made for the royal colleges) were specifically named as deserving to be resumed, exemptions from clerical taxation were to be abolished and all offices to which no real charge pertained were to cease to exist: *RP*, V, p. 301. The commons were to adjudicate any exemptions which the king might wish to make and all future recipients of any of the categories of grant now resumed were to be made liable under the statute of provisors (*RP*, V, p. 303). Other fiscal and bureaucratic arrange-

of government from that which normally obtained, and this was to be its weakness. The power of royal grace, which it attempted to remove, was integral to the monarchical polity: we have seen how the administration of justice, in particular, depended on it; but it was also, in a broader sense, the basis of the unity which effective kingship promoted.[268] Proposals such as those contained in the resumption bill effectively substituted conciliar rule, of a kind unfamiliar in England, for the supremacy of the king. This was the essence of their appeal to York in the circumstances in which he found himself, and, no doubt, a factor in their appeal to the commons, but it was also, perhaps, the source of their unattractiveness to the mass of the lords. Such far-reaching reforms threatened the *nexus* between king and nobility which was one of the most basic structures of the polity. In his efforts to assert himself at the expense of his royal rival, York threatened both the conventions of rule and the interests of his peers.

It was over this matter that the lords and the duke parted company.[269] There was, it seemed, a difference between endorsing a non-royal government created in response to the extraordinary circumstance of Henry VI's debility and accepting a thorough reshaping of monarchical authority. Almost certainly encouraged by partisans of the queen or of the household, most of whom had refused to co-operate with the post-St Albans regime, the lords revived the authority of the king as a means of resisting an unsuitable policy. The novel edifice of York's national protectorate, with its reshaping of government to appeal to the interests and attitudes expressed in parliament, rapidly disintegrated as noble support was withdrawn. In a way, the episode demonstrates the inexorable attachment of the nobility to the monarchical ideology: the lords could not dismantle royal power without dismantling their own as well.

> ments were to be standardised: the queen was to receive 10,000 marks dower (the precedent since 1399: Crawford 1981: pp. 41ff) even if she was currently receiving less than this sum (*RP*, V, p. 303). The spreading practice of granting offices in fee simple or tail was to be stopped, presumably to improve the accountability of officers (*RP*, v, p. 301: this had also been proposed in 1449–50 – *ibid.*, p. 184). Meanwhile, the new allocations for the household, proposed in the same parliament (*ibid.*, pp. 320–1), have been described as the most serious attempt of the reign to limit wardrobe preference to the crown's hereditary revenues: Harriss 1953: p. 171.
>
> [268] See above, pp. 74–80, 97–101, and note the telling comment in the king's reply to the resumption bill that his power to issue provisos to the act was part and parcel of 'the egalte and reason' that he had to do his people (*RP*, V, p. 303).
>
> [269] 'Benet's Chron.', p. 216. The lords cannot have been entirely opposed to the main bill of resumption since this was introduced in the first session and was passed, albeit with clauses saving the king's prerogative of grace and exempting a large number of people: *RP*, V, p. 303. Their anxieties were no doubt aroused by the more extreme clauses of this bill, but the trigger may have been another bill, apparently introduced in mid-February, which proposed the resumption of all liberties and franchises granted since 1422, and was actually endorsed 'huic bille domini non concensierunt' (*ibid.*, p. 328). The lords also refused, probably about the same time, a bill proposing the resumption of all grants of wards and marriages (*ibid.*, p. 330). See also Johnson 1988: p. 173.

York's enterprise had brought them to a point where they could begin to see what stark choices lay ahead. Not surprisingly, they stepped back. What conclusion the duke himself might have drawn from this *dénouement* is anyone's guess. It is clear that the representation of the lords, whether alone or, by their consent, with the afforcement of the commons, did not provide him with an adequate authority. Only a truly national and independent jurisdiction, conferred and confirmed by the unanswerable claims of royal blood, would suffice for the rule of the realm. This felicity was wasted on Henry VI. The 'March' claim was the obvious solution to the problem of the governance of England: had the moment arrived when it would be practicable to pursue it?

THE RULE OF THE LORDS IN THE 1450S

Before continuing with the narrative, it is worth pausing to consider some of the implications of the rule of the lords which became the dominant feature of the polity in the mid- to late 1450s. A pre-eminent role for the lords in the rule of Henry VI's realm was not, of course, unprecedented: it has been shown that all the regimes which had governed England since 1422 were fundamentally conciliar and depended for what practical authority they could muster on the support of the nobility. However, it should be clear that, from 1449–50, the lords had a heightened consciousness of their own role in preserving civil authority, not only as the executives or counsellors of the crown, but as its sole components. This consciousness was partly checked by the efficient rule of Somerset and, more importantly, by the spectre of popular rebellion and the assaults of the duke of York, which helped to hold the 'crown' together and to ensure that it continued to rest on the head of Henry VI. As a result, the real collapse of public authority, as far as the nobility were concerned, did not come until 1453. The inadequacy of royal justice, which drove the lords to help themselves in the shires, made them realise that they had only themselves to look to for help at the centre. This realisation was assisted by the simultaneous departure of the king's sanity, but it is important to recognise that the ties of loyalty had already been substantially loosened. By the time the king returned to health, the principal problem facing the body of lords had changed. In 1455, the question was no longer how to make the rule of Henry VI effective, but rather, how to find an adequate basis for a comprehensive authority.[270] It is this distinction which makes it possible to identify the years which followed as a period of rule by the

---

[270] It is possible that Henry never made a full recovery from his madness of 1453: Griffiths 1981: pp. 717–18, 775–6; Wolffe 1981: pp. 301–3, 312; *Crowland*, p. 424. It is not clear that this would have made any difference to the political and governmental

lords, in which the principle articulated in 1427 – that they enjoyed, corporately, the 'execucion' of an incompetent king's sovereignty – re-emerged, albeit rather tacitly.[271] As a result, the regimes of these years explicitly, and increasingly, depended on the highly conditional support of the mass of peers.

Upon what, principally, was this support conditional? As the account of 1453–4 has suggested, it was not a simple expectation that their personal and local interests would be satisfied that decided the nobility. Partly because the balance of power rested with the majority of lords, many of whom were not involved in uncontainable disputes, wider interests became a factor in the calculations of the belligerents.[272] If the forthright enmity of Nevilles and Percies forced the uncommitted mass to take account of the existence of division, for example by agreeing to the imprisonment of Somerset in November 1453, it is equally clear that the neutrality of the mass limited the extent to which the regimes that belligerents supported could or would satisfy their interests. Although the first protectorate gave willing support to the Nevilles against the Percies, for instance, it did not give the earl of Devon satisfaction against Lord Bonville.[273] When Somerset returned to power in 1455, he persisted in an even-handed treatment of the dispute in the South-West and did not fully restore the duke of Exeter.[274] In other words, using central authority to obtain local victory was not always – perhaps even often – a viable policy. What conditioned the peers, as a group, to give or withdraw enough support to make or break governments was less the matter of

problems of the later 1450s, however, since the king had possessed scarcely any personal authority for some time.

[271] It was evidently difficult to present Henry VI as incompetent to rule without provoking calls for his deposition, and these could not be entertained: above, pp. 263–5. Even so, the appointment of a governing council in 1455, for example, was made in language reminiscent of the arrangements of 1437: the task of government was 'to his moost noble persone full tedious and grete to suffre and bere'; the council would be very much 'for the wele and ease of his said persone' (*RP*, V, pp. 289–90). See above, pp. 115–17 and 133–5 for 1427 and 1437, respectively.

[272] Examples of lords who were not generally involved in such disputes include the duke of Buckingham, the earls of Arundel, Westmorland, Oxford, Worcester, Wiltshire, Shrewsbury, Pembroke and Richmond, Viscounts Bourgchier and Beaumont and a good number of others, including, let us remember, nearly all the bishops, who played an important part in the noble councils of these years, in the creation of the sense of a noble community and in the attribution of public status to ruling regimes.

[273] Above, p. 311.

[274] Cherry 1981b: p. 296. On 3 March, Bonville and his associates were granted the custody of Lostwithiel and a series of other boroughs and manors in Cornwall, which had been farmed by the duke of Exeter since the last resumption (*CFR, 1452–61*, p. 122; *CFR, 1445–52*, pp. 241–2). This reflects the cloud of disapproval which continued to hang over Exeter, even as the new regime made arrangements for his release (see Payling 1989: pp. 904–5). Note, too, that Somerset seems to have done nothing about cancelling the bonds which had been imposed on the Percies by the protectorate: these were still outstanding in 1458 (see below, p. 344 n. 351).

whether or not individual interests had been satisfied, than the matter of whether or not these governments were sufficiently representative to be regarded as 'public', because it was only thus that peace could be maintained or imposed. As a rule, of course, it was the king who supplied this public representativeness, but Henry VI's lords, as they were now well aware, had only themselves to look to.

As the decade progressed, it became increasingly difficult for successive regimes to establish a comprehensive, and therefore public, authority. Against the background of Henry VI's madness, York had achieved an almost complete representation of the lords through his recognition of Prince Edward and his acceptance of the principle of 1427. The duke's apparent commitment to what might be called the common weal of the nobility enabled him to govern effectively on a platform of noble unity. The king's recovery appeared to present Somerset with an opportunity to revive royal authority in opposition to the protectorate consensus, although, in fact, when the divisive nature of his intentions became clear, most of the lords held back. The ensuing secession of York and the Nevilles, now openly identifying themselves with good and politic govern-ment by the lords, damaged Somerset more than themselves. Their efficient victory at St Albans permitted the establishment of another reasonably authoritative regime, focused fairly explicitly on noble 'oonhede' and noble counsel. When, however, York tried to revive his popular and communal constituency, in the interests of providing himself with a source of rule which was independent of the community of the lords, tensions were generated; and his enemies, gathered about the queen, exploited them. They were, even so, unable to replace York with any adequate authority of their own: even more than in early 1455, the principle on which they removed York – noble unity – would not permit it. Rule devolved once again upon the lords corporately, who provided for the continuation of conciliar rule under the headship of the king only to find that unless their regime of unity was backed by a more effective source of lordship, they could not compel the participation of their peers. So it was that in 1456, the polity entered a new phase, in which no central authority truly existed and the strength of the idea of noble unity as the essential prescription for rule prevented such an authority from being established.[275]

This raises some important points about the rule of the lords as an ideal. Apparently innocuous, it could actually provide a basis for revolt, if detached from the king in whom it was conventionally realised.[276] In the

---

[275] The politics of 1456–61, dealt with summarily here, are discussed in full in the succeeding sections of the chapter.

[276] Interestingly enough, a foretaste of this appears in the discussions of 1427, viz. that if

later 1450s, such a development was partly averted by the fact that Henry VI was the acknowledged head of the loosely conciliar regimes which aimed to maintain noble unity. However, the situation was complicated by the fact that the king's headship was also claimed by those opposed to the rule of the lords: the queen, the prince and a growing body of support grouped around them. This group sought to resolve the crisis of authority by demanding unconditional allegiance to the crown, as represented by themselves. There are various reasons why they did so. Their attitude had been an element in the posture struck by Somerset, whose sometime constituency, comprising the queen herself, the royal household and the lords who had suffered from 'Yorkist' rule, now looked to Margaret for direction.[277] At the same time, the authority of the king was the greatest, perhaps the only, constitutional resource at the queen's disposal: unlike Somerset, she was not a lord and was thus unable to pull off his earlier coup of uniting noble counsel with the interests gathered around the king's person; of uniting, in fact, representation with authority. She was forced to oppose the rule of the lords not only because it directly removed her from political agency, but also because it meant that the royal person was reconstituted under the control of those whose good will was by no means clear and whose plans may have included her destruction, or, perhaps, that of her son.[278]

The queen's sponsorship of a division designed to revive an independent royal authority undermined the king's effectiveness and validity as a focus for the rule of the lords. Instead, the true representatives and, ultimately, guarantors, of the ideal of noble 'oonhede' were actually York and the Nevilles. The concept had empowered them in the past and it

the lords were not given the power to execute the king's authority, they would 'falle in ayenst the king' (*PPC*, III, p. 234).

[277] See below, for more details, and Morgan 1987: pp. 49–53 for the changes in the tone and purpose of the household at this time. The emergence of the 'household' as a power bloc removed from even the king's person represents the culmination of the process which began with the focusing of its loyalties on the duke of Somerset in the early 1450s: see above, pp. 293–4, 304–5.

[278] If the recognition of the prince had been the key to York's acquisition of power in 1454, it was by no means certain that Edward's authority would always be so highly regarded. After all, in 1460, a substantial gathering of lords was to set aside his interests, even as it protected those of his father: below, pp. 359–60. It would not be unreasonable for Margaret to have feared that something of this kind could happen earlier. At the same time, she herself was in perpetual danger of being marginalised, even by a body of lords which chose to recognise the prince. Queen Katherine had been edged out of the upbringing of Henry VI from about 1428 and left the royal household in 1430: see Griffiths 1981: pp. 52, 60–1. Before that, Henry IV's queen, Joan of Navarre, had actually been imprisoned as a witch by her step-son, apparently in order to use her dower to meet the costs of an overstretched government: Harriss 1985b: pp. 49–50. If the queen had any ambition to wield power herself – and, to judge by her regency proposals of 1453 (above, p. 305), she did – she could not afford to allow power to rest with the body of lords.

now protected them from destruction as traitors. It was, in fact, towards
the Yorkism of 1453–6 that 'noble unity' inevitably led, and this became
increasingly clear from the summer of 1457.[279] Before considering the
implications of this for the vast majority of lords, who supported a noble
unity which they believed to be protected by the passive lordship of
Henry VI, let us look at the meaning of 'Yorkism' in this period and how
it differed from what came before and after.

Duke Richard's interventions in the early 1450s had rested on his
claims to speak for a national constituency. In advancing these claims,
the duke's title to the succession through his uncle of York had been an
important element. It was York's royal status which seemed to fit him, in
the popular (perhaps even 'parliamentary') mind, for the stewardship of
the common weal of the realm. Ultimately, however, this stewardship
belonged only to the king and, in the conflict of authorities which
resulted from York's actions, it was Henry VI who provided the most
continual resort of noble unity and who consequently emerged victorious. When Duke Richard returned to power, in 1453–4, his high blood
was no longer the principal feature of his platform.[280] In this period,
York tacitly exchanged his claim to represent the common weal of the
nation for a claim to represent the common interest of the nobility. As
he did so, the basis of his authority ceased to be the quasi-regality he
had enjoyed as the leading prince of the blood and became, instead, his
capacity to provide good government in association with the 'oonhede'
of the lords, a 'oonhede' which was focused (rather abstractly) on the
king and prince. This is very important in the evaluation of his relations
with the Nevilles: Warwick and Salisbury took part with York in
governments of noble unity; their attachment was not to the duke
personally, but to the common interest of the peers who had gathered,
conditionally, under his lordship.[281] This was made plain when York
tried to give his power a more independent basis, by reviving his
representation of the national common weal in the 1455–6 protectorate.
The Nevilles opted for noble unity and the council of lords in preference

---

[279] See below, pp. 341ff.
[280] It must, even so, have been among the reasons why he was invited to the 1453 council,
why he was considered eligible to be protector and why he became a pole of allegiance.
See above.
[281] This is partly illustrated by the view of de Waurin, *Croniques*, V, p. 267, that the Nevilles
had agreed to help York in 1455 only if the person of the king received no 'molleste'.
This does seem to reflect their attitude and that of other lords at that time, an attitude
which York, having emphasised his loyalty and belief in noble unity, was forced to
accommodate. See below, pp. 356–9, for the similar situation of 1460.

to the duke's adventures. In the ensuing years, they and York went their separate ways.[282]

As will become clear in the next section, however, the rule of the lords could not be maintained without York's assistance, whilst the determination of the queen to re-establish independent royal authority drove her to sustain an atmosphere of division which not only threatened York and the Nevilles individually, but drove them back together, by reviving, perhaps accidentally, the issue of St Albans. When Salisbury and his men resolved to take 'ful partie' with York in November 1458, it was almost certainly with the intention of restoring a workable authority of lords: an authority led by the duke, perhaps, but nominally headed by the king.[283] Right up to 1460, the common weal of the nobility remained the leading theme of Yorkist enterprise. Whether these priorities were shared by York himself, as consensus receded in the later 1450s, is not clear. To begin with, he seems to have been prepared to maintain a posture of obedience to the king and co-operation with the lords in keeping with his policy since 1453.[284] On the other hand, the lack of central authority in these years may, as in 1450, have restored to public consciousness the duke's other identity as an alternative and independent source of lordship over the realm as a whole. The essence of this lordship could no longer be the 'York' claim, which was set aside by the birth of the prince, but, rather, the 'March' claim, which seems to have achieved a greater public currency in these years.[285] Just as the queen sought to re-erect the king as an independent royal authority, so York had the means to do the same for himself. We do not know if the duke did anything to encourage this revival of his more controversial claims at this stage, but he certainly returned to them during the exile of 1459–60, when the queen succeeded in annexing the unity of the lords to herself.[286] Moreover, when the victorious Lancastrians publicised their version of the events of 1459 at the Coventry parliament, they identified dynastic ambition as the true

---

[282] See below, pp. 333–4, 345.

[283] Pollard 1976: p. 52.

[284] See below and note that, unlike Salisbury, York had only a small force of household men with him in London in January/February 1458 (PL, III, p. 125).

[285] Pedigrees showing the 'March' claim became common in the period 1455–8, which may explain why the government chose to make veiled references to it at the Coventry parliament (Allan 1981: pp. 267–8; below, n. 287).

[286] See below, pp. 357ff, for York's use of his March claim in the autumn of 1460. There is every reason to doubt James II of Scotland's assertion that, some time before the end of June 1456, York had asked him for assistance in support of the 'clarum jus quod habet ad coronam et dyadema Anglie' (CSP Milan, I, p. 23; Letters and Papers, I, p. 324): see Dunlop 1950: p. 167.

cause of the duke's rebellion.[287] A new Yorkism was emerging, with or without York's own prompting.[288]

It emerges from the above that noble unity, realised in the rule of the lords, was a problematic and unrealistic concept. On the one hand, what might be identified as the crown interest – Margaret, the prince and the old Somerset connection – repudiated it until late 1458. On the other hand, while the lords attempted to focus their rule on the person and crown of Henry VI, the natural supporters of that form of rule – York, Warwick and Salisbury – found themselves in opposition to both the queen and, logically and reputedly, if not actually, to the king. As a result, none of the possible configurations of power could work. Government by the lords threatened the queen, because, in practice, it tended towards the displacement of the king by an authoritative council headed by York. It could not, as a result, command the united support of the peerage which was its basic justification. Government by the queen, meanwhile, over-looked the lords' corporate power to execute royal authority; and, even were this drawback to be overcome somehow, it threatened to precipitate civil war by excluding the Yorkists. Government by the king, finally, which seemed to reconcile noble unity with royal authority, was, in practice, a fiction. The rule of Henry VI was no longer a matter of monarchical power. The components of the crown – lordship, representa-tion, the executive and even the household – were no longer united and focused on King Henry himself. Lordship came from the irreconcilable poles of York and Margaret. Representation was carried out through a series of fragile councils which could not afford to give full recognition to the lordship of either of these authorities if real unity was to be maintained.[289] The executive, overlapping with these councils, acted upon both the authority of the lords corporately and, from the autumn of

---

[287] In the attainder document, the duke's return in the autumn of 1450 was linked to the fact that Cade's rebels had intended to 'have exalted the seid Duc, ayenst all reason, lawe and trouth, to the estate that God and nature hath ordeyned You and youre succession to be born to' (*RP*, V, p. 346). That York had shared their intent was signalled by a reference to the Yorkists' 'moost unresonable appetite of such estate, as of reason ought not to be desired nor had by noon of theym, nor to noon erthely creature but to You alone, and to youre succession' (*ibid.*, p. 347). Meanwhile, the wording of the oath of allegiance at the same parliament made it quite plain that dynastic threat was in the air: see below, p. 353 n. 388. It does not seem to have occurred to the royalists that by publicising York's dynastic claims, they ran the risk of legitimising his rebellion: see below.

[288] In fact, however, the 'Yorkism' of 1453–6 had successfully, surprisingly and perhaps unbeknown to York been resuscitated by the lords coming from Calais in the summer of 1460: this gave the noble unity of Henry VI a last brief efflorescence (see below, pp. 355ff).

[289] And if something closely resembling real unity was *not* maintained, these councils had no authority: see above, pp. 116–17, 313–14, 325ff.

1456, that of the queen.[290] The household, now a bloc all but discrete from the king's person, provided the queen with a means of power and finance.[291] The unpalatable choice facing the lords was therefore between anarchy under the king and/or a 'Yorkist' noble unity, on the one hand, and civil war under the opposing forces of the queen and the new Yorkist legitimism, on the other. They can hardly be blamed for making every effort to avoid the latter, even if the former was hardly less disastrous.[292]

The mass of the nobility were thus placed in a situation of profound uncertainty. Instead of the familiar pattern of relations with the crown which they could follow unreflectingly, and the more demanding but still comparatively simple choices which had faced them earlier in the 1450s, they now confronted a bewildering array of possible positions, of roughly equivalent legitimacy, which they could adopt for the fulfilment of their interests, both corporate and individual. At the same time, adopt them they must, because the lords, as we have seen, were not autonomous agents. Behind them were the men of their countries, who were more immediately concerned with local rule, in both senses of the word, than with its national counterpart.[293] This imposed complex obligations on the lords, particularly when the queen set about the creation of a regional power-base in the north-west Midlands. Under these circumstances, the magnates of the region – men like Buckingham and Shrewsbury, who apparently saw the preservation of noble unity as the best chance of politic rule – were forced to participate in Margaret's prevailing local lordship, whatever their feelings about her national ambitions.[294]

It is for reasons of this sort that the impression of a 'middle party' – perhaps comprising Buckingham and the Bourgchiers, who were so prominent in the politics of 1455–6 – is rather misleading.[295] Local power and national power were not closely related in this period: indeed precious little of the latter existed. Margaret's vast aggregation of regional support in the later 1450s did not bring her the rule of the realm. Conversely, the

---

[290] The conch in Golding's *The Lord of the Flies* seems an appropriate analogy for the position of the clerical and financial offices in this period: anyone who could control them could exercise public power, but the impact of this power was profoundly conditioned by the strength or weakness of the authority behind it.

[291] See below, p. 348.

[292] See McFarlane 1981f: pp. 237–40.

[293] For a nice illustration of the kinds of calculations made by gentlemen, note the case of Sir Thomas Harington of Hornby, a follower of the earl of Salisbury, who, in 1458 or 1459, enfeoffed his lands to several of Salisbury's enemies so that he could be sure of preserving his property, regardless of how the impending crisis was resolved (see Pollard 1990: p. 276). For an important discussion of how the gentry of Warwickshire responded to the worsening state of politics in the later 1450s, see Carpenter 1992: pp. 475–87 and chs. 16 and 17.

[294] For more details of the queen's party, see below, pp. 337ff.

[295] See e.g. Woodger 1974: pp. 63–95, *passim*. Griffiths 1981: p. 798 criticises the idea on different grounds from those proposed here.

Yorkist or implicitly Yorkist regimes of noble unity which met in London between 1456 and 1461 did not exercise power in the regions: in fact, as the battle of Wakefield was to demonstrate, they did not necessarily exercise power even in the 'countries' of the lords who composed them.[296] As a consequence, it was for some time possible to offer conditional allegiance to potentially conflicting authorities: one regional, sectional, and claiming legitimacy through queen, prince and, often, king; the other national, corporatist, and claiming legitimacy through the representation of the lords, accompanied, intermittently, by the king. In this anarchy, more or less all the lords were in a 'middle party', retaining dual allegiances until it became necessary, or preferable, to commit themselves to the armed defence of one lord or another.[297] This began to be feasible from the autumn of 1458, when the queen seems to have managed to gain comprehensive control, retaining her hold over regional loyalties in the Midlands, whilst acquiring the public authority of the rule of the lords in London. Even then, it was probably Yorkist insurrection, rather than Lancastrian repression, which finally produced civil war. The concept of a 'middle party' distinct from the nobility as a whole in the later 1450s presupposes that a single government existed to receive its moderating counsels and, implicitly, that this government was based in Coventry and led by the queen. In fact, as will be becoming clear, the situation was very much more complicated than that. How it came to be resolved into the clearer divisions of civil war is the subject of the next section.

THE ANARCHY, 1456–1459

Most accounts of the 1450s are so entirely dominated by the dispute between Somerset and York that the period from the end of the second protectorate to the coronation of Edward IV, which lasted nearly as long, has been comparatively neglected.[298] In large part, this is due to the shortage of evidence: in the later 1450s, the documentation of governmental activity in all spheres, including justice and finance, all but broke down. This makes the history of central authority very difficult to write; but, even so, given that the conflict between York and Somerset was a symptom of fundamental problems in Henry VI's polity, rather than the

---

[296] Below, p. 361 n. 423.

[297] For a graphic illustration of the slowness with which the nobility, in general, took up arms, see Richmond 1977. See also Gillingham 1981: pp. 183–4 for some interesting comments about the similar conditions of 1470–1.

[298] Storey 1966 is perhaps the most dramatic example, spending about a hundred and thirty pages on 1450–6 and about fifteen on the ensuing five-year period which actually covered the 'end' of the dynasty.

straightforward and external, or fortuitous, cause of its collapse, it seems important to make a real attempt to discover and understand what happened when this conflict was no longer the main item on the political agenda. The fact that in 1459 York and the Nevilles again rose up against a government supported by the sons of Somerset and Northumberland has tended to suggest that the personal and familial disputes which helped to produce St Albans had not gone away. This may be true, although the extent to which these disputes can be used to explain the wider politics of the period should be questioned. The real mystery is why the progression from Yorkist hegemony to outright division under the revived crown took three and a half years. Why, when the issues were apparently clear in 1456, if not 1455, or even 1453, was the resort to violence not more immediate? Some answers to this question have been advanced in the preceding section. What remains to be done is to explore them in relation to the rather mystifying events of the period.

York was removed from office, in late February 1456, by the confluence of two streams of thinking. First of all, it seems likely that associated with the lords' resistance to the resumption was a deep-seated concern about both the fact and consequences of York's usurpation of the royal power. Although the events of the preceding years seemed to justify a conciliar form of rule, with Somerset dead there was no particular reason why it had to be conducted under York's protection: the demands of unity and good government might be better served by a council operating under royal, rather than ducal, headship.[299] This was the form of government which emerged in the spring of 1456.[300] In many ways, it was the logical outcome of the St Albans campaign as York had presented it, a point which serves to show that the interests of 'Yorkism' were not

---

[299] A desire to restore unity was reflected by the abandonment of the trials of both Exeter and Devon in early 1456. Exeter was due to be tried in parliament in January 1456 (KB9/149/1, m. 39), but was instead released under bonds to come and answer if summoned (*CCIR, 1454–61*, p. 109). Three of his mainpernors were non-partisan figures – Buckingham, Oxford and Berners (the other was Richmount-Grey, who had been associated with the court since 1450) – which suggests that the move commanded the sympathy of the lords in general. We know less of Devon's circumstances, only that the proposal to try him was 'countermaundid' by 9 February: *PL*, III, p. 76. As with the ending of the protectorate itself, if the restoration of Devon and Exeter had been proposed by a group opposed to York, it suited the more moderate plans of the lords as a whole.

[300] Conciliar rule continued for the time being, and this is signalled by the fact that councillors went on signing issues of government. There were few royal signs manual and none at all in the sources I have looked at before 16 March (C81/1546/109). The relationship between royal headship and the establishment of a non-partisan, but effectively governing, council is to some extent evoked by a peculiar practice, current in March 1456, in which the king himself handed instruments witnessed by listed lords of the council to the chancellor for engrossing (e.g. C81/1465/1–5). Note the recorded view of the chancellor, in late March, that 'the rule is amendid heer': *PL*, III, p. 79.

always those of Duke Richard himself: he and the Nevilles had had their justice on the battlefield; now, the 'politique governaunce' they had sought was to be provided by a substantial council, in which York, alongside others, was welcome to take part.[301] Running against these considerations, meanwhile, but also helping to shape the lords' behaviour, was a second line of thought, which issued from the queen and the same coalition of interests which had revived the rule of Somerset in 1455. As later became clear, this view amounted to a repudiation of the post-St Albans settlement, and focused not on the preservation of unity but on the meting out of justice to a new set of 'traitors': York and his erstwhile allies.[302] It may have been from this perspective that Margaret's supporters among the lords opposed both resumption and protectorate.[303] The opposition of such men could have convinced lords otherwise sympathetic to York that there was no chance of peace without bringing back the king. Even so, it seems that the lords as a whole were not prepared to see a repetition of the 'royalist' and revanchist coup of March 1455. They stood by the broadly based, but pro-Neville, council, merely substituting the king for York as its head.[304] As a result, while the protectorate fell, the

---

[301] A Paston correspondent recorded the view of a great lord that the king wished York to remain as 'chief and princepall counceller' during pleasure, but not to be protector, or to be as independent of royal power as the parliamentary appointment had implied (*PL*, III, p. 75). This seems to have been the consensus view among the lords, implying both the continuation of the council as a means of realising royal power and York's permitted participation in its activities, albeit on a less exalted footing. York attended meetings on 3 and 6 March (C81/1465/2; E28/87/31) and perhaps on 9 March when he received payment for his wages during the first protectorate: *CPR, 1452–61*, p. 278 (cf. Johnson 1988: p. 173). For other signs of continued favour towards York, see *ibid.*, p. 175. He even seems to have played a part in the appointment of a new treasurer of the household in May: Harriss 1953: p. 171.

[302] Below, pp. 345ff.

[303] The activities of such a group cannot be firmly demonstrated from the records, but *PL*, III, p. 75, and *Loci e Libro*, p. 204, suggest that the queen and a number of lords were involved in the attack on the resumption and the suspension of the protectorate. A number of lords who were to be associated with the queen in the ensuing period – notably Shrewsbury and Wiltshire – had not attended either council or parliament in the autumn of 1455 (note that both were present at a meeting of 24 January 1456: *PPC*, VI, p. 286. Perhaps, as in 1455, changes to the composition of the body of lords at the centre was both a symptom and a cause of York's waning influence). Their participation in York's downfall is suggested by the fact that they, together with the Nevilles, Buckingham, Pembroke and a host of courtier barons – Moleyns, Sudeley, Welles, Beauchamp, St Amand, Rivers Stanley and Dudley – were exempted from the resumption (*RP*, V, pp. 308ff). A large number of household men also received exemptions.

[304] Records for attendance at the council in the spring and summer of 1456 show that Salisbury was one of the busier participants (see E28/87/*passim* and C81/1465/1, 2 and 6). Other councillors attending at this time include the Bourgchiers, Archbishop Booth, Waynflete, Warwick, Say and Wenlock: a group characteristic of the protectorate period. Neville influence is suggested by Salisbury's succession to the dead Cromwell's chief stewardship of Lancashire and the north parts of the duchy on 15 February (Somerville 1953: pp. 421, 492: the timing may suggest an accommodation between the

consensus which had underpinned it survived, guaranteeing Warwick the captaincy of Calais, and precipitating the departure of the queen for her estates by the end of April.[305] If Margaret's withdrawal from London was a sign of her hostility to the new government, it did not go unnoticed.[306]

In the meantime, the council seems to have taken its responsibility to maintain the unity of the lords seriously.[307] Even so, its efforts were undermined by a lack of authority. As the immediate crisis of the end of the protectorate passed, noble commitment to the council diminished.[308] To restore order to London in the wake of the anti-Lombard riots of April 1456, the government was forced to use personal appearances by the king in an attempt to bolster its power, and even this was insufficient to secure convictions.[309] When, in the late summer, York's men rose up in Wales and seized control of the southern part of the principality, the lords about the king seem to have realised that, alone, they possessed no firm base for maintaining the public authority of Henry VI against what may have appeared to be the opening moves in a new rebellion by the duke.[310] It was surely in order to afforce royal authority, and so to counter this threat, that they decided to reunite the king with the queen in late August 1456.[311] It seems unlikely that York's western men had the

earl and York's opponents, or an attempt by the protector to retain the support of one of his most important allies: who controlled duchy patronage at this time is far from clear); by Warwick's acquisition of Calais (next note) and by the exclusion of both Neville earls from the act of resumption (last note).

[305] Warwick may have pressed for the continuation of the protectorate until it was clear that he would indeed obtain this post: see *PL*, III, p. 75; Harriss 1960: pp. 45–6. For Margaret's departure, see *Town Chrons.*, p. 110.

[306] Note the increasing interest shown by contemporary correspondents in the queen's movements from 1456 onwards: *PL*, III, pp. 86–7, 92 etc. This would seem to suggest that she was increasingly recognised to be a source of authority, and one at odds with some, at least, of the lords (*ibid.*, pp. 75, 86).

[307] This is shown by its appointment of broadly based commissions, judicial and otherwise: e.g. that of 30th April against the anti-Lombard riots contained Exeter, Buckingham, Pembroke, Stafford (Buckingham's son and heir), Salisbury, Northumberland, Worcester, Bourgchier, Sudeley, Berners, Stanley and Fortescue (*CPR, 1452–61*, p. 306); the oyer and terminer sent to Kent in June was headed by Pembroke, Arundel, Salisbury, Northumberland, Bourgchier, Bergavenny and Rivers (*ibid.*, p. 307). A Kent commission of array in August included Lord Clinton, who had joined York at St Albans (*ibid.*, p. 311).

[308] It was reported that only the Bourgchiers and Salisbury were in London for the start of a great council in early June: *PL*, III, p. 92.

[309] The king was moved into London, from Windsor, for judicial sessions in the first week of May: *PL*, III, p. 86. On 5 May, two dukes, five earls and the chief justice sat as judges, together with others (KB9/289, m. 45). The fact that, even under such a demonstration of authority, nothing but trespasses was presented by the juries seems to have prompted unease on the part of the duke of Buckingham, who was perhaps the most prominent lay lord in the government: *PL*, III, p. 86.

[310] For the rising of Herbert and Devereux, see Griffiths 1981: pp. 779–80; Johnson 1988: pp. 176–9.

[311] Wolffe 1981: pp. 303–4, 370; Storey 1966: p. 180 (cf. the views of contemporary chroniclers, some of whom linked the king's departure to the riots against the Lombards: *Town Chrons.*, p. 110; *Brut*, p. 523. It is interesting that when Henry prepared to return

subversion of the realm in mind: the point is rather that this episode helped to demonstrate to the lords that the rule of the king was no rule and that control of the administration did not confer control of the realm. The real sources of lordship lay outside the structures which had grown up since the protectorate: York, who was making royal power work against the Scottish king;[312] and the queen, who was preparing to realise the potential of the royal lands in the north and west Midlands.[313] As we have seen time and again, the provision of effective lordship was an integral part of preserving unity and exercising authority.

The formal authority supplied by the king's presence was all that Margaret needed to transform her lordship into national power. Gaining an immediate stake in the control of the executive with the appointment of her chancellor, Laurence Booth, as keeper of the privy seal,[314] she contrived the summons of a great council to Coventry in early October 1456 and made the earl of Shrewsbury treasurer just before it met.[315] The queen may have expected the assembly to provide her with a chance to proceed against her enemies using the public authority of the king and lords. In doing so, perhaps, she would be able to annexe that authority to herself. If she could damage York, she could also discredit the council which had been created under his rule and persuade the lords that a more meaningful royal power, underpinned by her and those who supported her, offered the best chance of unity. A show trial seems to have been planned and indeed something of this kind did take place, though whether at this council or at a second assembly held at Coventry six months later

to London, in the autumn of 1457, letters from both the king and the chancellor to the corporation made reference to the fact that the city had now convinced the government of its loyalty: Sharpe, 1894–5:, III, pp. 382–3).

[312] King James had opportunistically invaded the North. The government despatched angry letters from Henry VI at Windsor (Williams, (ed.) *Correspondence of Bekynton*, II, pp. 141–2), but it seems to have been York himself who took personal action against the Scottish king. He wrote from Durham, ostensibly at Henry's command, but under his own seal and sign manual and in his own words, inviting the king to face him and, implicitly, his army in open combat: *ibid.*, II, pp. 142–4. It is difficult to know whether York was acting on orders from the council or, as if still protector, on his own initiative. In either case, the duke's deeds, even when couched in terms of emphatic loyalty (four references to 'my sovereign lord' in a short credence – *ibid.*), brought to light the fragmentation of authority and his own fitness to rule.

[313] The impression of York and the queen as the two sources of real authority in the realm is neatly conveyed by a record of how they waited upon each other in early June, even though they were based some distance apart (at Sandal and Chester, respectively): *PL*, III, p. 92.

[314] Griffiths 1981: p. 773.

[315] See *ibid.*, though note that it seems that the council opened on 7 October, two days after Shrewsbury's appointment (*PL*, III, p. 103; *CPR, 1452–61*, p. 324). It is interesting that the patent was reissued when the council gathered, with slightly more specific terms: *ibid.* This may reflect the superior authority of the gathering of king and lords. For Shrewsbury's connections with the queen, see below, at n. 331.

is not clear.[316] In the event, however, it appears that the assembled lords had a different approach to managing York from that envisaged by the queen. Perhaps once, perhaps twice, the duke was made to swear a version of the oath he had sworn in 1452. On one occasion, he was reminded by Buckingham that nothing but royal grace protected him from destruction. But, beyond this, no action was taken.[317] While these steps amounted to a public invocation of full royal authority, with its branding of York (and perhaps Warwick) as rebellious, the effect was severely undermined by the readiness of the peers to support, and indeed to supervise, the exercise of mercy.[318] It seems, therefore, that, although the queen was able to change the great officers, this availed her little: she did not have the exclusive claim on their loyalties which her policies demanded.[319] The right of the lords

[316] The dating of the submissions discussed in this paragraph is not clear: Johnson 1988: pp. 178–9 and Wolffe 1981: pp. 309–10 prefer the spring of 1457, and their arguments are persuasive, though not conclusive. Even so, it seems very likely that the queen had intended to take action on the first occasion, if not also on the second. Herbert and Devereux were apparently summoned to appear before the council of October 1456 (*CClR, 1454–61*, pp. 158, 174) and anti-Yorkist bills, posted in London in September, implied that the duke's downfall was assured (see Johnson 1988: pp. 176–7 for details).

[317] *RP*, V, p. 347, and cf. *PL*, III, p. 108 (which, in its description of Buckingham's behaviour, could be offering a more honest, but also more ignorant, account of the same event), 'Benet's Chron.', p. 217, and *Chrons. of London*, p. 167. According to the near-contemporary copy of the 1452 oath in BL, Add. MS 48031A, fol. 129r, it was 'sworen wones at Westm. and another tyme at Coventre at several tymes and in sundre yeres'.

[318] Note that even the 1459 account of York's submission, which might be expected to emphasise the role of the king in proceedings, casts the assembled lords as protagonists. The view of James Gresham (*PL*, III, p. 108), echoed by some of the chronicles, that York was in 'good conceyt' with the king should be taken to mean that he enjoyed the sympathy of the peers as a whole: note that other lords, besides Buckingham, the half-brother of the dismissed Bourgchiers, were concerned at the drift of the queen's policy (*ibid.*). The roll of the 1459 parliament records that Warwick was made to swear the same oath that York had sworn, or a very similar one (*RP*, V, p. 347). He was apparently present at the 1456 Coventry council, but there is no evidence for his attendance at the 1457 one, and neither he nor Salisbury was summoned to it, although York was ('Benet's Chron.', p. 217; *PPC*, VI, pp. 333–4).

[319] Waynflete, the new chancellor, was closely connected with the foundations (above, p. 168) and had been a regular attender of the council under Somerset, but there is not much else to link him with the queen. Both he and Shrewsbury had been members of the protectorate councils. This may be part of the reason why they returned to London soon after their appointment: Waynflete was back in the capital by mid-October (e.g. *CPR, 1452–61*, p. 329: briefly back in Coventry on 9 December – ibid., p. 331); Shrewsbury was certainly back by January 1457 (C81/1546/114) and probably before then. Obviously, the chancellor, when in London, would hardly disobey privy seals coming from Coventry. The point is that he would also be under pressure to seal instruments issuing from whichever lords continued to meet there as a council. We do not know as much about the whereabouts of the keeper of the privy seal, but there is no evidence to suggest that he was in London while the king and queen were in the Midlands, except on one occasion in June 1459 (E28/88/58: and note that on 21 June 1458, Booth was to be found sealing letters at Kenilworth, presumably with the queen, while the king was certainly in London – E404/71/2/72). It is interesting that it was the former chancellor, Archbishop Bourgchier, who was expected to oversee the appointments of sheriffs in November 1456: another suggestion that something of a conciliar authority continued to exist (*PL*, III, p. 109).

corporately to execute the king's power when his personal authority was in abeyance seems to have triumphed over the pull of the queen's lordship and the possibilities it offered (that Henry's authority *was* in abeyance is suggested by the fact that although the king remained, on the queen's advice, in the North-West, the chancellor and most of the lords appear to have returned to London within a matter of weeks).[320] The queen had succeeded in capturing some important positions, but, because she had not found a settlement, she had not won the war: the exercise of government and the authority of the crown remained dispersed.

Undaunted, Margaret pressed ahead with other measures to broaden her authority.[321] These concerned the prince, not the king. Between the autumn of 1456 and the early spring of 1457, the queen made a series of appointments to create a *familia* and administration for the young Edward.[322] Whether or not the queen was using Herbert's and Devereux's recent usurpation of royal authority in the prince's lands as the pretext for these moves, it is clear that she derived considerable benefit from them.[323] In this way, her lordship acquired a bureaucratic and constitutional reality independently of the authority of the king – now inconveniently reposing in the wider body of lords – which had undermined her success in the autumn.[324] She was using the authority of the prince as York had used it before, to turn a dubious or downright private lordship and a disparate, uncertain or conditional fund of support into a quasi-public party of unimpeachable loyalty.[325] If this party was all too obviously an aggregation of local power, this was perhaps justified by the

---

[320] 'Benet's Chron.', p. 217; *PL*, III, p. 109. We only have records of two council meetings at Westminster in the ensuing months, one on 29 November 1456, the other on 31 January 1457, both endorsed 'rex de avisamento consilii' (C81/1546/112, 114). The attendance was small and did not include any of the greater lay lords except Shrewsbury, though Waynflete attended on both occasions. See also above, n. 319.

[321] Because of the conviction of the chroniclers that Margaret was the major architect of royal policy at this time (see e.g. *Loci e Libro*, p. 205; *Collections*, p. 209), it is easy to overlook the fact that the queen still had to stake her claim to the exercise of public authority. Such a claim could not be made on her own behalf, only on that of her husband or son (above, p. 326; although note that this did not stop her letting it be known to the corporation of Coventry that she expected to be treated by them with the same honour as the king received: Harris (ed.), *Coventry Leet Book*, pp. 298–9).

[322] It is worth noting that the letters appointing a chancellor and receiver-general for the prince must have been among the first items to be sealed by Laurence Booth following his appointment as keeper: *CPR, 1452–61*, p. 323 (26 September). See Griffiths 1981: pp. 781–2 for the other appointments which followed.

[323] The appointment of a chancellor seems particularly germane, given Herbert's abuse of the seal of the principality at Aberystwyth a month before (*ibid.*, p. 780). For the political value of the councillors – Archbishop Booth, Bishops Waynflete, Boulers and Stanbury, the earls of Stafford, Wiltshire and Shrewsbury, Viscount Beaumont and Lords Stanley and Dudley – see Griffiths 1981: pp. 781–2.

[324] The warrants of the prince's council required the formal assent of the queen: *ibid.*, pp. 781–2 at nn. 68–9; also *CPR, 1452–61*, p. 515.

[325] The queen had begun to use royal favour to build up a party as soon as she acquired a

headship of the prince, whose lordship was regional as well as national.[326] It seems too much to suggest that the queen envisaged a formal new centre of authority based in the Midlands, but it may be that she perceived what the lords as a group did not, that her husband's polity had disintegrated and that the time had come to build a new one, focused on her son, even if this meant war.[327]

As a result, the main beneficiaries of Margaret's good lordship were leading magnates: the need to exert control over the king's household, which had preoccupied and ultimately defeated Suffolk, was much reduced now that the king's personal authority was once again a matter of totemic, rather than practical, importance.[328] The men whom the queen attracted were a sizeable and mixed group: misfits, such as Devon and Exeter,[329] *habitués* of the court, such as Wiltshire and

partial control of the administration in the autumn of 1456. See Griffiths 1991k: pp. 214–15 for her activities in Wales as early as October.

[326] Obviously the queen had withdrawn to the Midlands in 1456 because this was where her own Lancastrian estates and the patrimony of the prince were concentrated. For the geopolitical importance of the men Margaret attracted to her service, see Griffiths 1981: p. 784 and Carpenter 1992: pp. 476, 484 (also Rowney 1981: pp. 12–16 for the convenient location of Dudley's estates; and Bennett 1983: pp. 215–23 and Griffiths 1991c: pp. 177–8 for Stanley's power in the North-West). Note that Coventry itself was a town with close associations with the prince's county of Chester (Griffiths 1981: p. 777).

[327] The Yorkist 'English Chronicle' printed by Davies has the queen 'makyng pryve menys to some of the lordes of Englond for to styre the kyng that he shulde resygne the croune to hyre sone'. It is interesting that 'she coude nat bryng her purpos aboute': the king remained the publicised focus of lordly government (*English Chron.*, p. 80). Note also that, if war did break out, control of the Midlands could, strategically at least, provide the key to victory: see Goodman 1981: pp. 26, 30, 36, 39–40, while access to the superior impressment capacity of Marcher lords – such as Buckingham and, in a sense (Cheshire), Stanley – would also be important: Carpenter 1992: pp. 483–4.

[328] The household was scarcely starved of patronage (see e.g. Griffiths 1981: p. 803), but it appears to have been its more territorially substantial figures who received most. Given the split-site nature of the government at this time, it is, of course, difficult to know at whose authority ministers were acting. Sometimes, the only way to distinguish what might be assessed as a partisan policy on the part of the queen from a deliberately non-partisan policy on the part of a council which was probably open to wider influences, is by looking closely at the dating of grants. For example, on 9 July 1456, Exeter was committed the custody of Calstock, Trematon and Saltash, duchy of Cornwall lands which had long been kept by the Hollands (*CFR, 1452–61*, p. 163). This would seem to be the work of the council. On 24 September 1456 – the very day Booth became keeper of the privy seal – Exeter, together with his courtier associate John Trevilian, received the custody of Lostwithiel, Camelford and a series of Cornish manors, which, although they had been in his hands in the past, had been kept by Lord Bonville until the resumption (*CFR 1445–52*, pp. 241–2; *CFR, 1452–61*, pp. 122, 179). Bonville had been more or less in favour with the conciliar regimes of 1455 and 1456, but the queen apparently had her eye on the earl of Devon (see below). For these reasons, this grant is likely to have been her work.

[329] See Griffiths 1981: pp. 802–3 for these two. Note that Devon may have been with the queen when he died in February 1458 (*English Chron.*, p. 75) and that his executors were men closely linked to her: William Booth, Waynflete, Shrewsbury and Fortescue (*CClR, 1454–61*, pp. 357–8). For a new link between Exeter and the Percies in 1457, see *CClR, 1454–61*, p. 223.

Beaumont;[330] men who had endorsed the Yorkist protectorates, such as
Shrewsbury and Pembroke;[331] and, most famously, of course, the heirs
and associates of those killed at St Albans, Somerset, Northumberland
and, perhaps to a lesser extent, Clifford and Egremont.[332] Some of
these were drawn in at once, others in the course of 1457 and 1458,
and it is true that the creation of a 'royalist' party was to some extent a
two-way process as the lords began to despair of conciliar unity as an
alternative source of power; but, even so, the queen was clearly not a
passive bystander.[333] These lords exercised real territorial dominance,
and not only in the royal heartland of the north-west Midlands. The
power of this increasingly effective confederation of noblemen may even
have been a factor in the apparent reduction of local strife in these
years, although this must be regarded as a highly tentative suggestion,

[330] See Griffiths 1981: pp. 784, 803. These two, both significant powers in the area of the
queen's Leicestershire estates, had long been associated with her (Somerville 1953:
p. 340; Ross 1974: p. 75; Acheson 1992: pp. 20–1; Carpenter 1992: pp. 326, 411, 413;
above, pp. 294n, 305n). Together with Shrewsbury, the two were identified as the
Yorkists' most extreme and mortal enemies in 1460 (*English Chron.*, p. 88). Wiltshire
became treasurer in succession to Shrewsbury in October 1458 (*CPR, 1452–61*, p. 459:
and see pp. 352, 419, 478, for other patronage). Other former 'courtier' lords who now
embraced Margaret were Lords Rivers, Roos and Welles. Rivers received the keeping of
Rochester Castle in 1457 and a commission to investigate the activities of Warwick in
1458 (*CPR, 1452–61*, pp. 394, 443). Roos headed, with Scales, Tuddenham, Daniel
and others, a commission to Norfolk to investigate treasonable words spoken against the
king, queen and prince in 1457 (*ibid.*, p. 404) and he and Somerset got a wool licence in
the same year (*DKR*, XLVIII, p. 421). He was a mainpernor for Exeter in 1459 (*CClR,
1454–61*, p. 350). Rivers and Roos were among those sent to support Somerset's
retinue outside Calais in 1459–60 (*Three Chrons.*, p. 72; *English Chron.*, p. 84). Welles
joined the garter in 1457, Wiltshire in 1459 (Anstis (ed.), *Register of the Garter*, II,
pp. 158, 163).
[331] See Griffiths 1981: pp. 780–1, 803–4; Pollard 1968: pp. 77–80; *CPR, 1452–61*,
pp. 360, 391, 394–5, 428, 433, 485, 486–7, 497; *CFR, 1452–61*, pp. 209–10, 231.
Shrewsbury's dismissal from the treasury in 1458 does not seem to have been a mark of
disgrace: he was handsomely rewarded for his service (E404/71/3/36). It may have been
the failure of York's lordship, particularly locally in Wales and Shropshire, which
encouraged both peers to desert to the rising force of the queen.
[332] Somerset received licence to enter his father's lands under age and a series of other
perks in March 1457, some six months after he had apparently tried to attack York at
Coventry (*CPR, 1452–61*, p. 355; *Town Chrons.*, p. 159; *PL*, III, p. 108). For other
rewards and grants, see *CPR, 1452–61*, pp. 390–1, 423, 485–6; *CClR, 1454–61*,
pp. 236–7, 248; E404/71/2/12 (£100 reward). For Northumberland, see Pollard 1990:
p. 267 and *CClR, 1454–61*, p. 227 (a wool licence granted in April 1457). There is
almost no evidence for Clifford, but he clearly benefited from the loveday and became
warden of the West March after the attainders of 1459 (Pollard 1990: pp. 272–3).
Egremont, meanwhile, seems to have remained under a cloud until the loveday of 1458.
This episode, which may have played an important part in reviving division and
increasing the queen's lordship, is discussed below, pp. 343ff.
[333] Note that in a poem of 1458, which uses 'ship of state' imagery, the 'royalist' party is
identified as the prince, the dukes of Exeter, Somerset and Buckingham, the earls of
Pembroke, Devon, Northumberland, Shrewsbury and Wiltshire, Viscount Beaumont
and Lords Grey of Ruthin, Beauchamp, Scales, Roos, Clifford, Egremont, Welles and
Rivers – substantially the men listed above: Robbins (ed.), *Historical Poems*, no. 78.

given the state of the evidence.[334] All the same, it is clear that Margaret had begun to establish a 'pale' of royal (or, in fact, princely) authority in which lordship may have functioned more or less as it should have.[335] How was this to be reconciled with the public structures of the wider realm which she was effectively repudiating?

The answer came in a second council summoned to Coventry in February and March 1457.[336] This seems to have been another attempt by the queen to exploit her possession of the king to obtain more public support, but its results were, if anything, more disappointing than on the previous occasion. If Margaret wanted the recognition of the wider political community, then she had to invite broadly based counsel. In doing so, however, her independent power was to a large extent dissolved in the overwhelming authority attached to the *persona publica* of her husband: an authority whose execution belonged to the lords. This meant that, in practice, she was forced to defer to assemblies founded on a principle of noble unity, which – on past form – were likely to favour compromise. The position of those who had been working all along for noble unity, on the other hand, was the very obverse of that of the queen.

---

[334] Record keeping generally was diminishing in the later 1450s, owing to the confusion over who or what constituted the government. It is also possible that normal judicial processes were disrupted by the divisions at the centre, resulting in the suspension of sessions, destruction of records, diminishing recourse to law and so on. Avrutick 1967: p. 132 observes that less use was made of oyer and terminer commissions after 1454, arguing that the absence of sufficient central authority encouraged the abandonment of judicial processes in favour of a resort to arms by all those who could exercise any lordship. See Carpenter 1992: pp. 478–81 for a discussion of how cross-factional gentry groupings helped to preserve the peace in Warwickshire at this time.

[335] In connection with this, the issuing of a series of commissions, on 16 July 1457, to a small number of magnates, nearly all of whom were closely associated with the court, is most interesting. These included orders to ride with the sheriffs and county posses of most of the Midland counties: see Griffiths 1981: p. 801; *CPR, 1452–61*, pp. 370–1. Their comprehensiveness, and the almost total absence of gentry members (only Sir John Barre), invites the suspicion that these were not (as was claimed) issued in response to actual risings, but were instead to provide the occasion for displays of force by loyalist lords in their own 'contrees'. The lords concerned were Suffolk, Lovell, Beaumont, Welles, Buckingham, Sudeley, Beauchamp, Shrewsbury, Audley, Grey of Ruthin and Rivers. Suffolk later became attached to York, but there was no reason to expect that at this stage. During his long minority, the De La Pole interest in the Thames Valley had probably been managed by William, Lord Lovell, who seems to have supported Somerset (see above, p. 282 n. 96). Lovell's son, named here, regarded Viscount Beaumont, whose daughter he had married, as his very good lord (*PL*, III, p. 143). Audley had begun to be appointed to royal commissions in the early part of 1457 (*CPR, 1452–61*, pp. 347, 348–9) and was, together with Shrewsbury, one of the crown's alternative sources of lordship in the Yorkist-dominated Welsh March.

[336] Harris, *Coventry Leet Book*, pp. 297–8; *PPC*, VI, pp. 333–4. Its attendance seems to have been fairly representative, though the Nevilles were not summoned and Norfolk, the Bourgchiers and, more surprisingly, Pembroke and Wiltshire were apparently absent. York was present. The summonses were issued on 27 January, the day before the appointment of the prince's council, and this may suggest that it was the recognition of this body by a council of lords that the queen was seeking.

To acquire an effective practical authority, they had to take account of Margaret and her growing party; especially when the king, symbol of their own unity, was with her. So it was that the second Coventry council, like its predecessor, was a highly ambivalent affair. Its acts, insofar as these can be assessed, appear to have included measures to satisfy not only the interests of the queen and her supporters, but also those of York.[337] Despite her growing following among them, Margaret had not succeeded in persuading the lords to accept the inevitability of division, nor had she been able to transfer the seat of government to Coventry. Rather as before, it seems that the chancellor and a number of lords returned to London after the council,[338] although it is true, and perhaps significant, that others – notably Buckingham – remained in the Midlands to escort the king and attend the sessions at Hereford.[339] Division may have been gaining ground, but it is clear that the principle that the governmental aspects of royal authority reposed in the united body of the lords remained highly influential.

This was borne out a few months later, at the end of August 1457, when a French raid on Sandwich raised the possibility that the realm was faced with a threat of invasion.[340] The circumstances of national

---

[337] Since all the authorities in the polity were gathered together in the same place, it seems reasonable to assume that the grants and appointments which follow were made by mutual agreement, or at least knowledge. The queen received ratification of her estate in the lands granted to her at Bury and of the prince's estate in lands granted to him by the parliament of 1455: *CPR, 1452–61*, pp. 339–40, 357–8. Some further appointments were made for the prince's household. An oyer and terminer commission, comprising an impressive array of lords, was secured against Devereux and Herbert and the latter was officially declared a rebel (*ibid.*, pp, 348–9; *CClR, 1454–61*, p. 158); Northumberland was reappointed to the wardenship of the East March at an increased wage (E404/71/1/77: and see Pollard 1990: p. 267 for an attack on Neville rule in Richmondshire); and York, who may have faced the pseudo-trial described above on this occasion (pp. 335–6), was induced to surrender his estate in the South Wales castles to Pembroke (*CPR, 1452–61*, p. 340). At the same time, however, York was awarded compensation for the surrender of the Welsh castles and reappointed to the lieutenancy of Ireland, a post which others (notably Wiltshire: above, p. 308 n. 208) may have coveted, for a further ten years. *CPR, 1452–61*, p. 341; Johnson 1988: p. 179.

[338] *CPR, 1452–61*, pp. 335, 347. The duke of Norfolk appeared before the council at Westminster on 1 May 1457 (BL Add. MS 18,612, fols. 63v–64r): we do not know who attended on this occasion, but it seems likely that the presence of a number of magnates would have been required for proceedings concerning a peer and held in the absence of the king.

[339] We only have one record of who sat at Hereford in April: KB9/35, m. 61 (Buckingham, Shrewsbury, Beaumont, Audley and the judges). Buckingham and Shrewsbury remained with the king and queen at Hereford for the rest of April (*PL*, III, p. 118). Buckingham, Beaumont, Beauchamp and Rivers were with Henry in May (Anstis (ed.), *Register of the Garter*, II, p. 161). Buckingham, Stafford, Stanbury, Beaumont, Tunstall and others accompanied the king and queen into Coventry in June (Harris (ed.), *Coventry Leet Book*, p. 300).

[340] See Griffiths 1981: pp. 815–16. Storey 1966: p. 184, makes the threat of war the major reason for the attempted reconciliation among the nobility which followed. See also the

necessity led to the prompt return of the king to London and, in association, the revival of an authoritative council of lords, meeting in the capital.[341] The queen, unwilling or unable to resist the trend of events, lost the initiative. Having followed the king out of her Midland stronghold, she was perhaps reduced to something more like her normal status, leaving her party fragmented and more susceptible to the call of noble unity.[342] Although it was a crisis of national security that had brought about this change in the distribution of power, the new authority seems quickly to have taken root. The council rapidly took charge of affairs, organising defence plans, inaugurating measures to improve the king's finances and, perhaps, preparing the way for an attempt to restore good relations among the lords the following January.[343] Quite what made this new firmness of purpose possible is not clear: strong as the pull towards unity was, it usually required some sort of lordship for this kind of authoritative realisation. The lords did, of course, have the king to look to, but his headship was scarcely sufficient in itself, especially as this regime appeared to be able to take

poem on the loveday in Robbins (ed.), *Historical Poems*, no. 79, sts. 2–3, for a possible reference.

[341] See Wolffe 1981: p. 371, for Henry's movements (and pp. 310–11, for a different interpretation of them). *PPC*, VI, p. 290, indicates that a great council met at Westminster during the Michaelmas term (see also *Registrum Whethamstede*, I, pp. 265, 268, and Sharpe 1894–5: III, pp. 383–4). It seems plausible that it may have gathered before the issuing of commissions of array to most of the southern and Midland counties on 25–27 September: *CPR, 1452–61*, pp. 401–3. The commissions were even-handed, including York (in Suffolk, Essex and Northampton) and a number of his men (Burley in Shropshire, Devereux in Herefordshire, for example) alongside Buckingham, the Bourgchiers and some members of the queen's party. The Nevilles, Percies, Somerset, Wiltshire, Devon and Bonville do not appear: except in the case of the last two, this is most likely to be because no commissions were issued for the North, Somerset and Dorset.

[342] Her supporters continued to receive items of royal patronage at this time, however, just as they had at Coventry in the spring. We do not know how many of them participated in the council of this period, as no evidence of attendance has survived.

[343] See Johnson 1988: pp. 180–1 for the council in general and Griffiths 1981: p. 805 for the scheme to raise the archers voted in 1453. A second series of commissions was issued almost three weeks after the council was prorogued (*PPC*, VI, p. 292; *CPR, 1452–61*, pp. 407–9), but perhaps under its influence, to broadly based groups of notables. That for Yorkshire, for example, included York, Salisbury, Greystoke, Fitzhugh, Sir William Plumpton (a Percy connection: above, p. 235n), Sir Robert Ughtrede (a household man: Arnold 1984: p. 116), John Thwaytes (a Percy man: *Plumpton*, pp. lxiii, lxvi) and others. Exeter, Devon, Bonville and Somerset, interestingly, were not appointed to any commissions. As far as finance was concerned, a committee was appointed on 2 November to study proposals shown to the king, which would allegedly enable him to repay his creditors in good coin within a few years: *CPR, 1452–61*, p. 390 (note that it was due to report back to king and council on 2 February 1458, which shows that a continuing conciliar government was envisaged). The need to rebuild good relations may have become apparent in the course of the council (see *PPC*, VI, pp. 290–1). It was perhaps with this in mind that the earl of Salisbury, who had apparently kept away from the centre since the summer of 1456, was summoned to London in mid-November (*CPR, 1452–61*, p. 428).

some controversial steps.[344] Moreover, unlike the assemblies in Coventry, it seems to have held together for more than a few weeks. It is tempting to speculate that the source of its strength was York, but, in the absence of any corroborating information, we cannot know.

It was surely in the work of this council, rather than the whimsy of the king, that the inspiration for the famous loveday of March 1458 is to be found.[345] By attempting a general reconciliation, the less committed lords may have imagined that they could recreate an adequate public authority. Unfortunately, but perhaps inevitably, the attempt at peace-making reopened the question of what had happened at the battle of St Albans, and the answers which emerged did less to smother division than to sharpen it. In many ways, as we have seen, the enterprise of preserving noble unity went hand in hand with the Yorkist view of St Albans as a thoroughly regrettable event which had been caused by sectional and inadequate government. This approach removed the divisive, and genuinely secondary, matter of feuding among the magnates from further consideration.[346] In the loveday award, however, these feuds were given a prominent place and ascribed, moreover, to the results, rather than the causes, of the battle: almost all the specific terms of the document were tailored to the settlement of private and personal differences arising from the 'obviationem et insultationem' done, implicitly by the Yorkists, at St Albans.[347] This redefinition of events had important consequences for the political position of York and the Nevilles. Not only were they presented as more at fault than their dead opponents (because they had been the first to resort to arms in such an uncompromising fashion), but also the entire public dimension which had served both to legitimise their activities at St Albans and to underpin the reforming regime of 1455–6 – the misgovernment of the realm, the misleading of the king, the unavailability of justice – was pushed out of

---

[344] In an appointment which overrode the claims of the duke of Exeter, as admiral (see *PL*, III, p. 125, for his anger at the move), the earl of Warwick was commissioned, by advice and assent of the council, to keep the sea and fight the king's enemies upon it on 3 October 1457: *CPR, 1452–61*, pp. 390, 413. The indentures were drawn up on 26 November 1457 and arrangements for pay devised on 27 December: a further suggestion that conciliar influence continued after the formal end of the great council (see n. 343, above). Interestingly, Exeter seized upon the separation of king and lords over the Christmas period to achieve compensation. A privy seal warrant, dated Abingdon, 30 December 1457, referred to Exeter's recent appointment by advice of council to go to sea and awarded him 400 marks: E404/71/2/41.

[345] Cf. Griffiths 1981: pp. 806–7; Johnson 1988: pp. 179ff. Once the king had opened the council, at the end of January, he withdrew: 'Benet's Chron.', p. 221; *PL*, III, pp. 126–7.

[346] Above, pp. 305–6, 316–17.

[347] The loveday award (printed in *Registrum Whethamstede*, I, pp. 298–308: translated version in Holinshed's chronicle) focused on variances between York and the Nevilles on the one hand and Somerset, the Percies and Clifford on the other and suggested that these had been caused by the deaths at St Albans (pp. 298–9).

the picture.[348] The award was thus a triumph for their enemies. By drawing attention to the personal elements in the feuds of the early 1450s, it undermined all the Yorkists' larger claims. At the same time, by providing a new arbitration explicitly under the aegis of the king and queen, it asserted the authority of the crown against that of the peers corporately, emphasising that the right to act publicly was the king's alone and that no one else could usurp it.[349] The episode must therefore be seen as a move in the queen's struggle for hegemony, a point neatly demonstrated by the fact that it was her hand, and not Somerset's, which York was holding as the loveday procession left St Paul's.[350]

It is unlikely that this outcome was planned by the lords at the outset. They probably meant to devise a forward-looking settlement among themselves and impose it upon the Percies and Nevilles, whom they seem to have identified as the major obstacles to rebuilding 'oonhede' among the lords.[351] They failed in their attempt because they had overestimated the effectiveness of their jurisdiction. Neither Nevilles nor Percies were willing to submit to judgement, even from an apparently representative

---

[348] See Johnson 1988: pp. 183–4 for details of the terms. Almost the only crumb of comfort for York and the Nevilles was the declaration that they were to be regarded as the king's true lieges, but the force of this was dented by the fact that it followed a similar, and more detailed, certification of the three lords who had died at St Albans, a step which countered the accusations which York and the others had made against Somerset, at least, and removed their justification for rising up (*Registrum Whethamstede*, I, p. 302). The only member of the opposing faction to face any sanctions at all was Egremont, who was to be bound to keep the peace towards the Nevilles, but he was released from the damages of 1453 all the same and not punished for his escape from prison (pp. 304–5).

[349] The award was said to be made by the king, albeit on the advice of counsel, and any breaches of its terms were to be referred to him (*Registrum Whethamstede*, I, pp. 299–301, 306–7). See above, p. 44, for the expression of similar ideas in the tract 'Somnium Vigilantis'.

[350] Noted by Johnson 1988: p. 184. The queen had allegedly played a central part in arranging the settlement: *Registrum Whethamstede*, I, p. 301. Perhaps significantly, she had been brought down to London by Buckingham and his son Stafford, who was a member of the prince's council (above, n. 323).

[351] A sense that tension between the Percies and the Nevilles was the main obstacle to peace may be revealed by the fact that, unlike York, Somerset and Exeter (and, in fact, Clifford), the principals in the Percy–Neville dispute (viz. Northumberland, Egremont, Warwick and Salisbury) were not summoned to the council due to meet in January 1458 (*PPC*, VI, pp. 333–4). We do not know anything about the state of the North at this time although, to judge by the silence of the sources, Percy–Neville rivalry was more muted than in 1453–4. The main reason why the feud may have been seen as the main threat to unity is the matter of the vast damages still owed by Egremont to Salisbury and his family for the outrages of 1454: see Storey 1966: p. 149. Although Egremont had escaped from Newgate, where these debts had placed him, Richard Percy was probably still there in 1457–8 (see *CCIR, 1454–61*, p. 223, and *Registrum Whethamstede*, I, p. 304). This matter could perfectly easily have been settled without returning to the events at St Albans. The pacific intentions of the lords may be indicated by the issue of pardons, presumably on conciliar authority, to men as diverse as York, Warwick and Wiltshire in January 1458: E159/234, *communia*, Hil., rot. 4, 7, and Eas., rot. 35.

body of peers.[352] This fatally weakened the lords' claims to authority and made consensus impossible. It also made the revival of the divisions of 1453-4 inevitable as both Nevilles and Percies sought out the protection of those who had supported them before. Since the fall of the protectorate York, Warwick and Salisbury had been united only by their common experience of hostility from the queen and from the heirs of the St Albans dead.[353] Now, it seems, they drew closer together, as it became clear that this hostility was officially recognised, if not actually encouraged. So it was that Salisbury and Warwick aligned themselves not only with York, but also, perhaps, with the council of lords as the form of authority best suited to the defence of their past behaviour and present interests.[354] At the same time, the Percies, Exeter and Somerset reinforced their ties with the king and queen.[355] When a settlement emerged, therefore, in late March, it took account not so much of the broader interests of lords or realm, but of the existence of two organised forces, one of which was, in basic terms, considerably more powerful than the other.

If this result drew the lords closer to outright division, it also clarified

[352] The four lords came to the capital despite the lack of summons, and they came heavily armed: *PL*, III, pp. 125-6; *Chrons. of London*, p. 168. The civic authorities feared that a battle would ensue: *ibid.*; *Three Chrons.*, p. 71; *Town Chrons.*, pp. 111-12.

[353] Both York and Warwick faced threats or actual assaults from the young lords over the eighteen months between the end of the protectorate and the loveday: Johnson 1988: p. 177; *Town Chrons.*, p. 160. Salisbury, who appears to have remained in the North from the summer of 1456 until February 1458 (absent from all three councils held in this time, and still apparently resisting summons in January 1458: above, nn. 318, 343; *PL*, III, pp. 121-2), was threatened by the redirection of patronage and financial resources in the North, though it is interesting to note that Bishop Booth of Durham sought to remain on good terms with him (Pollard 1990: pp. 266-9). Note that, in this time, only York was unmistakably charged with disloyalty, though Warwick apparently had to swear an oath like that of 1452 on one occasion (above, n. 318). See above, pp. 332ff for the diverging interests of York and the Nevilles in the early part of 1456.

[354] The chronicles are inclined to suggest that York and the Nevilles came with smaller forces or, at least, in search of peace (e.g. *Three Chrons.*, p. 71; *English Chron.*, p. 77). This could be the product of bias, though it is probable that York himself *did* come with only a small force (*PL*, III, p. 125). It is not impossible that the three lords came to London with the aim of working with the council of peers (albeit in order to defend their interests), while the Percies and others who were already in the queen's orbit may have come to oppose it. This would certainly reflect the behaviour of each group (or its antecedents) in 1453 (above, p. 311) and could help to explain why it was York, Warwick and Salisbury who were in the city and their enemies who were outside it. See also below, n. 359.

[355] See *PL*, III, pp. 126-7. Even so, the Percy-Beaufort-Holland group apparently agreed in late February to bind themselves to accept a 'throw peace final by means of all the Lords' (*ibid.*, p. 126). Note that Ralph Percy was granted the keeping of Bamburgh Castle on 16 March (*CFR, 1452-61*, p. 205). On the day of the award itself (24 March), Northumberland's petition for payment was settled and he received a wool licence (E28/88/12; *CClR, 1454-61*, pp. 238-9). The following day, the king granted the keeping of Sandgate Castle to Andrew Trollope (PSO1/20/1020), an ominous instance of direct interference in Warwick's Calais establishment, in favour of a man of Beaufort loyalties (see Griffiths 1981: p. 822).

the options facing them. The loveday demonstrated that if the way of noble unity was still upheld by anyone, it was by York and the Nevilles: their opponents now plainly sought justice first, together with the restoration of royal authority focused on the queen and prince as much as the king.[356] This distribution of attitudes was to be very important in the crisis of 1460, but, in the shorter term, it shaped the events of the rest of 1458. For some months, a semblance of unity was preserved, with king and government apparently staying in London and representing the interests of the Yorkist lords as much as those of anyone else.[357] There is some evidence to suggest that this was not because peace had broken out,[358] but because York and the Nevilles, reunited by the loveday, had substantially recaptured the initiative in its wake and that they were using what time they had to lay foundations for their self-defence in the future.[359] What permitted them to do this is not clear. One possibility is that the queen's lords had once again withdrawn from London, inevitably changing the balance of the council in the Yorkists' favour.[360] Another is

---

[356] Note that York and the Nevilles did make efforts to fulfil their obligations under the terms of the loveday: *CPR, 1452–61*, p. 424.

[357] There are various signs that York and the Nevilles were regarded as acceptable by the ruling lords. (1) Perhaps in association with the loveday, a marriage was arranged in May 1458 between the queen's ward, Isabella Ingaldesthorpe, and Sir John Neville, Salisbury's son (*CCIR, 1454–61*, pp. 300–1; *CPR, 1452–61*, p. 507). (2) When Lord Fauconberg was taken to task for piracies in the same month, the commissioners of inquiry were Buckingham and Warwick (*ibid.*, p. 438). In a display of unity and moderation reminiscent of the minority, these two joined Viscount Bourgchier and Sir Thomas Neville in recognisances of 500 marks to ensure that Fauconberg would answer. He did so and was quit (*CCIR, 1454–61*, pp. 227–8). Even during his spell of imprisonment, he continued to receive payments for the custody of Windsor Castle (*CPR, 1452–61*, pp. 424–5). (3) In July, Shrewsbury, Beaumont and one of the younger Cliffords were appointed to arrest a number of men of Nottinghamshire and to hold them until they found security not to harm Salisbury's second son, Thomas Neville (*CPR, 1452–61*, pp. 440–1). (4) York was assigned 1,000 marks of arrears of his pensions in Trinity Term 1458 (Johnson 1988: p. 185) and was named as a witness to the surviving royal charters up to July 1459 (C53/190/16, 12, 10, 9 (all dated at Westminster)). (5) Warwick, meanwhile, kept his commission on the sea and received commissions against piracy in April (*CPR, 1452–61*, pp. 436–7). He was a charter witness on 22 December 1458 (C53/190/12). Rather less is known about the position of Salisbury, but it is most unlikely that he alone was excluded.

[358] Note that when Warwick rode through London on 9 May 1458, he apparently did so with a large fellowship: *Town Chrons.*, p. 146.

[359] It seems likely that York and the Nevilles had already captured the leadership of the council *before* the loveday. Meeting with Waynflete, Chedworth, Lyhert and the Bourgchiers on 4 March, they made arrangements to pay Warwick £500 out of the hanaper, immediately, for the keeping of the sea. They also ordered that the duchy feoffees should reimburse the hanaper, which suggests that this council was fairly confident of its authority (*PPC*, VI, pp. 294–5). In addition, Salisbury was, unusually in this period, named as a charter witness on 20 March 1458 (C53/190/16).

[360] The queen seems to have returned to Warwickshire, although this scarcely removed her share of administrative power. Whilst the king was at the Tower of London on 17 June 1458 (E404/71/2/71), Laurence Booth, still keeper of the privy seal, was at Kenilworth on 21 June (*ibid.*/72).

that the lords still in the capital were coming to accept that the principle of noble or conciliar rule was now a divisive one which only the Yorkists were disposed to defend, but, equally, that the time had come to make positive choices. At any rate, it appears that York, Warwick and Salisbury were able to direct the government's foreign policy, treading a thin line between public and private interests.[361] Simply to exert themselves in government gave them some political advantage, and it may have been on their initiative that, in August 1458, a council was summoned to meet the following October.[362] Many of those invited to attend had participated in the protectorate councils and most of the queen's more partisan supporters – Exeter, Somerset, Devon, Northumberland, Clifford and perhaps Pembroke – were not summoned.[363] The purpose of the assembly is far from clear. The summonses spoke of a general obligation to attend to the king's counsels in term-time, but added that 'suche matiers as concerne specially oure honeure and worship' required particular attention. This form of words may suggest that the council was inspired by the Yorkists' enemies and intended to cut them down to size (perhaps by removing Warwick from the captaincy of Calais), but, if so, its rather moderate

---

[361] See Wolffe 1981: pp. 313–15. It seems that the lords were pursuing two sets of negotiations simultaneously: while Sir John Wenlock discussed proposals for a peace with France and a series of marriages that autumn, Bishop Beauchamp of Salisbury attempted to open a private dialogue with Charles VII on behalf of York, Warwick, Salisbury and Norfolk (and possibly others). York had already tried to enlist the French king's aid against the queen earlier in the year, it seems (ibid., p. 314). On 14 May 1458, Warwick, Salisbury, Bourgchier and Wenlock had (again publicly) been appointed to treat with the duke of Burgundy over breaches of the truce (Roskell 1981–3: II, p. 250; Town Chrons., p. 146). Discussions actually covered 'aucuns autres secrets entendements', if Chastellain is to be believed (Thielemans 1966: p. 370). The result of all this diplomacy seems to have been to generate suspicions between the French and Burgundians and doubts on the part of each about the standing of Henry VI in his own kingdom (ibid., pp. 373–4; Wolffe 1981: p. 315).

[362] PPC, VI, p. 297. The summonses were sent out as arrangements for Wenlock's autumn embassy were being made. It was perhaps hoped that he would be ready to report back by mid-October, when the council was due to be in session.

[363] Those summoned were the archbishops, Bishops Kemp, Boulers, Chedworth, Grey and Beauchamp, Stanbury and Lyhert, the dukes of York, Buckingham and Norfolk, the earls of Warwick, Salisbury, Oxford, Shrewsbury and Wiltshire, Viscounts Beaumont and Bourgchier, the prior of St Johns, Lords Grey of Ruthin, Welles, Scales, Sudeley, Fauconberg, Dudley, Rivers, Beauchamp, Stourton and Stanley, Sir John Wenlock, the dean of St Severin's and John Say. Bishop Grey, Stanley and Fauconberg attended during the second protectorate. Stanbury and Grey of Ruthin attended then and after. Welles, who seems to have been closely associated with the court, had been present at a council meeting at Westminster on 31 January 1457 (C81/1546/114), and may have attended more often in the period following the protectorate. Beauchamp had not attended a recorded meeting since he was treasurer in the early 1450s, but was being paid wages as a councillor at this time (E404/71/3/33). The remainder had all been councillors under York from 1454, though not all of them are known to have attended. The fact that the chancellor and keeper were not summoned is probably conventional: they would have been expected to attend and both apparently did so (to judge from the dating clauses in the patent rolls and privy seal warrants for issue).

composition seems surprising. An alternative explanation is that York and the Nevilles were hoping to revive the council of 1455–6, preserving the king's 'honeure and worship' by resuming the execution of his authority.[364]

If so, they had over-reached themselves. The planned council, or something similar, actually met, but it did so under changed circumstances.[365] These may have been created by the queen. Returning to London in the autumn, she seems to have set about reviving the atmosphere of division, presumably counting on the sheer size of her party among the lords to undermine the Yorkist annexation of the broader noble constituency.[366] Far from establishing a conciliar authority, the government in these months took a series of steps which reflected the particular interests of the Coventry regime, rather than what the Yorkists and their associates in London must have claimed to be the general interests of the realm. Its initiatives fell in three main areas. First of all, the foundations of a new financial system were apparently laid down: it was from this time that the crown abandoned its traditional role as fisc of the realm and instead funded its activities through private connections and patrimonial resources.[367] The money raised by these means was put to the maintenance of the citadel of royal power: not the rule and defence of the realm, but of the new Lancastrian affinity and 'pale'.[368] Second, a series of defensive measures was launched. In this, the lead had, perhaps, been taken by the Yorkists,[369] but now the crown made no bones about gathering its defences against rebellion.[370] This was brought home in the

---

[364] For the possibility that the council tried to remove Warwick from Calais, and that this had been its purpose, see Wolffe 1981: p. 315.

[365] The king removed to Westminster between mid-October and early December: Wolffe 1981: p. 371. Unfortunately, there are no records of this council and we do not have much idea who attended. Warwick was in London at this time (see below, n. 371), but Salisbury was apparently at Middleham in November 1458: Pollard 1976: p. 52, though he may have been in London earlier in the month (see below, n. 371). Of York's whereabouts we have no knowledge.

[366] See *English Chron.*, p. 78, for the queen's presence in London.

[367] Among the methods adopted were a systematic exploitation of the financial resources of the shrievalties (Harriss 1953: p. 184; Jeffs 1960: pp. 146–7). These, together with crown leases, were increasingly concentrated in curialist hands and provided a significant proportion of the sources of assignment (Harriss 1953: pp. 184–6 and 176–200, generally). New treasurers were appointed (Griffiths 1981: p. 789) and their personal wealth exploited (e.g. E404/71/2/77–85, and E404/71/4/30).

[368] See Morgan 1987: pp. 50–1, for the crown's retreat into its 'demesne interest'.

[369] A warrant for issue dated 1 September 1458, when the Yorkists may have had the upper hand in London, referred to a need for additions to the royal ordnance, to the fitting out of a new gun at Calais and to the transfer of a large amount of military equipment at Kenilworth to London: E404/71/3/1.

[370] See Wolffe 1981: p. 315 for measures taken early in December (shortly before this, various items of ordnance had been delivered to the sea coasts, possibly with the intention of resisting Warwick who had probably returned to Calais in mid-November: E404/71/3/43). When commissions of array were appointed for the southern and eastern

third series of measures, which amounted to a deliberate harrying of the Yorkist lords. These centred on attempts to remove Warwick from Calais – by murder, if necessary – but also affected the rest of the Neville family.[371] Their result was to drive Warwick and Salisbury, and probably York, out of London before the end of 1458, not to return until 1460.

The revival of conciliar authority in 1457 had, despite the setback of the loveday, brought York and the Nevilles back to a meaningful participation in central government. No less than in 1456, however, their pre-eminence brought to the surface the fact that the unity of the lords was almost as divisive a goal as the pursuit of sectarian justice. If many of the lords who were not directly associated with the queen found the explicit consultativeness of the Yorkist approach attractive, they were not yet prepared to commit themselves to its defence. When Margaret and her lords appeared in London in the autumn of 1458, patently hostile to Warwick and probably to his father and uncle as well, the remainder were presented with a difficult choice. In the capital, with the king and her sizeable magnate following at her side, the queen too offered a form of unity. When the Yorkists left London on this occasion, they did as the Percies had done in 1453, as they themselves had done in 1455 and as Margaret had done in 1456: they distanced themselves from the authority established there, and, in doing so, more or less excluded themselves from the community of lords on which it rested.[372] The choices for members of

coastal counties in February 1459, no one from the York–Neville interest was included in what were otherwise broadly based bodies (*CPR, 1452–61*, pp. 494–5: it was usual for Bergavenny to be appointed in Kent and for York to be appointed in Essex and Suffolk, but this time they were not).

[371] See Wolffe 1981: p. 315 for the treament of Warwick. Note that by December 1458, the government had reached an agreement with the council of the Staple, under which £4,000 per year was to be lent for the expenses of the household in return for tax-free shipping: *CPR, 1452–61*, pp. 500–1. This was significant because Warwick's captaincy rested to a considerable extent on the financial goodwill of the Staplers (Harriss 1960: pp. 40–52) and this may have been an attempt to draw them away from him. November 1458 seems to be a likelier date than February 1459 for the attempt of the household men on Warwick's life (as in e.g. *English Chron.*, p. 78). It fits better with the other events mentioned in this note, with what may have happened at the council of autumn 1458 (Wolffe, 1981: p. 315 and *Letters and Papers*, I, p. 369) and with the earl of Salisbury's decision to convene his men at Middleham and take 'ful partie' with the duke of York (above n. 365; Warwick said goodbye to his father and left for Calais soon after the attack: *Town Chrons.*, p. 113). Note that at the end of November, Fauconberg was removed from his share in the custody of Windsor Castle (*CPR, 1452–61*, p. 470) and that, on the 20th, Sir William Oldhall was subpena'd to be before the king in chancery a few days later: C253/35/73. Various Neville satellites were removed from the Kent commission of the peace in early December (*CPR, 1452–61*, p. 668): Lords Bergavenny and Clinton (the latter had fought for York at St Albans) and Robert Hoorn and John Fogge, who were two of the three Kent notables who defected to the Yorkists at Canterbury in June 1460 (Searle, 'Chron. of John Stone', p. 79).

[372] Although even in March 1459, orders were despatched to arrest ships for Warwick's use (*CPR, 1452–61*, p. 494), whilst as late as June 1459 the government was willing to send Salisbury over £1,500 towards his wages as warden: Griffiths 1981: p. 813.

political society had at last become clear: to support York and the Nevilles, in their now-inevitable rebellion; or to support the queen, who, for the first time, seemed to offer all the major ingredients of public authority.

What had happened between 1456 and 1459, then, was not so much that the lords lost faith in corporate resolutions to their shared problem, as that Queen Margaret found herself in a position to effect her claim that only through adherence to rigorous royal authority was corporate action possible. York (and perhaps the Nevilles) might have to be excluded from the common body if the reconciliation of noble unity and royal authority were to be a success, but there were grounds for claiming that, by their actions, these lords had effectively excluded themselves. If the queen could offer an authority which was convincingly public, as well as fully royal, she might succeed in persuading the lords that the abandonment of York was the precondition for peace. In the months following the council of autumn 1458, she stayed in London, conducting what remained of the business of government, and preparing for the final showdown.[373] In early May, she and the king set out for Coventry[374] and, it appears, for a great council which the Yorkists did not attend.[375] The circumstances of 1455 were more or less repeated: gathering in arms, and recognising their exclusion, the Yorkists set out to meet the king and defend themselves.

THE COMMON WEAL AND THE CROWN, 1459–1461

In some ways, the civil war which marked the last two years of Henry VI's sorry reign was a continuation of the struggle between the different

---

[373] There may not have been many lords in London at this time (see e.g. *Letters and Papers*, I, pp. 367–8). Even so, the forms of public authority were maintained. When the duke of Exeter seized one of the king's justices in Westminster Hall, in January or February 1459, he was properly sent off to prison (on pain of £10,000) and bound over to keep the peace (Payling 1989: p. 883; *CCIR, 1454–61*, pp. 318, 350). A great council of all the parliamentary peers was summoned on 20 February to meet at Westminster on 2 April to appoint an embassy to the church council at Mantua (*PPC*, VI, pp. 298–9). This may have assembled, since the king was in Westminster in April and mid-May (Wolffe 1981: p. 371) and, when trouble broke out between the men of Fleet St and those of the household in mid-April, the Bourgchiers and Lord Fauconberg were among the lords helping to restore calm ('Benet's Chron.', p. 223: a number of the queen's adherents were also present). For royal defence preparations in April and May, see Wolffe 1981: p. 317.

[374] Wolffe 1981: p. 317. A number of lords remained in the capital, but it is unlikely that they constituted anything of an alternative authority: see E28/88/58 for a meeting on 7 June 1459, attended by Archbishop Booth, Bishops Waynflete, Kemp, Lyhert and Laurence Booth, the earl of Wiltshire, the dean of St Severin's and Lord Dudley, all of whom, except Kemp and the dean, were closely linked to the queen.

[375] See Johnson 1988: pp. 185–6. Besides York and the Nevilles, the absentees included Archbishop Bourgchier, Viscount Bourgchier, Bishop Grey and the earl of Arundel. According to 'Benet's Chron.', which may have aimed to supply the Yorkists with a justification for what they did next, the non-attenders were indicted of treason, whereupon the crown gathered large forces and set off for Nottingham.

attributes of the crown which had characterised the preceding period of uneasy peace: a struggle, in effect, between its readiness to provide the lords with comprehensive representation, which was emphasised by the Yorkists, and the exceeding authority of its judgements, which was emphasised by the queen. What now made war possible, however, was the fact that each of the combatant parties sought, with some success, to reassemble the whole itself; claiming, also with some success, that their opponents were rebels or traitors and thus undeserving of representation. As a result, the anarchy of the later 1450s to some extent gave way to a politics shaped by effective (but contending) authorities. The queen was increasingly prepared to modify the tone of her lordship in order to add the communal support of the lords to the personal authority of the crown which she was in the process of rebuilding. At the same time, while the familiar Yorkist commitment to noble 'oonhede' and consultative government had always borne with it an expressed loyalty to the king, March, Warwick and Salisbury were actually to make good their claim by defending Henry VI's tenure of the crown against York himself. While there were differences in the ideological accent of the two parties, then, it is clear that each was nonetheless gathering up the main threads of public rule. By the end of 1460, if not before, there were two equally legitimate powers struggling for control of the same polity. The circumstances of 1455 were more or less restored, and, in the months following the queen's declaration of war, the battle of St Albans was several times refought. On three occasions, victory ushered in a new and quite convincing government – at Ludford in 1459, at Northampton in 1460, at Towton in 1461.[376] It was against this background that the Yorkists, who started with the odds against them, acquired a series of advantages external to the polity of Henry VI, which eventually gave them victory.

In the autumn of 1459, as York and the Nevilles assembled their forces at Ludlow, it was plain that the trend of events was very much against them. They were joined by almost no one in their resistance to the renascent royal authority.[377] Even more than in 1455, the fact that they represented little more than themselves meant that the published rationale for their rising must have fallen rather flat. They had revived the claims they made at St Albans – the need to take steps for their own defence and to protect the common weal from the king's intimates – but, while they protested their loyalty to the king and the 'good and worthy lordes' about

---

[376] Clearly enough, no battle was actually fought at Ludford, but the skirmish at Blore Heath, in which Lord Audley was killed, lent credibility to the government's claims that war had been raised against the king and had only been averted fortuitously. The débâcle which followed for the Yorkists could thus be regarded as a kind of victory by the Lancastrians.

[377] Griffiths 1981: pp. 821–2.

him, they could hardly escape from the fact that they had risen in arms against them all.[378] The king was not surrounded by traitors, but by magnates, and magnates who, it seems, were coming to believe that the acceptance of authority – rather than the advancement of consultation – was the main priority for restoring order, unity and the common weal. It was thus not only the uncongenial balance of military power that dictated the flight of the lords during the night of 12–13 October, but, rather as in 1452, the impossibility of the Yorkist political position. Capitulation was a possibility, but – particularly in the wake of the unplanned and bloody skirmish at Blore Heath – a sympathetic response could scarcely be counted on.[379] A posture of defiance, mounted from the Yorkist bases in Ireland and Calais, must have seemed preferable.

The parliament at Coventry, which followed the events at Ludlow, set the seal on the ideological victory which the queen had already achieved.[380] The ignominious flight of the Yorkists before an army which contained the majority of leading magnates had demonstrated that the king, with Margaret's assistance, was the true defender of the common weal.[381] The assembly, which was well attended and, it seems, properly constituted, provided a significant endorsement of the queen's policies.[382] In the lengthy denunciation which preceded their attainder, the Yorkist lords were identified as rebels of long standing, their feigned concern for the common weal merely a front for the satisfaction of their own covetous interests.[383] The king, on the other hand, was portrayed as an active and

---

[378] The Yorkists' position is set out in *English Chron.*, pp. 81–3, and in a series of articles, allegedly distributed by Warwick, as he returned from Calais in 1459 (BL, Harley MS 543, fols. 164–5, abstracted in Giles, *Chronicles of the White Rose*, pp. lxviii–ix). Note that Andrew Trollope and the men from the Calais garrison, whose defection probably played the largest part in causing the Yorkist withdrawal (see e.g. Johnson 1988: p. 188), protested that they had been brought to England to protect the king, only to find that they were expected to fight for York (*Crowland*, p. 454; *Collections*, p. 205). We need not assume that Warwick had lied, only that the Yorkist idea that the king could, and should, be protected from his closest associates had lost its power to convince.

[379] Because of Blore Heath, Salisbury had been excluded from the offers of pardon made two weeks later (*RP*, V, p. 348). The other two lords had sworn to stand by him (*English Chron.*, p. 81).

[380] Note that the writs of summons were despatched on 9 October, before the final confrontation took place (*CClR, 1454–61*, pp. 420–2). Since York, his sons and the Nevilles were not summoned, it is clear that the queen was aware that she had scored a political victory even before her military triumph.

[381] See Goodman 1981: p. 28 and Richmond 1977: p. 74 for the king's supporters; also *Crowland*, p. 454 for the observation that more and more support accrued to the king in the course of the rebellion.

[382] Roskell 1956: p. 195 comments on the good attendance of lords at the parliament. Payling 1987 shows that the elections to the commons were conducted normally. The oath of allegiance to the king was sworn by as many as sixty-six peers, including Norfolk and Viscount Bourgchier (*RP*, V, pp. 351–2; Johnson 1988: p. 192).

[383] *RP*, V, pp. 346–9. The matter of Yorkist enthusiasm for the common weal was treated

competent ruler: his grace and, now, his justice were shown to be the true and proper sources of authority in the realm.[384]

Even so, the very emphasis on the king's grace in the parliament suggests that something of the old noble enthusiasm for 'oonhede' and compromise had survived.[385] The door was not entirely closed on the Yorkists: just as pardons had been offered to all but Salisbury before the battle,[386] so now the king retained 'his prerogatyf to shewe such mercy and grace as shall please his Highnes' to anyone named in the act.[387] This must have been more than a mere form of words. The Yorkists were, after all, still at large, and it would be entirely characteristic of the consensual tendency among the lords that peace might best be effected by negotiation rather than warfare: this was certainly reflected in the behaviour of some of them the following summer. Margaret was on the horns of a familiar dilemma: she could acquire the unity which gave her comprehensive authority, but only at the price of accepting consultation, compromise and the assertion of a quasi-independent corporate interest on the part of the lords.[388] It seems

rather obliquely at Coventry (e.g. references to York's 'crafty labours': p. 346), perhaps because it was rather a tender issue, especially when the queen was at pains to stress the absolute nature of royal authority. In the contemporaneous 'Somnium', however, Yorkist claims on this basis were attacked directly (see above, pp. 43ff).

[384] *RP*, V, pp. 346–7. The king was presented as having been behind most of the initiatives of central government during the preceding decade. In 1450, for example, his reply to York's bills had been full of 'the spiret of wisdome of God', driving the duke away in confusion. In 1452, his 'knyghtly corage' had forced York to capitulate. In 1456, he had treated the Yorkists mercifully, forgiving them for their outrage at St Albans (now presented as an act of murder and treason, falsely sanctioned by a 'mervelous' act of parliament). In 1458, he had arranged the loveday and, most recently, in 1459, he had again shown martial leadership and renewed clemency. See above, pp. 58–9, for the emphasis on Henry's royal virtues in the attainder document (also discussed by Kekewich 1987: pp. 293–6).

[385] The attainder document emphasised the king's continual preference for mercy before justice. Direct reference was made to the fact that Lord Grey of Powis, Walter Devereux and Sir Henry Retford had come to ask the king's pardon and so were not to be included in the attainder (*RP*, V, pp. 349–50: the petition wanted them to lose their lands all the same, but the king dissented). Another example of the king's grace was given when a petition attempting to impeach Lord Stanley was defeated, even though his behaviour had hardly been loyal and would have contradicted the oath of allegiance sworn in the parliament (*ibid.*, pp. 369–70).

[386] Above, n. 379.   [387] *RP*, V, p. 350.

[388] Something of this emerges in the oath of allegiance, which amounted to a parliamentary recognition of Henry's title. Its first clause demanded that the swearer 'knowleche You ... Kyng Herry the VIte, to be my moost redoubted Soverayne Lord, and rightwesly by succession borne to reigne upon me': *ibid.*, p. 351. It went on to demand an explicit commitment to the succession of Prince Edward. This is rather different from the oath of 1455, which had made no reference to the king's right to the crown, a matter which was then above consideration, evidently: *ibid.*, p. 282. It is interesting that the familiar debate over whether or not there was ever a parliamentary title to the crown has overlooked this episode (see e.g. Chrimes 1936: pp. 23–34). True enough, in 1459 the crown was not explicit about what it was doing (as Henry IV had been in 1399 or 1406). Even so, the fact remains that Henry's leading subjects were being asked to endorse his title, something which had never been asked of them before. It was thus

that in 1459 she was ready to pay that price. As a result, the Coventry assembly, far from being a 'parliament of devils', was the start of a national settlement on the model of the parliament of July 1455.[389]

We have very little information about the activities of Margaret's government in the six months which followed, but it is fairly clear that it exercised a genuine public authority. If defence remained its chief preoccupation, it seems nonetheless to have aimed at a broad base of support[390] and even to have undertaken some minor reforms.[391] At least among landowners, there is no evidence of widespread dissatisfaction or of enthusiasm for the departed Yorkists. Had the exiled lords been purely dependent on support from within the English polity – and particularly from the nobility – it is likely that attempts to continue their rebellion would not have met with success. In fact, however, the Yorkists had three sources of power which were more or less external to the political situation of the preceding few years and which enabled them to overturn the emerging consensus. The first of these was their tenure of overseas bases, and particularly Calais which provided them not only with security but

open to the lords to infer that they had some choice in the matter. In the circumstances of 'Lancastrian' victory, this choice was abstract, but it need not remain so.

[389] This is certainly the impression the author of the poem *Knyghthode and Bataile* (ed. Dyboski and Arend) was trying to create. Its editors suggest that this reworking of Vegetius was written between 1457 and 1460 (p. xxiii), but references to the king's triumphal entry to London on 1 March (sts. 1–3) and, more obliquely, to the attainder of the Yorkists (lines 30–2, where the writer repeats the official line that the lords were nothing but rebels, even though 'Ypocrisie her faytys [i.e. deeds] peynte'), enable us to narrow the dating down to 1460. The entire conceptual basis of the post-Ludford crown seems to be contained in lines 23–4: 'Now prosperaunce and peax perpetuel / Shal growe – and why? For here is Unitas' (cf. the text taken by Waynflete at Coventry: 'Gratia vobis et pax multiplicetur': *RP*, V, p. 345). There were important differences between the parliaments of 1455 and 1459, all the same. The Yorkists had held the former at Westminster, for example: something which the queen was unwilling, perhaps afraid, to do. Moreover, in 1455, Somerset, Thorpe and Joseph were not attainted for what they had allegedly done at St Albans (a punitive bill against them was submitted, but refused: *RP*, V, pp. 332–3).

[390] Although major military commissions were given to trusted men (e.g. Somerset, Roos and Audley, son of the baron murdered by Salisbury, were sent to Calais in the autumn of 1459: *English Chron.*, p. 84), almost every other member of the nobility who was in the realm at the time received a commission of some kind during the period between Ludford and the Yorkist landing. The comparison with the commissions of July 1457 (above, p. 340 n. 335), is instructive. There are some startling examples of the width over which the government cast its net: Lord Bergavenny, Warwick's uncle, was appointed to head a commission of array in Kent in the wake of the Yorkists' Sandwich raid, for example (*CPR, 1452–61*, p. 563); the duke of Norfolk, who was appointed to various commissions, often in the company of his lifelong enemies Tuddenham and Heydon (*ibid.*, pp. 566, 606), was ordered to stay at Caister and keep his county against the earl of Warwick at Easter 1460: *PL*, III, p. 212.

[391] See Griffiths 1981: pp. 826–7 for the discretion exercised by the government in the handling of its new landed resources. Its determination to preserve this bounty, in order to restore royal finances, evokes the 'newe ffundacion' recommended by Fortescue (above, pp. 46–9 and n. 189). A resumption, directed (like that of 1453) against those who had recently rebelled but not been attainted, no doubt pleased the commons.

also with a source of men, funds, shipping and foreign support.[392] This support was most important, perhaps, in conferring a public – indeed international – significance upon the Yorkists and their resistance, which must have helped to counteract the pragmatic defection of English sympathy for them.[393] It was an external authorisation of this kind that characterised their second source of power: the papal legate, Francesco Coppini, who had been sent to restore peace to England.[394] He was impressed by the familiar themes of the Yorkist position – loyalty to Henry VI, concern for the common weal, demands for just treatment – and accordingly proclaimed that their actions were legitimate, undermining the royal claim that the crown and its ministers were the sole source of valid authority.[395] Whether he had a specific value to the Yorkists as an *entrée* to the support of the prelates, or, given his powers of indulgence and excommunication, to the recruitment of the populace, cannot be known, but it does not seem unlikely.[396]

The third source of Yorkist power was the fund of popular, and probably gentle, sympathy which the lords seem to have elicited in Kent and maybe London.[397] This was, no doubt, partly due to a residual

---

[392] See Harriss 1960.

[393] The fact that the duke of Burgundy sent a delegation to the Yorkist lords at the beginning of November 1459 (Thielemans 1966: p. 375) must have been a valuable mark of recognition. With this sort of backing, the Yorkists could indeed present the appearance of 'an alternative government' (Harriss 1960: p. 52).

[394] Griffiths 1981: p. 862.

[395] *CSP Venice*, I, pp. 89–91. The legate's view that it was for Henry, 'in your own person, wherein everyone places trust', to throw off the advice of the lords who were suspected by the Yorkists and to agree to negotiations was obviously informed by the perspective of the Calais lords (see e.g. the June 1460 manifesto in *English Chron.*, pp. 88–9). In a like way, other observations of Coppini's, though justifiable from a Yorkist – or even 'neutral' – perspective, ran against royal authority as it was normally conceived in England and, specifically, as Margaret was trying to present it at the time. Note, for example, his comment to the king that 'Scripture says that recourse must be had to arms when justice cannot otherwise be obtained from adversaries', which would have begged the question that it was for the king to dispense justice to the disputants within his realm (*CSP Venice*, I, p. 90); and, even more startling, the warning that 'Should you not hearken [to his advice], no one can say you are justified in fighting against your subjects now advancing' (*ibid.* and cf. York's posture at St Albans, five years earlier: *PL*, III, pp. 26–7). It is not altogether surprising that, two years later, the pope accused Coppini of having supported rebels: *CPL*, XI, pp. 675–6.

[396] Convocation was meeting in London when the Yorkists arrived at the city and its sympathies may have played a part in facilitating their entry: e.g. *Three Chrons.*, pp. 73–4; *English Chron.*, pp. 94–5. See *CSP Venice*, I, pp. 92–3, for Coppini's strenuous denials that he had used his powers of excommunication (cf. 'Benet's Chron.', p. 225). He does refer to a letter written by him to the clergy and people of the land, however: it could have been influential.

[397] See Harvey 1991: pp. 183–4 and note also the following. The *Brut*, pp. 528–9, claims that supporters flocked to Calais throughout 1459–60. The pseudo-Worcester reports the hanging of a number of Londoners who wanted to join Warwick in February 1460: *Letters and Papers*, II, ii, p. 772. A preacher at St Paul's Cross who urged people not to pray for the Yorkist lords received 'lytyl thank' from his audience (*PL*, III, p. 196). The

enthusiasm in these areas for communal disaffection, which the Yorkists stimulated with a volley of bills from Calais,[398] but it is likely that local support for the exiled lords was increased by Warwick's inspiring defence of the sea.[399] It is even possible that, by concentrating their rule in the Midlands, the Lancastrians had to some extent lost the rule of the South-East, rather as Edward IV found it difficult to impose his will upon the North in the early 1460s.[400] Whatever the cause, it is quite clear that their opportunistic descent on Sandwich brought the Yorkists an immediate wave of support, which, in a matter of days, swept them to the gates of London.[401] Stressing their loyalty to Henry VI, backed by the legate and all the time gathering a broader following, they began to resemble a public authority equivalent to that of the queen, the prince and the lords in the Midlands, who seem to have been paralysed by the speed of the Yorkist advance.[402] It was surely for these reasons that London admitted them, so adding another token of representativeness to their growing lordship.[403] When they arrived before the king at North-ampton, March and Warwick were accompanied by a large force, its public nature confirmed by a bevy of bishops and a patent willingness to

---

English Chron., p. 91, reports that the men of Kent, fearing tyrannous impositions and judicial measures, sent to Warwick, begging him to invade, promising assistance. The duke of Exeter, encountering Warwick in mid-sea did not dare to attack him, because he knew his men favoured the earl more than himself (*Chrons. of London*, p. 171; Leland, *De Rebus*, p. 494). The murder of John Judde, the king's master of ordnance, near St Albans on 2 June (before the Yorkist landing), may further suggest widespread dissent among the non-noble classes in the South-East (*Three Chrons.*, p. 73; *Town Chrons.*, p. 149). There was pro-Yorkist popular activity even in Coventry in early 1460 and it was perhaps for this reason that the town later gave support to the Calais lords, even after they had lost the king (Harris (ed.), *Coventry Leet Book*, pp. 309, 313–15).

[398] Harvey 1991: p. 183; *Collections*, p. 206. The Yorkists exploited local feeling by recirculating one of Cade's manifestoes (Harvey 1991: p. 188). The government responded by sending orders on 11 and 23 June 1460 to the sheriffs of the southern counties, telling them to proclaim that the Yorkists were not, as had been rumoured, in the king's grace, and the telling idea that 'his said Highness was not privy nor assenting to th'Act of Attaindre of theym' was not true: *Foedera*, V, II, p. 97.

[399] See e.g. *Town Chrons.*, p. 147, and Goodman 1981: pp. 33–4. Cf. Searle and Burghart 1972: pp. 380ff, 386 for possible parallels in 1381.

[400] See Goodman 1981: p. 33.

[401] Griffiths 1981: pp. 859–60. Three Kent esquires, Hoorn, Scotte and Fogge, sent to resist the Yorkist invasion, decided to join the lords instead: Searle, 'Chron. of John Stone', p. 79.

[402] Goodman 1981: p. 36.

[403] Warwick recited the Yorkists' concern for the misgovernment of the realm to the bishops assembled in convocation at St Paul's and swore their loyalty to Henry VI: Johnson 1988: p. 205; Barron 1981: p. 96. Among the grounds on which the Londoners dispensed with the services of Lord Scales, who had been left behind to guard the city, was the telling one that they were strong enough to defend themselves if the Yorkists proved not to intend the weal of the king and the commons (*Town Chrons.*, p. 150). Note that Salisbury's subsequent appointment as ruler and governor of London was putatively made by common assent (*English Chron.*, p. 95).

negotiate.[404] In circumstances once again reminiscent of St Albans,[405] Yorkist demands for justice were decisively rejected by royalists headed by Buckingham; battle was joined; and the victory of the earls, which followed, was marked by handsome submissions to Henry VI.[406]

After Northampton and the ensuing capture of the Tower of London, the Yorkists found themselves in a similar position to that of the queen after Ludford.[407] They were now the public authority and their enemies became rebels. Victory, however, did not give them a free hand, even if it did remove some of their more persistent enemies. They continued to be bound by those ties of emphatic loyalty to Henry VI and the common weal of his lords which had given them both their constituency and their victory.[408] This is the key to understanding their reaction when, a few months after the battle, the duke of York returned to England intending to make himself king.[409] It is quite likely that in taking this step, York was pursuing a policy agreed with the Calais lords before their astonishingly successful landing, or at least known to them before October 1460.[410]

[404] The attainted lords arrived at Northampton with Viscount Bourgchier, Archbishop Bourgchier, Bishop Neville and the legate (*Three Chrons.*, p. 74), Bishops Kemp, Beauchamp, Chedworth and Grey (*Registrum Whethamstede*, I, p. 372), the prior of St Johns, Bishop Lowe and Lords Audley, Bergavenny, Saye and Sele and Scrope of Bolton (*English Chron.*, p. 95). The presence of so many non-combatants, in particular, must have reinforced Yorkist claims to represent something greater than themselves. For the Yorkist willingness to negotiate, see *English Chron.*, pp. 96–7 (the detailed account may make this more than propaganda) and *Registrum Whethamstede*, I, pp. 372–3.

[405] As before, the Yorkists could justify their appearance in arms with reference to the need to defend themselves (*CSP Venice*, I, p. 90), though it was additionally clear that they were ready to fight Shrewsbury, Beaumont, Wiltshire and their adherents, who – like Somerset in 1455 – were blamed for misgovernment on the grounds of their accroachment of the royal power, and even of tyranny (*English Chron.*, pp. 88–9, arts. 9 and 10). Note that the king, even more than at St Albans, was absolved of all responsibility: 'nother assentyng ne knowyng therof' (p. 89).

[406] See Jack 1960 for full details.

[407] Writs for a parliament were sent out soon after the Tower of London was subdued, on 30 July 1460: *CClR, 1454–61*, pp. 462–3. In August, Coppini commented to the duke of Milan that England was 'newly reformed': *CSP Venice*, I, p. 91.

[408] See n. 403 above and note Coppini's comment that it was 'on account of [Warwick's] sincere inclination to the king, I principally came' (*CSP Venice*, I, p. 94). The lords affirmed their loyalty to Henry in various ways in the ensuing months: note, for example, the pilgrimage to Canterbury which the king undertook at the beginning of August 1460, in the company of Bishops Kemp, Neville and Arundel of Chichester and the earls of March, Salisbury and Warwick (Searle, 'Chron. of John Stone', p. 81).

[409] See Johnson 1988: pp. 210–18 for details.

[410] It is perfectly possible that the Calais lords had not expected the support of the commons of Kent and London, and then of the lords, to accrue to them as rapidly as it did (see *CSP Venice*, I, pp. 89–90), or that their professions of loyalty should have proved so effective. We know that York and Warwick met and conferred in Ireland and it is almost certain that they agreed some sort of common policy there: Johnson 1988: pp. 195–6. Some aspects of the behaviour of the Calais lords in the period between Northampton and York's return suggest that they knew what he was going to do: the king was not, for example, taken to Westminster Palace at any time before the opening

There were certainly good reasons for reviving York's claim to the throne. It had been tacitly laid aside since the early years of the decade, but when, in 1459, the royalists took up the theme of noble unity which had provided York with an alternative source of legitimacy since 1453, it may have seemed worth publishing his blood-right as a justification for further opposition.[411] If York was the true king, then he had no duty of obedience to Henry VI: he was not a rebel, but a contender in a just war.

It is also possible that York had realised, perhaps as a result of his 1455–6 protectorate, that the restoration of public authority depended not on counsel, or on artificial means of sustaining unity, but on the absolute replacement of Henry VI by an effective ruler. What he may have overlooked, however, was that it was very difficult to repudiate Henry VI without repudiating the body of lords who had struggled for so long to hold themselves together in order to give his name some credibility. What guarantees of security could York offer them? While the headship of Henry VI offered the last chance of a common platform with their peers around the queen – who, like the Yorkists in December 1459, were still free men – was it not essential to maintain it? Concerns like these, bound to be prevalent amongst a wide body of lords, many of whom had had no prior connection with York and who had joined a campaign for unity under the king against the sectarianism of the queen, must have carried the day.[412] Whether or not York would have made a good king was not in question: it was simply impossible for Henry VI's lords, gathered in his parliament, to depose him in the autumn of 1460.[413]

<hr />

of parliament, which may be significant (Wolffe 1981: p. 371) and John Stone noted that he did not go crowned to the assumption day vespers at Canterbury (Searle, 'Chron. of John Stone', p. 81). By mid-September, Warwick, at least, knew what was going to happen (Johnson 1988: pp. 211–12).

[411] *Vox populi* played an important part in this. De Waurin's account of the acclamation of York's title by the people of Ludlow in September 1460 evokes the scenes in London six months later, when Edward was made king. The people are asked by York to advise him what he should do. They announce that they are 'grandement esmerveilles comment vostre droit heritage vous laissies ainsi aller'. York thanks them and summons various lords of Wales to give him counsel. They agree with the people and swear to help him and accompany him to London (de Waurin, *Croniques*, V, pp. 311–12). For York's ceremonious progress to London, see *Collections*, p. 208. He entered the city with sword erect and borne before him: *Chrons. of London*, p. 171; Johnson 1988: pp. 213–14.

[412] The lords had to accommodate York: he was inescapably their leader, and his forthright behaviour shows that he was in earnest. Even so, their attitude seems to have been all along that they should try to find workable arguments against York's claim, according to the royal order to them, which they must themselves have fabricated (*RP*, V, p. 376).

[413] It seems almost certain that the duke had not intended to submit his claim to parliament, but to gain control of the situation using his armed men and, as Henry IV had before him, present political society with a *fait accompli* (see Johnson 1988: pp. 212–16 and McFarlane 1972: pp. 52–5). Note that York was later to point out that if Henry IV had had the crown 'by title of enheritaunce, discent or succession', he would not have needed or wanted an act of this kind: *RP*, V, p. 377.

Just as York had to behave as he did in order to assert the 'regal' pre-eminence of his authority, so the Calais lords, aware of the 'political' basis which their power actually possessed, had to resist him.[414]

The parliamentary accord of 31 October nonetheless reflected much of the justice of York's position.[415] It was, in essence, an attempt to reconcile the polity of Henry VI, with the right of the man who was its true leader in both a *de iure* and a *de facto* sense. While the disinheritance of the prince ensured the continued enmity of the queen and risked the alienation of the lords around her,[416] the really important point about the accord was that it betrayed none of the promises made by the Calais lords since their return and helped to commit other lords, who had joined them in the interests of unity, to the defence of a particular, and certainly, Yorkist settlement.[417] The fortunes of the Lancastrian commonwealth, as it

[414] It was under pressure from these lords – March, of course, among them – that York agreed to put his claim to the peers: see Johnson 1988: pp. 214–15 for this point and for some of the considerations they had in mind.

[415] *RP*, V, pp. 378–9.

[416] Not only was the prince removed from the line of succession, but, more immediately important, the principality of Wales, together with the earldom of Chester and the duchy of Cornwall, were granted to York (*RP*, V, pp. 380–1), threatening the regional hegemonies of some of the queen's supporters: see n. 423, below. Note too that, having lost the king, the queen's party had tended to refocus its allegiances upon the prince: it was, for example, observed that the army which captured Henry at the second battle of St Albans was clad in the prince's livery (*Collections*, p. 212); it was the prince who acted as judge at the 'trial' of Bonville, immediately after the battle (*English Chron.*, p. 108); it was rumoured that when the battle was over, the queen and Somerset induced the king to resign the crown to his son, which he did 'out of his good nature': *CSP Milan*, p. 55.

[417] We do not know who attended the 1460 parliament. The triers of petitions included, apart from the bishops, Warwick, Bourgchier, the prior of St Johns, Grey of Ruthin, Dacre (presumably Richard Fiennes), Fitzwarin, Salisbury, Scrope of Bolton, Bonville, Berners and, rather surprisingly, Richmount-Grey. Other lords in London during the period of the parliament (including January and early February 1461) were Stourton, Dudley and Stanley (*PPC*, VI, p. 307) and the newly ennobled John Neville, Lord Montague (*ibid.*, pp. 308–10), together, presumably, with the new Lords Scales (Anthony Woodville) and Cromwell (Humphrey Bourgchier). Norfolk, Welles and Rivers were also present – at a garter meeting – and Arundel may have been (Anstis (ed.), *Register of the Garter*, II, pp. 166–7: all the rest of those receiving votes are known to have been in London at this time, hence Arundel). The young Viscount Beaumont, who was admitted to his lands without suit in November (*CPR, 1452–61*, p. 632) and was a charter witness in December (C53/190/1), was very probably in London at this time. Note that a possible indicator of the attitudes of the lords of this parliament is the reappointment of the duchy feoffees, who were to include outright partisans of the queen, such as Pembroke, Laurence Booth and Lord Welles, together with familiar figures from the court such as Lords Sudeley and Beauchamp, and Bishops Waynflete, Lyhert and Stanbury. Lyhert and Beauchamp, removed from the board of feoffees in 1459, were actually restored by these 'Yorkists' (*RP*, V, pp. 384–7, 352–6). The legate Coppini, writing to a friend in the queen's camp in January 1461, identified two reasons why the people of London and the South-East favoured peace (and, implicitly, the Yorkist lords about the king): *CSP Venice*, I, p. 93. One was that the queen's army had acquired a reputation for cruelty and vindictiveness, whilst the Yorkists had not been cruel and had taken in all who would join them. The other was that it was known that

appeared to the lords in London, were, by this act, welded to the house of York.[418] Partly as a result, the death of the duke himself at Wakefield did not break up his following, or, in fact, protect them from the wrath of the queen. When the king himself fell into her hands at the second battle of St Albans, it was almost as if he had resigned his crown as the act prescribed.[419] In terms of the frame of reference prevailing in London, the coronation of Edward of March was now both acceptable and inevitable.[420]

It remains to consider the fortunes of the queen in these last few months of Lancastrian rule and, specifically, why it was that her recapture of the king and subsequent appearance at the gates of London with a vast army headed by a large number of magnates did not precipitate another *bouleversement*. Had the ingredients of public authority changed, or was Margaret's failure purely strategic? It is almost certain that the six odd months of division between Northampton and the queen's arrival at London undermined the faith of the lords in the possibility of reviving national unity. The queen's professions of clemency as she sought entry to the city may have convinced few.[421] The crucial factor, however, may be that the sense of ideological conflict or dynastic rivalry had more or less given way to the perception of a war between North and South.[422] The origins of this view are to be found in the later 1450s, with the queen's withdrawal from London, but the decisive moment came after

the king and his adherents (i.e. the Yorkists) were disposed to a fair and honourable peace. These same perceptions are likely to have influenced lords as well as men. Note that of those listed as present in London between the opening of parliament and the second battle of St Albans, only Welles, Richmount-Grey and the young Viscount Beaumont defected to the queen (Ross 1974: pp. 37, 46, 66; Richmond 1977: p. 76).

[418] Tellingly, it was for 'the wele, rest and prosperite of this lande' that York agreed to Henry VI's continued tenure of the throne: *RP*, V, p. 378.

[419] A view echoed in Gregory's chronicle, with the observation that, at the battle, the king 'for-soke alle hys lordys, ande truste better to [the queen's] party thenne unto hys owne lordys' (*Collections*, p. 212). In *Three Chrons.*, p. 76, also, it is the king's 'trewe lordis' who are deserted by him at St Albans, a perspective which cannot altogether be accounted for by post-1461 bias.

[420] *Crowland*, II, p. 456, reports that the council considered Edward released from his oath of allegiance under the terms of the act (see also *Town Chrons.*, pp. 166–7; Leland, *De Rebus*, p. 498). The crowning of Edward was the fruit of common policy in a way that his father's initiative had not been. Note that it was all completed in a matter of days (Edward arrived on 26 February and was king by 4 March: Ross 1974: pp. 32–4). It was the chancellor, George Neville, who preached the king's title at St Paul's Cross (*English Chron.*, p. 108). It may be significant that the papal legate was overseas at this time (in the Low Countries from 10 February) and unable to raise objections: *CSP Venice*, I, p. 98.

[421] The queen's letters to London carried an official denial that she intended the city any harm: BL, Add. MS 48031A, fol. 30v; *CSP Milan*, I, p. 50. See n. 425, below, for the reaction of the Londoners.

[422] In *Crowland*, I, pp. 421–3, for example, the 'enemy', from Wakefield onwards, is the men of the North, not the queen or the Lancastrians, or anything to do with the prior political and dynastic conflicts. See also *PL*, III, p. 250.

the battle of Northampton, when the queen and prince regrouped in the North. A combination of the collapse of Yorkist lordship in the area, and the demise of the queen's power in the Midlands and South-East, made the North the natural focus of resistance to the new regime in London.[423] At the same time, the lords of the South, the Marches and the Midlands were increasingly drawn into the royal government of the Calais lords.[424] Whilst it is unlikely that the *topos* of the wild northerner affected the way in which the nobility dealt with each other, it may have encouraged the resistance of the London mob, and this was a decisive factor in the refusal of the civic authorities to admit the queen.[425] What is most important, however, is that in those six months Margaret became indelibly associated

[423] The Midlands ceased to be a suitable base for the queen for two main reasons, perhaps. First, the deaths of Buckingham, Shrewsbury and Beaumont – the first two leaving child heirs – and the flight of Wiltshire meant that the queen lost the leading figures of her affinity in the area: see above, pp. 338–9. Second, almost all the major duchy offices in the Midlands and North-West went to the Nevilles in the autumn of 1460 (the chief stewards of the north and south parts and of Lancashire, the stewardships of Tutbury, Leicester and Bolingbroke: Somerville 1953: pp. 421, 429, 493, 540, 572, 576). In tandem with the deaths of the previous incumbents, this might well have influenced local loyalties away from the 'Lancastrian' party. Only three major territorial magnates remained about the queen: Northumberland, Pembroke and Devon. Devon was a relatively junior figure and faced the reviving Bonville–Fitzwarin–Courtenay of Powderham alliance in his 'country' (Cherry 1981a: pp. 139–40). Pembroke seems to have had quite a difficult time in Wales after 1459 and his influence may have been largely restricted to the Principality, particularly after Mortimer's Cross (see Thomas 1971: pp. 180–91). Northumberland, on the other hand, must have exercised a certain dominance in the North after Ludford (although see Pollard 1990: pp. 272 and 274 for some important qualifications). Apart from the crown, as duke of Lancaster, the northern baronage – Clifford, Greystoke, Fitzhugh, Neville of Brancepeth, Dacre – simply had no other source of lordship to look to (although it is interesting to note that Fitzhugh and Greystoke, who had assisted the Nevilles in the conflict of 1453–4, were regarded with suspicion by the other adherents of the queen and Percies: Pollard 1990: p. 275). Wakefield itself was a demonstration of how the balance of power in the North had changed. York and Salisbury seem to have thought they were in friendly territory. York's confident bearing during this expedition is well attested: *English Chron.*, p. 106; *Crowland*, I, p. 421; *Town Chrons.*, p. 152. Salisbury had been steward of Pontefract, so it is all the more striking that *English Chron.*, p. 107, should report that the common people in the town hated him and that it was they who took him from the castle and cut off his head.

[424] A document listing, in two columns, what appear to be the committed supporters of the Yorkists on the one hand and neutrals ('newtri [e?]galis') on the other, and datable to late January or early February 1461 (see Griffiths 1981: p. 880) includes only lords from the South, Centre and Marches in the former category (apart from the Nevilles and March and the single exception of Scrope of Bolton): viz. Norfolk, Berners, Bourgchier, Bonville, Grey of Powis, Bergavenny, Clinton, Fitzwater, La Warre, Saye and Sele, Stanley, Grey of Ruthin and, probably, Cobham ('dns de Comhom'): E163/28/5. It is significant that, among the neutrals only the northerners, Beaumont, Greystoke and Willoughby (*Letters and Papers*, II, ii, p. 776; Ross 1974: p. 66), fought against the Yorkists up to and including Towton (unless 'dns henriceus' is Henry, Lord Fitzhugh), while the remainder come from the South and the west Midlands.

[425] For the importance of the attitudes of the mob, see Barron 1981: p. 89; also *English Chron.*, p. 109, and *Chrons. of London*, p. 173. The evidence suggests that popular hatred and fear of the coming army was difficult to contain: e.g. *CSP Milan*, I, p. 50.

with an interest which was patently more regional than national: a fate
which has never, in the course of English history, befallen the men of
London and the home counties. Having failed to gain entry to the capital,
the king and queen had no choice but to return to the North and await the
assault of an increasingly credible public authority.[426] This authority
belonged to Edward of York. Until he had won the battle of Towton –
and, to some extent, even after that – his claims to the representation of
the realm were not incontrovertible, but they were already over-
whelming.[427] The polity of Henry VI had come to an end.

[426] Commenting on the withdrawal of king and queen to the North, the pseudo-Worcester
remarked, 'Et hoc fuit destructio regis Henrici et reginae suae' (*Letters and Papers*, II, ii,
p. 776). Other chroniclers explained Edward's succession in similar terms, e.g. *Three
Chrons.*, p. 155; *Crowland*, I, p. 424; *Chrons. of London*, p. 215, which emphasises the
role of popular acclamation, saying that the Londoners declared that they were free to
forsake the man who had forsaken their city.

[427] See Wolffe 1976: particularly pp. 372 and 374, for some important comments
concerning Edward's problems in the 1460s.

8

CONCLUSION

T HE STARTING-POINT of this book was a desire to look more closely at the workings of political society in fifteenth-century England, and, in particular, to explore the framework of expectations and beliefs which governed the operations of Lancastrian kingship. It will now, I hope, be clearer than ever that the nobility of later medieval England moved in a world shaped as much by common principles and structures as by individual interests and relationships. Under Henry VI, their behaviour and their fate were in almost every case determined by the workings of their system of government. If this has not always been sufficiently emphasised before, it is surely because that system was – in theory, as well as in practice – rather different from how it has traditionally been presented. The real centrepiece of public life for these men was not, as the Victorians imagined, parliament; nor, as has been implicit since, was it the formal agencies of the royal administration. It was the king, and the king in person. There was, in fifteenth-century England, no necessary antithesis between the public and the personal: the virtuous lord – be he king or magnate – was, in his person, the normal, ideal and in fact single bearer of the essentially public function of government. Men certainly placed a premium on counsel, because this was one key ingredient in the process of representation, which was what lordship was for – and, to a large extent, what it was. But they did not willingly promote councils, because these disrupted the exercise of will on which the efficacy of counsel and the preservation of order and unity finally depended. The nobility supported free royal power because it was in the public interests of the realm, as they understood these interests, to do so. That they spent the large majority of Henry VI's reign trying simultaneously to maintain conciliar modes of rule reflects the peculiar and difficult circumstances which the king's inadequacy created.

'Weak kingship' was indeed the central problem of the reign, and, as McFarlane long ago proposed, it was a personal and not a constitutional undermightiness which was its essence. The power of the fifteenth-century English king was constitutionally upheld; it accrued to him naturally in the proper performance of his representative duties. Later medieval monarchy was a sophisticated and flexible system, designed to provide the same communal services, no matter who the man beneath the crown, but it did demand two basic commitments from the person of the king. The first of these was to listen to counsel; the second to exercise will. If we are going to use the term 'weak kingship' at all, it can only mean a prolonged and repeated failure to meet the second of these demands, and it is in this sense that it can be applied to Henry VI. The study of his government and its impact has shown that, in Henry, the monarchical system was unable to function normally and that the cause of this malfunction was clearly not royal wilfulness.

At the same time, it must now be clear that 'weak kingship' is a phenomenon considerably more complicated, for both historians and contemporaries, than its obverse, tyranny. Henry VI was never blamed for the failure of his rule, even though this failure was entirely of his own making. It was up to the users of the system, and, principally, the nobility, to identify what was wrong with it, and it was in this respect that Henry's flaws were so peculiarly destructive. Kingship was characteristically a corporate enterprise, but there was very little that the lords could do to create and preserve an authority capable of leading them in unity, unless the king would do his small but necessary part. Yet it is clear, even so, that Henry VI's greatest subjects did everything they could. Far from fighting among themselves – until the impossibility of restoring 'rule' either locally or nationally made this absolutely unavoidable – they strove to hold together, and responded to the king's inertness by taking up a more extensive 'execucion' of his authority than would normally be necessary. Their corporate accroachment of the royal power, so long regarded as the acme of overmighty behaviour, can thus be seen as an attempt to preserve, not to frustrate, the power of the crown. The lords spoke the truth when, in 1427, they observed that 'the same autoritee resteth and is at this day in [the king's] persone that shal be in him at eny tyme hereafter'. While Henry VI grew physically, and perhaps mentally, he never came to perform the role expected of an adult king. In certain respects, therefore, the lords did indeed find themselves having to cope with 'forty years of virtual minority'.[1] Deprived of the independent will which, in the longer term, was the only guarantee of their unity and well-being, they were surely doomed to failure; but we should not be blind to the persistence of their common effort.

[1]   For McFarlane's lapidary description of the reign, see 1973: p. 284 (and, for the comments on personal undermightiness, mentioned above, 1981f: pp. 238-9).

Where the joint enterprise of Henry's kingship was successful, most notably in the creation and maintenance of a broad noble consensus from the early 1420s to the later 1440s, it did not occur to the lords to question it. Its failure to meet the wider needs of the realm was in part invisible and in part inexplicable. When, in 1450, France was lost and those outside the charmed circle of the nobility forcefully demonstrated that the king had not satisfied what they understood to be the common interest, the response of the lords was confused. Only now was the realisation dawning that their involvement in the 'execucion' of the king's authority had been too great and that it had drawn them away from the representation of the needs of the *communitas* which was, in a sense, their proper task.

By itself, however, this realisation was little help. In the atmosphere of crisis sparked off by popular ferment and the interventions of Richard of York, the preservation of unity among the lords was of pressing importance: the maintenance of civil rule depended on it. The king provided the obvious focus for this unity and this goes a long way towards explaining how he was able to survive such a clear demonstration of his utter inadequacy. But unity, whatever its focus, was only sustainable through the exercise of public authority, and, in practical terms, this authority came not, as was normal, from the king, but, as it had since 1422, from the lords themselves. The assaults of York could be resisted while he stood, as Gloucester had done, for the irreconcilable principles of loyalty and opposition, but they could not be authoritatively suppressed. Meanwhile, when a series of regional disputes broke out between the leading magnates, and York shifted his position to what was, in a sense, the old Beaufort platform of the common interest of the lords, the chances of reaching agreement about where the focus of unity should be located receded. The authority necessary for the preservation of Henry's polity no longer had a single source: the crown had fragmented, its power of will was in the hands of York and the queen, its representativeness shared out among the indecisive lords. The lords were in a hopeless position: the restoration of full, politic, public rule depended on the enthronement of a functioning king, but, as long as some of the nobility accepted the lordship of queen and prince, this was an end which could only be reached through a willingness to countenance unwelcome divisions. Civil war was the only possible resolution.

A coherent thread thus runs through the reign of Henry VI, linking the periods of optimistic noble consensus, of personal rule in the king's court, and of bitterness, enmity and mistrust: the absence of a fully independent royal authority. The great lords of Henry's reign – Bedford, Gloucester, Beaufort, Suffolk, York, Somerset and the queen – were, as Wolffe suggested, neither fools nor knaves, nor, for that matter, were they heroes: they were victims, driven by the hideous logic of a dysfunctional system to the fruitless creation and defence of an authority which could not be exercised. The crisis of Henry VI's reign was not brought about by overmighty subjects, by the misapplication of patronage, by defeat in war, by dynastic struggle, or by financial insolvency. Its fundamental cause was truly constitutional: the inability of monarchy, a means for the satisfaction of the public interest in the body of a single man, to adjust to one of the possible extremes of human frailty.

BIBLIOGRAPHY

UNPRINTED PRIMARY SOURCES

Cambridge: University Library

MS Ee.iii.61

London: British Library

Additional Charters
Additional MSS
Additional Rolls
Cotton Charters
Cotton MSS
Egerton Rolls
Harley MSS
Lansdowne MSS
Sloane MSS

London: College of Arms

Arundel MS xlviii.

London: Public Record Office

C47 (Chancery, miscellanea)
C49 (Chancery, parliamentary and council proceedings)
C53 (Chancery, charter rolls)
C81 (Chancery, warrants for the great seal, series 1)
C253 (Chancery, *sub pena*s)
C266 (Chancery, cancelled letters patent)
E28 (Exchequer, Treasury of Receipt, council and privy seal)
E101 (Exchequer, KR, accounts various)
E159 (Exchequer, KR, memoranda rolls)
E163 (Exchequer, KR, miscellanea)
E404 (Exchequer, warrants for issue)

KB9 (King's Bench ancient indictments)
PSO1 (Privy Seal Office, warrants for the privy seal)
SC1 (Special Collections, ancient correspondence)
SC8 (Special Collections, ancient petitions)

PRINTED PRIMARY SOURCES

Allmand, C. T., 'Documents relating to the Anglo-French Negotiations of 1439', *Camden Miscellany XXIV*, Camden Soc., 4th ser., IX, (London, 1972), pp. 79–149.

Anstey, H. (ed.), *Epistolae Academicae Oxonienses*, 2 vols., Oxford Historical Soc., nos. 35 and 36 (Oxford, 1898).

Anstis, J. (ed.), *Register of the Most Noble Order of the Garter*, 2 vols. (London, 1724).

Bateson, M. (ed.), *George Ashby's Poems*, EETS, extra ser., no. 76 (London, 1899).

Beaucourt, G. L. E. du F. de (ed.), *Chronique de Mathieu d'Escouchy*, 3 vols. (Paris, 1863–4).

Bornstein, b. (ed.), *The Middle English Translation of Christine de Pisan's Livre du Corps de Policie* (Heidelberg, 1977).

Brewer, D. S. (ed.), *Malory: The Morte Darthur* (London, 1968).

Brewer, J. S., and Bullen, W. (eds.), *Calendar of the Carew Manuscripts*, VI, (Book of Howth) (London, 1871).

Brie, F. W. D. (ed.), *The Brut, or The Chronicles of England*, 2 vols., EETS, orig. ser., nos. 131, 136 (London, 1906–8).

Bull, G. (ed.), *Niccolo Machiavelli: The Prince*, 3rd edn (Harmondsworth, 1983).

Byles, A. T. P. (ed.), *The Book of Fayttes of Armes and of Chyvalrye*, 2nd edn, EETS, orig. ser., no. 189 (London, 1937).

Calendar of the Charter Rolls, 6 vols., HMSO (London, 1903–27).

Calendar of the Close Rolls (for Henry VI's reign), 6 vols., HMSO (London, 1933–9).

Calendar of the Fine Rolls, XV–XIX, HMSO (London, 1935–9).

Calendar of . . . Papal Letters, XI, ed. W. H. Bliss, HMSO (London, 1893).

Calendar of the Patent Rolls (for Henry VI's reign), 6 vols., HMSO (Norwich, 1901–10).

Calendar of State Papers and Manuscripts . . . of Milan, I, ed. A. B. Hinds, HMSO (London, 1912).

Calendar of State Papers and Manuscripts . . . of Venice, I, ed. R. Brown, HMSO (London, 1864).

Calendarium Inquisitionum Post Mortem, 4 vols., Record Com. (London, 1806–28).

Cartularium Abbatiae de Whiteby, 2 vols., Surtees Soc., LXIX and LXXII (Durham, 1879, 1881 1879).

Chrimes, S. B., 'The Pretensions of the Duke of Gloucester in 1422', *Enlish Historical Review*, 45 (1930), pp. 101–3.

Chrimes, S. B. (ed.), *Sir John Fortescue: De Laudibus Legum Anglie* (Cambridge, 1942).

Crotch, W. J. B. (ed.), *The Prologues and Epilogues of William Caxton*, EETS, old ser., no. 176 (London, 1928).

Davies, J. S. (ed.), *An English Chronicle...*, Camden Soc., old ser., LXIV (London, 1856).

Denholm-Young, N. (ed.), *Vita Edwardi Secundi* (London, 1957).

D'Entreves, A. P. (ed.), *Aquinas: Selected Political Writings* (Oxford, 1959).

A Descriptive Catalogue of Ancient Deeds..., 6 vols., HMSO (London, 1890–1915).

Dillon (Viscount) and St John Hope, W. H., 'Inventory of the Goods and Chattels belonging to Thomas, Duke of Gloucester ...', *Archaeological Journal*, 54 (1897), pp. 275–308.

Dyboski, R., and Arend, Z. M. (eds.), *Knyghthode and Bataile*, EETS, old ser., no. 201 (London, 1935).

Ellis, H. (ed.), *The Chronicle of John Hardyng* (London, 1812).

Hall's Chronicle (London, 1809).

Three Books of Polydore Vergil's English History, Camden Soc., old ser., XXIX (London, 1844).

English Historical Documents, III, ed. H. Rothwell (London, 1975).

English Historical Documents, IV, ed. A. R. Myers (London, 1969).

Erdmann, A. (ed.), *Lydgate's Siege of Thebes*, EETS, extra ser., no. 108 (London, 1911).

Flenley, R. (ed.), *Six Town Chronicles of England* (Oxford, 1911).

Flugel, E., 'Eine Mittelenglische Claudian-Übersetzung (1445)', *Anglia*, 28 (1905), pp. 255–99.

Fortescue, T., Lord Clermont (ed.), *Sir John Fortescue, Knight, his Life, Works and Family History*, 2 vols. (London, 1869).

Furnivall, F. J. (ed.), *The Fifty Earliest English Wills*, EETS, orig. ser., no. 78 (London, 1882).

Hoccleve's Works, iii. The Regement of Princes, EETS, extra ser., no. 72 (London, 1897).

Gairdner, J. (ed.), *The Historical Collections of a Citizen of London*, Camden Soc., new ser., XVII (London, 1876).

The Paston Letters, Library edn, 6 vols. (London, 1904).

Three Fifteenth-Century Chronicles, Camden Soc., new ser., XXVIII, (London, 1880).

Genet, J. P. (ed.), *Four English Political Tracts of the Later Middle Ages*, Camden Soc., 4th ser., XVIII, (London, 1977).

Giles, J. A. (ed.), *Chronicles of the White Rose of York* (London, 1845).

Incerti Scriptoris Chronicon Angliae... (London, 1848).

Gilson, J. P., 'A Defence of the Proscription of the Yorkists in 1459', *English Historical Review*, 26 (1911), pp. 512–25.

Griffiths, R. A., 'The King's Council and the First Protectorate of the Duke of York, 1453–4', in Griffiths 1991a: pp. 305–20.

'The Winchester Session of the 1449 Parliament: A Further Comment', in Griffiths 1991a: pp. 253–63.

Halliwell, J. O. (ed.), *A Chronicle of the First Thirteen Years of the Reign of King Edward IV, by John Warkworth*, Camden Soc., old ser., X (London, 1839).

Hardy, W., and E. L. C. P. (eds.), *Recueil des Croniques et Aunchiennes Istories de la Grant Bretaigne . . . par Jehan de Waurin*, 5 vols., Rolls ser. (London, 1864–91).

Harris, M. D. (ed.), *The Coventry Leet Book*, EETS, old ser., nos. 134, 135, 138, 146 in one vol. (London, 1907–13).

Harriss, G. L., and M. A. (eds.), 'John Benet's Chronicle for the Years 1400–62', *Camden Miscellany XXIV*, 4th ser., IX (London, 1972), pp. 151–233.

Harvey, J. H. (ed.), *William Worcestre: Itineraries* (Oxford, 1969).

Hector, L. C., and Harvey, B. F. (eds.), *The Westminster Chronicle, 1381–1394* (Oxford, 1982).

Hellot, A. (ed.), *Les Cronicques de Normendie* (Rouen, 1881).

Hingeston, F. C. (ed.), *John Capgrave. Liber de Illustribus Henricis*, Rolls ser. (London, 1858).

Historical Manuscripts Commission, 3rd Rept App., 8th Rept App., 10th Rept App., 11th Rept. App.

Inquisitions and Assessments relating to Feudal Aids, 6 vols., HMSO (London, 1899–1920).

Jacob, E. F., *The Register of Henry Chichele*, 4 vols., II (Oxford, 1937).

James, M. R., *Henry the Sixth. A Reprint of John Blacman's Memoir* (Cambridge, 1919).

Kail, J. (ed.), *Twenty-Six Political and Other Poems*, EETS, orig. ser., no. 124 (London, 1904).

Kempe, A. J., *Historical Notices of the Collegiate Church . . . of St Martin-le-Grand* (London, 1825).

Kingsford, C. L. (ed.), *Chronicles of London* (Oxford, 1905).

English Historical Literature in the Fifteenth Century (Oxford, 1913).

The Song of Lewes (Oxford, 1890).

The Stonor Letters and Papers, 2 vols., Camden Soc., 3rd ser., XXIX–XXX (London, 1919).

Leadam, I. S., and Baldwin, J. F. (eds.), *Select Cases before the King's Council, 1243–1482*, Selden Soc., no. 35 (Cambridge, Mass., 1918).

Leland, J., *De Rebus Britannicis Collectanea*, ed. T. Hearne, 6 vols. (London, 1770).

Moisant, J. (ed.), *De Speculo Regis Edwardi III* (Paris, 1891).

Monro, C. (ed.), *Letters of Queen Margaret of Anjou . . .*, Camden Soc., old ser., no. LXXXVI, (London, 1863).

Myers, A. R., 'The Household of Queen Margaret of Anjou, 1452–3', *Bulletin of the John Rylands Library*, 40 (1957–8), pp. 79–113 and 391–431.

'A Parliamentary Debate of the Mid-Fifteenth Century', *Bulletin of the John Rylands Library*, 22 (1938), pp. 388–404.

'A Parliamentary Debate of 1449', *Bulletin of the Institute of Historical Research*, 51 (1978), pp. 78–83.

Nederman, C. J. (ed.), *John of Salisbury. Policraticus* (Cambridge, 1990).

Nichols, J., *A Collection of All the Wills . . . of the Kings and Queens of England*, Soc. of Antiquaries (London, 1780).

Nichols, J. G. (ed.), *The Boke of Noblesse*, Roxburghe Club (London, 1860).

Nicolas, N. H. (ed.), *A Journal by One of the Suite of Thomas Beckington . . .* (London, 1828).

Proceedings and Ordinances of the Privy Council of England, 7 vols., Record Com. (London, 1834–7).

Plummer, C. (ed.), *The Governance of England ... by Sir John Fortescue, Knight* (Oxford, 1885).

Pollard, A. F. (ed.), *The Reign of Henry VII from Contemporary Sources*, 3 vols. (London, 1913–14).

Rawcliffe, C., 'Richard Duke of York, the King's "Obeisant Liegeman": A New Source for the Protectorates of 1454 and 1455', *Bulletin of the Institute of Historical Research*, 60 (1987), pp. 232–9.

Report of the Deputy Keeper of the Public Records, XLVIII, HMSO (London, 1887).

Riley, H. T. (ed.), *Ingulph. Chronicle of the Abbey of Crowland* (London, 1854).

Registrum Abbatiae Johannis Whethamstede, 2 vols., Rolls ser. (London, 1872–3).

Robbins, R. H. (ed.), *Historical Poems of the XIVth and XVth Centuries* (New York, 1959).

Rogers, J. E. T. (ed.), *Thomas Gascoigne. Loci e Libro Veritatum* (Oxford, 1881).

Ross, C. (ed.), *The Rous Roll. John Rous* (Stroud, 1980)

Rotuli Parliamentorum, 6 vols., Record Com. (n.p., n.d.).

Rous, J., *Historia Regum Angliae*, ed. T. Hearne, 2nd edn (Oxford, 1745).

Rymer, T. (ed.), *Foedera, Conventiones, Literae ...*, 3rd edn, 10 vols. (The Hague, 1745).

Samaran, C. (ed.), *Thomas Basin. Histoire de Charles VII*, 2 vols. (Paris, 1933–44).

Searle, W. G. (ed.), 'Chronicle of John Stone', *Christ Church, Canterbury* pt I, (Cambridge, 1902).

Sharpe, R. R. (ed.), *Calendar of the Letter Books ... of the City of London. Letter Book I* (London, 1909).

Sheppard, J. B. (ed.), *Literae Cantuarienses: The Letter Books of the Monastery of Christ Church Canterbury*, 3 vols., Rolls ser. (London, 1887–9).

Stanley, A. P., *Historical Memorials of Westminster Abbey*, 3rd edn (London, 1869).

Stapleton, T. (ed.), *Plumpton Correspondence*, Camden Soc., old ser., IV (London, 1839).

Steele, R. R. (ed.), *Three Prose Versions of the Secreta Secretorum*, EETS, extra ser., no. 74 (London, 1898).

Stevenson, J. (ed.), *Letters and Papers Illustrative of the Wars of the English in France during the Reign of Henry VI*, 2 vols. in 3, Rolls ser. (London, 1861–4).

Strong, P., and Strong, F., 'The Last Will and Codicils of Henry V', *English Historical Review*, 96 (1981), pp. 79–102.

Thomas, A. H., and Thornley, I. D. (eds.), *The Great Chronicle of London* (London, 1938).

Thorne, S. E. (ed.), *Prerogativa Regis* (New Haven, 1949).

Todd, H. J., *Illustrations of the Lives and Writings of Gower and Chaucer* (London, 1810).

Whittaker, W. J. (ed.), *The Mirror of Justices*, Selden Soc., no. 7 (London, 1895).

Williams, G. (ed.), *Official Correspondence of Thomas Bekynton*, 2 vols., Rolls ser. (London, 1872).

Wright, T. (ed.), *Political Poems and Songs*, 2 vols., Rolls ser. (London, 1859–61).

SECONDARY SOURCES

Acheson, E., 1992, *A Gentry Community: Leicestershire in the Fifteenth Century, c.1422–c.1485*, Cambridge.

Adams, S., 1984, 'Eliza Enthroned? The Court and its Politics', in C. Haigh (ed.), *The Reign of Elizabeth I*, Basingstoke/London, pp. 55–77.

Allan, A. R., 1981, 'Political Propaganda Employed by the House of York in England in the Mid-Fifteenth Century, 1450–71', unpubl. PhD thesis, Wales at Swansea.

Allmand, C. T., 1967, 'The Anglo-French Negotiations, 1439', *Bulletin of the Institute of Historical Research*, 40, pp. 1–33.

    1983, *Lancastrian Normandy, 1415–50*, Oxford.

Archer, R. E., 1984a, 'The Mowbrays: Earls of Nottingham and Dukes of Norfolk, to 1432', unpubl. DPhil thesis, Oxford.

    1984b, 'Rich Old Ladies: The Problem of Late Medieval Dowagers', in Pollard (ed.) 1984: pp. 15–35.

Armstrong, C. A. J., 1960, 'Politics and the Battle of St Albans', *Bulletin of the Institute of Historical Research*, 33, pp. 1–72.

Arnold, C. E., 1984, 'A Political Study of the West Riding of Yorkshire, 1437–1509', unpubl. PhD thesis, Manchester.

Asch, R. G., 1991, 'Introduction: Court and Household from the Fifteenth to the Seventeenth Centuries', in *idem* and Birke, A. M. (eds.), *Princes, Patronage and the Nobility: The Court at the Beginning of the Modern Age, c.1450–1650*, Oxford, ch. 1.

Avrutick, J. B., 1967, 'Commissions of Oyer and Terminer in Fifteenth Century England', unpubl. MPhil thesis, London.

Bailey, F. G., 1965, 'Decisions by Consensus in Councils and Committees', in *Political Systems and the Distribution of Power*, A. S. A. Monographs ser., 2, London, pp. 1–20.

Baldwin, J. F., 1913, *The King's Council in England During the Middle Ages*, Oxford.

Barnie, J., 1974, *War in Medieval Society*, London.

Barron, C. M., 1981, 'London and the Crown, 1451–61', in Highfield and Jeffs (eds.) 1981: pp. 88–109.

    1985, 'The Art of Kingship – Richard II', *History Today*, 35 (June), pp. 30–7.

    1990, 'The Deposition of Richard II', in J. Taylor and W. Childs (eds.), *Politics and Crisis in Fourteenth-Century England*, Gloucester, pp. 132–49.

Bean, J. M. W., 1958, *The Estates of the Percy Family, 1416–1537*, Oxford.

    1984, 'The Financial Position of Richard, Duke of York', in J. Gillingham and J. C. Holt (eds.), *War and Government in the Middle Ages*, pp. 182–98.

Beaucourt, G. L. E. du F. de, 1881–91, *Histoire de Charles VII*, 6 vols., Paris.

Bellamy, J. G., 1970, *The Law of Treason in England in the Later Middle Ages*, Cambridge.

Bennett, H. S., 1946–7, 'The Production and Dissemination of Vernacular Manuscripts in the Fifteenth Century', *The Library*, 5th ser., 1, pp. 167–78.

Bennett, M. J., 1983, *Community, Class and Careerism: Cheshire and Lancashire Society in the Age of 'Sir Gawain and the Green Knight'*, Cambridge.

Black, A. J., 1970, *Monarchy and Community*, Cambridge.

Born, L. K., 1928, 'The Perfect Prince: A Study in Thirteenth- and Fourteenth-Century Ideals', *Speculum*, 3, pp. 470–504.

Brown, A. L., 1954, 'The Privy Seal in the Early Fifteenth Century', unpubl. DPhil thesis, Oxford.

 1964a, 'The Authorization of Letters under the Great Seal', *Bulletin of the Institute of Historical Research*, 37, pp. 125–56.

 1964b, 'The Commons and the Council in the Reign of Henry IV', *English Historical Review*, 79, pp. 1–30.

 1969a, *The Early History of the Clerkship of the Council*, Glasgow.

 1969b, 'The King's Councillors in Fifteenth-Century England', *Transactions of the Royal Historical Society*, 5th ser., 19, pp. 95–118.

 1981, 'Parliament, *c.* 1377–1422', in Davies and Denton (eds.) 1981, ch. 5.

 1989, *The Governance of Late Medieval England, 1272–1461*, London.

Burns, J. H., 1985, 'Fortescue and the Political Theory of Dominium', *Historical Journal*, 28, pp. 777–97.

Burrow, J. W., 1981, *A Liberal Descent*, Cambridge.

Cam, H. M., 1962a, *Law-Finders and Law-Makers in Medieval England*, London.

 1962b, 'The Theory and Practice of Representation in Medieval England', in Cam 1962a: ch. IX.

Campbell, J., 1988, *Stubbs and the English State*, Stenton Lecture no. 21, Reading.

Carey, H. M., 1992, *Courting Disaster: Astrology at the English Court and University in the Later Middle Ages*, London.

Carpenter, C., 1980, 'The Beauchamp Affinity: A Study of Bastard Feudalism at Work', *English Historical Review*, 95, pp. 515–32.

 1983a, 'Fifteenth-Century English Politics', *Historical Journal*, 26, pp. 963–7.

 1983b, 'Law, Justice and Landowners in Late Medieval England', *Law and History Review*, 1, pp. 205–37.

 1992, *Locality and Polity: A Study of Warwickshire Landed Society, 1401–99*, Cambridge.

Carpenter, D. A., 1990, *The Minority of Henry III*, London.

Castor, H. R., 1993, 'The Duchy of Lancaster in the Lancastrian Polity, 1399–1461', unpublished PhD thesis, Cambridge.

 1995, 'New Evidence on the Grant of Duchy of Lancaster Office to Henry Beauchamp, Earl of Warwick, in 1444', *Hisorical Research*, 68, pp. 225–8.

Catto, J., 1985a, 'The King's Servants', in Harriss (ed.) 1985: ch. IV.

 1985b, 'Religious Change under Henry V', in Harriss (ed.) 1985: ch. V.

Champion, P., 1911, *Vie de Charles d'Orléans*, Paris.

Cherry, M., 1979, 'The Courtenay Earls of Devon: The Formation and Disintegration of a Late Medieval Aristocratic Affinity', *Southern History*, 1, pp. 71–97.

 1981a, 'The Struggle for Power in Mid-Fifteenth-Century Devonshire', in Griffiths (ed.) 1981: pp. 123–44.

 1981b, 'The Crown and the Political Community in Devonshire, 1377–1461', unpubl. PhD thesis, Wales at Swansea.

Chrimes, S. B., 1936, *English Constitutional Ideas in the Fifteenth Century*, Cambridge.

1956, 'Richard II's Questions to the Judges, 1387', *Law Quarterly Review*, 72, pp. 365–90.

1963, 'The Fifteenth Century', *History*, 48, pp. 18–27.

1964, *Lancastrians, Yorkists and Henry VII*, London.

1972, *Henry VII*, London.

Chrimes, S. B., Ross, C. D., and Griffiths, R. A. (eds.), 1972, *Fifteenth Century England*, Manchester.

Clanchy, M. T., 1974, 'Law, Government and Society in Medieval England', *History*, 59, pp. 73–8.

1983a, 'Law and Love in the Middle Ages', in J. A. Bossy (ed.), *Disputes and Settlements*, Cambridge, pp. 47–67.

1983b, *England and its Rulers, 1066–1272*, Oxford.

Clarke, M. V., 1936, *Medieval Representation and Consent*, London.

Clayton, D. J., Davies, R. G., and McNiven, P. (eds.), 1994, *Trade, Devotion and Governance: Papers in Later Medieval History*, Stroud.

Cokayne, G. E., 1910–40, *The Complete Peerage*, ed. H. V. Gibbs, *et al.*, 13 vols., London.

Condon, M. M., 1979, 'Ruling Elites in the Reign of Henry VII', in Ross (ed.) 1979: pp. 109–42.

1986, 'An Anachronism with Intent? Henry VII's Council Ordinance of 1491/2', in Griffiths (ed.) 1986: pp. 228–53.

Coss, P. R., 1989, 'Bastard Feudalism Revised', *Past and Present*, 125, pp. 27–64.

Crawford, A., 1981, 'The King's Burden?: The Consequences of Royal Marriage in Fifteenth-Century England', in Griffiths (ed.) 1981: pp. 33–56.

Crowder, C. M. D., 1986, 'Peace and Justice around 1400: A Sketch', in Rowe (ed.) 1986: pp. 53–81.

Davies, R. G., 1974, 'The Episcopate in England and Wales, 1375–1443', unpubl. PhD thesis, Manchester.

Davies, R. G. and Denton, J. H. (eds.), 1981, *The English Parliament in the Middle Ages*, Manchester.

Davis, V., 1987, 'William Waynflete and the Educational Revolution of the Fifteenth Century', in J. T. Rosenthal and C. F. Richmond (eds.), *People, Politics and Community in the Later Middle Ages*, Gloucester, pp. 40–59.

Doe, N., 1990, *Fundamental Authority in Late Medieval English Law*, Cambridge.

Doyle, A. I., 1983, 'English Books In and Out of Court from Edward III to Henry VII', in Scattergood and Sherborne (eds.) 1983: pp. 163–81.

Duby, G., 1973, 'Les Origines de la Chevalerie', in *idem*, *Hommes et Structures*, Paris, ch. XIX.

Dunbabin, J., 1988, 'Government', in J. H. Burns (ed.), *Cambridge History of Medieval Political Thought*, Cambridge, ch. 16.

Dunlop, A. I., 1950, *The Life and Times of James Kennedy, Bishop of St Andrews*, Edinburgh.

Edward, A. S. G., 1977, 'The Influence of Lydgate's Fall of Princes, c.1440–1559: A Survey', *Medieval Studies*, 39, pp. 424–39.

Edwards, J. G., 1964, 'The Emergence of Majority Rule in English Parliamentary Elections', *Transactions of the Royal Historical Society*, 5th ser., 14, pp. 175–96.

1970, 'The *Plena Potestas* of English Parliamentary Representatives', in E. B. Fryde and E. Miller, *Historical Studies of the English Parliament*, I, Cambridge.

Elder, A. J., 1964, 'A Study in the Beauforts and their Estates, 1399–1450', unpubl. PhD thesis, Bryn Mawr.

Elton, G. R., 1958, 'Henry VII: Rapacity and Remorse?', *Historical Journal*, 1, 1, pp. 21–39.

1983, 'Tudor Government: The Points of Contact. III. The Court', in *idem*, *Studies in Tudor and Stuart Politics and Government*, III, Cambridge, pp. 38–57.

Emden, A. B., 1957–9, *A Biographical Register of the University of Oxford to A.D. 1500*, 3 vols., Oxford.

Ferguson, A. B., 1960, *The Indian Summer of English Chivalry*, Durham, NC.

1965, *The Articulate Citizen and the English Renaissance*, Durham, NC.

Ferguson, J. T., 1972, *English Diplomacy, 1422–61*, Oxford.

Fryde, E. B., *et al.* (eds.), 1986, *Handbook of British Chronology*, 3rd edn, London.

Genet, J. P., 1981, 'Political Theory and Local Communities in Later Medieval France and England', in Highfield and Jeffs (eds.), 1981: pp. 19–32.

Gillespie, J. L., 1979, 'Sir John Fortescue's Concept of Royal Will', *Nottingham Mediaeval Studies*, 23, pp. 47–65.

Gillingham, J., 1981, *The Wars of the Roses*, London.

1987, 'Crisis or Continuity? The Structure of Royal Authority in England, 1369–1422', in R. Schneider (ed.), *Das Spatmittelalterliche Konigtum im Europaischen Vergleich*, Vortrage & Forschungen ser., XXXII, Sigmaringen, pp. 59–80.

1988, 'War and Chivalry in the History of William the Marshal', in P. R. Coss and S. D. Lloyd (eds.), *Thirteenth Century England II*, Woodbridge, pp. 1–13.

Given-Wilson, C., 1986, *The Royal Household and the King's Affinity*, New Haven.

1987a, *The English Nobility in the Later Middle Ages*, London.

1987b, 'The King and the Gentry in Fourteenth-Century England', *Transactions of the Royal Historical Society*, 5th ser., 37, pp. 87–102.

Goodman, A., 1981, *The Wars of the Roses*, London.

1986, 'John of Gaunt', in W. M. Ormrod (ed.), *England in the Fourteenth Century*, Woodbridge, pp. 67–87.

1988, *The New Monarchy. England 1471–1534*, Oxford.

1992, *John of Gaunt*, Harlow.

Gransden, A., 1982, *Historical Writing in England: c. 1307 to the Early Sixteenth Century*, London.

Green, J. A., 1986, *The Government of England under Henry I*, Cambridge.

Green, R. F., 1980, *Poets and Princepleasers*, Toronto.

Griffith, M. C., 1940–1, 'The Talbot–Ormond Struggle for Control of the Anglo-Irish Government, 1414–47', *Irish Historical Studies*, 2, pp. 376–97.

Griffiths, R. A., 1981, *The Reign of King Henry VI*, London.

1991a, *King and Country. England and Wales in the Fifteenth Century*, London.

1991b, 'The King's Court during the Wars of the Roses: Continuities in an Age of Discontinuities', in Griffiths 1991a: pp. 11–32.

1991c, 'Patronage, Politics and the Principality of Wales, 1413–61', in Griffiths 1991a: pp. 161–78.

1991d, 'Gruffydd ap Nicholas and the Rise of the House of Dinefwr', in Griffiths 1991a: pp. 187–99.

1991e, 'Duke Richard of York's Intentions in 1450 and the Origins of the Wars of the Roses', in Griffiths 1991a: pp. 277–304.

1991f, 'Local Rivalries and National Politics: The Percies, the Nevilles and the Duke of Exeter, 1452–55', in Griffiths 1991a: pp. 321–64.

1991g, 'Public and Private Bureaucracies in England and Wales in the Fifteenth Century', in Griffiths 1991a: pp. 137–59.

1991h, 'Richard of York and the Royal Household in Wales, 1449–1450', in Griffiths 1991a: pp. 265–76.

1991i, 'The Sense of Dynasty in the Reign of Henry VI', in Griffiths 1991a: pp. 83–101.

1991j, 'The Trial of Eleanor Cobham: An Episode in the Fall of Duke Humphrey of Gloucester', in Griffiths 1991a: pp. 233–52.

1991k, 'Gruffydd ap Nicholas and the Fall of the House of Lancaster', in Griffiths 1991a: pp. 201–19.

Griffiths, R. A. (ed.), 1981, *Patronage, the Crown and the Provinces*, Gloucester.

1986, *Kings and Nobles in the Later Middle Ages*, Gloucester.

Guenée, B., 1971, 'The History of the State in France at the End of the Middle Ages, as Seen by French Historians in the Last Hundred Years', in P. Lewis (ed.), *The Recovery of France in the Fifteenth Century*, London and Basingstoke.

Guth, D. J., 1977, 'Fifteenth-Century England: Recent Scholarship and Future Directions', *British Studies Monitor*, 7.2, pp. 3–50.

Guy, J. A., 1986, 'The King's Council and Political Participation', in *idem* and A. Fox *Reassessing the Henrician Age*, Oxford, pp. 121–47.

1988, *Tudor England*, Oxford.

Haines, R. M., 1976, 'A Contemporary Preacher's View of King Henry V', *Medieval Studies*, 38, pp. 85–96.

Hanson, D. W., 1970, *From Kingdom to Commonwealth*, Cambridge, MA.

Harcourt, L. W. V., 1907, *His Grace the Steward and Trial of Peers*, London.

Harding, A., 1973, *The Law Courts of Medieval England*, London.

Harriss, G. L., 1953, 'The Finance of the Royal Household, 1437–60', unpubl. DPhil thesis, Oxford.

1960, 'The Struggle for Calais: An Aspect of the Rivalry Between Lancaster and York', *English Historical Review*, 75, pp. 30–53.

1975, *King, Parliament and Public Finance in Medieval England to 1369*, Oxford.

1981, Introduction to McFarlane 1981a.

1982, review of Wolffe 1981, *English Historical Review*, 97, pp. 840–2.

1985a, 'Introduction: The Exemplar of Kingship', in Harriss (ed.) 1985: ch. I.

1985b, 'The King and his Magnates', in Harriss (ed.) 1985: ch. II.

1986, 'Marmaduke Lumley and the Exchequer Crisis of 1446–9', in Rowe (ed.) 1986, pp. 143–78.

1988, *Cardinal Beaufort: A Study of Lancastrian Ascendancy and Decline*, Oxford.

1993, 'Political Society and the Growth of Government in Late Medieval England', *Past and Present*, no. 138, pp. 28–57.

Harriss, G. L. (ed.), 1985, *Henry V: The Practice of Kingship*, Oxford.

Harvey, I. M. W., 1991, *Jack Cade's Rebellion of 1450*, Oxford.

Hexter, J. H., 1967, 'Claude de Seyssel and Normal Politics in the Age of Machiavelli', in C. S. Singleton (ed.), *Art, Science and History in the Renaissance*, Baltimore, pp. 389–415.

Hicks, M. A., 1991a, *Richard III and his Rivals*, London.

1991b, 'Idealism in Late Medieval English Politics', in Hicks 1991a: pp. 41–59.

1991c, 'Bastard Feudalism: Society and Politics in Fifteenth-Century England', in Hicks 1991a: pp. 1–40.

1991d, 'Attainder, Resumption and Coercion, 1461–1509', in Hicks 1991a: pp. 61–77.

1991e, 'Chantries, Obits and Almshouses: The Hungerford Foundations, 1325–1478', in Hicks 1991a: pp. 79–98.

Highfield, J. R. L., and Jeffs, R. M. (eds.), 1981, *The Crown and the Local Communities*, Gloucester.

Holmes, G., 1975, *The Good Parliament*, Oxford.

Holt, J. C., 1960–1, 'Rights and Liberties in Magna Carta', in C. Robbins (ed.), *Album H. M. Cam*, 2 vols., Louvain, I, pp. 57–69.

1963, *King John*, Historical Association pamphlet, London.

1981, 'The Prehistory of Parliament', in Davies and Denton (eds.) 1981, pp. 1–28.

1985, *Magna Carta and Medieval Government*, London.

Horrox, R., 1989, *Richard III: A Study of Service*, Cambridge.

1992, 'Local and National Politics in Fifteenth-Century England', *Journal of Medieval History*, 18, pp. 391–403.

Huizinga, J., 1960, 'The Political and Military Significance of Chivalric Ideas in the Late Middle Ages', in *idem, Men and Ideas*, tr. J. S. Holmes and H. van Marle, London, pp. 196–206.

Ives, E. W., 1983, *The Common Lawyers of Pre-Reformation England*, Cambridge.

Jack, R. I., 1960, 'A Quincentenary: The Battle of Northampton, July 10th 1460', *Northamptonshire Past and Present*, 3, pp. 21–5.

Jacob, E. F., 1953, *Essays in the Conciliar Epoch*, 2nd edn, Manchester.

1962, 'Archbishop John Stafford', *Transactions of the Royal Historical Society*, 5th ser., 12, pp. 1–23.

1967, *Archbishop Henry Chichele*, London.

1968, 'Founders and Foundations in the Later Middle Ages', in *idem, Essays in Later Medieval History*, Manchester, ch. VIII.

Jalland, P., 1972, 'The Influence of the Aristocracy on Shire Elections in the North of England', *Speculum*, 47, pp. 483–507.

James, L. E., 1979, 'The Career and Political Influence of William de la Pole, First Duke of Suffolk, 1437–50', unpubl. BLitt thesis, Oxford.

James, M., 1978, *English Politics and the Concept of Honour, 1485–1642*, Past and Present Supplements, no. III.

Jeffs, R. M., 1960, 'The Later Medieval Sheriff and the Royal Household', unpubl. DPhil thesis, Oxford.

Johnson, P. A., 1981, 'The Political Career of Richard, Duke of York, to 1456', unpubl. DPhil thesis, Oxford.

1988, *Duke Richard of York, 1411–60*, Oxford.

Jolliffe, J. E. A., 1955, *Angevin Kingship*, London.

Jones, M. K., 1981, 'John Beaufort, Duke of Somerset, and the French Expedition of 1443', in Griffiths (ed.) 1981: pp. 79–102.

1982, 'The Beaufort Family and the War in France, 1421–50', unpubl. PhD thesis, Bristol.

1989a, 'Somerset, York and the Wars of the Roses', *English Historical Review*, 104, pp. 285–307.

1989b, 'War on the Frontier: The Lancastrian Land Settlement in Eastern Normandy', *Nottingham Medieval Studies*, 33, pp. 104–21.

Joubert, A., 1880, 'Les Négociations Relatives à l'Evacuation du Maine par les Anglais (1444–8)...', *Revue Historique et Archéologique du Maine*, 8, pp. 221–40.

Judd, A., 1961, *The Life of Thomas Beckynton*, Chichester.

Kaeuper, R. W., 1988, *War, Justice and Public Order: England and France in the Later Middle Ages*, Oxford.

Kaminsky, H., and Van Horn Melton, J., 1992, introduction to O. Brunner, *Land and Lordship. Structures of Governance in Medieval Austria*, Philadelphia, PA.

Kantororwicz, E. H., 1957, *The King's Two Bodies: A Study in Medieval Political Theology*, Princeton.

Keen, M. H., 1962, 'Brotherhood in Arms', *History*, 47, pp. 1–17.

1973, *England in the Later Middle Ages*, London.

1984, *Chivalry*, New Haven.

1989, 'The End of the Hundred Years War: Lancastrian France and Lancastrian England', in M. Jones and M. Vale (eds.), *England and her Neighbours, 1066–1453. Essays in Honour of Pierre Chaplais*, London, pp. 297–311.

Keen, M. H., and Daniel, M. J., 1974, 'English Diplomacy and the Sack of Fougères in 1449', *History*, 59, pp. 375–91.

Kekewich, M. L., 1982, 'The Attainder of the Yorkists in 1459: Two Contemporary Accounts', *Bulletin of the Institute of Historical Research*, 55, pp. 25–34.

1987, 'Books of Advice for Princes in Fifteenth-Century England, with Particular Reference to the Period 1450–1485', unpubl. PhD thesis, Open University.

Kennedy, E., 1988, 'The Quest for Identity and the Importance of Lineage in Thirteenth-Century French Prose Romance', in C. Harper-Bill and R. Harvey (eds.), *The Ideals and Practice of Medieval Knighthood*, Woodbridge, pp. 70–86.

Kern, F., 1939, *Kingship and the Law in the Middle Ages*, tr. S. B. Chrimes, Oxford.

Kingsford, C. L., 1925, 'The Policy and Fall of Suffolk', in *idem*, *Prejudice and Promise in Fifteenth Century England*, Oxford, ch. VI.

Knoop, D., and Jones, G. P., 1933, 'The Building of Eton College, 1442–1460', *Transactions of the Quatuor Coronati Lodge, London*, 46, pp. 70–114.

Laffan, R. G. D., 1959, article on Queens' College, in *VCH, Cambs.*, III, pp. 408–15.

Lander, J. R., 1958, 'The Yorkist Council and Administration, 1461–85', *English Historical Review*, 73, pp. 27–46.

1960–1, 'Henry VI and the Duke of York's Second Protectorate, 1455–6', *Bulletin of the John Rylands Library*, 43, pp. 46–69.

1969, *Conflict and Stability in Fifteenth Century England*, London.

1989, *The Limitations of English Monarchy in the Later Middle Ages*, Toronto.

Lawton, D., 1987, 'Dullness and the Fifteenth Century', *English Literary History*, 54, pp. 761–99.

Leach, A. F., 1908, 'Schools', in *VCH Bucks.*, II, pp. 145–221.

Leader, D. R., 1988, *A History of the University of Cambridge*, I, Cambridge.

Leguai, A., 1967, 'Les "Etats" Princiers en France à la Fin du Moyen Age', *Annali della Fondazione Italiana per la Storia Amministrativa*, 4, pp. 133–57.

Lewis, P. S., 1968, *Later Medieval France: The Polity*, London.

1985a, *Essays in Late Medieval French History*, London.

1985b, 'Sir John Fastolf's dispute over Titchwell, 1448–55', in Lewis 1985a: pp. 215–34.

1985c, 'Two Pieces of Fifteenth-Century Political Iconography', in Lewis 1985a: pp. 188–92.

Lovatt, R., 1981, 'John Blacman: Biographer of Henry VI', in R. H. C. Davis and J. M. Wallace-Hadrill (eds.), *The Writing of History in the Middle Ages...*, Oxford, pp. 415–44.

1984, 'A Collector of Apocryphal Anecdotes: John Blacman Revisited', in Pollard (ed.) 1984: pp. 172–97.

McCulloch, D., and Jones, E. D., 1983, 'Lancastrian Politics, the French War, and the Rise of the Popular Element', *Speculum*, 58, pp. 95–138.

McFarlane, K. B., 1936, 'The Lancastrian Kings', in *Cambridge Medieval History*, VIII, Cambridge, ch. 11.

1938, review of Chrimes 1936 in *English Historical Review*, 53, pp. 707–10.

1972, *Lancastrian Kings and Lollard Knights*, Oxford.

1973, *The Nobility of Later Medieval England*, Oxford.

1981a, *England in the Fifteenth Century*, Oxford.

1981b, 'At the Deathbed of Cardinal Beaufort', in McFarlane 1981a: ch. VI.

1981c, ' "Bastard Feudalism" ', in McFarlane 1981a: ch. II.

1981d, 'Henry V, Bishop Beaufort and the Red Hat, 1417–21', in McFarlane 1981a: ch. V.

1981e, 'Parliament and "Bastard Feudalism" ', in McFarlane 1981a: ch. I.

1981f, 'The Wars of the Roses', in McFarlane 1981a: ch. XII.

1981g, 'William Worcester: A Preliminary Survey', in McFarlane 1981a: ch. X.

McKenna, J. W., 1974, 'Piety and Propaganda: The Cult of Henry VI', in B. Rowland (ed.), *Chaucer and Middle English Studies*, London, pp. 72–88.

1979, 'The Myth of Parliamentary Sovereignty in Late Medieval England', *English Historical Review*, 94, pp. 481–506.

McKisack, M., 1959, *The Fourteenth Century*, Oxford.

Maddern, P. C., 1992, *Violence and Social Order. East Anglia 1422–1442*, Oxford.

Maddicott, J. R., 1981, 'Parliament and the Constituencies, 1272–1377', in Davies and Denton (eds.) 1981: ch. 3.

Maitland, F. W., 1911, 'The Corporation Sole', in H. A. L. Fisher (ed.), *The Collected Papers of Frederic William Maitland...*, 3 vols., III, Cambridge, pp. 210–43.

Martin, C., 1951, 'Some Medieval Commentaries on Aristotle's *Politics*', *History*, 36, pp. 29–44.

Mathew, G., 1948, 'Ideals of Knighthood in Late Fourteenth-Century England', in R. W. Hunt *et al.*, *Studies in Medieval History Presented to F. M. Powicke*, Oxford, pp. 354–62.

Maxwell-Lyte, H. C., 1899, *A History of Eton College*, 3rd edn, London.

1926, *Historical Notes on the Use of the Great Seal of England*, HMSO, London.

Meekings, C. A., 1975, 'Thomas Kerver's Case, 1444', *English Historical Review*, 90, pp. 331–46.

Mitchell, R. J., 1938, *John Tiptoft*, London.

Moore, S., 1912, 'Patrons of Letters in Norfolk and Suffolk, *c.* 1450', *Proceedings of the Modern Languages Association of America*, 27, pp. 188–207.

Morgan, D. A. L., 1973, 'The King's Affinity in the Polity of Yorkist England', *Transactions of the Royal Historical Society*, 5th ser., 23, pp. 1–25.

1987, 'The House of Policy: The Political Role of the Late Plantagenet Household, 1422–85', in Starkey *et al.* 1987, pp. 25–70.

Morris, C., 1972, *The Discovery of the Individual*, New York.

Murray, A., 1978, *Reason and Society in the Middle Ages*, Oxford.

Myers, A. R., 1959, *The Household of Edward IV*, Manchester.

Nederman, C. J., 1984, 'Bracton on Kingship Revisited', *History of Political Thought*, 5, pp. 61–77.

Nicholson, R., 1965, *Edward III and the Scots, 1327–35*, Oxford.

Oakley, F., 1968, 'Jacobean Political Theology: The Absolute and Ordinary Powers of the King', *Journal of the History of Ideas*, 29, pp. 323–46.

1973, 'Celestial Hierarchies Revisited: Walter Ullmann's Vision of Medieval Politics', *Past and Present*, 60, pp. 3–48.

Orme, N., 1984, *From Childhood to Chivalry*, London.

Ormrod, W. M., 1985, 'Edward III and the Recovery of Royal Authority in England, 1340–60', *History*, 72, pp. 4–19.

1990, *The Reign of Edward III*, New Haven and London.

Osberg, R., 1986, 'The Jesse Tree in the 1432 London Entry of Henry VI: Messianic Kingship and the Rule of Justice', *Journal of Medieval and Renaissance Studies*, 16, pp. 213–31.

Otway-Ruthven, A. J., 1939, *The King's Secretary and the Signet Office in the Fifteenth Century*, Cambridge.

Palmer, J. J. N., 1971 'The War Aims of the Protagonists and the Negotiations for Peace', in K. A. Fowler (ed.), *The Hundred Years War*, London, pp. 51–74.

Passingham, W. J., 1937, *A History of the Coronation*, London.

Payling, S. J., 1987, 'The Coventry Parliament of 1459: A Privy Seal Writ concerning the Election of the Knights of the Shire', *Historical Research*, 60, pp. 349–52.

1989, 'The Ampthill Dispute: A Study in Aristocratic Lawlessness and the Breakdown of Lancastrian Government', *English Historical Review*, 104, pp. 881–907.

1991, *Political Society in Lancastrian England*, Oxford.

Peters, E., 1970, *The Shadow King: Rex Inutilis* in Medieval Law and Literature, New Haven and London.

Petit-Dutaillis, C., and Lefebvre, G. (eds.), 1919, *Studies and Notes Supplementary to Stubbs' Constitutional History*, III, Manchester.

Plucknett, T. F. T., 1918, 'The Place of the Council in the Fifteenth Century', *Transactions of the Royal Historical Society*, 4th ser., 1, pp. 157–89.

1924, 'The Lancastrian Constitution', in R. W. Seton-Watson (ed.), *Tudor Studies Presented to A. F. Pollard*, London, pp. 161–81.

Pochoda, E. T., 1971, *Arthurian Propaganda: Le Morte Darthur as an Historical Ideal of Life*, Chapel Hill, NC.

Pocock, J. G. A., 1967, *The Ancient Constitution and the Feudal Law*, Cambridge.

1972, 'Languages and their Implications', in *idem, Politics, Language and Time*, London, ch. 1.

1973, 'Verbalising a Political Act: Toward a Politics of Speech', *Political Theory*, 1, pp. 27–45.

1975, *The Machiavellian Moment*, Princeton.

Pollard, A. J., 1968, 'The Family of Talbot, Lords Talbot and Earls of Shrewsbury in the Fifteenth Century', unpubl. PhD thesis, Bristol.

1976, 'The Northern Retainers of Richard Nevill, Earl of Salisbury', *Northern History*, 11, pp. 52–69.

1979, 'The Richmondshire Community of Gentry during the Wars of the Roses', in Ross (ed.) 1979: pp. 37–59.

1983, *John Talbot and the War in France, 1427–1453*, London.

1988, *The Wars of the Roses*, London.

1990, *North-Eastern England during the Wars of the Roses*, Oxford.

Pollard, A. J. (ed.), 1984, *Property and Politics*, Gloucester.

Post, G., 1964a, 'Status Regis', in W. M. Bowsky (ed.), *Studies in Medieval and Renaissance History*, I, Lincoln, Nebraska, pp. 1–103.

1964b, review of Wilks 1963, in *Speculum*, 39, pp. 365–72.

Postan, M. M., 1933, 'The Economic and Political Relations of England and the Hanse, from 1400 to 1475', in *idem* and E. Power (eds.), *Studies in English Trade in the Fifteenth Century*, London, pp. 91–153.

Powell, E., 1984, 'Settlement of Disputes by Arbitration in Fifteenth-Century England', *Law and History Review*, 2, pp. 21–43.

1989, *Kingship, Law and Society: Criminal Justice in the Reign of Henry V*, Oxford.

1994, 'After "After McFarlane": The Poverty of Patronage and the Case for Constitutional History', in Clayton *et al.* (eds.) 1994: pp. 1–16.

Powicke, F. M., 1936, 'Reflections on the Medieval State', *Transactions of the Royal Historical Society*, 4th ser., 19, pp. 1–18.

Pugh, T. B., 1972, 'The Magnates, Knights and Gentry', in Chrimes, Ross and Griffiths (eds.) 1972: pp. 86–128.

1986a, 'Richard Plantagenet (1411–60), Duke of York, as the King's Lieutenant in France and Ireland', in Rowe (ed.) 1986: pp. 107–41.

1986b, 'The Southampton Plot', in Griffiths (ed.) 1986: pp. 62–89.

Pugh, T. B. (ed.), 1971, *Glamorgan County History*, III, Cardiff.

Quillet, J., 1988, 'Community, Counsel and Representation', in J. H. Burns (ed.), *Cambridge History of Medieval Political Thought*, Cambridge, ch. 17, pt I.

Ramsay, J. H., 1892, *Lancaster and York. A Century of English History*, 2 vols., Oxford.

Ramsay, N., 1985, 'Retained Legal Counsel, *c*.1275–*c*.1475', *Transactions of the Royal Historical Society*, 5th ser., 35, pp. 95–112.

Rawcliffe, C., 1978, *The Staffords, Earls of Stafford and Dukes of Buckingham, 1394–1521*, Cambridge.

Rawcliffe, C., and Flower, S., 1986, 'English Noblemen and their Advisers: Consultation and Collaboration in the Later Middle Ages', *Journal of British Studies*, 25, pp. 157–77.

Reynolds, S., 1984, *Kingdoms and Communities in Western Europe, 900–1300*, Oxford.

Richardson, H. G., 1941, 'The English Coronation Oath', *Transactions of the Royal Historical Society*, 4th ser., 23, pp. 129–58.

Richmond, C. F., 1977, 'The Nobility and the Wars of the Roses, 1459–61', *Nottingham Mediaeval Studies*, 21, pp. 71–85.

1983, 'After McFarlane', *History*, 68, pp. 46–60.

1990, *The Paston Family in the Fifteenth Century*, Cambridge.

Rosenthal, J. T., 1965, 'The Estates and Finances of Richard, Duke of York, 1411–60', in W. M. Bowsky (ed.), *Studies in Medieval and Renaissance History*, II, Lincoln, NB, pp. 117–204.

1967, 'The King's "Wicked Advisers" and Medieval Baronial Rebellions', *Political Science Quarterly*, 82, pp. 595–618.

1987, 'Kings, Continuity and Ecclesiastical Benefaction in Fifteenth-Century England', in *idem* and C. F. Richmond (eds.), *People, Politics and Community in the Later Middle Ages*, Gloucester, pp. 161–75.

Roskell, J. S., 1953, 'The Office and Dignity of Protector of England, with Special Reference to its Origins', *English Historical Review*, 68, pp. 193–233.

1954, *The Commons in the Parliament of 1422*, Manchester.

1956, 'The Problem of the Attendance of the Lords in Late Medieval Parliaments', *Bulletin of the Institute of Historical Research*, 29, pp. 153–204.

1963–4, 'Perspectives in English Parliamentary History', *Bulletin of the John Rylands Library*, 46, pp. 448–75.

1965, *The Commons and their Speakers in English Parliaments, 1376–1523*, Manchester.

1981–3, *Parliament and Politics in Late Medieval England*, 3 vols., London.

Ross, C. D., 1951, 'The Yorkshire Baronage, 1399–1435', unpubl. DPhil thesis, Oxford.

1974, *Edward IV*, London.

Ross, C. D. (ed.), 1979, *Patronage, Pedigree and Power*, Gloucester.

Rowe, B. J. H., 1934, 'The Grand Conseil Under the Duke of Bedford, 1422–35', in F. M. Powicke (ed.), *Oxford Essays in Medieval History Presented to H. E. Salter*, Oxford, pp. 207–34.

Rowe, J. G. (ed.), 1986, *Aspects of Late Medieval Government and Society: Essays Presented to J. R. Lander*, Toronto.

Rowney, I. D., 1981, 'The Staffordshire Political Community', unpubl. PhD thesis, Keele.

1983, 'Government and Patronage in the Fifteenth Century: Staffordshire 1439–59', *Midland History*, 8, pp. 49–69.

Russell, F. H., 1975, *The Just War in the Middle Ages*, Cambridge.

Saltmarsh, J., 1959, article on King's College in *VCH, Cambs.*, III, pp. 376–407.

Saul, N., 1981, *Knights and Esquires: The Gloucestershire Gentry in the Fourteenth Century*, Oxford.

1986, *Scenes from Provincial Life. Knightly Families in Sussex, 1280–1400*, Oxford.

Scattergood, V. J., 1971, *Politics and Poetry in the Fifteenth Century*, London.

1983, 'Literary Culture at the Court of Richard II', in Scattergood and Sherborne (eds.) 1983: pp. 29–43.

Scattergood, V. J., and Sherborne, J. W. (eds.), 1983, *English Court Culture in the Later Middle Ages*, London.

Schofield, A. N. E. D., 'England and the Council of Basel', *Annuarium Historiae Conciliorum*, 5, pt i, pp. 1–117.

Searle, E., and Burghart, R., 1972, 'The Defence of England and the Peasants' Revolt', *Viator*, 3, pp. 365–88.

Sharpe, R. R., 1894–5, *London and the Kingdom*, 3 vols., London.

Sinclair, A., 1987, 'The Great Berkeley Law Suit Revisited, 1417–39', *Southern History*, 9, pp. 34–50.

Skinner, Q., 1969, 'Meaning and Understanding in the History of Ideas', *History and Theory*, 8, pp. 3–53.

1974, 'The Principles and Practice of Opposition: The Case of Bolingbroke *vs* Walpole', in N. McKendrick (ed.), *Historical Perspectives: Studies in English Thought and Society*, London, pp. 93–128.

1978, *The Foundations of Modern Political Thought*, 2 vols., Cambridge.

1981, *Machiavelli*, Past Masters ser., Oxford.

1986, 'Ambrogio Lorenzetti: The Artist as Political Philosopher', *Proceedings of the British Academy*, 72, pp. 1–56.

1988, 'Some Problems in the Analysis of Political Thought and Action', in J. Tully (ed.), *Meaning and Context. Quentin Skinner and his Critics*, Cambridge, pp. 97–118.

Smith, A. R., 1982, 'Aspects of the Career of Sir John Fastolf (1380–1459)', unpubl. DPhil thesis, Oxford.

1984, 'Litigation and Politics: Sir John Fastolf's Defence of his English Property', in Pollard (ed.) 1984: pp. 59–75.

Somerville, R., 1953, *History of the Duchy of Lancaster*, 1 vol., I, London.

Stansfield, M. M. N., 1987, 'The Holland Family, Dukes of Exeter, Earls of Kent and Huntingdon, 1352–1475', unpubl. DPhil thesis, Oxford.

Starkey, D. R., 1973, 'The King's Privy Chamber, 1485–1547', unpubl. PhD thesis, Cambridge.

1981, 'The Age of the Household: Politics, Society and the Arts, *c.*1350–*c.*1550', in S. Medcalf (ed.), *The Later Middle Ages*, London, pp. 225–90.

1986, 'Which Age of Reform?', in *idem* and C. Coleman (eds.), *Revolution Reassessed*, Oxford, pp. 13–27.

1987a, 'Introduction: Court History in Perspective', in Starkey *et al.* 1987: ch. 1.

1987b, 'Intimacy and Innovation: the Rise of the Privy Chamber, 1485–1547', in Starkey *et al.* 1987: ch. 3.

Starkey, D. R., *et al.*, 1987, *The English Court*, Harlow.

Storey, R. L., 1957, 'The Wardens of the Marches of England towards Scotland, 1377–1489', *English Historical Review*, 72, pp. 593–615.

1966, *The End of the House of Lancaster*, London.

1970, 'Lincolnshire and the Wars of the Roses', *Nottingham Mediaeval Studies*, 14, pp. 64–83.

Stubbs, W., 1875–8, *The Constitutional History of England in its Origin and Development*, 2nd edn, 3 vols., Oxford.

Thielemans, M.-R., 1966, *Bourgogne et Angleterre*, Brussels.

Thomas, R. S., 1971, 'The Political Career, Estates and Connection of Jasper Tudor . . .', unpubl. PhD thesis, Wales at Swansea.

Tierney, B., 1963, 'Bracton on Government', *Speculum*, 38, pp. 295–317.

Tout, T. F., 1937, *Chapters in the Administrative History of Medieval England*, 6 vols., Manchester.

Tuck, A., 1973, *Richard II and the English Nobility*, London.

1985, *Crown and Nobility, 1272–1461*, London.

Twigg, J., 1987, *A History of Queens' College, Cambridge, 1448–1986*, Woodbridge.

Vale, J., 1982, *Edward III and Chivalry*, Woodbridge.

Vale, M. G. A., 1974, *Charles VII*, London.

1981, *War and Chivalry*, London.

Vanderjagt, A., 1981, *'Qui sa Vertu Anoblist': The Concepts of Noblesse and Chose Publicque in Burgundian Political Thought*, Groningen.

Vaughan, R., 1970, *Philip the Good*, London.

Vickers, K. H., 1907, *Humphrey, Duke of Gloucester*, London.

Virgoe, R., 1964–5, 'The Death of William de la Pole, Duke of Suffolk', *Bulletin of the John Rylands Library*, 47, pp. 489–502.

1970, 'The Composition of the King's Council, 1437–61', *Bulletin of the Institute of Historical Research*, 43, pp. 134–60.

1972–3, 'William Tailboys and Lord Cromwell: Crime and Politics in Lancastrian England', *Bulletin of the John Rylands Library*, 55, pp. 459–82.

1973, 'The Cambridgeshire Election of 1439', *Bulletin of the Institute of Historical Research*, 46, pp. 95–101.

1981, 'The Crown, Magnates and Local Government in Fifteenth-Century East Anglia', in Highfield and Jeffs (eds.) 1981, pp. 72–87.

1990, 'Aspects of the County Community in the Fifteenth Century', in M. A. Hicks (ed.), *Profit, Piety and the Professions in Later Medieval England*, Gloucester, pp. 1–13.

Walker, S. K., 1990, *The Lancastrian Affinity, 1361–1399*, Oxford.

Warren, W. L., 1987, *The Governance of Norman and Angevin England, 1086–1272*, London.

Watts, J. L., 1990, *'De Consulatu Stiliconis*: Texts and Politics in the Reign of Henry VI', *Journal of Medieval History*, 16, pp. 251–66.

1991, 'The Counsels of King Henry VI, *c.*1435–45', *English Historical Review*, 106, pp. 279–98.

1994, 'When Did Henry VI's Minority End?', in Clayton *et al.* (eds.) 1994: pp. 116–39.

Wedgwood, J. C., 1936, *History of Parliament. Biographies of the Members of the Commons House, 1439–1509*, HMSO, London.

Weiss, M., 1976, 'A Power in the North? The Percies in the Fifteenth Century', *Historical Journal*, 19, pp. 501–9.

Weiss, R., 1957, 'Humphrey, Duke of Gloucester and Tito Livio Frulovisi', in D. J. Gordon (ed.), *Fritz Saxl, 1890–1948. Knowledge and Learning...*, London, pp. 218–27.

Wilkinson, B., 1948–58, *Constitutional History of Medieval England, 1216–1399*, 3 vols., London.

  1964, *Constitutional History of England in the Fifteenth Century (1399–1485)*, London.

Wilks, M., 1963, *The Problem of Sovereignty in the Later Middle Ages*, Cambridge.

Willard, J. F., and Morris, W. A. (eds.), 1940, *The English Government at Work, 1327–1336*, I, Cambridge, Mass.

Wolffe, B. P., 1958, 'Acts of Resumption in the Lancastrian Parliaments, 1399–1456', *English Historical Review*, 73, pp. 583–613.

  1971, *The Royal Demesne in English History*, London.

  1972, 'The Personal Rule of Henry VI', in Chrimes, Ross and Griffiths (eds.) 1972: pp. 29–48.

  1976, review of Ross 1974, in *English Historical Review*, 91, pp. 369–74.

  1981, *Henry VI*, London.

Woodger, L. S., 1974, 'Henry Bourgchier, Earl of Essex, and his Family (1408–83)', unpubl. DPhil thesis, Oxford.

Wright, S. M., 1983, *The Derbyshire Gentry in the Fifteenth Century*, Derb. Record Soc., no. 8, Chesterfield.

Wylie, J. H., and Waugh, W. T., 1929, *The Reign of Henry the Fifth*, III, Cambridge.

INDEX